Sensors Expo & Conference 2021

San Jose, California, USA
21-23 December 2021

ISBN: 978-1-7138-3934-7

Printed from e-media with permission by:

Curran Associates, Inc.
57 Morehouse Lane
Red Hook, NY 12571

Some format issues inherent in the e-media version may also appear in this print version.

Questex Media Group, Inc.
275 Grove Street, Suite 2-130
Newton, Massachusetts 02466
USA

Phone: (617) 219-8300

info@questex.com

Additional copies of this publication are available from:

Curran Associates, Inc.
57 Morehouse Lane
Red Hook, NY 12571 USA
Phone: 845-758-0400
Fax: 845-758-2633
Email: curran@proceedings.com
Web: www.proceedings.com

TABLE OF CONTENTS

Sensors Converge

Using Sensors and AI to Improve Human Health and Address Climate Change: **One Smart Building at a Time**

Aditya Dayal, Ph.D.
View Inc.

September 21-23, 2021 | San Jose, CA

#SensorsConverge

Outline

- Real Estate Industry Trends
- Introduction to smart glass
- Heat and glare control
- Smart Glass Intelligence
- Sensor data and insights

#SensorsConverge Aditya Dayal Sensors Converge

Real Estate Trends

Experience
- Humans spend 90% of time inside buildings
- Greater focus on Inside-Out vs. Outside-In

Sustainability and Efficiency
- Buildings consume 40% of all energy
- Imperative for buildings to be more energy efficient

Health
- Indoor space quality is the next frontier in health
- COVID has accelerated awareness

Computing and Digitization
- Interactive, smart buildings with sensors
- Digital Twins drive operational efficiencies

#SensorsConverge

View Smart Glass Technology

Smart Glass
- Dynamic tinting
- More natural light
- Heat and glare protection

+

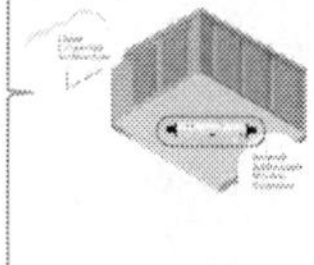

Network
- High bandwidth data and power
- Individual IGU control
- Smart Building OT Network

+

Software
- Predictive tinting algorithms
- Remote monitoring and management
- Data accessible through APIs

Aditya Dayal

View Smart Glass - Facts

600	100K+	90M	85M	2B	700B
Projects completed (**250** in progress)	Active Windows	Building SF	Complete Transitions (2020)	Measurements per Day	Measurements per Year

#SensorsConverge

Aditya Dayal

Glare and Heat Control

Traditional Glass

Smart Glass

#SensorsConverge

Aditya Dayal

Eliminate glare, maintain views

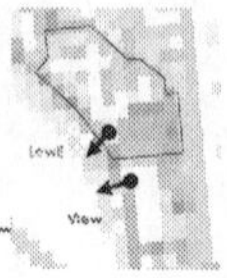

Traditional Glass (LowE + Shades)

View Smart Glass

#SensorsConverge Aditya Dayal Sensors Converge

Control Heat

6F lower interior temperatures with View Smart Glass

LowE + Shades

View Smart Glass

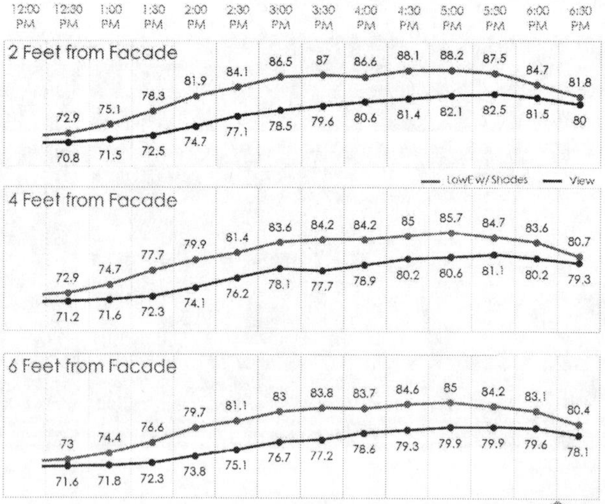

#Senso Aditya Dayal Sensors Converge

Glass Intelligence – optimized for user comfort

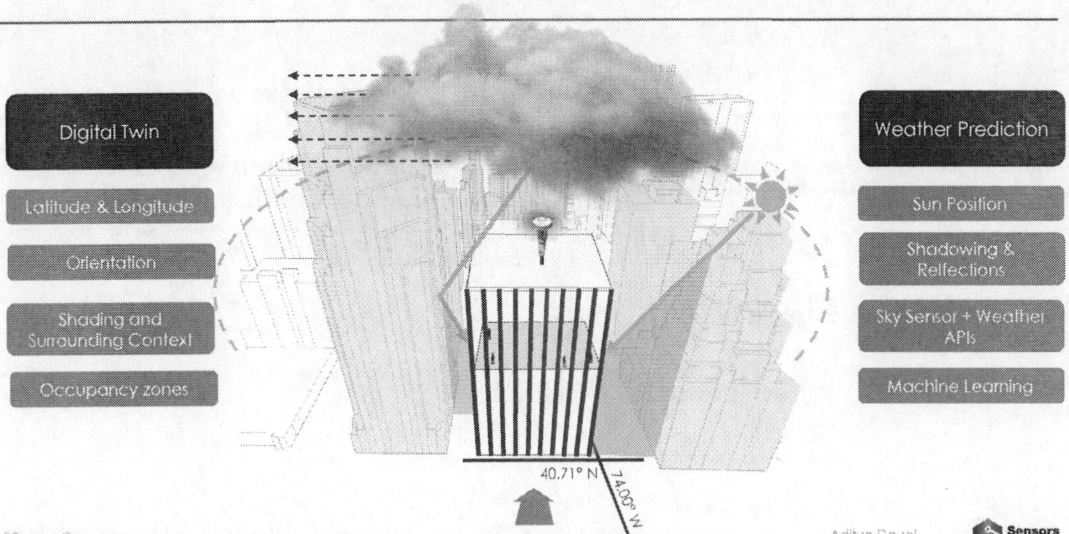

#SensorsConverge

Aditya Dayal

Predicting dynamic weather with ML

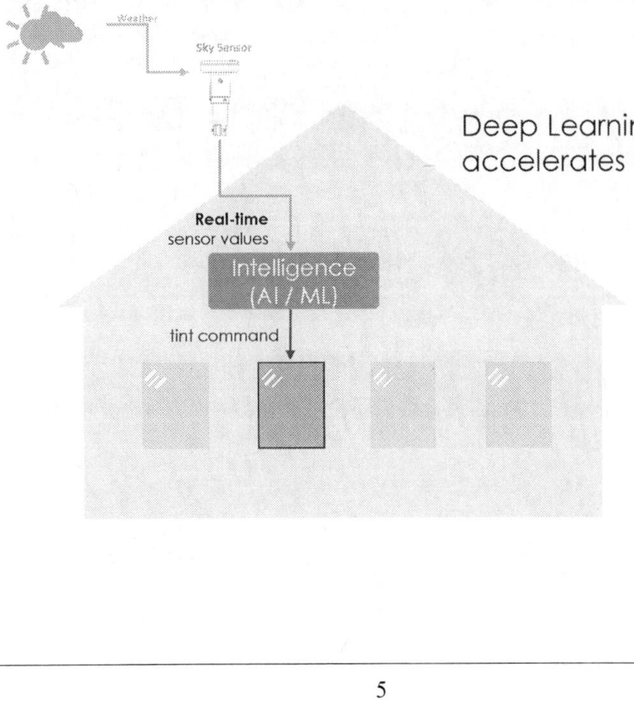

Deep Learning Application accelerates glass tint decisions

#SensorsConverge

Aditya Dayal

Indoor Air Quality

HARVARD T.H. CHAN SCHOOL OF PUBLIC HEALTH

Office air quality may affect employees' cognition, productivity

https://www.hsph.harvard.edu/news/press-releases/office-air-quality-may-affect-employees-cognition-productivity/

Forbes

Isn't It Time We Talked About Indoor Air Quality?

https://www.forbes.com/sites/jamiehailstone/2021/08/10/isnt-it-time-we-talked-about-indoor-air-quality/?sh=396817ed777e

The New York Times

THE WELL NEWSLETTER

Is Bad Indoor Air Dulling Your Brain?

https://www.nytimes.com/2021/09/16/well/air-quality-brain-function.html

#SensorsConverge

Aditya Dayal

Sensors Converge

Sensors for monitoring indoor environments

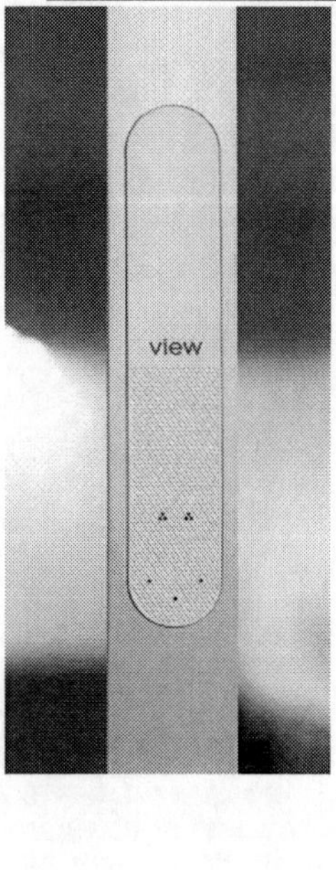

BREATHE FEEL HEAR SEE

1 View Sense EQ
Environmental Quality
CO_2 | tVOC | Temp | RH
Lux | CCT | SPL

2 View Sense PM
Particulate Matter
PM_1 | $PM_{2.5}$ | PM_{10}

3 View Sense AO
Advanced Occupancy
Detect | Count
Space Utilization

Aditya Dayal

Sensors Converge

Track spatial and temporal variations

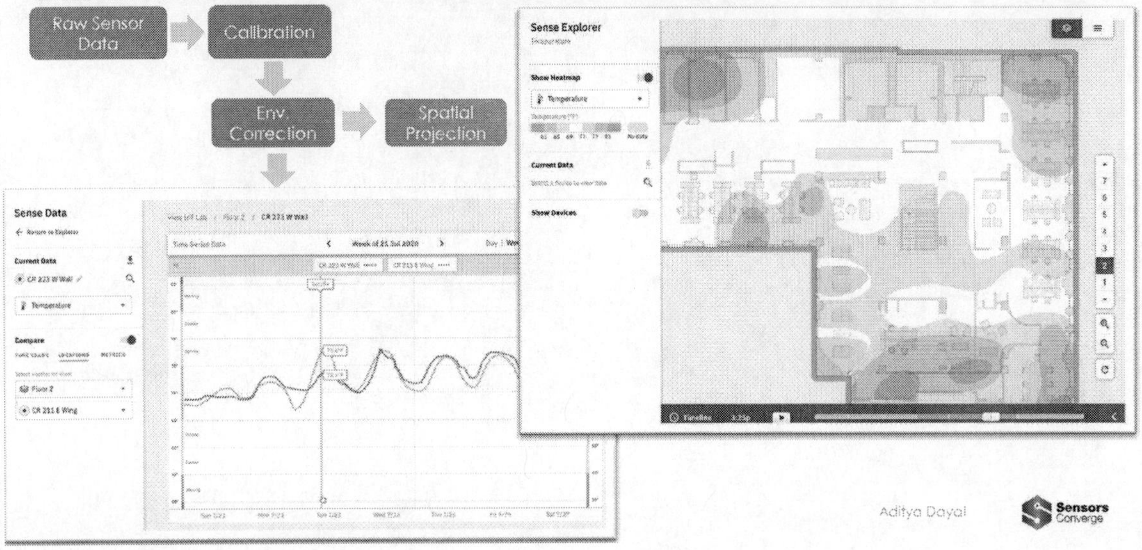

Aditya Dayal

Sensors Converge

CO_2 data overview

Predictable daily pattern

24 devices, Avg. CO_2 range: 550-600 PPM

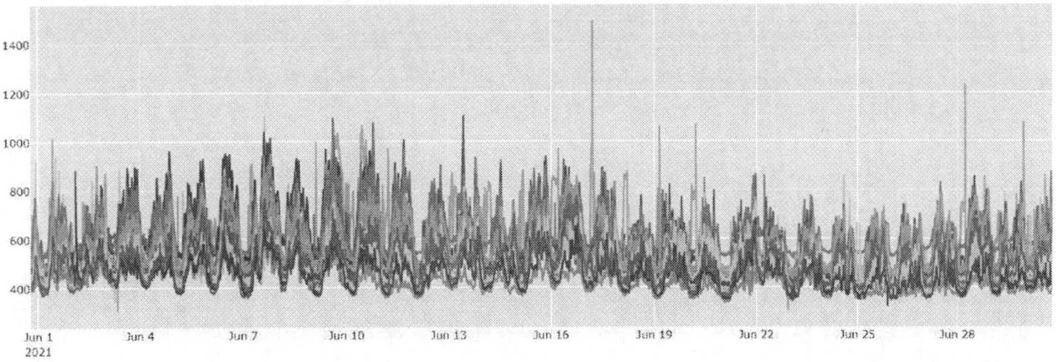

#SensorsConverge

Aditya Dayal

Sensors Converge

CO_2 insights: peaks correlated with occupancy

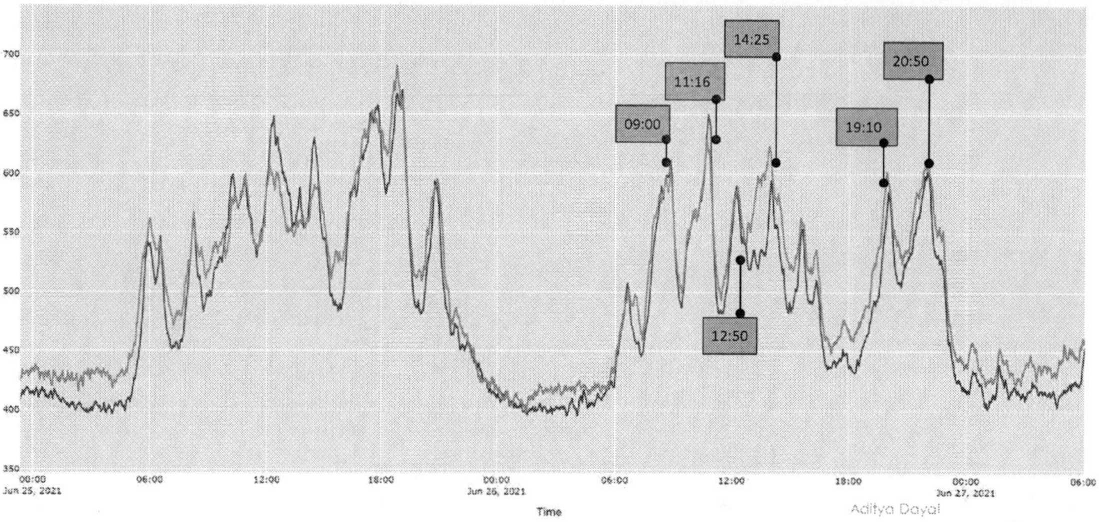

Aditya Dayal

Temperature data

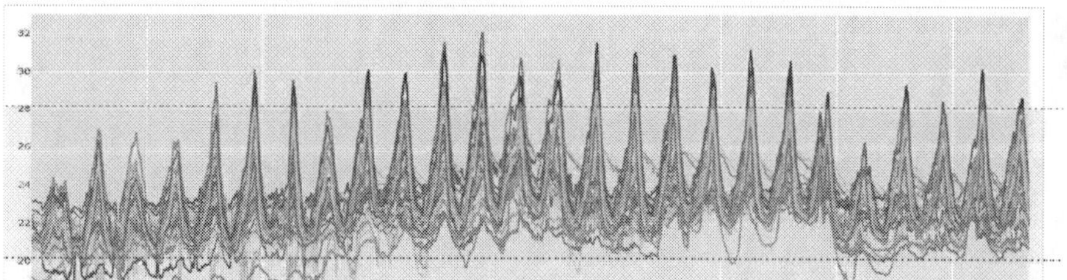

Interior Temperature

☺

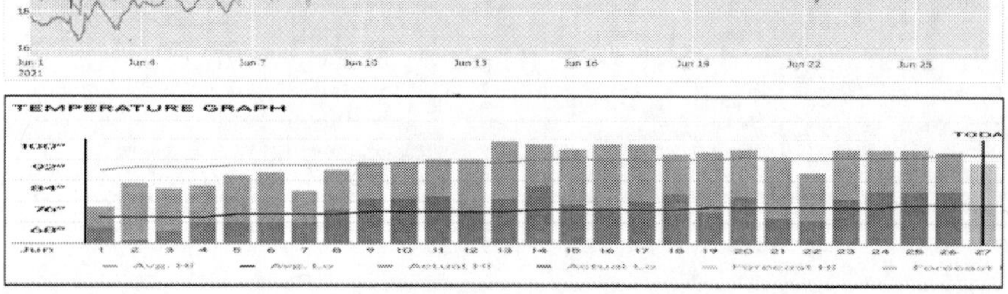

Outside Temperature

#SensorsConverge

Aditya Dayal

Sensors Converge

Temperature map

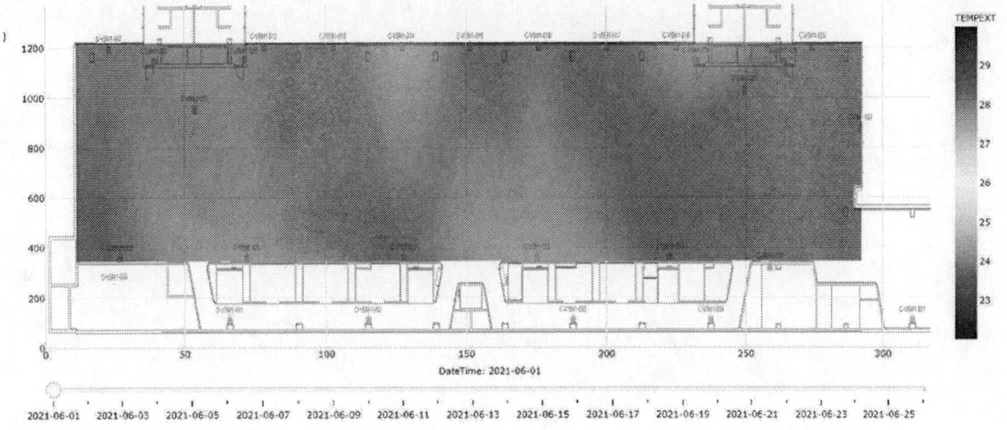

#SensorsConverge

Aditya Dayal

Temperature insights

Identify spatial "hotspots" → provide feedback to HVAC system

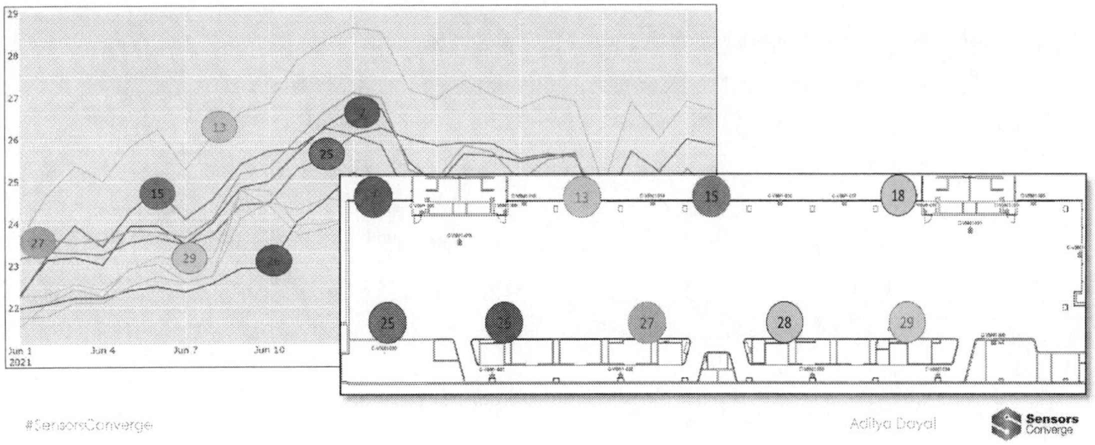

#SensorsConverge

Aditya Dayal

Occupancy Insights

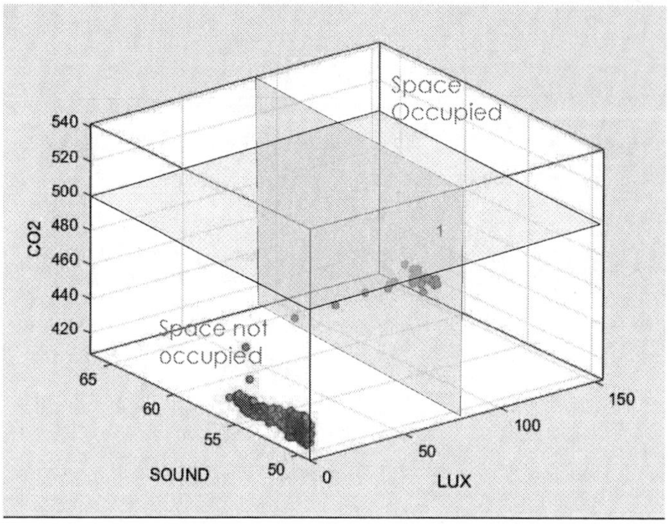

#SensorsConverge

Aditya Dayal

Sensors Converge

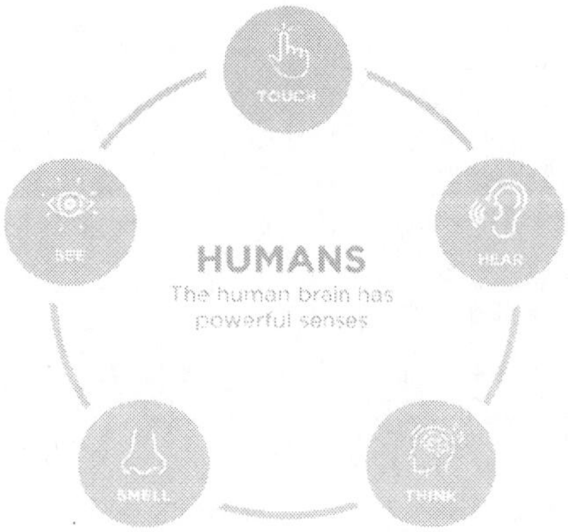

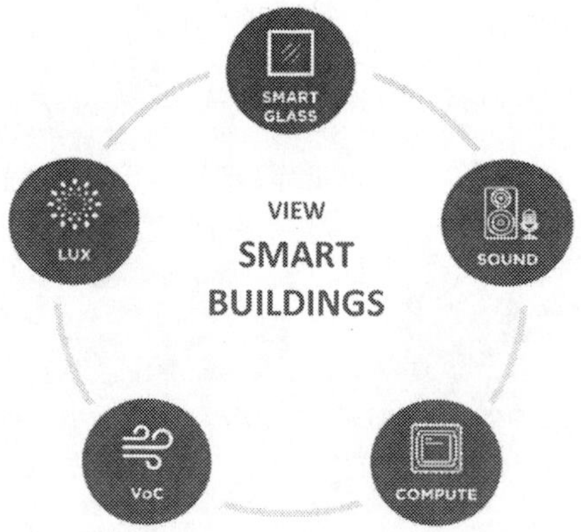

#SensorsConverge

Aditya Dayal

Sensors Converge

Thank You – Q/A

#SensorsConverge

Aditya Dayal

Sensors Converge

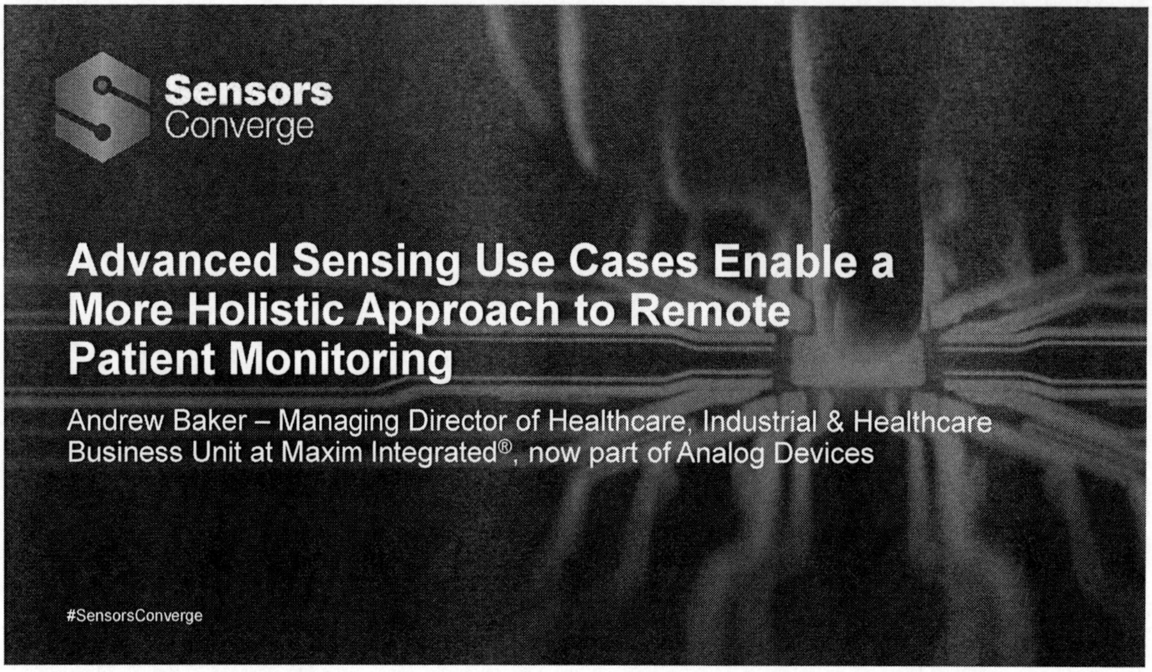
Sensors
Converge
Advanced Sensing Use Cases Enable a More Holistic Approach to Remote Patient Monitoring
Andrew Baker – Managing Director of Healthcare, Industrial & Healthcare Business Unit at Maxim Integrated®, now part of Analog Devices
#SensorsConverge

Decentralized Healthcare Enables Better Outcomes at Lower Cost
Earlier detection
Patient convenience
Data driven decisions
#SensorsConverge
Sensors
Converge

Healthcare is Becoming More Personalized

Wearable Health and Wellness devices Market

- 347Mu in 2019
- 754Mu in 2025
- 14% CAGR '19 to '25

Global wearable market shipments (million units)

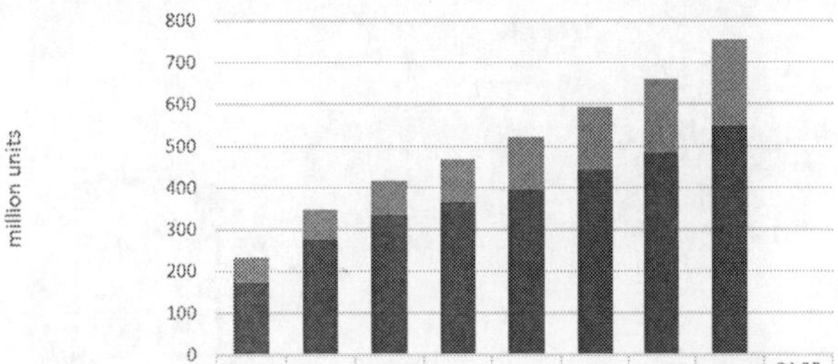

	2018	2019	2020e	2021e	2022e	2023e	2024e	2025e	CAGR 19-25
Medical wearables	59	71	85	104	126	150	177	207	19%
Consumer wearables	173	275	332	363	396	442	483	547	12%
Total	232	347	417	467	521	592	660	754	14%

Source: Wearables in Consumer and Medical Applications report, Yole Développement (Yole), 2020

#SensorsConverge

Sensors Converge

A Holistic Approach to Remote Healthcare

Wearables of the future need multiple Vital Signs Monitoring

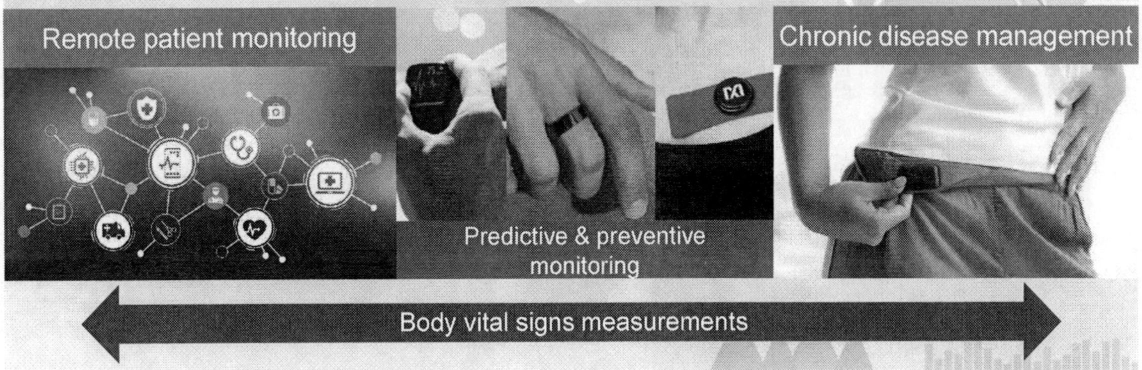

#SensorsConverge

Sensors Converge

Wearables Improve How We Detect & Manage Chronic Conditions

Identify onset of critical conditions to mitigate risk of costly hospitalization

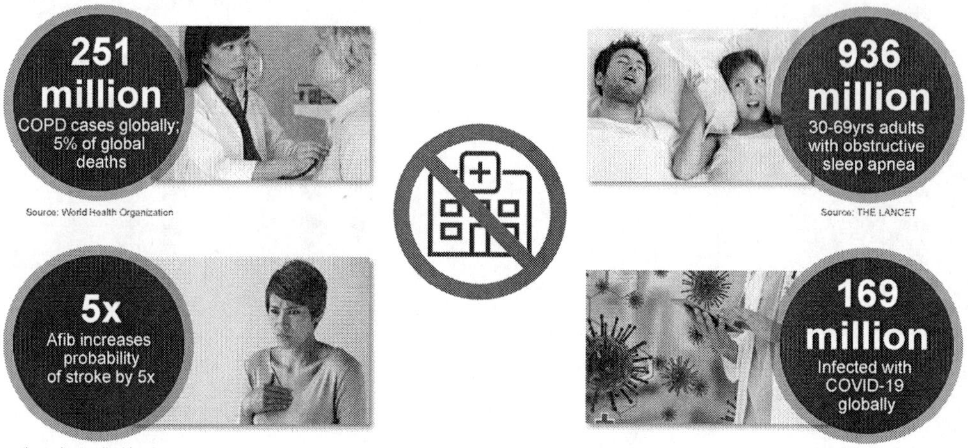

#SensorsConverge

Sensors Converge

Use Case Example: Body-Worn Healthcare Patch

Collects vital signs data & uploads it to cloud for clinician (remote patient monitoring)

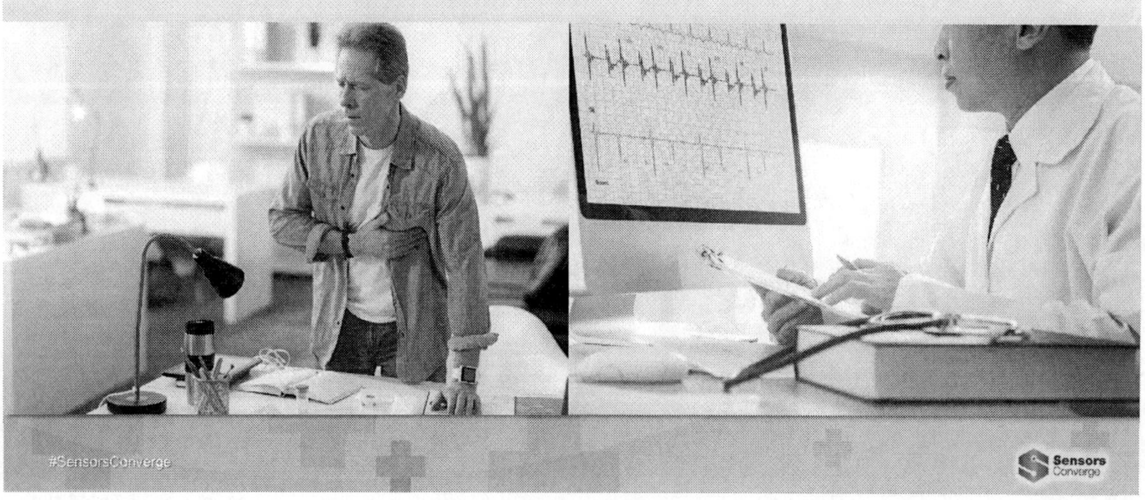

#SensorsConverge

Sensors Converge

MAX86178 Clinical-Grade AFE for Remote Patient Monitoring

- Single-chip AFE with 3 measurement sub-systems
  > PPG offers clinical-grade SpO_2 oximetry
    - Up to 115dB SNR using Burst Mode
  > Clinical-grade biopotential channel for HR and arrythmia detection
    - IEC60601-2-47 compliant
  > Flexible bioimpedance channel
    - Supports ICG, BIA/BIS, GSR/EDA
- Simplifies design of complex multi vital sign systems accelerating time to market
- Shrinks devices by 30% improving user experience
- High level of configurability for use case optimization (e.g. battery life)

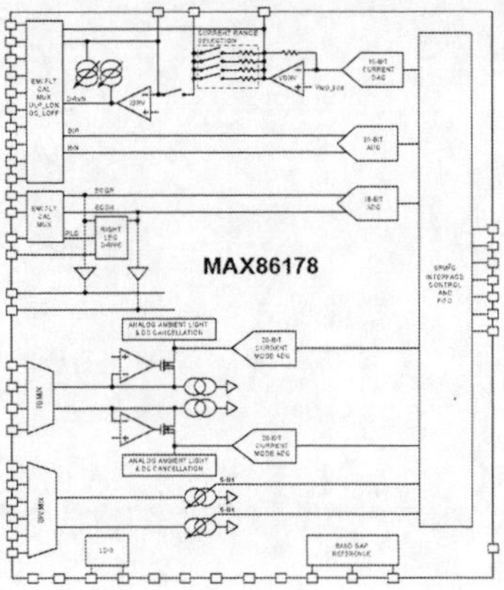

#SensorsConverge

Sensors Converge

4 Critical Vital-Sign Measurements

Vital Sign	Use Cases
Blood-oxygen saturation (SpO_2)	Monitor pulmonary function, sleep disorders
Respiration rate (using BioZ)	Monitor respiration trends
Heart rate (ECG or optical PPG)	Monitor heart rate trends
Electrocardiogram (ECG or EKG)	AFib detection, cardiac health

#SensorsConverge

Sensors Converge

Typical Remote Monitoring Patch System Block Diagram

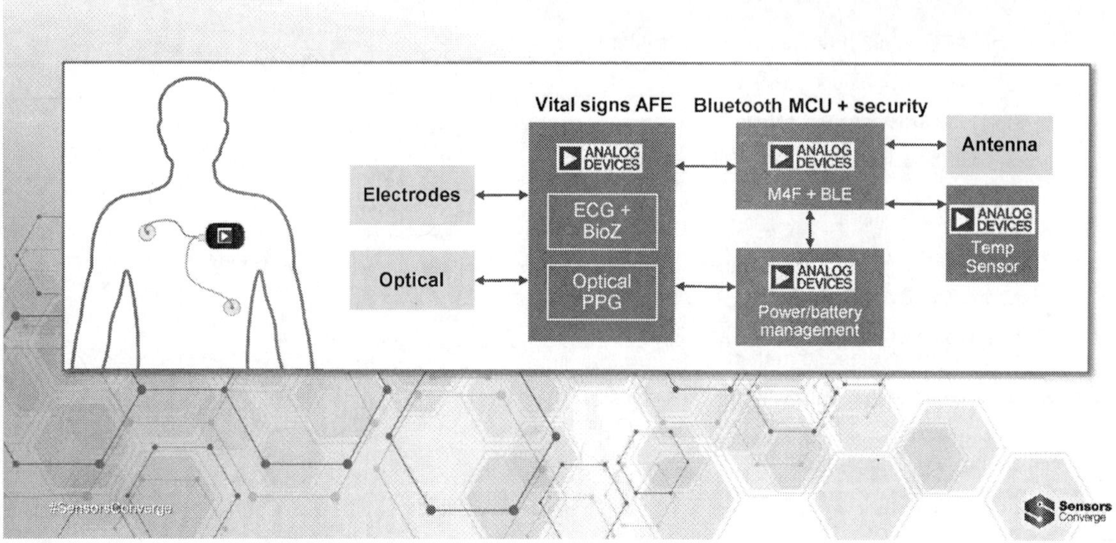

The Future of Wearable Healthcare is Accelerating

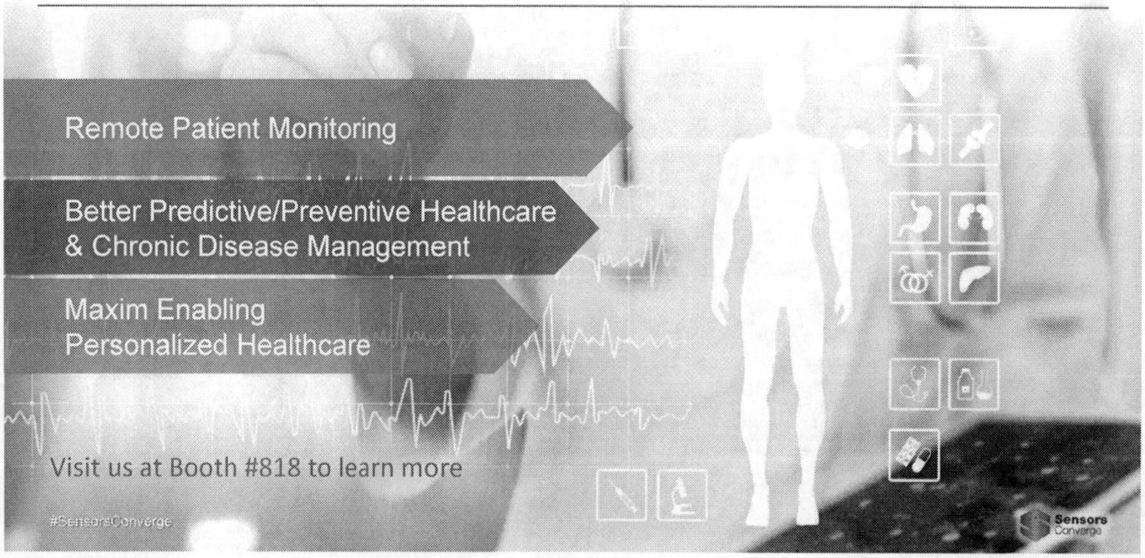

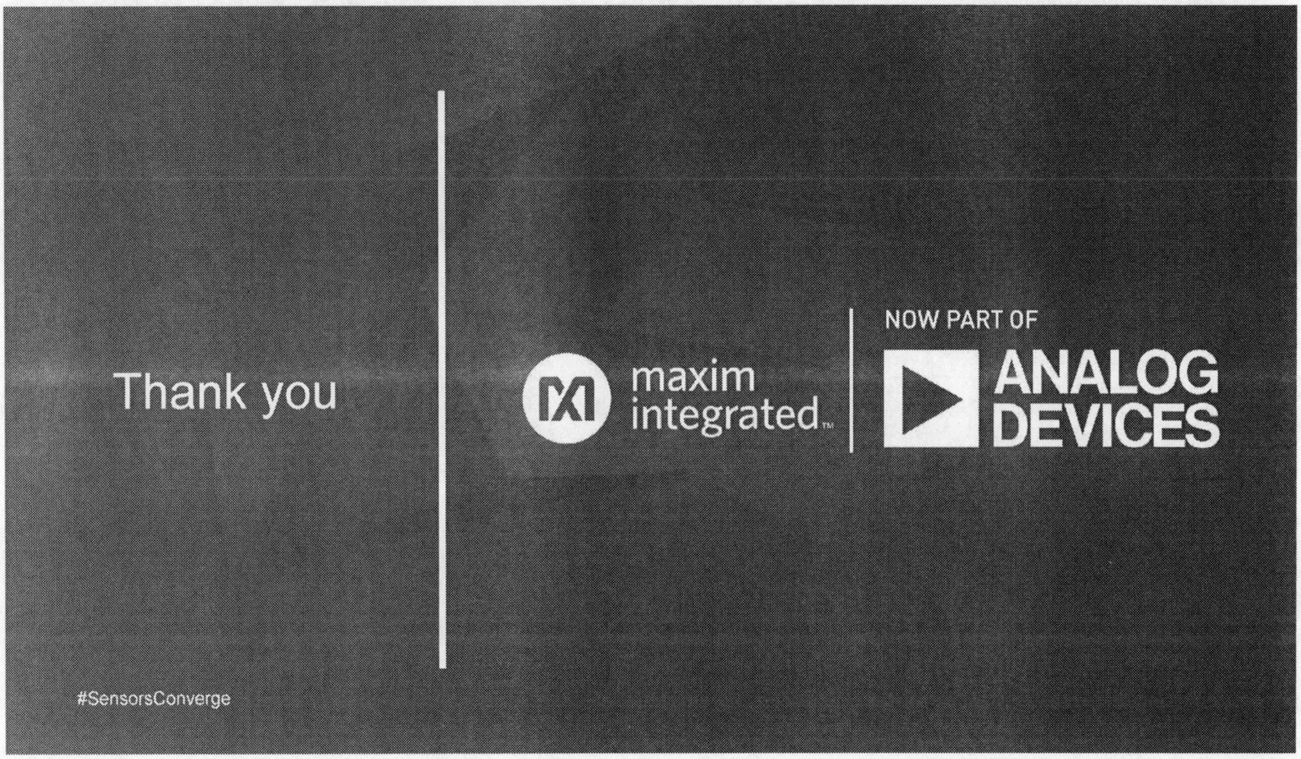
Thank you
maxim
integrated
NOW PART OF
ANALOG
DEVICES
#SensorsConverge

Sensors Converge

Achieving Accurate and Affordable IoT Asset Tracking

September 21-23, 2021 | San Jose, CA

#SensorsConverge

Company Snapshot LINK LABS

- ✓ **Founded** in 2014
- ✓ **Core Products**: AirFinder OnSite and AirFinder Everywhere – seamless indoor/outdoor IoT platform
- ✓ **Over 100,000** infrastructure devices deployed and managed (and growing)
- ✓ **Over 1 billion** events processed per month (and growing)
- ✓ **Tier 1** global partner network
- ✓ **60+ FTEs**
- ✓ **Nearly 30 patents**

Indoor Infrastructure Deployments

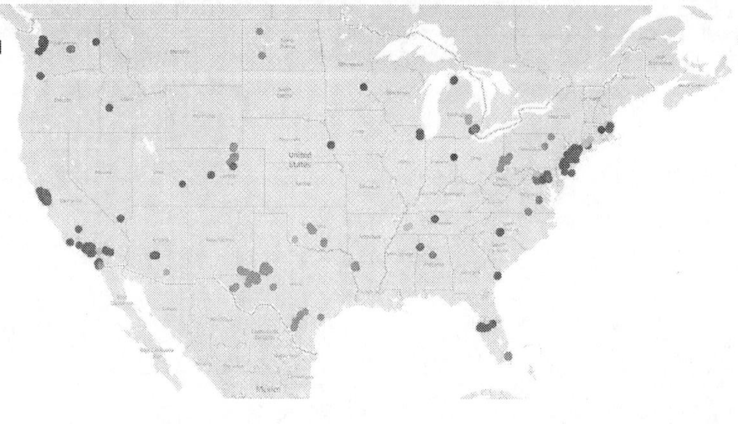

#SensorsConverge

Sensors Converge

Agenda

- Motivation (market perspective)
- Why phase ranging with Bluetooth LE chipsets?
- Practical considerations
- Technical approach
- Results
- Solution implementation
- Use cases

#SensorsConverge

Sensors Converge

Motivation Part I

IoT Asset Tracking is About Cost

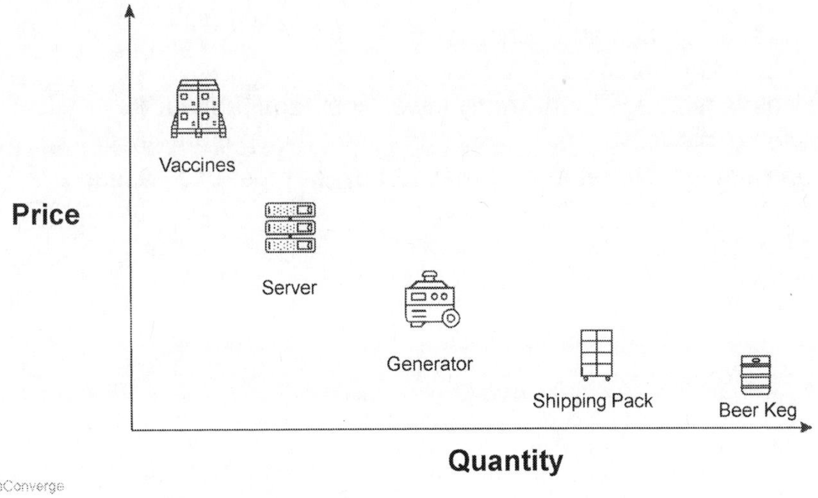

#SensorsConverge

Sensors Converge

Motivation Part II

Cost and Location Accuracy Trade-off

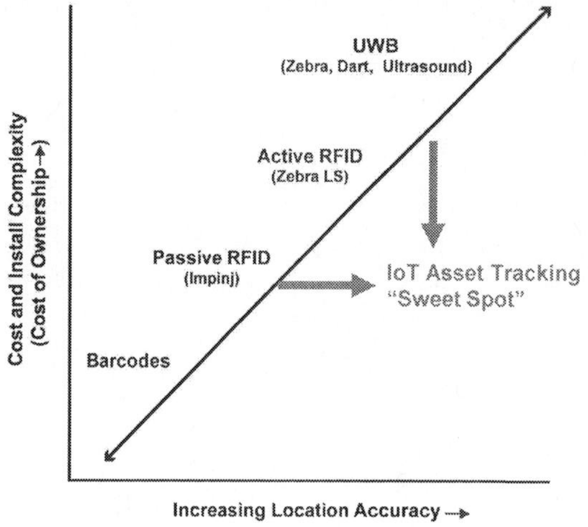

#SensorsConverge

Sensors Converge

What Motivates the Selection of Bluetooth LE?

- Mass customization of tags and sensors
- All at mass production volumes (= low cost)
- Sustainable cost advantage: inherently lower cost tags than UWB due to processing intensity
- Sufficient bandwidth for "great enough" accuracy for most use cases (i.e. sub-meter)
- Robust supplier ecosystem
- Global standard

#SensorsConverge

Sensors Converge

Bluetooth LE Localization Approaches

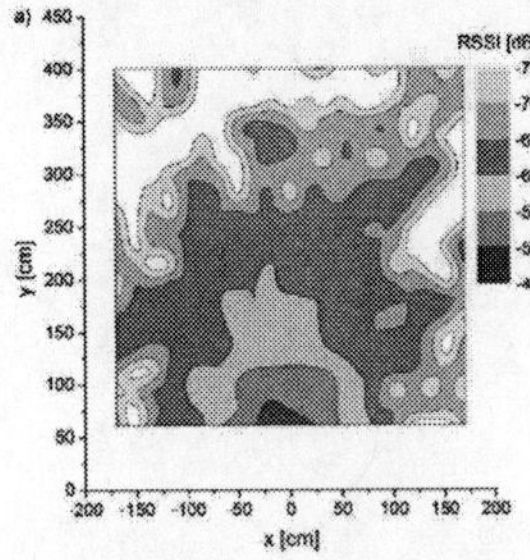

Signal Strength-Based

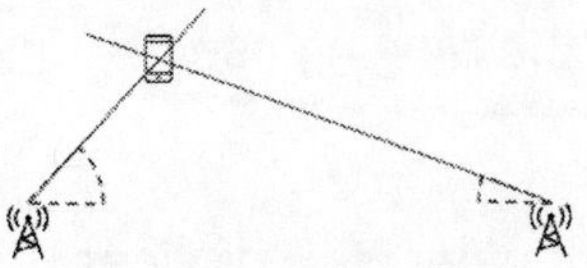

Angle-Based (BLE5.1)

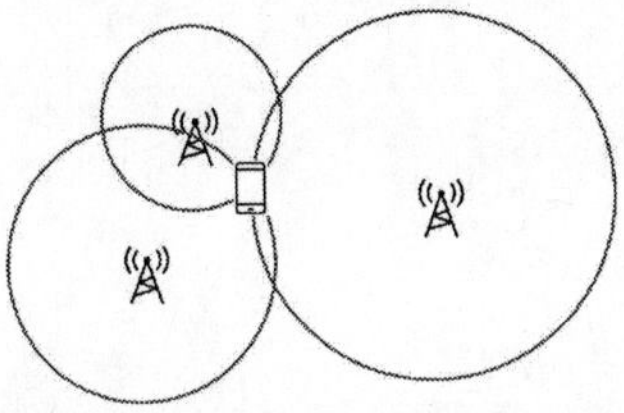

Phase Ranging i.e. Time-Based (similar to UWB or GPS)

#SensorsConverge

Sensors Converge

Appeal of Phase Ranging + Edge Processing

- Sufficient bandwidth for ~1 meter accuracy
- Phase ranging a proven performant technology with both GPS and UWB
- Far easier install: no critical antenna orientation or proximity dependencies
- Potential for high multipath tolerance
- Ease and low cost of backhaul
  - Edge processing (i.e. on the BLE chipset) limits backhaul data needs
  - More power efficient as well, extending tag operating life

#SensorsConverge

Sensors Converge

Practical Considerations

- How to perform the ranging itself!
- Power efficiency
- Interference from other BLE devices
- Scalability

#SensorsConverge

Sensors Converge

Classic Approach to RF Ranging Not Possible

- With ToF ranging, resolution is proportional to bandwidth
- 'Classical' approach: transmit a wide bandwidth signal [UWB for example]
- Problem: requires high speed/power ADCs, hefty processing [i.e., need bigger batteries to get long operational life]

#SensorsConverge

Sensors Converge

Solution: Multi-Carrier Phase Ranging

Synthesize wide bandwidth signal with multitude of narrowband tones on Bluetooth LE chipset

Low sampling rate => can be done on existing processor

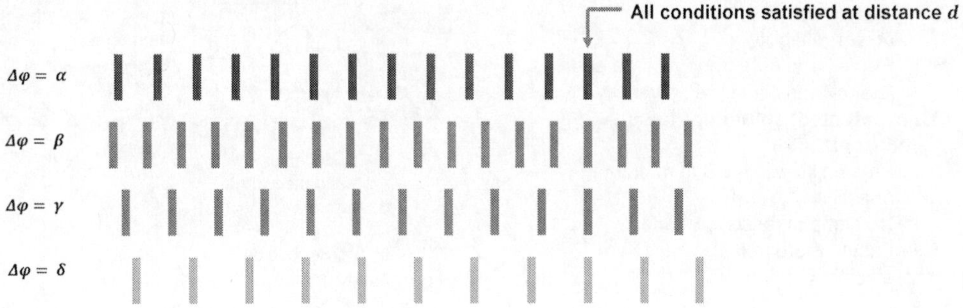

#SensorsConverge

Common Implementation

Oversimplified, idealized case

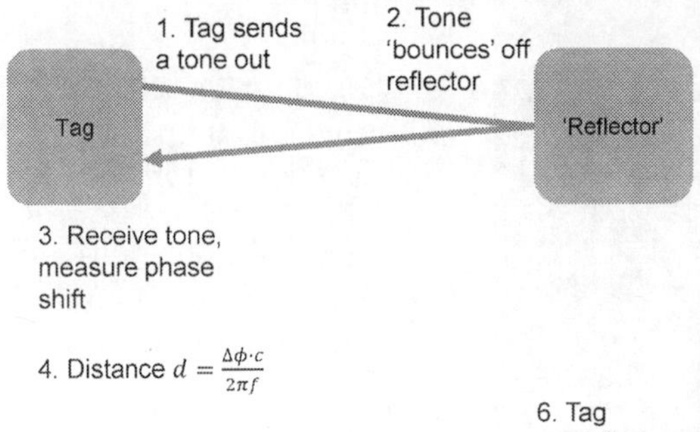

Common implementation designed to overcome the practical difficulty of handling phase/frequency difference between tag and beacon

Common Implementation

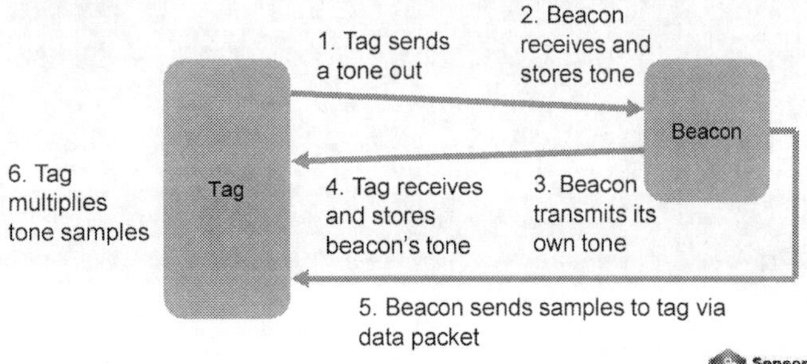

#SensorsConverge

Link Labs Approach

- **Sending samples from beacon to tag is not ideal**
  - 256B – 512B of data
  - Transmitting data is inherently more dependent on a quality link than reading tones
  - Lower reliability
  - Retries add data transmit time add latency and consume power
- **Our (patented) solution: Phase Synchronization**
  - Beacon slews its LO to match tag phase
  - No sample transfers needed
  - Faster, more reliable and power efficient ranging

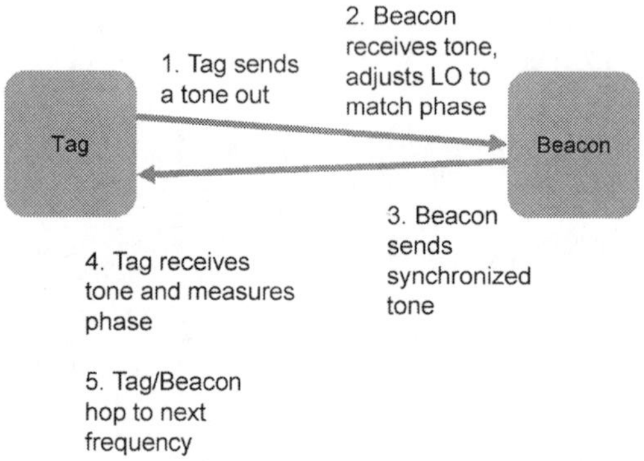

Phase Ranging Results

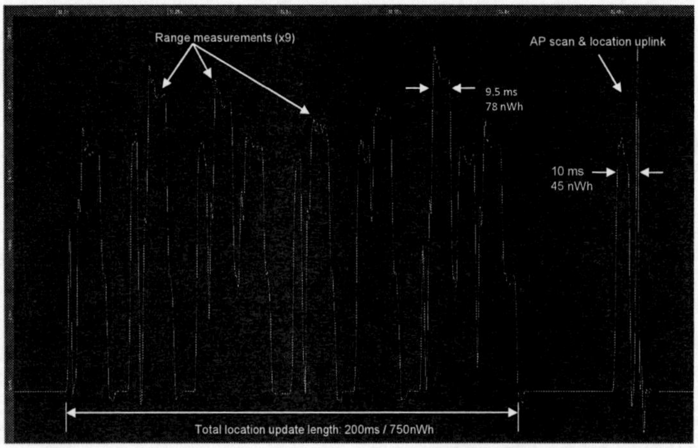

- **Timing**
  - Range duration: 9ms
  - 'Fix' duration: 200ms
- **Energy Consumption**
  - Fix energy: 750nWh
  - CR2477 coin cell battery→2,500,000+ fixes
  - Uplink energy: 45nWh
- **Location Accuracy**
  - Dependent on environment
  - Normal conditions: < 1 m

Power-Efficiency Results

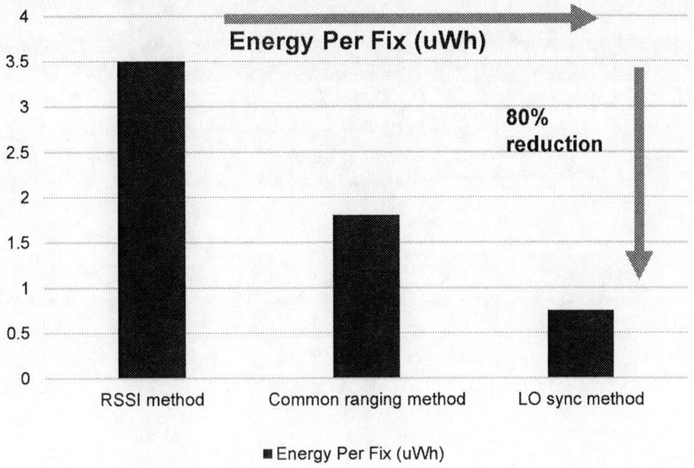

#SensorsConverge

Sensors Converge

System Results: Accuracy

What's in the UI

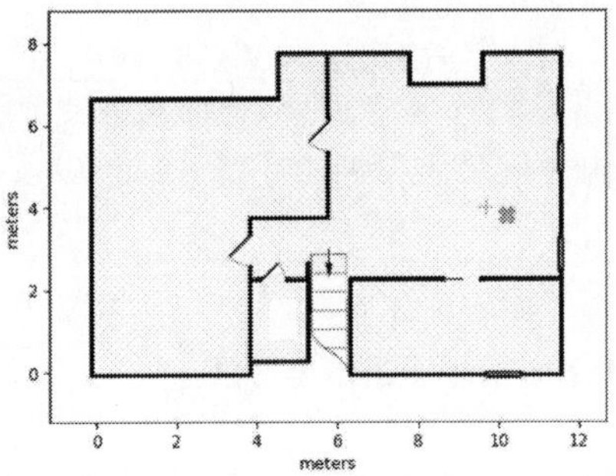

What's happening behind the scenes

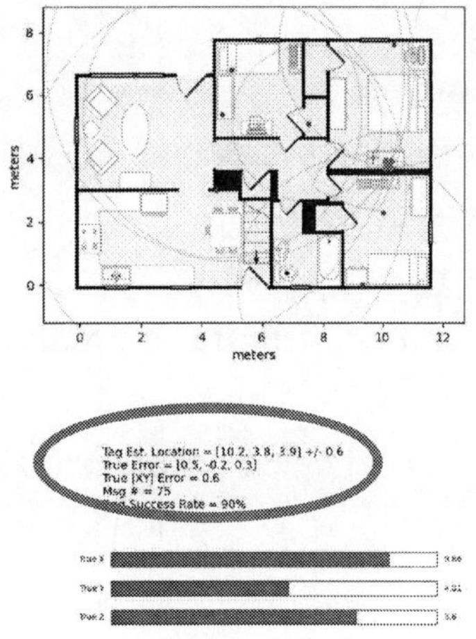

#SensorsConverge

Sensors Converge

Overall Performance Evaluation

	Ultrawideband (UWB)	BLE 5.1 AoA	Phase Ranging
Location Accuracy	A+	B+	A-
Power Consumption (ranging only)	A	A	A
Multipath Performance	A+	C+	A-
Ease, cost of Install	B+	C+	A-
Cost	D	B	A+

#SensorsConverge

Sensors Converge

Interference Mitigation and Scalability

- **Common techniques improve performance**
- **Interference mitigation: high reliability in challenging environments achievable**
  - Scanning/avoidance
  - Interpolation
  - Retries
- **Scalability: hundreds of *simultaneous* tags, thousands TBD**
  - Adding location beacons adds capacity
  - Channel coordination with known/common interference sources
  - Algorithms for distributing retries

#SensorsConverge

Sensors Converge

Link Labs Solution: AirFinder OnSite XLE

Components

XLE Tags

Attach to assets and transmit locations to access points
Battery

Location Beacons & Access Points

Mount beacons in a grid-like pattern for equal coverage within a zone; access points receive data from tagged assets and send data to gateway.
110 Power

Gateway

Receive data from access points via AirFinder's standalone Symphony Link network and sends data to cloud platform.
110 Power

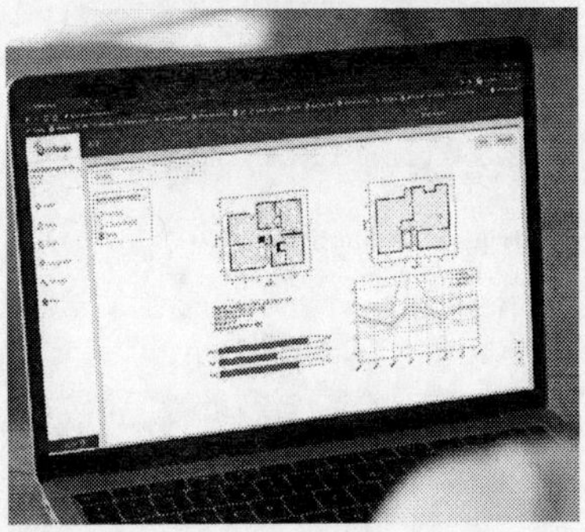

The location beacon to access point ratio for XLE is around 4:1

#SensorsConverge

Sensors Converge

AirFinder XLE in Action

#SensorsConverge

Sensors Converge

Use Case Examples

Supply chain/logistics
1. Closed loop container tracking—totes, cradles, etc.
2. Pallets
3. Trailers
4. Glass racks
5. Beer kegs

Production Through-put
6. Parts/materials tracking
7. Calibration/paperwork tracking
8. "Outbox"/"Inbox" alerts

Cold Chain/Temp Monitoring
9. Pharma/drugs
10. Retail environments
11. Food sourcing/distribution

Outdoor/indoor mobile items
12. Bike sharing
13. Scooter sharing
14. Airport tarmac equipment
15. Luggage and grocery carts

Equipment/tool tracking
16. Tools/templates in industrial environments
17. R&D facility equipment
18. Rental/leased equipment utilization and management
19. Tax savings—leased equipment used across state lines
20. Calibration/maintenance (hospital equipment)
21. Theft prevention
22. Shared hospital equipment across facilities

Commercial consumables
23. Auto glass
24. Gas cylinders
25. Lubricants/adhesives
26. Spare parts

Vehicles with equipment
27. Service vehicle on-board equipment
28. Ambulatory on-board equipment

People tracking
29. Contractors in oil/gas, construction, agriculture—contract compliance
30. Safety for emergency response—banking, hotels, refineries
31. Labor planning and staffing optimization for operational excellence (fast food)
32. Maintenance turns in manufacturing for capacity release
33. Visitor tracking in large facilities
34. Patient tracking in hospitals, same day surgery centers
35. Office space utilization/optimization
36. Elder care/wander management

Other
37. Marketing displays for retail
38. Agricultural equipment

Sensors Converge

Questions?

LINK LABS

bob.proctor@link-labs.com

#SensorsConverge

Sensors Converge

Sensors Converge

C-V2X: Tomorrow's Smart City Connected Infrastructure Is Today's Reality in Peachtree Corners

September 21-23, 2021 | San Jose, CA

#SensorsConverge

C-V2X: Tomorrow's Smart City Connected Infrastructure Is Today's Reality in Peachtree Corners

45,000 + Residents
45,000 + Jobs

Tech Park Housing Some of the World's Most Disruptive Technology Companies

Close Proximity to World's busiest Airport

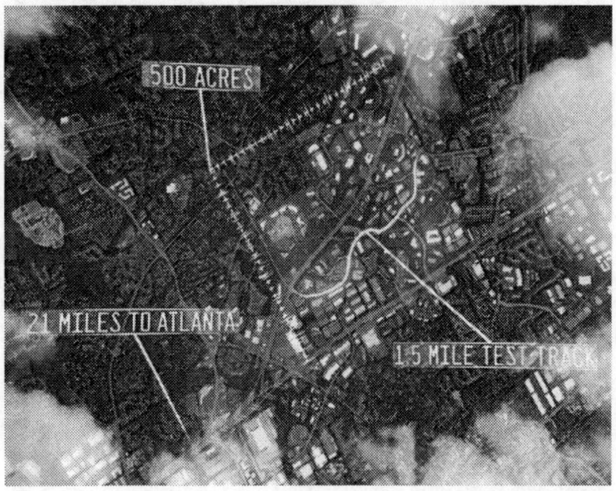

#SensorsConverge

Sensors Converge

C-V2X: Tomorrow's Smart City Connected Infrastructure Is Today's Reality in Peachtree Corners

Who Are We? The Heart of #SiliconOrchard

3-Mile Public Autonomous Test Track
(4.82 kilometer / 4828.03 meter)

Mobility Test Platform
Connected Infrastructure/V2X Test Platform

City Street of the Future
State-of-the-art smart city infrastructure

Innovation Center
Home of innovative companies

#SensorsConverge

Sensors Converge

C-V2X: Tomorrow's Smart City Connected Infrastructure Is Today's Reality in Peachtree Corners

#SensorsConverge

Sensors Converge

C-V2X: Tomorrow's Smart City Connected Infrastructure Is Today's Reality in Peachtree Corners

Innovation Center

- Technology Incubator for growing & scaling early-stage startups
- Corporate Innovation Space
- 25,000 square feet of flexible space

#SensorsConverge

Sensors Converge

C-V2X: Tomorrow's Smart City Connected Infrastructure Is Today's Reality in Peachtree Corners

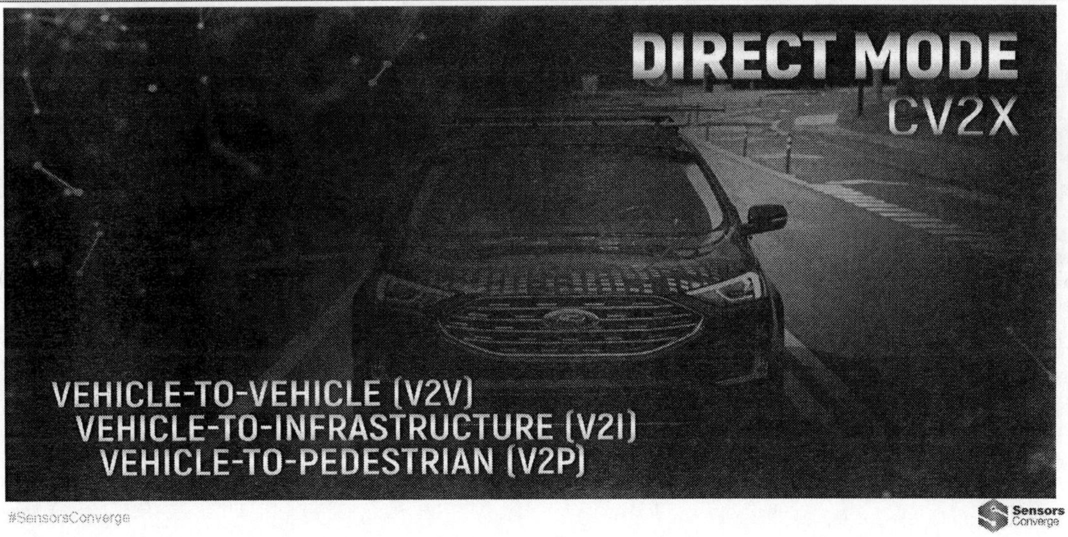

#SensorsConverge

Sensors Converge

C-V2X: Tomorrow's Smart City Connected Infrastructure Is Today's Reality in Peachtree Corners

#SensorsConverge

Sensors Converge

C-V2X: Tomorrow's Smart City Connected Infrastructure Is Today's Reality in Peachtree Corners

#SensorsConverge

Sensors Converge

C-V2X: Tomorrow's Smart City Connected Infrastructure Is Today's Reality in Peachtree Corners

#SensorsConverge

Sensors Converge

C-V2X: Tomorrow's Smart City Connected Infrastructure Is Today's Reality in Peachtree Corners

Autonomous Shuttle Deployment

- Hundreds of actual residents transported
- Critical data and real-world environment learnings generated
- CV2X Testing on Multiple OEM's

#SensorsConverge

Sensors Converge

C-V2X: Tomorrow's Smart City Connected Infrastructure Is Today's Reality in Peachtree Corners

E-Mobility

- The world's first fleet of teleoperated e-scooters with automated repositioning
- Updating to include CV2X applications

#SensorsConverge

Sensors Converge

C-V2X: Tomorrow's Smart City Connected Infrastructure Is Today's Reality in Peachtree Corners

Unlike Any Other Smart City Environment on Earth

- Live 5G wireless environment
- City government owns all infrastructure: quick approvals and decisions
- No charge for the use of the ecosystem/infrastructure
- No intellectual property rights required
- Respect and guarantee of security for proprietary data
- NIST-171 Compliant Facility
- General liability insurance for driven traffic and driverless traffic

#SensorsConverge

Sensors Converge

C-V2X: Tomorrow's Smart City Connected Infrastructure Is Today's Reality in Peachtree Corners

Some of Our Partners

CISCO

ASHRAE

T Mobile

BOSCH

GT

AUVSI
ALL THINGS UNMANNED

GAMA
Georgia Automotive Manufacturers Association

IATL

Cynamics

Georgia Power

OVHcloud

METRO ATLANTA CHAMBER

#SensorsConverge

Sensors Converge

C-V2X: Tomorrow's Smart City Connected Infrastructure Is Today's Reality in Peachtree Corners

International Partners

Israel

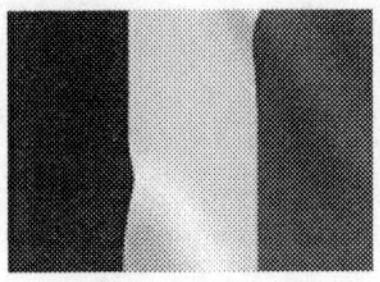

France

United Kingdom

Taiwan

Canada

#SensorsConverge

Sensors Converge

C-V2X: Tomorrow's Smart City Connected Infrastructure Is Today's Reality in Peachtree Corners

Questions?

Curiosity Lab
at Peachtree Corners

#SensorsConverge

Sensors Converge

Sensors Converge

TUTORIAL –

The Path to 1T Sensors Before 2025: An Exploratory Tutorial focused on Energy Consumption

Wednesday, September 22, 2021 | San Jose, CA

Brian Zahnstecher, Principal, IEEE Senior Member

Chair, *SF Bay IEEE Power Electronics Society (PELS)*
[Interim] Chair, *PELS Technical Committee (TC) 7*
Co-chair, *PSMA Energy Harvesting Committee*
Co-chair, *PSMA Reliability Committee*
Co-chair, ***IEEE 5G Initiative Roadmap, Energy Efficiency WG***
Co-chair, *IEEE Future Networks Initiative (FNI) Webinar Series*
Co-chair, *IEEE 5G Energy Efficiency Tutorial*
Board of Directors, *Power Sources Manufacturers Association (PSMA)*

Power to ™
1125 S Baywood Ave., San Jose, CA 95128
LinkedIn: www.linkedin.com/in/zahnstecher
bz@powerrox.com (508) 847-5747
www.powerrox.com Twitter: @PowerRoxLLC

#SensorsConverge

Dedication

This talk and work are dedicated to the memory of Earl McCune Jr.

He worked for a technologically advanced yet more energy efficient world, and the contents of the INGR and associated work are a tribute to that vision. Rest in peace, Earl!

2

Food for Thought

the ONION | HOME LATEST POLITICS SPORTS LOCAL ENTERTAINMENT THE TOPICAL OGN

NEWS IN BRIEF

Nation's Monster Truck Rally Organizers Vow To Crush 100% Electric Cars By 2030

HOUSTON—Claiming the move was the only way to guarantee a fully renewable future of adrenaline-charged metal smashing, the nation's monster

IMAGE CREDIT: *"Nation's Monster Truck Rally Organizers Vow To Crush 100% Electric Cars By 2030," The Onion, March 1, 2021. [Online]. Available: https://www.theonion.com/nation-s-monster-truck-rally-organizers-vow-to-crush-10-1846366255.*

Progress?!?

☺

The 5G Virtuous Circle

IMAGE CREDIT: *M. Hayes and B. Zahnstecher, "The Virtuous Circle of 5G, IoT and Energy Harvesting [Cover Story]," in IEEE Power Electronics Magazine, vol. 8, no. 3, Sept. 2021.*

Progress!!!

A Quick Poll

Raise your hand if you think it is critical to mitigate losses of…

…1 W?

…1 mW?

…1 μW?

Disclaimer

There is neither any sponsored promotion nor bias toward any of the products/organizations mentioned in this talk.

Any vendor-specific content is provided for example purposes only.

The INGR Energy Efficiency Working Group

Much of this work is the result of the Energy Efficiency Working Group (EE WG) of the International Network Generations Roadmap (INGR).

Co-chairs: Francesco Carobolante, IoTissimo
Brian Zahnstecher, PowerRox

Contributors (alphabetically):

Steve Allen, pSemi/Murata
Mohamed-Slim Alouini, KAUST
Anirban Bandyopadhyay, GlobalFoundries
Emil Björnson, KTH Royal Institute of Tech
Kirk Bresniker, Hewlett Packard Enterprise
Rick Booth, Eridan Communications
Frederica Darema, former NSF & AFOSR
Paul Draxler, Stonecrest Consulting
Doug Kirkpatrick, Eridan Communications
Laurence McGarry, pSemi/Murata
Lin Nease, Hewlett Packard Enterprise
Bruce Nordman, Lawrence Berkeley National Lab
Magnus Olsson, Huawei

IMAGE CREDIT: IEEE Future Networks Initiative - Energy Efficiency Working Group, "Energy Efficiency, 2021 Edition" International Network Generations Roadmap (INGR), Apr. 9 2021.

Presenter

Brian Zahnstecher

Principal, PowerRox

bz@powerrox.com | www.PowerRox.com | (508) 847-5747 | Twitter: @PowerRoxLLC

LinkedIn: www.linkedin.com/in/zahnstecher

San Jose, CA

Brian Zahnstecher is a Sr. Member of the IEEE, Chair (Emeritus) of the IEEE SFBAC Power Electronics Society (PELS) awarded 2017 Best Chapter awards at the local/national/worldwide levels concurrently (an unprecedented achievement), sits on the Power Sources Manufacturers Association (PSMA) Board of Directors, is Co-founder & Co-chair of the PSMA Reliability Committee, Co-chair of the PSMA Energy Harvesting Committee, and is the Principal of PowerRox, where he focuses on power design, integration, system applications, OEM market penetration, market research/analysis, and private seminars for power electronics. He Co-chairs the IEEE Future Directions (formerly 5G) Initiative webinar series and is the founding Co-chair of the IEEE 5G Roadmap Energy Efficiency Working Group, authored the Group's position paper, and has lectured on this topic at major industry conferences.

He has successfully handled assignments in system design/architecting, AC/DC front-end power, EMC/EMI design/debug, embedded solutions, processor power, and digital power solutions for a variety of clients. He previously held positions in power electronics with industry leaders Emerson Network Power (now Advanced Energy), Cisco, and Hewlett-Packard, where he advised on best practices, oversaw product development, managed international teams, created/enhanced optimal workflows and test procedures, and designed and optimized voltage regulators. He has been a regular contributor to the industry as an invited keynote speaker, author, workshop participant, session host, roundtable moderator, and volunteer. He has over 15 years of industry experience and holds Master of Engineering and Bachelor of Science degrees from Worcester Polytechnic Institute.

Overview

- **Rx** The Global Energy Footprint
- **Rx** The Path to 1T Sensors
- **Rx** A Focus on Utilization
- **Rx** The True Cost of Power at the Edge
- **Rx** The 5G Energy Gap
- **Rx** The "Universal Currency" of Energy
- **Rx** Summary & Conclusions
- **Rx** Q & A

The Global Energy Footprint

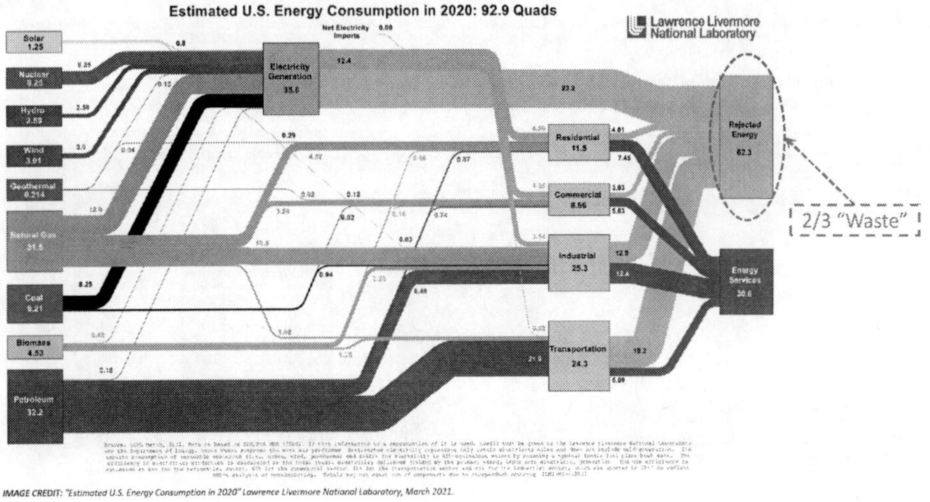

IMAGE CREDIT: "Estimated U.S. Energy Consumption in 2020" Lawrence Livermore National Laboratory, March 2021.

The Global Energy Footprint

Rx The Global Energy Pie

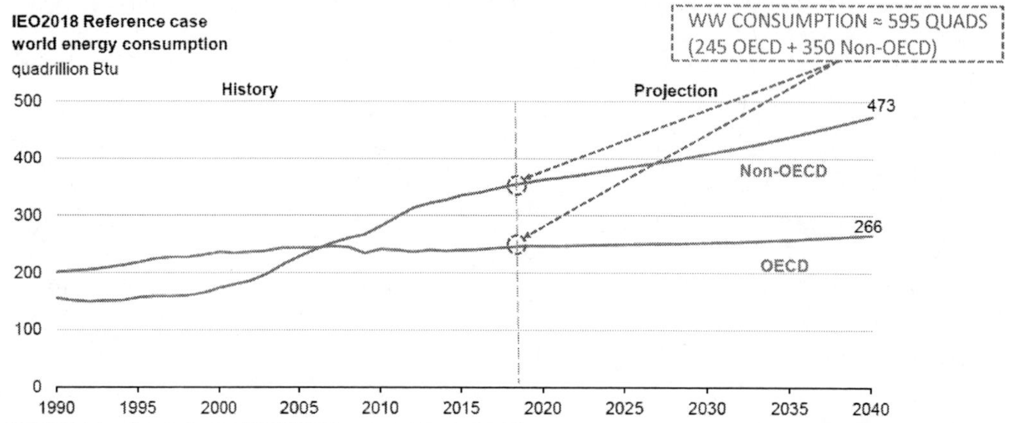

IMAGE CREDIT: Linda Capuano, "International Energy Outlook 2018 (IEO2018)," U.S. Energy Information Administration, July 24, 2018.

#SensorsConverge PowerRox © POWERROX LLC 2021 ALL INFORMATION SHALL BE CONSIDERED SPEAKER PROPERTY UNLESS OTHERWISE SUPERSEDED BY ANOTHER DOCUMENT. Sensors Converge 11

The Global Energy Footprint

Rx The Global Energy Pie

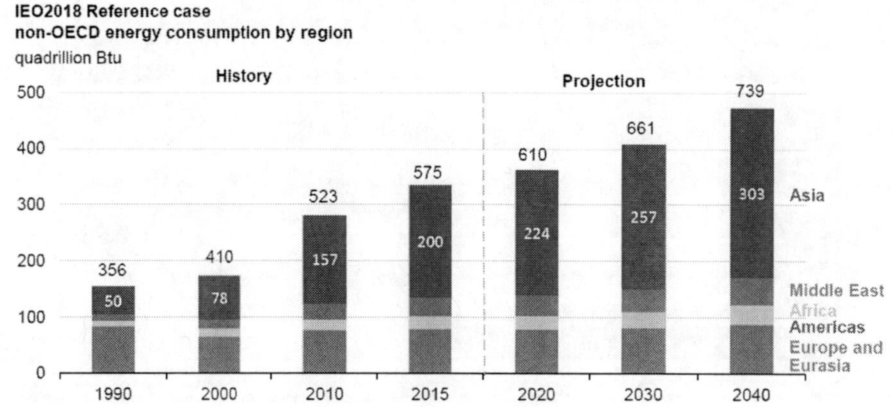

IMAGE CREDIT: Linda Capuano, "International Energy Outlook 2018 (IEO2018)," U.S. Energy Information Administration, July 24, 2018.

#SensorsConverge PowerRox © POWERROX LLC 2021 ALL INFORMATION SHALL BE CONSIDERED SPEAKER PROPERTY UNLESS OTHERWISE SUPERSEDED BY ANOTHER DOCUMENT. Sensors Converge 12

The Global Energy Footprint

℞ The Global Telecom Energy Pie

- The Network's Slice
  - WW ≈ 1,050 TWh ≈ 3.6 Quads ≈ 0.6% WW Energy

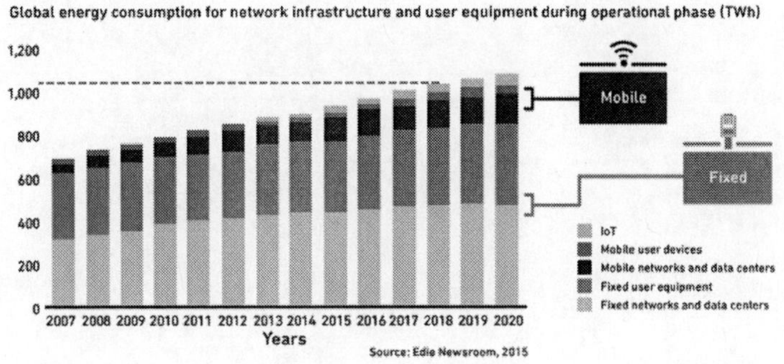

IMAGE CREDIT: David Schnaufer "Energy Efficiency In The Telecommunications Network," RF Globalnet, Posted 20 Jul 2016.

qorvo

The Global Energy Footprint

℞ The Global Telecom Energy Pie

- The Network's Pieces
  - A Generalization from 2011

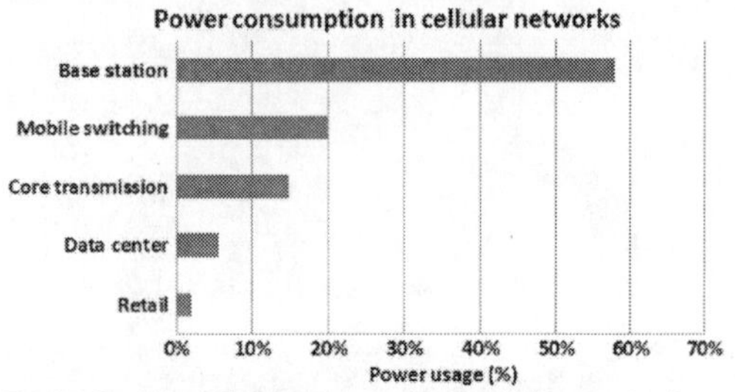

Fig. 1. Breakdown of energy consumption in cellular networks (Source: Vodafone [12]).

IMAGE CREDIT: J. Wu, Y. Zhang, M. Zukerman and E. K. Yung, "Energy-Efficient Base-Stations Sleep-Mode Techniques in Green Cellular Networks: A Survey," in IEEE Communications Surveys & Tutorials, vol. 17, no. 2, pp. 803-826, Second Quarter 2015.

ALL INFORMATION SHALL BE CONSIDERED SPEAKER PROPERTY UNLESS OTHERWISE SUPERSEDED BY ANOTHER DOCUMENT.

The Global Energy Footprint

R_x The Global Telecom Energy Pie

- The Network's Footprint

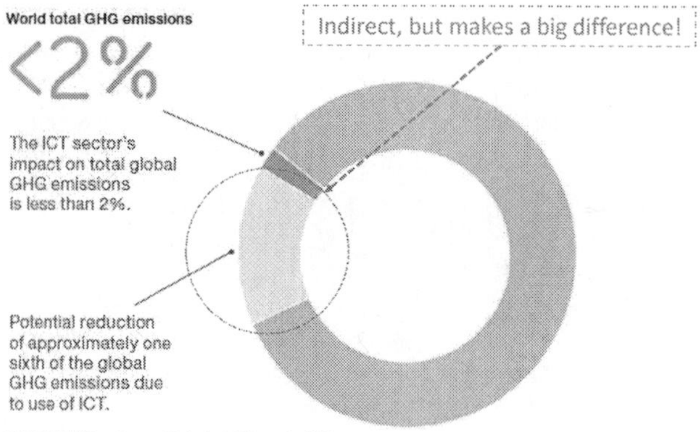

IMAGE CREDIT: "Ericsson Energy and Carbon Report," Ericsson, June 2014.

The Path to 1 T Sensors

R_x The Gratuitous 5G Slide

- The "Promise of 5G"

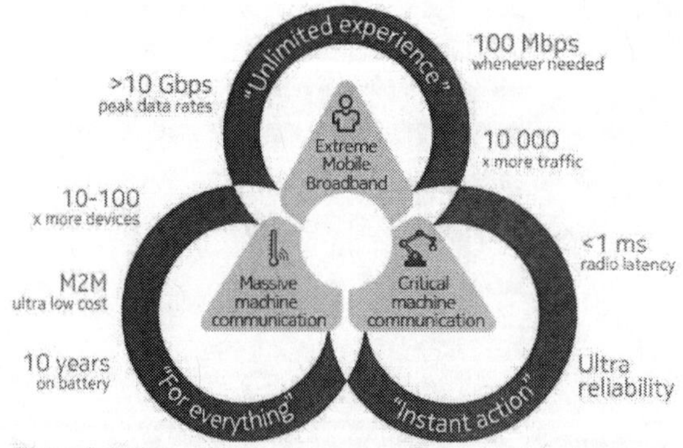

Figure 2. Heterogeneous use cases – diverse requirements

IMAGE CREDIT: "5G masterplan - 5 keys to create the new communications era," Nokia, 2016.

The Path to 1T Sensors

- **Rx** IoT provides comprehensive applications of new 5G technologies, promoting progress for all society.
- **Rx** Billions or Trillions of Edge Devices
  - Mobile Edge Computing (MEC)
  - Wireless Sensor Networks (WSN)
  - Internet of Things (IoT)
  - Industrial IoT (IIoT)
- **Rx** Cost of Power
  - CAPEX
  - OPEX (e.g. – fuel)

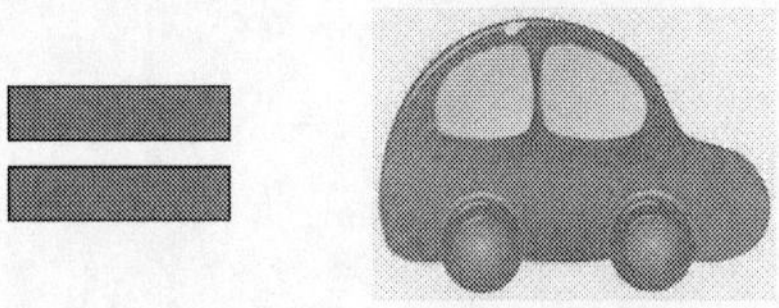

...much more to come on this.

The Path to 1T Sensors

- **Rx** Sensor Needs
  - 20-50 B IoT Devices, 1 T IoT Devices?!?...A *REALLY* Big Number
    - Not getting into IoT semantics here, but most folks agree there will be a whole lot of devices, sensor networks, etc. connected to some form of web/cloud interface.
    - A battery is commonly the limiting factor so the more energy that can be harvested from an ambient source, the more sensor/IoT device applications are enabled. 1T too LOW a number???
  - Accessibility
    - Harsh Environments
    - Inaccessible / Difficult to Access Sensors / Batteries
    - Monitoring Data on Steroids
    - Truly Permanent Installations

The Path to 1T Sensors

Rx Additional Goals

- Battery Mitigation
  - Garbage / Hazardous Materials
  - Replacement Efforts
    - Push For Rechargeable (Or Secondary) Battery Applications
  - Overall Design Effort (i.e. – Redundancy, Overprovisioning, Etc.)
  - Short-, Near-, & Long-Term Strategies

All we need is improved battery storage technology so we can go a really long time without having to plug-in and recharge, right?

WRONG!!!

#SensorsConverge PRx PowerRox © POWERROX LLC 2021 *ALL INFORMATION SHALL BE CONSIDERED SPEAKER PROPERTY UNLESS OTHERWISE SUPERSEDED BY ANOTHER DOCUMENT.* Sensors Converge 19

The Path to 1T Sensors

Rx Additional Goals

- Energy Harvesting
  - Waste = Opportunity
  - Many Energy Sources
  - Put Reclaimed Energy To Better Use
  - Reduce Infrastructure / CAPEX

"There is no such thing as waste heat…just underutilized energy recycling opportunities."

– Brian Zahnstecher

#SensorsConverge PRx PowerRox © POWERROX LLC 2021 *ALL INFORMATION SHALL BE CONSIDERED SPEAKER PROPERTY UNLESS OTHERWISE SUPERSEDED BY ANOTHER DOCUMENT.* Sensors Converge

The Path to 1T Sensors

R_x Application Challenges

- Size, Weight, & Power Consumption (SWaP)
- Motor Drives / Electrified Power Train
- Cost
- Amount of Data
  - VALUE of Data
- Security
- Slow Development / Qualification
- Mature Supply Chains

The Path to 1T Sensors

R_x Application Challenges

- Migration to the Gig Economy
  - Zero Ownership Model
  - Refurbishment
  - Increased Wear Out

The Path to 1 T Sensors

Rx Major Application Areas

- Autonomous Vehicles (AV)
  - The ultimate case study!
- Industrial Automation
- IoT / IIoT
- Smart Factory
- Smart Cities/Structures
- BLE Beacons

The Path to 1 T Sensors

Rx Autonomous Vehicles (AV)

- Data Analytics *(e.g. – Data Center)*
- Broadband Integration *(e.g. – Base Station)*
- On-board Sensor Networks *(e.g. – Ubiquitous Sensing)*
- Infotainment / IoT *(e.g. – Theater)*

The Path to 1T Sensors

*R*ₓ Autonomous Vehicles (AV)

- Really V2x

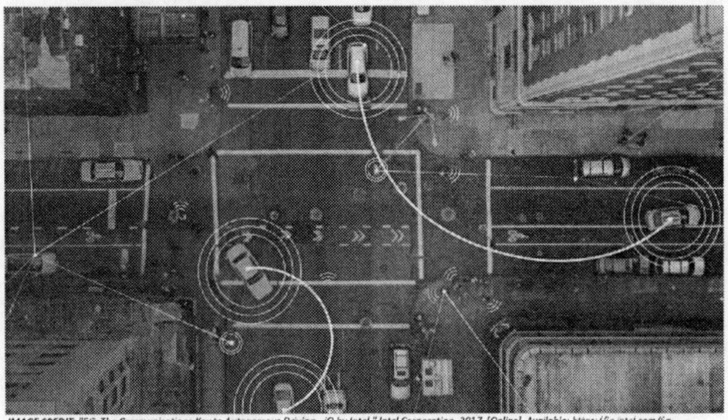

IMAGE CREDIT: "5G: The Communications Key to Autonomous Driving - iQ by Intel," Intel Corporation, 2017. [Online]. Available: https://iq.intel.com/5g-communications-key-autonomous-driving/.

The Path to 1T Sensors

*R*ₓ Autonomous Vehicles (AV)

- Data Analytics *(e.g. – Data Center)*
  - Artificial Intelligence (AI) / Machine Learning (ML)
    - Good? Bad? Both?!?
    - TinyML

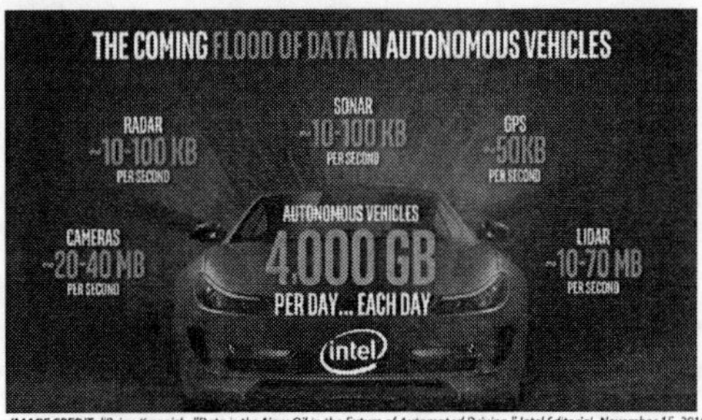

IMAGE CREDIT: "Brian Krzanich, "Data is the New Oil in the Future of Automated Driving," Intel Editorial, November 15, 2016.

Would you be willing to give up 30% range in exchange for your steering wheel?

The Path to 1 T Sensors

Rx Autonomous Vehicles (AV)

- Broadband Integration *(e.g. – Base Station)*
  - o Power Scales with Size of Base Station
  - o Smaller Power = More Dynamic
  - o React to Real-Time Traffic, Not Statistical Traffic Patterns
  - o V2V Vs. V2x
- FYI – Base Stations Consume 60-80% of the Global Energy Footprint of All ICT Equipment
  - o Dominated By Power Amplifier (PA)

IMAGE CREDIT: CDMA spectral efficiency - Wikipedia, 2016. [Online]. Available: https://en.wikipedia.org/wiki/CDMA_spectral_efficiency.

#SensorsConverge PowerRox © POWERROX LLC 2021 ALL INFORMATION SHALL BE CONSIDERED SPEAKER PROPERTY UNLESS OTHERWISE SUPERSEDED BY ANOTHER DOCUMENT. Sensors Converge 27

The Path to 1 T Sensors

Rx Autonomous Vehicles (AV)

- On-board Sensor Networks *(e.g. – Ubiquitous Sensing)*
  - o Radar / Lidar
  - o Tire Pressure Monitoring System (TPMS)
  - o Oil/Water Temperatures
  - o Cameras
  - o Fuel Level
  - o Passenger Telemetry
  - o Driver Monitoring
  - o Environmental Monitoring
  - o Preventative Maintenance

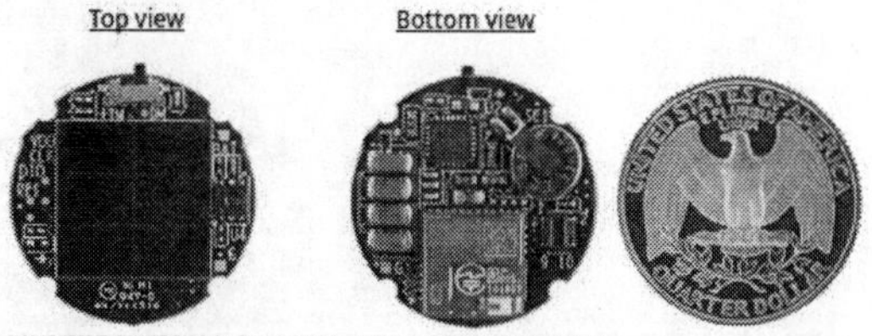

IMAGE CREDIT: CYALKIT-E02 Solar-Powered BLE Sensor Beacon Reference Design Kit (RDK) = http://www.cypress.com/documentation/development-kitsboards/cyalkit-e02-solar-powered-ble-sensor-beacon-reference-design.

#SensorsConverge PowerRox © POWERROX LLC 2021 ALL INFORMATION SHALL BE CONSIDERED SPEAKER PROPERTY UNLESS OTHERWISE SUPERSEDED BY ANOTHER DOCUMENT. Sensors Converge 28

The Path to 1 T Sensors

*R*x Autonomous Vehicles (AV)

- On-board Sensor Networks *(e.g. – Ubiquitous Sensing)*
  - Not All Applications Low Latency and/or High Bandwidth
    - ➢ Infrequent, Low Bandwidth System Data = Low Power
      - Many low power, low bandwidth protocols.
    - ➢ Sleep Mode Vs. Subthreshold Micros
    - ➢ More Power Vs. Latency Discussion/Data Required
  - *Keeping the Data at the Edge*

The Path to 1 T Sensors

*R*x Autonomous Vehicles (AV)

- Infotainment / IoT *(e.g. – Theater)*
  - Mobile Edge Computing (MEC) OR "The Edge"
    - ➢ User Equipment (UE) / IoT Devices
    - ➢ Edge Buffering

IMAGE CREDIT: https://www.youtube.com/watch?v=YVOdp9qf7uu

No, that is *THE* Edge!

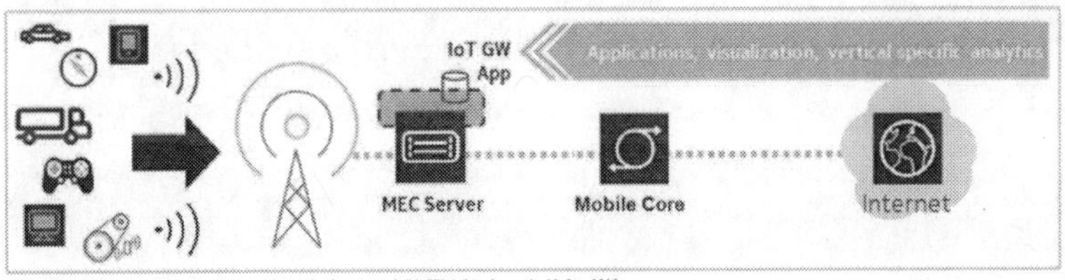

IMAGE CREDIT: ETSI, Mobile Edge Computing, A key technology towards 5G, ETSI White Paper No. 11, Sep. 2015.

PowerRox © POWERROX LLC 2021
ALL INFORMATION SHALL BE CONSIDERED SPEAKER PROPERTY UNLESS OTHERWISE SUPERSEDED BY ANOTHER DOCUMENT.

The Path to 1T Sensors

Rx The 5G (& Beyond) Perfect Storm

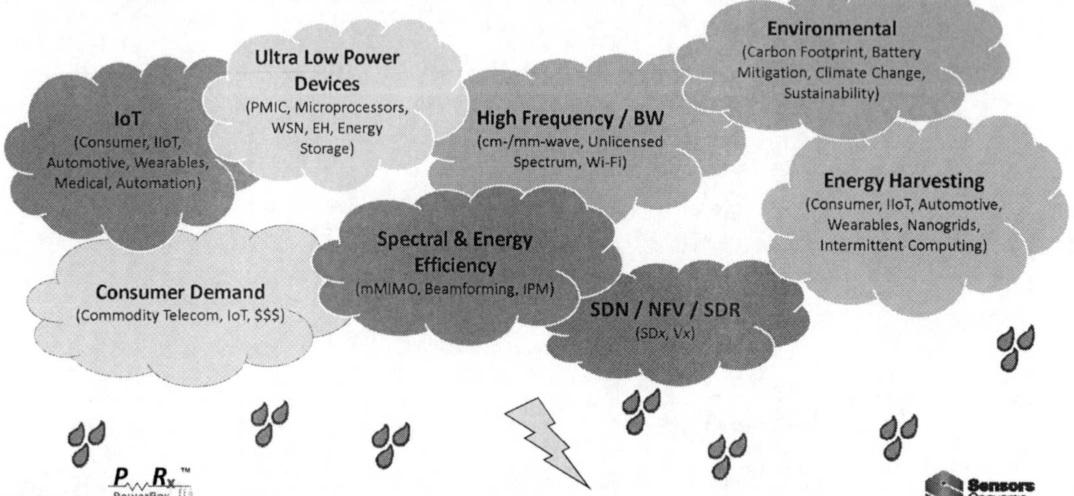

A Focus on Utilization

Rx It is all about utilization!

- Rarely Does Your Peak Power Occur at the Peak Point on the Efficiency Curve
- Even if it Does, Your Load is Typically Transient in Nature
- The Real Low-Hanging Fruit is Intelligent Power Management (IPM)
  - Characterize Your Systems/Loads To Understand Where Operating on Load Curve
    - More Accurate Thermal Modeling (*and everything that comes with it*)
  - Put the Maniacal Focus on *Reducing* the System Power Budget
  - Do NOT Put the Maniacal Focus on *Increasing* the Available Power

A Focus on Utilization

Rx Defining IPM

- Google to the Rescue:
  - "Intelligent Power Management (IPM) is a combination of hardware and software that optimizes the distribution and use of electrical power in computer systems and data centers." (http://searchdatacenter.techtarget.com/definition/intelligent-power-management-IPM)
- This is More of a Frame of Mind Than Anything Else

#SensorsConverge PowerRox © POWERROX LLC 2021 ALL INFORMATION SHALL BE CONSIDERED SPEAKER PROPERTY UNLESS OTHERWISE SUPERSEDED BY ANOTHER DOCUMENT. Sensors Converge 33

A Focus on Utilization

Rx An In-Depth Look at Power Supply Efficiency

- If optimizing efficiency is important, ...
  - ...then utilization (area under the efficiency curve) is what counts!
  - ...then you can more realistically predict/model power usage.
  - ...then you have a better idea of what improvements in system-level power conversion have actual value.
  - ...then you are better enabled to provide cost benefit analyses at all levels.
  - ...then you will have much better input for your SW people to implement more intelligent power management algorithms.

FYI: If this point is getting redundant to the point of nausea, then GOOD, we are making progress!

#SensorsConverge PowerRox © POWERROX LLC 2021 ALL INFORMATION SHALL BE CONSIDERED SPEAKER PROPERTY UNLESS OTHERWISE SUPERSEDED BY ANOTHER DOCUMENT. Sensors Converge 34

A Focus on Utilization

℞ All Roads Lead to $$$
- CAPEX, OPEX, Application
- Everything ends up in *SOMEONE's* profit/loss columns eventually.
- Decision-making from the smallest system design all the way to the worldwide IT) architectural level must take this into consideration.

℞ Who is your customer?
- *HINT*: this is a loaded question.
- Perhaps a better way to state:
  - o *What are their motivations?*
    - ➤ *FYI – the answer to this nearly always leads back to $$$*
  - o *How do they align (or not) with yours?*

A Focus on Utilization

Does anyone know what THE MOST efficient power conversion solution in the world is?

(FYI – this is not a subjective question.)

CLUE: A better question "Does anyone know which power conversion device dissipates the least heat?"

Does anyone know what THE SECOND MOST efficient power conversion solution in the world is?

The True Cost of Power at the Edge

*R*x Time for a Quick Thought Experiment

- What is the TRUE cost of 1 W?
- What is the TRUE cost of 1 mW?
- The Big Picture

The True Cost of Power at the Edge

*R*x What is the TRUE cost of 1 W?

NOTE: # % represents efficiency loss due to power conversion stage.

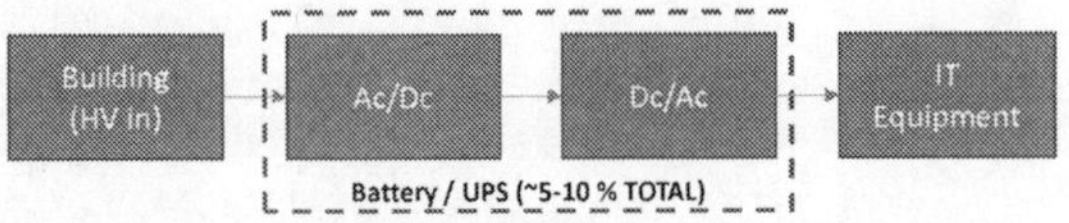

You have lost ~5-10 % of your power just getting from the door to your system.

EFFICIENCY FOR THIS STAGE = ~95 % (BEST-CASE)

SERVER EXAMPLE (Ac Input)

You have lost ~15-32 % of your power getting from the system input to the load.

EFFICIENCY FOR THIS STAGE = ~85 % (BEST-CASE)

FROM POWER PLANT TO LOAD = 0.92 x 0.95 x 0.85 = ~74 % (BEST-CASE)
FYI = ~53 % (WORST-CASE)

The True Cost of Power at the Edge

Rx What is the TRUE cost of 1 W?

- So for each 1 W burned at the IT load alone, 1.4-1.9 W need to be generated at the power plant.

- When you do the rest of the calculations for typical data to account for the infrastructure, there is an additional cost of 1.1-2.5 W. (In general, infrastructure equipment efficiency will be worse than IT equipment.)

So the true cost of *EACH 1 W* of IT load requires 2.5-4.4 X of power generated at the power plant!!!

The True Cost of Power at the Edge

Rx What is the TRUE cost of 1 mW?

- Now, let us consider a tiny, wireless IoT device.
  - o Transmission of Power in Base Station
    - ➢ From Grid to RF Transmitter
  - o Transmission of Data to UE (i.e. – Smartphone)
    - ➢ From Base Station RF Transmitter to UI RF Receiver

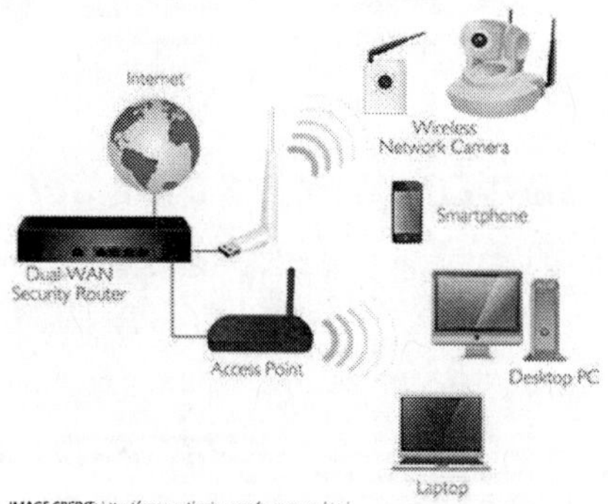

IMAGE CREDIT: http://www.eetherika.com/ip_camera.html

The True Cost of Power at the Edge

$\underline{R_x}$ What is the TRUE cost of 1 mW?

BASE STATION EXAMPLE

POWER (~20-25 %) → OVERHEAD (~10-20 %) → BASEBAND UNIT (BBU) (~20-30 %) → POWER AMP (PA) (~80-90 %) → Tx ANTENNA (~50 %) =

[Combined Power Solution & Cooling]

You have lost ~94-98 % of your power getting from grid to the transmitting antenna.

EFFICIENCY FOR THIS STAGE = ~6 % (BEST-CASE)

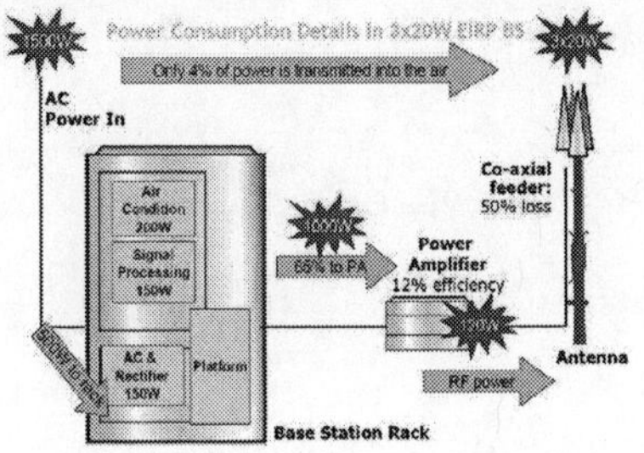

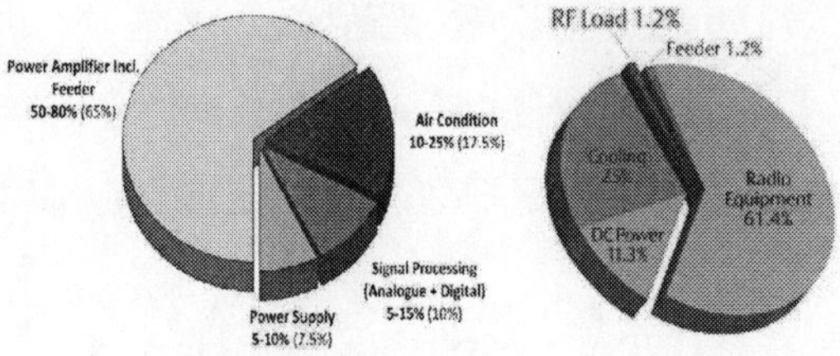

IMAGES CREDIT: Alberto Conte, "Power consumption of base stations," Alcatel-Lucent Bell Labs France, TREND Plenary meeting, Ghent, 14-15/02/2012

#SensorsConverge PowerRox © POWERROX LLC 2021 *ALL INFORMATION SHALL BE CONSIDERED SPEAKER PROPERTY UNLESS OTHERWISE SUPERSEDED BY ANOTHER DOCUMENT.* Sensors Converge 41

The True Cost of Power at the Edge

$\underline{R_x}$ What is the TRUE cost of 1 mW?

SMARTPHONE EXAMPLE

(Modified) Friis Transmission Equation

$$P_R = \frac{P_T G_T G_R c^2}{(4\pi R f)^2}$$

SOURCE: Friis Equation - (aka Friis Transmission Formula) = http://www.antenna-theory.com/basics/friis.php

- 0 dBm = 1 mW reference
- 10 dBm per power order of magnitude
- *Rx power falls dramatically with distance and/or frequency*

IMAGE CREDIT: https://commons.wikimedia.org/wiki/File:Base_transceiver_station.jpg

IMAGE CREDIT: https://www.flickr.com/photos/alpat/8789930518

You have lost ~99.9 % of your power transmitting from base station to smartphone.

EFFICIENCY FOR THIS STAGE = ~0.1 % (BEST-CASE)

#SensorsConverge PowerRox © POWERROX LLC 2021 *ALL INFORMATION SHALL BE CONSIDERED SPEAKER PROPERTY UNLESS OTHERWISE SUPERSEDED BY ANOTHER DOCUMENT.* Sensors Converge 42

The True Cost of Power at the Edge

Rx What is the TRUE cost of 1 mW?

- So for each 1 mW of received power at the device (i.e. – edge, mote, etc.), *1-2 W* need to be transmitted by the base station.
- Each 1 W of transmit power will draw of *16.7-50 W* at the input of the base station.
- From the utility grid, we lose 8-15 % of our power in transmission from power plant to the base station.

So the true cost of *EACH 1 mW* of received data at the edge requires *~18,000 x-60,000 x (18-60 W)* of power generated at the power plant! plant!

Now, multiply that by 10s of billions or even 1 T devices!!!

The True Cost of Power at the Edge

Rx What is the Entire Power Value Chain (PVC)?

- The Complete Power Picture from End-to-End
- Some Examples:
  - Chip → Power Subsystem → Battery → Adapter → Home → Grid → Power Plant
  - Display → PMIC → Battery → Adapter → Home → Grid → Power Plant
  - Antenna → SoC → PMIC → Battery → Adapter → Home → Grid → Power Plant
  - ASIC → Power Subsystem → System → Rack → Data Center → Grid → Power Plant
  - ASIC → Advanced Non-isolated DC/DC (i.e. – VRM) → Upstream Non-isolated DC/DC → Isolated DC/DC → Front-end → PDU → UPS → Grid/Generator → Power Plant
  - ASIC → Advanced Non-isolated DC/DC (i.e. – VRM) → Upstream Non-isolated DC/DC → Battery → Alternator → Motor → Motor Drive → FUEL (fossil or renewable)

The True Cost of Power at the Edge

$\underline{R}_x$ What is the Entire Power Value Chain (PVC)?

- The Complete Power Picture from End-to-End

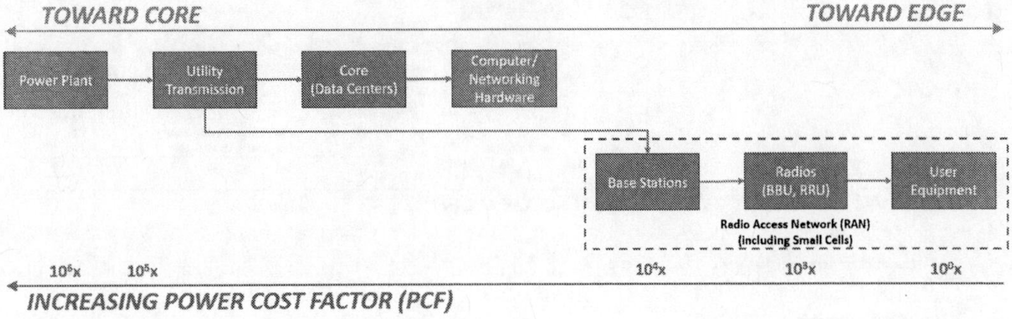

IMAGE CREDIT: *B. Zahnstecher, "The 5G Energy Gap [Expert View]," in IEEE Power Electronics Magazine, vol. 6, no. 4, pp. 64-67, Dec. 2019.*

The True Cost of Power at the Edge

$\underline{R}_x$ The Power Value Chain (PVC)

- *Energy flow across all the distribution/conversion steps between source and source and load.*

$\underline{R}_x$ The Power Cost Factor (PCF)

- *Unitless number to assess the overall cost of energy utilization at any given given point within the PVC.*

The True Cost of Power at the Edge

Rx The 5G PVC

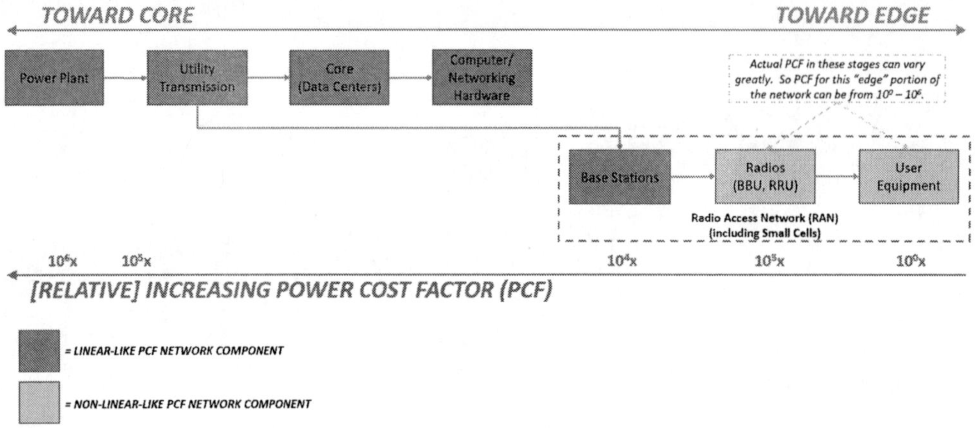

IMAGE CREDIT: IEEE Future Networks Initiative - Energy Efficiency Working Group, "Energy Efficiency - 1st Edition White Paper," International Network Generations Roadmap (INGR), Apr. 2020.

The 5G Energy Gap

Rx The Disproportionate Impact of Tiny Power on Big Power

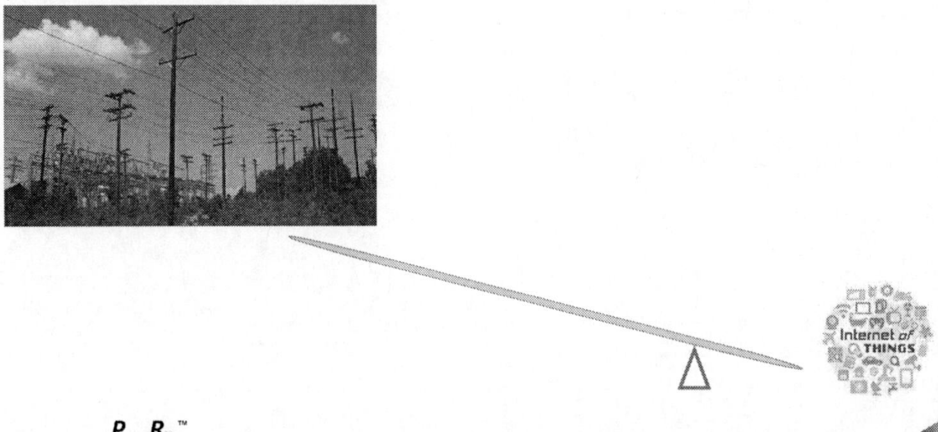

The 5G Energy Gap

Rx The 5G Energy Gap (5GEG)

- *Disparity between available energy (i.e. – sources) and demand (i.e. – loads) loads) of the [mostly] "micro-power" devices representing the majority of majority of "things" in the highly-scalable edge space of the network.*

Rx The 5G Economic Gap (5GEcG)

- *Disparity between available power a system can deliver (i.e. – system allocation) and the increasing load demands on its outputs.*

So hold on a second...what is the difference between the two of these?

The 5G Energy Gap

Rx The 5G Energy Gap (5GEG)

- *Power Cost Factor (PCF)* is what the 5G Energy Gap is all about...read the press!

IMAGE CREDIT: Monroe, Jazz, "Public Enemy Announce New Album, Return to Def Jam," Pitchfork, August 28, 2020. [Online]. Available: https://pitchfork.com/news/public-enemy-announce-new-album-return-to-def-jam/.

Expert View

by [redacted]

The 5G Energy Gap

There is no shortage of hype and excitement when it comes to discussions about the next-generation cellular network, now in the process of production deployment worldwide, known as *5G* (or *5G New Radio* or the *Third Generation Partnership Project Release 15 standard* [1], to be more accurate). Combine this with all of the marketing projections for the many billions of (or even trillions, depending on your definition) smart devices, wearables, trackers, marriage of a massive network with an explosion of devices to reshape our daily lives. But hold on a second: Almost every marketing projection and "killer app" (apologies for this overused buzzword) starts with an assumption that has the potential to be an absolutely fatal flaw. It certainly makes this author

Like most things in the world of electronics, the viability of the application eventually leads to power requirements and energy utilization.

most situations, these critical factors are not given serious, proper consideration until far too late in the deployment process, and 5G is no exception to that. The fatal flaw is that most of the folks in the information and communications technology ecosystem, from mobile network operators to those deploying

IMAGE CREDIT: B. Zahnstecher, "The 5G Energy Gap [Expert View]," in IEEE Power Electronics Magazine, vol. 6, no. 4, pp. 64-67, Dec. 2019.

The 5G Energy Gap

*R*x The 5G Derate Factor (5GDF)

- *Scaling factor for the application of technical and economic risk factors to the factors to the ideal 5G network deployment model that will reduce the optimal, maximum designed capabilities of a network due to energy-limited limited (5GEG) and/or economically-limited (5GEcG) and/or socioeconomically-limited (5GEqG) factors.*

Remember Power Usage Effectiveness (PUE) from the data center world?

The 5G Energy Gap

*R*x The 5G Derate Factor (5GDF)

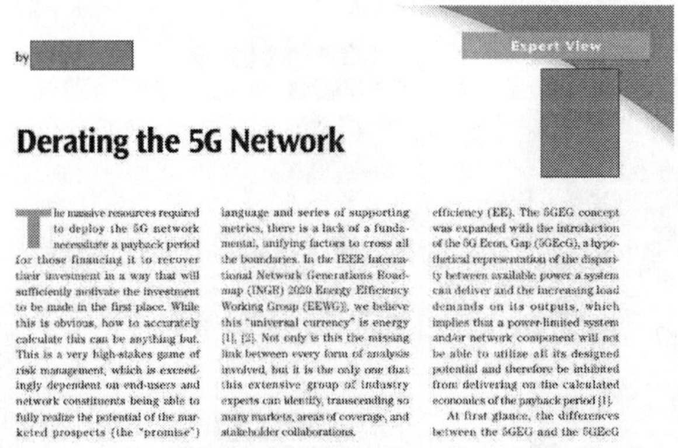

by [redacted]

Expert View

Derating the 5G Network

The massive resources required to deploy the 5G network necessitate a payback period for those financing it to recover their investment in a way that will sufficiently motivate the investment to be made in the first place. While this is obvious, how to accurately calculate this can be anything but. This is a very high-stakes game of risk management, which is exceedingly dependent on end-users and network constituents being able to fully realize the potential of the marketed prospects (the "promise") language and series of supporting metrics, there is a lack of a fundamental, unifying factors to cross all the boundaries. In the IEEE International Network Generations Roadmap (INGR) 2020 Energy Efficiency Working Group (EEWG), we believe this "universal currency" is energy [1], [2]. Not only is this the missing link between every form of analysis involved, but it is the only one that this extensive group of industry experts can identify, transcending so many markets, areas of coverage, and stakeholder collaborations.

efficiency (EE). The 5GEG concept was expanded with the introduction of the 5G Econ. Gap (5GEcG), a hypothetical representation of the disparity between available power a system can deliver and the increasing load demands on its outputs, which implies that a power-limited system and/or network component will not be able to utilize all its designed potential and therefore be inhibited from delivering on the calculated economics of the payback period [1].

At first glance, the differences between the 5GEG and the 5GEcG

IMAGE CREDIT: B. Zahnstecher, "Derating the 5G Network [Expert View]," in IEEE Power Electronics Magazine, vol. 8, no. 1, pp. 69-73, Mar. 2021.

The 5G Energy Gap

Rx The 5G Equality Gap (5GEqG)

- *Socioeconomic disparity between those able to adapt to unanticipated underperformance due to energy-limited (5GEG) and/or economically-limited limited (5GEcG) factors, and those that will not have the resources to do so. do so.*

The "Universal Currency" of Energy

Rx In the beginning...

- a block diagram was created to facilitate working with other working groups (WG) to clearly illustrate relationships between key stakeholders and network constituents.

Rx This became...

- the IEEE INGR EE WG Systems-of-Systems (SoS) Block Diagram.

Rx Thus resulting in...

- a tool to drive the EE WG roadmap chapter creation methodology.

The "Universal Currency" of Energy

- **Rx** How can all the black boxes "talk" to each other?
  - Given the full spectrum of stakeholders and contributors to the SoS, we cannot connect a variety of technical, business, and legislative black boxes in a meaningful way to form a PVC for analysis.
  - ...or can we?!?
- **Rx** We Must Find a "Universal Currency"
  - Need Metric(s) Translating Random Inputs Into Common Outputs
  - $$$ is a good one...
  - ...but ENERGY is better!!!

Summary & Conclusions

- **Rx** Tiny Devices at Scale Can Cause BIG Problems, Especially Combined in the Connected Vehicle
- **Rx** Driving energy efficiency optimization is not a "nice-to-have" and can be critical to enabling many applications.
- **Rx** Metrics such as PCF and 5GDF can help simplify complex analyses and enable stakeholders to collaborate constructively.
- **Rx** In the 5G world, normalizing all to the "common currency" of energy is the only way to enable complex technical/business analyses to coexist.

Summary & Conclusions

...and never forget the true motivation and importance of improved efficiency and power savings...

...I know I never do!

A Closing Poll

Raise your hand if you think it is critical to mitigate losses of...

...1 W?

...1 mW?

...1 μW?

Q & A

P Rx ™
PowerRox

Thanks a lot for your time and attention!

Any questions and/or comments?

References

- "Nation's Monster Truck Rally Organizers Vow To Crush 100% Electric Cars By 2030," The Onion, March 1, 2021. [Online]. Available: https://www.theonion.com/nation-s-monster-truck-rally-organizers-vow-to-crush-10-1846366255.
- M. Hayes and B. Zahnstecher, "The Virtuous Circle of 5G, IoT and Energy Harvesting [Cover Story]," in IEEE Power Electronics Magazine, vol. 8, no. 3, Sept. 2021.
- IEEE Future Networks Initiative - Energy Efficiency Working Group, "Energy Efficiency, 2021 Edition" International Network Generations Roadmap (INGR), Apr. 9 2021.
- "Estimated U.S. Energy Consumption in 2020," Lawrence Livermore National Laboratory, March 2021.
- Linda Capuano, "International Energy Outlook 2018 (IEO2018)," U.S. Energy Information Administration, July 24, 2018.
- David Schnaufer "Energy Efficiency In The Telecommunications Network," RF Globalnet, Posted 20 Jul 2016.
- J. Wu, Y. Zhang, M. Zukerman and E. K. Yung, "Energy-Efficient Base-Stations Sleep-Mode Techniques in Green Cellular Networks: A Survey," in IEEE Communications Surveys & Tutorials, vol. 17, no. 2, pp. 803-826, Second Quarter 2015.
- "Ericsson Energy and Carbon Report," Ericsson, June 2014.
- "5G masterplan - 5 keys to create the new communications era.," Nokia, 2016.
- *"5G: The Communications Key to Autonomous Driving - iQ by Intel," Intel Corporation, 2017. [Online]. Available: https://iq.intel.com/5g-communications-key-autonomous-driving/.*
- Brian Krzanich, "Data is the New Oil in the Future of Automated Driving," Intel Editorial, November 15, 2016.
- CDMA spectral efficiency - Wikipedia, 2016. [Online]. Available: https://en.wikipedia.org/wiki/CDMA_spectral_efficiency.
- CYALKIT-E02 Solar-Powered BLE Sensor Beacon Reference Design Kit (RDK) = http://www.cypress.com/documentation/development-kitsboards/cyalkit-e02-solar-powered-ble-sensor-beacon-reference-design.
- ETSI, Mobile Edge Computing, A key technology towards 5G, ETSI White Paper No. 11, Sep. 2015.
- Alberto Conte, "Power consumption of base stations," Alcatel-Lucent Bell Labs France, TREND Plenary meeting, Ghent, 14-15/02/2012.
- Friis Equation - (aka Friis Transmission Formula) = http://www.antenna-theory.com/basics/friis.php
- B. Zahnstecher, "The 5G Energy Gap [Expert View]," in IEEE Power Electronics Magazine, vol. 6, no. 4, pp. 64-67, Dec. 2019.
- IEEE Future Networks Initiative - Energy Efficiency Working Group, "Energy Efficiency - 1st Edition White Paper," International Network Generations Roadmap (INGR), Apr. 2020.
- IEEE Future Networks Initiative - Energy Efficiency Working Group, "HOW TO UNDERSTAND AND APPLY THE IEEE INGR ENERGY EFFICIENCY (EE) WG SYSTEMS OF SYSTEMS (SoS) BLOCK DIAGRAM TEMPLATES," International Network Generations Roadmap (INGR) Guidance Document, Sept. 2020.
- B. Zahnstecher, "Derating the 5G Network [Expert View]," in IEEE Power Electronics Magazine, vol. 8, no. 1, pp. 69-73, Mar. 2021.

Sensors Converge

Practical Learnings Applying Edge AI/ML to Innovate Commercial IoT Sensing Devices

September 21-23, 2021 | San Jose, CA

Presenter: Chris Rogers, CEO/Founder - SensiML

#SensorsConverge

Introduction

- **SensiML is a software tools company for AI at the IoT edge**
  - Smart sensor models running directly on embedded processors
  - AutoML code-gen 'teaching' the desired output from labeled data
  - Models as small as 10KB executing on 8/16/32-bit platforms
- **Former Intel AI software tool and team now hardware independent**
  - Started in 2012, launched originally by Intel in 2016, spun-off in 2017
- **Experience across a broad array of embedded sensing applications**
  - Consumer IoT, Wearables, Industrial Sensing, Agriculture, Smart Building, Healthcare
  - Partners and supported platforms include Arm, Intel, NXP, Microchip Technologies, Nordic Semiconductor, QuickLogic, Silicon Labs, and ST Microelectronics
- **Chris Rogers - personal background**
  - Former test & measurement engineer now building ML sensor software
  - 20 years at Intel; 30-year passion for developing embedded sensing applications

#SensorsConverge

Sensors Converge

The Evolution of Sensor Processing

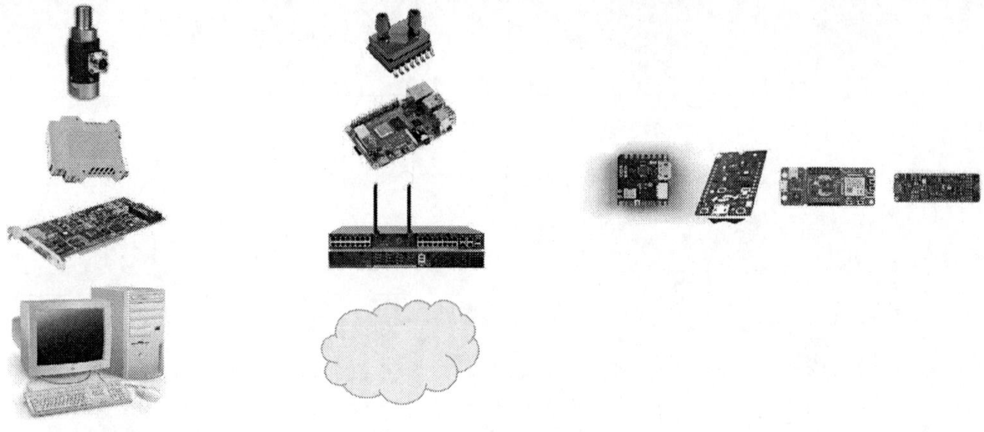

2000 **2015** **2020**

#SensorsConverge

Sensors Converge

Edge AI/ML Sensing Applications

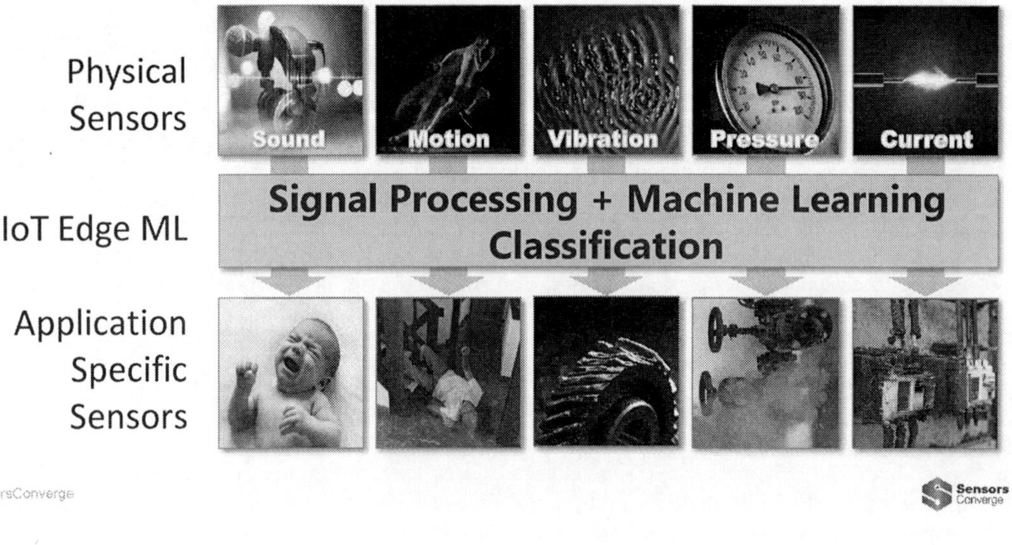

#SensorsConverge

Sensors Converge

Limitless Applications for ML at the IoT Edge

Below is just a sampling of those SensiML has worked on:

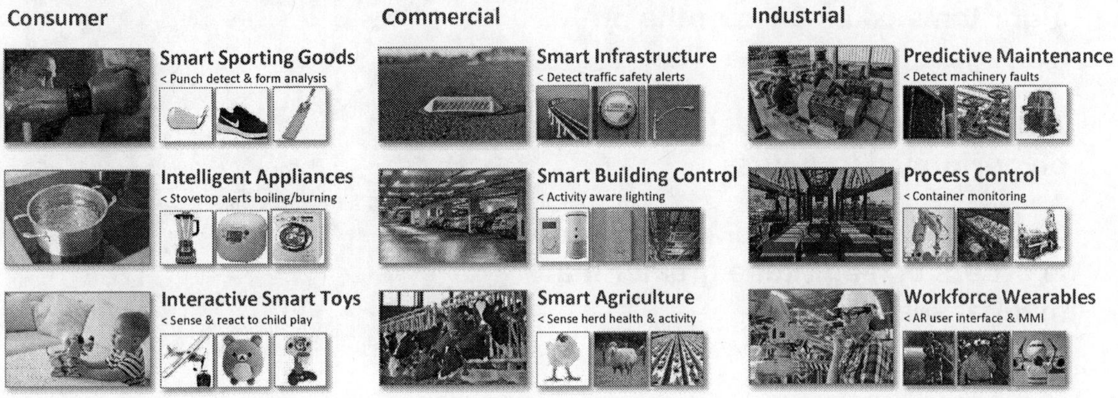

#SensorsConverge

Sensors Converge

Insight #1: ML Goes Deeper than Deep Learning

- **Deep Learning is just one class of ML algorithm**
- **Best algorithm: The one that provides desired accuracy for least computing resources**
- **Choosing an optimized ML algorithm is especially important for IoT edge applications**

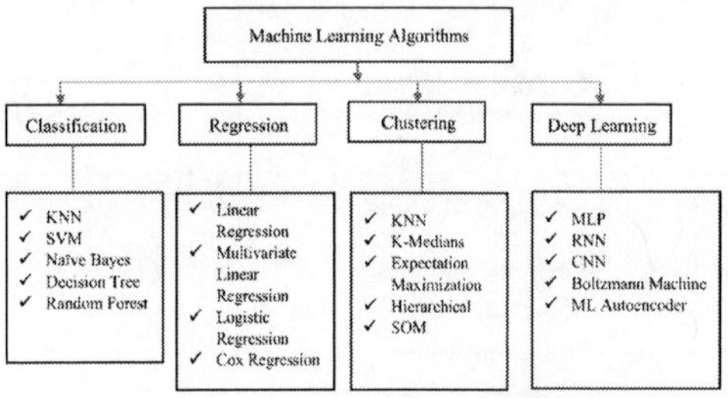

#SensorsConverge

Sensors Converge

Insight #2: AutoML will Supplant Hand-Coding

- **Hand-coding embedded sensor algorithms takes 6-9 months on average**
- **AutoML algorithm development can be performed in hours**
- **Search space for AutoML optimization is orders of magnitude greater than manual search**

#SensorsConverge

Sensors Converge

AutoML Machine Learning Model Development

Capture Data

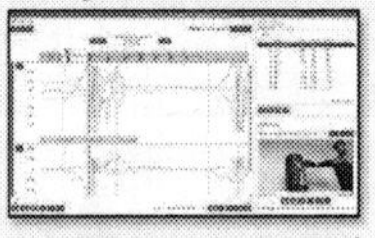

SensiML Data Capture Lab

Time: **Hours to Weeks**
(Depending on application data collection complexity)

Skill: **Domain Expertise**
(As required to collect and label events of interest)

Build Model

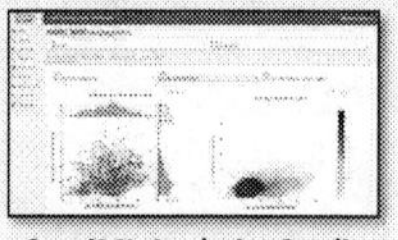

SensiML Analytics Studio

Time: **Minutes to Hours**
(Depending on degree of model control exerted)

Skill: **None**
(Full AutoML)
Basic ML Concepts
(Advanced UI tuning)
Python Programming
(Full pipeline control)

Test Device

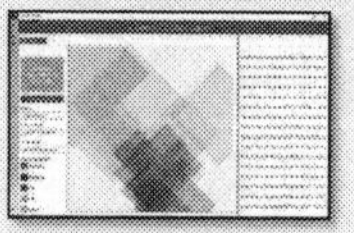

SensiML TestApp

Time: **Minutes to Weeks**
(Depending on app code integration needs)

Skill: **None**
(Binary firmware with auto generated I/O wrapper code)
Embedding Programming
(Integration of SensiML library or C source with user code)

#SensorsConverge

Sensors Converge

ML is Not Magic: Relies on High Quality Datasets

Common But Avoidable Issues:

- **Insufficient sample size**
- **Mislabeled data**
- **Insufficient metadata**
- **Overfitting**
- **Omitted conditions / variance**

#SensorsConverge

Sensors Converge

Example: Digital Pedometers in the Real-World

Digital Pedometer Step Counting: Lab algorithm didn't anticipate a number of real-world corner cases

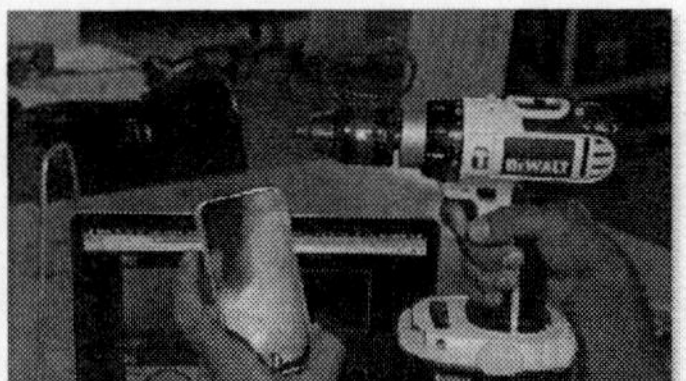

One major vendor had 60 engineers devoted to step counting sensor algorithm development at its peak

Imagine scaling this to many exercises and activities needed to differentiate today

#SensorsConverge

Sensors Converge

Example: Smart Factory Predictive Maintenance

- Customer sought to build a proof-of-concept for predictive maintenance, machine faults, and operational status
- Reconfigurable kit built to simulate many conditions
- Collected GBs of data
- Why? Failed to account for large assembly tolerances

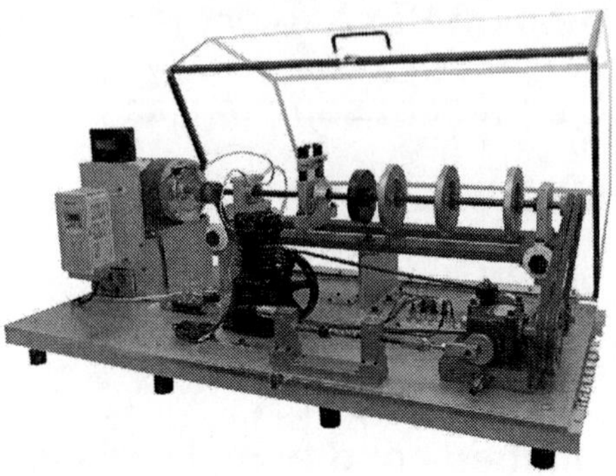

#SensorsConverge

Sensors Converge

Example: Simple Demo Application

- Simple self-contained demo
- Worked well in the lab, at customers, so we shipped kits to our worldwide sales teams…
- Geo teams reported the demo didn't work!
- What happened?
- Model behavior changed due to 100V/50Hz vs. 115V/60Hz AC power

#SensorsConverge

Sensors Converge

Insight #3: Prepare a Data Collection Plan Upfront

- **Consider all potential sources of variance for your application**
- **Systematically work through each variance source and how to account for it**
- **Include the application domain experts in the process**
- **Unaccounted variance often manifests as noise and error in your predictive model**
  - Reduces model accuracy
  - Increases training data requirements
- **Common issue for teams new to ML: Expecting too much from existing datasets**
  - Historical data rarely collected with supervised ML modeling in mind
  - Omits key information that explains input>output behavior
- **Equally problematic: Data collection without upfront test protocol planning**

#SensorsConverge

Sensors Converge

Smart Edge AI Test Plan Template

- **Desired Inference Classifications**
- **Intended Variance Sources**
- **Unintended Variance Sources**
- **Metadata**
- **Labels**
- **Sensor Input Details**

Smart Edge AI Test Plan: Rotating Machinery – Predictive Maintenance Smart Sensor		
Revision: 1.0	**Last Revised:** 09/15/2021	**By:** SensiML AE Team
Application Summary: Automated fault detection for industrial rotating machinery demonstrated on V-TEK MVAT-02 machine vibration analysis trainer.		

SensiML Test Plan Template 1.0, ©2020 SensiML Corporation

Desired Inference Classifications				
Categorical Variable (SensiML Event Group)	Class 1 (SensiML Event 1)	Class 2 (SensiML Event 2)	Class 3 (SensiML Event 3)	Class 4 (SensiML Event 4)
Must Include				
Bearing Fault	Good Bearing	Faulty Bearing		
Workload Rotor	None	Balanced	Imbalanced	Cocked
Machine State	Off	On		

Available at: https://sensiml.com/automl-whitepaper

#SensorsConverge

Sensors Converge

Insight #4: Stage Your Dataset Collection Effort

- Expect to learn something unexpected
- At SensiML, we always iterate data collection starting with 10-30 samples initially
- Don't try to cover all the variance at once
- Isolate as many variables as possible initially to reduce dimensionality
- Incrementally add them with each iteration of data collection
- Look at the data, run early models to explore results

Incremental data collection far better than assuming you have got it 100% right upfront

#SensorsConverge

Sensors Converge

Insight #5: Plan for Dataset Reuse

- Much time/effort will go into collecting your application-specific ML dataset
- Ensure it is enduring and reusable
- Consider sensor location changes which can impact signal response
- Use high resolution and sample rates
- Capture video of data collection
- Synchronize video to data

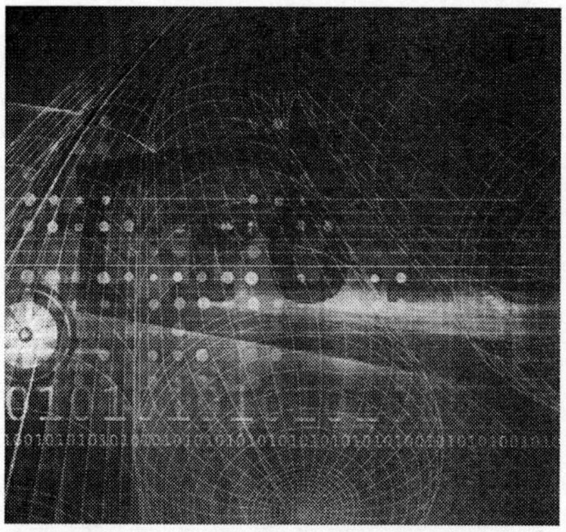

Collect data with a mindset of viewing it as an enduring IP asset, not a one-off

#SensorsConverge

Sensors Converge

Questions?

#SensorsConverge

Sensors Converge

Sensors Converge

Towards wearable physiological biosensor systems

Coralie Gallis, CTO, Wearable Start-up

September 21-23, 2021 | San Jose, CA

#SensorsConverge

Highlights

- State of the art
- Challenges
- Biosensors
- Sweat analysis
- Application

#SensorsConverge

Sensors Converge

World of wearables

A mix of healthcare, medical, fitness and wellness

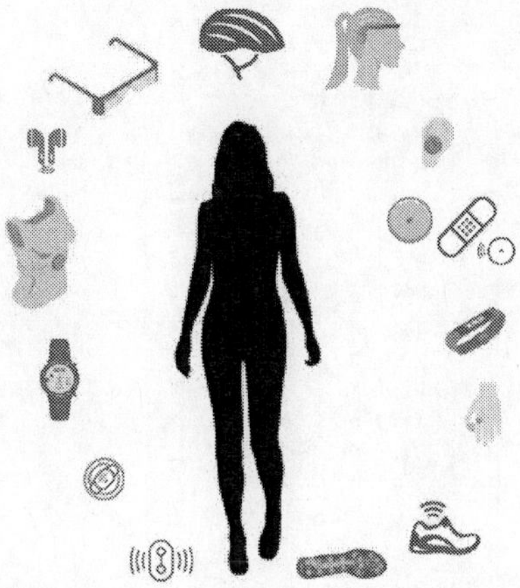

- Heart rate, HRV
- Respiration rate
- Blood pressure
- Blood oxygen levels
- Body temperature
- Skin pH level
- Sweat analysis
- Ions
- Glucose
- Lactate

To analyze and monitor
- Sleep
- Gait
- Steps count
- Distance
- Activity level
- Calorie
- Perspiration
- Cholesterol levels
- Performance
- Hydration
- Nutrition
- Emotion
- Anxiety/depression

#SensorsConverge

Sensors Converge

A little bit of Market Data

- **Global wearable technology market size valued at $37B in 2020 reaching $120B by 2028**
- **266.3M units shipped in 2020, projected to reach 776.23M units by 2026**
- **Annual growth rate of 16% from 2020 to 2027**
- **Rising the adoption of wearable to gather information about the overall health**

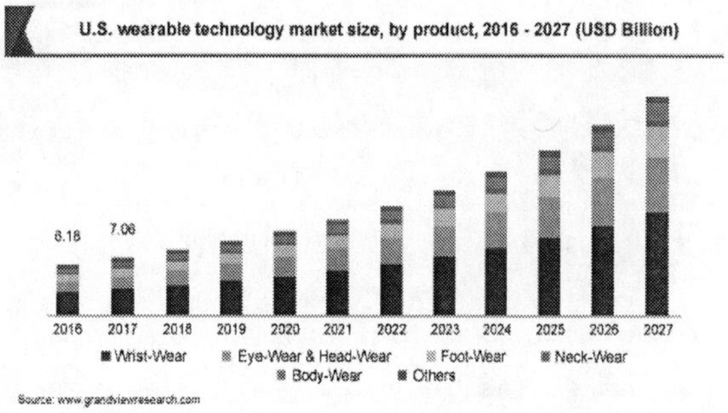

#SensorsConverge

Sensors Converge

Challenges of sensors

- **Miniaturization**

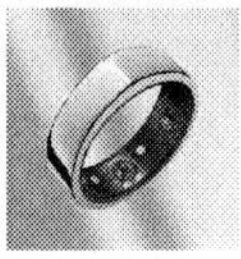

- **Flexibility / stretchability**

- **From physical sensor to biochemical sensor**

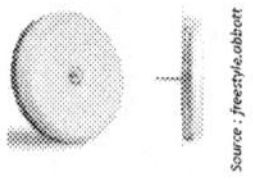

#SensorsConverge

Sensors Converge

Miniaturization examples

- **Smart Ring**

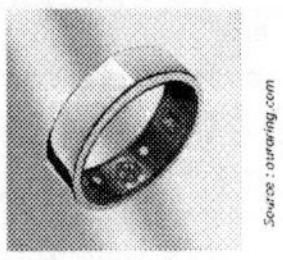

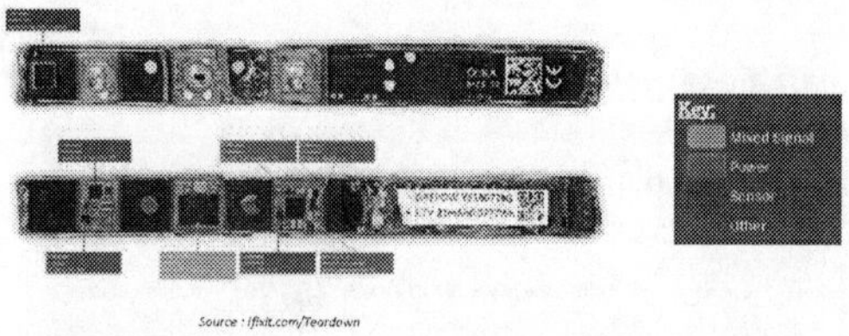

- **Earbuds**

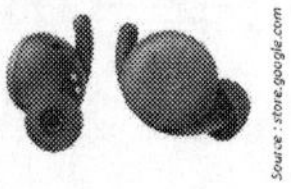

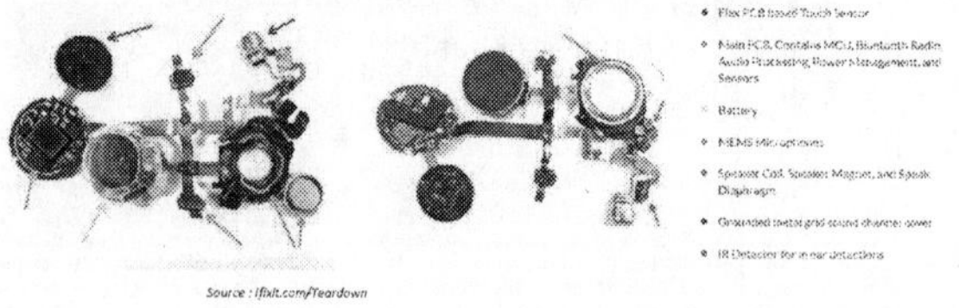

#SensorsConverge

Sensors Converge

Innovative biochemical sensors

#SensorsConverge

Sensors Converge

Electrochemical Sensors Technology

Imperial College London
Bioengineering

- **Principles** : Amperometric biosensors for small molecules

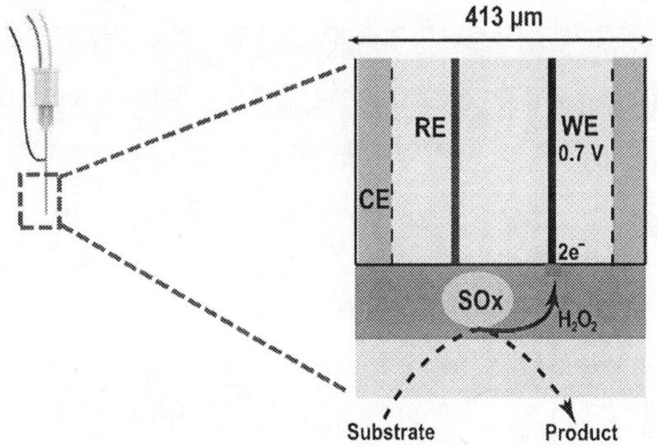

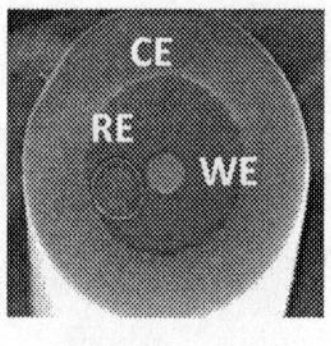

50 μm detector

1. Exclusion layer for selectivity
2. Enzyme hydrogel layer
   GOx for glucose
   LOx for lactate
3. Outer diffusion-limiting layer
4. Fluids being sweat, blood, saliva

#SensorsConverge

Sensors Converge

Electrochemical Sensors Technology

Imperial College London
Bioengineering

- Amperometric biosensors : signal output

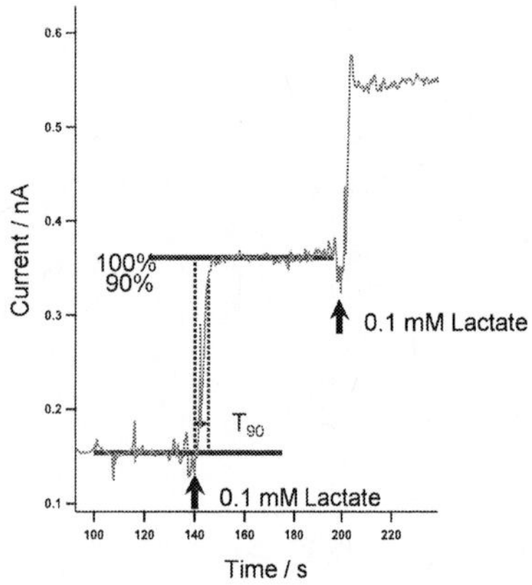

Lactate monitoring:

90% response time $T_{90\%}$: 3.6 s

Limit of detection: < 0.2 μM Lactate

Fast continuous signals

#SensorsConverge

Sensors Converge

Engineering biosensors to be under diffusion control

Imperial College London
Bioengineering

Biosensor without Diffusion control layer

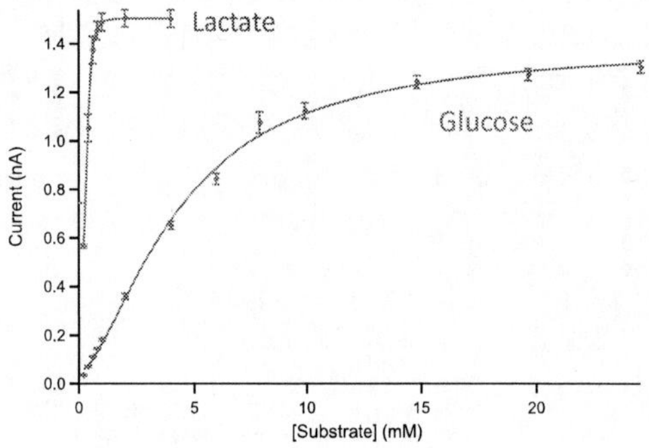

Current proportional to concentration

#SensorsConverge

Sensors Converge

Engineering biosensors to be under diffusion control

Imperial College London Bioengineering

Biosensor with Diffusion control layer

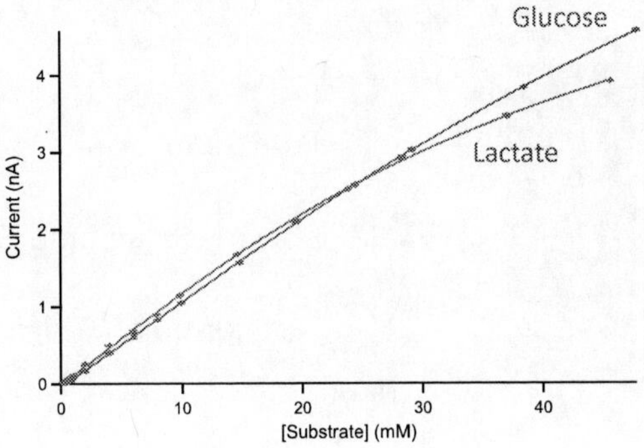

Current proportional to concentration

#SensorsConverge

Sensors Converge

Electrochemical Sensors Technology

Imperial College London Bioengineering

- **Principles** : Potentiometric ion sensors

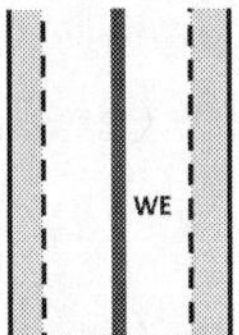

1. PEDOT - PSS conducting polymer
2. PVC membrane containing ionophore:
3. Fluids

K^+

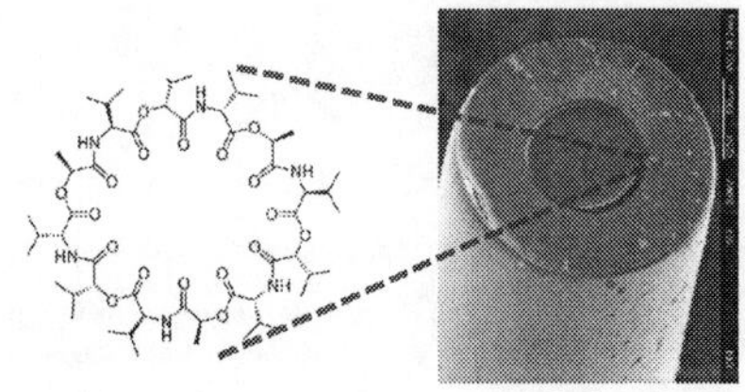

Valinomycin

#SensorsConverge

Sensors Converge

Electrochemical Sensors Technology

Imperial College London
Bioengineering

- Potentiometric Ion Sensors : signal output

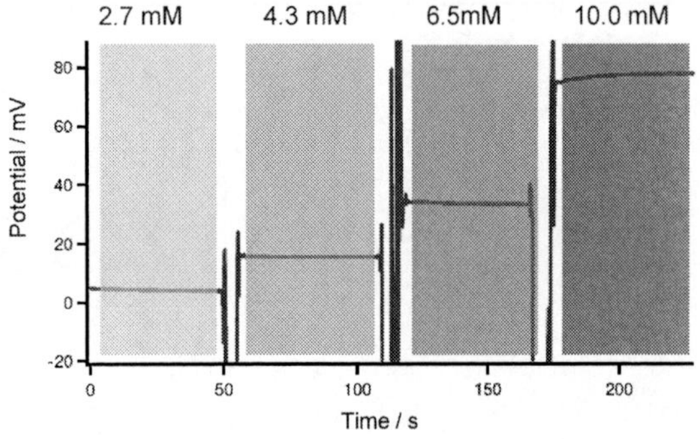

Potassium monitoring:

90% response time $T_{90\%}$: 4.8 s

Fast continuous signals

#SensorsConverge

Sensors Converge

Electrochemical Sensors Technology

Imperial College London
Bioengineering

Ion selective electrode

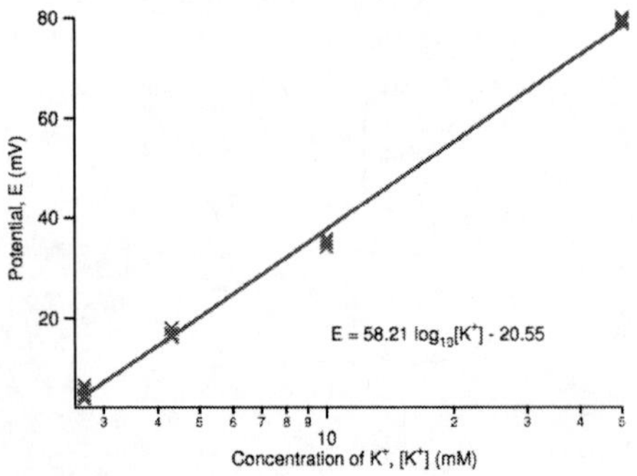

Voltage proportional to Log (concentration)

#SensorsConverge

Adapted from Gowers et al.; Lab Chip. 2019 19: 2537-48

Sensors Converge

Application Specific Integrated Circuit (ASIC)

Imperial College London
Bioengineering

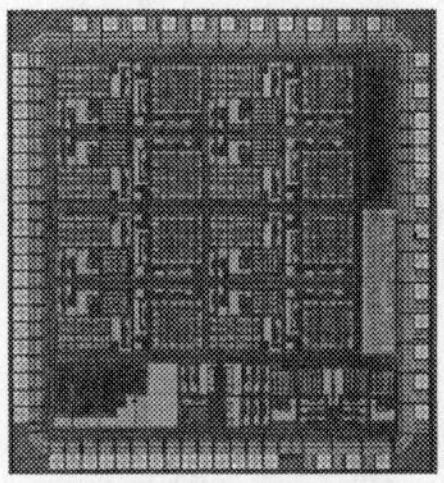

2 mm

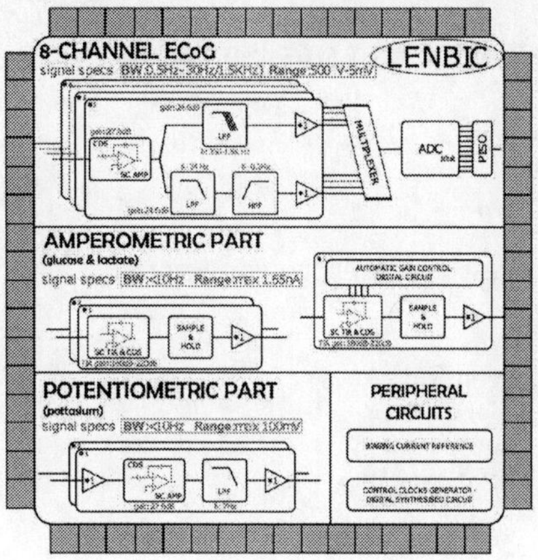

Pagkalos Iet al.. 2018. ChemPhysChem 19: 1215-25

Analyzing sweat

- Sweat is a bi-product of blood
- Various biomarkers can be measured in sweat (ions, small molecules)
- Non invasive, continuous measurement monitoring

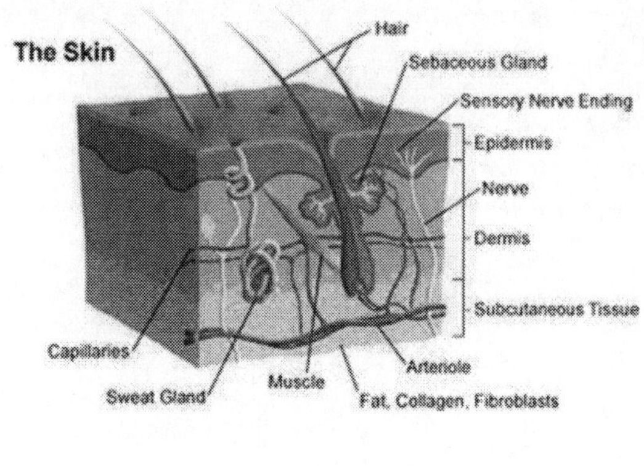

Applications

- Why monitoring ion or small molecules in sweat ?
  - Hydration
  - Sport/fitness performance optimization
  - Injury prevention
  - Nutrition / weight loss

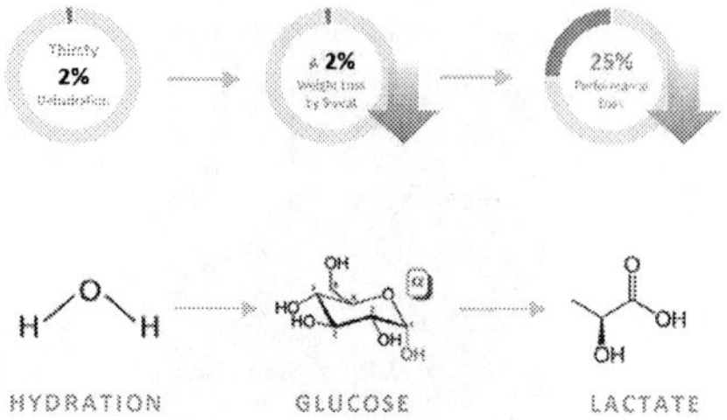

#SensorsConverge

Sensors Converge

Continuous Glucose Monitoring

- How does a Continuous Glucose Monitoring work ?

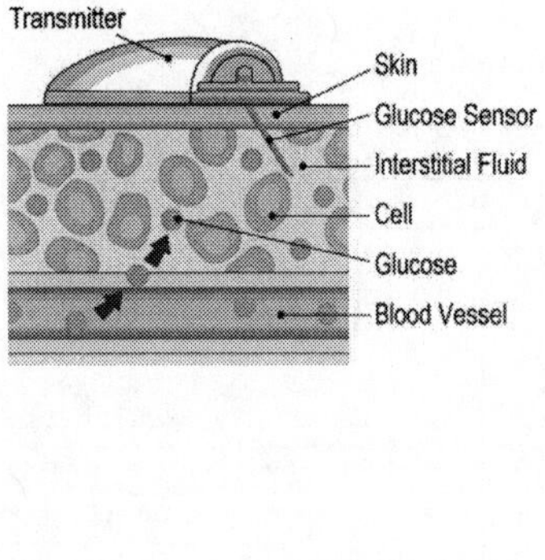

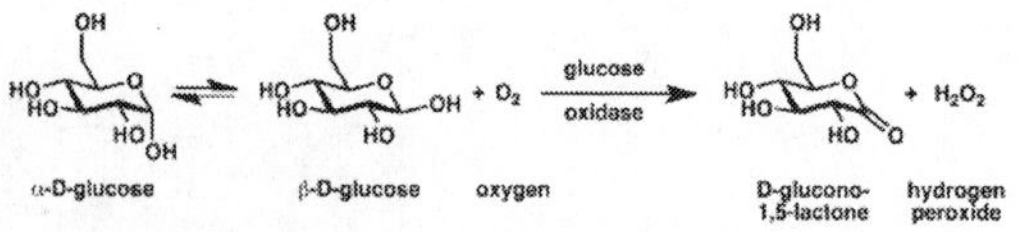

#SensorsConverge

Sensors Converge

Analysis

- Measure the effects of a stimuli on small molecules

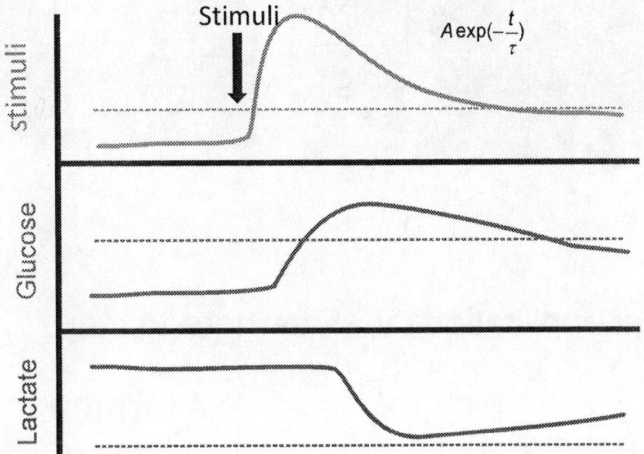

What do we need to do this?

#SensorsConverge

Sensors Converge

Key takeaways

- People are used to wearable sensor in a form of watches, or earbuds.
- One of the next opportunities of wearable sensors evolution is to expand the analysis of body fluids to monitor health indicators.
- **Smart patch** applications include **non-invasive** and **continuous** measurement of Glucose and Lactate levels using sweat analysis.

#SensorsConverge

Sensors Converge

New COVID-19 technologies and applications that are here to stay

David Jones
September 2021

Infineon

COVID-19 – What have we learned… and what do we not know?!

Infineon

› **We learned the word pandemic, but this has happened many times before…**

- 2009: Influenza A (H1N1) virus emerged
- 1968: Pandemic (H3N2 virus)
- 1957-1958: Pandemic (H2N2 virus)
- 1918: Pandemic (H1N1 virus)

› There are other pandemics and epidemics … in our lifetime to name a few **

1. Chikungunya
2. Cholera
3. Crimean-Congo hemorrhagic fever
4. Ebola virus disease
5. Hendra virus infection
6. Influenza (pandemic, seasonal, zoonotic)
7. Lassa fever
8. Marburg virus disease
9. Meningitis
10. MERS-CoV
11. Monkeypox
12. Nipah virus infection
13. Novel coronavirus
14. Plague
15. Rift Valley fever
16. SARS
17. Smallpox
18. Tularaemia
19. Yellow fever
20. Zika virus disease

This has led to:

a) Wearing Masks
b) Keeping Social Distancing
c) Enforcing Cleanliness Rules
d) Different way of working & Socializing

This is not going away!

** U.S News March 13th 2020

Let's take a look at how Sensors can help

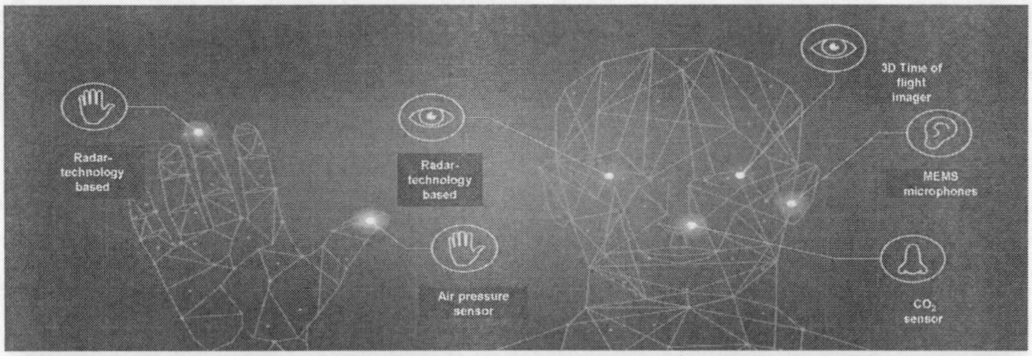

Today we can replicate the human senses

Question – Can we also use them to seamlessly & anonymously accelerate innovation to combat COVID-19?

Main smart home trends rely on using sensors today

	"Whole House" IoT simple & secure	Green & Energy consumption	Safety & Surveillance	Comfort & Convenience	Health & Wellness
	› Easy setup and interoperability › Built-in IoT security › Reliable, long range, connectivity	› Presence-based heating › CO2 based ventilation › Smart light/power switch	› Intrusion alarm › Children and seniors monitoring › Authentication	› Voice assistant ubiquity › Presence based wake-up › HMI & Gesture	› Sleep monitoring › Vital sensing › Air quality
Microphone			✓	✓	✓
Gas sensor		✓			✓
Pressure sensor		✓	✓		
Radar sensor		✓	✓	✓	✓
ToF sensor			✓		
Touch Screen Technology				✓	

Main smart home trends rely on using sensors today

"Whole House" IoT simple & secure
- Easy setup and interoperability
- Built-in IoT security
- Reliable, long range, connectivity

Green & Energy consumption
- Presence-based heating
- CO2 based ventilation
- Smart light/power switch

Safety & Surveillance
- Intrusion alarm
- Children and seniors monitoring
- Authentication

Comfort & Convenience
- Voice assistant ubiquity
- Presence based wake-up
- HMI & Gesture

Health & Wellness
- Sleep monitoring
- Vital sensing
- Air quality

Emerging Trends for sensor systems
- Human presence detection & localization
- Vital sensing
- Air quality monitoring

Let's start at the front door

Radar Entrance Counter
- Counts people in and out
- Wall or ceiling mount

- The latest 60GHz Radar with build-in antenna's in-package
  - It's possible to hide sensors
  - The size of a complete Radar Sensor system with all necessary compute and connectivity can be less than 1.5cm x 1.5cm
  - It can be hidden behind existing door material
  - Nobody even knows it is there!
- **Use Cases**
  - People Counting – keeping room building occupancy safe
  - Social distancing – For example, it can implement a "traffic light" system for a safe distance between people

Human Presence Detection (HPD) and localization with radar sensor systems enable tracking and tracing

Enabled use-cases in the prevention of COVID-19

- Room Occupancy Devices
- Device switch on/off
- Social Distancing
- Detection & Surveillance

Human Detection and localization

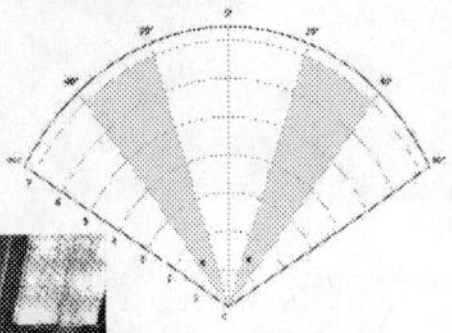

Features vs processor class

- Human localization & counting
- Human detection in zones
- AI/ML Presence (disturbers immunity)
- Human Presence Detection (HPD)
- Motion detection (PIR like)

...and protecting again COVID when inside

- Environmental Sensing is also shrinking with MEMS Sensor technology
- Makes it affordable to widely deploy environmental & gas sensing within buildings
- Protecting against COVID-19
  - Many reports have been published showing the link between CO2 & COVID-19:

Bazant et al. (2021). Monitoring carbon dioxide to quantify the risk of indoor airborne transmission of COVID-19. https://bit.ly/3gpgLnf

Blocken et al. (2021). Ventilation and air cleaning to limit aerosol particle concentrations in a gym during the COVID-19 pandemic. *Build Environ.* 193:107659. https://bit.ly/32Bn8f8

Hartmann, A., and Kriegel, M. (2020). Risk assessment of aerosols loaded with virus based on CO_2-concentration. Technische Universität Berlin. https://bit.ly/3gmfPQh

Pant et al. (2021). A Smart CO_2-Based Ventilation Control Framework to Minimize the Infection Risk of COVID-19 In Public Buildings. https://bit.ly/3avWdFT

Peng, Z., and Jimenez, J. L. (2021). Exhaled CO_2 as a COVID-19 Infection Risk Proxy for Different Indoor Environments and Activities, *Environmental Science & Technology Letters*, Article ASAP. https://bit.ly/3tvESo1

Schade, W., Reimer, V., Seipenbusch, M., and Willer, U. (2021). Experimental Investigation of Aerosol and CO_2 Dispersion for Evaluation of COVID-19 Infection Risk in a Concert Hall, *Int. J. Environ. Res. Public Health.* 18(6): 3037. https://bit.ly/2QG1fbx

Non Dispersive Infrared Light (NDIR) Technology

Photo Acoustic Spectroscopy (PAS) Technology

CO2 MEMS-based Sensor Example
> x4 Smaller than other solutions

Monitoring CO_2 levels in a school in Luxembourg.

Gas sensor systems enable air quality monitoring and smart ventilation

Market drivers

Covid raised air quality and ventilation awareness

Regulation pushing for better energy efficiency in buildings

Derived use-cases

Monitor CO2 and other unhealthy gas

Smart ventilation

Challenges solved by Environmental Sensors

- Simple, small, accurate & low-power connected multi-gas sensors

Running Venues Safely

- Many sensors can be used for:
  - RF Tagging
  - Camera with Face Recognition
  - Smart Entrance counters
  - Heat Detection Devices
  - Controlled Ventilation
- But what if there is problem?
  - Can extra safe guards be put in place?
  - Can we do contract tracing accurately?

ToF could be great technology to take us to the next level

- Can be used to create 3D point cloud images at an entrance
- Match point clouds to authorization i.e. tickets / RF tagging
- Get around privacy concerns with cameras
- No spoofing like some camera-based security systems

Sleep monitoring and vital sensing devices using sensor systems can help monitor the health & well-being of people during COVID-19

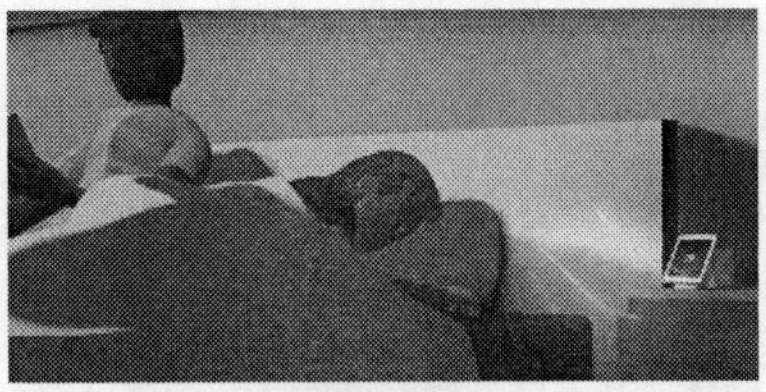

Sleep monitoring
Sleep detection, sleep quality, Apnea & snoring detection
(Radar and Microphone)

Vital sensing for home Fitness
Heart rate and breathing rate measurement
(person standing still after exercise)

What about a total touch free environment for going back to work>

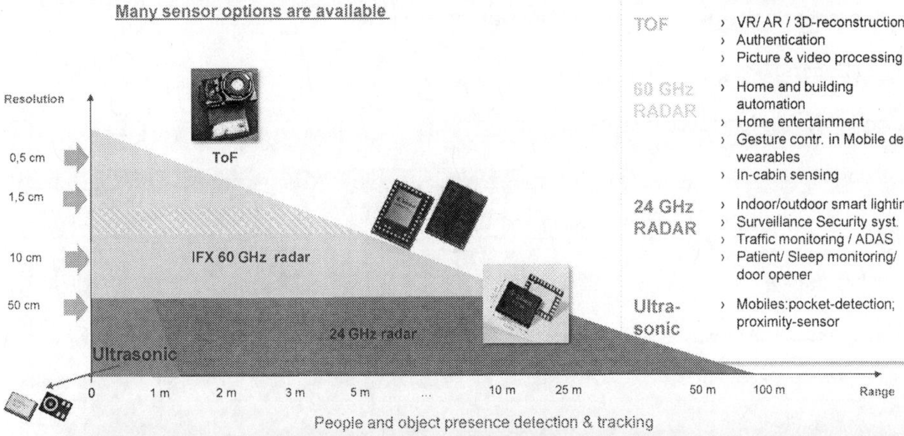

People and object presence detection & tracking

	Use-case	Capabilities
TOF	› VR/ AR / 3D-reconstruction › Authentication › Picture & video processing	High resolution 3D-point cloud
60 GHz RADAR	› Home and building automation › Home entertainment › Gesture contr. in Mobile dev / wearables › In-cabin sensing	Good in dust/fog/smoke; high accuracy; smaller formfactor
24 GHz RADAR	› Indoor/outdoor smart lighting › Surveillance Security syst. › Traffic monitoring / ADAS › Patient/ Sleep monitoring/ door opener	Good in dust/fog/smoke; lower bandwidth
Ultra-sonic	› Mobiles:pocket-detection; proximity-sensor	Additional Microphone function; one target

Resolution: ability to resolve two closely spaced objects
Range: distance of object
Additional technology differentiators: form factor, power consumption, robustness, privacy, aesthetics, price, sensitivity to light

Touchless Human Machine Interface Enabled by Sensors

Infineon

- Why touch any interface with day-to-day objects
- Safe Sanitary interface
- Could this be the next level of HMI?

- With sensor technology today holographic displays are a reality
- Fine gesture with figures can be detected
- Replace button with holographic images of button & use the features of the sensors to create touch "feelings"
- Applications everywhere with sensor fusion
    - Door entry push open / shut close
    - Vending Machines
    - Point of sales terminals
    - And the list goes on…

Infineon Proprietary

So what technologies are here to stay?

Infineon

- Smart Entrance Counter technologies over and above Cameras today that maintain privacy
- Environmental & Health Sensing being common place
- Touchless HMI / Holographic with real touch sensations
- Social Distancing monitoring
- Holographic Learning
- Its going to be an exciting change
- We may never truly wipe out COVID-19, but in the "new normal," we can live safely and more productively

Broadsens

Wireless Low-Power Sensor System Design and Applications

SENSE A BROADER WORLD

Dr. David C. Zhang

www.broadsens.com Email: david.zhang@broadsens.com

Sensors Converge

CONTENTS

Sensors Converge

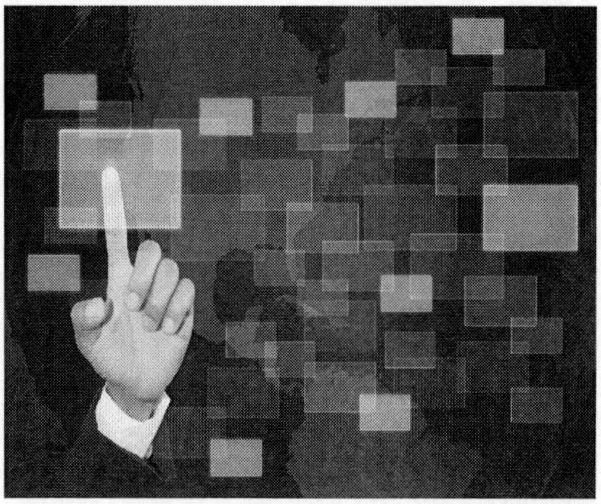

BROADSENS CORPORATION 2

Why Wireless Sensor System

Sensors Converge

- Easy installation
- Looks great, no messy wires
- Lower cost
- Natural choice for:
  - moving/rotating parts
  - Very high voltage applications
  - Wiring restriction areas
- Easy maintenance (if the battery lasts long enough)

Challenges of Wireless Applications

Sensors Converge

Battery Life	Size & weight	Security	Reliability	Distance	Throughput	Latency
Imagine to replace hundreds of batteries from wireless sensors	To extend battery replacement interval, wireless sensors tend to be bulky	Cyber security is getting more and more important	Interference from many wireless signals and internal bugs	Many applications need longer distance while consuming little power	Higher throughput may consume more power	Low power also means high latency

CONTENTS

Sensors Converge

Wireless Sensor System Design (Top-Down)

Sensors Converge

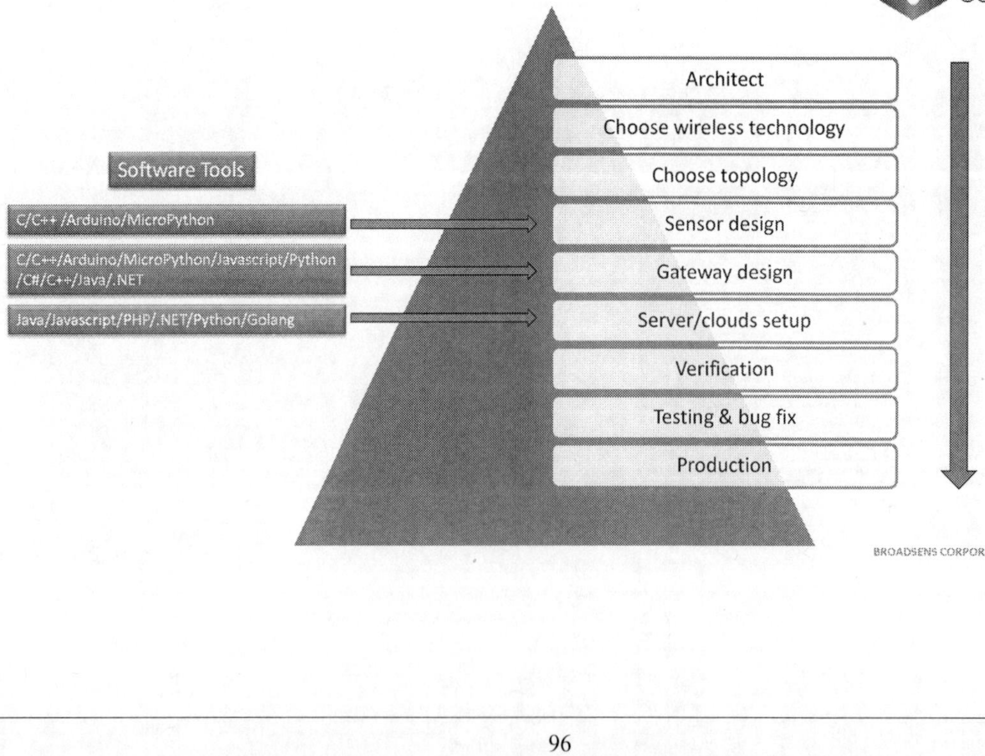

Wireless Technology Selection

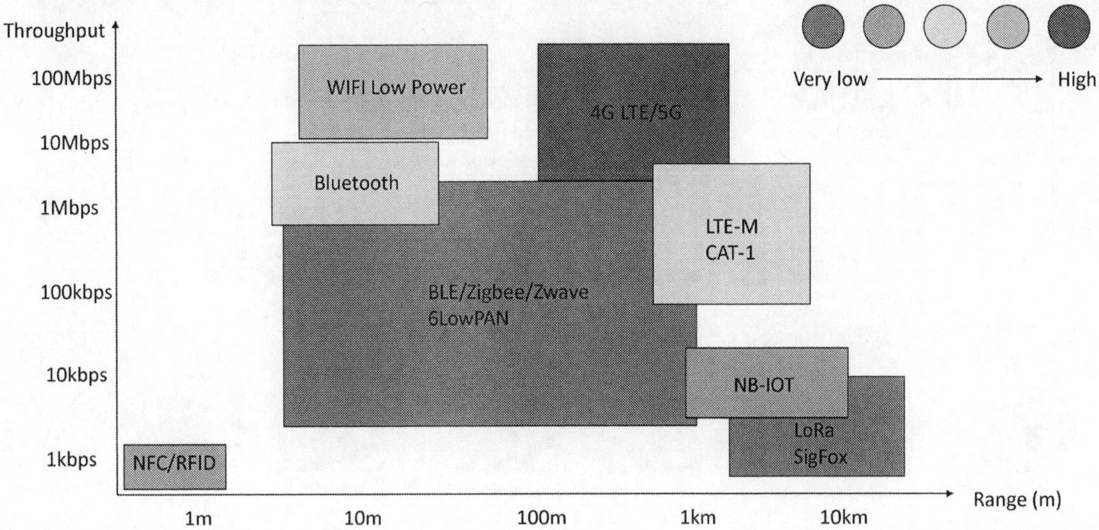

BROADSENS CORPORATION

Wireless Topology Selection

Sensors Converge

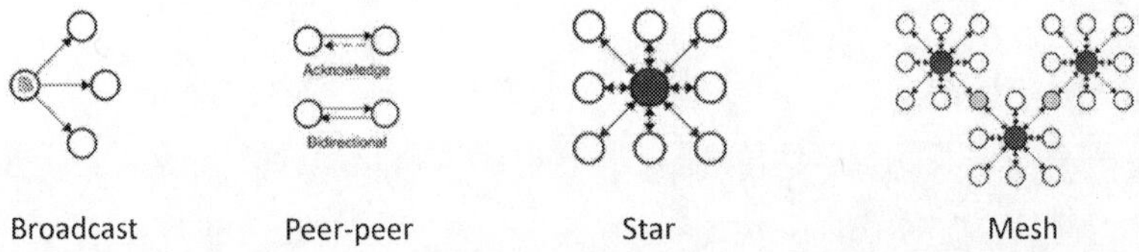

Topology	RFID/NFC	BLE/Zigbee/ Zwave	Bluetooth	WIFI	LTE-M/NB-IOT	4G/5G	LoRa/SigFox
Broadcast		√		√			√
Peer-peer	√	√	√	√	√	√	√
Star		√		√	√	√	√
Mesh		√		√			√

Picture credit: Digikey

BROADSENS CORPORATION

Low-Power Sensor Design

Sensors Converge

Low-power sensor Interface:
- Analog
  - Op-AMP selection (nA)
  - ADC selection (µA)
- Digital
  - One wire
  - I2C
  - SPI

Battery selection:
- Cell battery: 3.0v
- Lithium-thionyl Chloride (Li-$SOCl_2$): 3.6v
- Lithium sulfur dioxide (Li-SO_2): 2.8v
- Lithium-manganese dioxide (Li-MnO_2): 3.0v

Tools:
- Development kit
- Multimeter
- Oscilloscope
- Power profiler

Attention: DC-DC converter may be needed for 3.6v or higher voltage

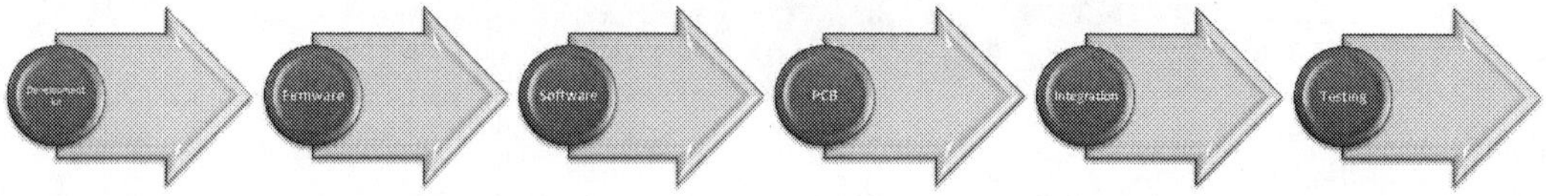

Example: Wireless Motion Detector

Sensors Converge

Up to 10 years battery life

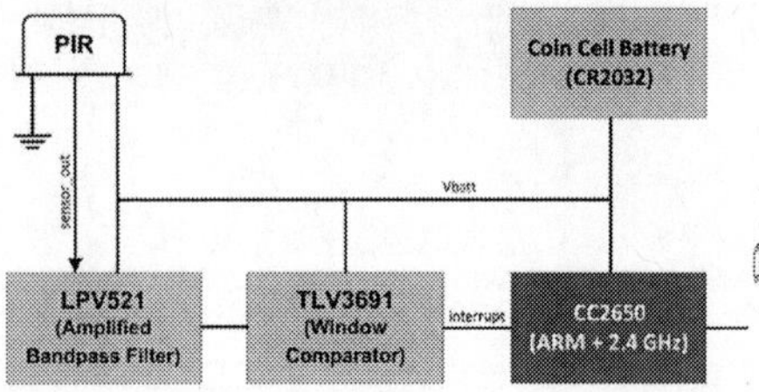

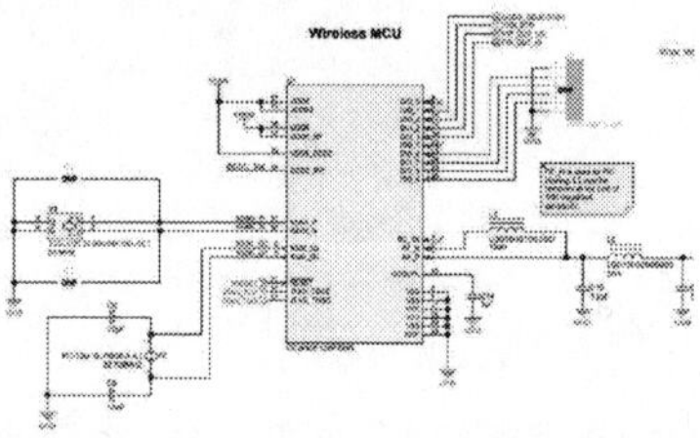

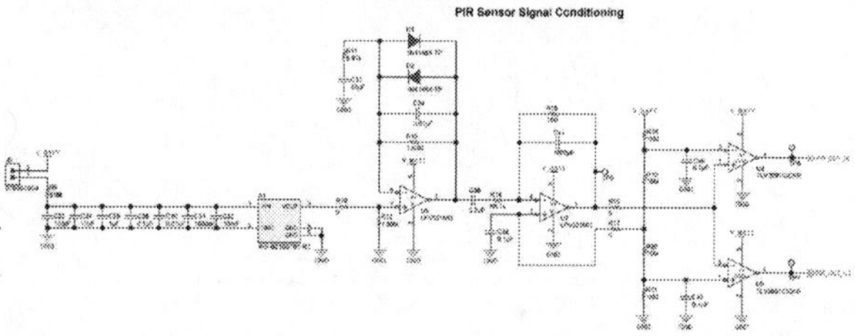

Credit: Texas Instruments
Link: https://www.ti.com/tool/TIDA-00759

Example: Moisture & Temperature Sensor

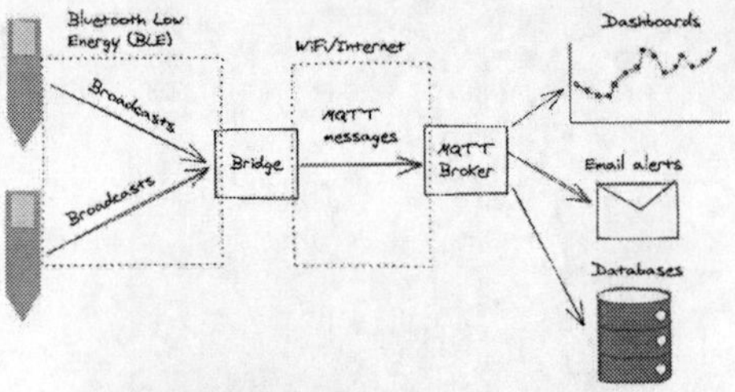

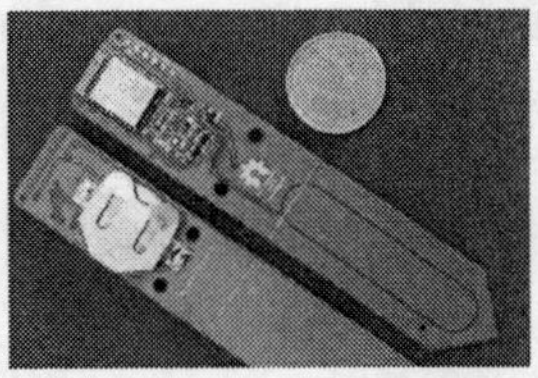

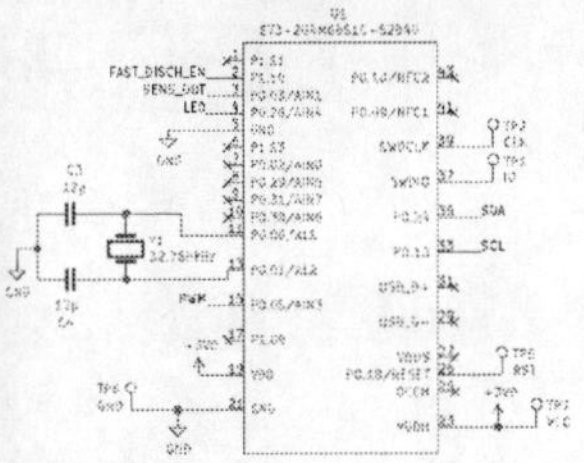

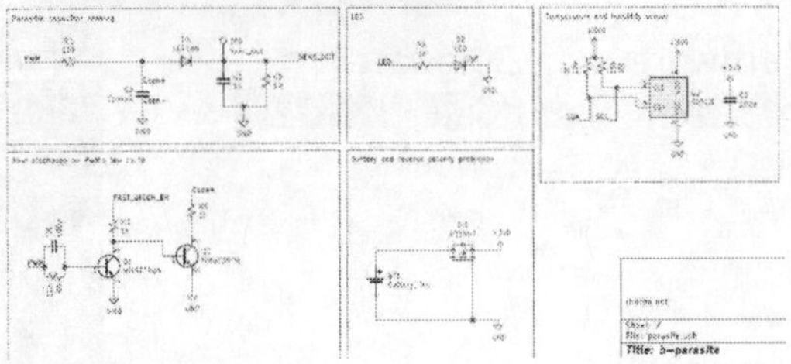

Credit: rbaron
Link: https://github.com/rbaron/b-parasite

Gateway Design

Select gateway proper role and design based on requirements

Basic
- Limited data storage
- Basic sensor configuration
- Powered by battery
- In sleep mode when not in usage
- Optional energy harvesting

Intermediate
- Added data storage
- Edge computing and analysis function
- File storage and management
- AC power with optional energy harvesting
- Power on all the time

Advanced
- Large data storage
- Edge computing, machine learning and advanced analysis function
- File system and optional compact database
- AC power
- Power on all the time

Example: Gateway with Edge Computing Ability

Block Diagram

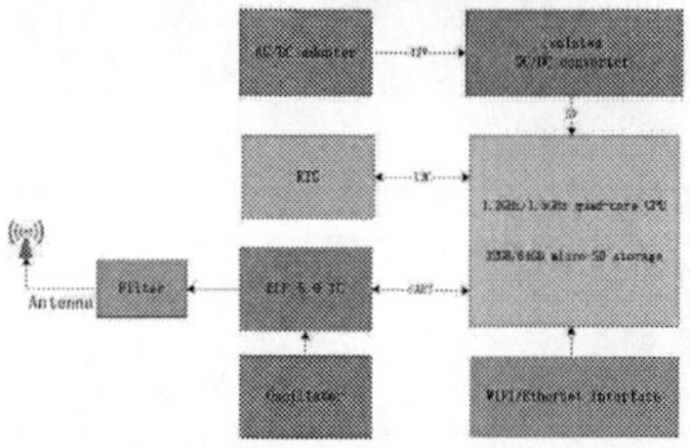

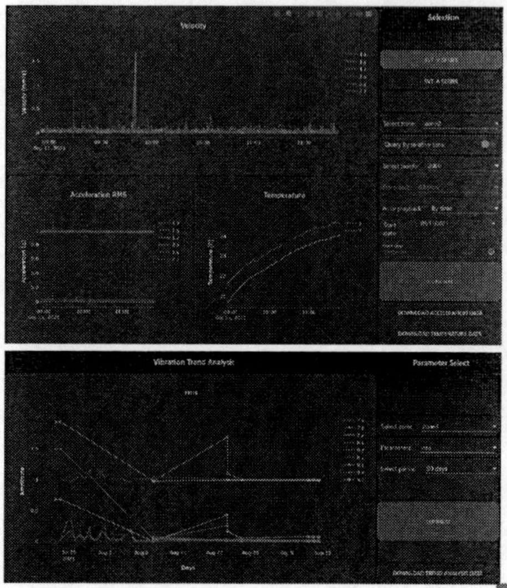

Hardware	Software
CPU: 1.2GHz	Linux Debian OS
RAM: 1GB	Node-RED
Data storage: 32GB	InfluxDB
Sensor interface: BLE 5.0	Mosquitto (MQTT)
Ethernet/USB/WIFI	

Local Server VS Clouds

Local server

Pros	Cons
Gives you physical control over your backup.	Requires a capital investment in hardware and infrastructure.
Keeps critical data in-house. No third party has access to your information.	Needs space in your office for a rack or server room/closet, in addition to dedicated IT support.
No need to rely on an Internet connection for access to data.	May be more susceptible to data loss during disaster situations due to its in-house location. How often you take the data offsite will reflect how much data you'll lose in an emergency.
Can be more cost-effective for small to mid-sized companies.	No uptime or recovery time guarantees

Clouds

Pros	Cons
No need for onsite hardware or capital expenses. Well-suited to smaller companies that may outgrow storage too quickly.	The costs of the data recovery could outweigh the benefits for companies that are not as dependent on uptime and instant recovery.
Storage can be added as needed. Solutions are often on-demand, so you only pay for what you need.	Organization may have a limit to data that can be stored in the cloud due to storage availability and cost.
Backup and restore can be initiated from anywhere, using any computer, tablet, or smartphone.	If the Internet goes down on your side or on your cloud provider's side, you won't have access to any of your information.
Data can be backed up in the cloud as regularly as 15-minute intervals, minimizing data losses in disaster situations. Small data set recovery time is improved.	Full data recovery could prove very time-consuming and impactful on systems. However, if a Datto is used, recovery can occur in minutes.

Credit: Sysgen
Link: https://sysgen.ca/cloud-vs-in-house-servers/

CONTENTS

Sensors Converge

01 Introduction

02 Wireless Technologies

03 Applications

04 Live Demo

BROADSENS CORPORATION 15

Industrial Case Study: Steel Mill

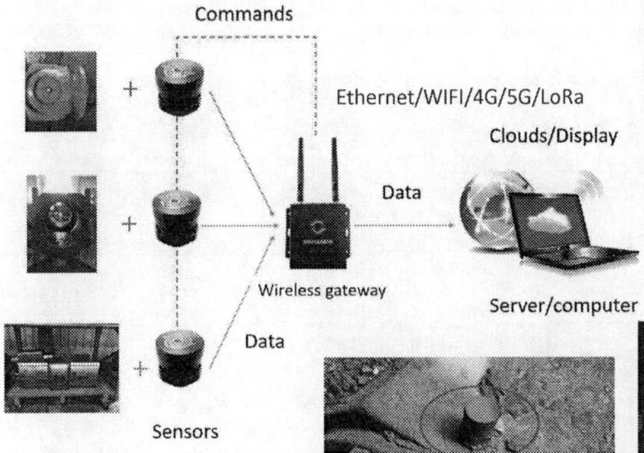

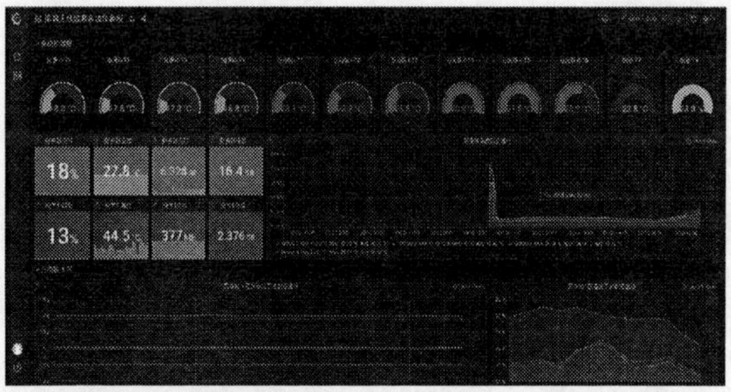

Dashboard

Sensor in harsh environments

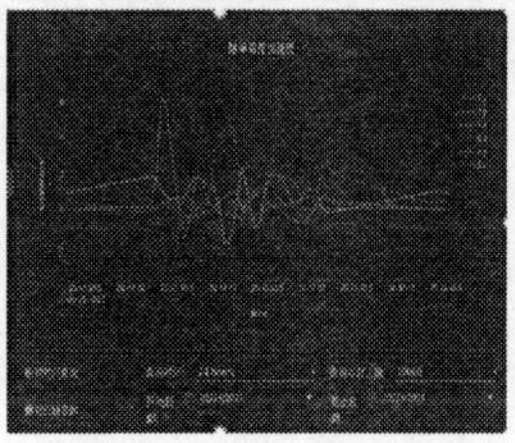

Data analysis

Easy config | Powerful | AES encryption | Data visualization

Improve operation time 30%

Increase life 10%

Reduce downtime 45%

Increase efficiency 20%

BROADSENS CORPORATION 16

Industrial Case Study: High-Voltage Transmission Line

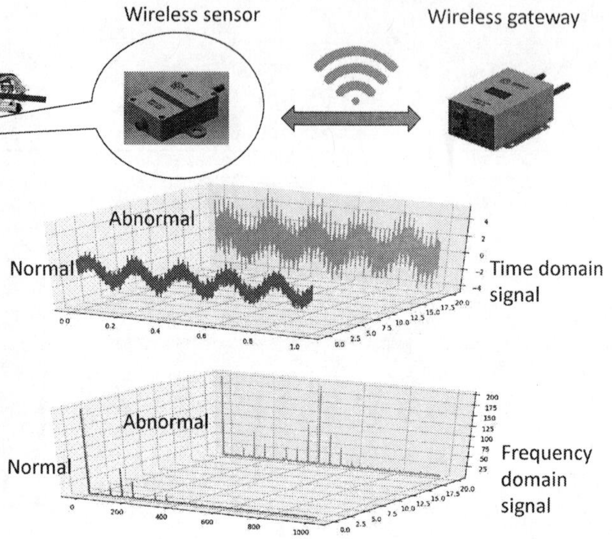

- Easy installation
- High voltage proof
- Cost Effective
- Easy maintenance

CONTENTS

Sensors Converge

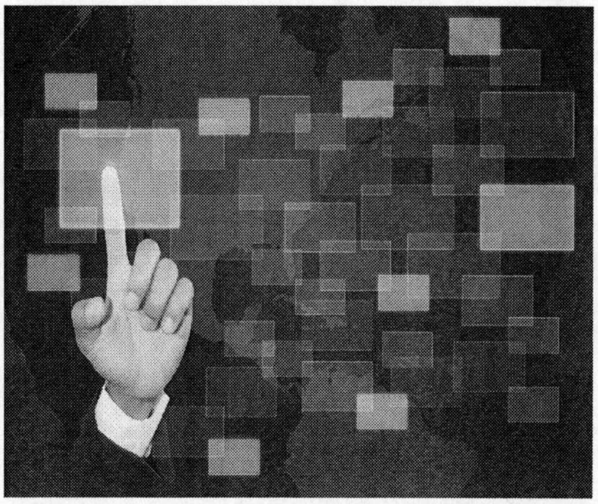

Live Demo Of Ultra-Low Power Wireless System

Sensors Converge

In this demo, we will learn:

- How to set up and use Node-RED basic functions
- How to set up a time-series database inside Node-RED
- How to set up data transfer to clouds/private server
- How to connect ultra-low power sensors
- How to operate ultra-low power sensors and draw live data

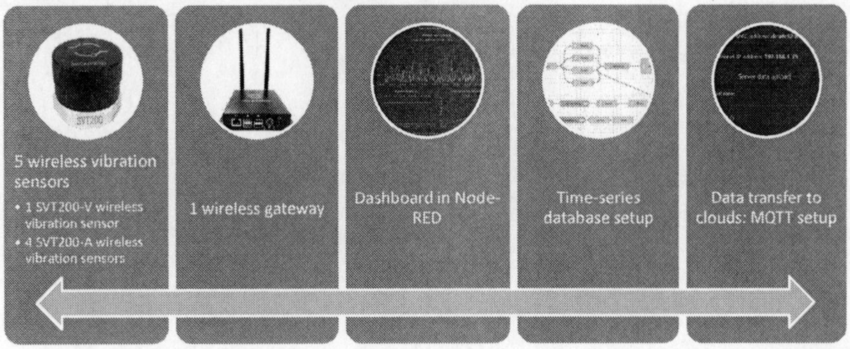

BROADSENS CORPORATION 19

Setup Node-RED, Database And Data Upoad

Sensors Converge

Node-RED

- Flow-based low-code programming tool
- Installation: https://nodered.org/docs/getting-started/
- Dashboard helps setup live data display

Database

- Time-series database ideal for IOT applications
- Setup InfluxDB: https://docs.influxdata.com/influxdb/v1.8/introduction/install/

Data Visualization

- Use Node-RED dashboard
- Advanced features

Data Transfer

- To local server
- To clouds

BROADSENS CORPORATION 20

Broadsens

SENSE A BROADER WORLD

Sensors Converge

Questions & Answers

Thank you

Email: david.zhang@broadsens.com

Web: https://www.broadsens.com

BROADSENS CORPORATION 21

1

Sensors Converge

Path to a Healthier More Productive Workforce While Keeping Insurance Premiums Flat

September 21-23, 2021 | San Jose, CA

#SensorsConverge

2

Presenter

David DiPaola

- Founder and CEO of Sensibly and a master certified wellness coach. He is a health, leadership and technology enthusiast with a passion for personal transformation. David is also Managing Director for DiPaola Consulting focused on medical sensing and formerly, held positions as VP of Global R&D for TT Electronics PLC (Asia, Europe and US) and engineering manager and technical staff at Texas Instruments, Sensata Technologies, and SMART Microsystems.

#SensorsConverge

Sensors Converge

3

Sick Care Society

Sensibly

68.5	78.9

(Scott et al., 2021)

In U.S.:

- $1.1 Trillion spent on chronic illness (Waters et al. 2018)
- 6 / 10 Adults have a chronic disease (CDC)
- Health care spending grew 4.6% in 2019, reaching $3.8 trillion or $11,582 / person (17.7% GDP, AMA 2020)

#SensorsConverge

Sensors Converge

4

Drivers of Cost

Sensibly

Annual Health Care Spend

- Top 1%: > $109,750 pp
- Top 5%: ~$50,000 pp
- 80 / 20 Rule - focus on top 15 – 20% first to reduce costs

Contribution to total health expenditures by individuals, 2016

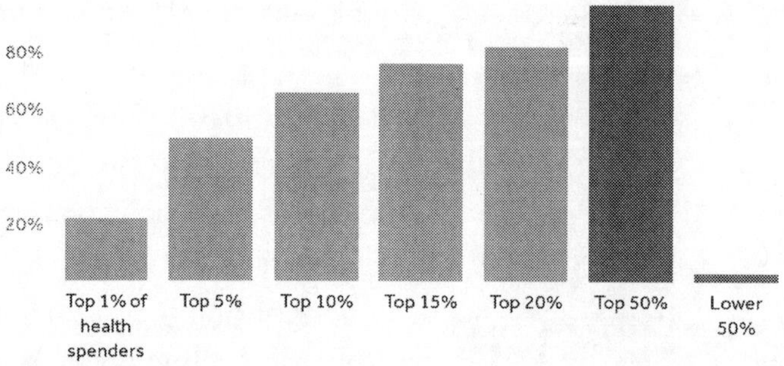

Source: Kaiser Family Foundation analysis of Medical Expenditure Panel Survey, Agency for Healthcare Research and Quality, U.S. Department of Health and Human Services

Peterson-KFF Health System Tracker

#SensorsConverge

Sensors Converge

5

Potential Value of Wellness Focus

Sensibly

Credit: Surface Unsplash

- ↑ $1920 / yr Chronic Disease Cost Savings*
- ↓ 66% drop in hospital admissions in year 7*
- – Potential for flat insurance premiums
  - ➢ National avg. increased 17 – 22% 2015 - 2020**
- ↑ Higher employee engagement / creativity
- ↑ 10% productivity increase***
- ↑ Higher customer and employee satisfaction
- ↓ Reduced employee turnover

#SensorsConverge

*Caloyeras et al. 2014, **Kaiser Family Foundation 2020, ***Krekel et al. 2019

Sensors Converge

6

Health Insurance Models

Sensibly

Fee for Service	Value Based	Self-Insured
• Most Prevalent model • Inherent inefficiencies	• Paid based on patient health outcomes	• Most flexibility for employers • Potentially higher risk • Potentially lower cost

#SensorsConverge

Sensors Converge

7

Self-Insured Health Insurance

Sensibly

- **Assumptions:** 100 Employees, $1000 / Employee / Month (Fully Insured)

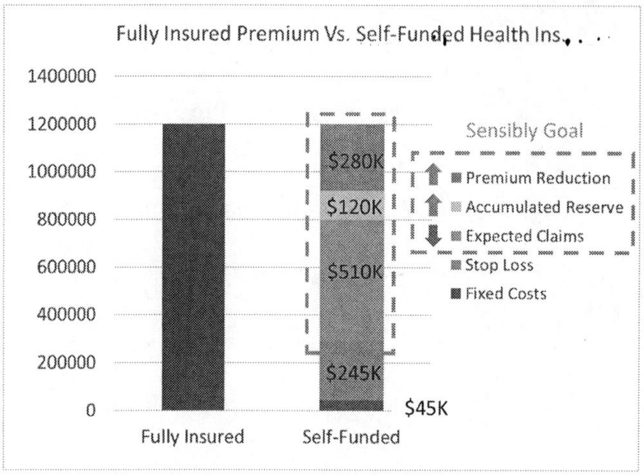

#SensorsConverge

Sensors Converge

8

Specific Examples of Risk

Sensibly

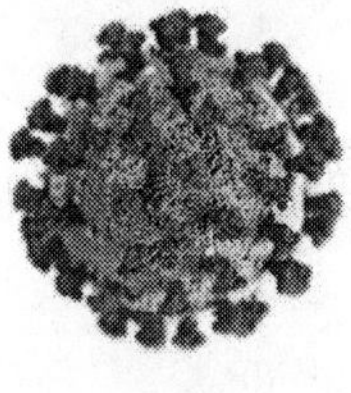

COVID
$2.5 K / $51 – 78 K
Outpatient / Average In-Patient Stay
(Healthcare Finance 2020)

Mental Health
$16 K Increase
in Health-care Spending w/ Chronic Disease
(Sporinova et al. 2019)

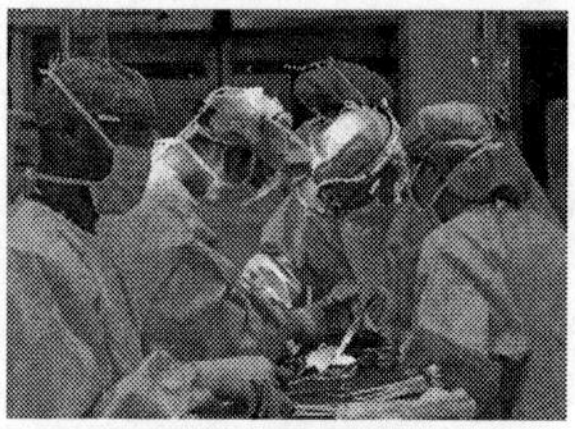

Heart Disease
$19 K / $27 K / $85 K
Mean / w/diabetes / 2nd CVD Hospitalization
(Nichols et al. 2010)

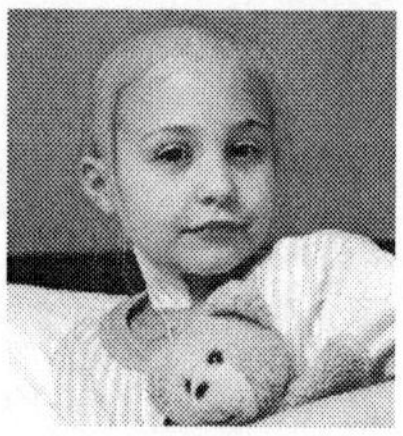

Cancers
$50 K / $120 K / $475 K
Radiation & Drug, Cell Based
(Johns Hopkins / Nature 2018)

#SensorsConverge

Image Credits - National Cancer Institute, Annie Spratt, Claudia Wolff, Unsplash

Sensors Converge

9

How to Lower Risk

Sensibly

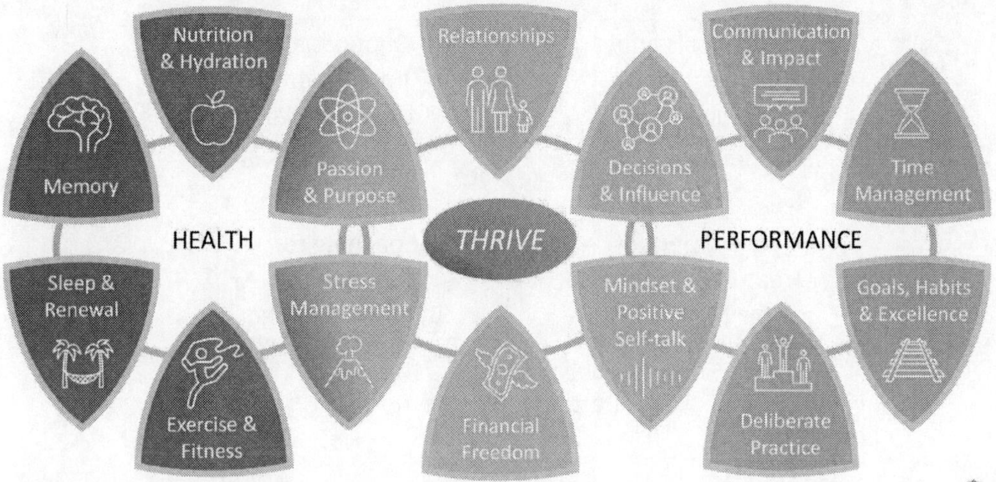

#SensorsConverge

Sensors Converge

10

How to Lower Risk

Sensibly

#SensorsConverge

Sensors Converge

11

How to Lower Risk and Improve Care

Sensibly

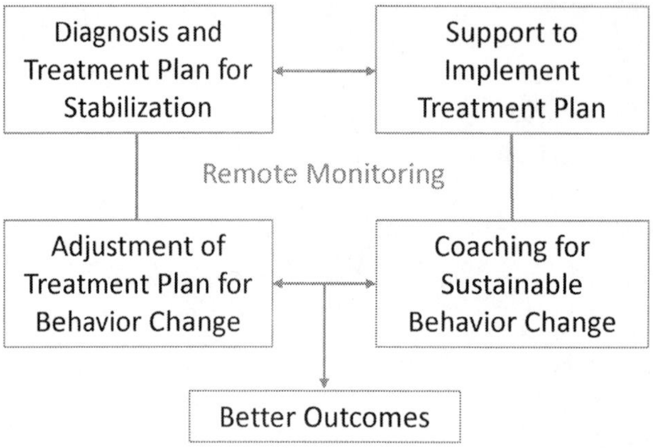

#SensorsConverge

Sensors Converge

12

Power of Coaching and Monitoring

Sensibly

2019 2021

#SensorsConverge

Sensors Converge

13

Monitoring Change

Sensibly

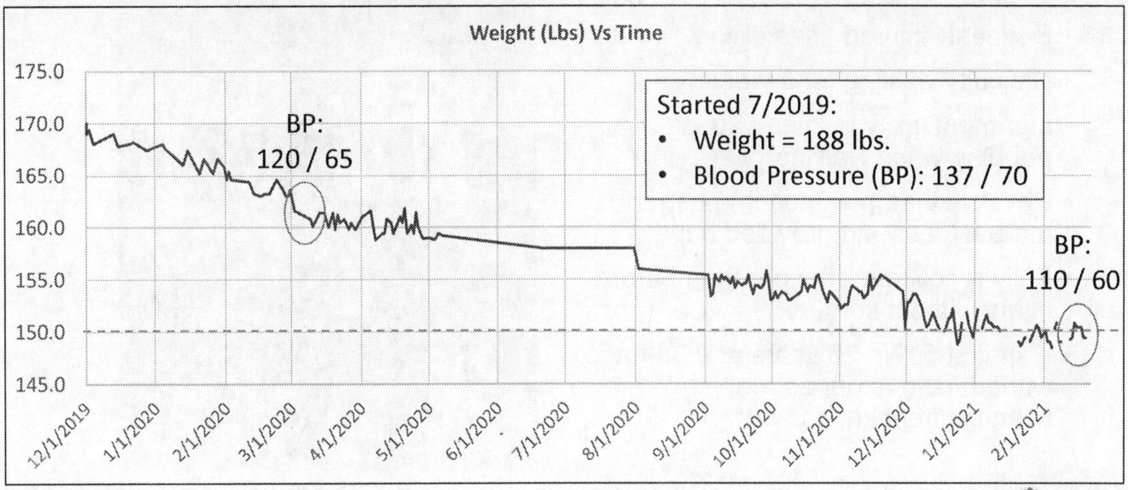

#SensorsConverge

Sensors Converge

14

Monitoring Change

Sensibly

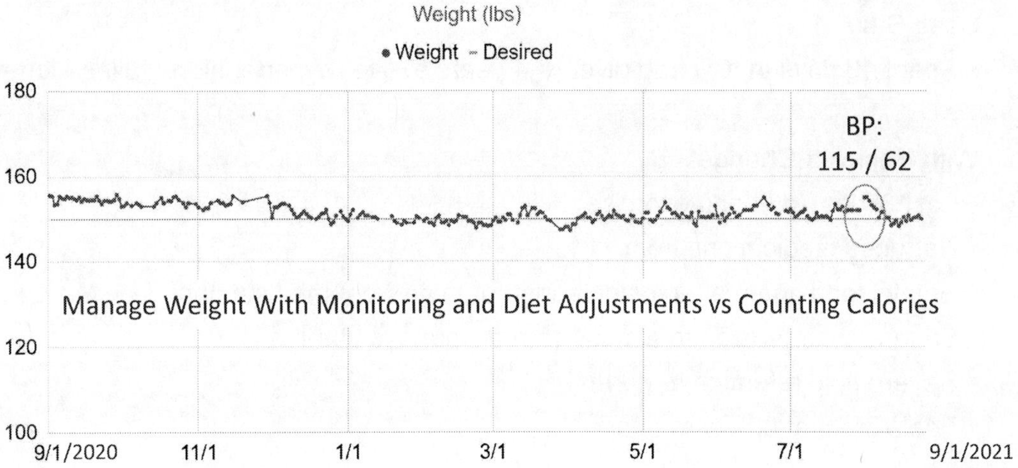

#SensorsConverge

Sensors Converge

15

Quality of Life Improvement

Sensibly

- Seriously injured knee skiing
- Difficulty walking for 3-weeks
- Ligament laxity in knee caused popping when walking
- Physical therapist (coach) pushed me past fear and provided hope
- Fully recovered stronger than before injury without surgery
- Ran first 5 K in 25 years at 9:38 pace without pain (stopped running in twenties from knee pain)

7/30/2021

#SensorsConverge

Sensors Converge

16

Power of Coaching and Monitoring

Sensibly

Case Study 1:

- Spent 13 days in ICU and given < 4 years to live (hypertension / failed kidneys)

With Behavior Change:

- Lost 38 lbs. (diet and exercise)
- Reduced medications from 11 to 1
- Enjoys food again after losing sense of taste from medications
- Severe hypertension to almost normal, kidneys stabilized
- Severe fluid retention to normal
- Feels great at 80 years of age

#SensorsConverge

Sensors Converge

17

Hypertension and Weight Improvement

Sensibly

HIPAA Release Provided

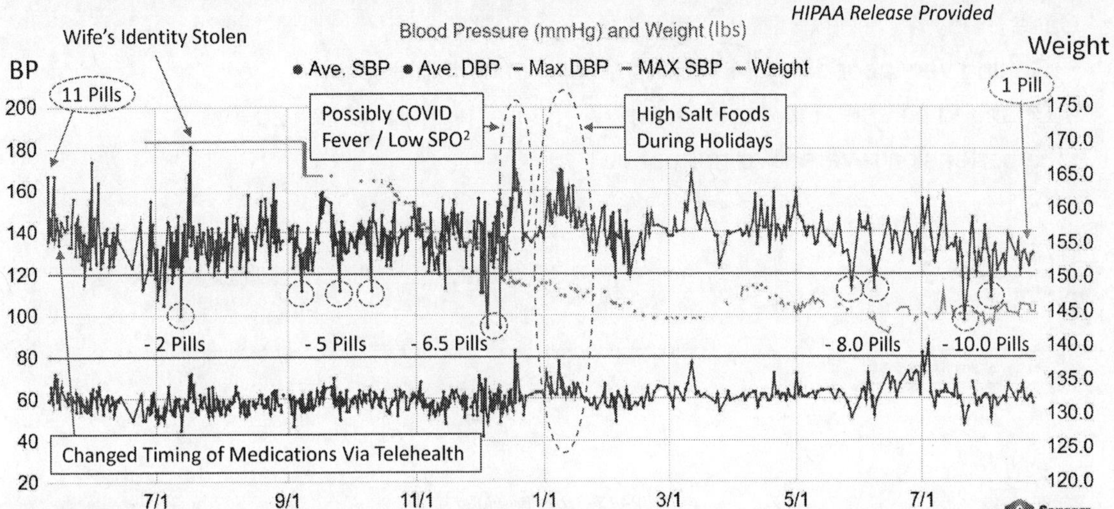

#SensorsConverge

Sensors Converge

18

Improvement in Health

Sensibly

Case Study 3 – Eliminated early signs of gout, improved hypertension w/ less meds

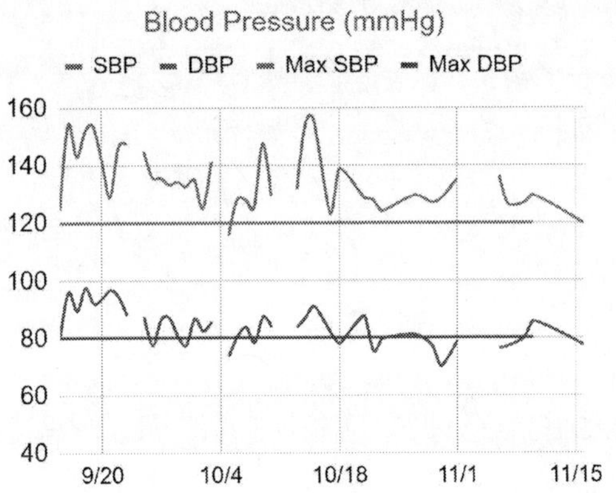

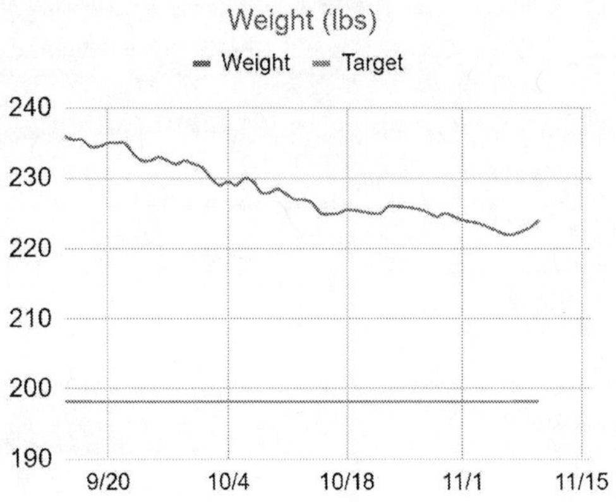

#SensorsConverge

HIPAA Release Provided

Sensors Converge

19

Hypertension and Weight Improvement

Sensibly

Case Study 4

- Getting very poor sleep (4 – 5 hrs / night) in high stress job
- Changed careers, increased sleep (7 - 8 hrs / night) and lost 20 lbs.
- Hypertension reversed to normal

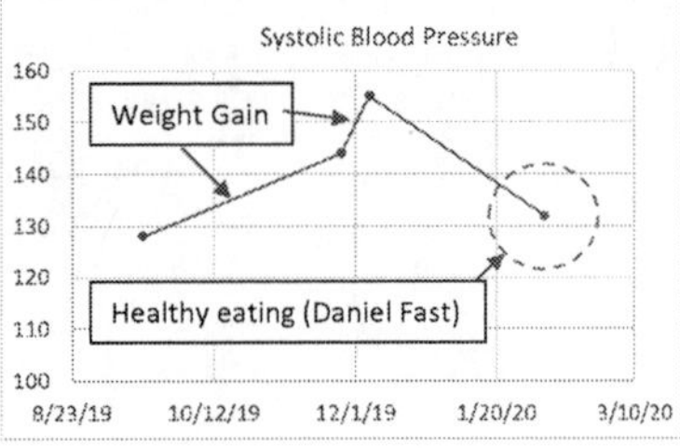

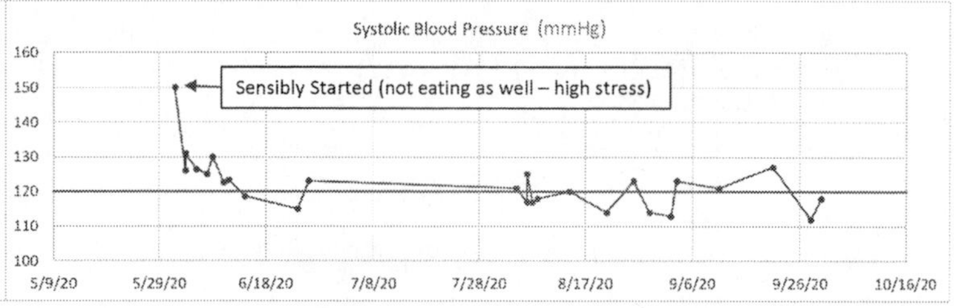

#SensorsConverge

HIPAA Release Provided

Sensors Converge

20

Monitoring of COVID Potential

Sensibly

- Case Study 5 – Helped keep patient at home and out of the hospital

In regular contact with Physicians during event

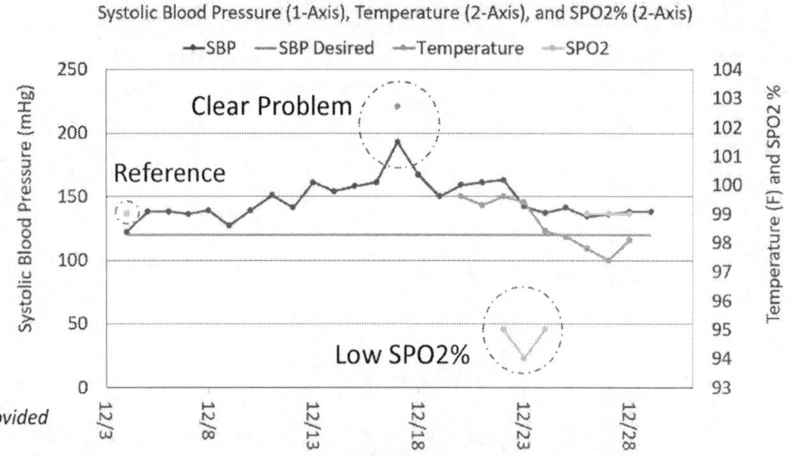

HIPAA Release Provided

#SensorsConverge

Sensors Converge

21

Flexibility to Implement Best Practices

Sensibly

Fee for Service	Value Based	Self-Insured
• Most Prevalent model • Encourages waste and sick care	• Paid based on patient health outcomes	• Most flexibility for employers • Manage risk • Potentially lower cost

Behavior Change Lowers Risk

#SensorsConverge

Sensors Converge

22

Conclusions

Sensibly

- A combination of remote monitoring and coaching can evoke intrinsic motivation for positive, sustainable behavior change
  - Key to improving healthy life expectancy and lower health cost burden
- Benefits to self-insured small businesses:
  - Managed risk
  - Potentially reduce cost and share saving with employees
  - A healthier, more productive, and satisfied work force
- Hope that chronic disease is reversable even for the elderly dramatically improving quality of life

What is your dream?

#SensorsConverge

Sensors Converge

23

References

- "Average cost of hospital care for COVID-19 ranges from $51,000 to $78,000, based on age." Healthcare Finance (2020).
- "Bringing Down the Cost of Cancer Treatment." Nature: Outlook (2018).
- Caloyeras, John P., Liu, Hangsheng, Exum, Ellen, Broderick, Megan, and Mattke, Soeren. "Managing Manifest Diseases, But Not Health Risks, Saved PepsiCo Money Over Seven Years" in Health Affairs Vol. 33, No. 1: Exploring Alternatives to Malpractice Mitigation (2014).
- 2020 Employer Health Benefits Survey. Kaiser Family Foundation (2020). https://www.kff.org/report-section/ehbs-2020-section-1-cost-of-health-insurance/
- Krekel, Christian, George Ward, Jan-Emmanuel De Neve, and Council Members: J. Harter, A. Blankson, A. Clark, C. Cooper, J. Lim, P. Litchfield, J. Moss, M. I. Norton, A.V. Whillans, and D. Cooperrider, and D. Mendelwicz. "Employee Well-being, Productivity, and Firm Performance: Evidence and Case Studies." Chap. 5 in *Global Happiness and Wellbeing Policy Report*, by Global Council for Happiness and Wellbeing, 72–94. New York: Sustainable Development Solutions Network, 2019.

#SensorsConverge

24

References

- Nichols, Gregory A., Bell, Timothy J., Pedula, Kathryn L., and Keeffe-Rosetti, Maureen. "Medical Care Costs Among Patients With Established Cardiovascular Disease". AJMC, 2010, https://www.ajmc.com/view/ajmc_10marnicholswebx_e86to93.
- Scott, A.J., Ellison, M. & Sinclair, D.A. "The economic value of targeting aging." Nature Aging 1, 616–623 (2021). https://doi.org/10.1038/s43587-021-00080-0
- Select Images, Unsplash.com
- Sporinova B, Manns B, Tonelli M, et al. "Association of Mental Health Disorders With Health Care Utilization and Costs Among Adults With Chronic Disease." JAMA 2019; 2 (8): e199910. doi:10.1001/jamanetworkopen.2019.9910
- "The Financial Impact of a Cancer Diagnosis." Johns Hopkins Medicine
- "Trends in health care spending." American Medical Association. (2020) https://www.ama-assn.org/about/research/trends-health-care-spending
- Waters, Hugh, Graf, Marlon. "The Costs of Chronic Disease in the U.S." Milken Institute (2018).

#SensorsConverge

Sensors Converge

Applications of Standards in Industry 4.0

Doug Sandy, CTO of PICMG

September 21-23, 2021 | San Jose, CA

#SensorsConverge

Topics to Cover

- PICMG Background
- Industry 4.0 Challenges
- PICMG IIoT Efforts
- Demonstration

#SensorsConverge

Sensors Converge

PICMG Background

"We enable our member companies and the markets they serve by providing quality open specifications for embedded computing."

PICMG®

#SensorsConverge

PICMG Overview

COM+HPC®

MicroSAM™

CompactPCI® Serial

COM Express®

μTCA®

AdvancedTCA®

CompactPCI®

SHB Express™

Modular

Scalable

Interoperable

Founded 1994 as a non-profit consortium

Deep engineering expertise in member companies

Rigorous Intellectual Property policies

Over 50 standards released to date

Membership comprised of ~140 companies from 20 countries

#SensorsConverge

Sensors Converge

Mars Curiosity Rover: PICMG CompactPCI®

High-Energy Physics: PICMG MicroTCA®

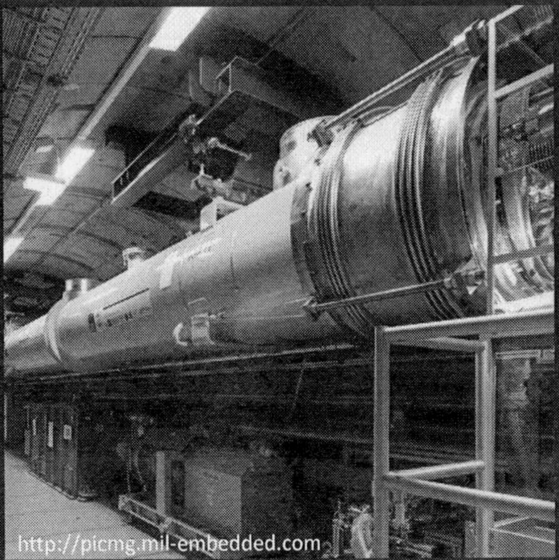

MicroTCA is increasingly being used in particle accelerators, plasma fusion, photon science for data acquisition and fast feedback:

LNLS (BR), CERN (CH), IHEP (CN), SINAP (CN), GSI/FAIR (DE), IPP (DE), ITER (FR), Soleil (FR), KEK (JAP), ESS (SWE), TARLA (TR), Diamond (UK), APS-U (USA), FRIB (USA), ORNL (USA), ...

Sensors
Converge

Industry 4.0 Challenges

#SensorsConverge

Factory Automation Evolution

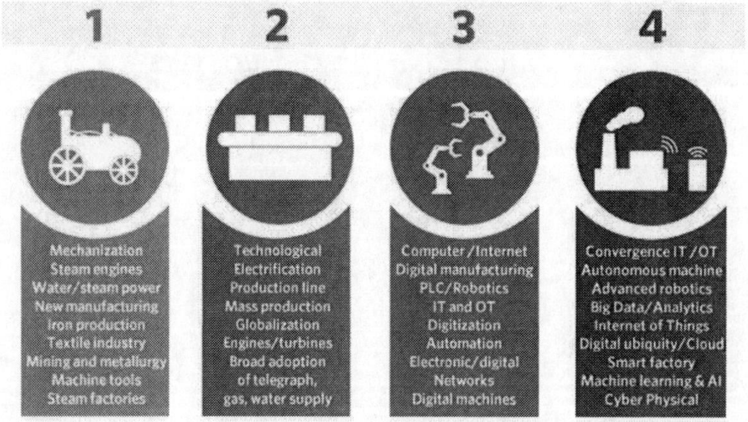

#SensorsConverge

From https://www.i-scoop.eu/industry-4-0/

Sensors
Converge

Implication: Shift to Distributed Control

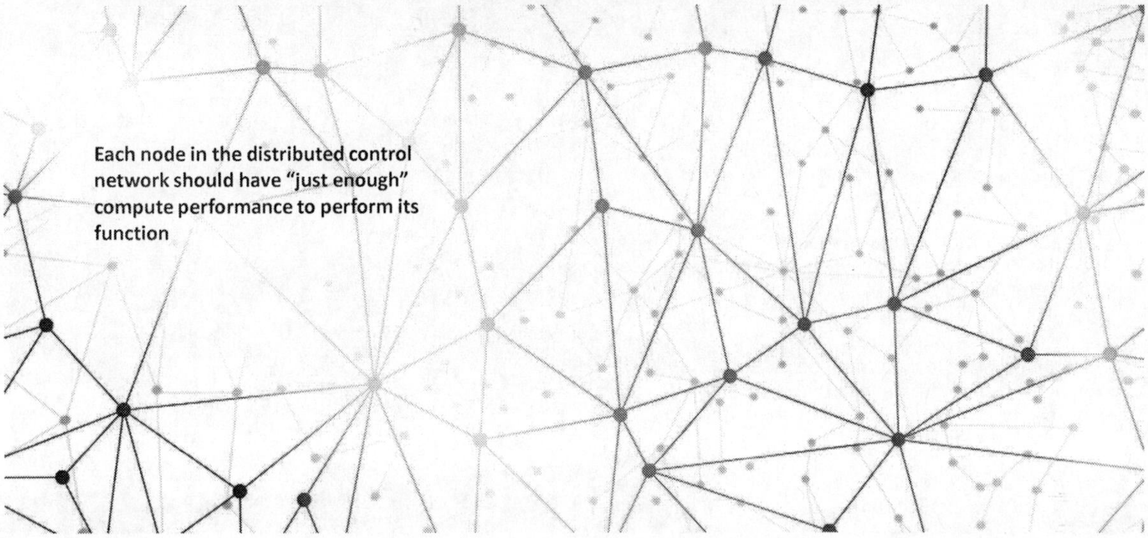

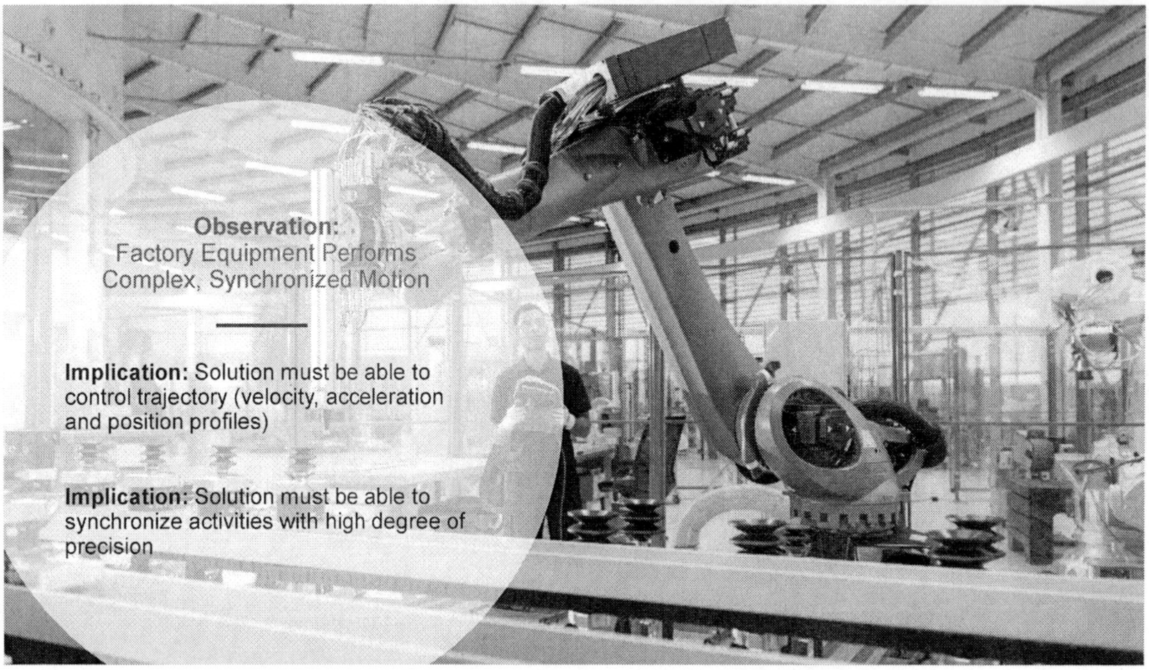
Observation:
Factory Equipment Performs Complex, Synchronized Motion
Implication: Solution must be able to control trajectory (velocity, acceleration and position profiles)
Implication: Solution must be able to synchronize activities with high degree of precision

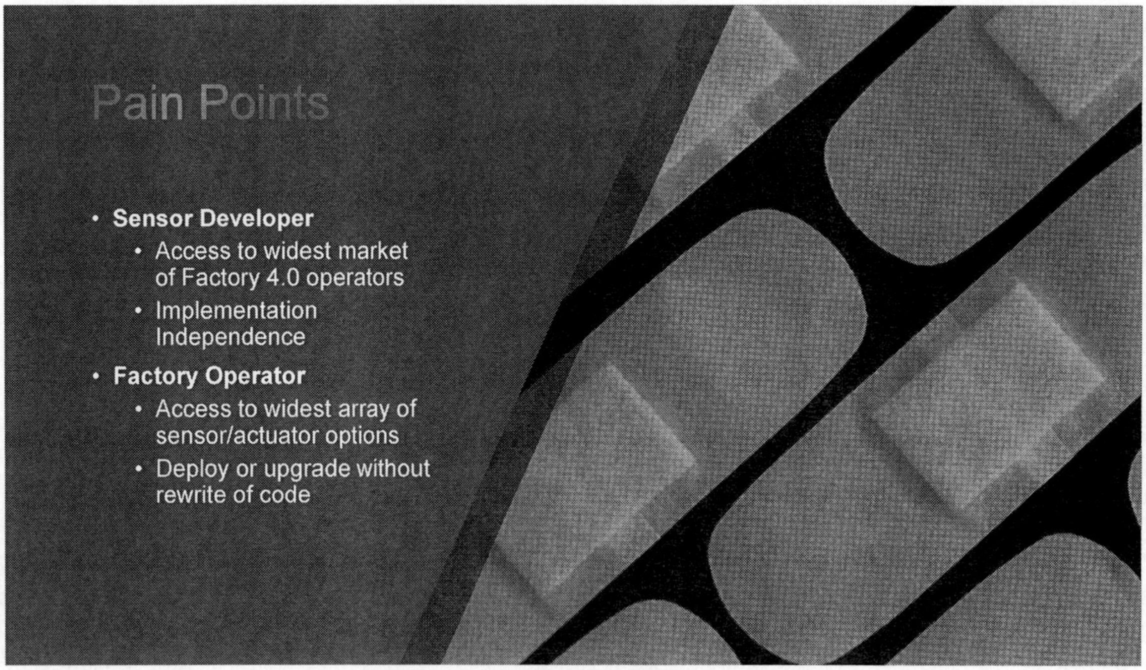
Pain Points
• Sensor Developer
• Access to widest market of Factory 4.0 operators
• Implementation Independence
• Factory Operator
• Access to widest array of sensor/actuator options
• Deploy or upgrade without rewrite of code

Plug and Play at the Sensor Domain
(the last foot of the network)

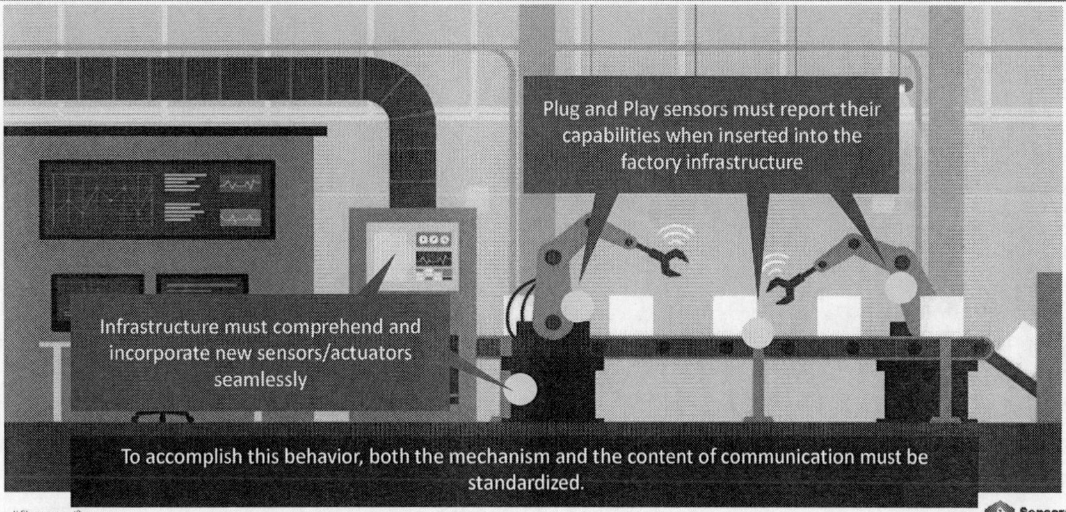

#SensorsConverge

Sensors Converge

Sensors Converge

PICMG IIoT Efforts

#SensorsConverge

Our Strategy

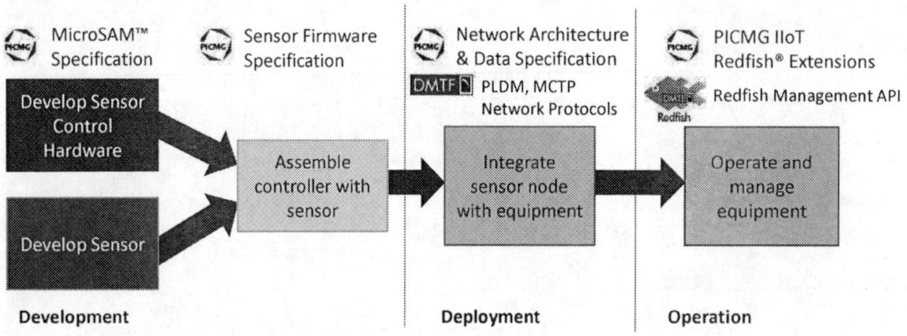

#SensorsConverge

PICMG IoT 1.1 Sensor Firmware Specification

- Leverages DMTF® PLDM and MCTP communications
- Supports multiple industry deployment scenarios for Smart Sensors
- Defines three data models for automation and control
- Defines codeless configuration
- Defines synchronization model
- Reference Code on Github Repository

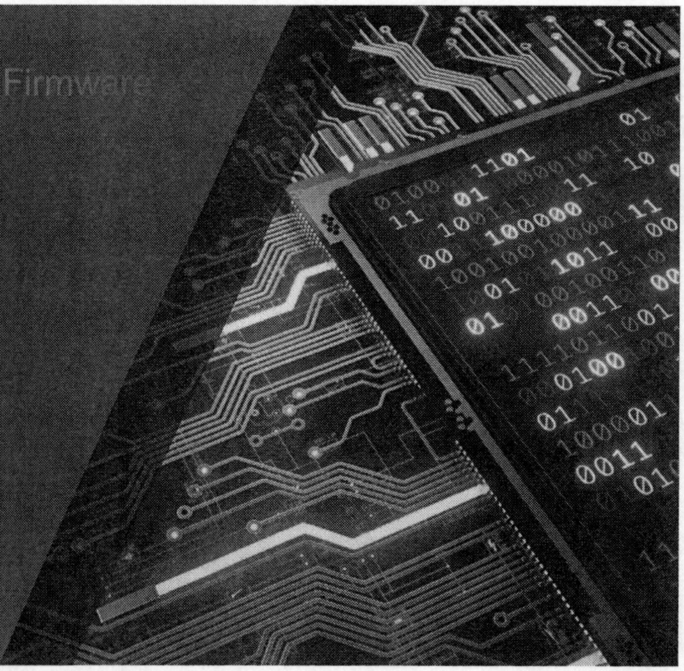

Codeless Configuration of Firmware

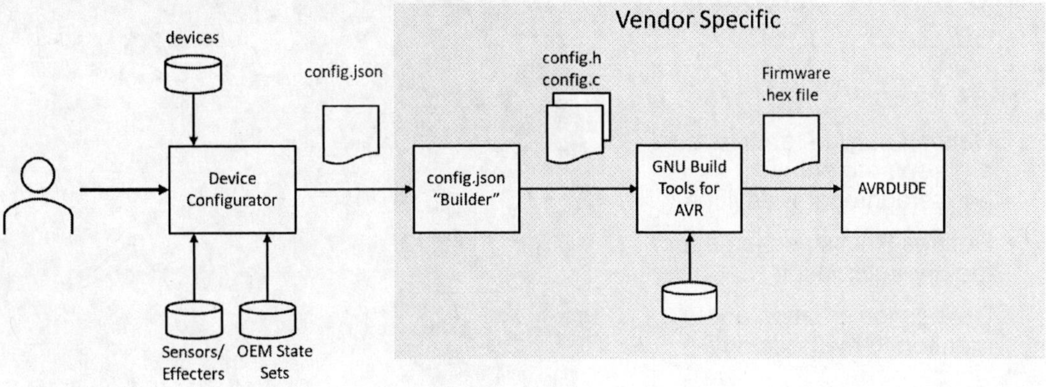

#SensorsConverge

Sensors Converge

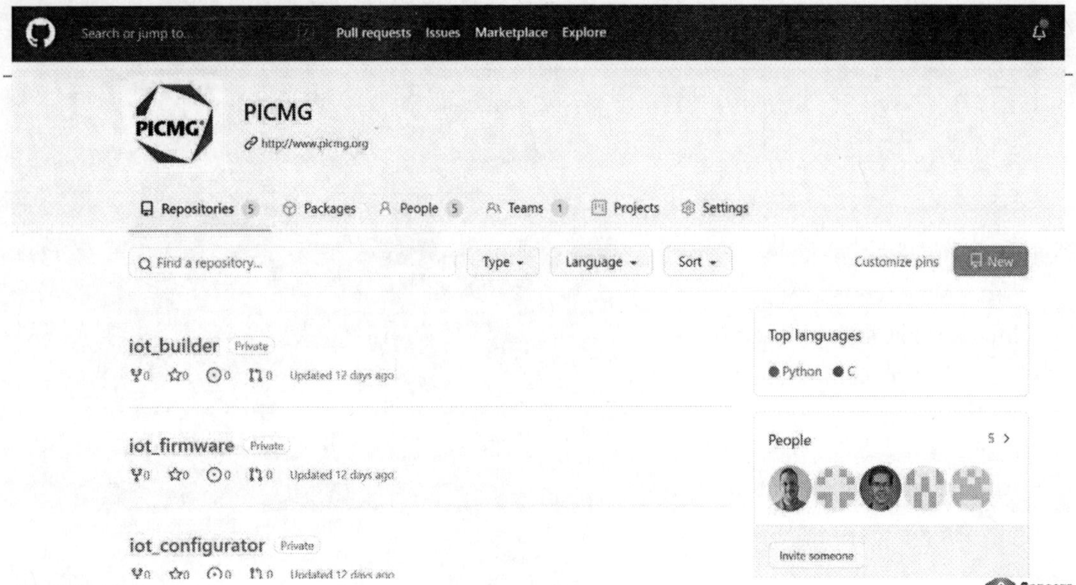

#SensorsConverge

Sensors Converge

Ongoing Work: IoT 1.2 Network Architecture and Data Model

- Defines network architecture and requirements for bridge/aggregator devices
- Defines Redfish schema for factory automation
- Defines job creation and monitoring methodology

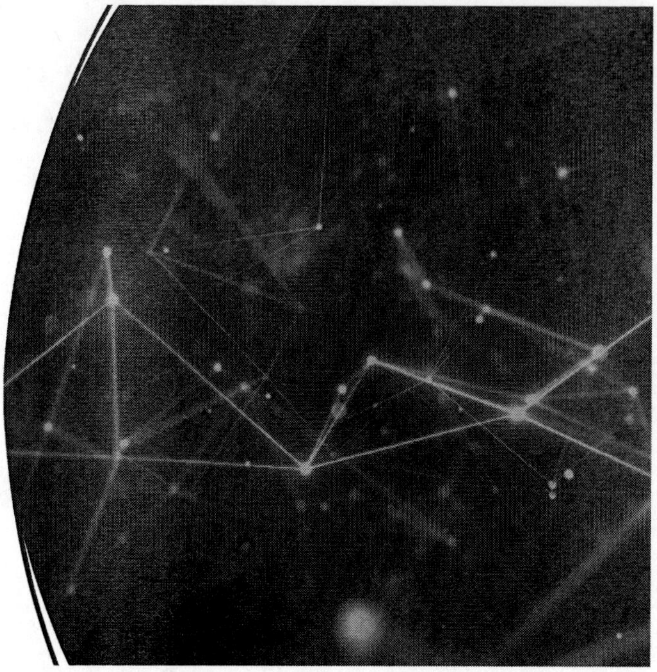

IoT 1.0 MicroSAM™ Specification

- 32mm x 32mm module
- Processor agnostic
- Multi-node synchronization
- Full industrial temperature range
- EMI/EMC
- Robust communications
- Locking connectors

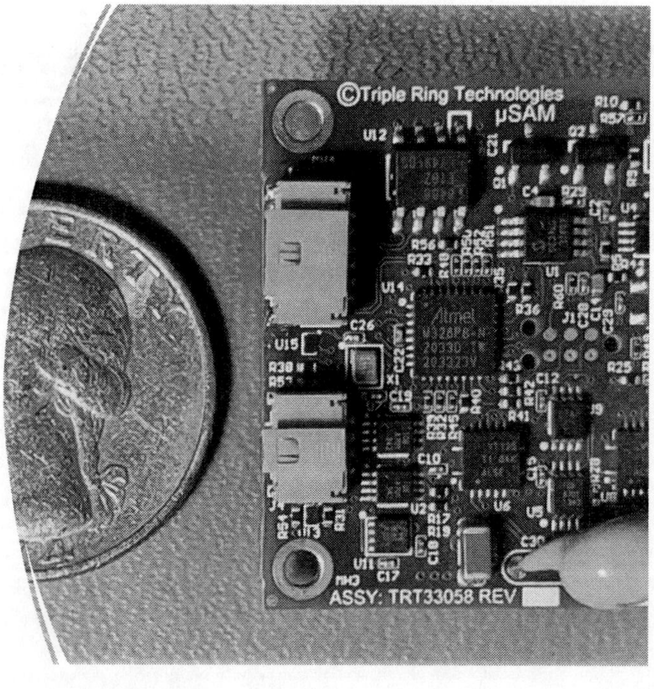

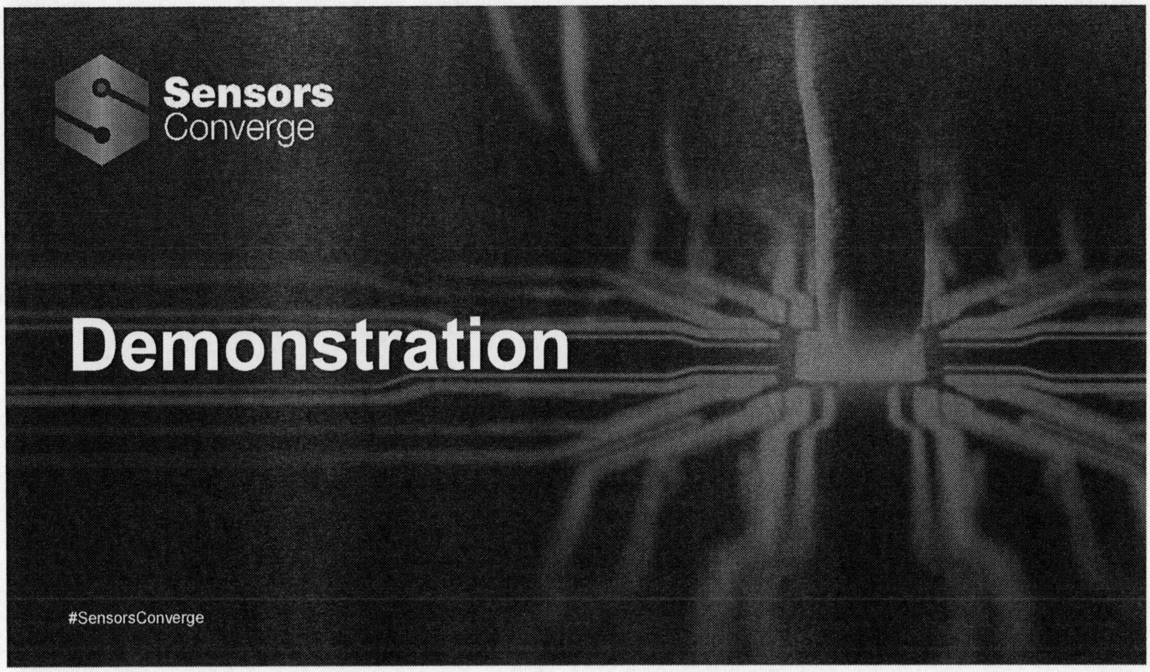
Sensors
Converge
Demonstration
#SensorsConverge

Sensors
Converge
Thank you
doug@picmg.org
LinkedIn: @picmg
PICMG®
#SensorsConverge

CONFIDENTIAL

Infineon pmd IMAGINE YOU CAN

Challenges Facing 3D Cameras for Consumer Applications

Time-of-Flight under the display and for long range applications

Edmund Neo, Senior Product Manager @Infineon

September 22, 2021

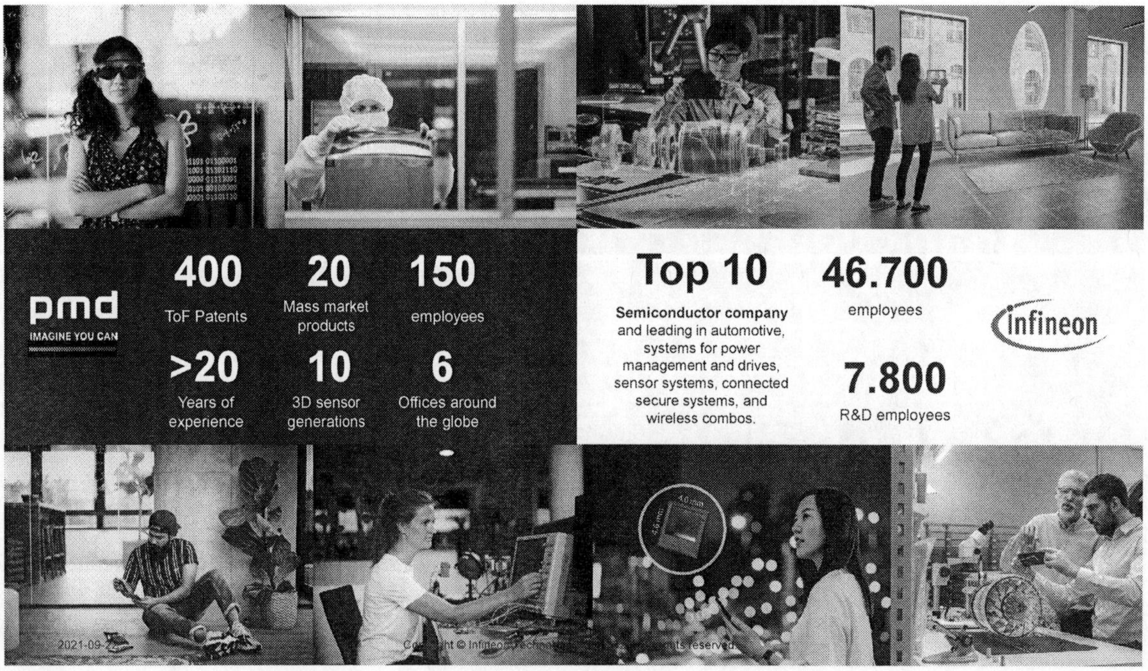

CONFIDENTIAL

Infineon and pmd
A strong and successful partnership

From Pixel to Final Product – a complete System Solution for the customer.

Pixel Design | Sensor Design | Reference Design | Software Development | Integration Support | Ramp Up

pmd and Infineon are pioneers in the ToF technology and trusted supplier to the smartphone industry

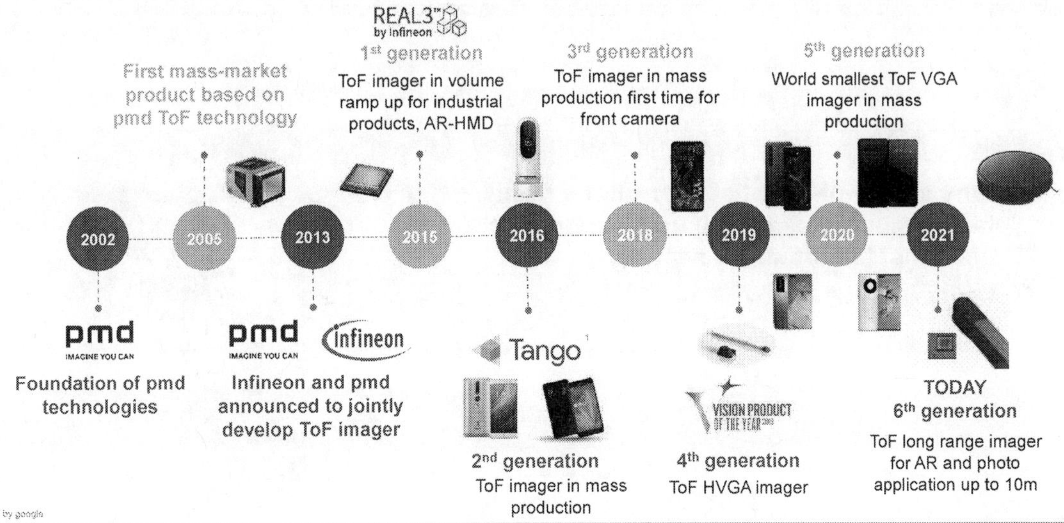

1) by google

CONFIDENTIAL

Time-of-Flight (ToF) Principle
Depth and amplitude is measured in every pixel

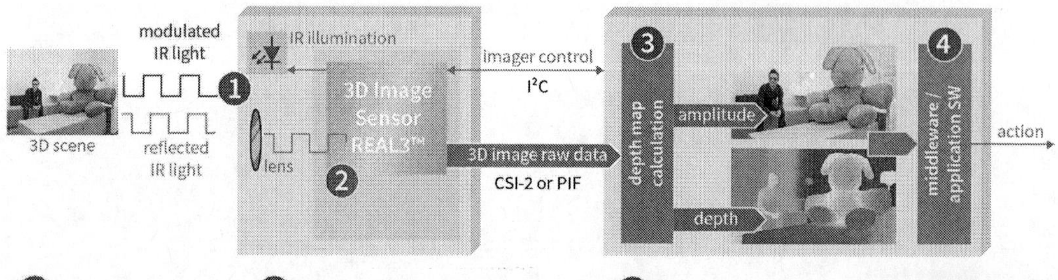

1 Active illumination › Modulated near infrared light › 850 or 940 nm	**2 Distance measurement in every pixel** Phase Shift transmitted reflected	**3 Processing** › Depth map calculation › Calibration data › Post processing	**High quality depth map** **4 Application algorithms**

2021-09-22

5

CONFIDENTIAL

3D ToF for Front-Facing Applications in Smartphones

Why a Time-of-Flight sensor on the front-facing side is key for the user experience and most important for security.

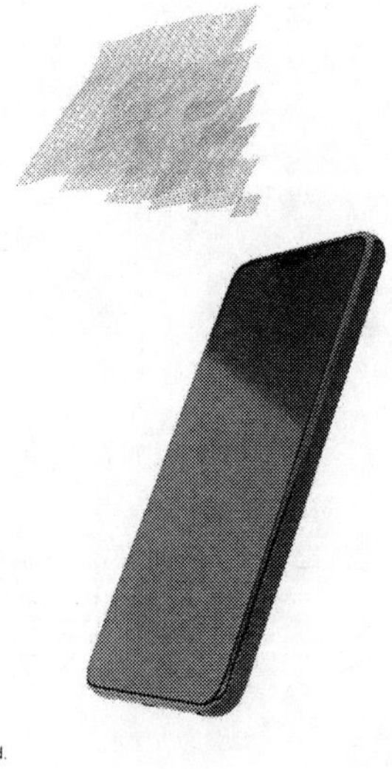

2021-09-22

6

CONFIDENTIAL

Technical press showed that 2D-Face ID is vulnerable to simple hacking

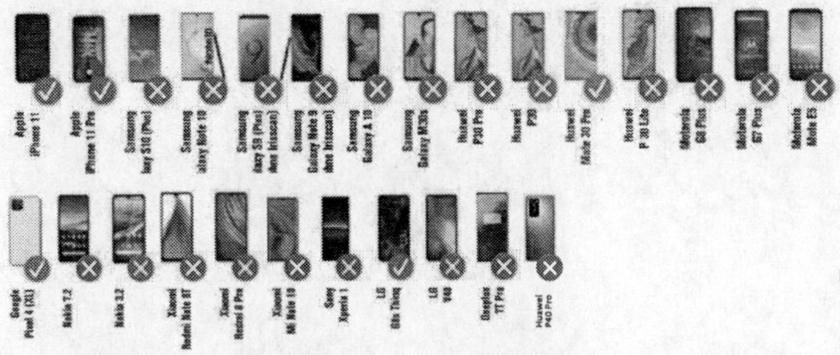

Test of FaceID from German ComputerBild magazine Q1'20

- 20 out of 25 smartphone models were able to be spoofed easily.
- **Only the 5 phones with 3D technology are secure.**

photo by phone

print by standard printer

test the phone

CONFIDENTIAL

What the customers wants:

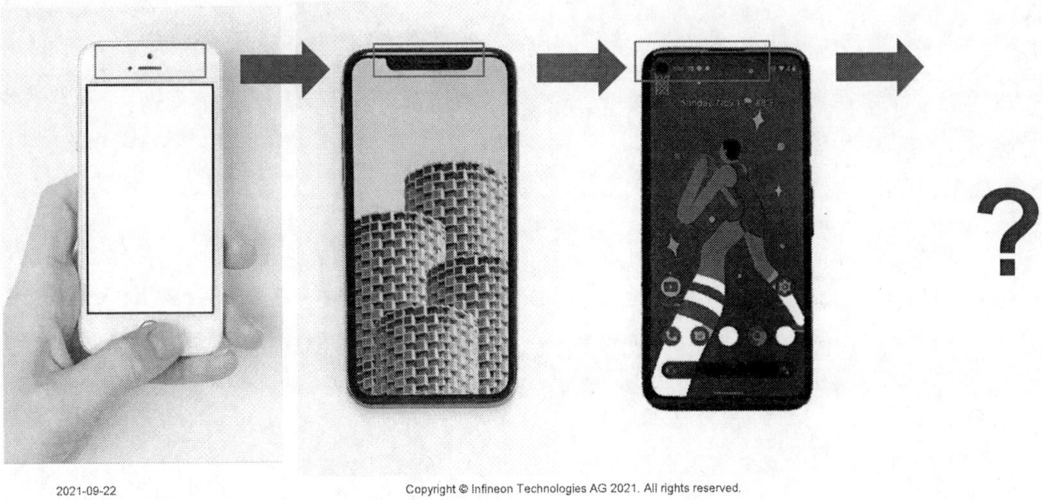

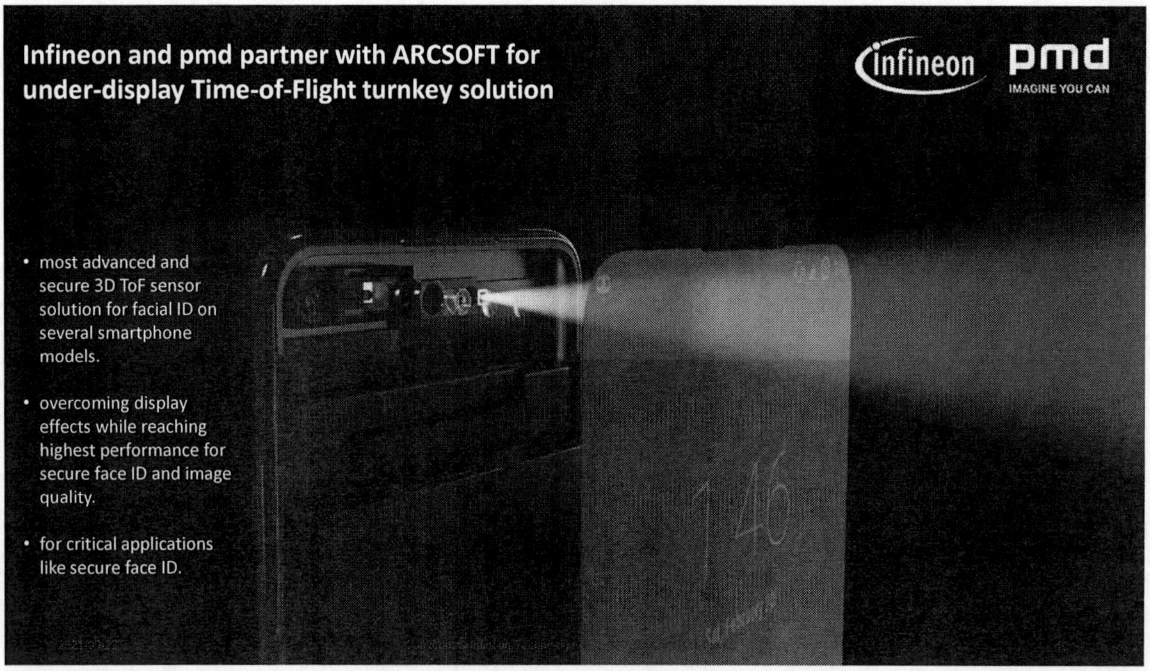
Infineon and pmd partner with ARCSOFT for
under-display Time-of-Flight turnkey solution
infineon
pmd
IMAGINE YOU CAN
• most advanced and secure 3D ToF sensor solution for facial ID on several smartphone models.
• overcoming display effects while reaching highest performance for secure face ID and image quality.
• for critical applications like secure face ID.

CONFIDENTIAL

Under Display pmd improvements

Infineon pmd IMAGINE YOU CAN

ToF UD Test Setup

- Rx & TX covered
- Display with 35% IR transmission
- Emitter: 2W VCSEL @ 940nm
- Receiver: IRS2877C
- Working range: >1m

Our goal: pmd and Infineon are enabling ToF operation under-display for secure FaceID based on propietary post-processing algorithms, which compensate display artefacts

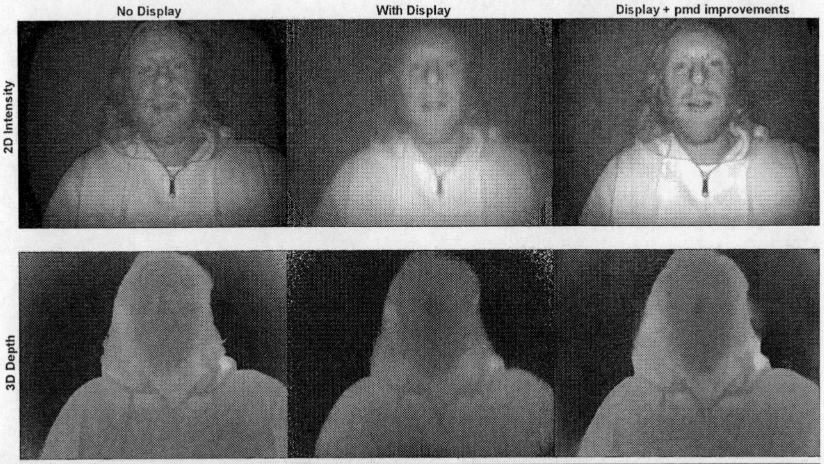

pmd improvements enable reliable facial landmark detection under display

2021-09-22 11

CONFIDENTIAL

And on the World-Facing side?

infineon pmd IMAGINE YOU CAN

Adding a world facing 3D imager to a smartphone improves the user experience and performance of the phones camera system!

CONFIDENTIAL

The new standard for high-end phones
Drivers for 3D depth imaging market & ecosystem growth

infineon pmd IMAGINE YOU CAN

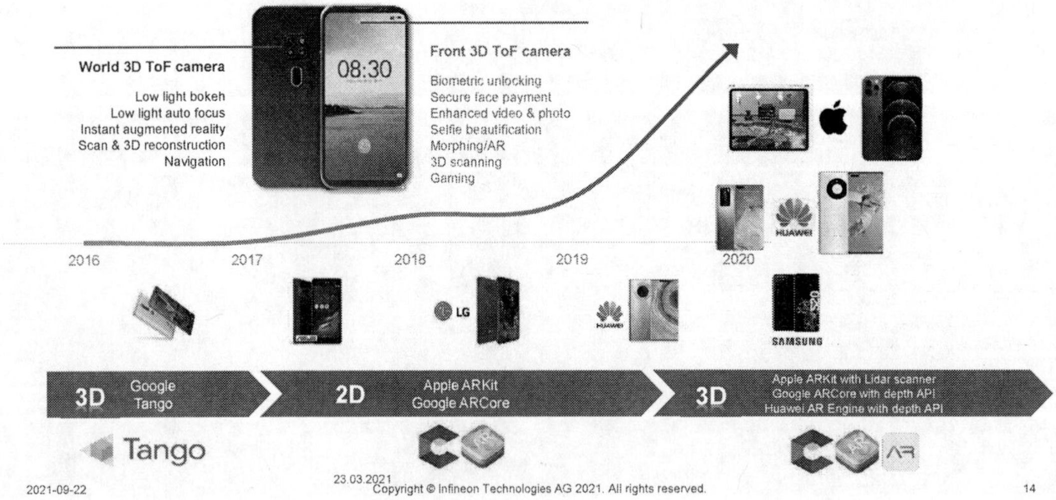

23.03.2021

CONFIDENTIAL

3D ToF camera enables differentiating applications
One sensor – many applications

infineon pmd IMAGINE YOU CAN

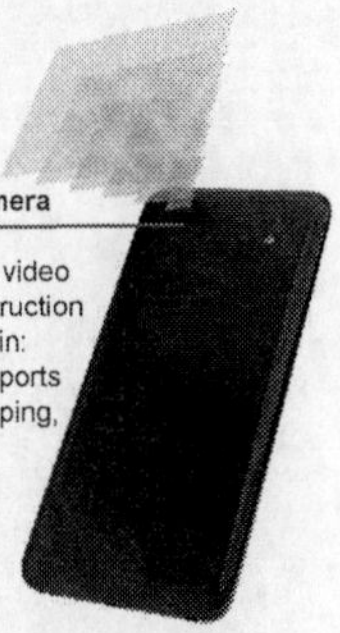

World 3D ToF camera

Enhanced photo & video
Scan & 3D reconstruction
Augmented reality in: education/leisure/sports
Navigation, e-shopping, gaming

The camera capabilities is key purchase criteria
REAL3 ™ ToF: Better camera, more applications, better user experience

2021-09-22

CONFIDENTIAL

3D ToF camera enables differentiating applications
One sensor – many applications

infineon pmd IMAGINE YOU CAN

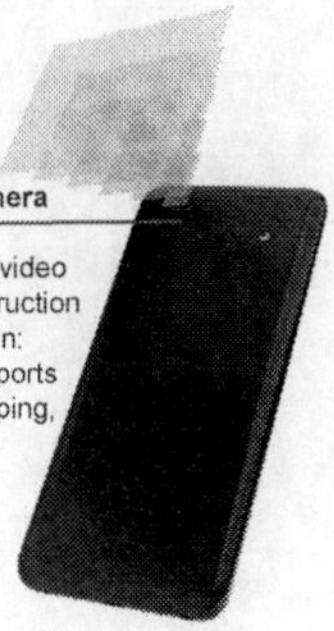

World 3D ToF camera

Enhanced photo & video
Scan & 3D reconstruction
Augmented reality in: education/leisure/sports
Navigation, e-shopping, gaming

TikTok AR filter using new depth sensing technology

The camera capabilities is key purchase criteria
REAL3 ™ ToF: Better camera, more applications, better user experience

2021-09-22

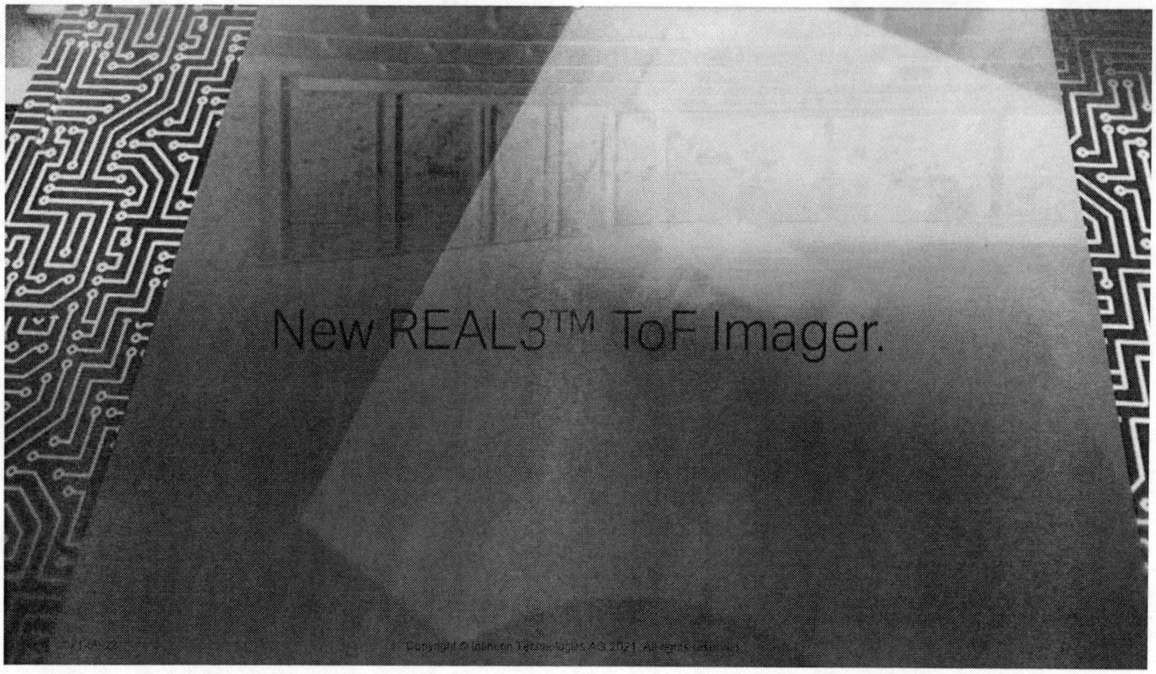
New REAL3™ ToF Imager.

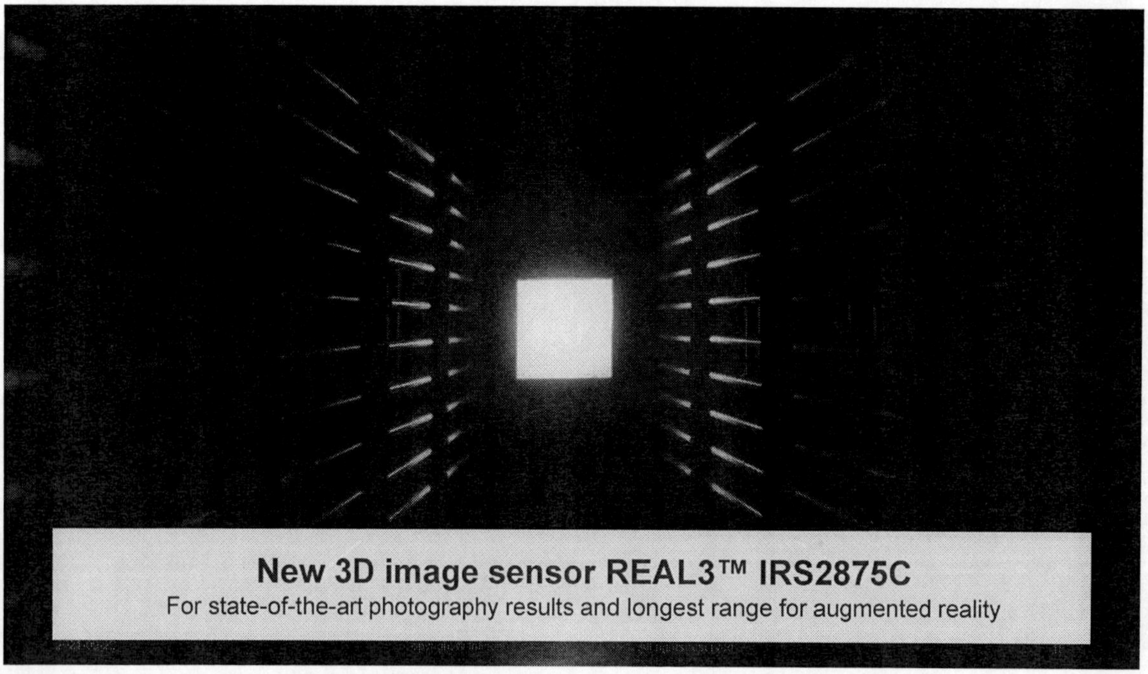
New 3D image sensor REAL3™ IRS2875C
For state-of-the-art photography results and longest range for augmented reality

CONFIDENTIAL

Specification IRS2875C

infineon pmd IMAGINE YOU CAN

- **IRS2875C Key Benefits**
  - HQVGA resolution 240 x 180
  - Improved CMOS technology for increased QE and DME
    - Smaller pixel → Same high performance
  - Highly integrated system and eye safety mechanisms
  - Lowest module BOM in combination with **IRS9102C** VCSEL driver
  - Availability: **Reference design available**
    Start of Delivery: **Mid 2021**

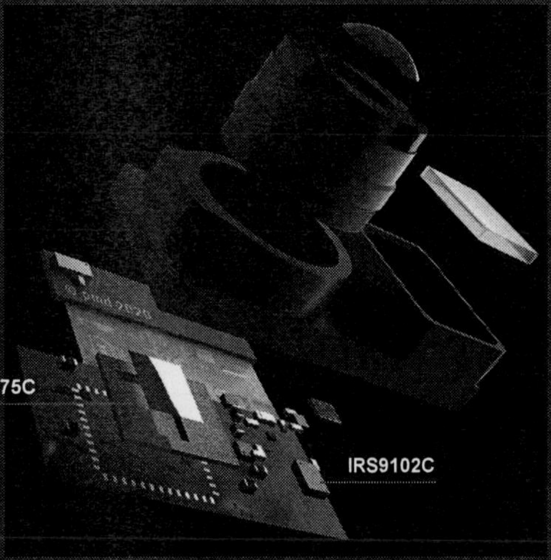

CONFIDENTIAL

IRS2875C optimized solution for world-facing applications

long range, low power, lowest BOM 3D camera

infineon pmd IMAGINE YOU CAN

- Long range up to **10 meters**
- High resolution up **to 43.2 k depth points**
- Lowest power, reduction of 40% at the imager
- Accurate and robust depth data under all light conditions
- Smallest 3D camera. **35% smaller footprint**
- **REAL3™** for lowest system BOM with Infineon's highly integrated **IRS2875C** imager and **IRS9100 / IRS9102C** VCSEL drivers

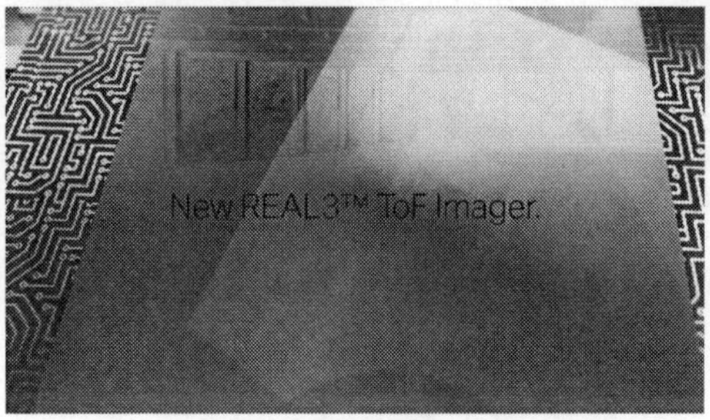

2021-09-22

20

CONFIDENTIAL

Hybrid Time of Flight

Infineon pmd IMAGINE YOU CAN

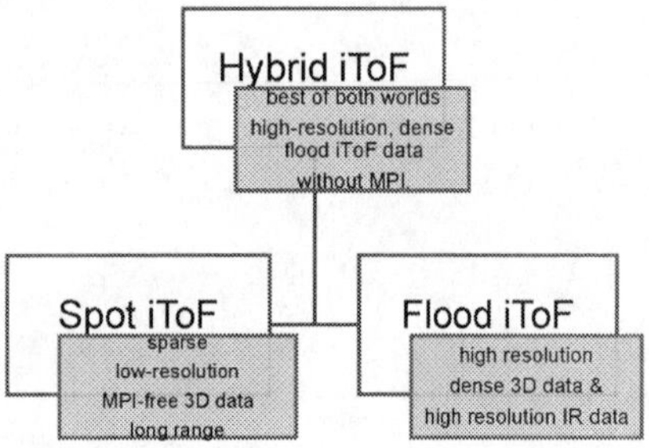

Infineon / pmd are working on a **hybrid flood / spot** time of flight system to combine the benefits of two worlds into one camera.

CONFIDENTIAL

Hybrid Illumination – Removing MPI

Infineon pmd IMAGINE YOU CAN

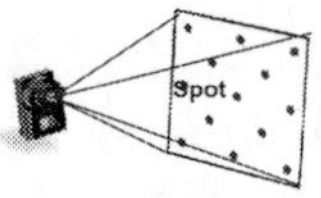

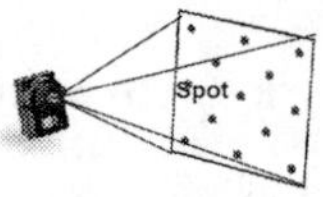

+ pmd

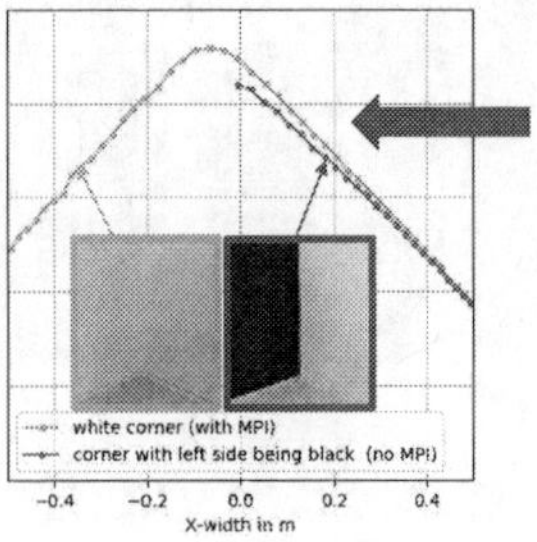

Difference between blue and orange 3D data due to MPI even with spot illumination;

blue = correct;
orange = with MPI

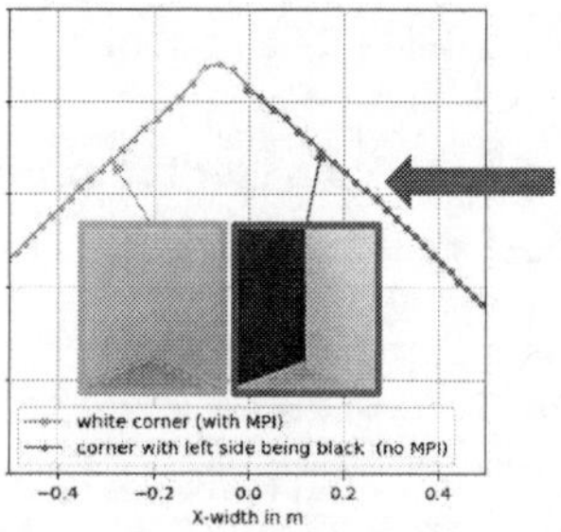

No difference between blue and orange 3D data due to pmd's **MPI correction algorithm**; pmd make's spot depth data significantly more correct

CONFIDENTIAL

Time of Flight

Spot iToF

[Spot Projection] [Spot iTOF greyscale]

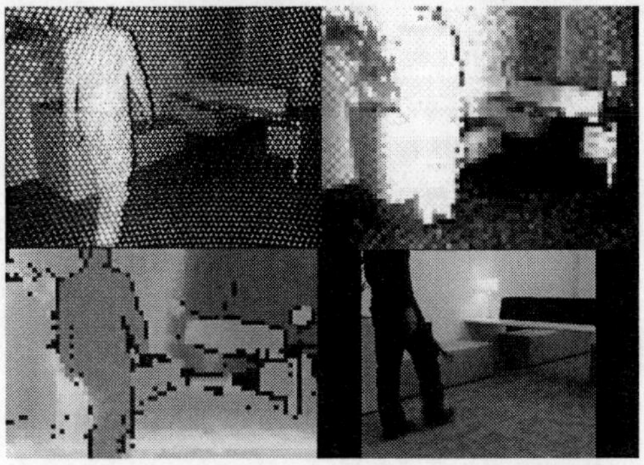

[Spot iTOF Depth Map] [RGB reference]

Impact on MPI – in corners

binned flood | spot, no correction | spot with correction

Higher Signal **Reduced MPI** **Lower resolution (~4k dots)**

CONFIDENTIAL

ToF is scalable to many applications and use cases

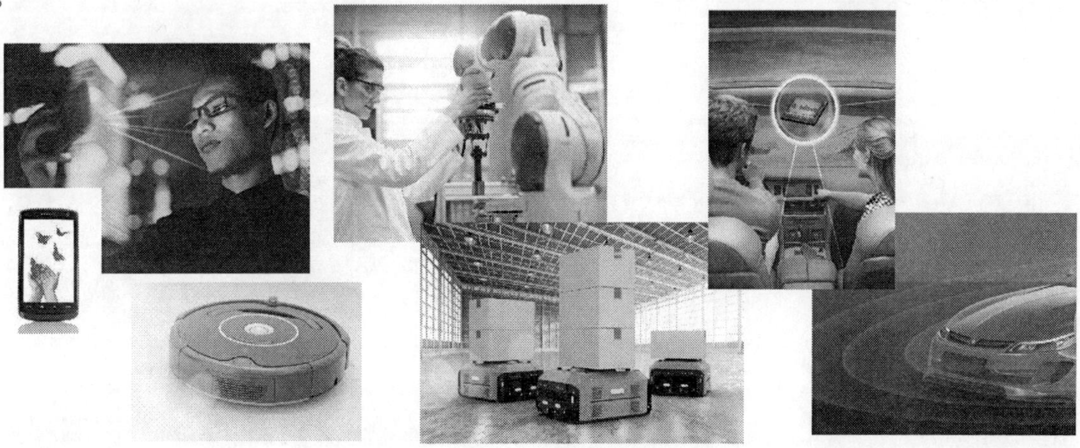

Mobile Phones | Consumer Electronics | Collaborative Robotics | Industrial Automation | Car in-cabin Sensing | Autonomous Driving

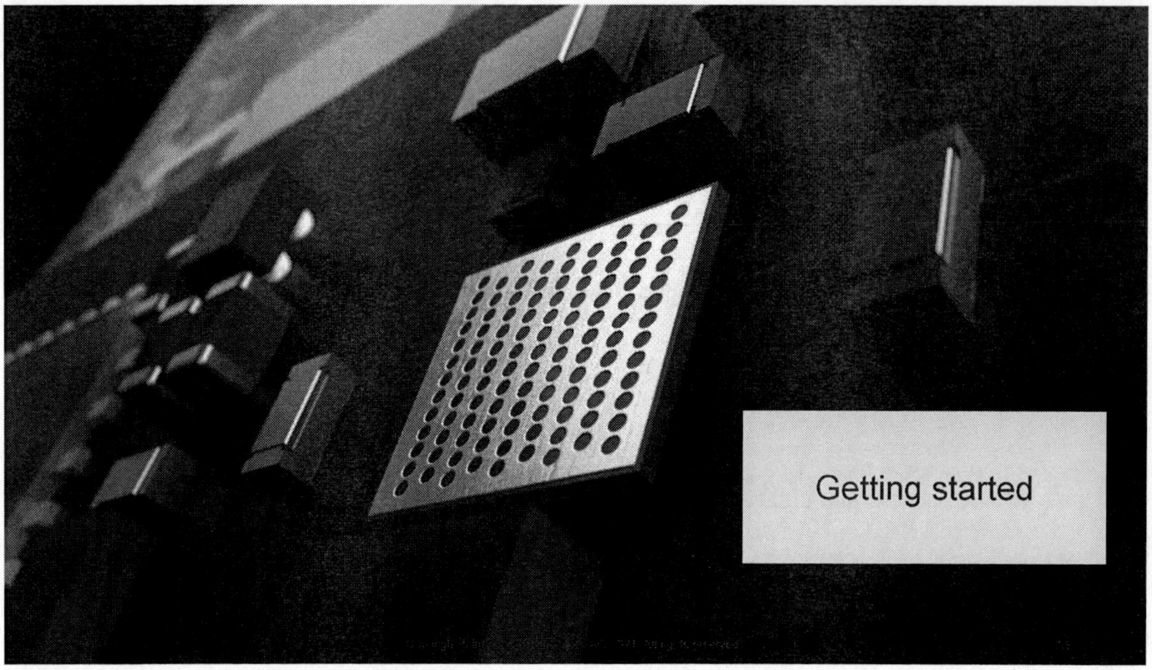

CONFIDENTIAL

3D Time-of-Flight Development Kit
Getting started

The System-On-Module (SOM) offers a small form factor development kit and comes with two mobile form factor Time of flight camera options:

- **A65** – 105° x 85° wide field of view; 224 x 172 pixel
- **MTP006** – 60° x 40° field of view; 224 x 172 pixel

These MIPI modules come as a **total ToF system solution** that can be used for either development, or as-is in a production device.

The SOM is shipped with a **pre-loaded** with **pmd's Spectre and Royale Software** in object code to provide the user with a quick an easy 3D depth map

CONFIDENTIAL

Summary

- **pmd/Infineon** as the **ToF pioneers** in phones are the **leading players** and shows already **multiple phones** with desired applications in **high volume**
- **Removing the bezel!** REAL3™ for secure under display face authentication
- **IRS2875C** imager and **IRS9102C** VCSEL driver to introduce a **new generation** of long range, low power, low BOM time of flight cameras
- **High resolution** flood and **high SnR** from spot illumination. Get **the best of two worlds** with a pmd / Infineon **hybrid time of flight system**

2021-09-22 27

CONFIDENTIAL

pmdtechnologies ag
www.pmdtec.com

Infineon Technologies AG
www.infineon.com

Thank you

2021-09-22 28

Questions
& answers
Gear 7-38
Copyright © Infineon Technologies AG 2021. All rights reserved.

Sensors Converge

Design Considerations for Medical Wearables

September 21-23, 2021 | San Jose, CA

#SensorsConverge

Introductions

Elizabeth Gomes
Biomedical Engineer
blümio Medtronic

Steve Braaten
Product Acceleration Lead
blümio cisco IBM

#SensorsConverge

Sensors Converge

Outline

- Wearable applications: medical vs. consumer
- Design considerations
  - Signal processing and biometric extraction
  - Selecting a transducer
  - Device design and integration
- Blood pressure monitoring as an example

Medical vs. Consumer Wearables

Two Different Product Paths

Whether your product is a medical wearable depends on the **diagnostic or treatment claims** you make and its **intended use**

Consumer Wearable or Medical Wearable?

Fitness Heart Rate Tracker

Wearable with Blood Pressure Measurements

#SensorsConverge

Sensors Converge

FDA Device Classification

Class I Low Risk

- Example: dental floss
- Typically only requires registration with the FDA
- Pathway takes about a month

Class II Moderate Risk

- Most medical wearables
- Typically only requires FDA clearance through 510(k)
- Pathway takes about 4-10 months

Class III High Risk

- Example: pacemakers
- Typically requires FDA approved clinical trial and FDA premarket approval (PMA)
- Pathway takes multiple years

#SensorsConverge

Sensors Converge

Keep in Mind

- A medical wearable is going to require more rigorous scientific and accuracy evidence
- A medical wearable may be subject to other regulatory agencies
- Consider that new technology tends to flow from the clinic to the consumer market

#SensorsConverge

Sensors Converge

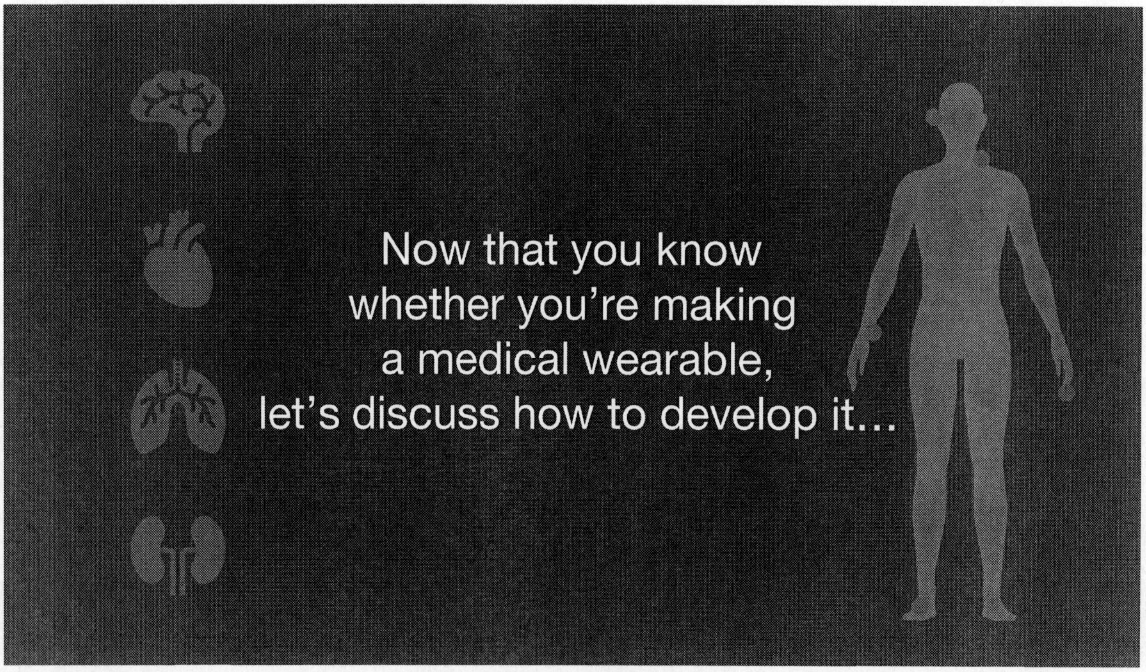

Outline

- Wearable applications: medical vs. consumer
- **Design considerations**
  - **Signal processing and biometric extraction**
  - **Selecting a transducer**
  - **Device design and integration**
- Blood pressure monitoring as an example

#SensorsConverge

Sensors Converge

Signal Processing and Biometric Extraction

#SensorsConverge

Sensors Converge

Starting with a Signal

- The pulse waveform contains a vast amount of health data
- The next step is to build up the algorithmic capability to tease out that health information

#SensorsConverge

Sensors Converge

Signal Quality Indices

- Why?
  - Establish quality indices to exclude poor quality measurements
- How?
  - Signal shape or spectra doesn't resemble that of a pulse waveform
  - Machine learning models to recognize low-quality waveforms
  - Biometric readings are outside of the realm of physiologically possible

Biometrics to Extract

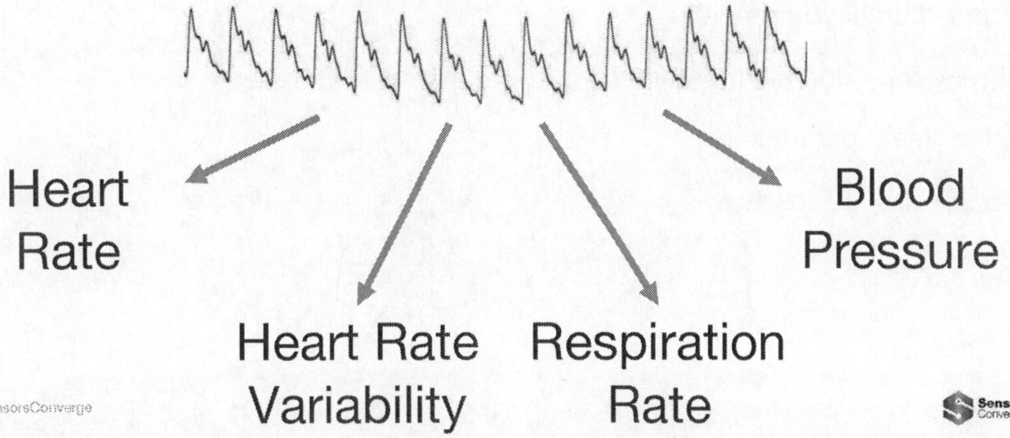

#SensorsConverge

Sensors Converge

Heart Rate

- Time-domain processing
- Frequency-domain processing

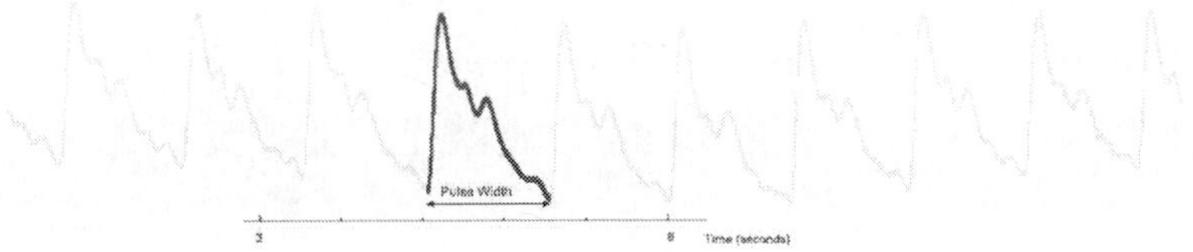

#SensorsConverge

Sensors Converge

Heart Rate Variability

- Short term (5 min) vs. long term (24 hr) heart rate variability
- Time-domain parameters
- Frequency-domain parameters
- Non-linear parameters

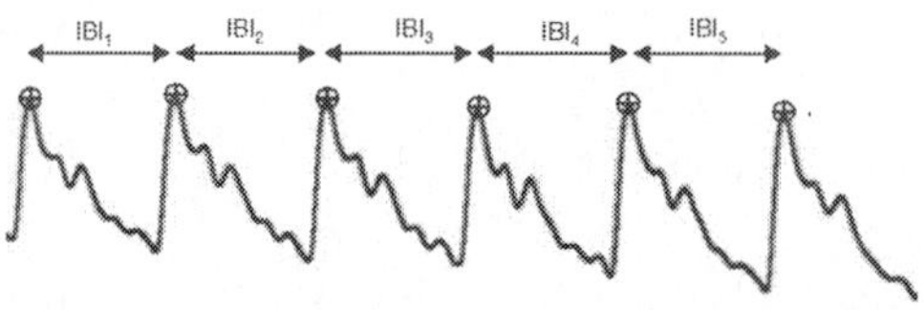

Shaffer F, Ginsberg JP. An Overview of Heart Rate Variability Metrics and Norms. Front Public Health. 2017;5:258. Published 2017 Sep 28. doi:10.3389/fpubh.2017.00258

#SensorsConverge

Respiration Rate

- Extract the respiratory signal with filtering methods
- Frequency domain processing

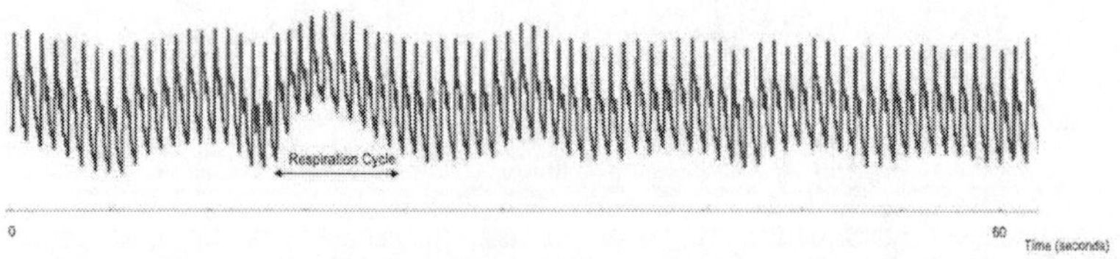

#SensorsConverge

Blood Pressure

- Pulse wave analysis or pulse decomposition analysis
- Pulse wave velocity, pulse travel time, or pulse arrival time
- Extract waveform features and build machine learning model

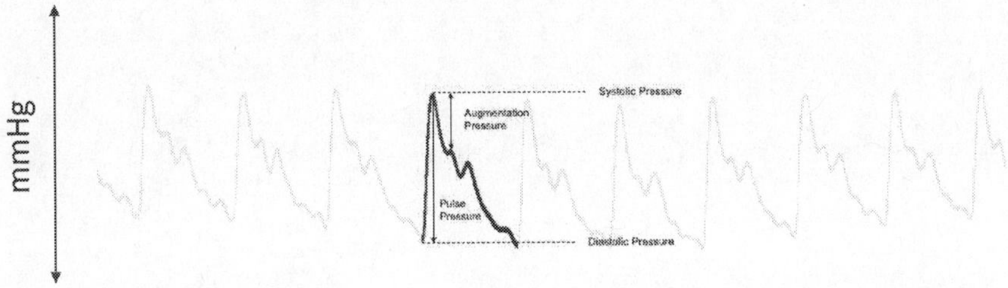

#SensorsConverge

Sensors Converge

Biometrics to Extract

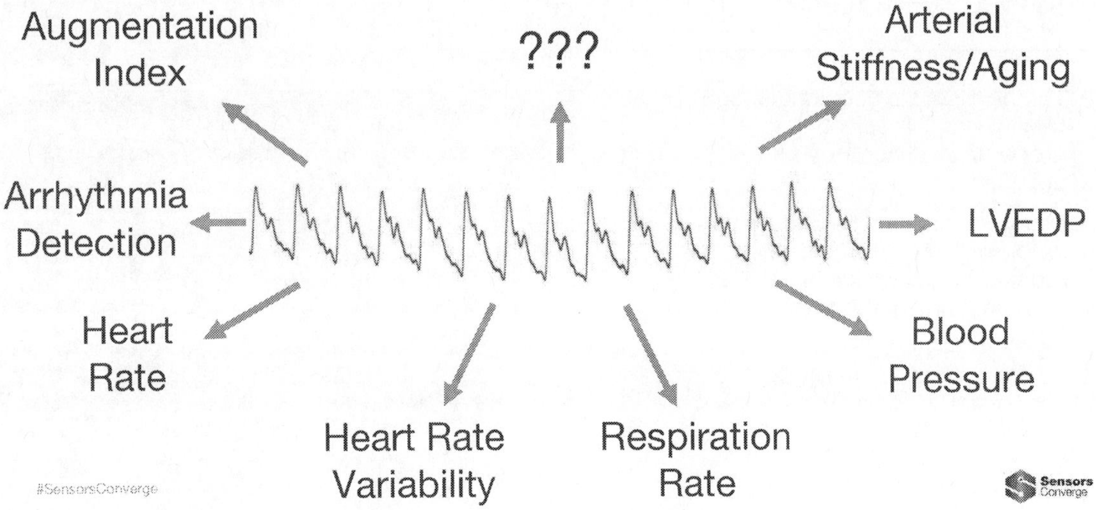

#SensorsConverge

Sensors Converge

Selecting a Transducer

#SensorsConverge

Sensors Converge

How to Acquire Your Signal

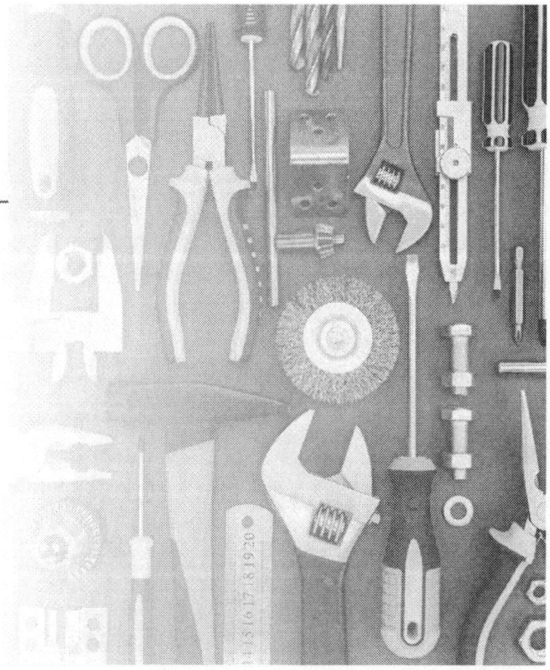

- The next step in acquiring a high-quality signal is selecting the proper transducer for your application
- Many transducers have been employed in cardiovascular monitoring, as well as fused combinations of those transducers

#SensorsConverge

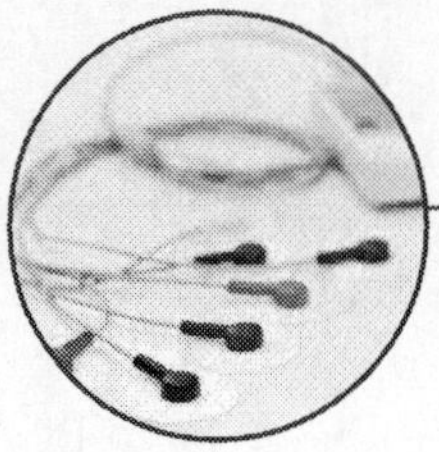

Electrocardiogram (ECG)

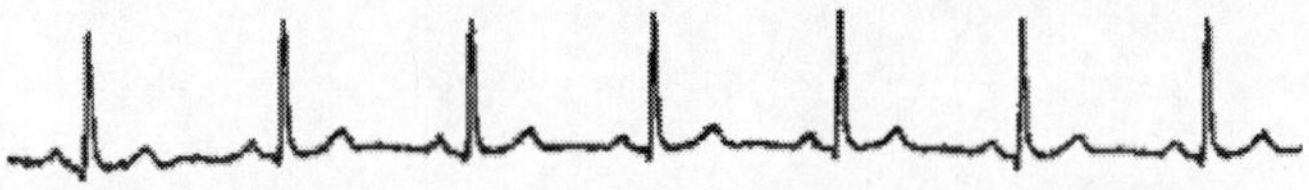

Modality	Electrical Activity
Requires Compression?	No
Continuous Sampling?	Yes
Cons	Requires multiple electrodes or points of contact.
Companies using this transducer	iRHYTHM, AliveCor

#SensorsConverge

Sensors Converge

Bioimpedance

Modality	Impedance
Requires Compression?	No
Continuous Sampling?	Yes
Cons	Requires multiple electrodes or points of contact.
Companies using this transducer	ATM

B. Ibrahim and R. Jafari, "Cuffless Blood Pressure Monitoring from an Array of Wrist Bio-Impedance Sensors Using Subject-Specific Regression Models: Proof of Concept," in IEEE Transactions on Biomedical Circuits and Systems, vol. 13, no. 6, pp. 1723-1735, Dec. 2019. doi: 10.1109/TBCAS.2019.2946661.

#SensorsConverge

Sensors Converge

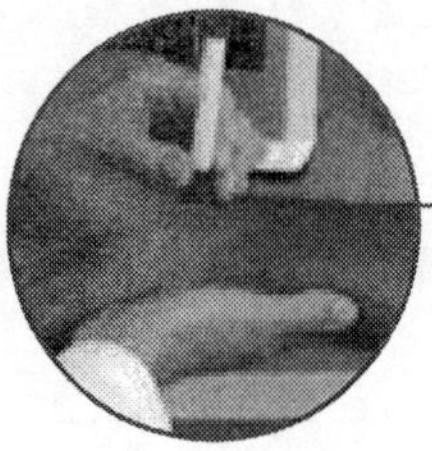

Applanation Tonometry

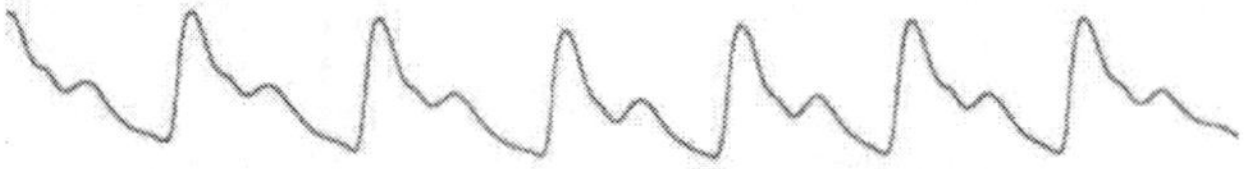

Modality	Force
Requires Compression?	Yes
Continuous Sampling?	No
Cons	Requires precise placement and constant pressure.
Companies using this transducer	BPro®

#SensorsConverge

Sensors Converge

Photoplethysmography (PPG)

Modality	Optical
Requires Compression?	No
Continuous Sampling?	Yes
Cons	Measures volume changes and not pressure.
Companies using this transducer	spry, RIVA HEALTH, AKTIIA

#SensorsConverge

Sensors Converge

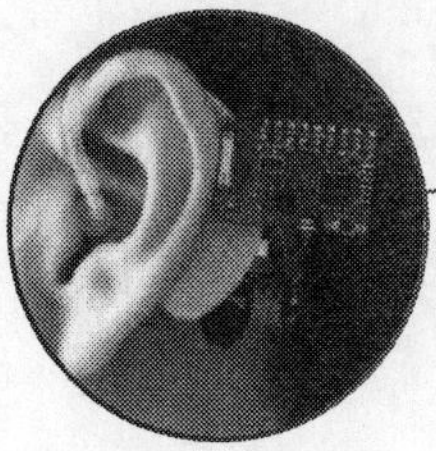

Ballistocardiography (BCG)

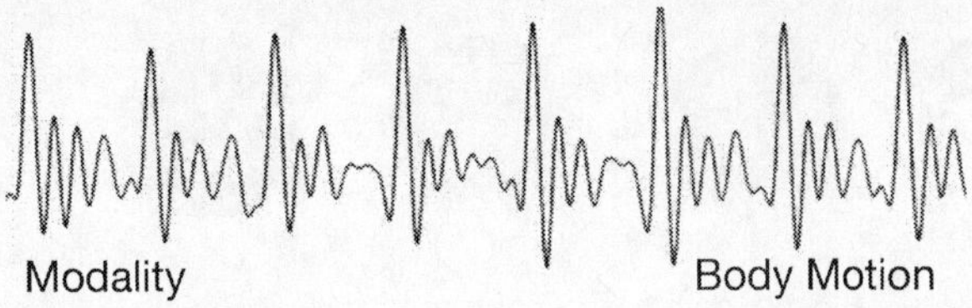

Modality	Body Motion
Requires Compression?	No
Continuous Sampling?	Yes
Cons	Suffers from gross motion artifacts.
Companies using this transducer	QUANTTUS

Winokur ES, He DD, Sodini CG. A wearable vital signs monitor at the ear for continuous heart rate and pulse transit time measurements. Annu Int Conf IEEE Eng Med Biol Soc. 2012;2012:2724-2727. doi:10.1109/EMBC.2012.6346527

#SensorsConverge

Sensors Converge

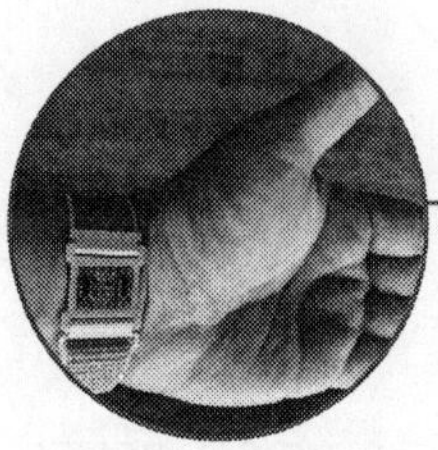

Radar (Radio Frequency)

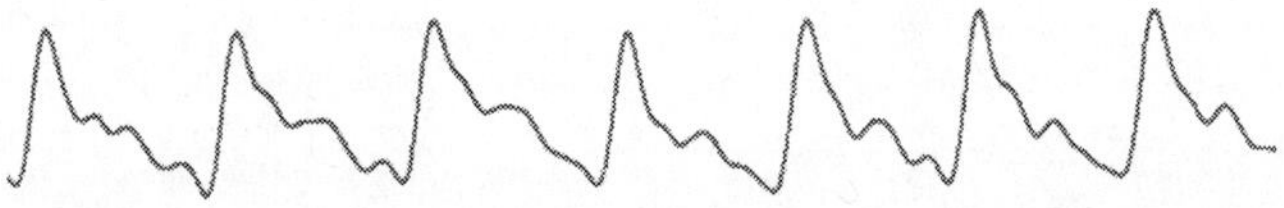

Modality	Skin Surface Motion
Requires Compression?	No
Continuous Sampling?	Yes
Cons	Suffers from gross motion artifacts.
Companies using this transducer	blümio

#SensorsConverge

Sensors Converge

Off-the-Shelf Transducers

	ECG	Bioimpedance	Tonometer	PPG	BCG	Radar
Modality	Electrical Activity	Impedance	Force	Optical	Body Motion	Skin Surface Motion
Pitfalls	Requires multiple electrodes or points of contact.	Requires multiple electrodes or points of contact.	Requires precise placement and constant pressure.	Measures volume changes and not pressure.	Suffers from gross motion artifacts.	Suffers from gross motion artifacts.
Companies using this transducer	iRHYTHM, Apple, AliveCor	ATM	BPro	spry, AKTIIA, RIVA HEALTH	QUANTTUS	blümio

Device Design and Integration

Design and Integration

- The design of your final device will be most greatly influenced by your:
  - Application of choice
  - Transducer of choice
  - Regulatory requirements

1. FDA Design Control Guidance For Medical Device Manufacturers
2. FDA Design Considerations for Devices Intended for Home Use
3. ISO 14971:2007 Medical devices – Application of risk management to medical devices

#SensorsConverge

Sensors Converge

Areas of Design

- Mechanical
- Data, Computation, and Storage
- Electrical and Power
- Connectivity
- Usability

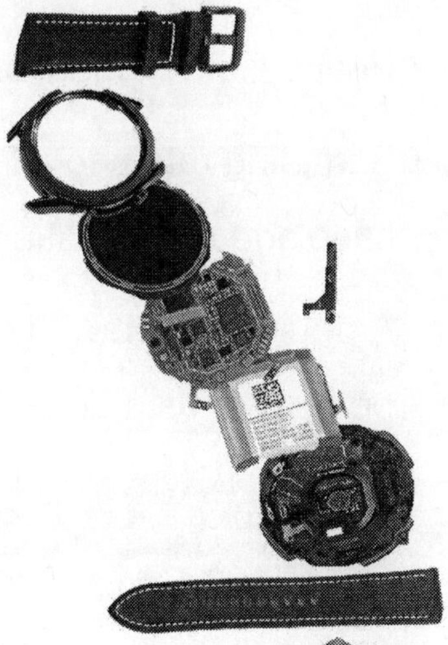

#SensorsConverge

www.ifixit.com

Sensors Converge

Mechanical

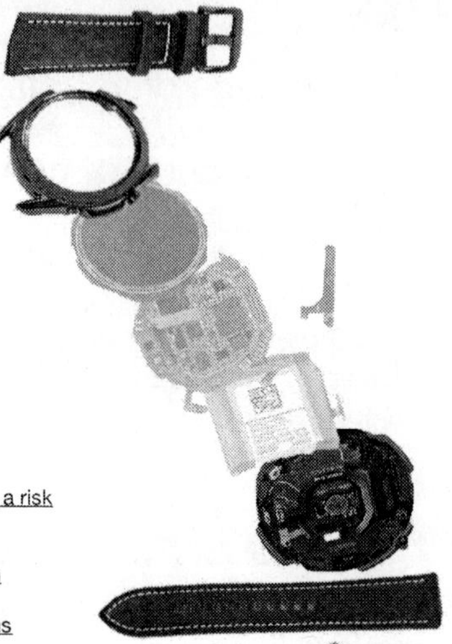

- Sufficiently protect components
- Secure sensor to wearer for duration of use
- Robust to sterilization
- Biocompatible

1. IEC 60601-1:2021 SER Medical electrical equipment
2. ISO 10993-1:2009 Biological evaluation of medical devices — Part 1: Evaluation and testing within a risk management process
3. ISO 10993-5:2009 Biological evaluation of medical devices — Part 5: Tests for in vitro cytotoxicity
4. ISO 10993-10:2010 Biological evaluation of medical devices — Part 10: Tests for irritation and skin sensitization
5. ASTM D4169-2014 Standard Practice for Performance Testing of Shipping Containers and Systems

#SensorsConverge

www.ifixit.com

Sensors Converge

Data, Computation, and Storage

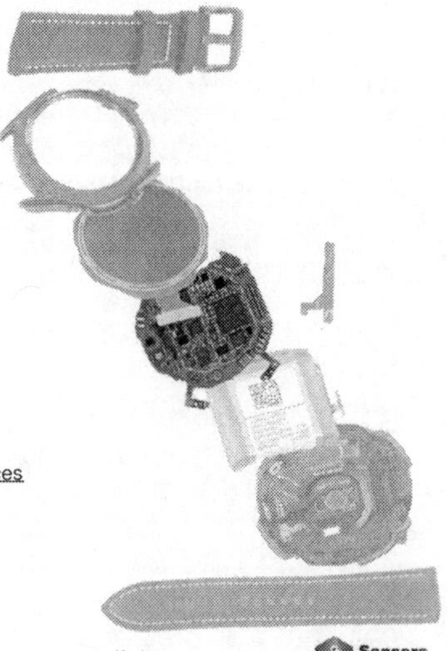

- Privacy, encryption, and security
- Sampling rate should be sufficient for your use-case and computational needs
- Amount of on-board storage and processing power will be a constraint

1. FDA Guidance for the Content of Premarket Submissions for Software Contained in Medical Devices
2. FDA Guidance on Off-the-Shelf Software Use in Medical Devices
3. FDA General Principles of Software Validation
4. FDA Content of Premarket Submissions for Management of Cybersecurity in Medical Devices
5. FDA Cybersecurity for Networked Medical Devices Containing Off-the-Shelf (OTS) Software
6. HIPAA Combined Regulation Text of All Rules
7. IEC 62304:2006 Medical device software — Software life cycle processes

#SensorsConverge

www.ifixit.com

Sensors Converge

Electrical and Power

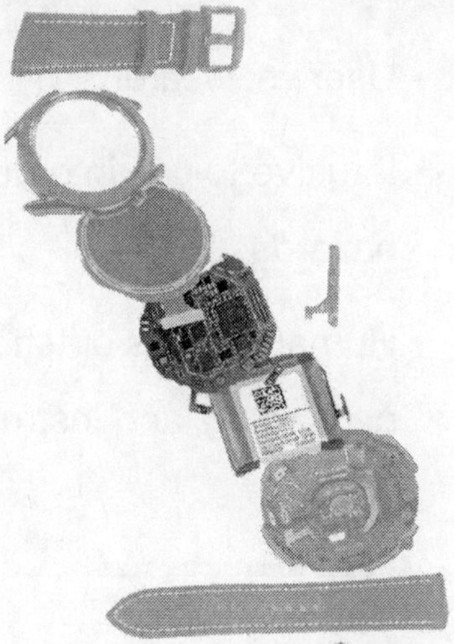

- Battery capacity will be a determining factor for many design choices
- Sampling rate, computation, and duration of use will inform power requirements

1. IEC 60601-1:2021 SER Medical electrical equipment

#SensorsConverge

www.ifixit.com

Connectivity

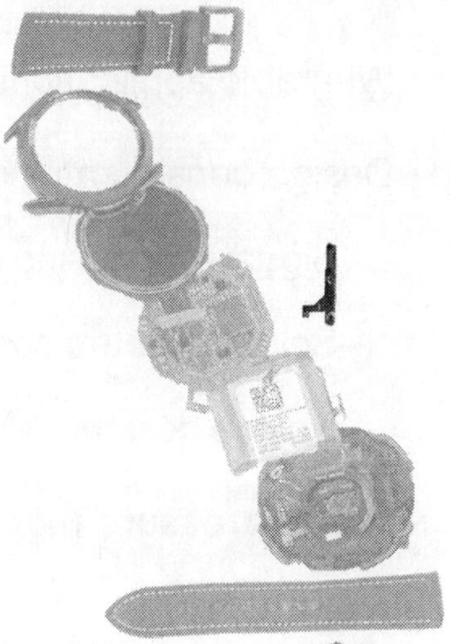

- Depends on whether being used inside or outside the clinic
  - Device interference
- Electronic medical record / electronic health record systems

1. IEC 60601-1:2021 SER Medical electrical equipment

#SensorsConverge

www.ifixit.com

Usability

- User vs. wearer
- Intuitive to use in order to minimize errors or hazards
- Human factors criteria in design, labeling, packaging, and instructions

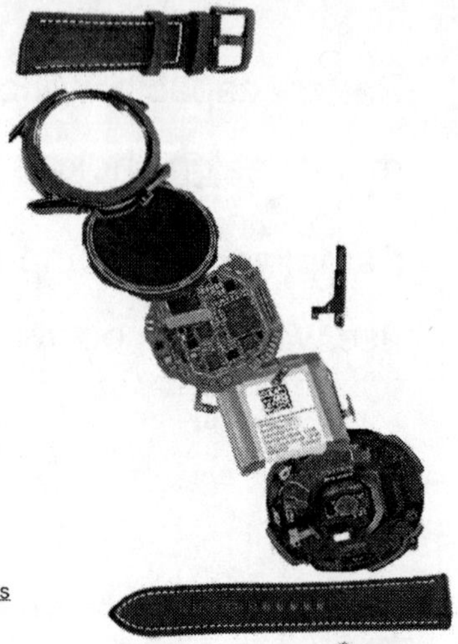

1. FDA Applying Human Factors and Usability Engineering to Medical Devices
2. IEC 62366-1:2015 Medical devices - Part 1: Application of usability engineering to medical devices

#SensorsConverge

www.ifixit.com

Sensors Converge

Outline

- Wearable applications: medical vs. consumer
- Design considerations
  - –Signal processing and biometric extraction
  - –Selecting a transducer
  - –Device design and integration
- **Blood pressure monitoring as an example**

#SensorsConverge

Sensors Converge

CASE STUDY

Building a wearable BP monitor

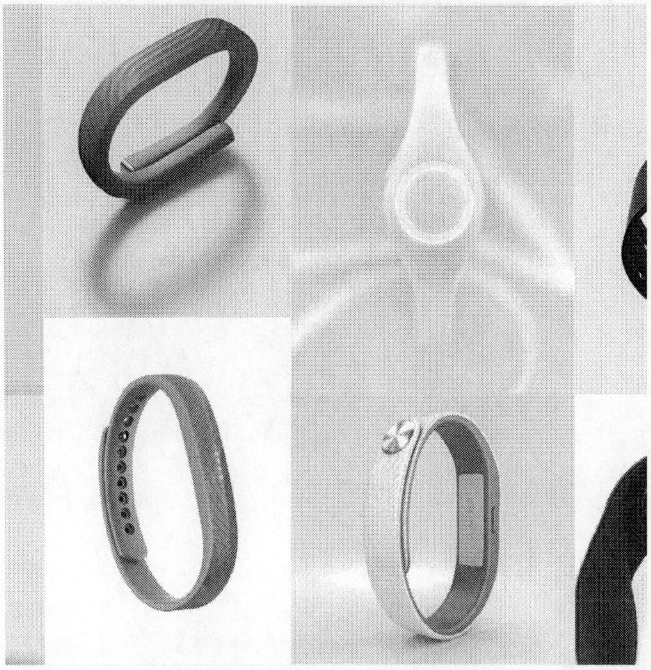

Continuous data solutions emerging, except for BP...

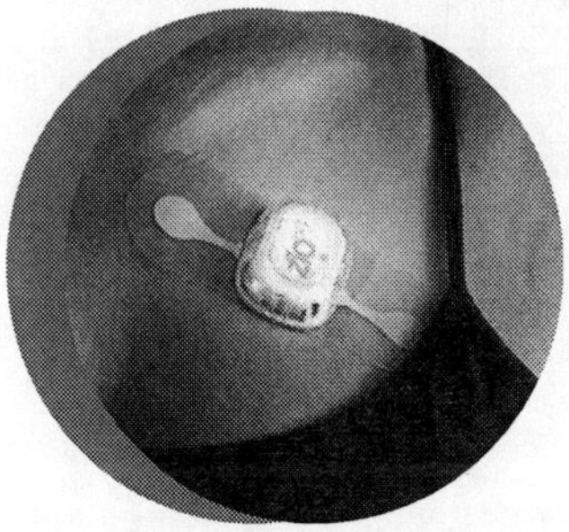

Arrhythmia

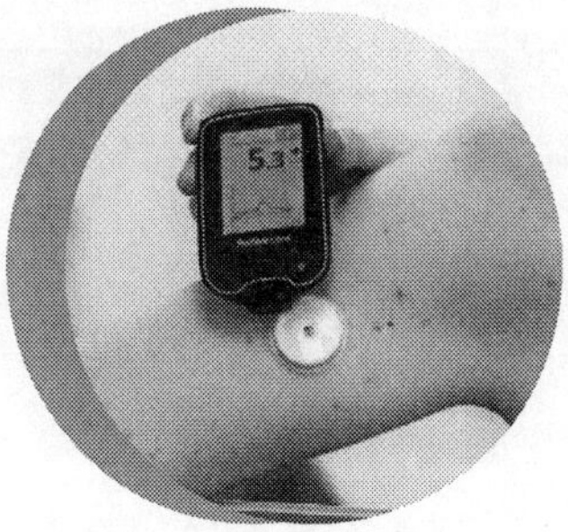

Glucose

Blood Pressure

#SensorsConverge

Sensors Converge

Unmet need in ambulatory BP monitoring (ABPM)

Increases the accuracy of hypertension diagnosis and reduces the costs of hypertension management.

Currently underserved by existing technologies.

55%	41%	17%
interfered with sleep	experienced pain	skin reactions

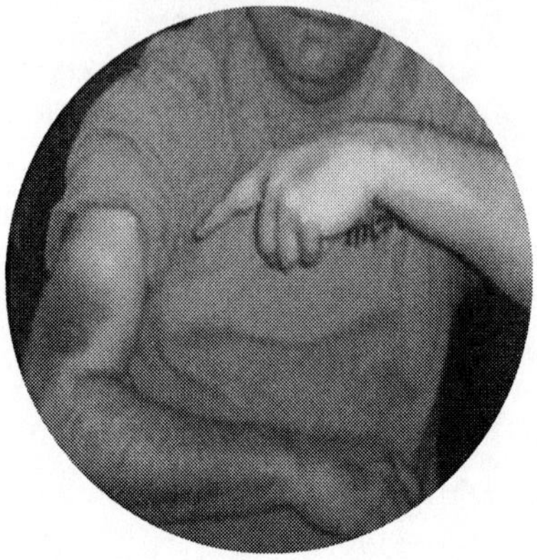

… at least not since the 1800s

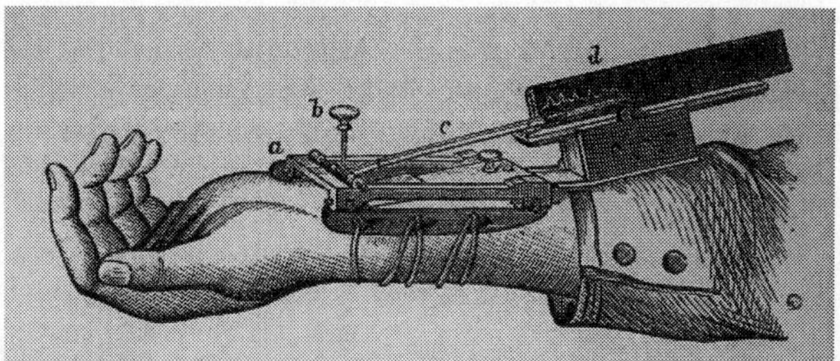

FIG. 83.—Marey's Sphygmograph in position. *a*, framework bound to the arm ; *b*, screw for adjusting pressure to the vessel ; *c*, lever, writing on smoked paper *d*.

Solution is a wearable, cuffless BP monitor

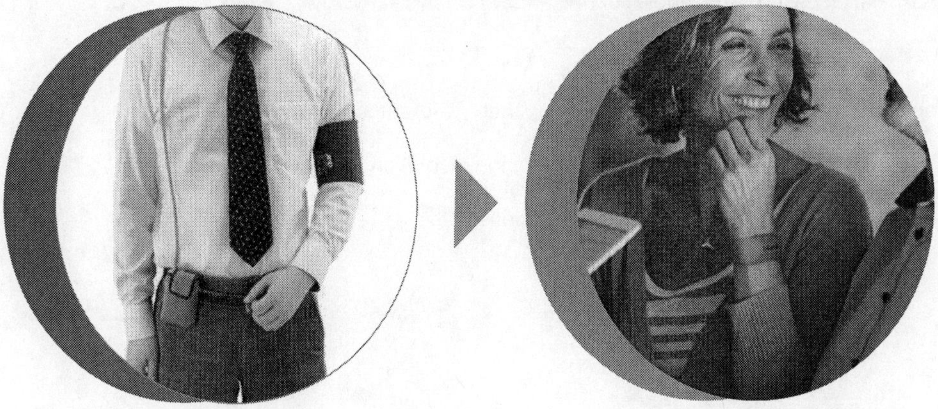

#SensorsConverge

Sensors Converge

Regulatory pathway for ABPM

Winner: Most Underappreciated Challenge

- FDA Class II regulated under **21 CFR 870.1130** and grouped under Product Code **DXN**.
- **510(k) Premarket Notification** - appropriate when the new device has the same intended use and substantially equivalent technological characteristics as one or more legally marketed predicate devices.
- Device-specific guidance document:
    - **Non-Invasive Blood Pressure (NIBP) Monitor Guidance**, March 10, 1997.
- Device-specific Standards
    - **IEC 80601-2-30:2018** Medical Electrical Equipment - Part 2-30: Particular requirements for basic safety and essential performance of automated non-invasive sphygmomanometers.
    - **IEC 81060-2:2018** Non-invasive sphygmomanometers - Part 2: Clinical investigation of automated measurement type.
    - **IEEE/ISO 11073-10407:2010** Health informatics - Personal health device communication - Part 10407: Device specialization - Blood pressure monitor.
- Caveat: FDA has not issued guidance for cuffless BP solutions ⍰ Critical to engage FDA early.

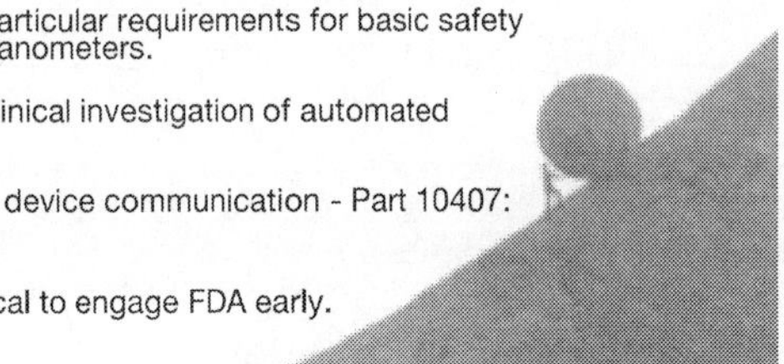

#SensorsConverge

Sensors Converge

ABPM Device Design

- BP determination based on principles of Pulse Wave Analysis (PWA)
- Custom-developed transducer using radar:
  - Compact radar IC available, allowing for a variety of form factors
  - Balance between signal-to-noise ratio and range resolution & high spatial sensitivity
- Patch-based design targeted for clinical applications.

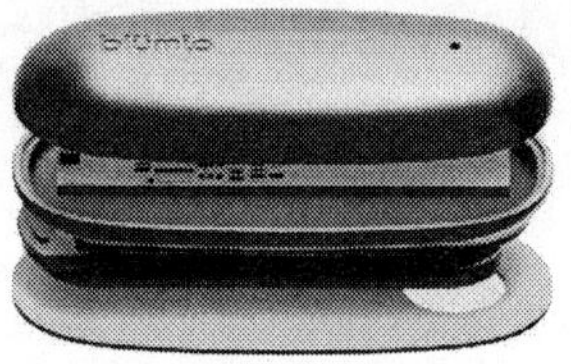

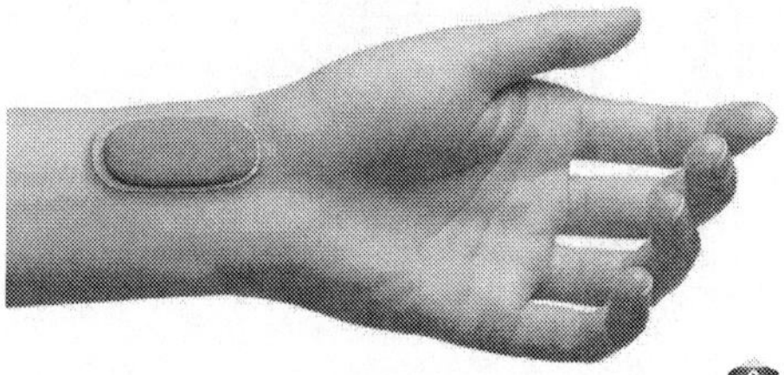

#SensorsConverge

Sensors Converge

Summary

- Wearable applications: medical vs. consumer
    * Medical wearable = FDA regulated medical device
- Design considerations
  - Signal processing and biometric extraction
    * Value is in your high-quality signal
  - Selecting a transducer
    * Many off-the-shelf options with different modalities
  - Device design and integration
    * Design is most influenced by the use-case, transducer, and regulatory requirements
- Blood pressure monitoring as an example

#SensorsConverge

Sensors Converge

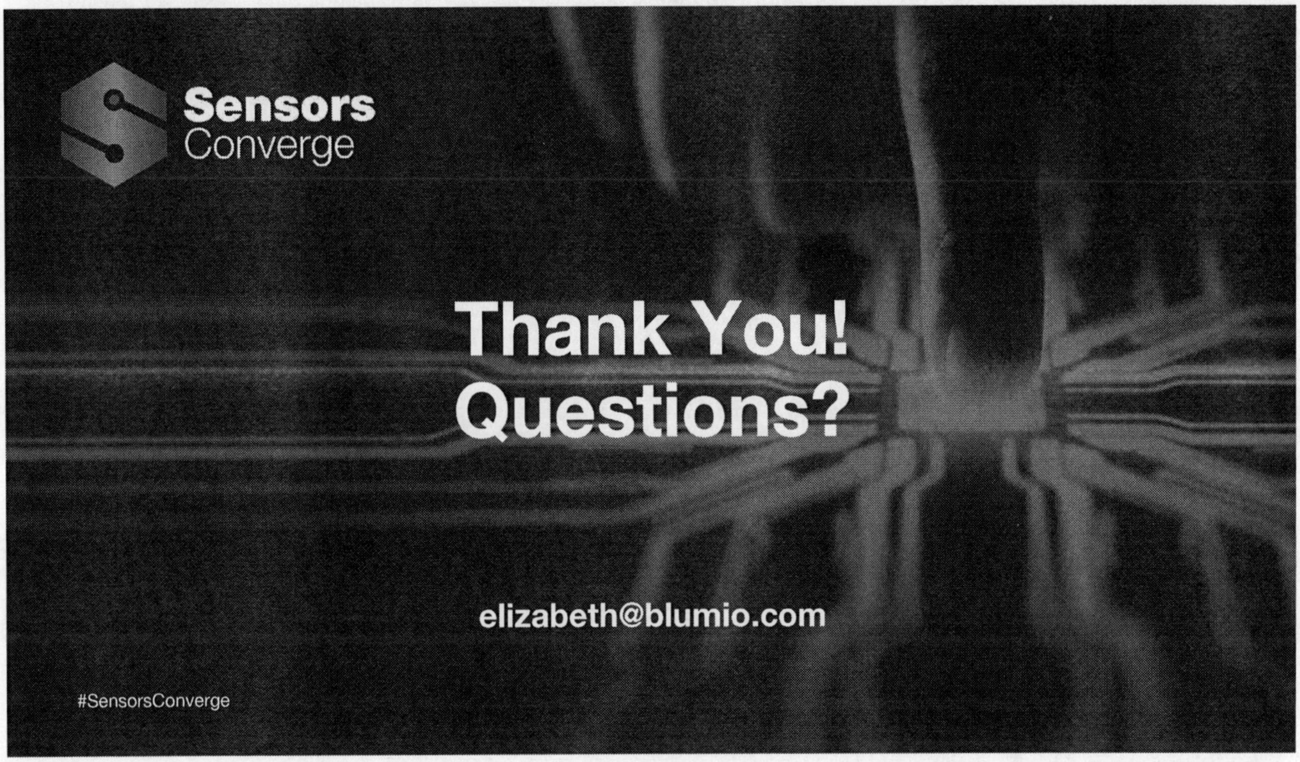
Sensors
Converge
Thank You!
Questions?
elizabeth@blumio.com
#SensorsConverge

Sensors
Converge

Simplifying Power Supply Selection for the Next Generation of Medical Optical Sensors

Gaurav Mital – Senior Principal Power Architect, Battery Power Solutions Business Unit
Maxim Integrated®, now part of Analog Devices

September 21-23, 2021 | San Jose, CA

#SensorsConverge

Agenda

Healthcare Wellness Transition
Wearable Eco-System
Power Your Wellness Device
What's Next?

#SensorsConverge

Sensors
Converge

Healthcare Wellness Transition

#SensorsConverge

Sensors Converge

Personalized Healthcare/Wellness Transition

Doctor's Clinic

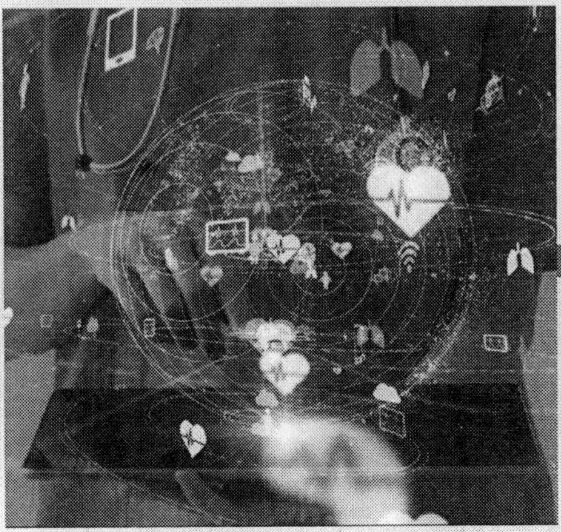

People's Wardrobe

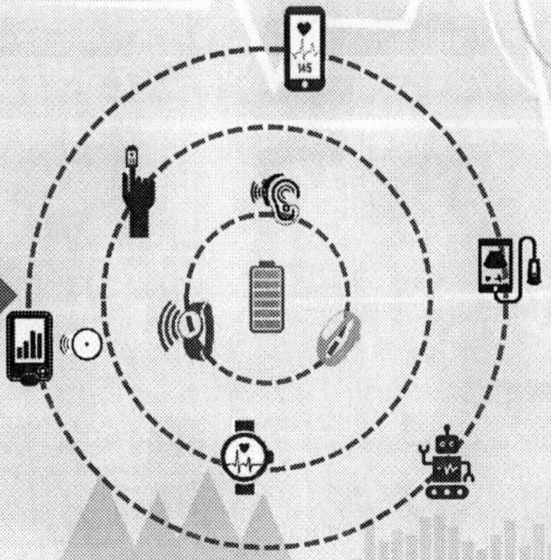

#SensorsConverge

Sensors Converge

Consumer & Medical Wearable Applications

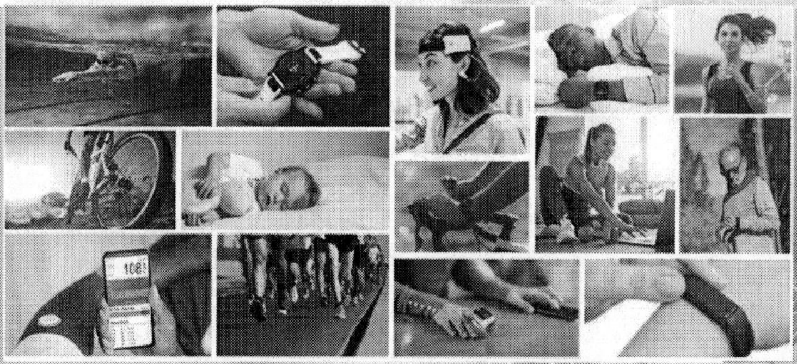

#SensorsConverge

Sensors Converge

Medical Devices Challenges

Predicting healthcare	Monitoring treatment	Ensuring recovery
Patients required to track heath continually	Non-invasive health monitoring	Continuous data after treatment

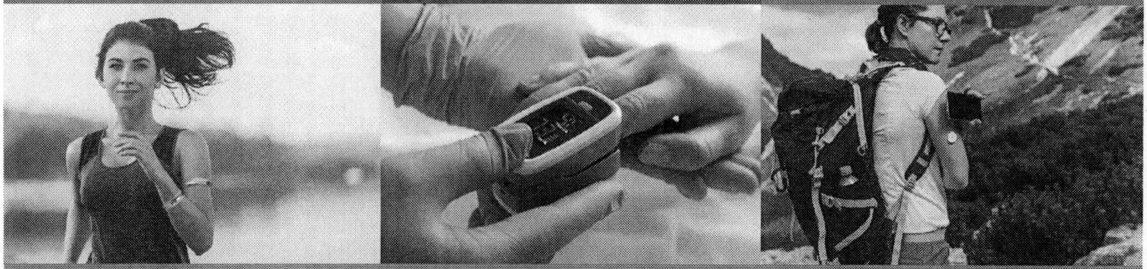

Compliance
Getting the user to wear a device

#SensorsConverge

Sensors Converge

Medical Device Compliance Challenges

Challenges	Solution Strategies
Comfort	Small/thin form factor
Accuracy	Precision measurements
Battery Life	High efficiency, longer battery life
Charging	Fast charging
Contextual Data	More integrated features

#SensorsConverge

Sensors Converge

Wearable Eco-System

#SensorsConverge

Sensors Converge

Wearable Device System

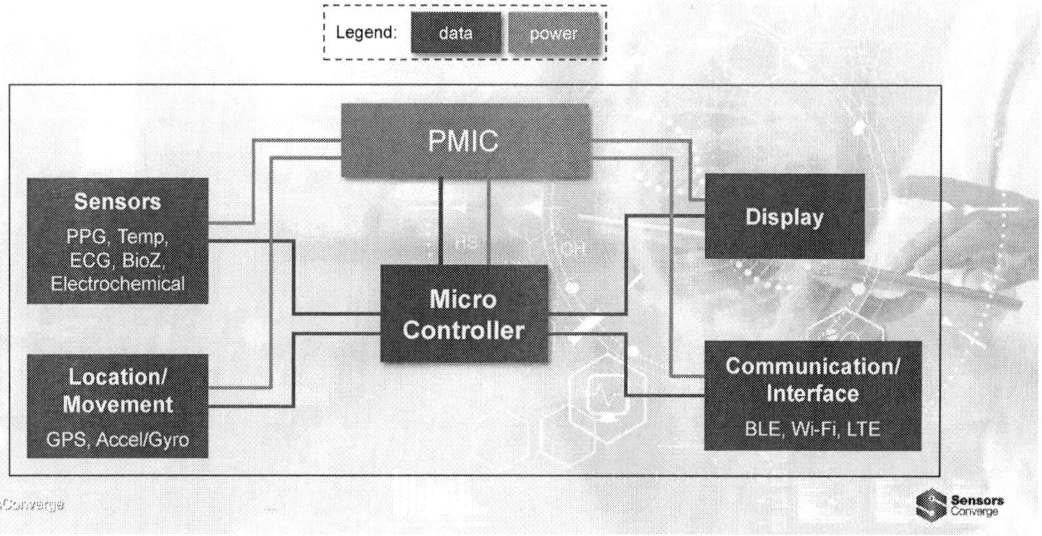

Wearable Device – Space Constrained

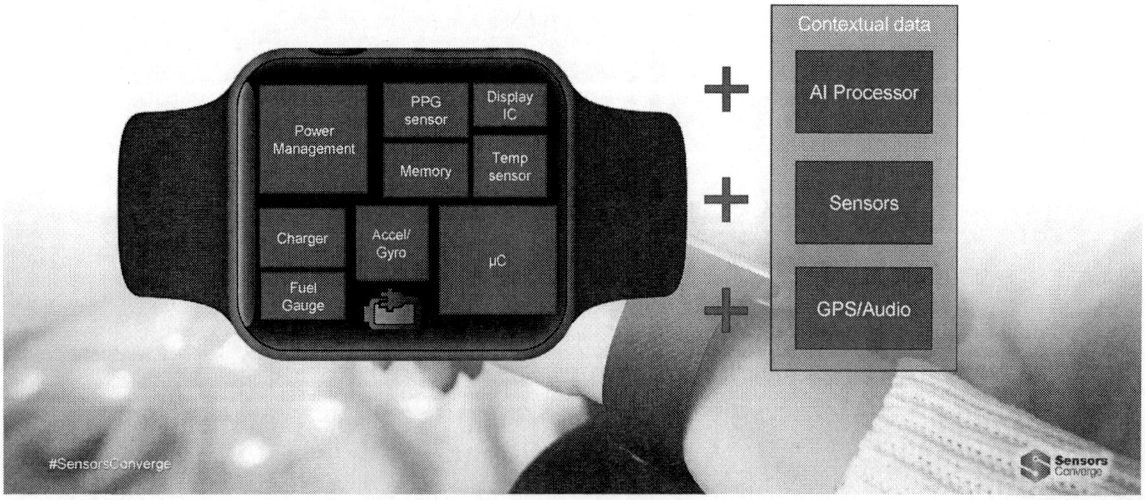

Optical Signal to Noise Ratio (SNR) Considerations

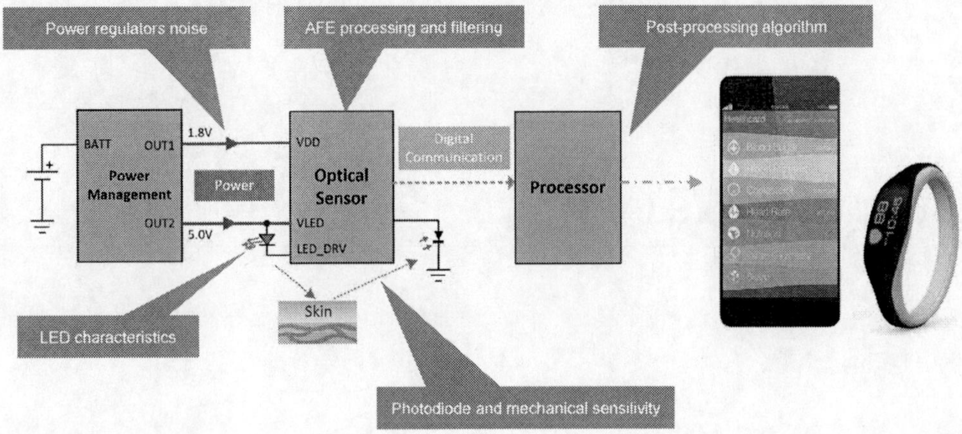

#SensorsConverge

Sensors Converge

PPG Sensor Optical Path

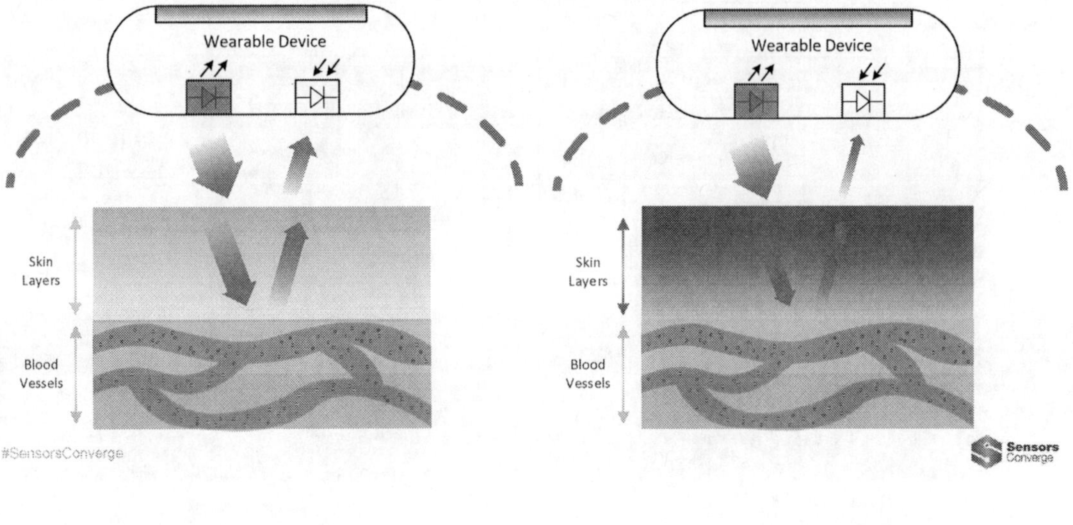

#SensorsConverge

Sensors Converge

Power Your Wellness Device

#SensorsConverge

Sensors Converge

Traditional Wearable Architecture

Lower computational power, large form factor

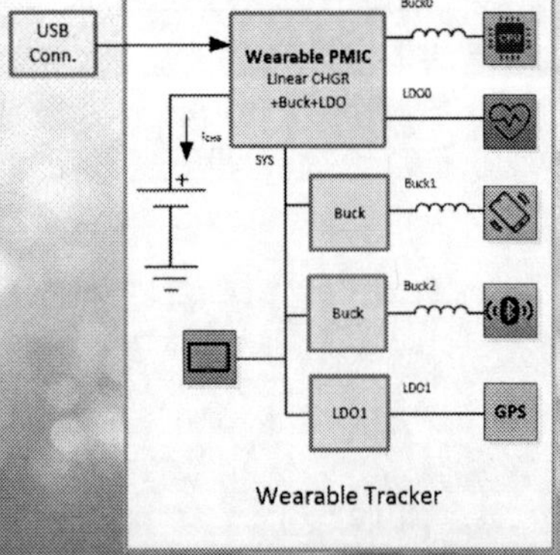

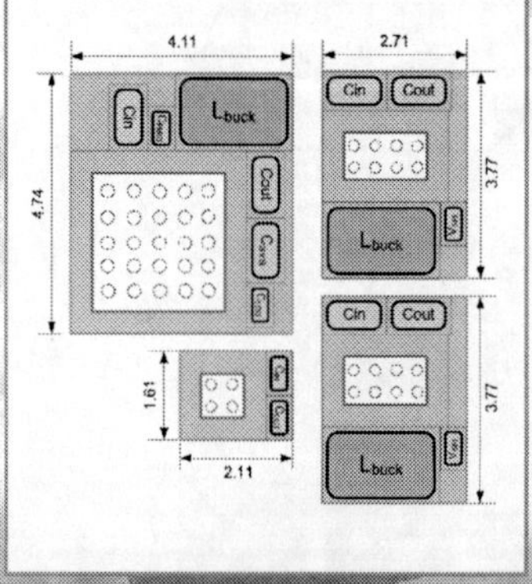

Solution Size:
43.31mm^2

Component Count: 20

#SensorsConverge

Sensors Converge

Next-Gen Wearable Architecture

Higher computational power for AI processing, half the form factor

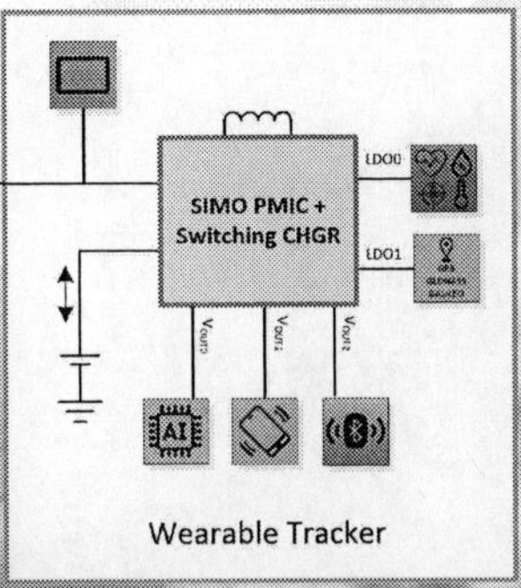

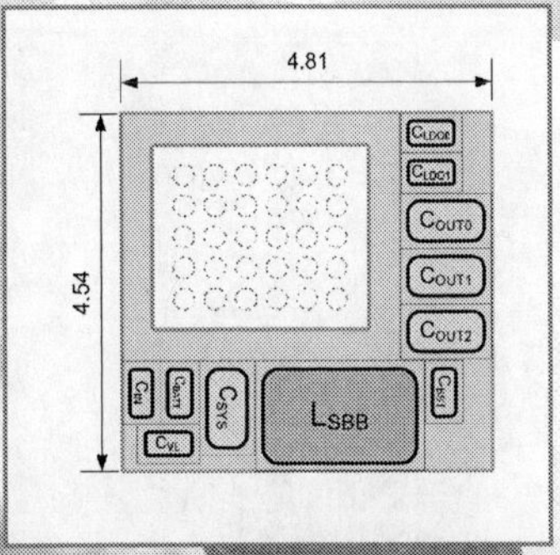

50% Smaller

Solution Size:
21.83mm²

Component Count: 12

40% Lower BOM Count

#SensorsConverge

Sensors Converge

Single Inductor Multiple Output (SIMO) Technology

SIMO Architecture

- 50% Smaller Solution
- 20% Longer Battery Life
- High Signal Integrity
- 4X Faster Charging

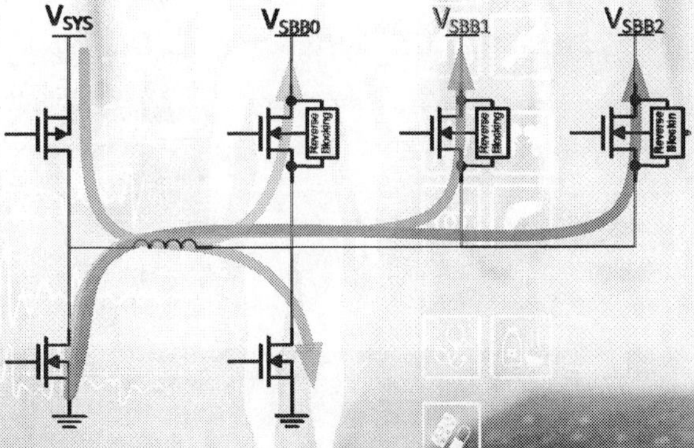

#SensorsConverge

Sensors Converge

SIMO PMIC Enabling More Integrated Features

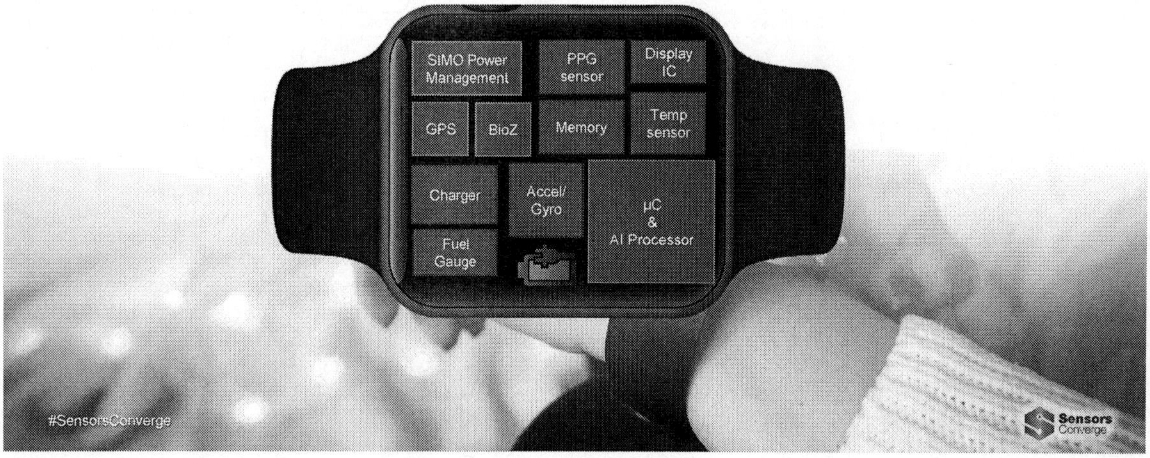

Increasing Battery Life by 20%

Traditional Solution
System Eff = 69.5%

SIMO Power Management
System Eff = 86.1%

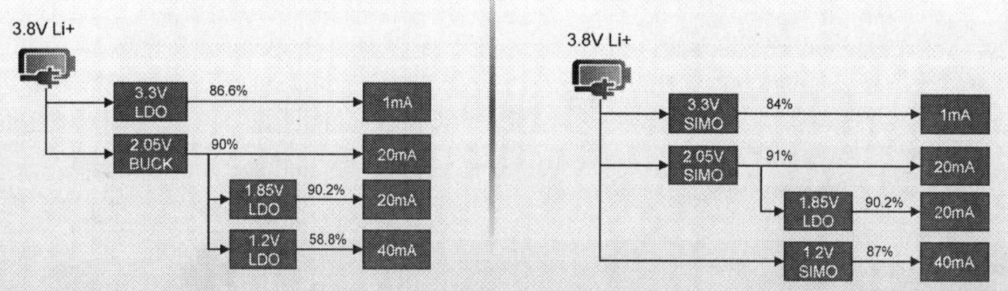

Key Parameters	Traditional Power Management	SIMO Power Management
BATT Current	49mA	39.5mA
System Efficiency	69.5%	86.1%

#SensorsConverge

Sensors Converge

Powering the PPG AFEs

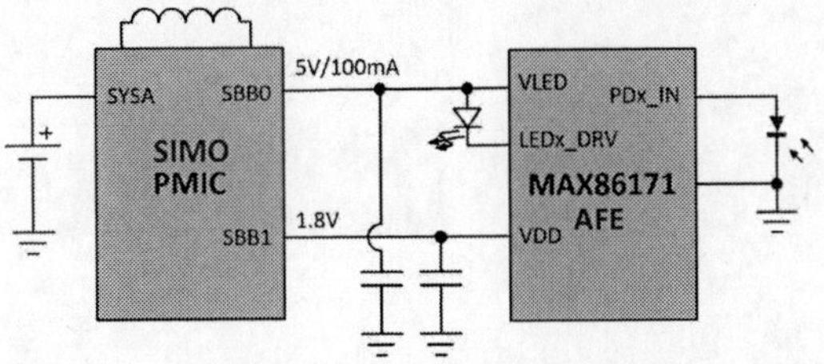

- **SNR:** Calibrated data after linear regression
- **SNR12:** Data from 1 filtered by a bandpass filter with passband between 0.5Hz and 12Hz
- **SNR4:** Data from 1 filtered by a bandpass filter with passband between 0.5Hz and 4Hz

Average: 1; PPG Offset: 0µA			
DUT	SNR	SNR12	SNR4
SIMO PMIC	90.9	97.2	101.9

#SensorsConverge

Sensors Converge

4x Faster Charging with SIMO Charger

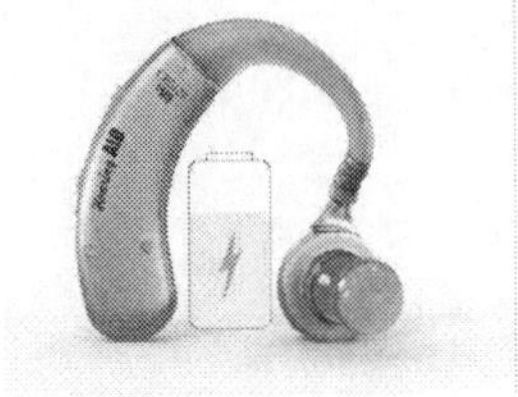

Existing Solution

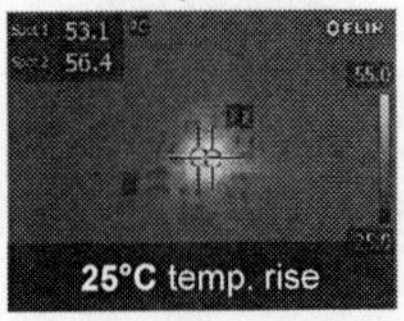

SIMO Switching Charger
MAX77659

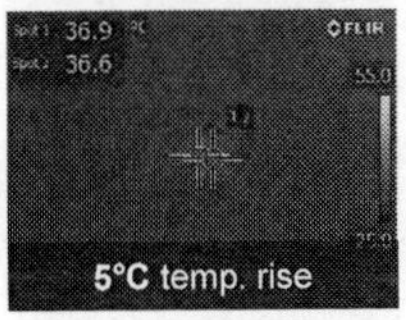

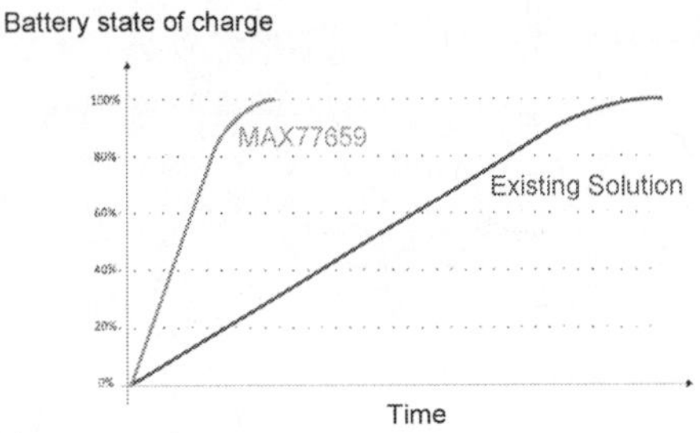

#SensorsConverge

Sensors Converge

Visit our booth to see an "on the go" vital monitoring demo featuring Analog Devices' low power SIMO PMIC, m5 Fuel Gauge, microcontroller and sensors.

Booth #818

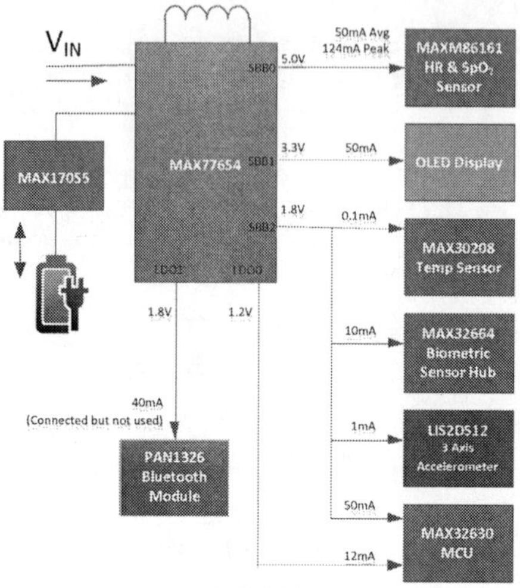

#SensorsConverge

Sensors Converge

What's Next?

#SensorsConverge

Sensors Converge

Future Trends – Digital Therapeutics

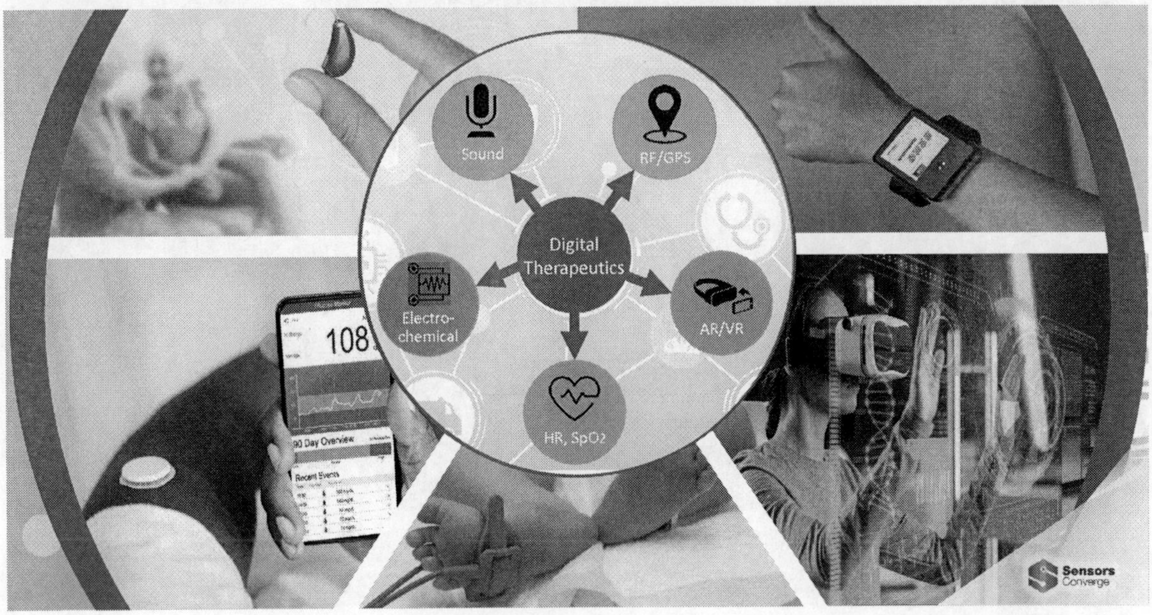

Thank you

NOW PART OF

maxim integrated

ANALOG DEVICES

Sensors Converge

Sensors Converge

The Importance of Sensing Technology in AR/VR/MR

Fundamental Optical Solutions LLC
Golshan Coleiny
Founder
September 21-23, 2021 | San Jose, CA

Fundamental Optical Solutions LLC

Outline

- Sensors Everywhere
- Sensors & Type of Sensors
- Optical Sensors
- Brief about AR VR MR (How Started)
- Augmented Reality (AR)
  - Technology, Applications, Markets
- Virtual Reality (VR)
  - Technology, Applications, Sensors
- Mixed Reality (MR)
  - Technology, Applications,
- Advanced Technologies
- RoadMap

Summary
Contact Info

Sensors Everywhere

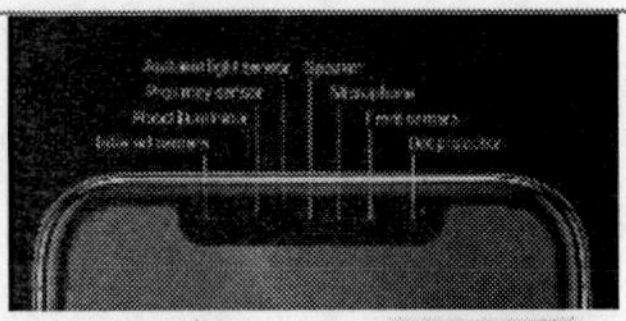

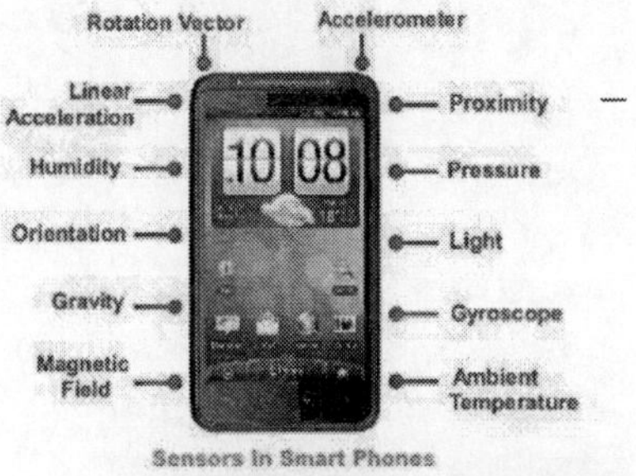

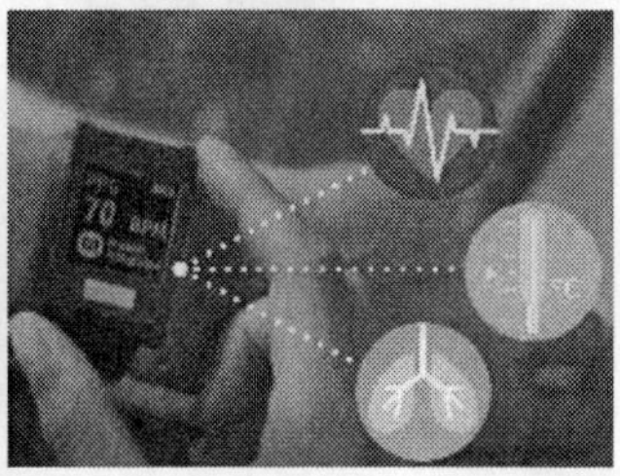

Fundamental Optical Solutions LLC

Sensors Converge

What Sensors Do & Type of Sensors

- Chemical Sensor
- Touch Sensor
- Humidity Sensors
- Light(Photon) Sensor (IR Sensors, Photodiode, CMOS, CCD, ,,,)
- Proximity Sensors
- Gas Sensors
- Acceleration Sensors
- Temperature Sensors
- Sound Sensors
- Ultrasonic Sensors
- ....

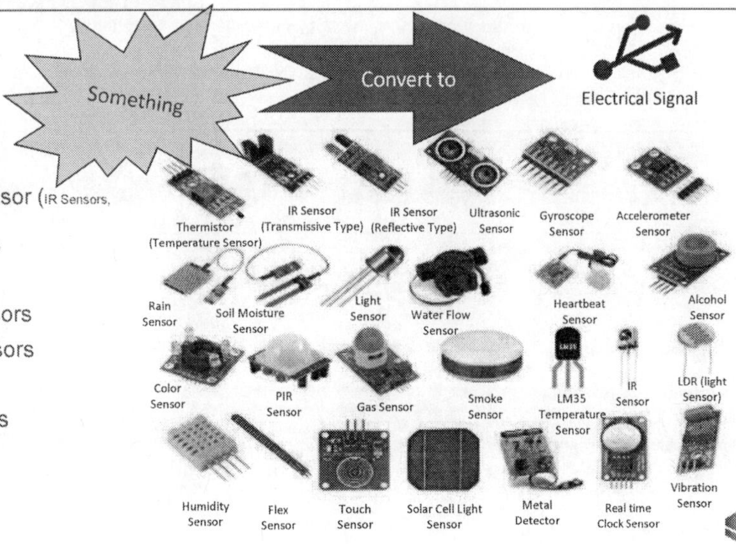

Fundamental Optical Solutions LLC

Sensors Converge

Optical Sensors

Optical or Light sensors are a device for detecting photons in wide range of light spectrum UV/VIS/IR in three different base:

- Intensity-Based Sensors
- Phase-Based Sensors
- Wavelength-Based Sensors

All are common being sensitive device to detect any change to photon status.

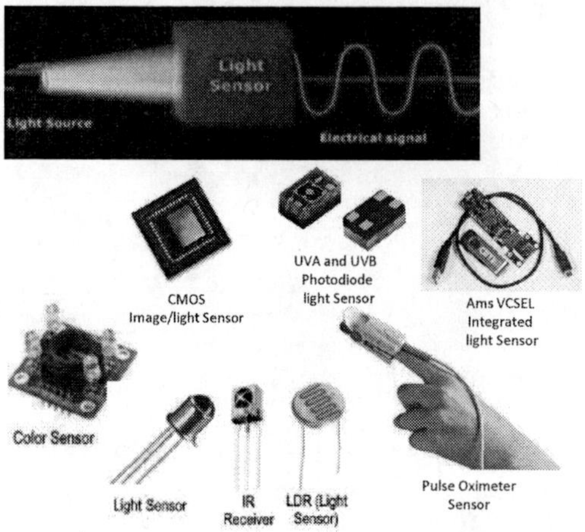

Fundamental Optical Solutions LLC

Sensors Converge

Optical/Light Sensors Evolutions

Optical or Light sensors are based on Semiconductors, the fast improvement are related to:

- Low cost, and high Yield Productions (Chip level)
- Science and technology progress of Micro, and Nano-structure development in Compound Semiconductor
- Integration Compact space packaging Technologies

Photodiodes & Phototransistors	Photodiodes W Integrated function	Intelligent Opto-sensors	Multi-function Opto-sensors	ALS-based Module	Color-based Modules	Advanced Modules	Future Solutions
	Light-Voltage Light-Freq.	Amplifiers Integrated A/Ds Digital Interface Interrupts	Photopic-Ambient light Sensing Color Sensing	Ambient light Sensing Proximity Detection IR LED	Ambient light Sensing Proximity Detection IR LED Color Sensing	Gesture Detection IR Remote Control Encode Emulation	Aperture Reduction Biosensors Advanced Color Sensing

Evolution of Light Sensor Integration (Optical Sensor in Smart Phone)

Fundamental Optical Solutions LLC

Sensors Converge

AR VR MR

How it was possible:

- Emerging Technol
  Digital immersion, overlay world, user interaction
- Consumer Deman
  Accelerating education, w environment, professiona remote access

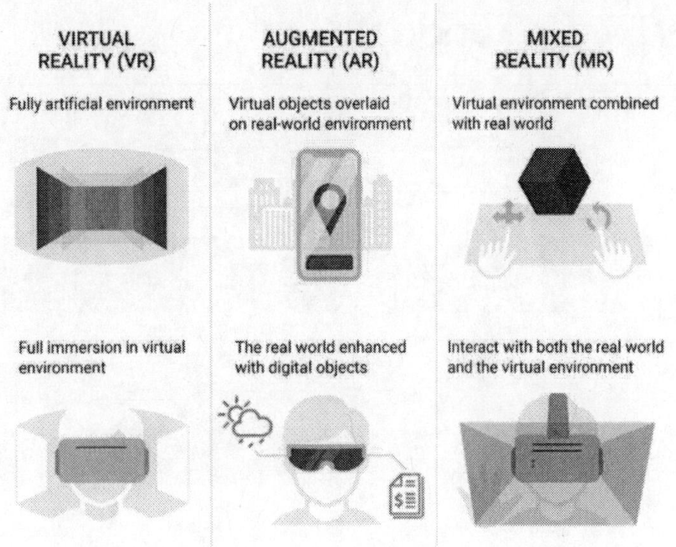

Fundamental Optical Solutions LLC

https://youtu.be/A2y12s7FHxA

Sensors Converge

ARVRMR Near-to-Eye Display

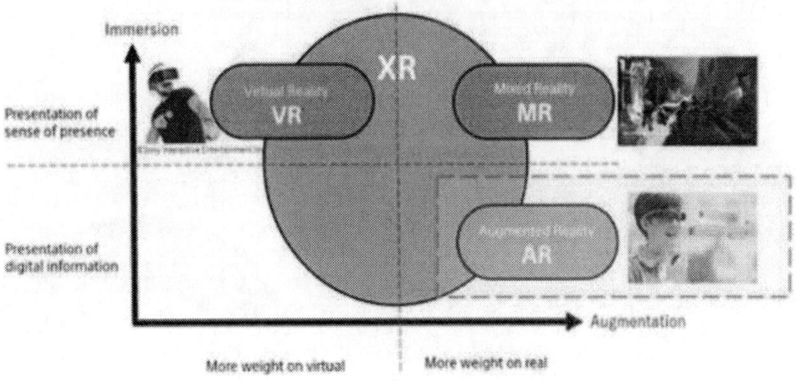

New ways to interact with the world around

AR VR MR Products

- Google
- Microsoft
- Facebook

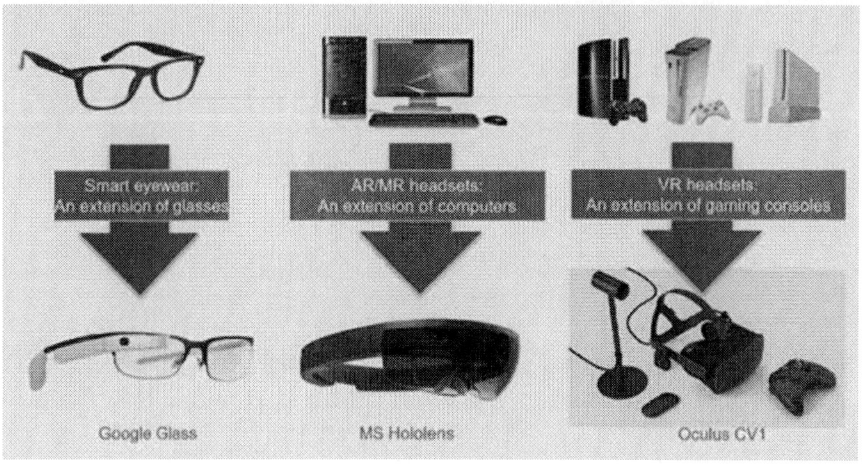

Fundamental Optical Solutions LLC

Sensors Converge

Augmented Reality (AR)

How it was possible:

Fast progress combinations of:

→ low cost, Fast response Sensors

→ Automated Technology

→ Decrease device size, thermal control

→ Design Improvements

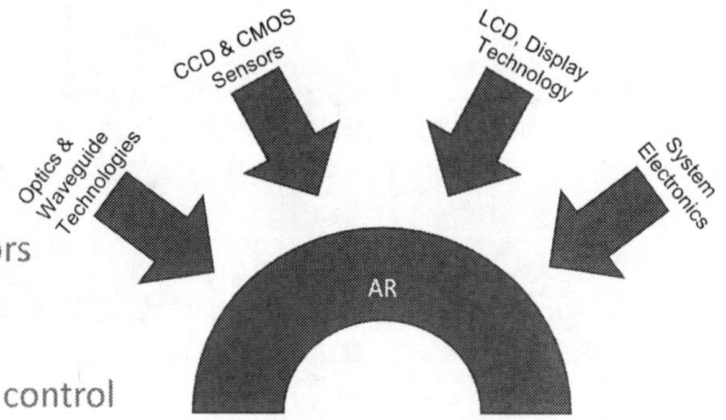

A Combination of four technological Dimensions

Fundamental Optical Solutions LLC

Sensors Converge

AR Global Market and Applications

The Augmented Reality Market has rapidly increased since 2016.

COVID 19, and performing jobs remotely are key acceleration of market and sales in many sectors.

Such as:

- Health Care (Telemedicine, virtual visit, virtual monitoring)
- Manufacturing (Remote Control, Test, and Monitoring)
- Robotics
- Game and entertainment

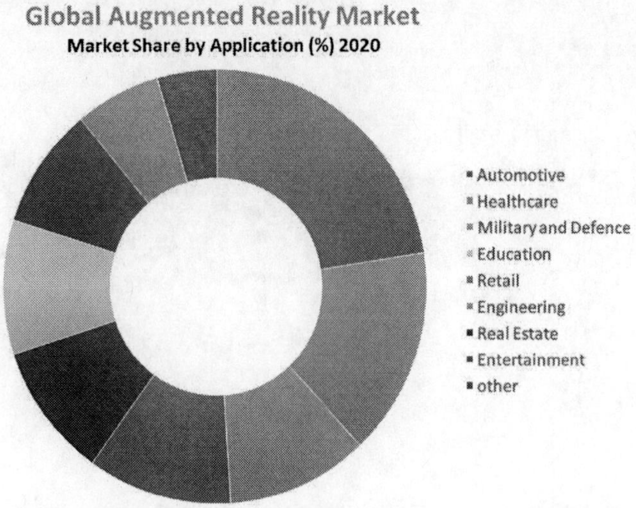

Fundamental Optical Solutions LLC

Sensors Converge

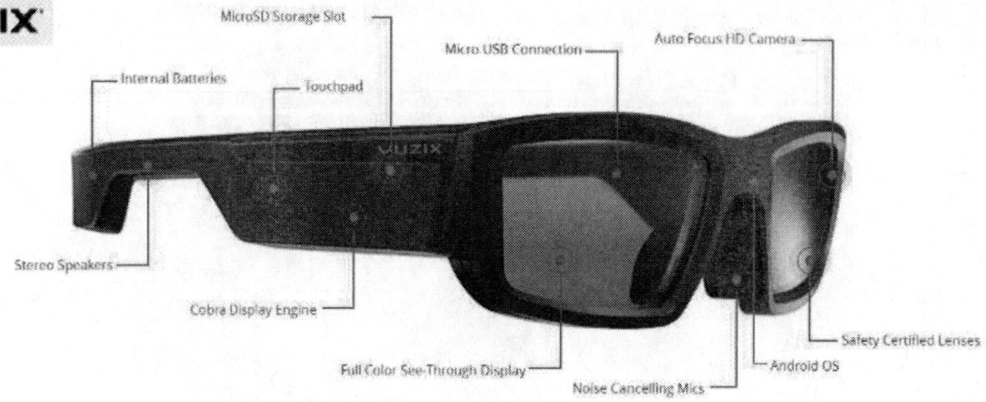

Virtual Reality (VR)

How it was possible:

Fast progress combinations of:

→ Miniaturization of Display

→ Computational Power Control

→ The simulated environment

→ The Computer-generated graphics

https://youtu.be/bCjWlPkJ19E

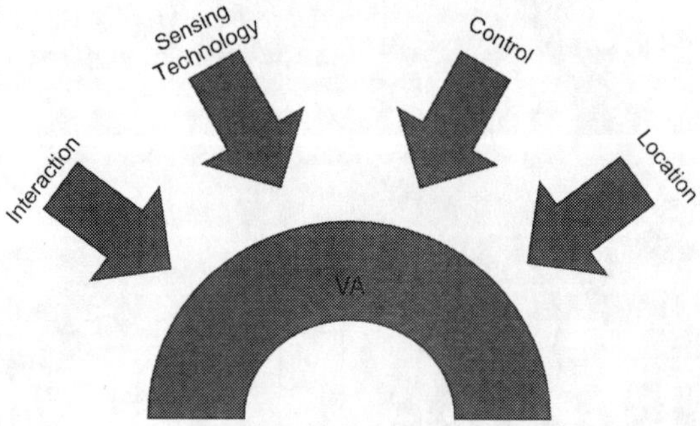

A Combination of four technological Dimensions

Fundamental Optical Solutions LLC

Sensors Converge

VR Applications, Sensors

100% Digital and Computer-Generated

Applications:

→ Education, Medical Training

→ Work Training

→ Game

→ Commercial Illustration (Ex. Real Estate)

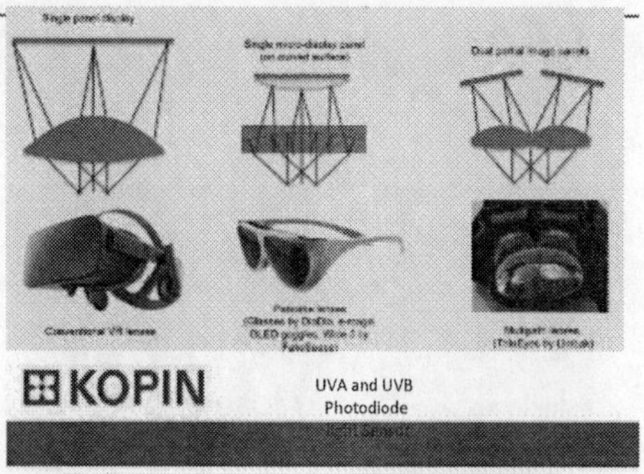

NVIS
High-fidelity VR headsets
Binocular hand-held displays,
and emulated CRT display
for training and simulation.

Fundamental Optical Solutions LLC

Sensors Converge

Mixed Reality (MR)

How it was possible?

Combinations of:

→ Computer interface

→ Miniaturization of Display

→ Computational Power Control

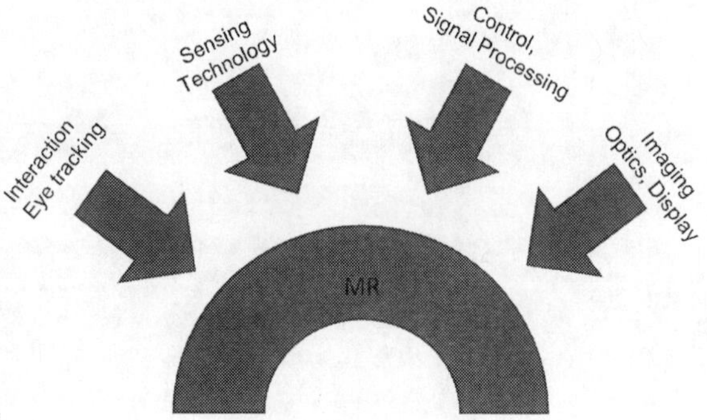

A Combination of four technological Dimensions

Fundamental Optical Solutions LLC

Sensors Converge

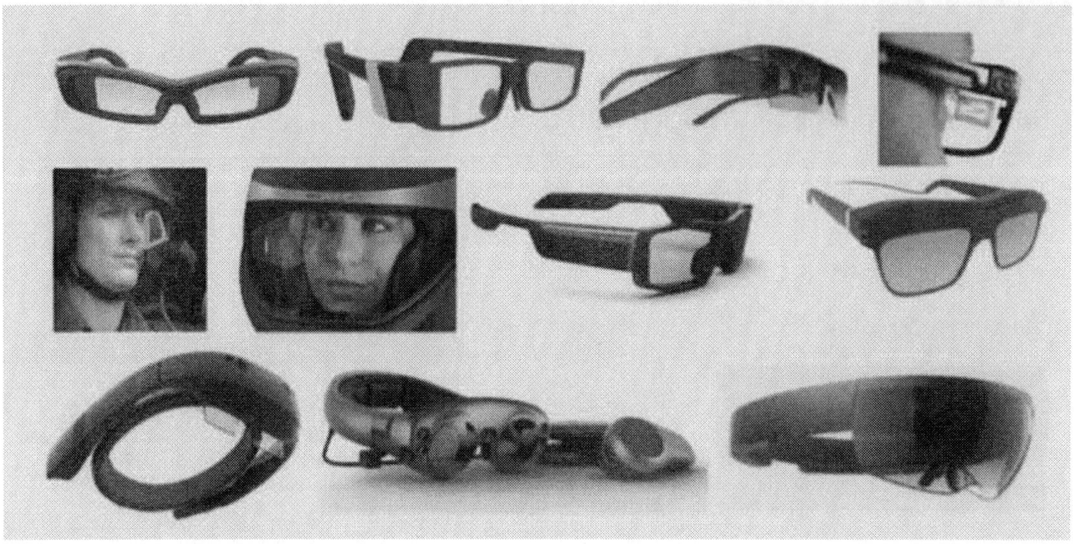

Mixed Reality (MR)

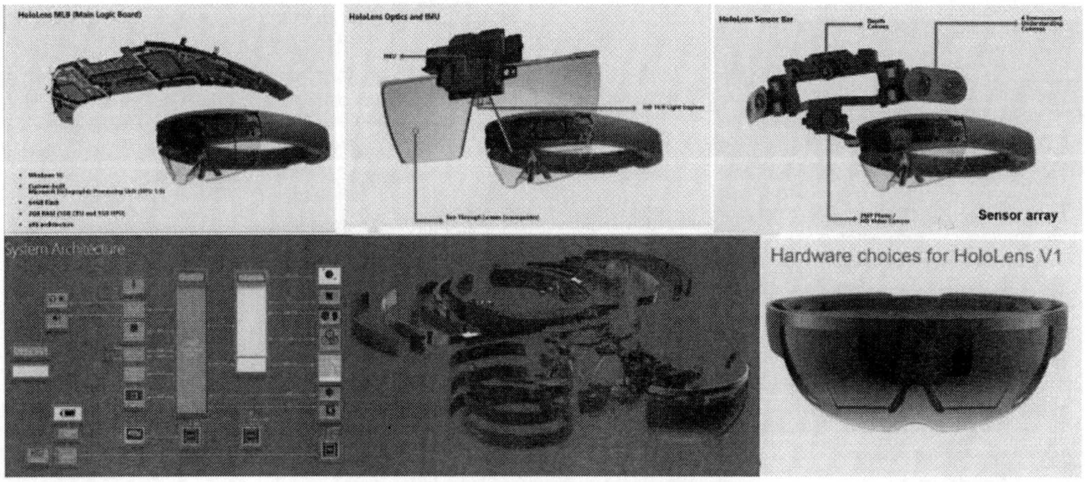

Hololens Mixed Reality (Microsoft)

Fundamental Optical Solutions LLC

Sensors Converge

MR Technologies, and Applications

What, Where are the technologies heading?

Combinations of:

- Computer interface → Higher Speed
- Miniaturization of Display → Smaller
- Sensors → More Sensors, the better the tracking

Microsoft's Hololens, As important AR tech in the emerging "MR" Market.
(AR/VR/MR focus summer 2021 optics.org)

Applications

Design	Education	Training	Entertainment	Healthcare	Remote Working

Fundamental Optical Solutions LLC

Sensors Converge

GLOBAL AR/VR MARKET GROWTH (2020-2024)

The Insight Partners Report (Sept. 2021):

$17.86Bn Virtual Reality and Augmented Reality in Retail Market (by 2028) Global Growth Forecast at 24.8% CAGR During 2021 to 2028 as impact of COVID

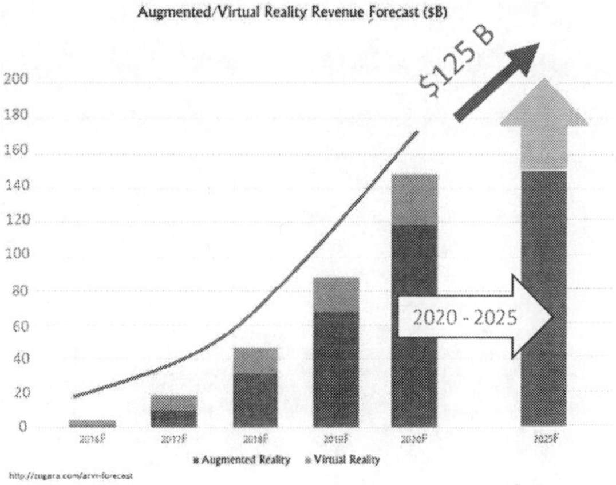

Fundamental Optical Solutions LLC

Sensors Converge

Why Sensors are important in AR/VR/MR?

Examples:

- GPS Systems can be linked to AR as location sensors
- Eye-Tracking sensors for human-centered Mixed Reality (MR)
- Motion and Gesture Sensors for visualization in VR
- Sony's 3D Time of Flight Sensing solution
- VCSELS for 3D Camera (Samsung + Huawei)
- Hololens (embed Azure AI + Sony intelligent vision sensor IMX500)
- MicroLED Displays for AR & VR (high brightness, low power RGB pixel arrays CMOS)

	Sensors (HoloLens (MR))
Head tracking	4 visible light camera
Eye tracking	2 IR cameras
Depth	1-MP time-of-flight (ToF) depth sensor
IMU	Accelerometer, gyroscope, magnetometer
Camera	8-MP stills, 1080p30 video

Fundamental Optical Solutions LLC

Sensors Converge

Advanced Technologies for Future of AR/VR/MR

As we move globally to Artificial Intelligent (AI) and Internet of things (IoT), advance technologies that effect on future of AR/VR/MR are:

- Cloud, Wireless, Data Management
- Eye tracking
- VCSEL
- Miniaturization of optics: Camera & Light Source, Display (Meta-surface Optics)
- Robotics
- Compound Semiconductor Devices

Ams Osram shrinks camera module. R&D Report, Aug. 2021

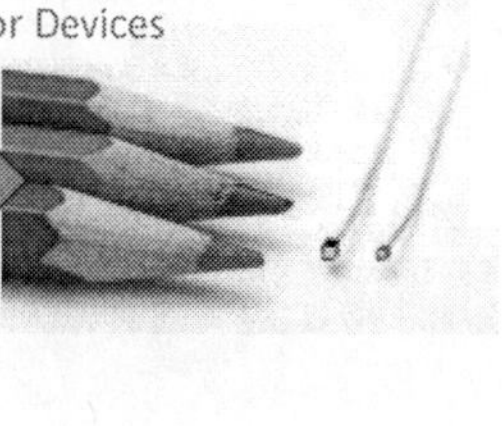

Meta-surface Optics

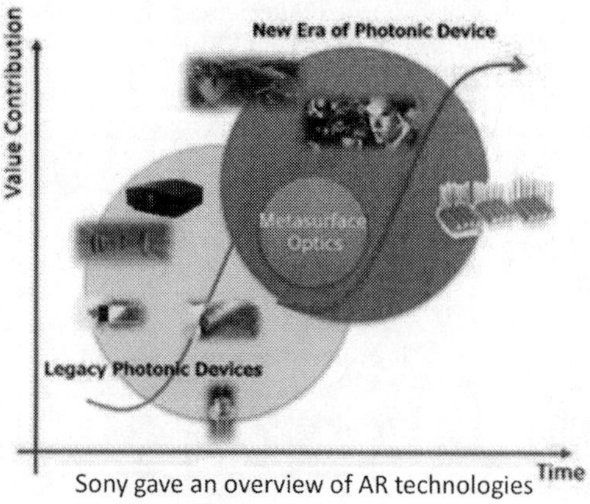

Sony gave an overview of AR technologies they are working on

(SPIE Digital Optical Technologies June 2021)

Fundamental Optical Solutions LLC

Sensors Converge

Advance Technologies for Future of AR/VR/MR

DARPA (IR) Camera-Based Project

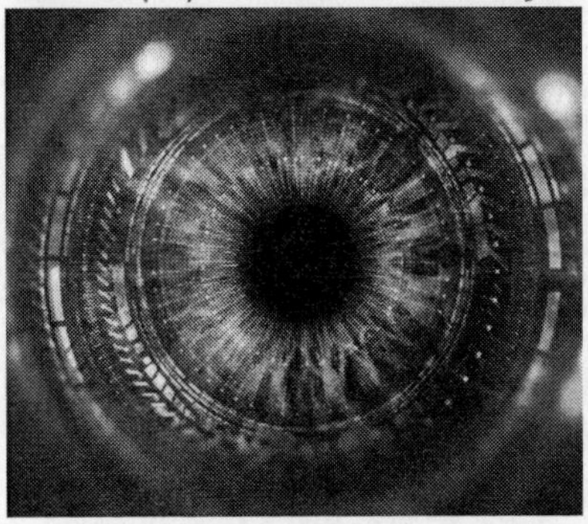

A team of DARPA, BAE Systems, and North Grumman Researchers are developing a new dynamic sensors based on infrared camera-neuromorphic technologies as an emerging class of sensors.

(AR/VR/MR focus summer 2021 optics.org)

Meta-form Optics

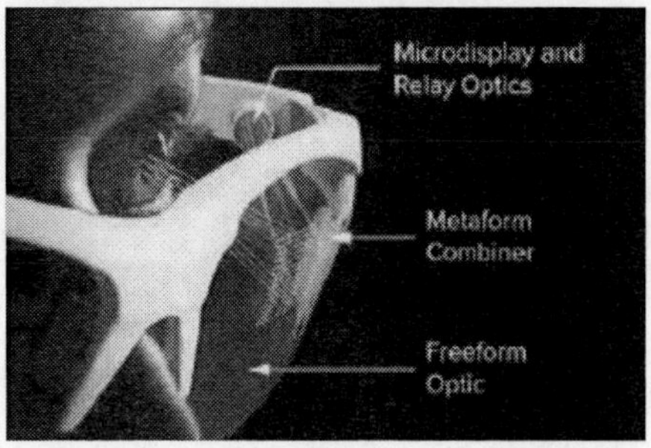

Researchers (Univ. of Rochester) have developed combination of meta-surface and freeform optics for compact high-resolution waveguide for AR optics.

(AR/VR/MR focus summer 2021 optics.org)

Fundamental Optical Solutions LLC

Sensors Converge

Roadmaps

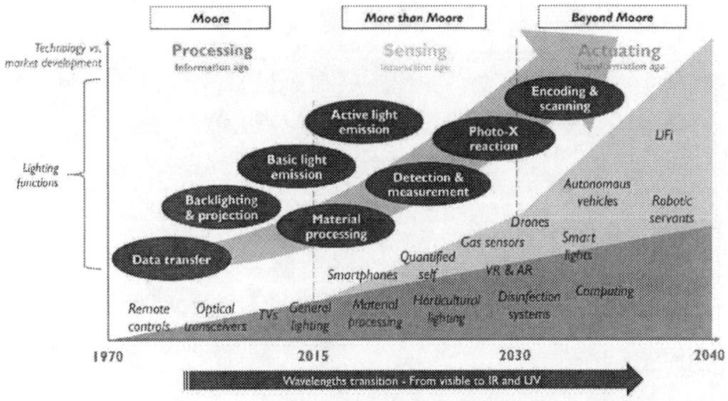

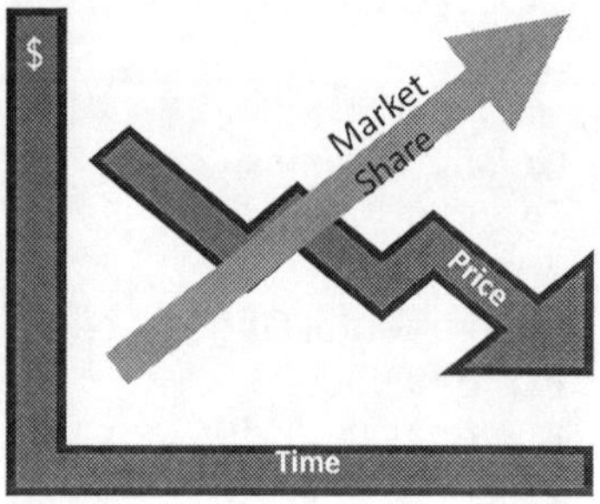

Headset → Smart Glass → Contact lens?

Fundamental Optical Solutions LLC

Sensors Converge

Summary

According to the international data corporation (IDT), the global market share of smartphones has remained the same in the last four quarters. The question is, with all these signs of progress in technologies, what is the next booming market?
As technology grows Globally towards automation, computer interface technologies such as Artificial Intelligent (AI), Cloud data, Internet of things (IoT), robotics, fast Internet, high cyber securities, and remote communications, technologies such as AR/VR/MR become essential to sustain such rapid growth.

Fundamental Optical Solutions LLC

Sensors Converge

Fundamental Optical Solutions LLC

Contact Information:

Golshan Coleiny
Founder - President

Fundamental Optical Solutions™, LLC
P.O. Box 990985
Boston, MA, 02199
Toll Free: (855) 481-2004
Email: info@fundamentalopticalsolutions.com

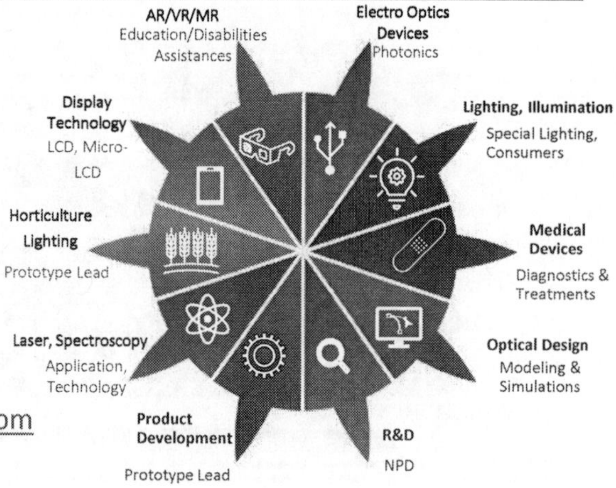

Fundamental Optical Solutions LLC

Sensors Converge

Thank you

Sensors Converge

September 21-23, 2021 | San Jose, CA

Fundamental Optical Solutions LLC

Sensors Converge

Managing Patient Care in the time of COVID-19 using Biosensors and Cassia's Bluetooth Gateways

September 21-23, 2021 | San Jose, CA

#SensorsConverge

Howard Doherty- VP Sales, Cassia Networks
Dr. Ravi Kuppuraj- Founding Chairman, nSensing Inc.

Managing Patient Care in the time of COVID-19 using Biosensors and Cassia's Bluetooth Gateways

Agenda:

- Challenges of COVID-19 transmission in hospitals and clinics
- Bluetooth technology and BLE medical devices for patient monitoring in the continuum of care
- An overview of the integration of Cassia's Bluetooth Gateways and Philips' biosensor
- Use cases
- Summary

#SensorsConverge

Sensors Converge

Challenges of COVID-19 transmission in hospitals and clinics

- Increases risk of cross infection
  (between patients and medical staff)
- Medical shortages (critical PPE)
- Reduces quality of patient care
- Can deter other patients from attending hospitals who may need urgent treatment for other conditions

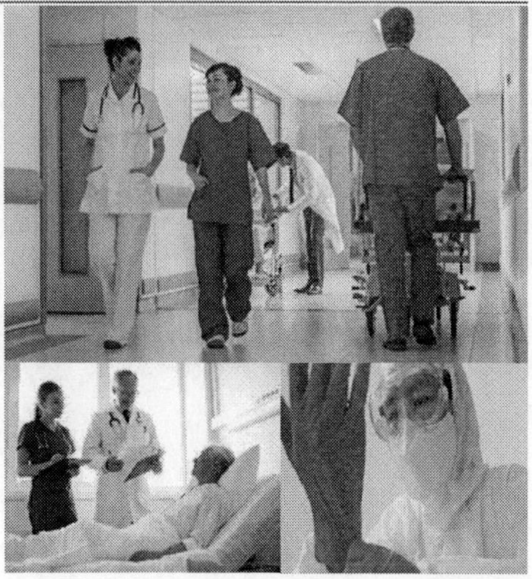

#SensorsConverge

Sensors Converge

The challenges of manual approaches for treating patients diagnosed with COVID-19

- Can result in inaccurate and inconsistent readings
- Restricts a patient's ability to move freely
- Not resource efficient, time consuming and costly

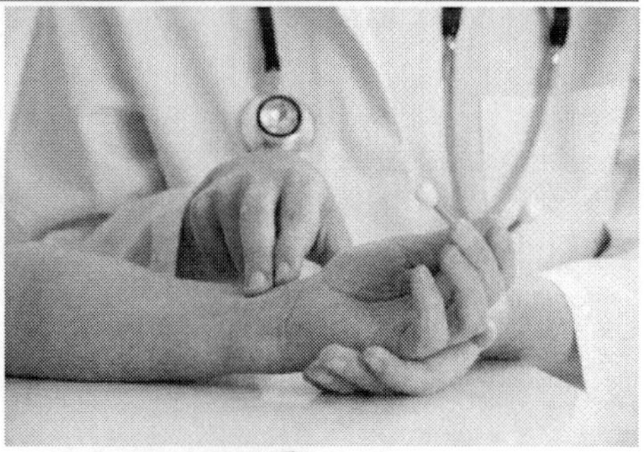

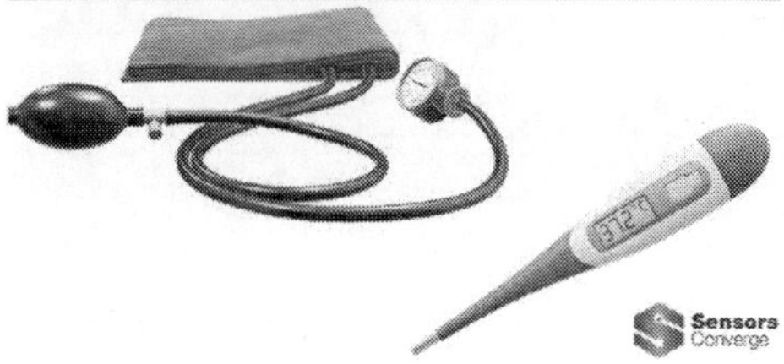

#SensorsConverge

Sensors Converge

Using Bluetooth technology and BLE medical devices for patient monitoring in the continuum of care

Key requirements for continuous patient monitoring in the continuum of care:

- A wireless solution to connect medical devices used in hospitals and clinics
- Ensuring patient data is safeguarded at all times
- Easy setup and management to improve clinician workflow

#SensorsConverge

Sensors Converge

Using Bluetooth technology and BLE medical devices for patient monitoring in the continuum of care

Why Bluetooth technology for healthcare?

- New deployments during the COVID-19 pandemic will boost the healthcare wearables market to nearly 100 million shipments by 2025*
- These wearables include connected blood pressure monitors, continuous glucose monitors, pulse oximeters, and electrocardiogram monitors
- The majority of smart medical devices (nearly 90%) use Bluetooth technology for connectivity

100 Million

Bluetooth® fitness and wearable trackers will ship annually by 2025

#SensorsConverge

Sensors Converge

Using Bluetooth technology and BLE medical devices for patient monitoring in the continuum of care

Why Bluetooth technology for healthcare?

Low power, Long battery life | **Low cost** | **Open** | **Universal**

#SensorsConverge

Sensors Converge

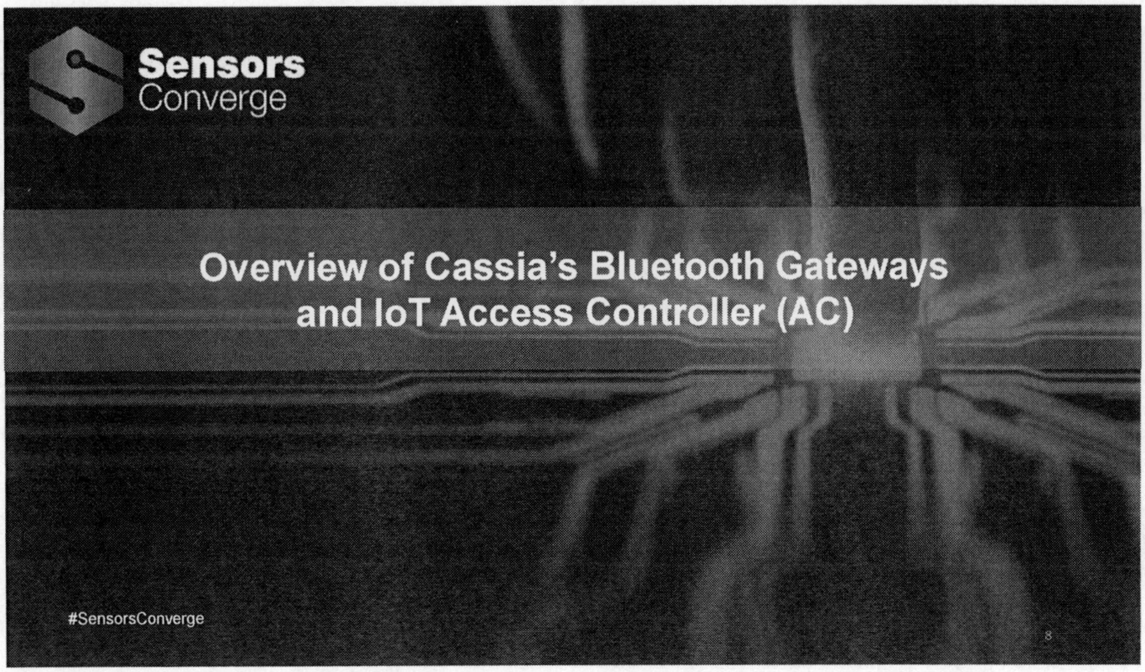

Overview of Cassia's Bluetooth Gateways for Digital Health IoT

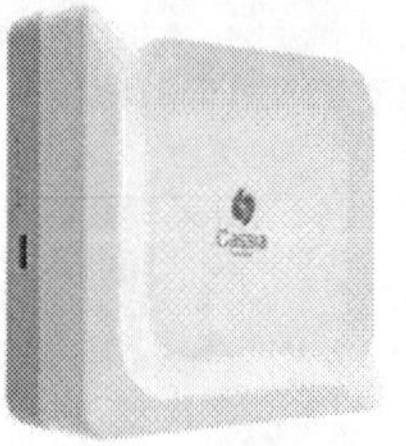

E1000
(indoor)

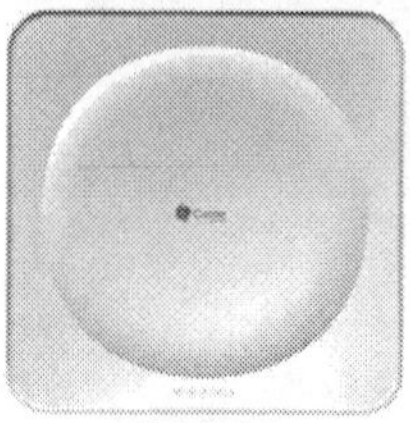

S2000
(indoor)

1. Long range, up to 400 m with Bluetooth 4, up to 1 km with Bluetooth 5.0*
2. One to many connections, up to 40 (E1000) and up to 20 (S2000)
3. Flexible backhaul and easy integration
4. Edge computing support

#SensorsConverge

Sensors Converge

Overview of Cassia's IoT Access Controller (AC)

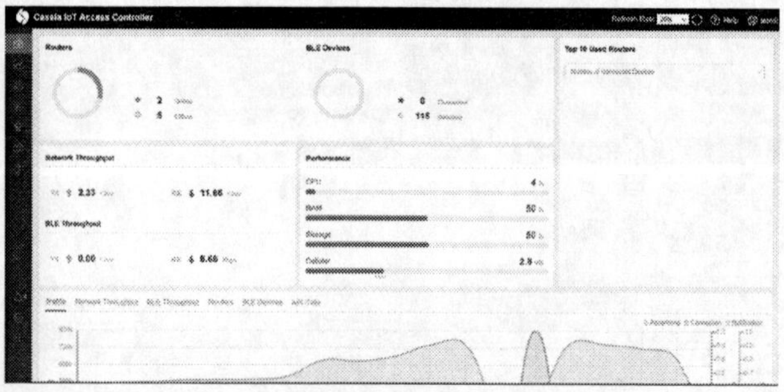

1. Easy and centralized management
2. End-to-end security
3. Easy integration and highly scalable
4. Supports Bluetooth roaming and positioning

#SensorsConverge

Sensors Converge

Sensors Converge

Overview of the Philips biosensor

#SensorsConverge

11

Overview of the Philips biosensor

- Medical-grade, battery operated wireless biosensor for continuous vital sign monitoring
- Provides data for two key early indicators
  1. Respiratory rate
  2. Heart rate
- Identifies subtle signs of patient deterioration hours before an adverse event
- Provides accurate data to drive early intervention

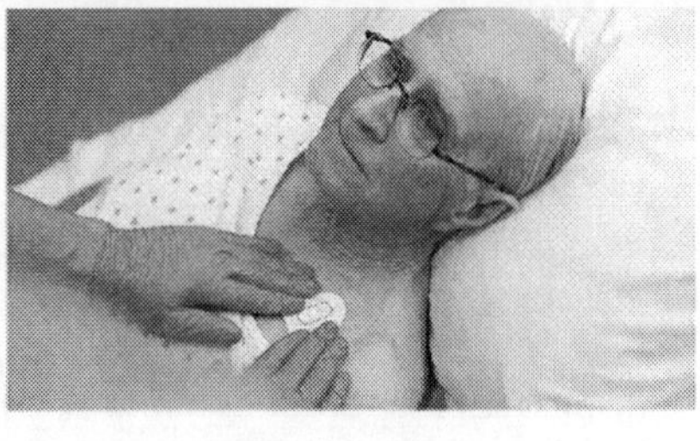

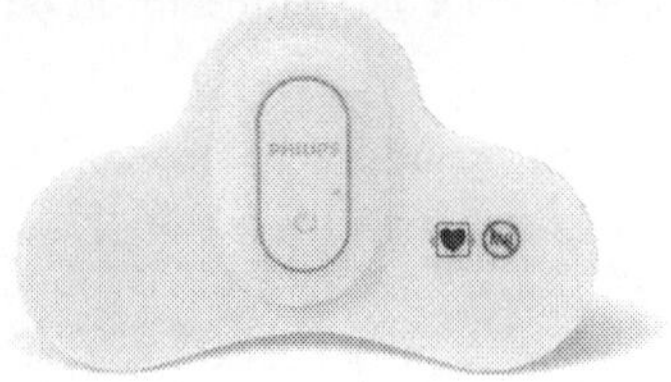

#SensorsConverge

Sensors Converge

Sensors Converge

Overview of the integration between the Philips biosensor and Cassia's Bluetooth Gateways

#SensorsConverge

13

Common challenges with traditional Bluetooth Sensors

- Lack of infrastructure to support multiple users
- Inability to scale large digital health IoT deployments
- Traditional Bluetooth sensors and end devices have been limited to single end-user applications
- Limited pairing, one-to-one device connections

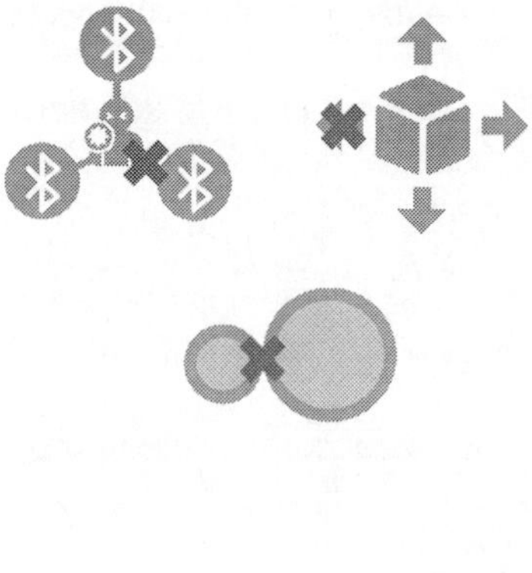

#SensorsConverge

Sensors Converge

Overview of the Philips biosensor and Cassia's E1000 Gateway

- Patient is equipped with the Philips biosensor sensor to collect, store and transmit vital sign data
- Cassia's E1000 gateways are used to transmit this data to a health management dashboard for further analysis
- As patients move freely in the hospital, a single Cassia gateway can connect up to 16 sensors

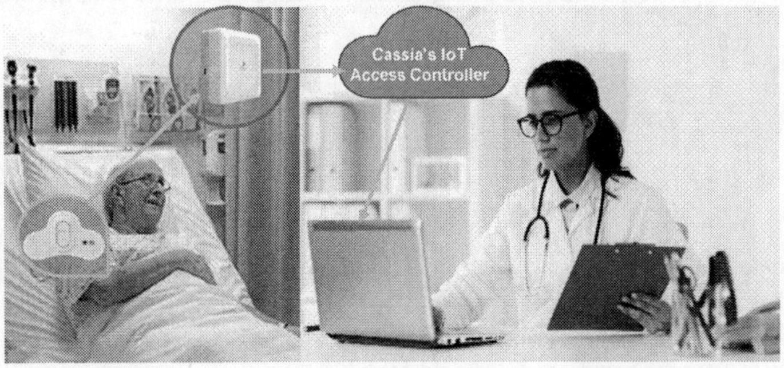

#SensorsConverge

Sensors Converge

The integration between the Philips biosensor and Cassia's Bluetooth Gateways

- Cassia's Bluetooth gateways provide seamless integration to support the deployment of the Philips biosensor
- The integration between the gateways and sensor are uniquely designed to function as one solution
- A mobile app and/or barcode reader from a patient's monitor is used for initial setup, pairing, and provisioning to the Philips biosensor

#SensorsConverge

Sensors Converge

The integration between the Philips biosensor and Cassia's Bluetooth Gateways

Benefits of the integration for hospitals and caregivers

- Seamless and secure integration between gateway and sensor
- Cost-effective and scalable vital sign monitoring solution
- Streamlines clinical workflows to improve efficiency for medical staff and caregivers

#SensorsConverge

Sensors Converge

The integration between the Philips biosensor and Cassia's Bluetooth Gateways

Benefits of the integration for patients

- Discrete, easy to use/wear, greater mobility for patients
- Patients remain connected without worrying about losing coverage and/or connectivity
- Improves patient satisfaction
- Minimizes risk of COVID-19 exposure between patients and medical staff

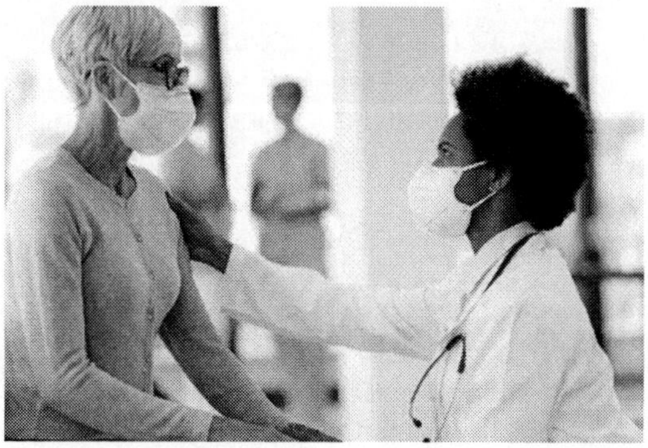

#SensorsConverge

Sensors Converge

Sensors Converge

Use Cases

#SensorsConverge

19

Use Case: Hospital in the Netherlands

- Deployed the Philips biosensor and Cassia's gateways to monitor patients in isolation
- The solution was used to monitor COVID-19 patients and minimize interactions with medical staff
- Provides early detection of patient deterioration with continuous, real-time data
- Significantly improved quality of patient care and reduced costs for the hospital

#SensorsConverge

Sensors Converge

Summary

- Challenges with traditional methods of treating patients diagnosed with COVID-19
- The benefits of using Bluetooth technology for remote patient monitoring
- How the integration between the Philips biosensor and Cassia's Bluetooth gateways work and the benefits to hospitals, caregivers and patients
- Use case discussion: hospital in the Netherlands deploys Cassia's Bluetooth gateways and the Philips biosensor to detect patient deterioration

#SensorsConverge

Sensors Converge

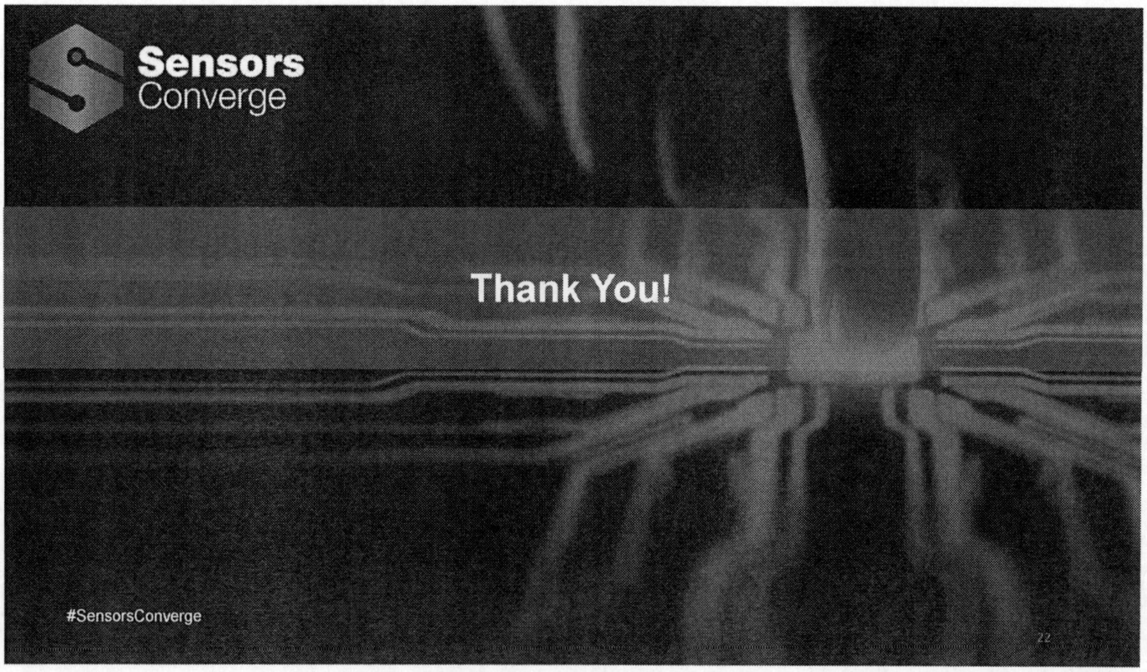

Columbia Laboratory for Unconventional Electronics CLUE chromation

Miniature Spectrometers: A Revolution in Sensing

Ioannis (John) Kymissis
Department of Electrical Engineering
Columbia University
johnkym@ee.columbia.edu
http://kymissis.columbia.edu
Nadia Pervez
Chromation, Inc.
http://www.chromation.com

PD OLED FET DBR PIEZO DNA

CLUE Columbia Laboratory for Unconventional Electronics

chromation

COLUMBIA UNIVERSITY IN THE CITY OF NEW YORK

Columbia Laboratory for Unconventional Electronics CLUE chromation

Columbia University…where are we?

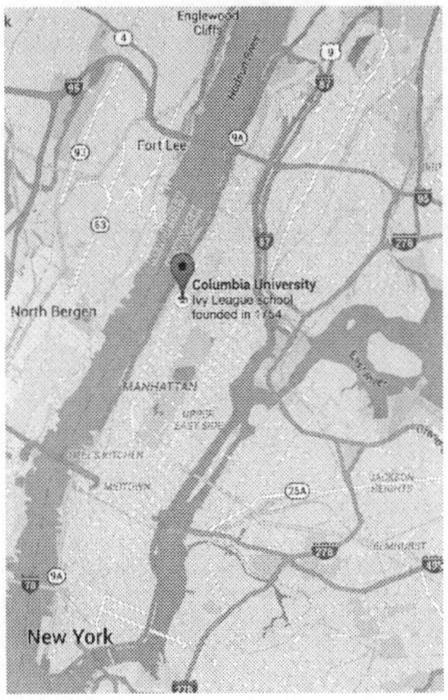

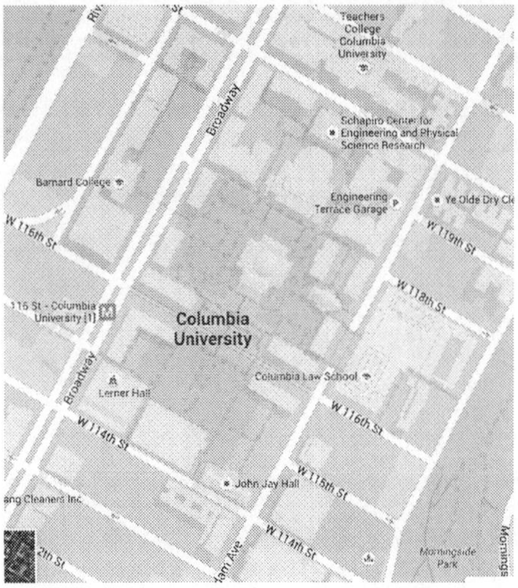

COLUMBIA UNIVERSITY IN THE CITY OF NEW YORK

Chromation …where are we?

Columbia Laboratory for Unconventional Electronics CLUE

chromation

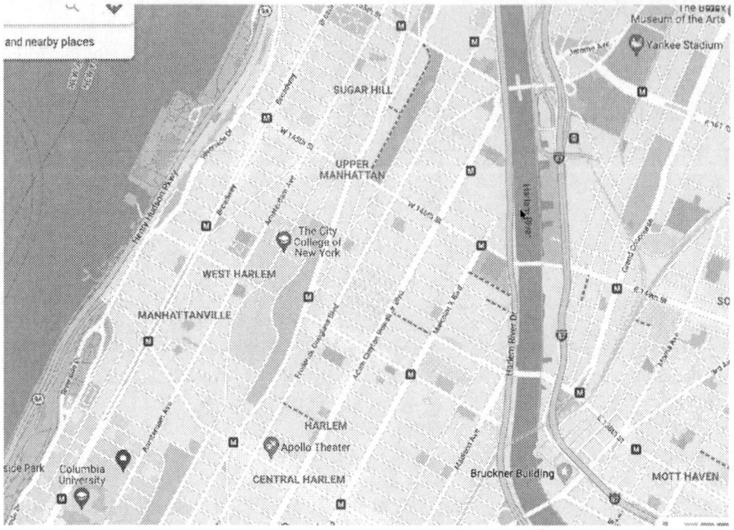

COLUMBIA UNIVERSITY IN THE CITY OF NEW YORK

What is a spectrometer?

Columbia Laboratory for Unconventional Electronics CLUE

- This is a little bit of a loaded question…
  - Measures the spectral content of light
- Beyond that … ?

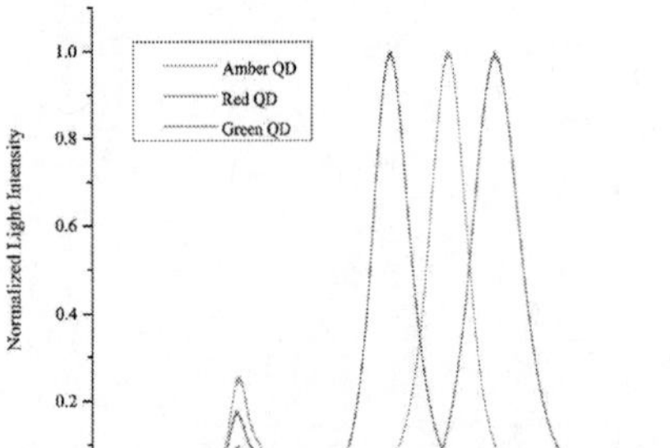

COLUMBIA UNIVERSITY IN THE CITY OF NEW YORK

What isn't a spectrometer?

- Also a loaded question
  - One or two filters + photodetector
  - A spectrophotometer (e.g. tunable light source)
- Not in contention for this discussion
  - If the light has to be guided in a single mode fiber, this is a different sort of instrument

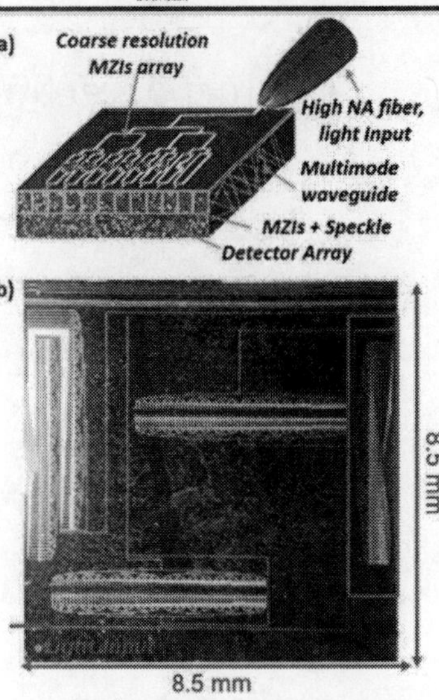

https://doi.org/10.1364/OE.388153

COLUMBIA UNIVERSITY IN THE CITY OF NEW YORK

In between?

- If we can offer 12 or 24 bands using filters, why not? How many bands are needed before we consider it a spectrometer?
- Use of (other) spectrally selective photodetectors?

COLUMBIA UNIVERSITY IN THE CITY OF NEW YORK

Major modes of use

- Direct detection of light
  - PAR, circadian active light,
- Use in a spectrophotometer
  - Reflectance, flourescence
- Raman spectroscopy
- "Other"
  - Lots of creative new modes are in play

COLUMBIA UNIVERSITY
IN THE CITY OF NEW YORK

Limiting the discussion to validated instruments

- There are a significant number of miniature spectrometers that work
- Spectrometers measure light, they do not perform any miracles or break the laws of physics

- Let's not let the promises / claims / etc. at the application level create disappointment in actual working systems

COLUMBIA UNIVERSITY
IN THE CITY OF NEW YORK

Major classes of miniature spectrometers

- Dispersive spectrometers
- Multi-filter devices
- MEMS/tunable filters
- Miniature FTIR
- Reconstruction approaches

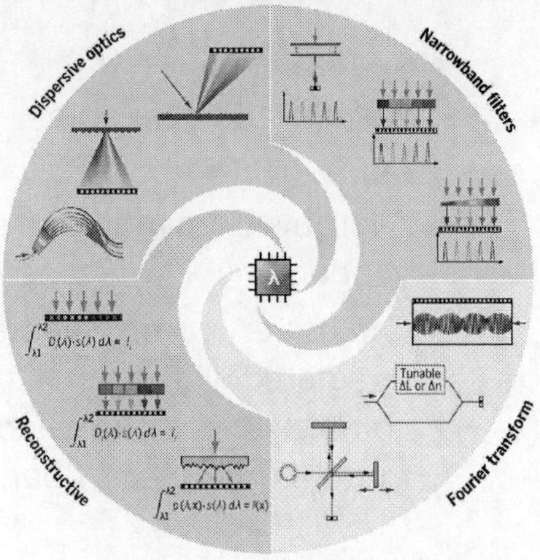

DOI: 10.1126/science.abe0722

COLUMBIA UNIVERSITY
IN THE CITY OF NEW YORK

Dispersive spectrometers

- This is what we usually think of as a spectrometer…using a grating, prism, etc. we spread the wavelengths of light
- Shrinking these devices has been performed a number of ways (photonic crystals, miniature molded optics, metasurfaces and flat lenses, etc.)

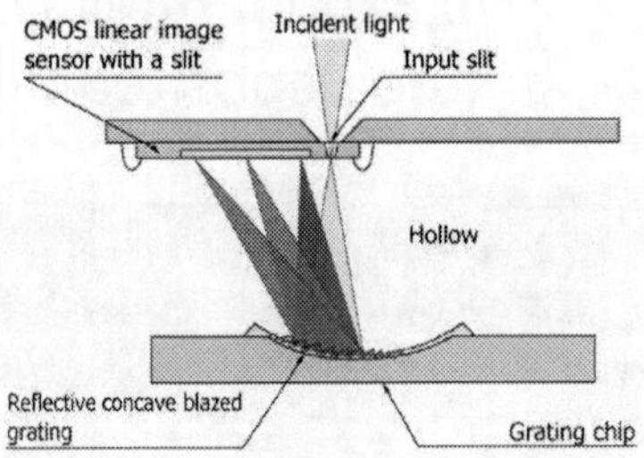

Hamamatsu, Inc.

COLUMBIA UNIVERSITY
IN THE CITY OF NEW YORK

Dispersive spectrometers

The good:

- Definite and definable performance metrics
- Available from multiple vendors
- Can be very compact and integrated with little complexity in a number of formats (free space, fiber, etc.)

The bad:

- Still (mostly) limited by the same scaling laws as regular spectrometers
- Array photodetectors limit cost scaling outside the visible

COLUMBIA UNIVERSITY
IN THE CITY OF NEW YORK

Multi-filter devices

- In a multi-filter system, multiple filters (e.g. LVF or multi-step deposited filters)

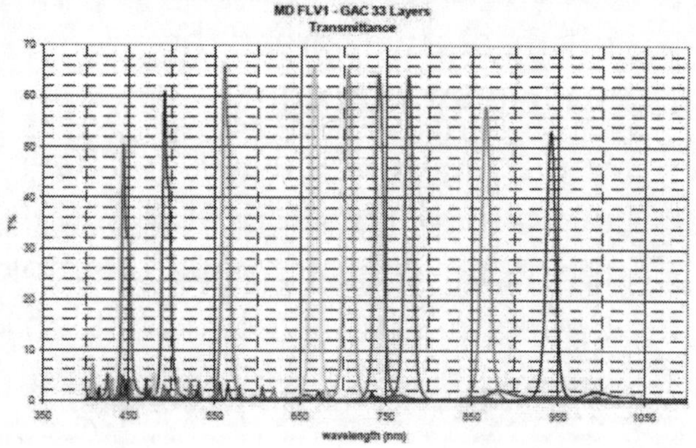

https://doi.org/10.1117/12.2309265

COLUMBIA UNIVERSITY
IN THE CITY OF NEW YORK

Multi-filter devices

Columbia Laboratory for Unconventional Electronics CLUE

The good:

- Definite and definable performance metrics
- Available from multiple vendors
- Broad spectral range, high level of stability

The bad:

- Power loss due to filters
- Depending on size of array may or may not converge on a spectrum
- Array photodetectors limit cost scaling outside the visible

COLUMBIA UNIVERSITY IN THE CITY OF NEW YORK

MEMS/tunable filters

Columbia Laboratory for Unconventional Electronics CLUE

- Using MEMS it is possible to make tunable filters that sweep the relevant measurement range
- Allows use of a single photodetector and optical path

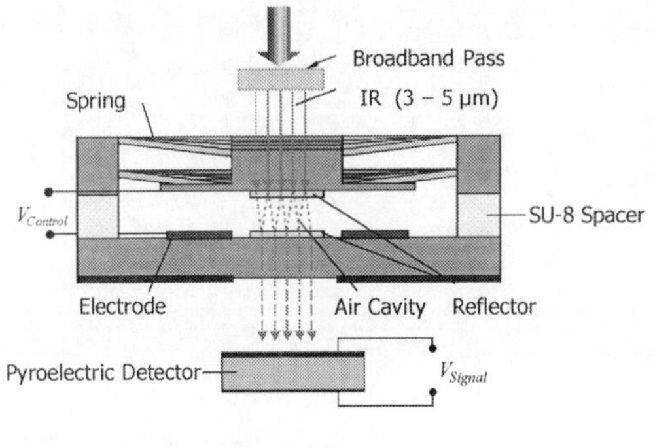

doi: 10.1117/1.2909206

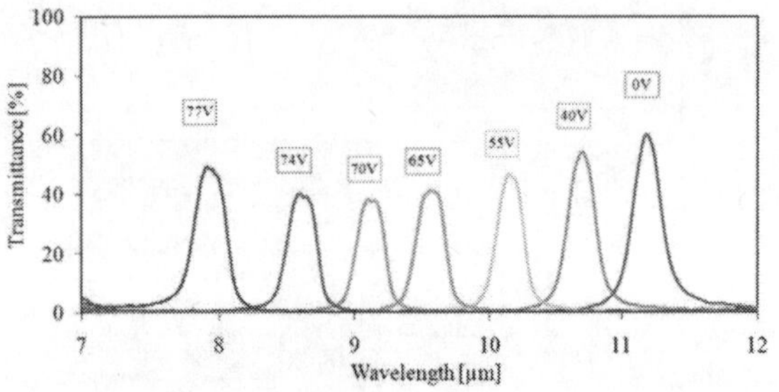

doi: 10.1109/ICSENS.2010.5690856.

COLUMBIA UNIVERSITY IN THE CITY OF NEW YORK

MEMS/tunable filters

The good:

- Definite and definable performance metrics
- Potentially very broad spectral range, high level of stability
- Can use a single photodetector
- Can have a large aperture/etendue

The bad:

- Power loss due to filters
- Cost scaling for MEMS

COLUMBIA UNIVERSITY
IN THE CITY OF NEW YORK

Miniature FTIR

- Miniature FTIR is a relative of the tunable filter, but uses an FTIR approach instead of producing a tunable filter

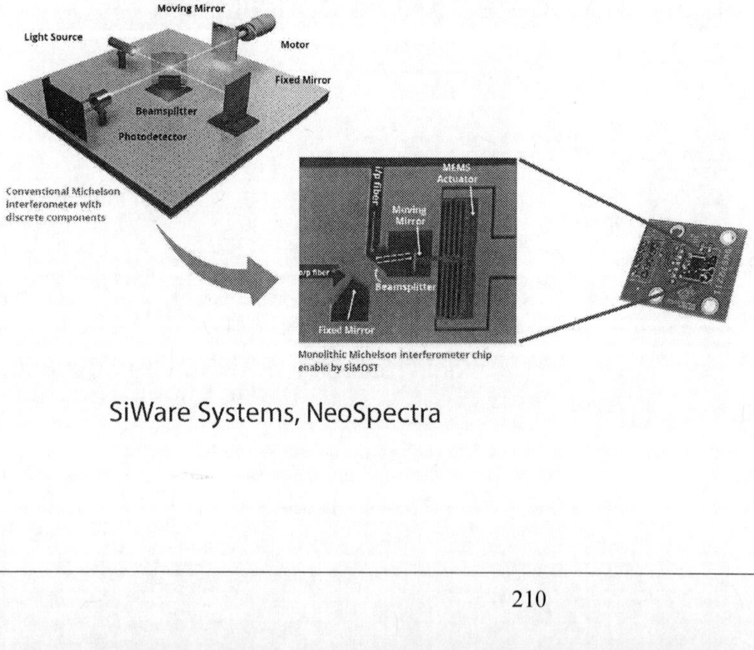

SiWare Systems, NeoSpectra

COLUMBIA UNIVERSITY
IN THE CITY OF NEW YORK

Miniature FTIR

The good:
- Definite and definable performance metrics
- Broad spectral range, high level of stability
- Can use a single photodetector
- Uses more of the light available

The bad:
- (Relatively) limited spectral range within scale
- Cost scaling for MEMS

COLUMBIA UNIVERSITY IN THE CITY OF NEW YORK

Reconstruction approaches

- Several approaches have been proposed that create a deterministic or random pattern (interference, plasmonics) and interpret this to create a spectrum

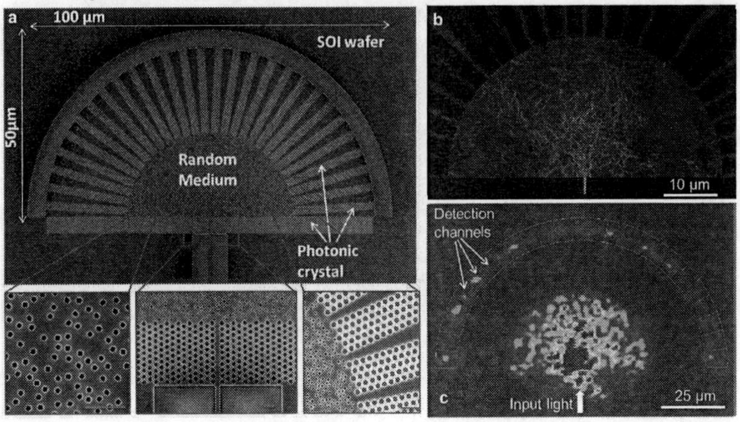

arxiv.org/pdf/1304.2951.pdf

COLUMBIA UNIVERSITY IN THE CITY OF NEW YORK

Reconstruction approaches

Columbia Laboratory for Unconventional Electronics CLUE

The good:

- Can have a large aperture/etendue
- Can offer better SNR for some mapping/ID applications
- Potentially applicable to a large spectral range

The bad:

- Indefinite performance metrics / convergence
- Some of these patterns can be expensive to scale

COLUMBIA UNIVERSITY IN THE CITY OF NEW YORK

Figures of merit to consider

Columbia Laboratory for Unconventional Electronics CLUE

- Resolution – is this definable? What does the instrument or application need?
- Etendue/responsivity – how is the light coming in? Is it free-space or fiber coupled? How is the system aligned and measured?
- Range – What wavelengths are important? Are some parts of the range more important than others (e.g. in fluorescence)?

COLUMBIA UNIVERSITY IN THE CITY OF NEW YORK

Planar geometry + integrated input optics

- Thin film folded optical path with photonic crystal
- Integrated input optics: low barrier to integration
- Wafer scale fab: precise and reproducible
- Simple alignment: stacked to detector

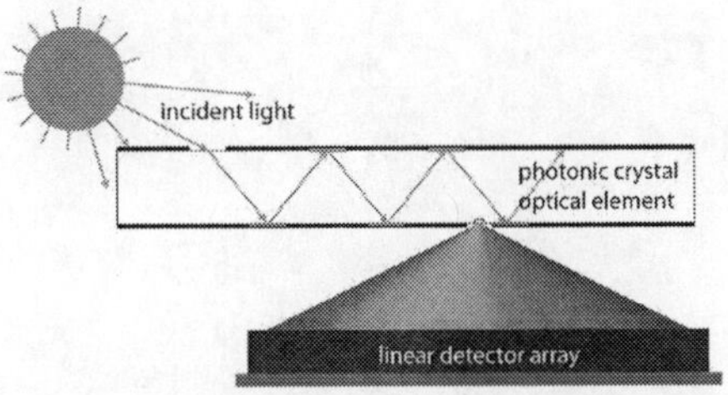

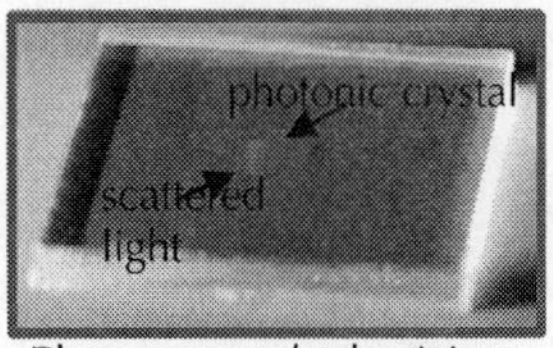

Planar spectral selectivity using photonic crystal

COLUMBIA UNIVERSITY
IN THE CITY OF NEW YORK

Performance

- 14nm FWHM in standard module,

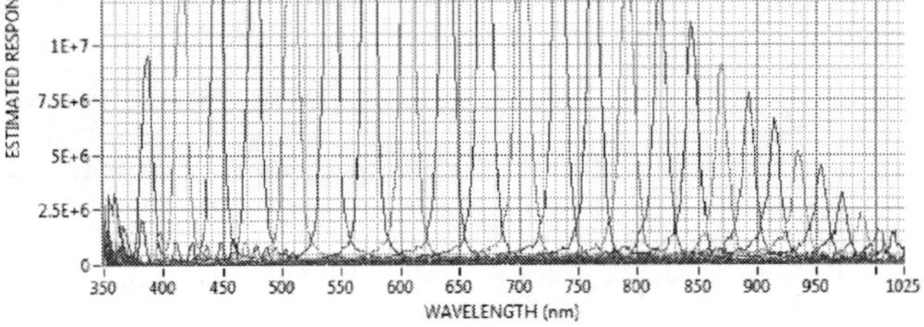

COLUMBIA UNIVERSITY
IN THE CITY OF NEW YORK

Current status of technology

Columbia Laboratory for Unconventional Electronics CLUE

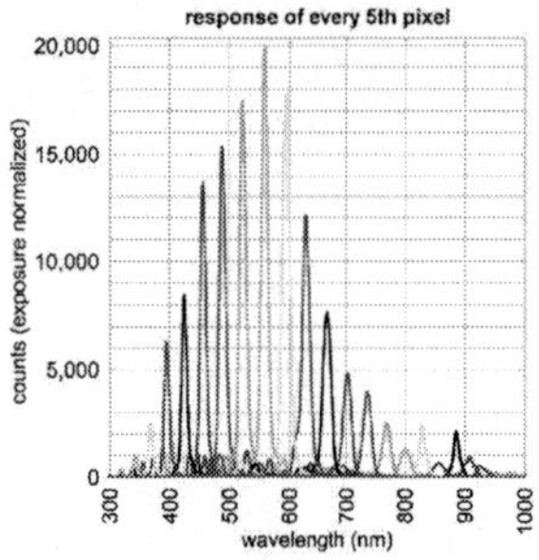

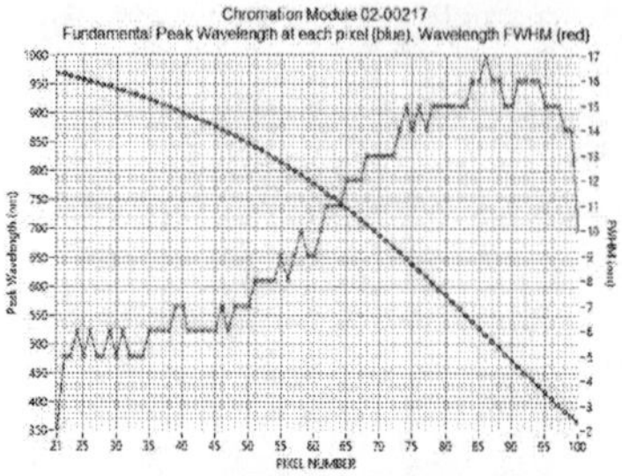

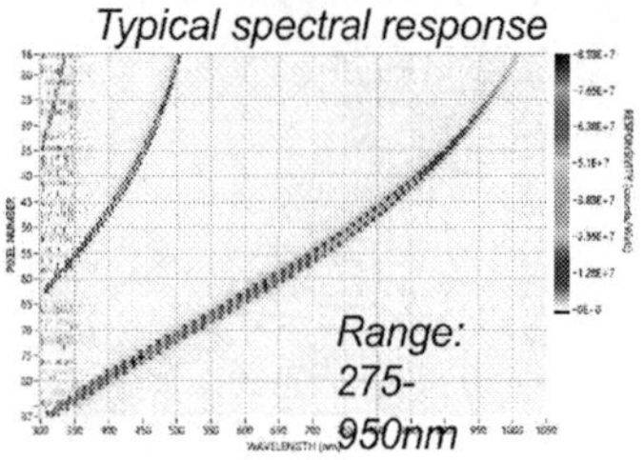

A UNIVERSITY
NEW YORK

Can it do IR?

Columbia Laboratory for Unconventional Electronics CLUE

- The spectral range is only limited by the detector in the system – base unit covers 350-950 UV/VIS/NIR range
- Photonic crystals can be designed with maximum extraction at any wavelength
- Operation has been demonstrated through the LWIR using the Hamamatsu G13913-256FG

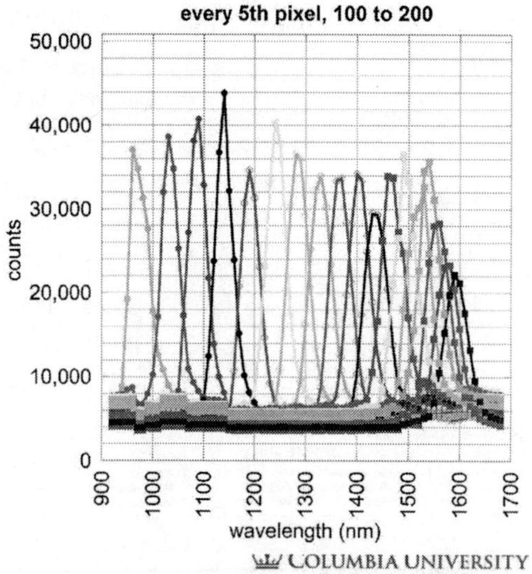

COLUMBIA UNIVERSITY
IN THE CITY OF NEW YORK

What are we looking for?

There are a number of options for miniuature spectrometers…but the really big question is what are we looking for and interested to prioritize?

- Cost?
- Performance?
  - What FOMs?
- Size?

COLUMBIA UNIVERSITY
IN THE CITY OF NEW YORK

One tradeoff: Cost vs. Capability

Example: Water testing instruments

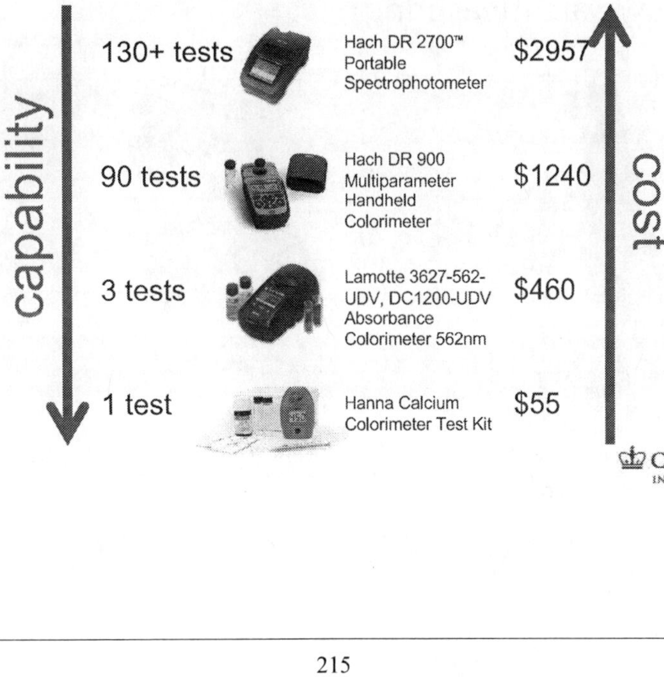

COLUMBIA UNIVERSITY
IN THE CITY OF NEW YORK

Problem: Spectral Sensing Gap

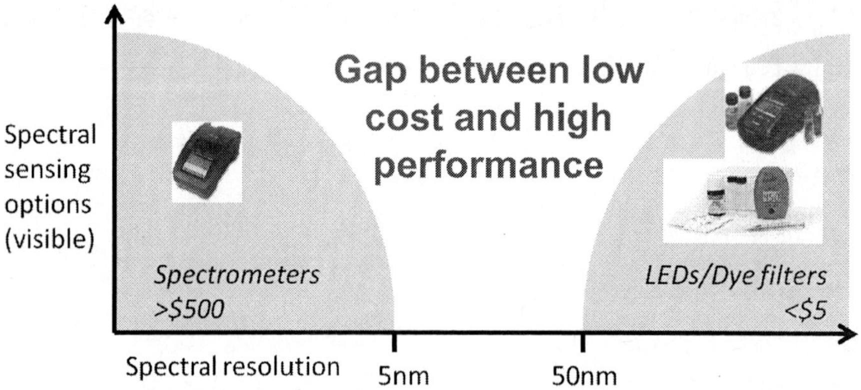

Spectrometers are too expensive

LEDs/Dye filters offer poor performance

COLUMBIA UNIVERSITY
IN THE CITY OF NEW YORK

A second tradeoff…size

- Do we really need a single chip/miniature solution? What is it that we are measuring?

Viavi

Gemchrom

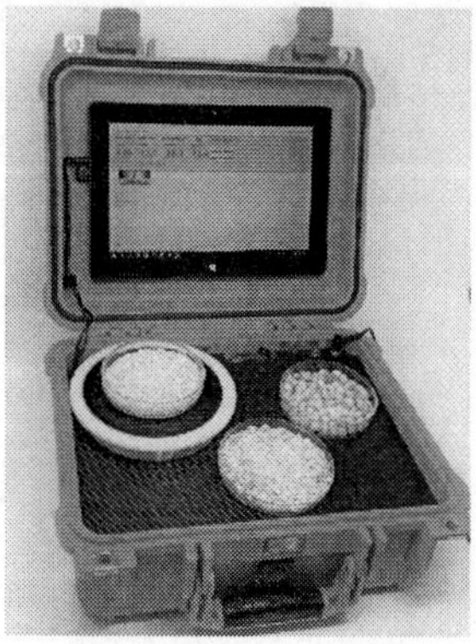

Stellarnet

COLUMBIA UNIVERSITY
IN THE CITY OF NEW YORK

Applications for miniature spectrometers

- Security
  - Quantitative and traceable analysis of colorimetric sensors (e.g. chemical weapons, drugs of abuse, explosives)
- Authentication
  - Security markers, currency, novel ink systems
- Color and lighting analysis
  - White point, lighting, feedback on displays, matching natural lighting
- Health applications
  - Whole spectrum pulse oximetry
  - Circadian rhythm
  - Integration in portable/POC healthcare systems
- Agriculture
  - Plant health, life-cycle spectral lighting control, PAR monitors

COLUMBIA UNIVERSITY
IN THE CITY OF NEW YORK

What applications will take off?

- There are no spectrometer applications that have taken off in consumer products, although there are many ideas
  - White point analysis
  - Monitoring circadian active light
  - Whole spectrum pulse/ox
  - Raman analysis
  - Colorimetry
  - Authenticity
- Why?

COLUMBIA UNIVERSITY
IN THE CITY OF NEW YORK

Conclusions

- There are a wide range of creative concepts for building new miniature spectrometers
- Depending on the application, a wide range of choices are available that can provide direct spectral sensing
- Significant progress has been made – and is continuing to be made – in cost and additional size scaling to bring these devices to the mainstream
- Moving spectroscopy into large volume/mainstream applications is still a developing area

COLUMBIA UNIVERSITY
IN THE CITY OF NEW YORK

Thanks!

johnkym@ee.columbia.edu

kymissis.columbia.edu

www. chromation.com

Sensors Converge

Importance of Stability and Accuracy in Pressure Sensors

September 21-23, 2021 | San Jose, CA
Jon Jachura | Product Manager | Dwyer Instruments

#SensorsConverge

About Dwyer

Dwyer

- USA sensor & instrumentation manufacturer
- Founded in 1931
- Michigan City, IN
- HVAC & process automation
- Dwyer calibration laboratory
  - ISO/IEC 17025:2017
  - ANSI/NCSL Z540-1-1994 (ANAB)
  - ANSI/NCSL Z540.3-2006 (ANAB)

ilac-MRA ANAB ACCREDITED CALIBRATION LABORATORY

#SensorsConverge

Sensors Converge

What is Accuracy?

- **Difference between the sensor's measurement and the actual value**
- **According to IEC, accuracy includes 3 types of errors**
  - **Hysteresis**
  - **Non-Repeatability**
  - **Non-Linearity**

#SensorsConverge *IEC = International Electrotechnical Commission*

Sensors Converge

Hysteresis

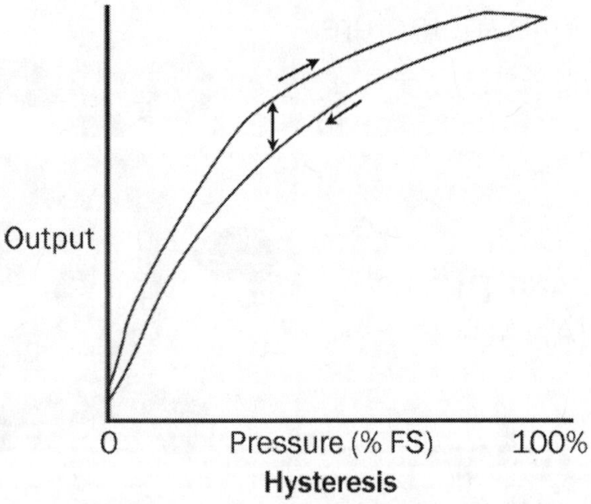

Hysteresis

- Measurement difference between an increasing input vs a decreasing input

#SensorsConverge

Sensors Converge

Non-Repeatability

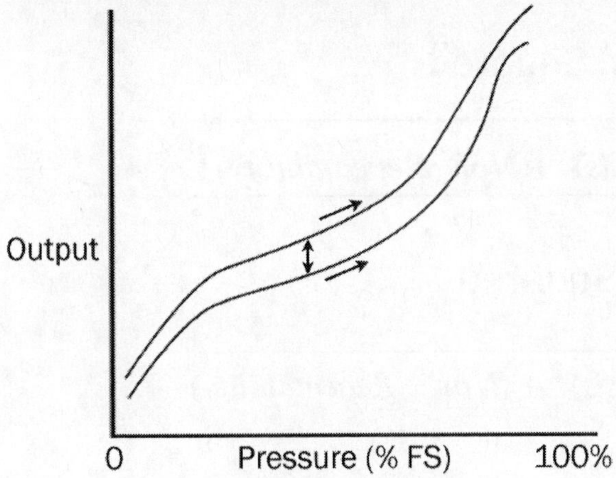

Non-Repeatability

- Under the same input conditions, measurement 1 differs from measurement 2

#SensorsConverge

Sensors Converge

Non-Linearity

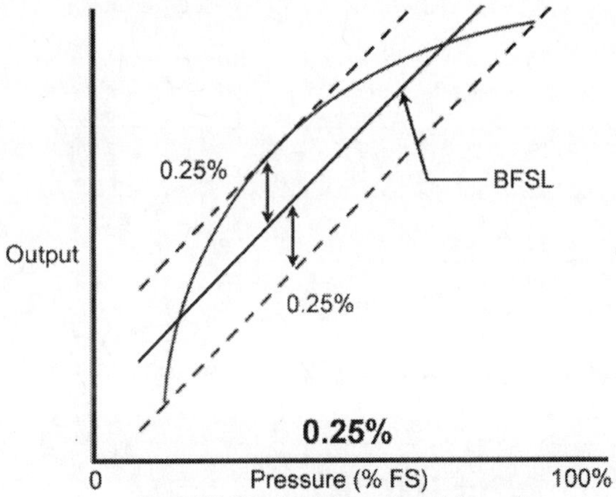

Best Fit Straight Line Non-Linearity

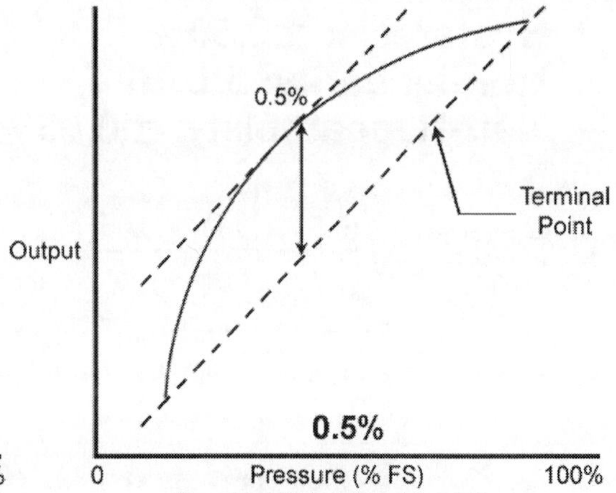

Terminal Point Non-Linearity

The same set of data can result in a vastly different error

#SensorsConverge

Sensors Converge

Calculating Accuracy

- **% RMS - Root of the Mean Squared**

$$\sqrt{\frac{(Non\text{-}Linearity)^2+(Hysteresis)^2+(Non\text{-}Repeatability)^2}{3}}$$

- **% RSS - Root of the Sum Squared**

$$\sqrt{(Non - Linearity)^2 + (Hysteresis)^2 + (Non - Repeatability)^2}$$

#SensorsConverge

Sensors Converge

Accuracy Calculation Comparison

- **Hysteresis: ±0.50%**
- **Non-Linearity: ±0.10%**
- **Non-Repeatability: ±0.05%**

- RMS: $\sqrt{\frac{(0.5)^2+(0.1)^2+(0.05)^2}{3}} = \pm 0.30\%$
- RSS: $\sqrt{(0.5)^2 + (0.1)^2 + (0.05)^2} = \pm 0.51\%$
- Worst Case: $0.5 + 0.1 + 0.05 = \pm 0.65\%$

#SensorsConverge

Sensors Converge

Stability

- The change in accuracy over a period of time
  - Poor stability causes greater inaccuracy over time
  - Drift specs illustrate stability, i.e. ±0.25%/year

Stability is more important than accuracy

#SensorsConverge

Sensors Converge

Comparison

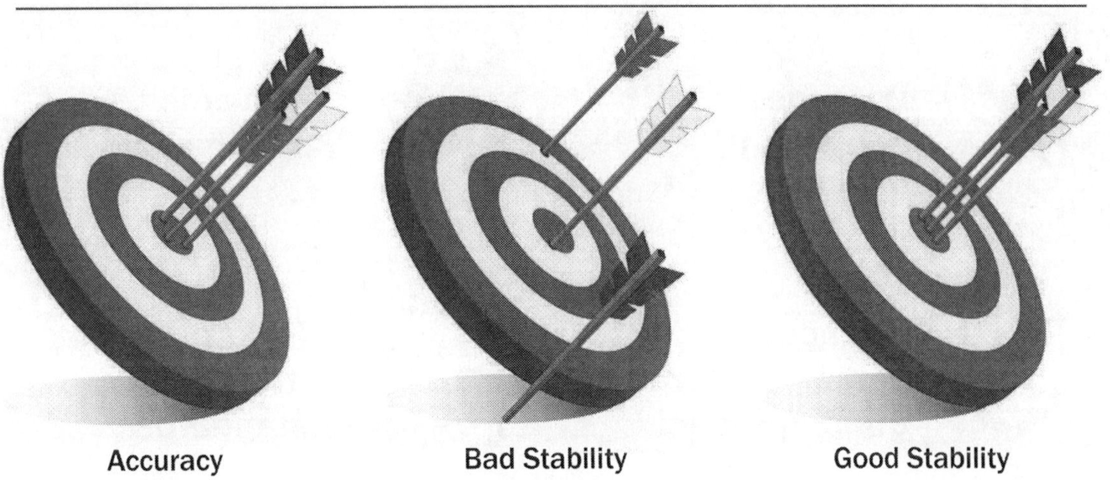

#SensorsConverge

Sensors Converge

Accuracy & Stability Benefits

Stable measurement
- Reduces re-calibration

Better efficiency
- Improves system performance
- Reduces cost & downtime associated with maintenance

Compliance & Safety
- Ensures safety standards are met
- Protects building occupants

#SensorsConverge

Sensors Converge

Poor Accuracy & Stability Risks

Damages equipment

Prevents occupancy

Reduced quality of manufactured goods/products

Failure to meet safety standards

#SensorsConverge

Sensors Converge

Accuracy & Stability in Applications

- **HVAC Systems**
  - Increases efficiency
  - Reduces maintenance
  - Keeps occupants happy

#SensorsConverge

Sensors Converge

Accuracy & Stability in Applications

- **Semiconductor Manufacturing**
  - Ensures proper relative humidity and temperature for ideal manufacturing conditions
  - Through proper pressurization control, ensures no infiltration of dust into manufacturing clean rooms

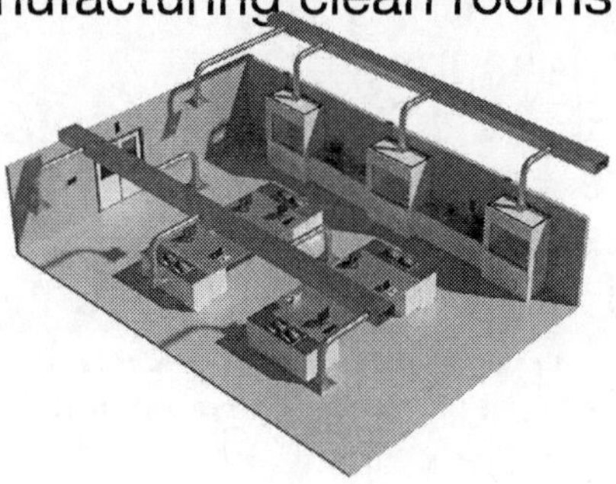

#SensorsConverge

Sensors Converge

Accuracy & Stability in Applications

- **Healthcare Facilities**
  - Ensures proper room pressure is maintained
  - Helps prevent spread of pathogens
  - Protects patients, staff, and visitors

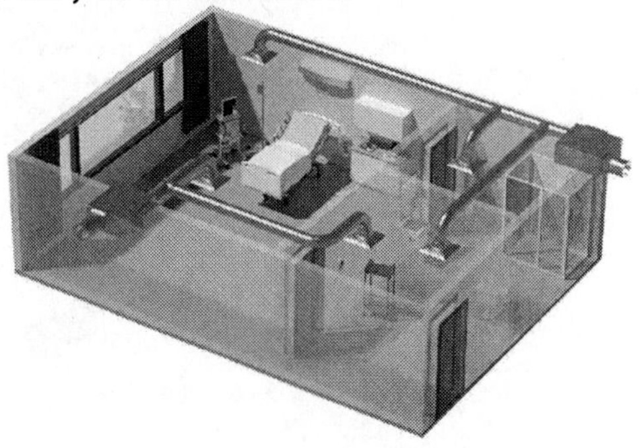

Industry Guidelines and Recommendations

- **ASHRAE 62.1 Standard for Ventilation for Acceptable Indoor Air Quality**
- Accuracy & stability of sensors help maintain ASHRAE 62.1 conformance by:
  - Controlling outdoor air delivery
  - Monitoring air flow
  - Measuring CO2
- **ASHRAE 170-2021 Ventilation of Health Care Facilities**
  - Isolation rooms: *-0.01" w.c*
  - Protective Environments: *+0.01" w.c.*
- **USP Compounding General Chapters**
  - Various pressure guidelines

USP ®

ASHRAE- American Society of Heating, Refrigerating and Air-Conditioning Engineers

USP - United States Pharmacopeia

Why is Accuracy & Stability So Important?

- Sensors provide a way to ensure a process is running correctly
- Accuracy ensures your measurements are correct
- Stability ensures your measurements *stay* correct

#SensorsConverge

Sensors Converge

Recap

- **Accuracy**: max difference between the sensor's measurement and the actual value
- **Stability**: change in accuracy over a period of time
- **Accurate and stable sensor benefits**
  - Saves time & money
  - Increases efficiency
  - Protects people
- Accuracy and stability helps with conformance to ASHRAE 62.1, ASHRAE 170-2021, USP, etc.

#SensorsConverge

Sensors Converge

Questions?

#SensorsConverge

Sensors Converge

Sensors Converge

Living on the Edge

Karthik Rau – CEO, Stoke Systems, Inc.
September 21-23, 2021 | San Jose, CA

#SensorsConverge

Agenda

- Introduction
- Remote monitoring challenge
- Prevailing system architecture
- Edge AI primer
- Edge AI applications and key benefits
- Case study
- Takeaways

Sensors Converge

Introduction

STOKE

FLICQ Atmel GainSpan intel

#SensorsConverge

Sensors Converge

What is Edge AI?

Source: Qualcomm

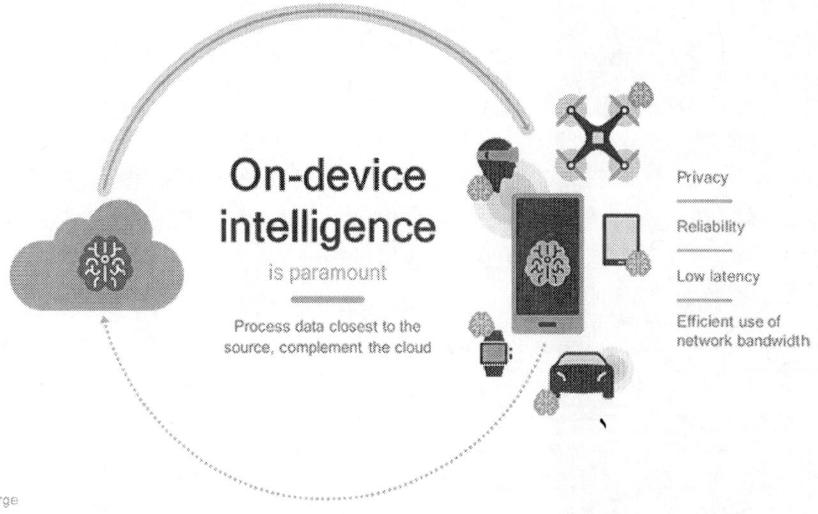

#SensorsConverge

Sensors Converge

Macro trend

Source: Qualcomm

#SensorsConverge

Sensors Converge

IoT technology stack

Source: IoT Analytics

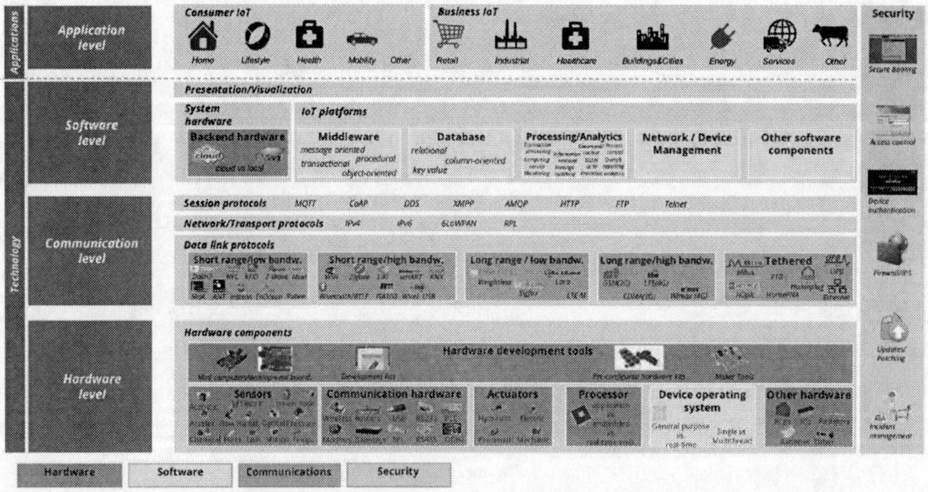

#SensorsConverge

Sensors Converge

Prevailing IIoT system architecture

Source: Microsoft

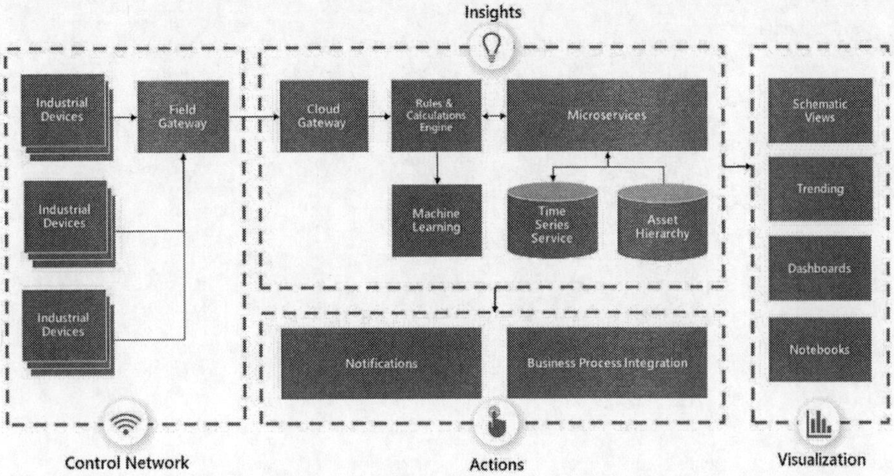

Sensors Converge

Edge AI vs Cloud AI

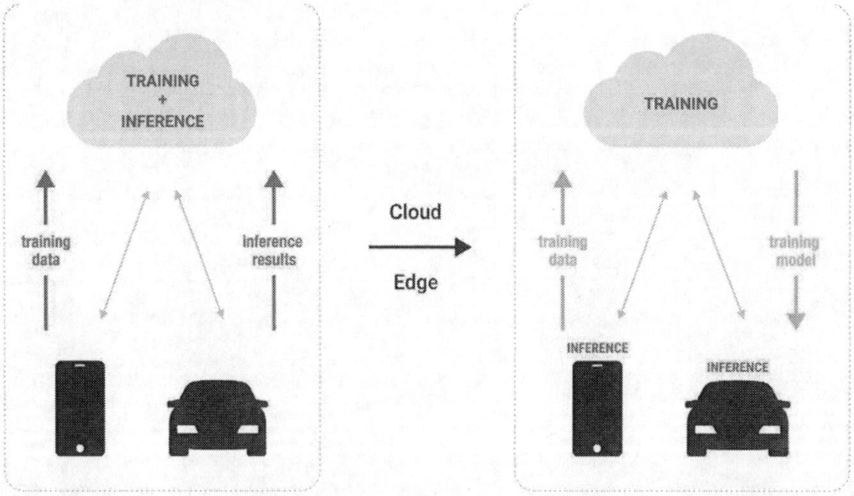

#SensorsConverge

Sensors
Converge

Edge AI vs Cloud AI

Source: Semi Engineering

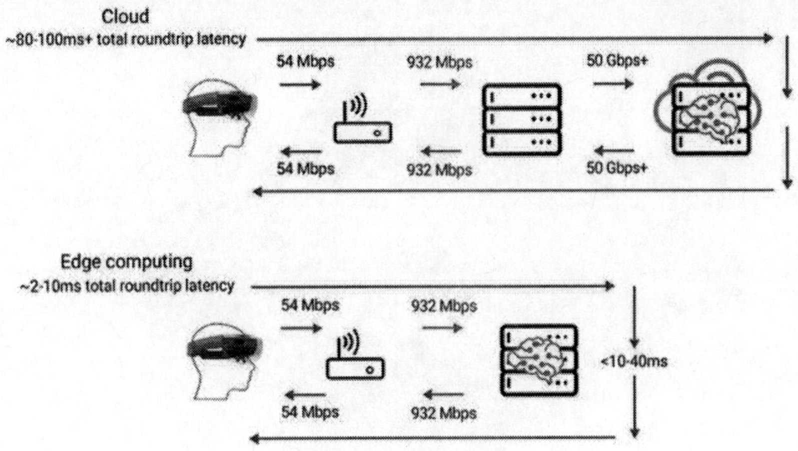

5x response time improvement in edge computing vs. cloud

#SensorsConverge

Sensors Converge

Edge AI benefits

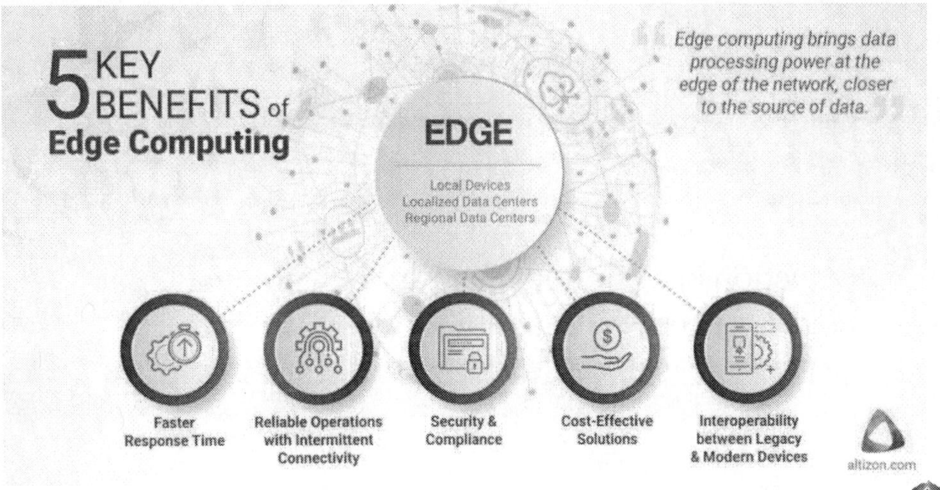

#SensorsConverge

Sensors Converge

Edge AI applications

Source: Axiomtek

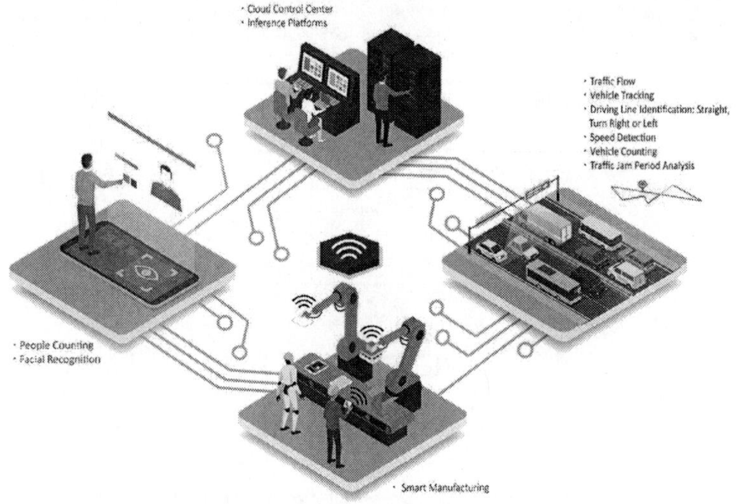

#SensorsConverge

Sensors Converge

Business case

Source: McKinsey

10%	20%	25%
Reduction in maintenance costs	Reduction in equipment downtime	Reduction in inspection costs

#SensorsConverge

Sensors Converge

Case study: Ensuring water supply for millions

#SensorsConverge

Sensors Converge

Case study: Ensuring water supply for millions

Assets: Water Pumps	Challenges	Stoke Impact
	• Maintenance is the company's second largest operational cost • Sending personnel to site for periodic monitoring is inefficient (expensive, time consuming) and potentially hazardous (remote locations)	• **Reduced maintenance costs** – site visits reduced by **80%** • **Improved productivity** – Edge AI reduced planned and unplanned downtime by predicting maintenance events

#SensorsConverge

Sensors Converge

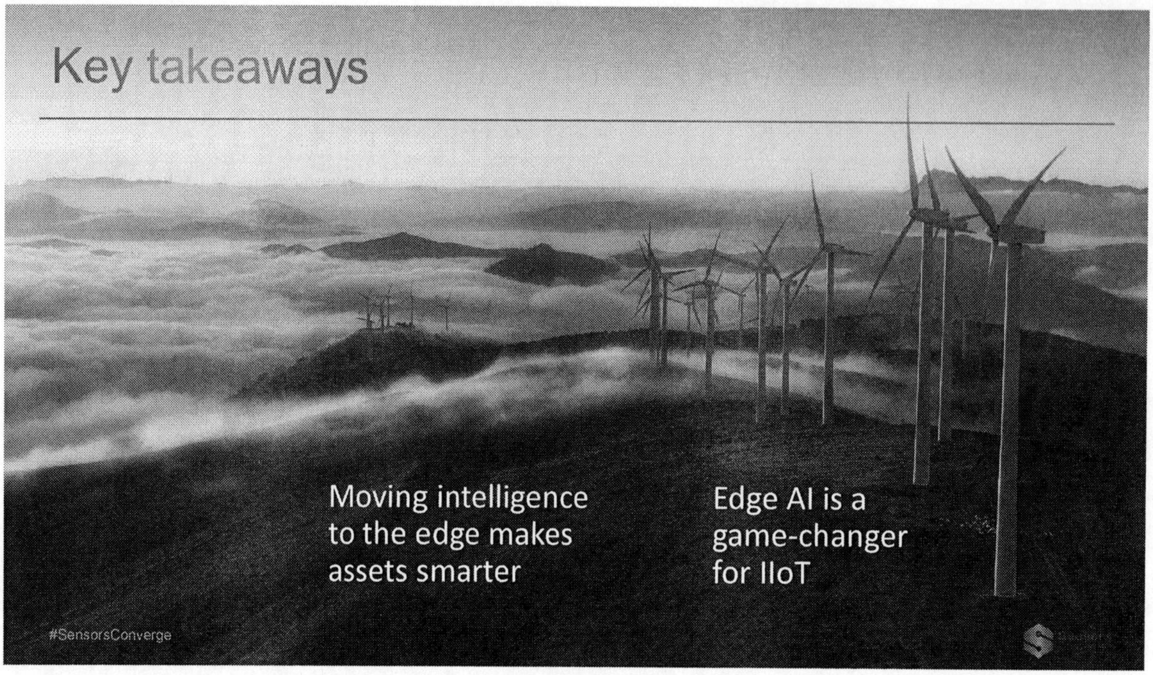
Key takeaways
Moving intelligence to the edge makes assets smarter
Edge AI is a game-changer for IIoT
#SensorsConverge

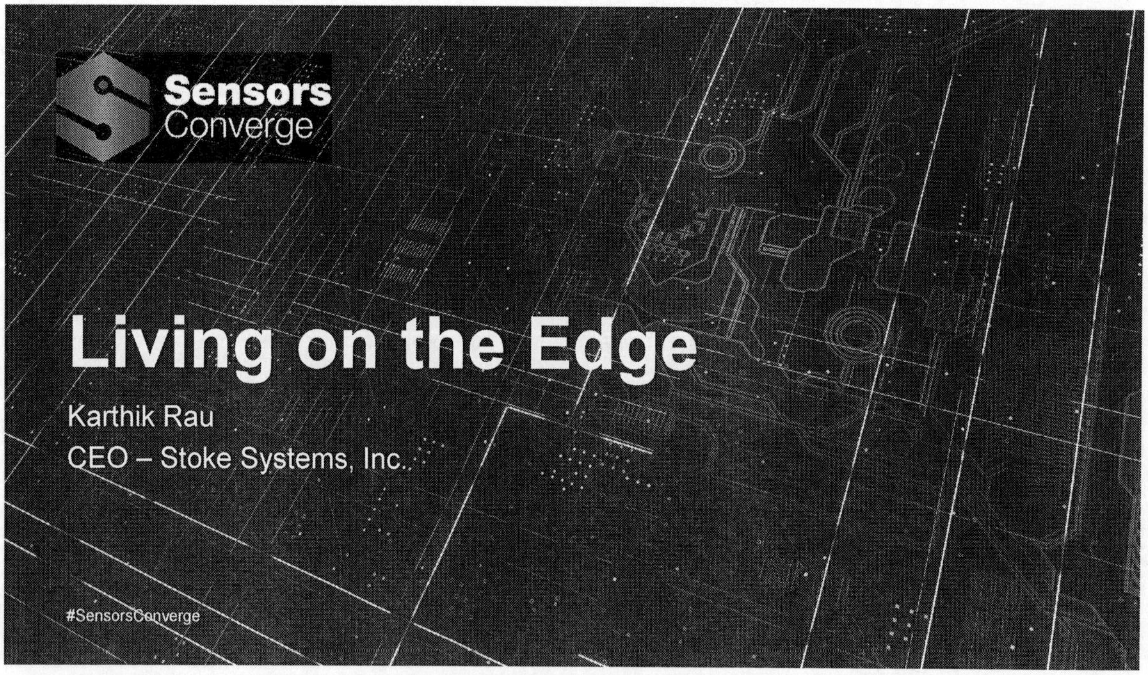
Sensors Converge
Living on the Edge
Karthik Rau
CEO – Stoke Systems, Inc.
#SensorsConverge

Sensors Converge

Reduce complexity in vision applications with a new standard sensor interface

September 21-23, 2021 | San Jose, CA

#SensorsConverge

Why should you care about this session?

- We are not going to be building a camera
- We will look to add vision sensing for a new system
- Explore how to avoid doing ALL of the work on your own

#SensorsConverge

Sensors Converge

Enhanced User Experience - Add Vision Capability

Automotive

Robotics

Industrial

Retail

How do we add basic vision to a system?

- Image sensor is an array of photodiodes sensitive to the 'visible light' portion of the electromagnetic radiation spectrum
- Most image sensors today are built using CMOS technology
  - Photodiode well filled with electrons
  - Each well is exposed and resulting charge value is read out

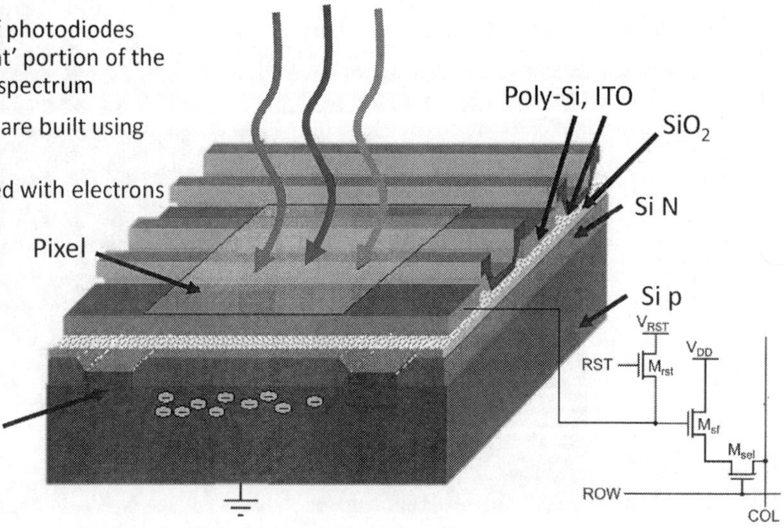

How do we add color vision to a system?

- Color image sensors use a Bayer filter mosaic
  - Array of pixels that are exclusively sensitive to red, green, or blue light
  - Data is processed into usable images

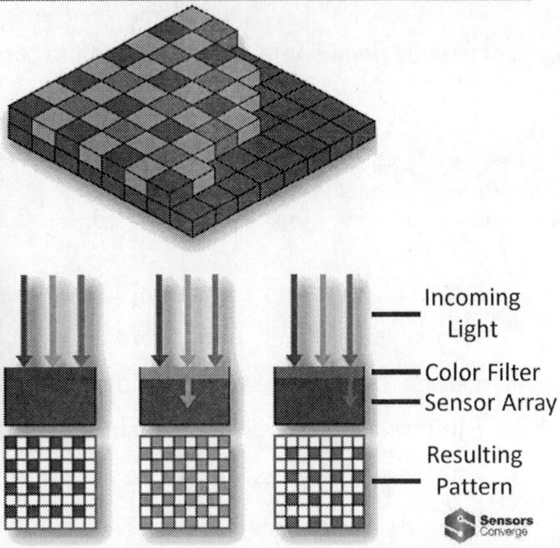

- Color sensors are not always the best choice
  - Monochrome sensors for machine vision

#SensorsConverge

How do you choose the right image sensor?

There are many variables to consider for image sensor selection:

1. Application: What end application, are specific features required?
2. Resolution: How many pixels do you want in your sensor?
3. Frame Rate: How fast does the sensor need to run?
4. Pixel Size: Does your application require low light sensitivity?
5. Chromacity: Is color suitable, is monochrome sensor a better fit?
6. Shutter Type: Do you require a global shutter sensor, or is rolling shutter sufficient?
7. Interface: What is your preferred interface to your host?
8. Additional Features: What else does the sensor need to do? High dynamic range?

#SensorsConverge

Once you choose the right image sensor

You usually need some additional optical components to complete your vision system:

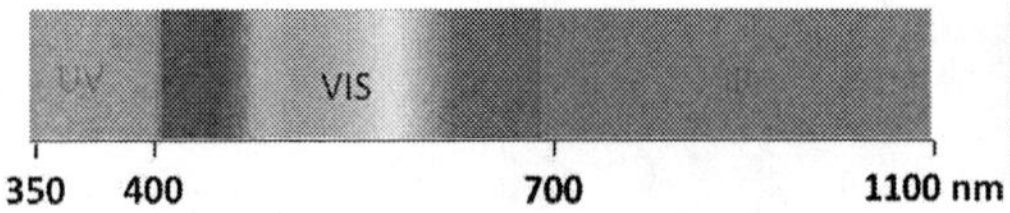

1. Lens: Do you require macro or fisheye view?
2. Focus: Can you rely upon Fixed Focus or do you need Auto Focus?
3. Filters: Do you need IR cut or other color filtering?
4. Mounting: How will your sensor and lens assembly be mechanically coupled?
5. Additional Features: What else does your vision system need to do?

#SensorsConverge

Sensors Converge

We used to provide examples of camera design

Hardware Overview

- PYTHON-1300 color sensor
  - 1280 x 1024 @ 210 frames/sec
  - 10 bits raw pixels (RGB bayer)
  - Pixel size = 4.8 µm x 4.8 µm
  - Global shutter and rolling shutter
- Optics
  - C mount lens (2/3" optical size, 8mm)
  - IR cut filter

AES-CAM-ON-P1300C-G

Reference Designs

- Camera Frame Buffer Tutorial

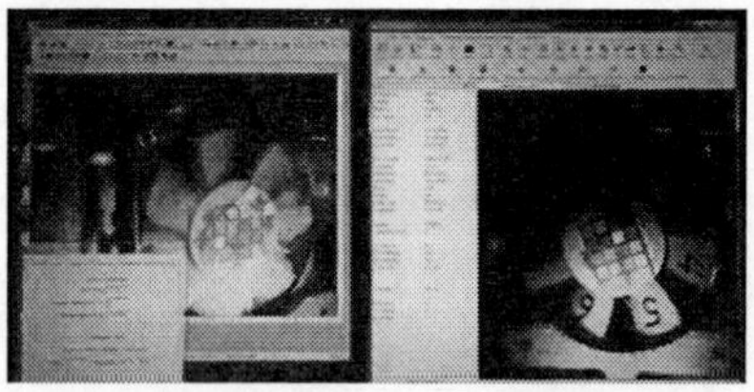

#SensorsConverge

Sensors Converge

Camera is assembled, how do you get data out?

Traditionally a wide parallel data bus to the Host CPU

Trend moving toward faster speed, higher pixel rate, serialized MIPI interface to Host CPU

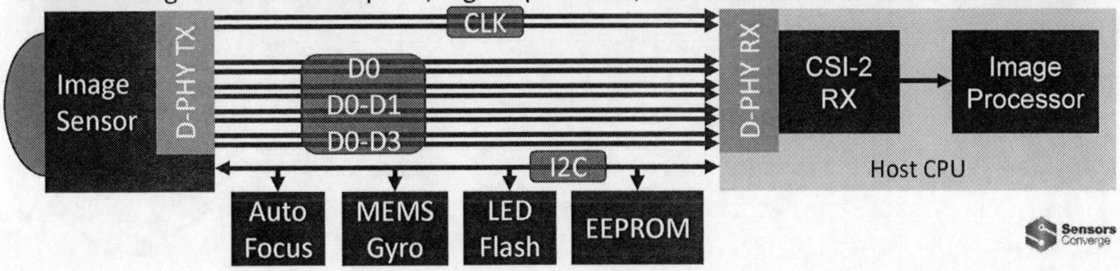

Sensors Converge

What is MIPI?

mipi alliance

MIPI = *Mobile Industry Processor Interface*

Most widely used camera interface: MIPI CSI-2

- Advantages
  - High performance, low power
  - Low EMI
- Use Cases
  - Imaging & Vision
  - Contextual awareness
  - Biometric recognition
  - Surveillance

For More Information:

https://www.mipi.org/specifications/csi-2

Sensors Converge

Introducing IAS - Imager Access System

- Many of the camera and vision design challenges already solved for you

onsemi

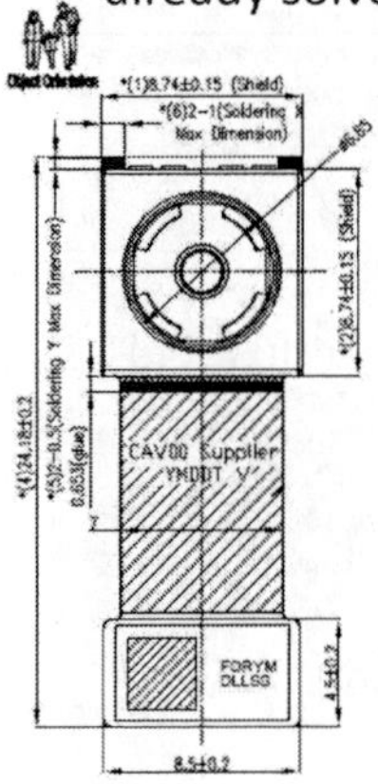

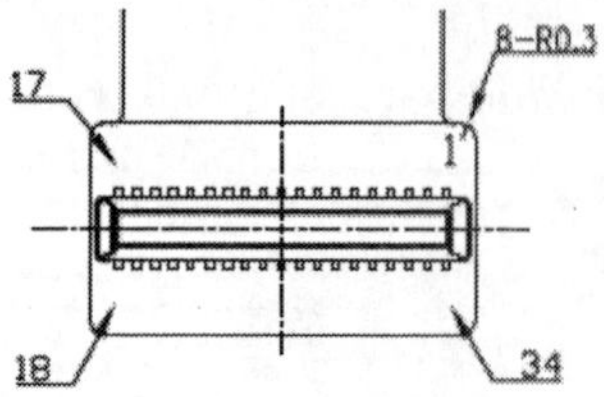

NO	NAME	TYPE	DESCRIPTION
1	ACTVDD	Power	VCM Power
2	ACTGND	Supply	VCM GND
3	DGND	Supply	Digital GND
4	DGND	Supply	Digital GND
5	RESET	Input	Reset and power down
6	MCLK	Input	Master Clock 6-48MHz
7	DGND	Supply	Digital GND
8	FLASH	I/O	Camera Shutter Flash
9	DATA3_N	Output	MIPI DATA
10	DGND	Supply	Digital GND
11	DATA3_P	Output	MIPI DATA
12	DATA1-N	Output	MIPI DATA
13	DGND	Supply	Digital GND
14	DATA1_P	Output	MIPI DATA
15	CLK_N	Output	MIPI Clock
16	DGND	Supply	Digital GND
17	CLK_P	Output	MIPI Clock
18	DOVDD	Power	IO VDD 1.8V
19	DGND	Supply	Digital GND
20	DGND	Supply	Digital GND
21	DATA2_N	Output	MIPI DATA
22	DATA0_N	Output	MIPI DATA
23	DATA2_P	Output	MIPI DATA
24	DATA0_P	Output	MIPI DATA
25	DGND	Supply	Digital GND
26	DGND	Supply	Digital GND
27	SDA	I/O	I2C DATA
28	SCL	I/O	I2C CLOCK
29	DGND	Supply	Digital GND
30	DVDD	Supply	DVDD 1.2V
31	DGND	Supply	Digital GND
32	DOVDD	Power	IO VDD 1.8V
33	AGND	Supply	Analog GND
34	AVDD	Power	Analog 2.8V

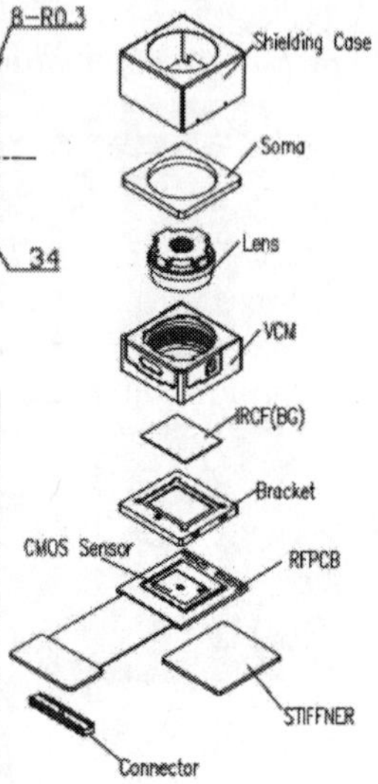

#SensorsConverge

IAS Camera Modules with onsemi Image Sensors

4K Imaging Solution with Auto-Focus

Part Number: **CAVBA-000A**

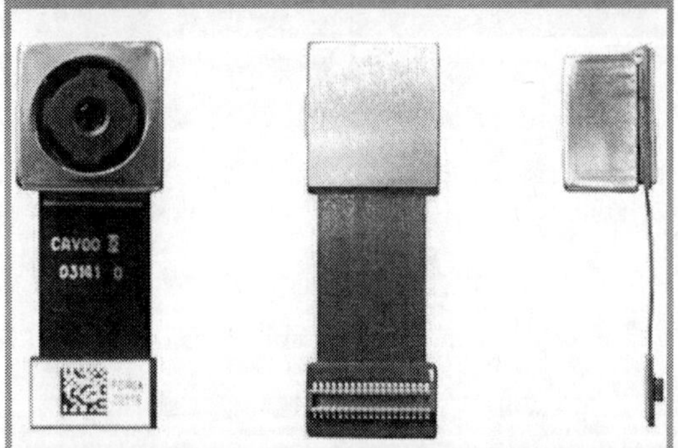

- Capable of 4k @ 30 Hz video
- 4208 x 3120 resolution (13 megapixels)
- Up to 30 FPS at full resolution
- Raw Bayer sensor (RGB color), MIPI interface
- 74 deg FOV lens with built-in VCM for auto-focus

onsemi

For More Information, Lead Time and Price Quote:
http://avnet.me/ias-camera-modules

#Se

IAS Camera Modules with onsemi Image Sensors

Compact Global Shutter Imaging Solution

Part Number: **CAV10-000A**

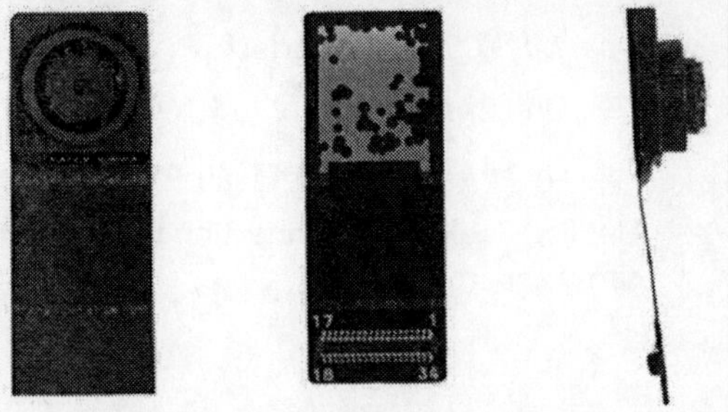

- Ideal for machine vision, industrial applications
- 1280 x 800 resolution (1 megapixel)
- Up to 60 FPS at full resolution
- Global shutter reduces motion artifacts, allows for system synchronization
- Monochrome for fast processing and better sensitivity
- 84 deg FOV lens, MIPI interface

onsemi™

For More Information, Lead Time and Price Quote:
http://avnet.me/ias-camera-modules

IAS Camera Modules with onsemi Image Sensors

Compact HD Imaging Solution

Part Number: **AS-AE0268ASAM1-50**

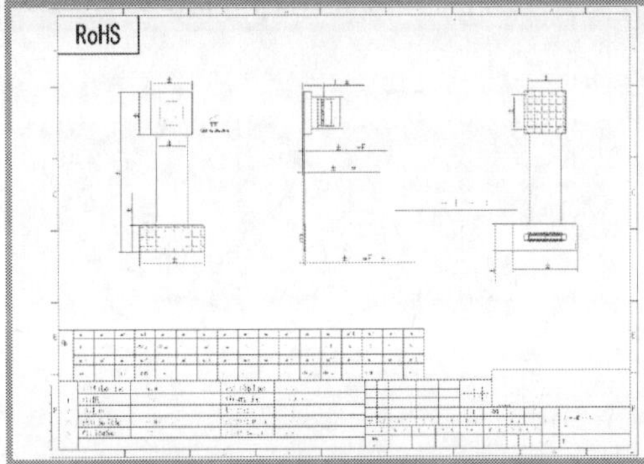

- Ideal for Edge AI applications
- 1920 x 1080 resolution (2 megapixel)
- Up to 30 FPS at full resolution
- 1.4-micron pixel technology, better low-light performance
- 80 deg FOV lens, MIPI interface

onsemi™

Coming Soon

Avnet Dual IAS Camera Adapter

- Two onsemi AR1335 IAS Camera Modules from Polight
- AP1302 Image Sensor Processor (ISP)
- Dual MIPI-CSI Host Interfaces
- One 2x interface for low-resolution
- One 4x interface for high-resolution
- Flat Foil Cable (FFC) connection to SMARC EP5 carrier board

onsemi™

#SensorsConverge

Sensors Converge

Camera is connected, how do you process the data?

How much data are we talking about and what needs to be done with it?

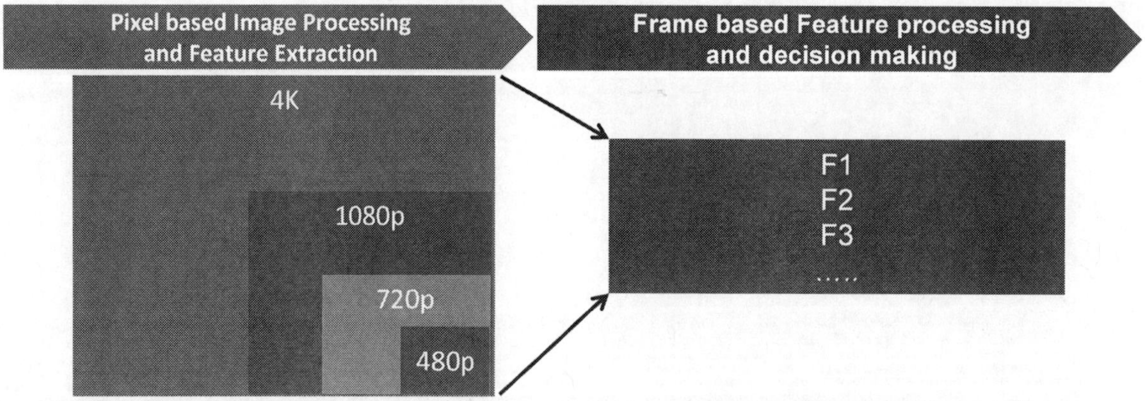

100's Ops/pixel →
8MPx100 Pixels / frame = 100's GOPS

10000's OPS/feature ->
1000's of features/sec = MOPS

Sensors Converge

AP1302 Image Signal Processor (ISP)

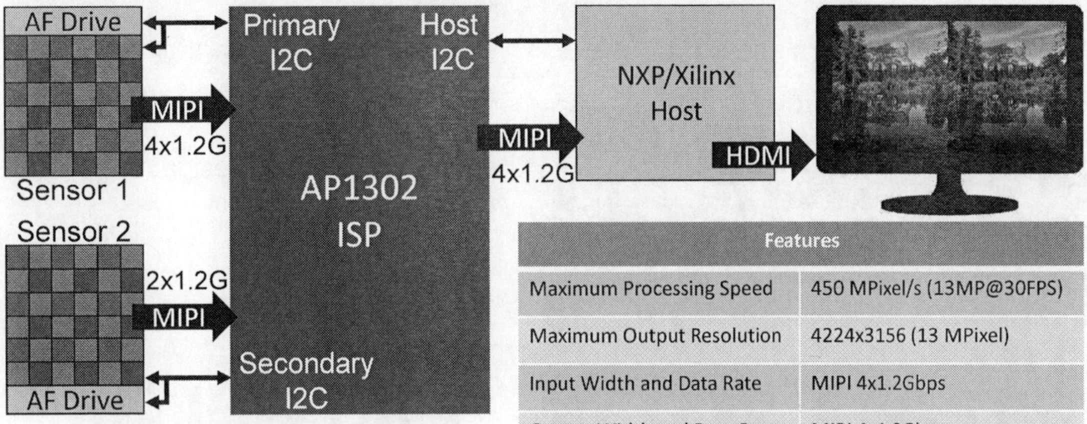

Features	
Maximum Processing Speed	450 MPixel/s (13MP@30FPS)
Maximum Output Resolution	4224x3156 (13 MPixel)
Input Width and Data Rate	MIPI 4x1.2Gbps
Output Width and Data Rate	MIPI 4x1.2Gbps
Package Size and Type	6.5 x 6.5 x 0.8mm VFBGA

onsemi

#SensorsConverge

Edge AI Kit

- **Markets Targeted**
  - Industrial, Retail, Medical
- **Kit Includes**
- Avnet i.MX 8M Plus SMARC SOM
- Avnet EP5 SMARC Carrier
- Dual Image Sensor
- 10.1 Inch Touch Display
- 12V Power Supply
- Quick-start instruction card
- Contact customize@avnet.com for volume pricing

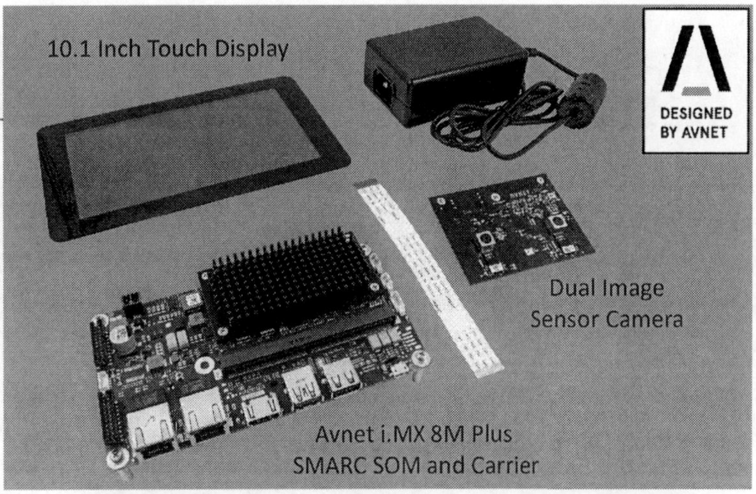

AES-IMX8MPLUS-EDGEAI-G
699USD*
http://avnet.me/imx8mplus-edgeai

*Single piece pricing, volume pricing available

18
#SensorsConverge
Sensors Converge

How to add embedded vision to FPGAs and SOCs?

- Start with Avnet Ultra96-V2 SBC
- Add-on a 96Boards Mezzanine with Vision Capability
- Ideally, have lots of design reuse and reference designs

#SensorsConverge

96Boards Dual Camera Mezzanine

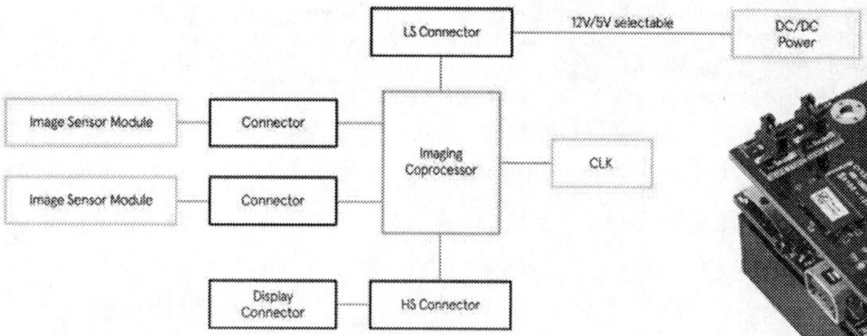

- Example designs based on Ultra96-V2
- Compatible with 96Boards Consumer Edition Mezzanine Specification
- Supports IAS Modules for vision components

#SensorsConverge

Dual Camera Mezzanine Details

ON Semiconductor imaging sensors and coprocessor

- Imaging sensors via modules from Avnet
- AP1302 imaging co-processor

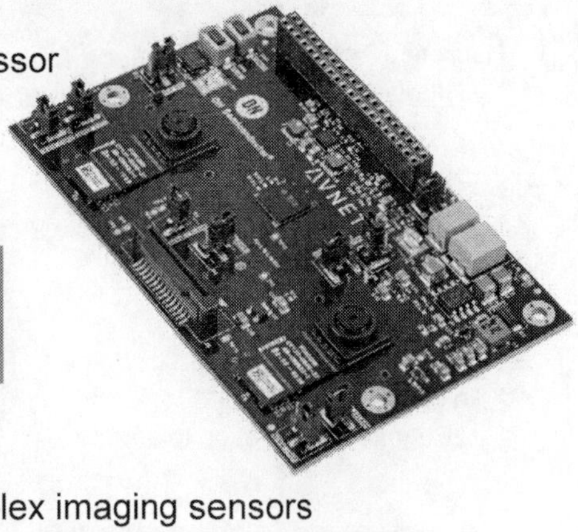

AES-ACC-U96-ONCAM-MEZ
199 USD
http://avnet.me/DualCameraMezz

Board supports up to 2 camera modules

- Platform allows for easier prototyping with complex imaging sensors
- Current design supports modules based on the AR0144 with global shutter

onsemi

#SensorsConverge

Sensors Converge

FPGA based Image Processing Pipeline

Avnet provided onsemi + Xilinx solution uses Programmable Logic resources to make an example Image Processing Pipeline which can be customized to suit application needs

onsemi

XILINX

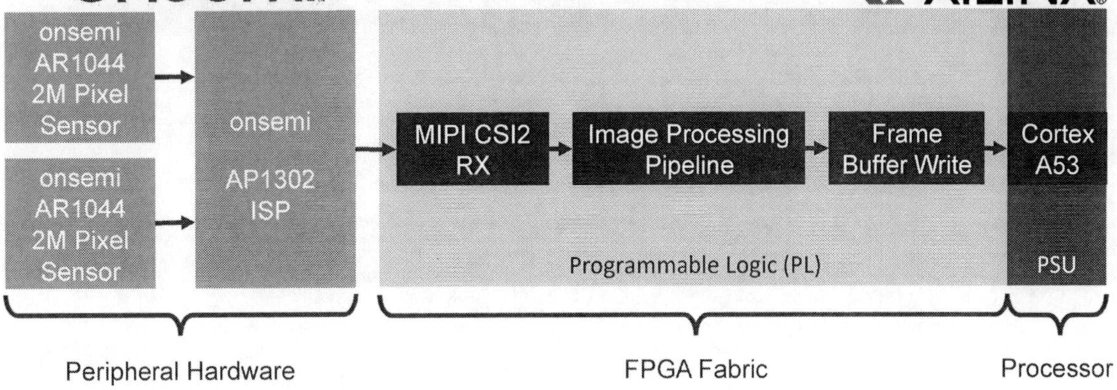

Real-Time Face Recognition on Ultra96-V2

- Hackster.IO project
  - http://avnet.me/vitis-ai-1.3-face-recognition
- Supported boards
  - Ultra96-V2
  - UltraZed-EV Starter Kit
  - UltraZed-EG Starter Kit
- Xilinx Developer Program
  - Requires registration to access

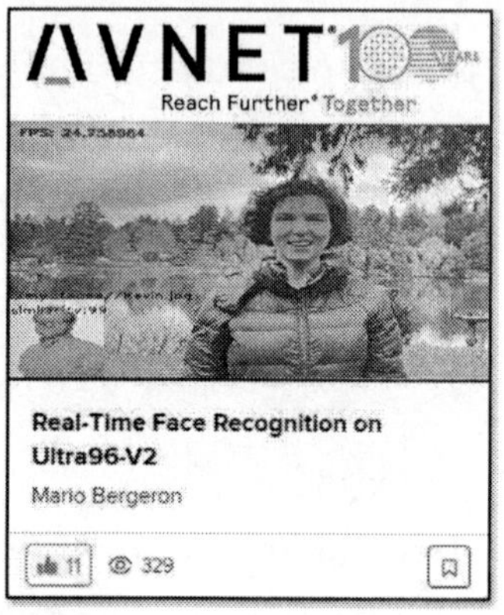

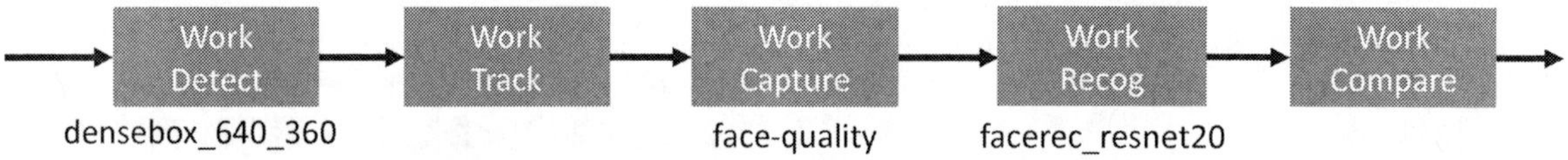

What else can you do with the image data?

https://xilinx.github.io/Vitis_Libraries/vision/2020.1/overview.html#getting-started-with-hls

Video Processing Functions

- Compatible with standard OpenCV functions

Video Functions			
AbsDiff	Duplicate	MaxS	Remap
AddS	→ EqualizeHist	Mean	→ Resize
AddWeighted	→ Erode	Merge	Scale
And	→ FASTX	Min	Set
Avg	→ Filter2D	MinMaxLoc	→ Sobel
AvgSdv	→ GaussianBlur	MinS	Split
Cmp	→ Harris	Mul	SubRS
CmpS	→ HoughLines2	Not	SubS
→ CornerHarris	→ Integral	PaintMask	Sum
→ CvtColor	InitUndistortRectifyMap	Range	Threshold
→ Dilate	Max	Reduce	Zero

#SensorsConverge

Sensors Converge

Why Dual Image Sensors?

Delivers more information about subject

- Depth maps from stereo images are used to determine disparity
- OpenCV code helps determine target distance

```
import numpy as np
import cv2
from matplotlib import pyplot as plt

imgL = cv2.imread('tsukuba_l.png',0)
imgR = cv2.imread('tsukuba_r.png',0)

stereo = cv2.createStereoBM(numDisparities=16, blockSize=15)
disparity = stereo.compute(imgL,imgR)
plt.imshow(disparity,'gray')
plt.show()
```

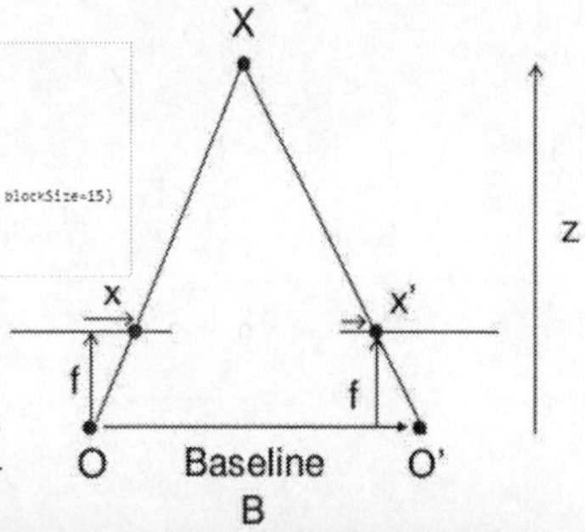

$$disparity = x - x' = \frac{Bf}{Z}$$

3D Authentication = Better positive ID security

- Detect live 3D faces
- Avoid 2D photo spoofing

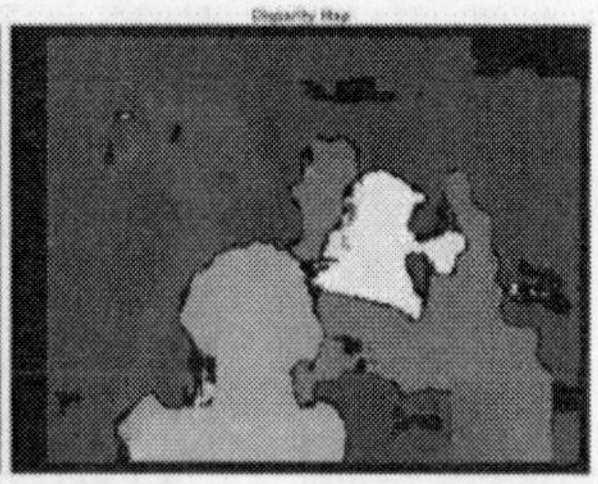

#SensorsConverge

For More Information

Element14 Webinar

- Show use of High Level Synthesis (HLS) to configure Field Programmable Gate Array (FPGA) logic
- Explain how to build the real-time video processing pipelines in Xilinx Vivado HLS
- Review the advantages of using FPGAs in vision systems

Embedded Vision on Xilinx FPGA

http://avnet.me/xilinx-vision

#SensorsConverge

Sensors Converge

27

Sensors
Converge

1

Game controller on your fingertip: Battery performance in a miniaturized wireless motion sensor

September 22, 2021 | San Jose, CA

Leland Smith, PhD
COO, Millibatt Inc.

#SensorsConverge

Agenda

2

- Battery fundamentals
  1. Energy > Run-time
  2. Power
     - Safety

- Case Study
  3. Power vs. data rate
  4. Fingertip-size real time motion tracker

#SensorsConverge

Sensors
Converge

3

1. Energy

Energy

4

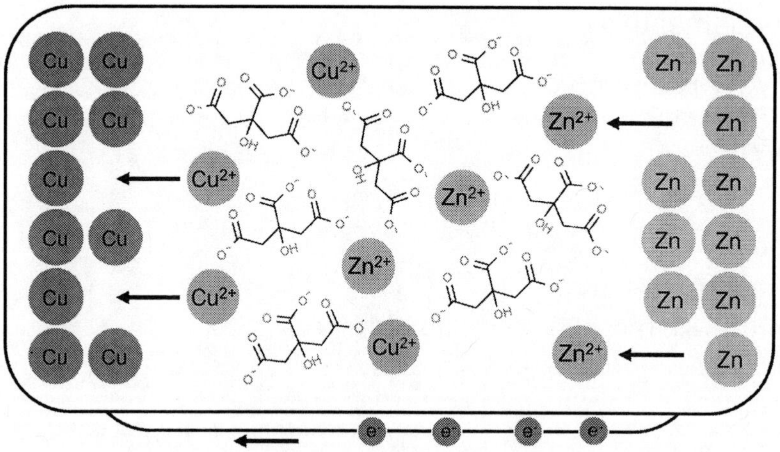

#SensorsConverge

Sensors Converge

Energy

5

The Periodic Table of the Elements

1	1 H 1.008																	2 He 4.003
	IA	IIA	IIIB	IVB	VB	VIB	VIIB	VIIIB			IB	IIB	IIIA	IVA	VA	VIA	VIIA	VIIIA
	1	2	3	4	5	6	7	8	9	10	11	12	13	14	15	16	17	18
2	3 Li 6.941	4 Be 9.012											5 B 10.81	6 C 12.01	7 N 14.01	8 O 16.00	9 F 19.00	10 Ne 20.18
3	11 Na 22.99	12 Mg 24.31											13 Al 26.98	14 Si 28.09	15 P 30.97	16 S 32.07	17 Cl 35.45	18 Ar 39.95
4	19 K 39.10	20 Ca 40.08	21 Sc 44.96	22 Ti 47.87	23 V 50.94	24 Cr 52.00	25 Mn 54.94	26 Fe 55.85	27 Co 58.93	28 Ni 58.69	29 Cu 63.55	30 Zn 65.38	31 Ga 69.72	32 Ge 72.64	33 As 74.92	34 Se 78.96	35 Br 79.90	36 Kr 83.80
5	37 Rb 85.47	38 Sr 87.62	39 Y 88.91	40 Zr 91.22	41 Nb 92.91	42 Mo 95.96	43 Tc (98)	44 Ru 101.1	45 Rh 102.9	46 Pd 106.4	47 Ag 107.9	48 Cd 112.4	49 In 114.8	50 Sn 118.7	51 Sb 121.8	52 Te 127.6	53 I 126.9	54 Xe 131.3
6	55 Cs 132.9	56 Ba 137.3	57-71 La-Lu *	72 Hf 178.5	73 Ta 180.9	74 W 183.8	75 Re 186.2	76 Os 190.2	77 Ir 192.2	78 Pt 195.1	79 Au 197.0	80 Hg 200.6	81 Tl 204.4	82 Pb 207.2	83 Bi 209.0	84 Po (209)	85 At (210)	86 Rn (222)
7	87 Fr (223)	88 Ra (226)	89-103 Ac-Lr #	104 Rf (267)	105 Db (268)	106 Sg (271)	107 Bh (272)	108 Hs (270)	109 Mt (276)	110 Ds (281)	111 Rg (280)	112 Cn (285)	113 Nh (286)	114 Fl (289)	115 Mc (289)	116 Lv (293)	117 Ts (294)	118 Og (294)

*	57 La 138.9	58 Ce 140.1	59 Pr 140.9	60 Nd 144.2	61 Pm (145)	62 Sm 150.4	63 Eu 152.0	64 Gd 157.3	65 Tb 158.9	66 Dy 162.5	67 Ho 164.9	68 Er 167.3	69 Tm 168.9	70 Yb 173.0	71 Lu 175.0
#	89 Ac (227)	90 Th 232.0	91 Pa 231.0	92 U 238.0	93 Np (237)	94 Pu (244)	95 Am (243)	96 Cm (247)	97 Bk (247)	98 Cf (251)	99 Es (252)	100 Fm (257)	101 Md (258)	102 No (259)	103 Lr (262)

#SensorsConverge

Sensors Converge

Energy

6

The Periodic Table of the Elements

1	1 H 1.008																	2 He 4.003
	IA	IIA	IIIB	IVB	VB	VIB	VIIB	VIIIB			IB	IIB	IIIA	IVA	VA	VIA	VIIA	VIIIA
	1	2	3	4	5	6	7	8	9	10	11	12	13	14	15	16	17	18
2	3 Li 6.941	4 Be 9.012											5 B 10.81	6 C 12.01	7 N 14.01	8 O 16.00	9 F 19.00	10 Ne 20.18
3	11 Na 22.99	12 Mg 24.31											13 Al 26.98	14 Si 28.09	15 P 30.97	16 S 32.07	17 Cl 35.45	18 Ar 39.95
4	19 K	20 Ca	21 Sc	22 Ti 47.87	23 V 50.94	24 Cr 52.00	25 Mn 54.94	26 Fe 55.85	27 Co 58.93	28 Ni 58.69	29 Cu 63.55	30 Zn 65.38	31 Ga 69.72	32 Ge 72.64	33 As 74.92	34 Se 78.96	35 Br 79.90	36 Kr 83.80
				40 Zr 91.22	41 Nb 92.91	42 Mo 95.96	43 Tc (98)	44 Ru 101.1	45 Rh 102.9	46 Pd 106.4	47 Ag 107.9	48 Cd 112.4	49 In 114.8	50 Sn 118.7	51 Sb 121.8	52 Te 127.6	53 I 126.9	54 Xe 131.3
				72 Hf 178.5	73 Ta 180.9	74 W 183.8	75 Re 186.2	76 Os 190.2	77 Ir 192.2	78 Pt 195.1	79 Au 197.0	80 Hg 200.6	81 Tl 204.4	82 Pb 207.2	83 Bi 209.0	84 Po (209)	85 At (210)	86 Rn (222)
				104 Rf (267)	105 Db (268)	106 Sg (271)	107 Bh (272)	108 Hs (270)	109 Mt (276)	110 Ds (281)	111 Rg (280)	112 Cn (285)	113 Nh (286)	114 Fl (289)	115 Mc (289)	116 Lv (293)	117 Ts (294)	118 Og (294)

57 La 138.9	58 Ce 140.1	59 Pr 140.9	60 Nd 144.2	61 Pm (145)	62 Sm 150.4	63 Eu 152.0	64 Gd 157.3	65 Tb 158.9	66 Dy 162.5	67 Ho 164.9	68 Er 167.3	69 Tm 168.9	70 Yb 173.0	71 Lu 175.0
89 Ac (227)	90 Th 232.0	91 Pa 231.0	92 U 238.0	93 Np (237)	94 Pu (244)	95 Am (243)	96 Cm (247)	97 Bk (247)	98 Cf (251)	99 Es (252)	100 Fm (257)	101 Md (258)	102 No (259)	103 Lr (262)

#SensorsConverge

Sensors Converge

Energy

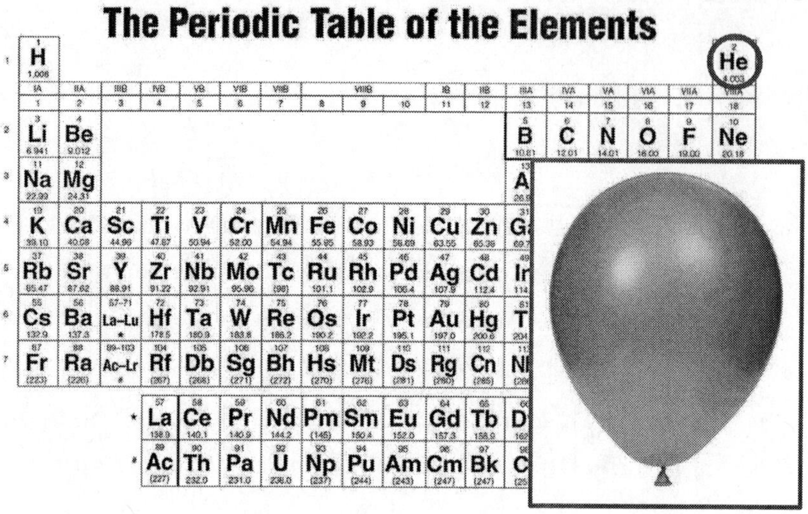

#SensorsConverge

Sensors Converge

Energy

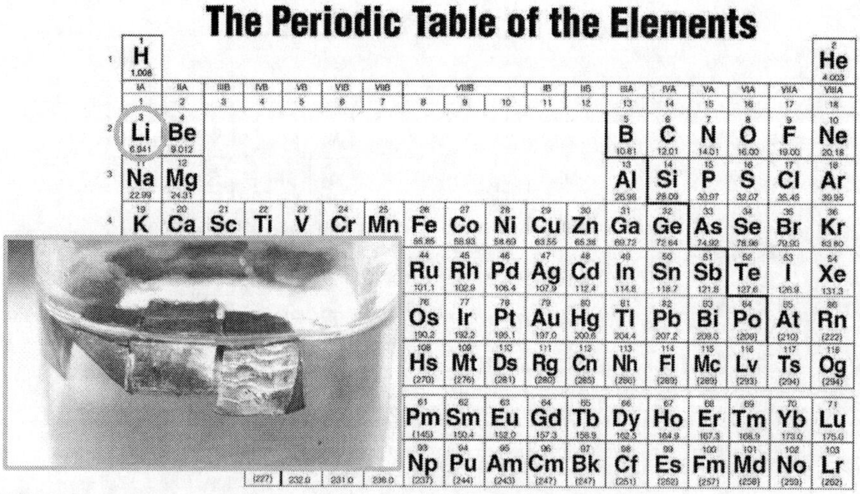

#SensorsConverge

Sensors Converge

Energy

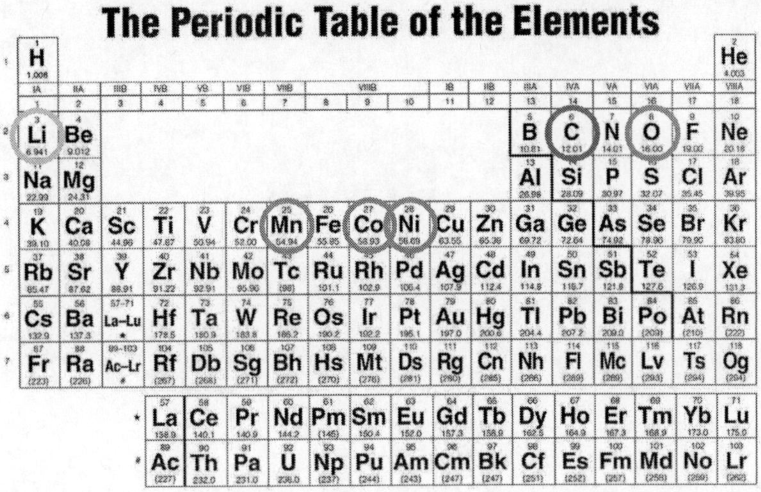

#SensorsConverge

Sensors Converge

Energy

ACS Energy Lett. 2020, 5, 11, 3544–3547
Publication Date:October 23, 2020
https://doi.org/10.1021/acsenergylett.0c02181

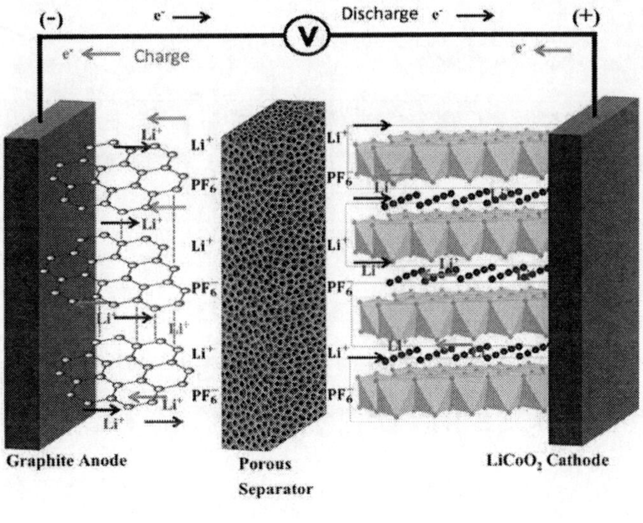

#SensorsConverge

Sensors Converge

11

2. Power

12

Power

Energy = E_{batt}

Power = $P_{batt} = \frac{dE_{batt}}{dt}$

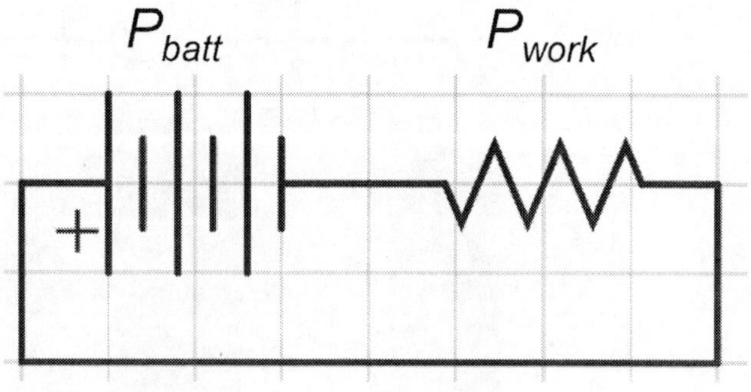

Conclusion: Chose the battery that stores the most energy

#SensorsConverge

Sensors Converge

Power

13

- Problems as P_{heat} ↑
  - Safety
  - Cycle life
  - Voltage drop (V_{heat})

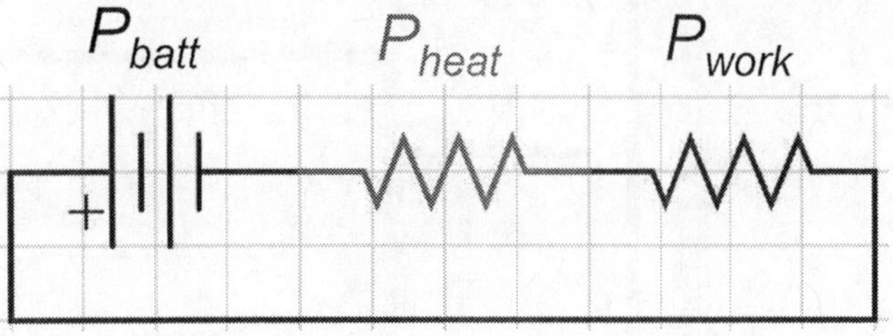

$$P_{heat} = i^2 \times R_{batt} = i \times V_{heat}$$

$$V_{work} = V_{batt} - V_{heat}$$

#SensorsConverge

Sensors Converge

Power

14

Battery "Resistance" is a conceptually useful AND fundamentally flawed analogy

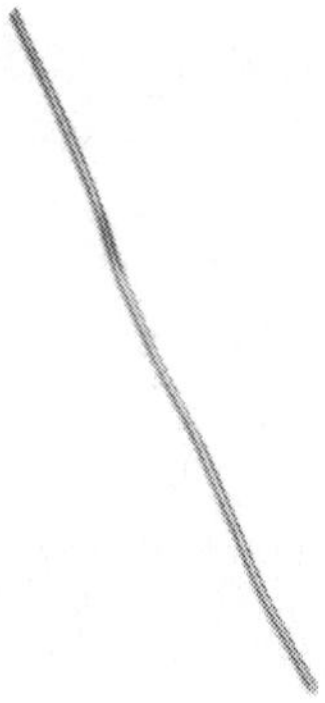

VS

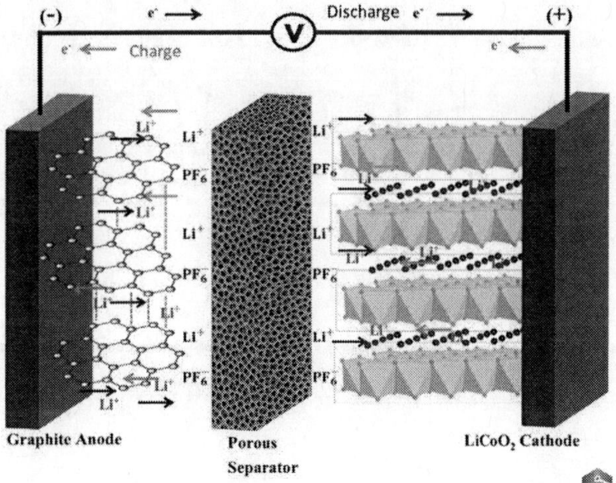

#SensorsConverge

Sensors Converge

Power

15

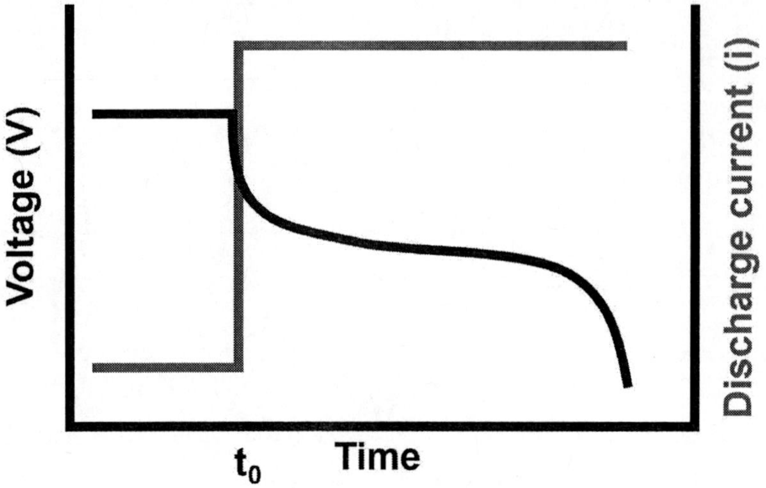

#SensorsConverge

Sensors Converge

Power

16

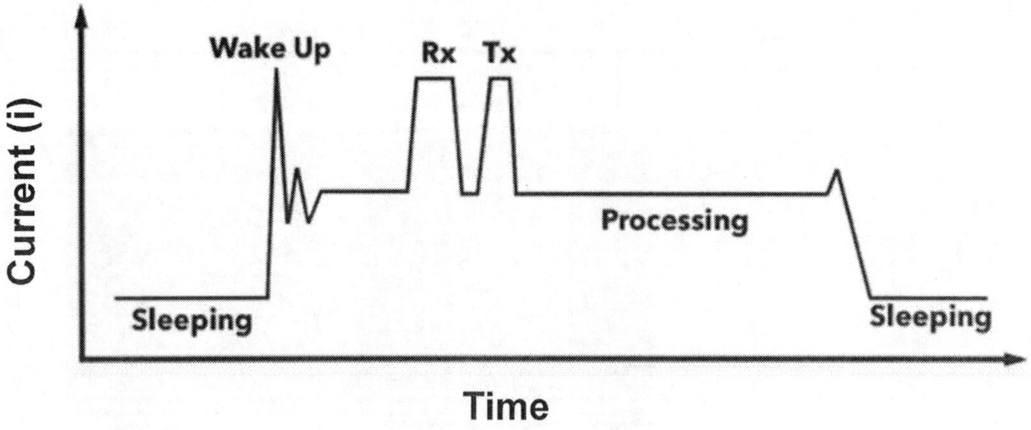

#SensorsConverge

Sensors Converge

3. Power vs. data rate

Power vs. data rate

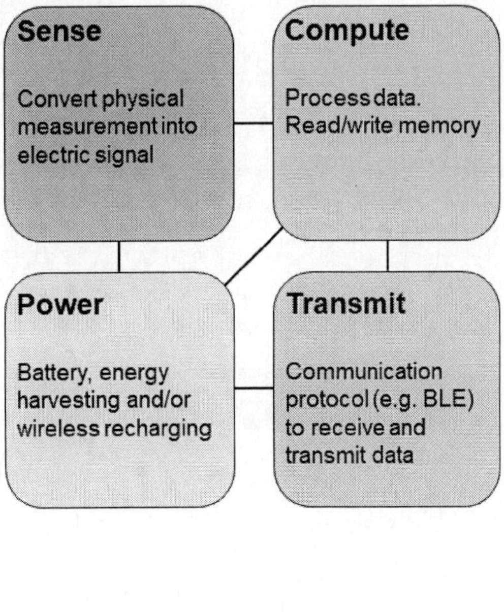

Power vs. data rate

19

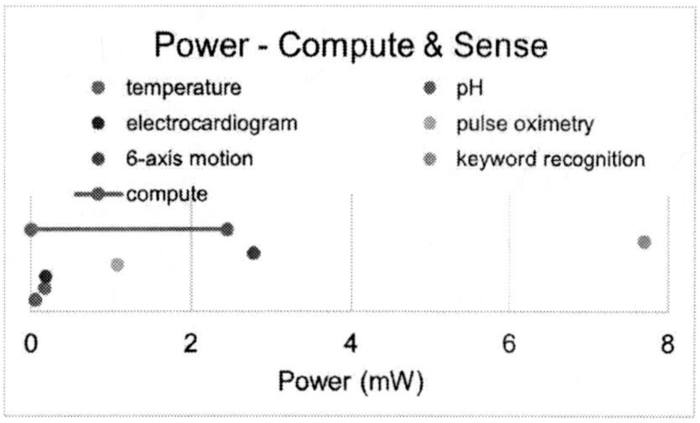

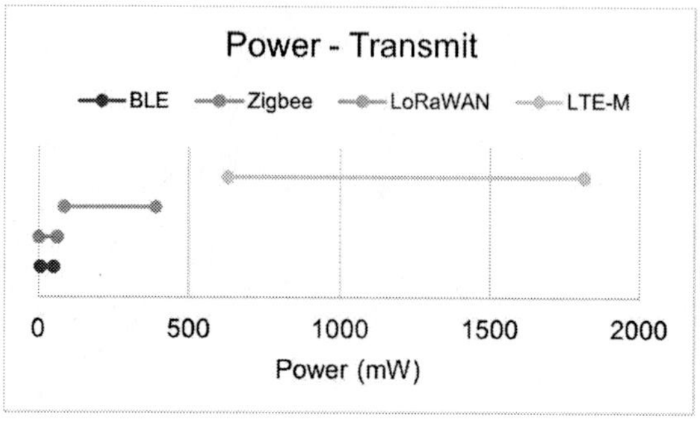

#SensorsConverge

Sensors Converge

20

4. Fingertip-size real time motion tracker

Fingertip-size real time motion tracker

#SensorsConverge

Sensors Converge

Fingertip-size real time motion tracker

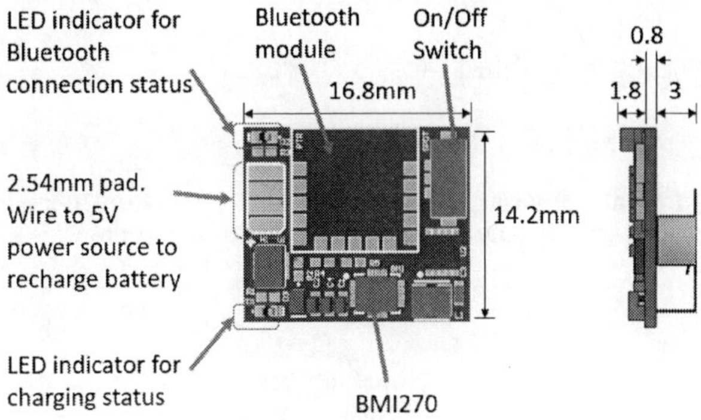

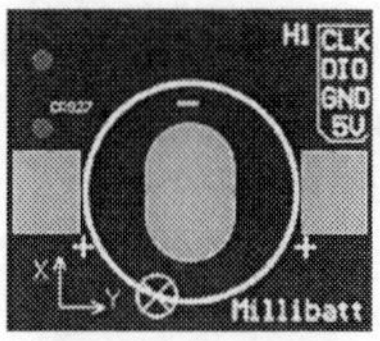

BOM / 10,000 units = $5.99

- Surface Mount component
- Durable and safe vs. tabs
- Battery integration and replacement in the field

#SensorsConverge

Sensors Converge

Fingertip-size real time motion tracker

23

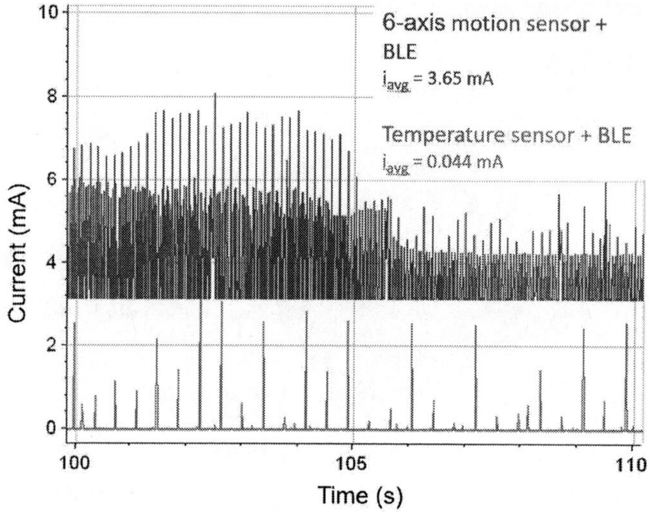

#SensorsConverge

Sensors Converge

Fingertip-size real time motion tracker

24

Head-to-head comparison of 9 mm rechargeable Li-ion coin cells

Battery	Nominal voltage (V)	Energy (mWh)	Energy Density (Wh/L)	Internal Resistance (Ohm, 1 kHz)	Run Time (min)
A	2.6	32	220	33	11
B	3.7	40	205	2	176

#SensorsConverge

Sensors Converge

Conclusions

25

- Energy AND power density of batteries contribute to achievable run-time for sensors
- High-power batteries produce less heat, are safer and longer-lasting
- Wireless sensing power demands are complex and dictated by the numerous processes occurring onboard
- Even an application with low *average* power consumption may have high *instantaneous* power draw
- Questions?

leland.smith@millibatt.com

MILLIBATT

#SensorsConverge

Sensors Converge

Sensors
Converge

Accelerating Sensor System Development with Reference Designs and Open Source Software

September 21-23, 2021 | San Jose, CA

#SensorsConverge

Abstract

- This tutorial will analyze the design and subsequent improvements made to an optical liquid analysis platform, focusing on the benefits of using standard hardware and open-source software frameworks to accelerate all phases of system design, from proof of concept to production.
  Application of these frameworks to other sensor technologies such as temperature, angular rate, acceleration, and general-purpose analog input / output, will also be presented and demonstrated.

- Target time: 20 Minutes

Underlying Theme: Maximize Usefulness

- Skill sets vary widely. Reference designs should be "as useful as possible, to as wide an audience as possible"
- Invent as little as possible – Leverage industry standards so you can focus on adding value

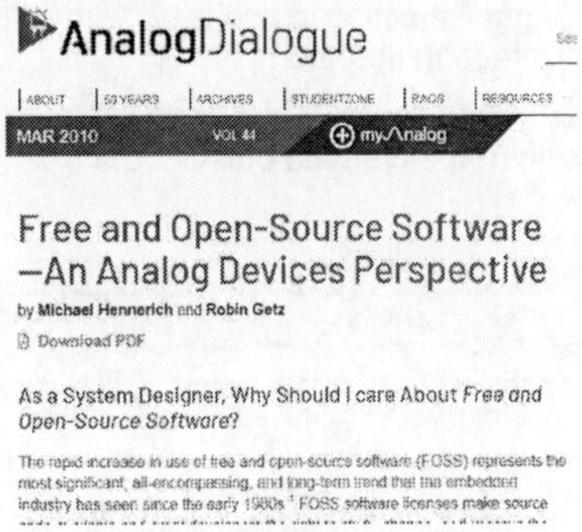
AnalogDialogue

ABOUT | 50 YEARS | ARCHIVES | STUDENTZONE | FAQS | RESOURCES

MAR 2010 VOL 44 myAnalog

Free and Open-Source Software —An Analog Devices Perspective

by Michael Hennerich and Robin Getz

Download PDF

As a System Designer, Why Should I care About *Free and Open-Source Software*?

The rapid increase in use of free and open-source software (FOSS) represents the most significant, all-encompassing, and long-term trend that the embedded industry has seen since the early 1980s.[1] FOSS software licenses make source

#SensorsConverge

History Lesson: Photometric Front-Ends

First Applications: Gesture Sensing and Triangulation

CN0409 Turbidity Meter

A Complete, Precision Optical Liquid Analysis Platform

Wearables – PPG, Sp02

Quinine Fluorescence Detector (cool intern project)

#SensorsConverge

Background: CN0503 electronic tricks to simplify optics

Optical Platform Block Diagram is almost a complete schematic. Bypass caps not shown, but there's not much more to it than this.

High Ambient Light Rejection is achieved with a Synchronous Detection method

Higher frequency light flicker rejection improved with short pulse width and increased pulse count

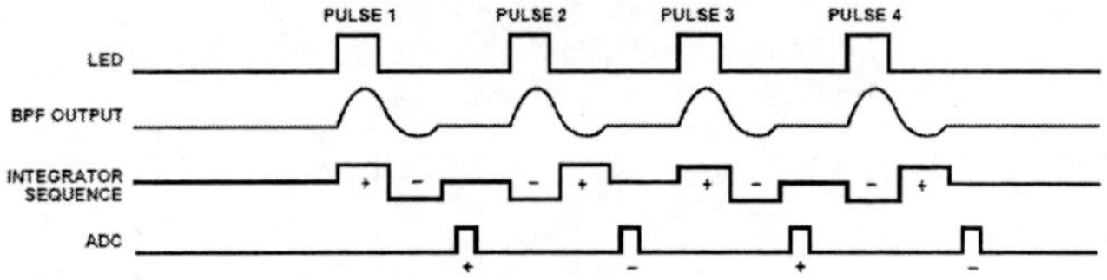

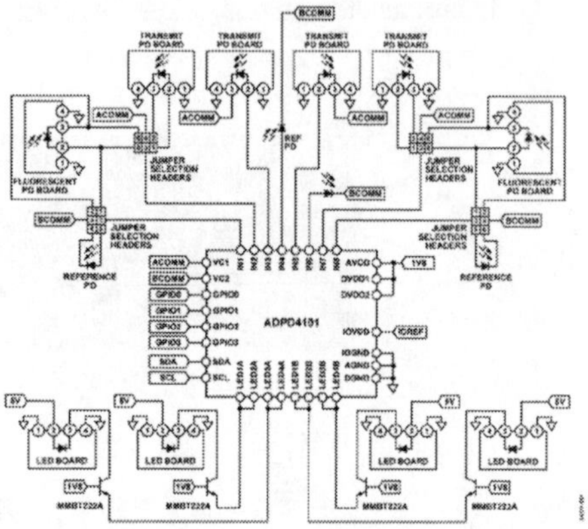

#SensorsConverge

Sensors Converge

Background: CN0503 Optical / Cuvette Holder

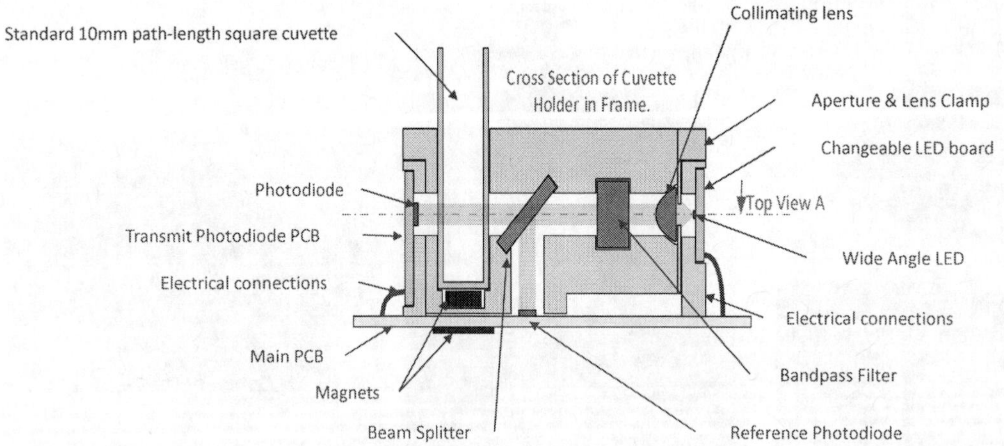

#SensorsConverge

Sensors Converge

Features for Reducing Noise and Drift

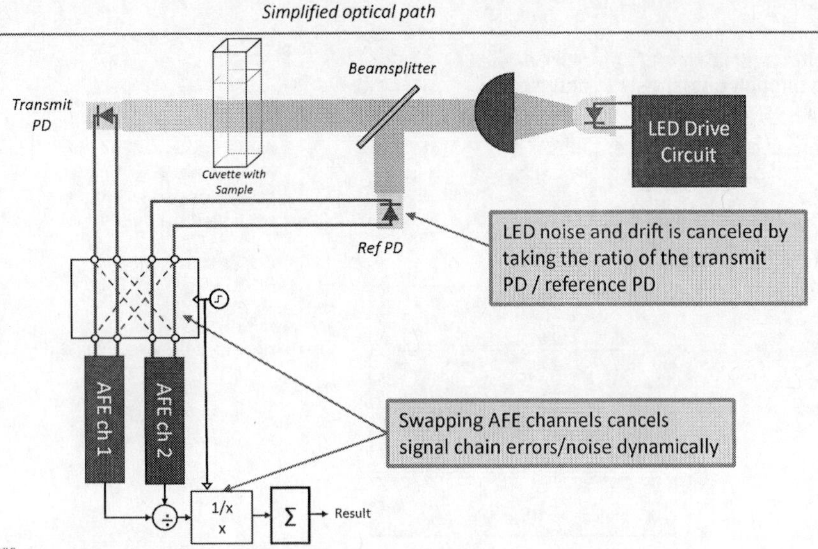

#SensorsConverge

Sensors Converge

It's also wicked complicated on the inside ☹

(If this doesn't scare you or put you to sleep, the next 48 pages will…)

#SensorsConverge

Sensors Converge

No-OS device drivers

- Take care of the "first layers" of complexity – no more digging through datasheets to figure out which bit to flip.
- Also takes care of dependent operations (required order of operations, mutually exclusive modes, etc.)
- Still need a main program to get off the starting line and start taking measurements.

```
#define ADPD410X_REG_FIFO_STATUS            0x0000
#define ADPD410X_REG_INT_STATUS_DATA        0x0001
#define ADPD410X_REG_INT_STATUS_LEV0        0x0002
#define ADPD410X_REG_INT_STATUS_LEV1        0x0003
#define ADPD410X_REG_FIFO_TH                0x0006
#define ADPD410X_REG_INT_ACLEAR             0x0007

#define ADPD410X_REG_LED_POW12(ts)     (0x0105 + (ts) * 0x20)
#define ADPD410X_REG_LED_POW34(ts)     (0x0106 + (ts) * 0x20)
#define ADPD410X_REG_COUNTS(ts)        (0x0107 + (ts) * 0x20)
#define ADPD410X_REG_PERIOD(ts)        (0x0108 + (ts) * 0x20)
#define ADPD410X_REG_LED_PULSE(ts)     (0x0109 + (ts) * 0x20)
```

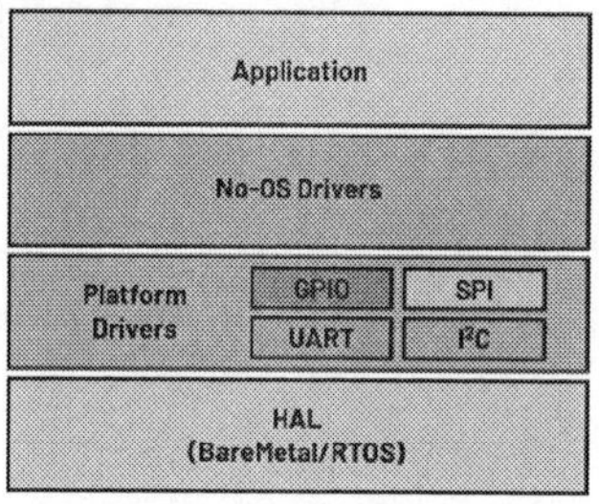

#SensorsConverge

Sensors Converge

Retrospective: CN0503 Existing Firmware Data Flow

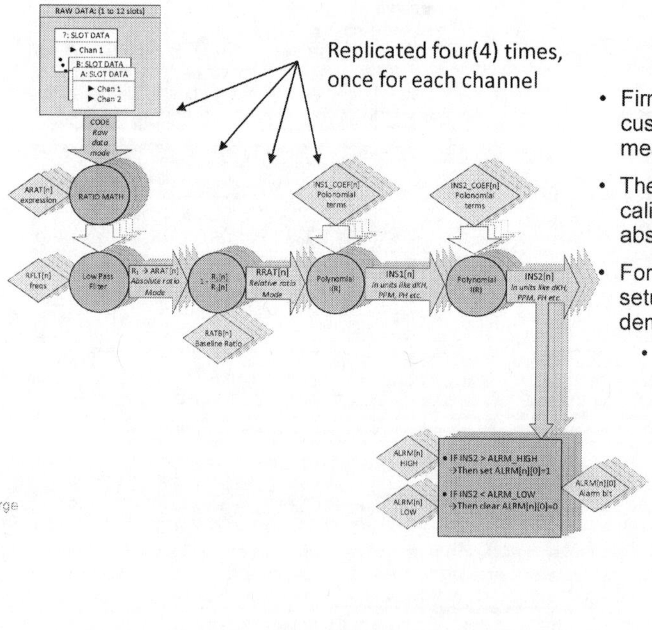

- Firmware allows for full customization of multiple optical measurement channels.
- The data flow includes the ability to calibrate into 1 or more sets of absolute measurement units.
- For more information and how to setup the hardware and software demo, see the software user guide:
  - https://wiki.analog.com/resources/eval/user-guides/eval-adicup3029/reference_designs/demo_cn0503

#SensorsConverge

Sensors Converge

Retrospective: CN0503 – Embedded Firmware CLI

- Ad-hoc "semi-human readable, semi-machine readable" protocol
- Often perfectly acceptable – if you're in a "closed ecosystem", and only have one, or a couple, of devices to support.
- Supporting multiple devices, across different platforms, across different teams, across long stretches of time, could benefit from some level of standardization…

Command	Description	Example
HELP	Display available commands.	
REG? XXX	Read an ADPD register. *<XXX>* = register address in hexadecimal	REG? 10A - read register 0x10A
REG XXX YYYY	Write an ADPD register. *<XXX>* = register address in hexadecimal *<YYYY>* = register new value in hexadecimal	REG 10A 301 - write 0x301 to register 0x10A
MODE?	Read the data display mode. Return a 4 character code: *CODE* - raw data is displayed; *ARAT* - absolute ratio is displayed; *RRAT* - relative ratio is displayed; *INS1* - data processed for instrument 1 is displayed; *INS2* - data processed for instrument 2 is displayed.	
MODE XXXX	Set the data display mode. *XXXX* = 4 character code to describe the data display mode. The options are: *CODE* - raw data is displayed; *ARAT* - absolute ratio is displayed; *RRAT* - relative ratio is displayed; *INS1* - data processed for instrument 1 is displayed; *INS2* - data processed for instrument 2 is displayed.	MODE CODE - set display mode to raw codes
STREAM X	Start calculating and displaying a stream of data. *X* = If 0 or not present enter continuous streaming mode; if X>0 stream data for X values.	STREAM 10 - stream for 10 values of the output.

#SensorsConverge

Sensors Converge

Retrospective: CN0503 Software Stack

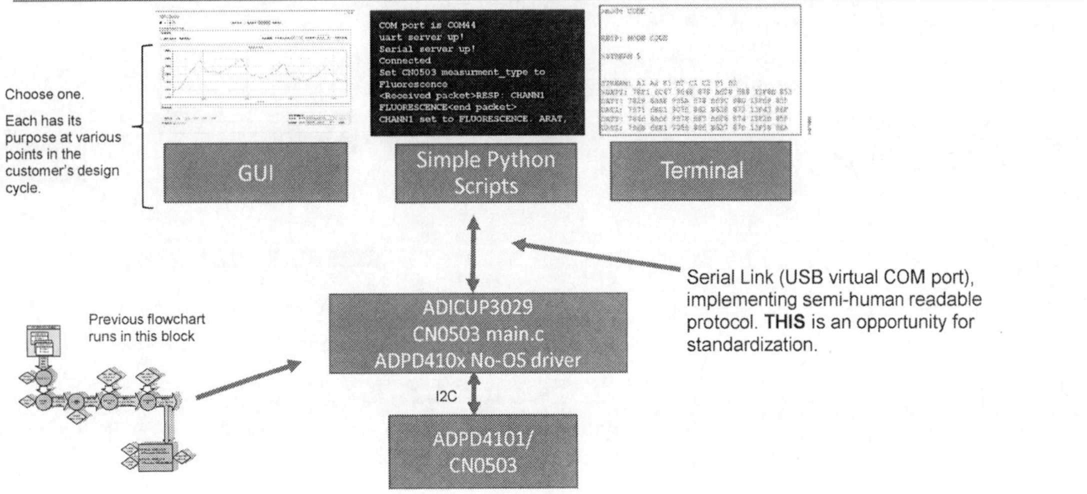

#SensorsConverge

Sensors Converge

Moving Forward: Leveraging the Linux IIO Framework

From kernel.org:

"The main purpose of the Industrial I/O subsystem (IIO) is to provide support for devices that in some sense perform either analog-to-digital conversion (ADC) or digital-to-analog conversion (DAC) or both."

New! Embedded IIO support

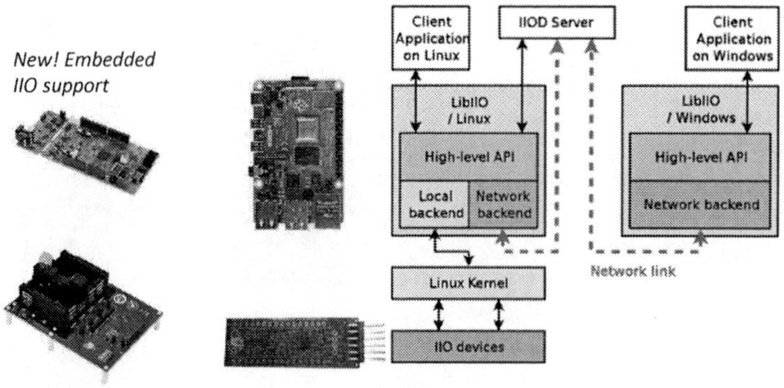

The Libiio:
Windows, Linux, Mac
C, C#, Python, MATLAB, and more

- Virtual network
- Direct USB
- Serial
- Mass Storage
- OTG

#SensorsConverge

Sensors Converge

IIO is a Linux Standard framework (not ADI)

- IIO is an industry standard, not ADI specific

index : kernel/git/torvalds/linux.git

Linux kernel source tree

about summary refs log tree commit diff stats

path: root/drivers/iio/adc

Mode	Name
-rw-r--r--	Kconfig
-rw-r--r--	Makefile
-rw-r--r--	ab8500-gpadc.c
-rw-r--r--	ad7091r-base.c
-rw-r--r--	ad7091r-be
-rw-r--r--	ad7091r5.c
-rw-r--r--	ad7124.c
-rw-r--r--	stx104.c
-rw-r--r--	sun4i-gpadc-iio.c
-rw-r--r--	ti-adc081c.c
-rw-r--r--	ti-adc0832.c
-rw-r--r--	ti-adc084s021.c
-rw-r--r--	ti-adc108s102.c
-rw-r--r--	ti-adc12138.c

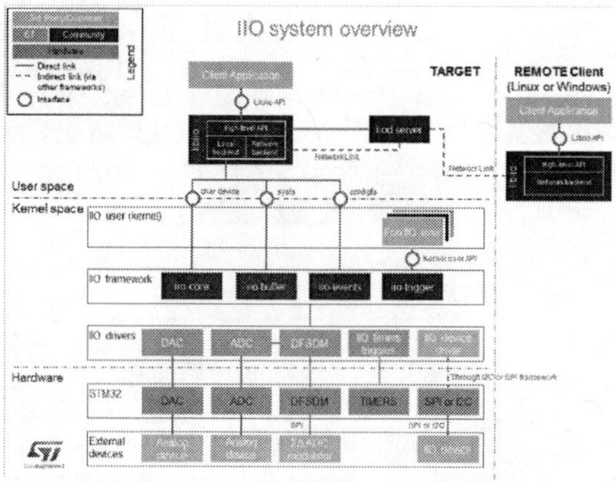

From https://wiki.st.com/stm32mpu/wiki/IIO_overview

#SensorsConverge

Sensors Converge

Tinyiiod: Extending IIO to Microcontroller/no-OS

But WHY?

- Hardware gurus, chemists, physicists, other subject matter experts can get started earlier, write code in their language of choice.
- Defer software development until AFTER the domain-specific bugs have been figured out.
- Re-use existing IIO tools
  - IIO-Oscilloscope for "signs of life"
  - The Libiio library is cross-platform (Win/Lin/Mac)
  - The Libiio library has bindings for C, C#, Python, MATLAB

The Libiio:
Windows, Linux, Mac
C, C#, Python, MATLAB,
and more

New! Embedded IIO support

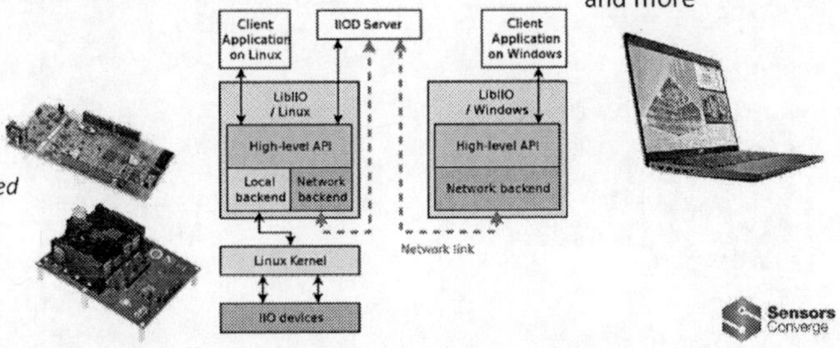

#SensorsConverge

Sensors Converge

ADPD410x Hardware and Software Evolution

A Complete ADPD4101 Python Application:

```
import adi
my_adpd410x = adi.adpd410x(uri="serial:COM20,115200")
reference = my_adpd410x.channel[0].raw
reading = my_adpd410x.channel[1].raw
my_measurement=my_formula(reference, reading)
print("My measurement: ", my_measurement)
del my_adpd410x
del adi
```

Application Output:

```
Channel  0 :  71705
Channel  1 :  1969
Channel  2 :  2030
Channel  3 :  2027
Channel  4 :  1935
Channel  5 :  1947
Channel  6 :  1724
Channel  7 :  1935
```

(non-CS) subject matter expert can now get to work.

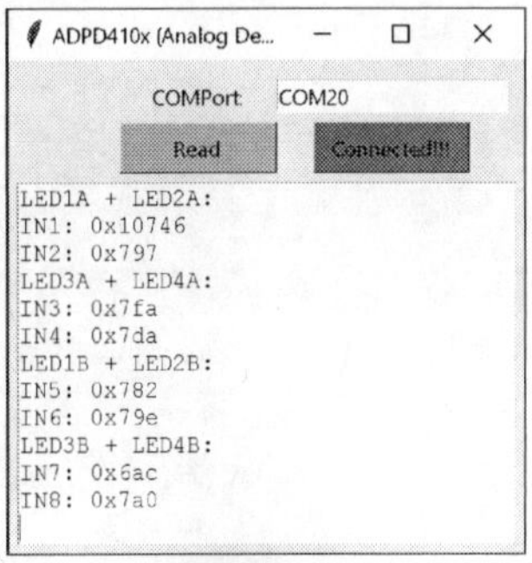

#SensorsConverge

Sensors Converge

Let's not forget about hardware…

- CN0503 – wonderful for prototyping optical liquid applications, big, expensive, for anything else.
- EVAL-ADPD4100 – great for developing wearable applications, difficult to adapt to anything else.

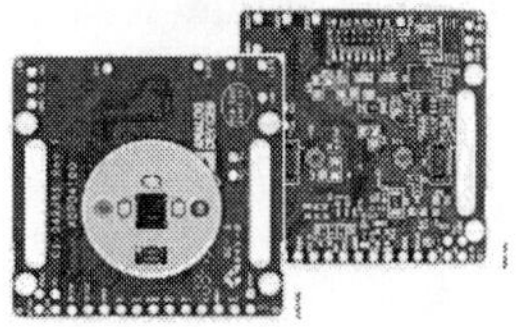

#SensorsConverge

Sensors Converge

ADPD410x was just one example…

Pick a Platform

Pick a Part

ADXRS290 Gyro

AD5791 DAC

AD7124 ADC

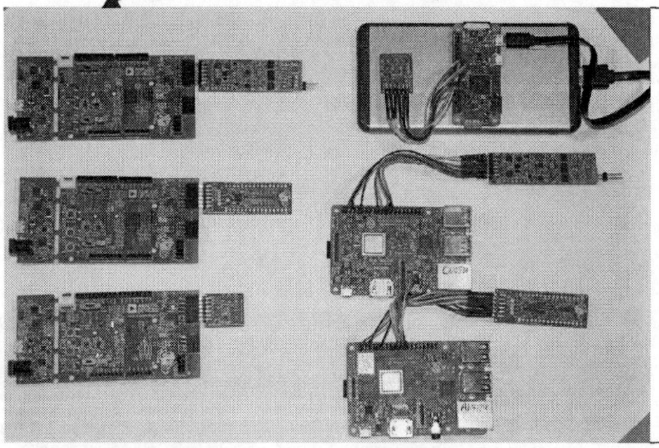

no-OS (µC, bare metal)

Linux

The libiio makes everything look nearly identical!

#SensorsConverge

Sensors Converge

Conclusion

- Hardware reference designs should be flexible, hackable, and use **standard** interfaces. Weigh popularity and community support against other factors (cost, size,… lack of ground pins?)
- Modular software built on **standard** frameworks addresses the needs of cross-functional teams:
    - Subject matter experts and scientists can evaluate performance instantly with provided example code.
    - System designers can translate science experiments into software requirements
    - Embedded programmers can use Linux and no-OS device drivers and examples to get a head start, and start adding value earlier.
- **YOU** can play with this stuff! Have a look at these easy, low barrier to entry tutorials:
    - https://wiki.analog.com/university/labs/software/precision_adc_toolbox
    - https://wiki.analog.com/university/labs/software/iio_intro_toolbox

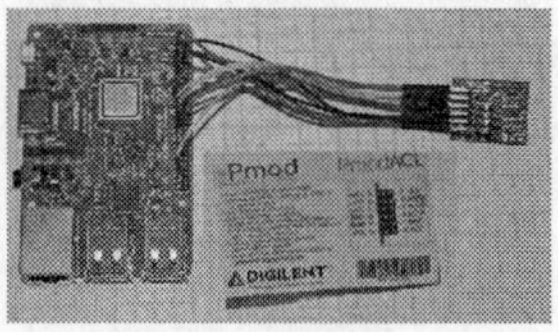


```
import adi
my_adpd410x = adi.adpd410x(uri="serial:COM26,115200")
reference = my_adpd410x.channel[0].raw
reading = my_adpd410x.channel[1].raw
my_measurement=my_formula(reference, reading)
print("My measurement: ", my_measurement)
del my_adpd410x
del adi
```

#SensorsConverge

Sensors Converge

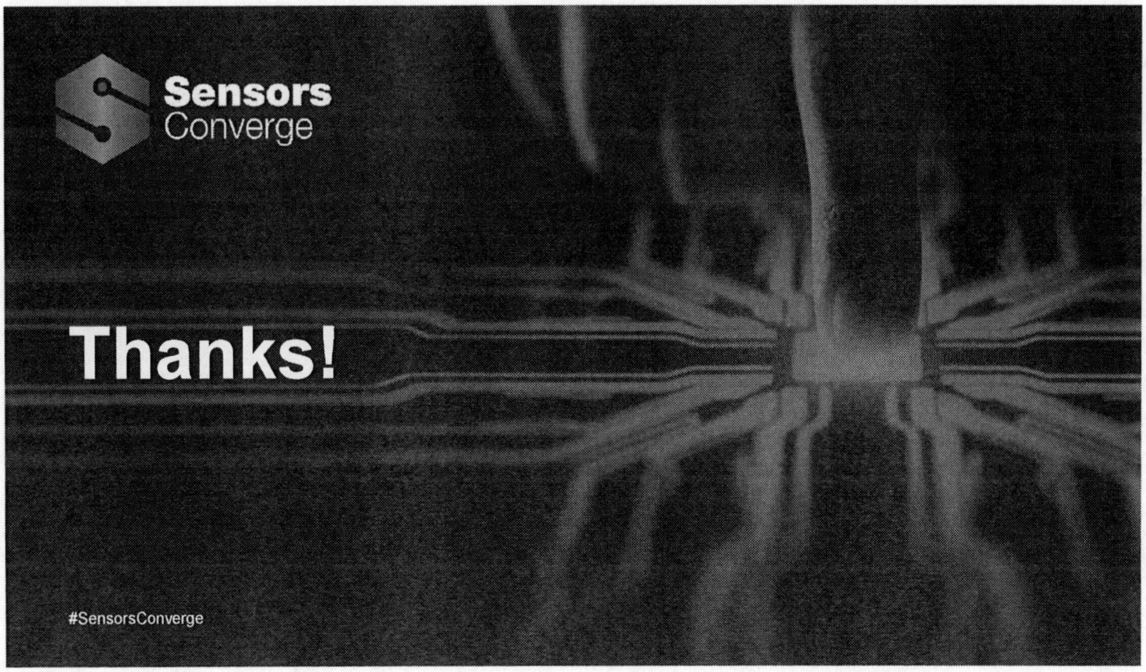

Accelerating Sensor System Development with Reference Designs and Open-Source Software

Sensors Converge

```
import adi
my_adpd410x = adi.adpd410x(uri="serial:COM20,115200")
reference = my_adpd410x.channel[0].raw
reading = my_adpd410x.channel[1].raw
my_measurement=my_formula(reference, reading)
print("My measurement: ", my_measurement)
del my_adpd410x
del adi
```

#SensorsConverge

CN0503 Python GUI

- Simplify interaction with CN0503
    - Load configuration files
    - Log data
    - Display data graphs
    - Configure channels and settings
    - Manage flash memory contents
    - Ease calibrations
- Optimized premade measurement configuration files
- Easy to configure measurement channel via dropdown selection
    - Turbidity
    - Absorption/colorimetry
    - Fluorimetry
- Download Python GUI
    - ftp://ftp.analog.com/pub/cftl/CN0503/

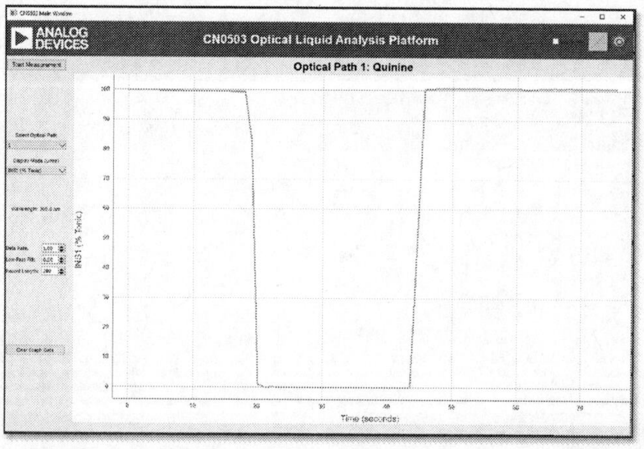

#SensorsConverge

Sensors Converge

Modularity

(Or, keeping most engineers on a multidisciplinary team reasonably happy)

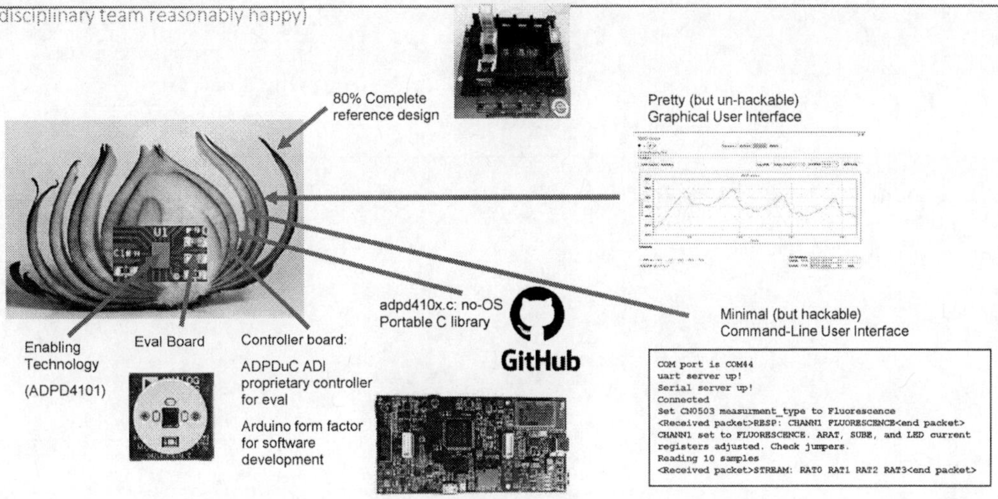

#SensorsConverge

Sensors Converge

CN0503 Python Script

- Same measurements as GUI (Colorimetry, Fluorescence, Turbidity) in easy to use and easy to modify form.
- Allows customers to quickly and easily test out their own measurements and algorithms
- Cross-platform: runs on Linux, Mac, Raspberry Pi
- Scripts included in firmware repo on Github
  - https://github.com/analogdevicesinc/EVAL-ADICUP3029/tree/master/projects/ADuCM3029_demo_cn0503/scripts

Typical Script Interaction

```
COM port is COM44
uart server up!
Serial server up!
Connected
Set display mode to absolute ratio
<Received packet>RESP: MODE ARAT<end packet>
ARAT
Configuring channel 0
Set CN0503 measurment_type to Fluorescence
<Received packet>RESP: CHANN1 FLUORESCENCE<end packet>
CHANN1 set to FLUORESCENCE. ARAT, SUBE, and LED current
registers adjusted. Check jumpers.
Please add distilled water
Press enter when ready ...
Reading 10 samples
<Received packet>STREAM: RAT0 RAT1 RAT2 RAT3<end packet>
<Received packet>>DATF: 2.9182E-04 1.1494E+00 1.21E+00 3.0E-
02<end packet>
<Received packet>DATF: 3.3336E-04 1.3793E+00 1.45E+00 3.61E-
02<end packet>
```

Raw data ready for further processing, averaging, displaying, etc.

#SensorsConverge

Sensors Converge

```
import adi
my_adpd410x = adi.adpd410x(uri="serial:COM20,115200")
for idx in range(8):
    print("Channel ", idx, ": ", my_adpd410x.channel[idx].raw)
del my_adpd410x
del adi
```

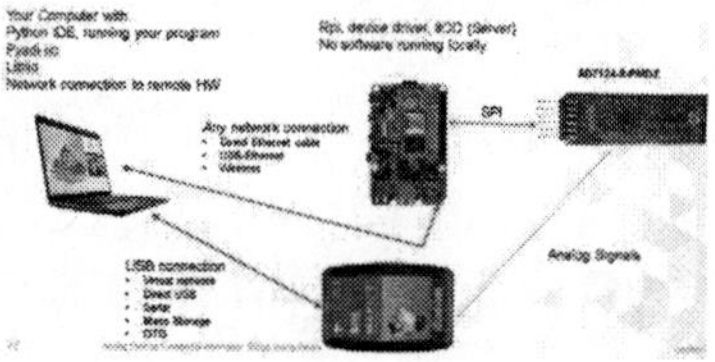

#SensorsConverge

Sensors Converge

Digital Twins for Sensor Design

September 21-23, 2021 | San Jose, CA

Mary Ann Maher
maryann@softmems.com

#SensorsConverge

softMEMS

Agenda

- **Digital Twin Definition**
- **Digital Twin Examples in MEMS**
  - Manufacturing- Yield enhancement- MEMS Foundry
  - Design- From Materials to Systems
  - Product- Digital Twins in Medical Products
- **Summary, Conclusions**

#SensorsConverge

softMEMS

Sensors Converge

What is a Digital Twin?

- **Digital Twins are software (digital) representations of assets and processes**
- **Used to understand, predict, and optimize performance and maintenance**
- **Digital twins originated from Automotive, Industrial, and Aircraft sectors**
- **Consists of three components**
  - A data model- 3D CAD, FEM (Finite Element Model), circuits
  - A set of analytics- software, algorithms
  - And knowledge- design rules, expert information

Source: Siemens

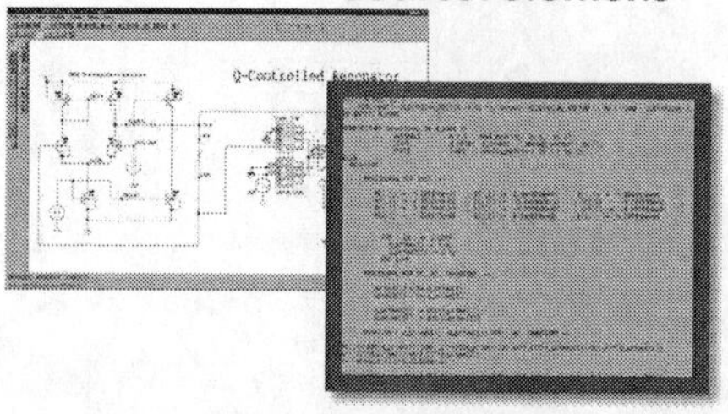

#SensorsConverge

softMEMS Sensors Converge

Digital Twin- Medical

- **Digital Twins are an alternative to invasive techniques**
- **Catheterization is an invasive procedure to measure blockages**
  - Catheter is inserted into an artery to find artery blockages
- **Digital Twin replaces catheterization:**
  - 3D model of artery created from CT scan data (non-invasive)
  - Blockage is estimated by simulation of the flow in the artificial artery using CFD-(computational fluid dynamics)
  - Digital Twin data accessed securely by doctors to decide if there is a blockage

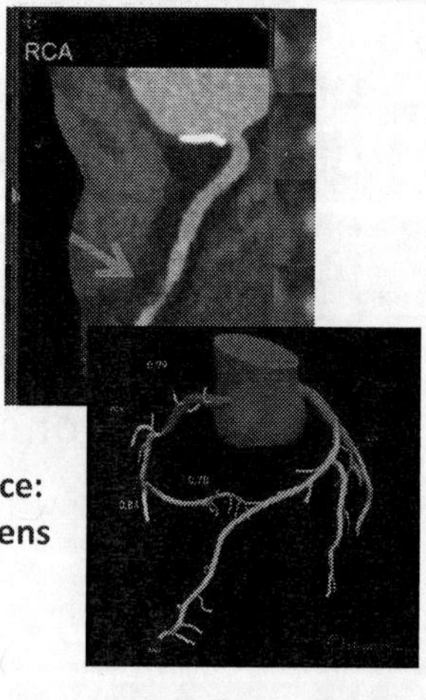

Source: Siemens

#SensorsConverge

softMEMS Sensors Converge

Digital Twin- Engineering

Source: Siemens

Connected and Interrelated Models

#SensorsConverge

softMEMS

Sensors Converge

Digital Twin- Engineering

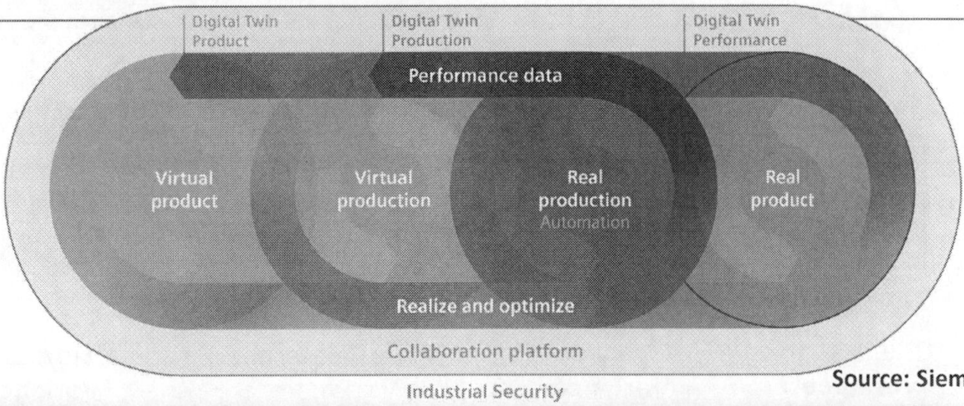

Source: Siemens

Feedback from real production, performance
Platform for Collaboration

#SensorsConverge

softMEMS

Sensors Converge

Digital Twins for MEMS Devices

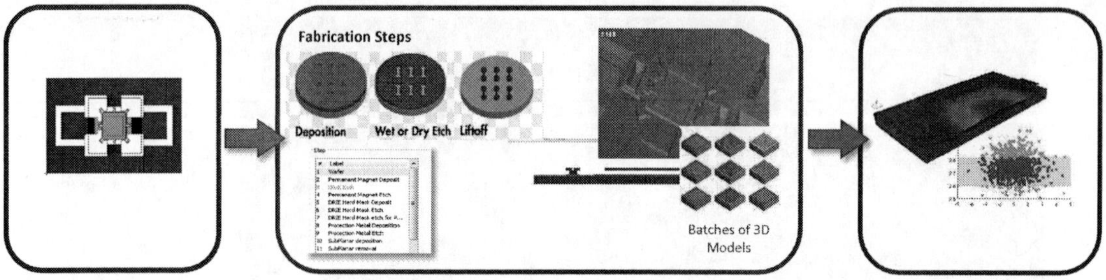

Digital Twin of Product/Design

Digital Foundry -Digital Twin of Fabrication/Production- Wafer based

Digital Twin of Performance & Yield

MEMS Digital Twins-Multiple companies- Fab, Design house, EDA Vendors

#SensorsConverge

softMEMS

Sensors Converge

Digital Foundry

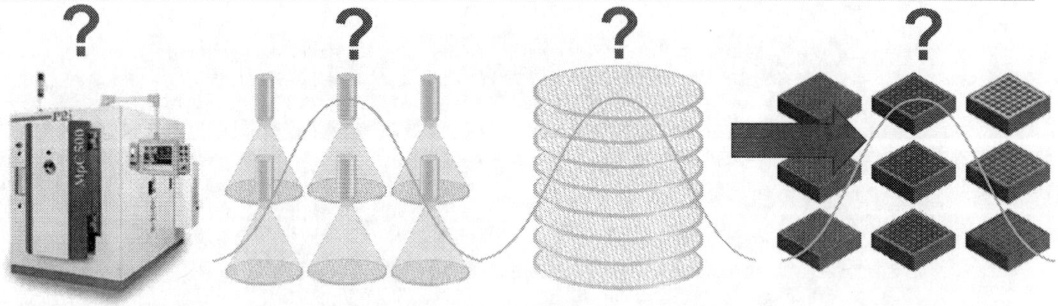

Equipment Variance

Process Variance

Wafer/Material Variance

Performance Variance Effects Yield

Use Digital Twin to relate manufacturing variation to performance variation

#SensorsConverge

softMEMS

Sensors Converge

Wafer Level Process Variation

Example Process:
Deposition

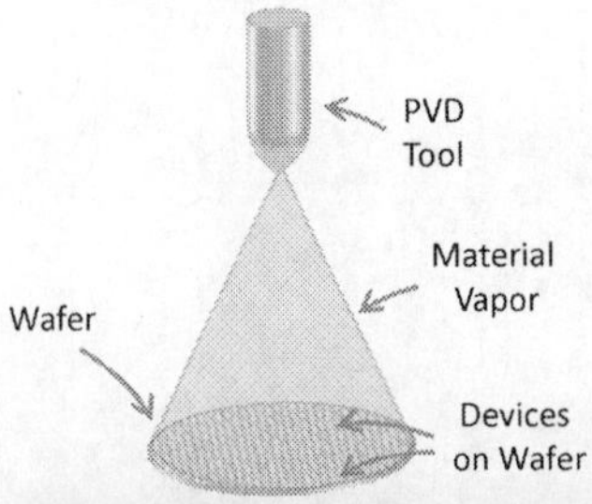

Deposition Thickness Variance: $t_1 < t_2$, and $var(t) = f(x)$

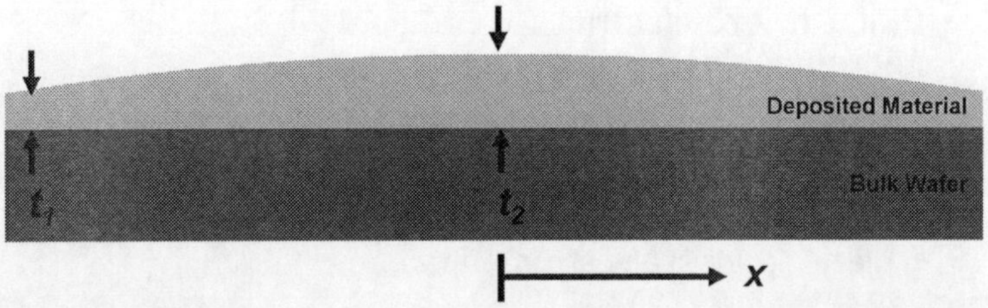

MEMS process variance can be radially dependent
Impacts device performance across the wafer
Others: mask dependent, edge dependent, scan dependent

#SensorsConverge

Digital Twin Example:
Manufacturing Variation

Collaboration – SilTerra, Siemens, SoftMEMS, OnScale and Polytec

#SensorsConverge

Example: SilTerra - Monolithic PMUTs

- **Digital Foundry Twin model for SilTerra's PMUT process**
- **PMUT (Piezo-electric Micromachined Ultrasonic Transducer)**
  - Consists of a membrane of piezo-electric material between 2 electrodes over a cavity
  - Piezo-electric material converts voltage to stress and vice versa
  - Stress creates bending in the membrane
  - Device Emits/Senses Ultrasound Waves

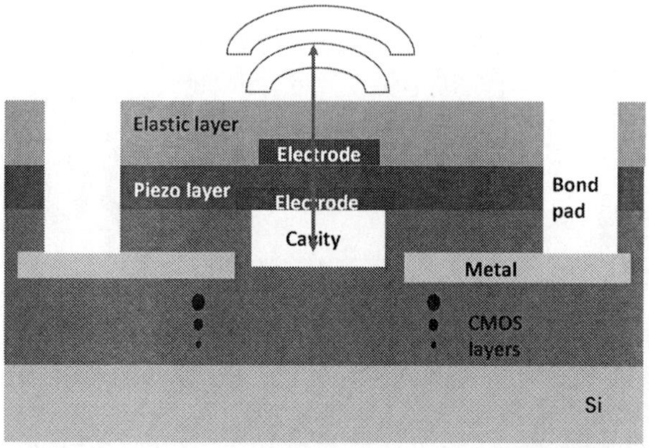

#SensorsConverge

softMEMS Sensors Converge

SilTerra - Monolithic PMUTs

- **MEMS on CMOS – MEMS and circuits on single wafer**
  - AlSCN – scandium doped aluminum nitride- piezo-electric layer
  - Elastic layer on top
  - Cavity created with sacrificial etch under bottom Al electrode
- **Integration Advantages**
  - Reduced footprint electrical connections
  - Better fill factor than 2 chip solutions
  - Better electrical performance
  - Reduced parasitics

Optical Image of Single PMUT
Fabricated using SilTerra MEMS on CMOS Process

#SensorsConverge

softMEMS Sensors Converge

PMUT Applications

- **Applications**
  - Finger-print sensors (biometrics)
  - Automotive- Range finding
  - Medical Imaging-Ultrasound arrays
  - Non-destructive testing (NDT), material characterization
  - A/R- V/R
  - Advantages in terms of size, weight, power and cost

PMUT 11 x 11 Array Digital Prototype:
Sensing and Imaging Applications

Digital Twin Creation

- **Design variables identified:**
  - Applications vary by resonant frequency
  - Resonant frequency depends on membrane size
  - Different membrane sizes to explore different frequencies
  - Nominal device- tolerances, mask biases

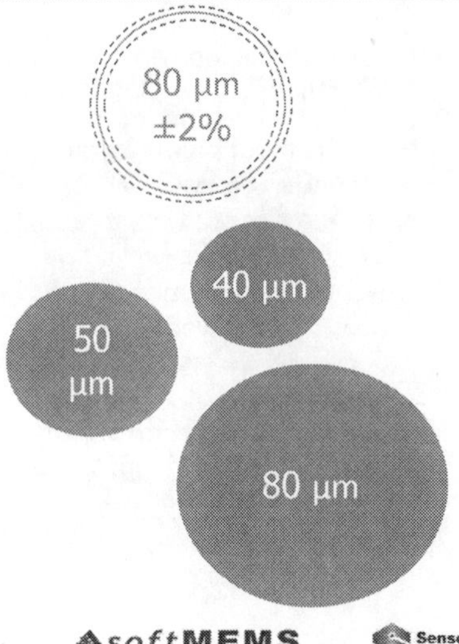

Digital Twin Creation

- **Material properties and variation**
- **Fab sequences**
  - Layer Thicknesses and uniformities
- **3D models generated from design test masks and process sequences passed to simulation**

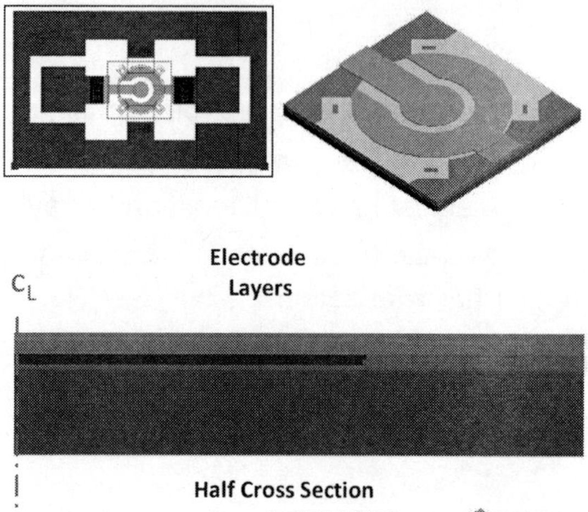

#SensorsConverge

softMEMS

Sensors Converge

Performance-Monte Carlo Results

- **Models simulated with high capacity, cloud-based FEM (Finite Element Model) from OnScale for performance estimates**
- **Example Input parameters:**
  - Thickness of piezo- layer
  - Thickness of elastic layer
  - 2% standard deviation from nominal
- **Output key performance indicators (KPIs):**
  - Resonance frequency
  - Sensitivity (displacement / input voltage)
  - Capacitance
  - Pass band 4% of nominal value
- **Digital Twins of Design, Manufacturing and Performance connected**

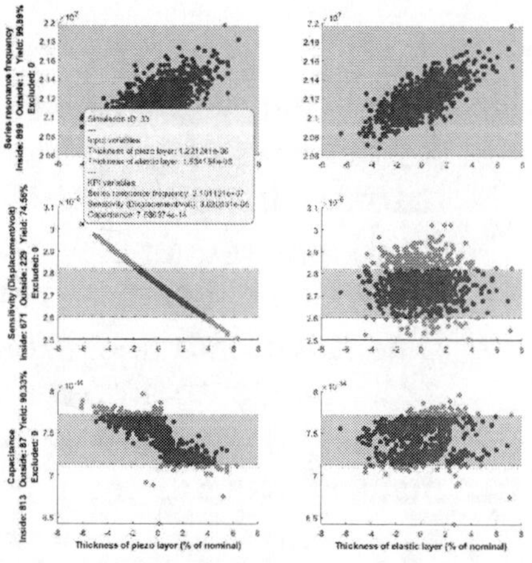

#SensorsConverge

softMEMS

Sensors Converge

Physical Test Results

- **Experimental Data to feedback to the Twin**
- **SilTerra Electrical Measurements**
  - Individual cells
  - Capacitance, Resonant Frequency, S parameters
  - Data vs position on wafer
- **Polytec MSA-600 Micro System Analyzer**
  - Array devices
  - Allows measurement of displacement
  - Uses Laser vibrometry
  - PMUT Array driven with broadband chirps covering the expected resonant frequency ranges
  - BW: 1.25 kHz to 10 MHz

SB15 – 40 µm

Inner electrode to Bottom electrode

X/Y (Co)	-3	-2	-1	0	1	2	3
2				0.069			
1				0.07			
0	0.071	0.0.076	0.076	0.072	0.072	0.071	NA
-1				0.07			
-2				0.07			
	Avg.	Std.	Max	Min	Range		

Outer electrode to Bottom electrode

X/Y (Co)	-3	-2	-1	0	1	2	3
2				0.146			
1				0.145			
0	0.144	0.145	0.146	0.145	0.145	0.147	NA
-1				0.145			
-2				0.144			
	Avg.	Std.	Max.	Min	Range		

SB15 – 50/80 µm

Inner electrode to Bottom electrode

X/Y (Co)	-3	-2	-1	0	1	2	3
2				0.097			
1				0.099			
0	0.096	0.097	0.097	0.099	0.097	0.099	NA
-1				0.096			
-2				0.096			
	Avg.	Std.	Max	Min	Range		

Outer electrode to Bottom electrode

X/Y (Co)	-3	-2	-1	0	1	2	3
2				0.208			
1				0.209			
0	0.207	0.207	0.207	0.212	0.210	0.212	NA
-1				0.208			
-2				0.207			
	Avg.	Std.	Max	Min	Range		

Source: SilTerra

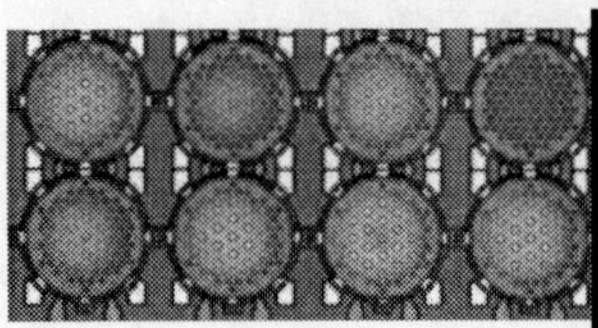

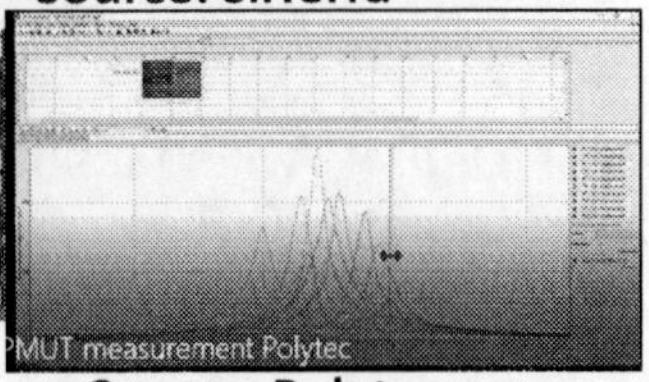

Source: Polytec

#SensorsConverge

softMEMS

Sensors Converge

Digital Twins for Device design

- **New products, New requirements:**
  - Medical Imaging, Wearables, Filters for 5G
  - Arrays/Multiple devices
  - Analyze complex interactions between devices
  - Position of array on wafer
  - Digital Twin must be more detailed- lots of simulations

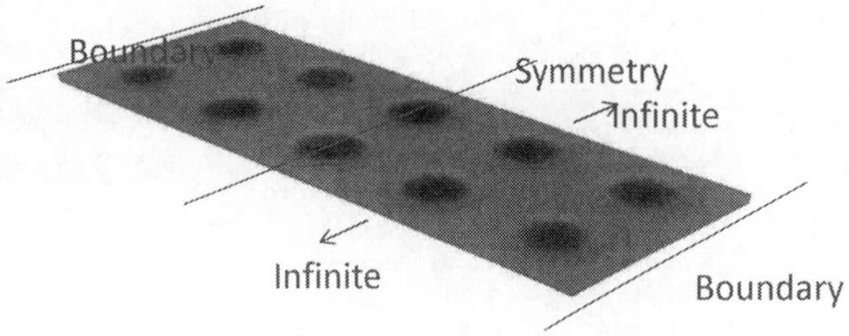

#SensorsConverge

softMEMS

Sensors Converge

Sensor Device + IC/Electronics + Packaging

- **MEMS and electronics can be combined in multiple ways**
- **Example: Medical Imaging Sensors**
  - MEMS and IC dies flip chipped and connected with through silicon vias (TSVs)
- **Interactions between physical sensor, electronics and packaging**
  - Places stress, thermal, electrical parasitics
  - Design constraints on all three
- **Digital Twins facilitate co-design of Sensor, IC/Electronics and Packaging**

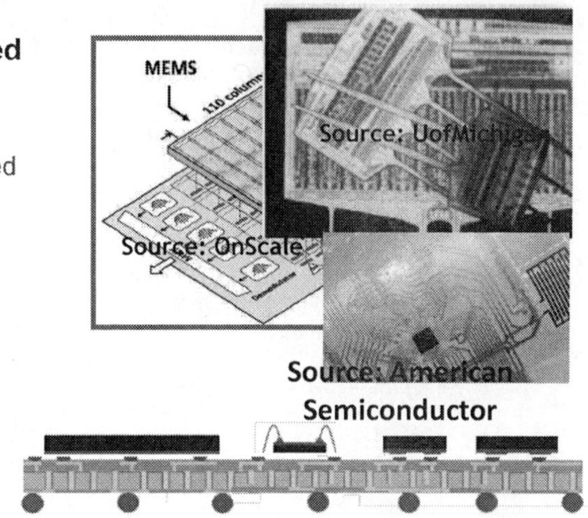

#SensorsConverge

softMEMS Sensors Converge

Digital Twins for Product Design

- **Digital Twins can also model the Materials the Sensor Interacts with:**
  - Medical devices interact with eye, skin, brain
  - Create Digital Twin-Tissue models
  - Sensor performance simulated with realistic environment
- **Organ Models for Testing Sensors**
  - Digital Twins made for hearts, lungs and other organs can be used for testing new devices
  - 3D printed device from a digital Twin of the heart
  - Simulation models being developed
  - Similar electrical signals, muscle contraction, pressure dynamics etc

Source: UW Medicine

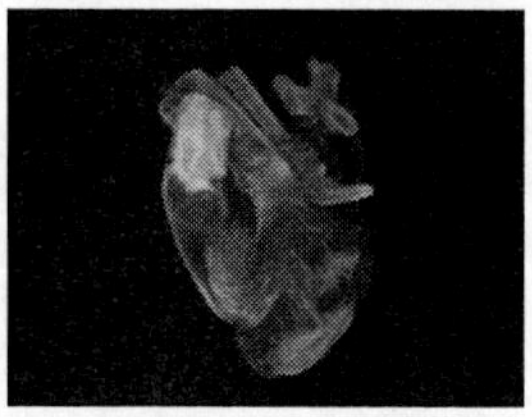

Source: Siemens Healthineers

#SensorsConverge

softMEMS Sensors Converge

Conclusions

- Digital Twins can be used in Sensor Product Design from material modelling to testing
- Digital Twins enable remote design collaboration
- Several types of Digital Twins used in device/product design
  - Sensor
  - Environment of Sensor- tissue, organ, patient
- Investments are required to make a good digital twin – computation power, good measurements

#SensorsConverge

softMEMS

Sensors Converge

Sensors Converge

KINEXON

COVID-19 and beyond
Using Sensor Technology for Workplace Safety, Public Health, and Automation

#SensorsConverge

FROM THE NFL TO ESSENTIAL BUSINESSES

KINEXON SafeZone

#SensorsConverge

Sensors Converge

LEADING THROUGH CRISIS: MAINTAINING OPERATIONS DURING A PANDEMIC

KINEXON SafeZone

Airgas. an Air Liquide company
alift
NETFLIX
BILL & MELINDA GATES foundation
Waters™
essity
MARS
Continental
BlackRock.
Henkel
MGM GRAND
UNITED
J.D. McCarty Center for children with developmental disabilities
Schluter Systems
BORUSAN MANNESMANN
oerlikon

#SensorsConverge

Sensors Converge

CONTACT WARNING & TRACING

KINEXON SafeZone

1. **PHYSICAL DISTANCING**
Maintaining a safe physical distance to those around you.

2. **CONTACT TRACING**
Rapid and accurate contact tracing that is available the moment someone tests positive.

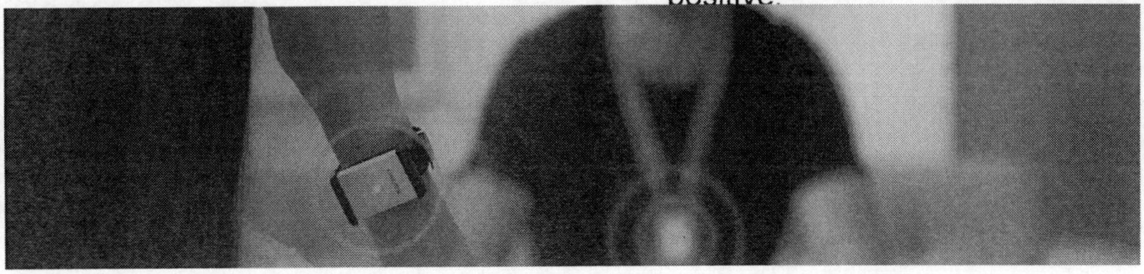

THE KINEXON SAFETAG

KINEXON SafeZone

- A lightweight wearable
- Centimeter-accurate precision (< 10 cm)
- Customizable audible and visual warnings
- Measures contact intensity: distance and time
- Sensors communicate with each other, no infrastructure required
- Privacy Compliant: Does not track movement or location

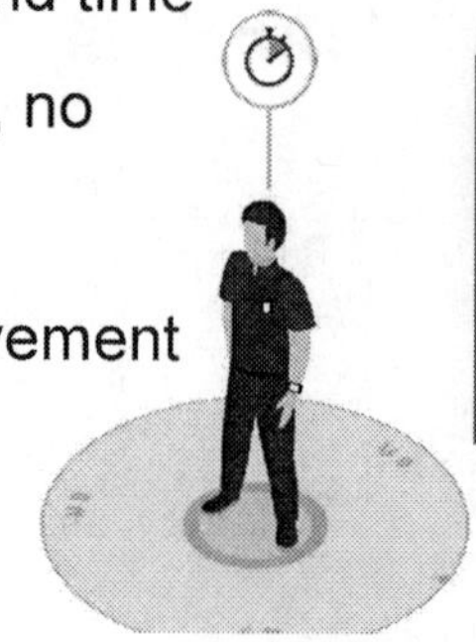

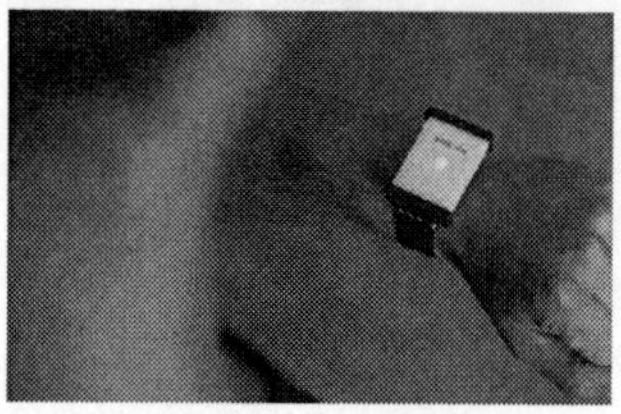

#SensorsConverge

Sensors Converge

CONTACT TRACING

KINEXON SafeZone

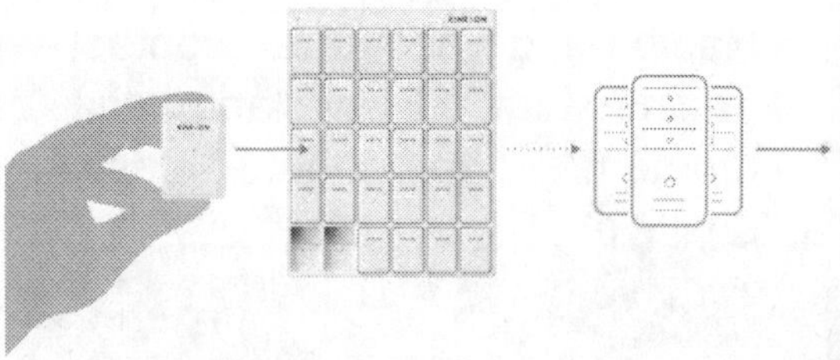

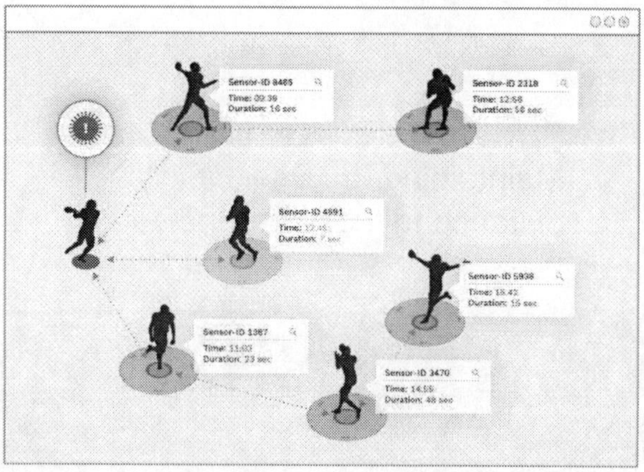

STORAGE OF CRITICAL CONTACT EVENTS

SOFTWARE ANALYSIS

#SensorsConverge

Sensors Converge

SOFTWARE SOLUTION

KINEXON SafeZone

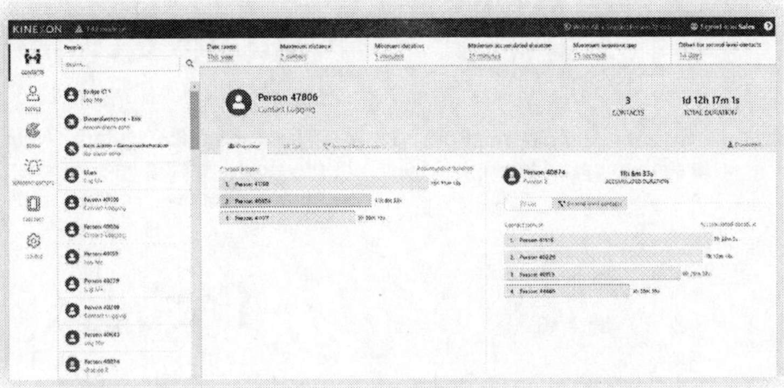

Integrate directly into your existing IT infrastructure

Multi-layer data protection

Only designated officials have access to the proximity recording data.

#SensorsConverge

Sensors Converge

SAFEZONE BY THE NUMBERS

KINEXON SafeZone

More than 1.6 million interactions every day rely on KINEXON SafeZone for precise contact warning and contact tracing.

↑75%

are falsely sent into quarantine in an interview-based tracing process.

~25min

is the average time to identify critical contacts with KINEXON SafeZone – from the real-time contact tracing to the time an employee is told to quarantine.

50%

of potentially critical contacts were actively avoided by users of the KINEXON SafeTag after only a few days.

↑70%

of critical contacts are missed without a digital solution in an interview-based tracing process.

3/4

users of KINEXON SafeZone stated that they feel safer in their daily work by wearing the SafeTag.

0.1 sec

is the time it takes for the KINEXON SafeTag to warn its user if a person gets too close.

#SensorsConverge

Sensors Converge

MEDIA VOICES

KINEXON SafeZone

CNBC

"If I ever leave my house again, I will definitely want one of these devices."

BUSINESS INSIDER

"Social distancing just got a technological leg-up..."

Chicago Tribune

"The benefits start with physical distancing. ...can help people adjust their actions."

StarTribune

"You used to check phone, keys, wallet. ...Now it's phone, keys, wallet, mask, proximity locator."

CNN

"That data is collected, making contact tracing easier if someone gets infected."

Forbes

"This societal crisis is shining a new light on the value of this kind of data."

#SensorsConverge

Sensors Converge

SECURING THE NBA BUBBLE

KINEXON SafeZone

- The NBA used KINEXON SafeZone to assist with physical distancing of players, staff, and media in the Orlando bubble as a part of its restart protocols.

- More than 2,300 SafeTags were used in the bubble to safely complete the season.

#SensorsConverge

Sensors Converge

SECURING BUSINESS CONTINUITY

KINEXON SafeZone

> *"Implementing KINEXON SafeZone has been a strong contributor in the success of our overall business continuity efforts. (...) Our experience tells us that SafeZone is an excellent solution to facilitate a safe return to the workplace."*

Thomas A. Wesley
Senior Director, Workplace Solutions

Waters™

#SensorsConverge

Sensors Converge

MOVING FORWARD

KINEXON SafeZone

- Supporting Business Continuity
- Supporting Safe Return-to-Office
- Supporting Major Events

- Connected Worker & Workplace Safety
- Workflow & Fleet Management
- Location-based Automation

#SensorsConverge

Sensors Converge

BEYOND THE PANDEMIC: LOCATION-BASED AUTOMATION

PRODUCTION & LOGISTICS

HOSPITALITY & EVENTS

RETURN TO OFFICE

MEDICAL

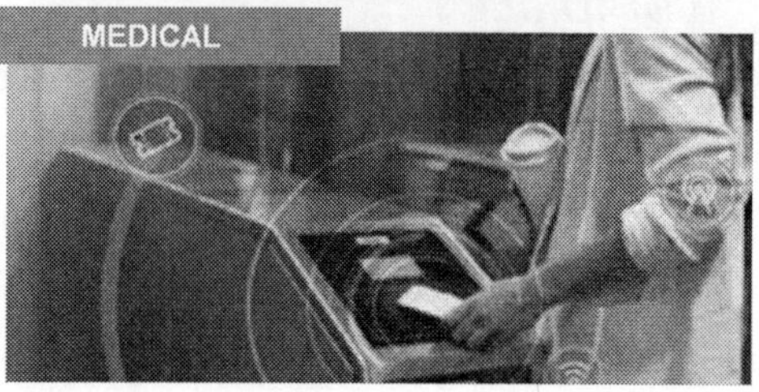

A COMPLETE SOLUTION

KINEXON SafeZone

PRECISE LOCALIZATION

REAL TIME

CONNECTIVITY

KINEXON CORE TECHNOLOGY

KINEXON SafeZone

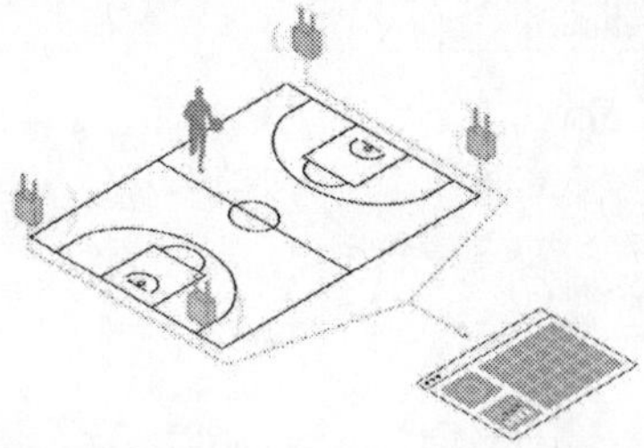

SPORTS

KINEXON provides performance and analytics solutions for more than 100 sports teams and leagues worldwide.

INDUSTRIES

KINEXON implements sensors and software for location-based automation for Industry 4.0.

#SensorsConverge

Sensors Converge

LOCATION-BASED AUTOMATION

KINEXON SafeZone

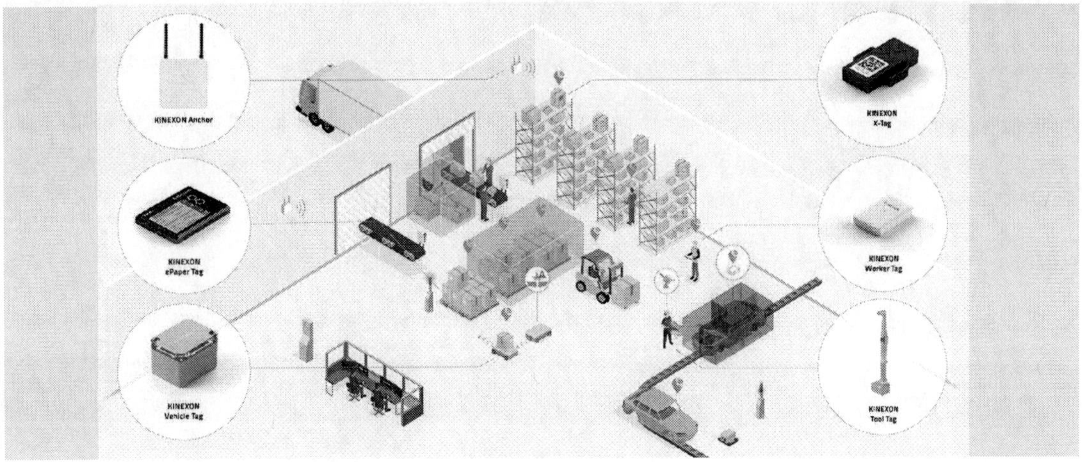

#SensorsConverge

Sensors Converge

GLOBAL TRANSPARENCY

KINEXON SafeZone

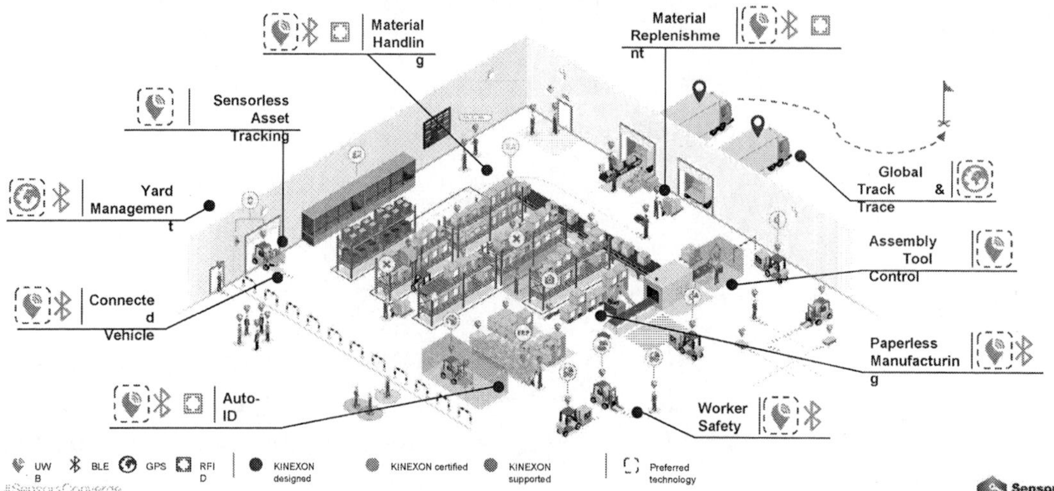

Sensors Converge

KINEXON

Visit us at BOOTH 432

MEHDI BENTANFOUS
CEO - North America, KINEXON Inc.

Sensors Converge

Sensors
Converge
KINEXON
LOCATION, LOCATION, LOCATION:
The Missing Piece of the Automation Puzzle
September 23, 2021 | San Jose, CA | Booth #432
#SensorsConverge

KINEXON
HBL
LIQUI
MOLY
HANDBALL-BUNDESLIGA

LOCATION-BASED INDUSTRIAL AUTOMATION

Leveraging Geolocation for the Smart Factory

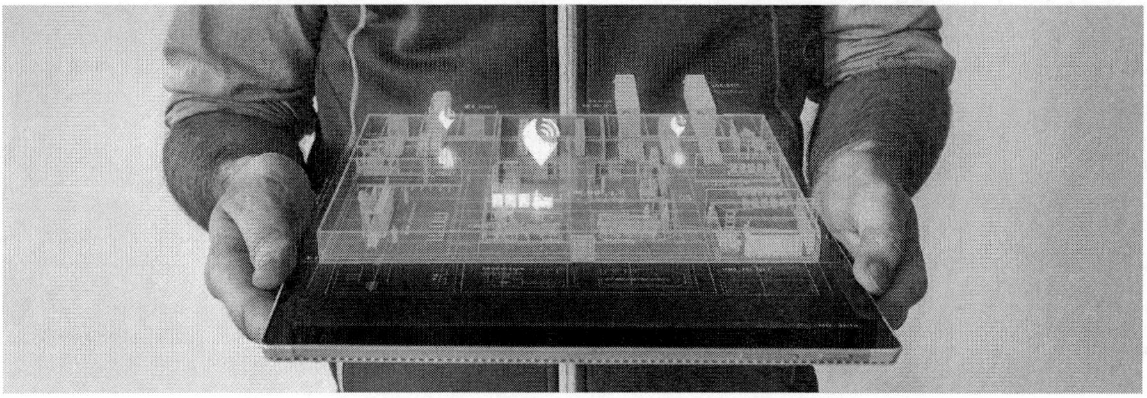

THE SMART FACTORY

A Goal and How to Get There

In a truly **smart factory**, all moving objects are connected and interact automatically in real time for a **"perfect flow."**

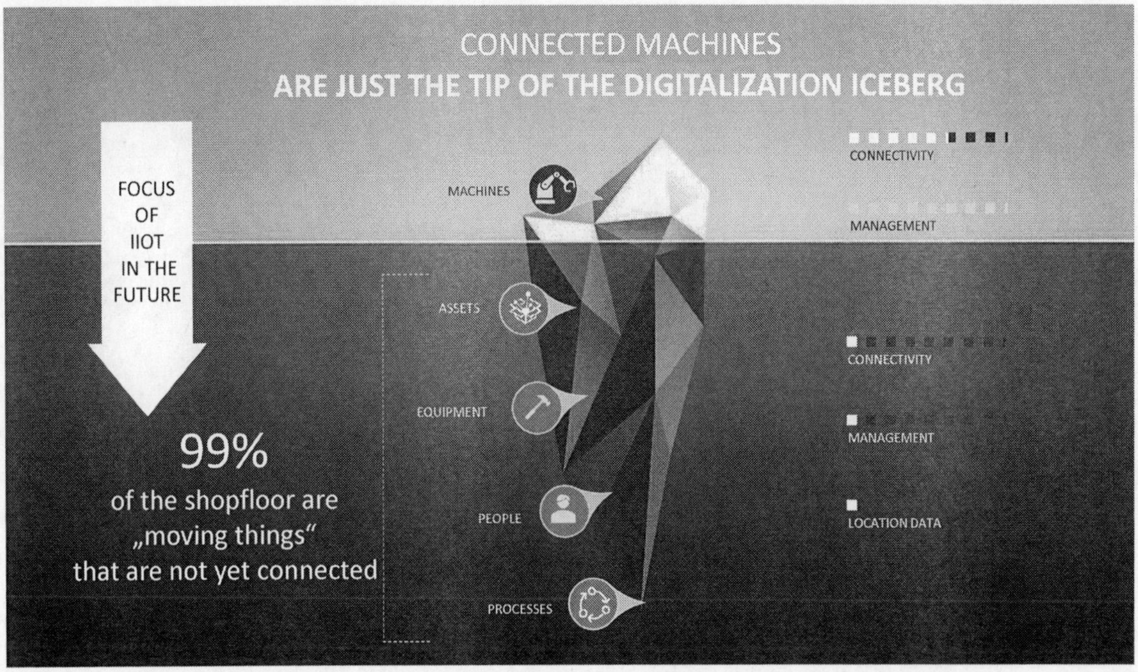

If you want to **automate** the dynamic physical world, it always comes down to one essential question:

"Where are the things?"

Thomas Strebin,
Lead for Shopfloor Digitization at BMW Group

1. Company and Market Highlights

IN A NUTSHELL

Location intelligence digitizes and automates dynamic physical worlds.

It ensures the smartest real-time orchestration of moving “things”: assets, processes and people

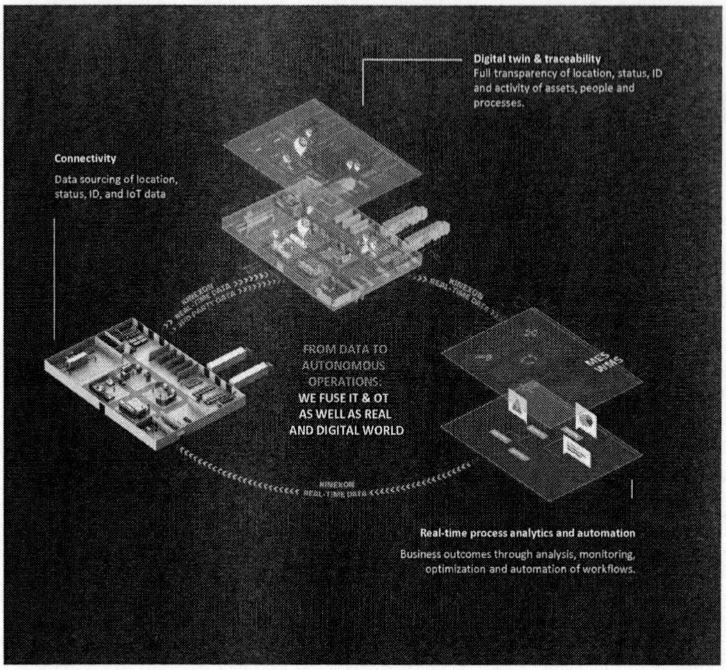

A NEW DIMENSION OF TRANSPARENCY

End-to-End Connectivity for all Moving Things on the Shop Floor

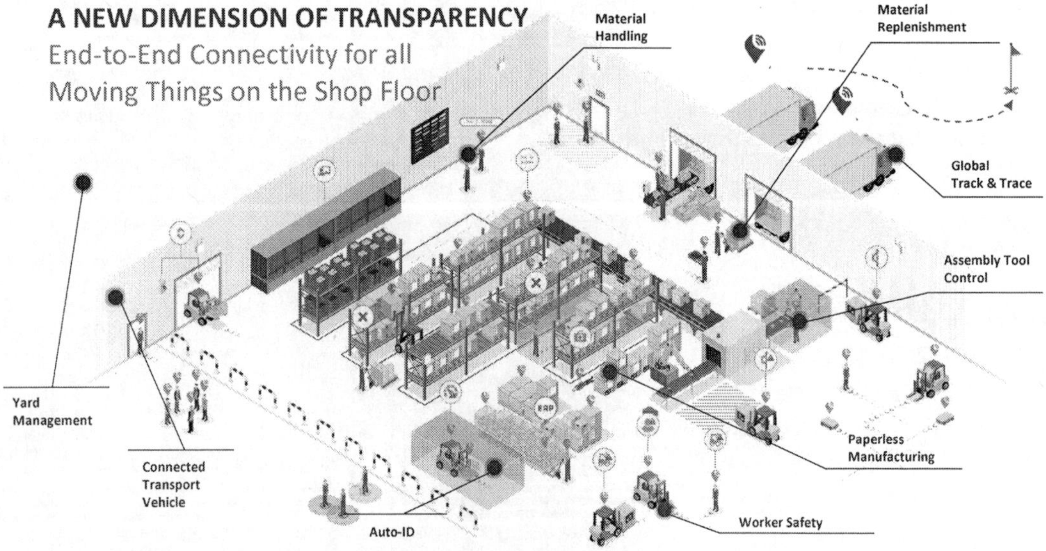

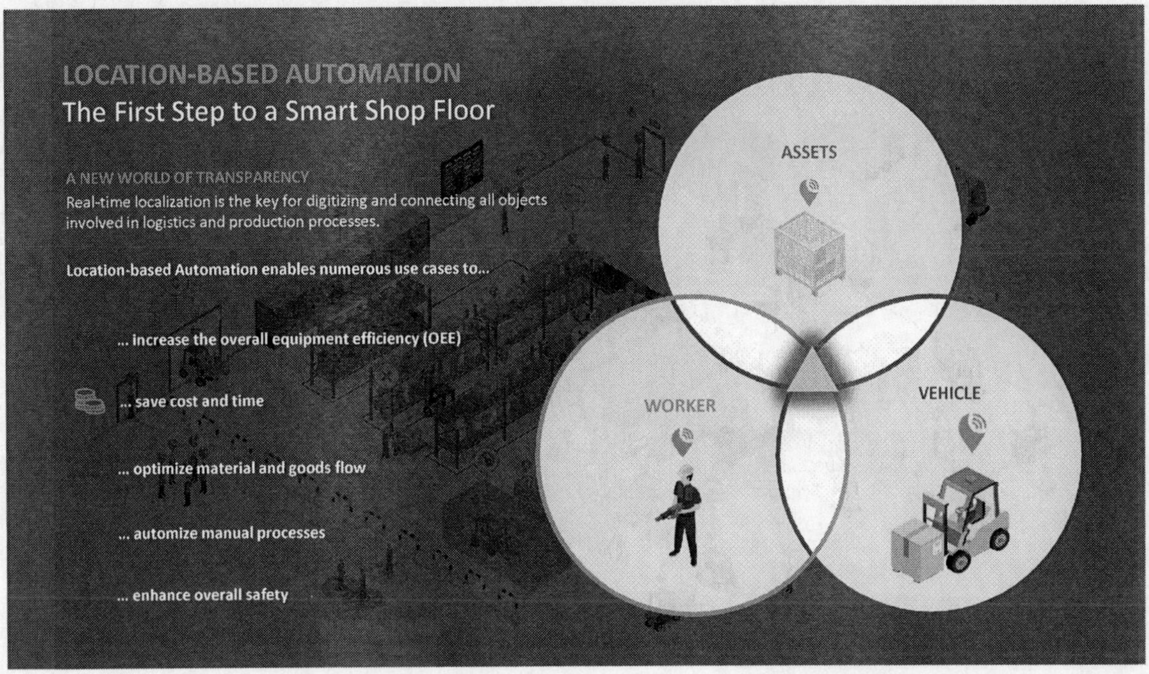
LOCATION-BASED AUTOMATION
The First Step to a Smart Shop Floor
A NEW WORLD OF TRANSPARENCY
Real-time localization is the key for digitizing and connecting all objects involved in logistics and production processes.
Location-based Automation enables numerous use cases to...
... increase the overall equipment efficiency (OEE)
... save cost and time
... optimize material and goods flow
... automize manual processes
... enhance overall safety
ASSETS
WORKER
VEHICLE

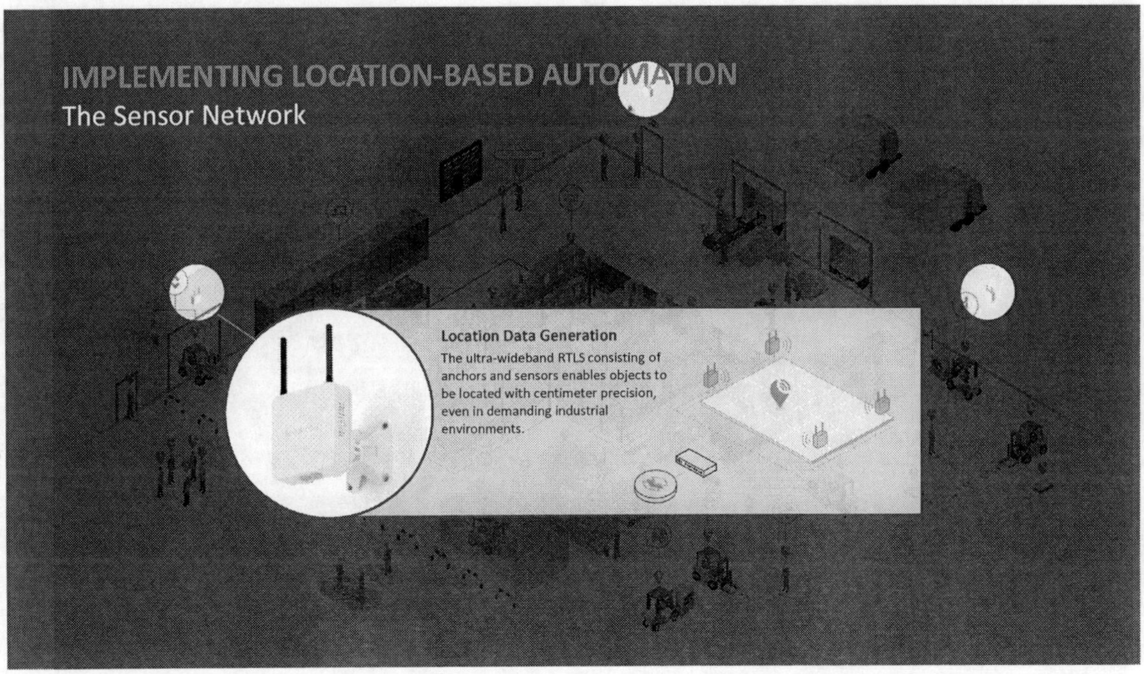
IMPLEMENTING LOCATION-BASED AUTOMATION
The Sensor Network
Location Data Generation
The ultra-wideband RTLS consisting of anchors and sensors enables objects to be located with centimeter precision, even in demanding industrial environments.

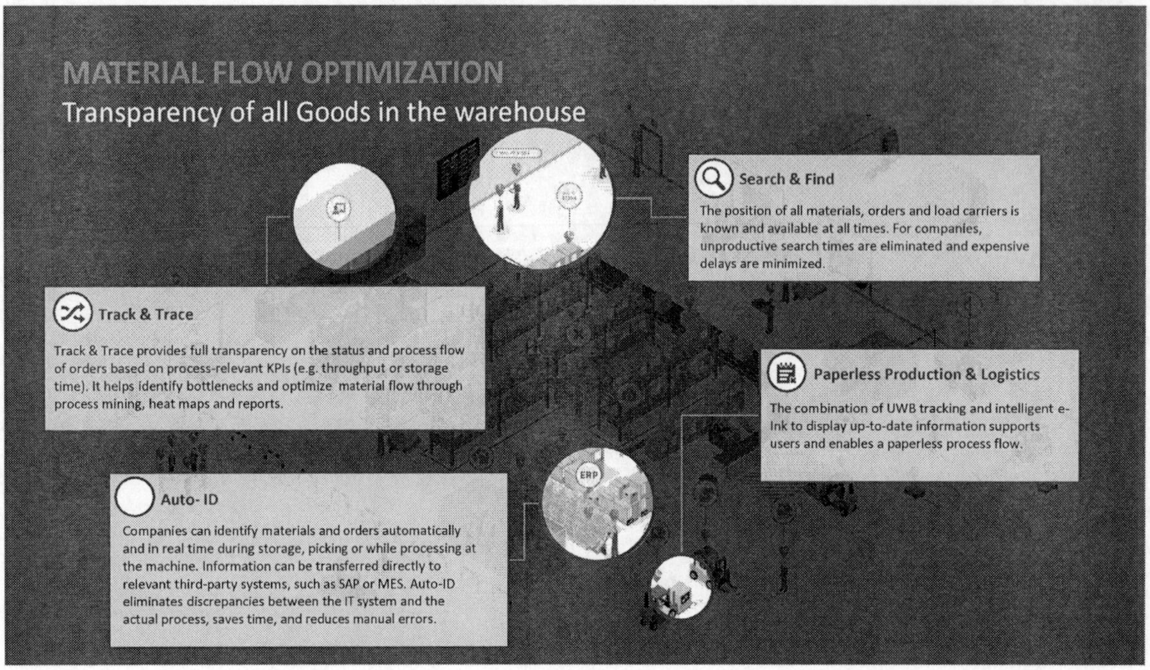
MATERIAL FLOW OPTIMIZATION
Transparency of all Goods in the warehouse
Search & Find
The position of all materials, orders and load carriers is known and available at all times. For companies, unproductive search times are eliminated and expensive delays are minimized.
Track & Trace
Track & Trace provides full transparency on the status and process flow of orders based on process-relevant KPIs (e.g. throughput or storage time). It helps identify bottlenecks and optimize material flow through process mining, heat maps and reports.
Paperless Production & Logistics
The combination of UWB tracking and intelligent e-Ink to display up-to-date information supports users and enables a paperless process flow.
ERP
Auto- ID
Companies can identify materials and orders automatically and in real time during storage, picking or while processing at the machine. Information can be transferred directly to relevant third-party systems, such as SAP or MES. Auto-ID eliminates discrepancies between the IT system and the actual process, saves time, and reduces manual errors.

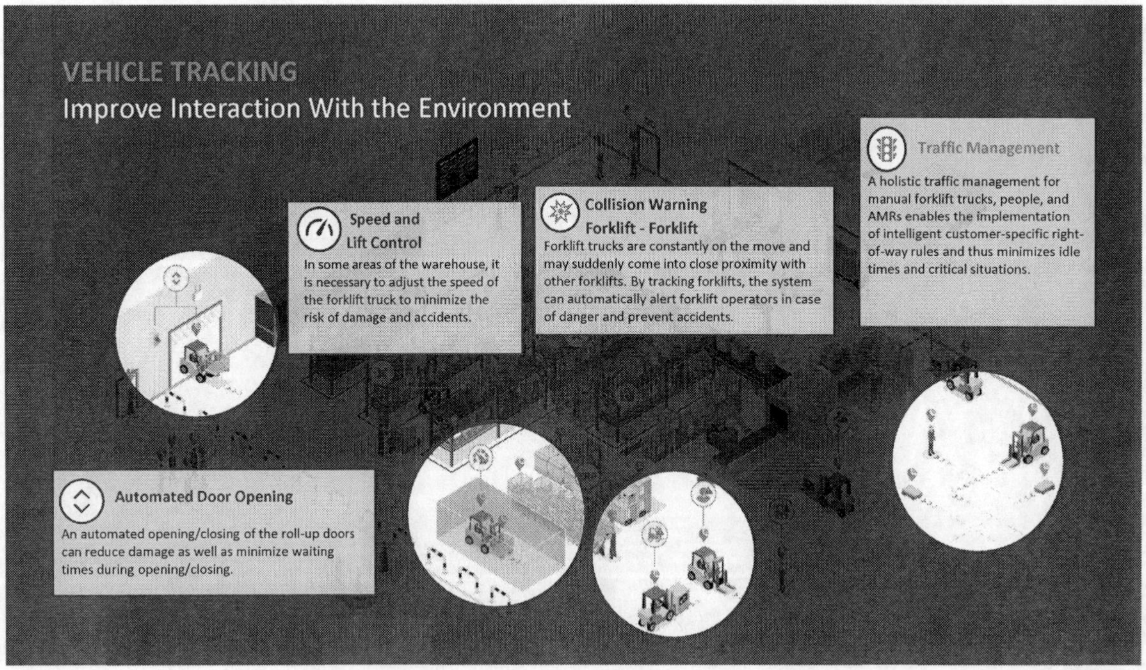
VEHICLE TRACKING
Improve Interaction With the Environment
Traffic Management
A holistic traffic management for manual forklift trucks, people, and AMRs enables the implementation of intelligent customer-specific right-of-way rules and thus minimizes idle times and critical situations.
Speed and Lift Control
In some areas of the warehouse, it is necessary to adjust the speed of the forklift truck to minimize the risk of damage and accidents.
Collision Warning Forklift - Forklift
Forklift trucks are constantly on the move and may suddenly come into close proximity with other forklifts. By tracking forklifts, the system can automatically alert forklift operators in case of danger and prevent accidents.
Automated Door Opening
An automated opening/closing of the roll-up doors can reduce damage as well as minimize waiting times during opening/closing.

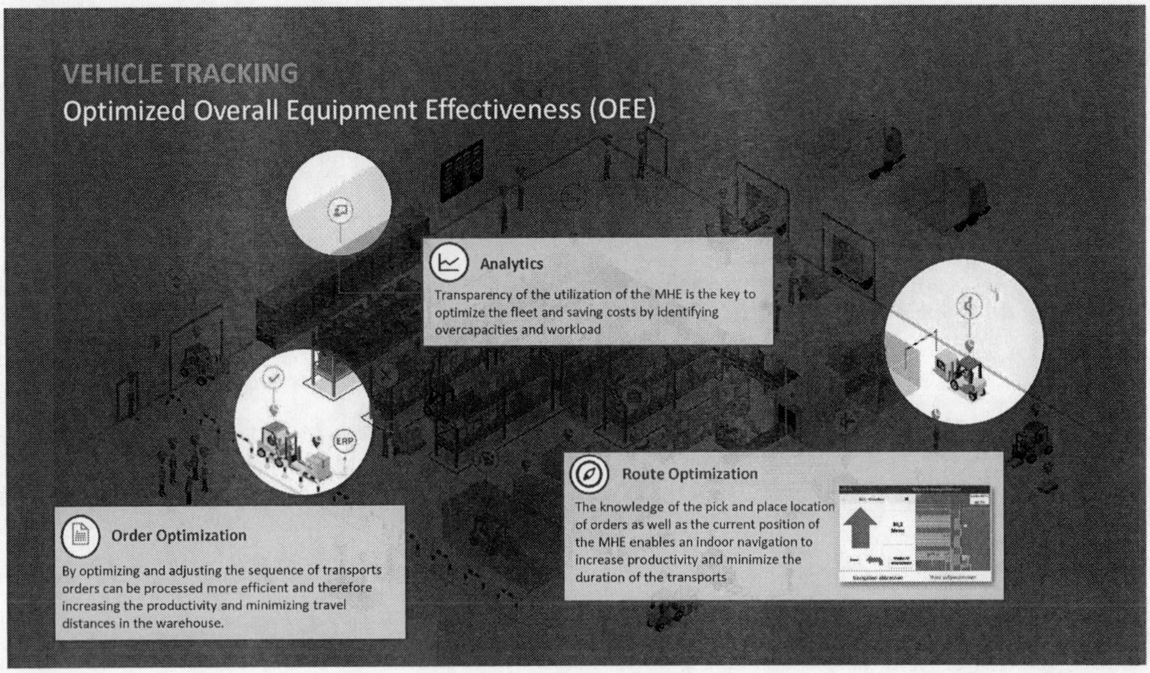
VEHICLE TRACKING
Optimized Overall Equipment Effectiveness (OEE)
Analytics
Transparency of the utilization of the MHE is the key to optimize the fleet and saving costs by identifying overcapacities and workload
Route Optimization
The knowledge of the pick and place location of orders as well as the current position of the MHE enables an indoor navigation to increase productivity and minimize the duration of the transports
Order Optimization
By optimizing and adjusting the sequence of transports orders can be processed more efficient and therefore increasing the productivity and minimizing travel distances in the warehouse.

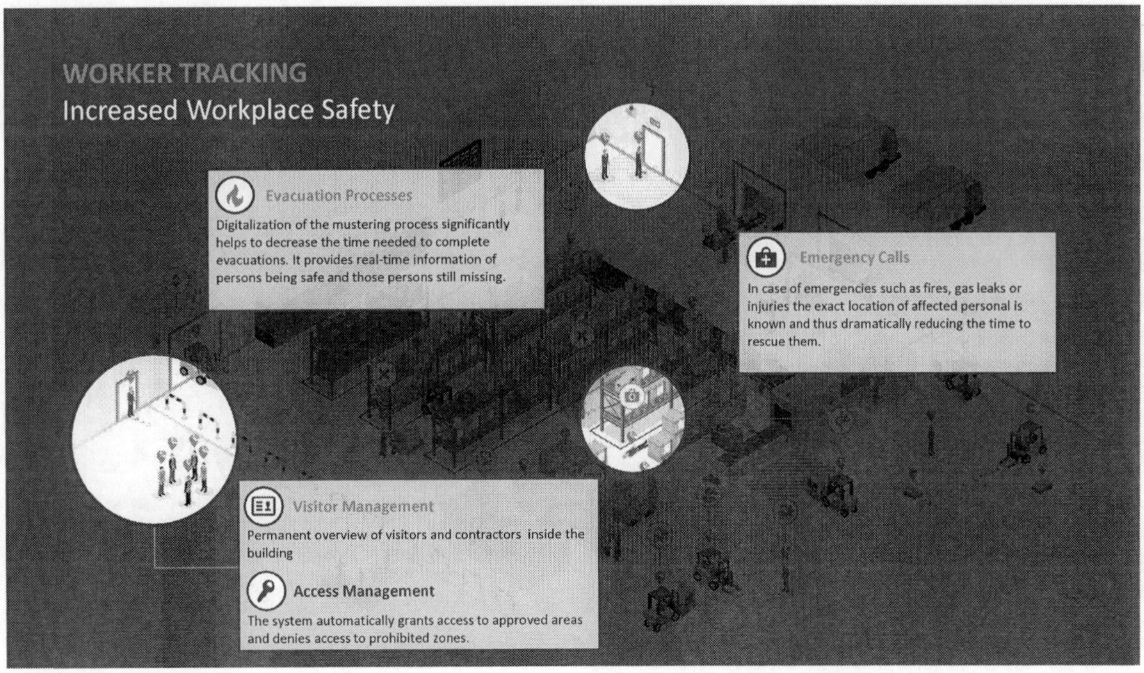
WORKER TRACKING
Increased Workplace Safety
Evacuation Processes
Digitalization of the mustering process significantly helps to decrease the time needed to complete evacuations. It provides real-time information of persons being safe and those persons still missing.
Emergency Calls
In case of emergencies such as fires, gas leaks or injuries the exact location of affected personal is known and thus dramatically reducing the time to rescue them.
Visitor Management
Permanent overview of visitors and contractors inside the building
Access Management
The system automatically grants access to approved areas and denies access to prohibited zones.

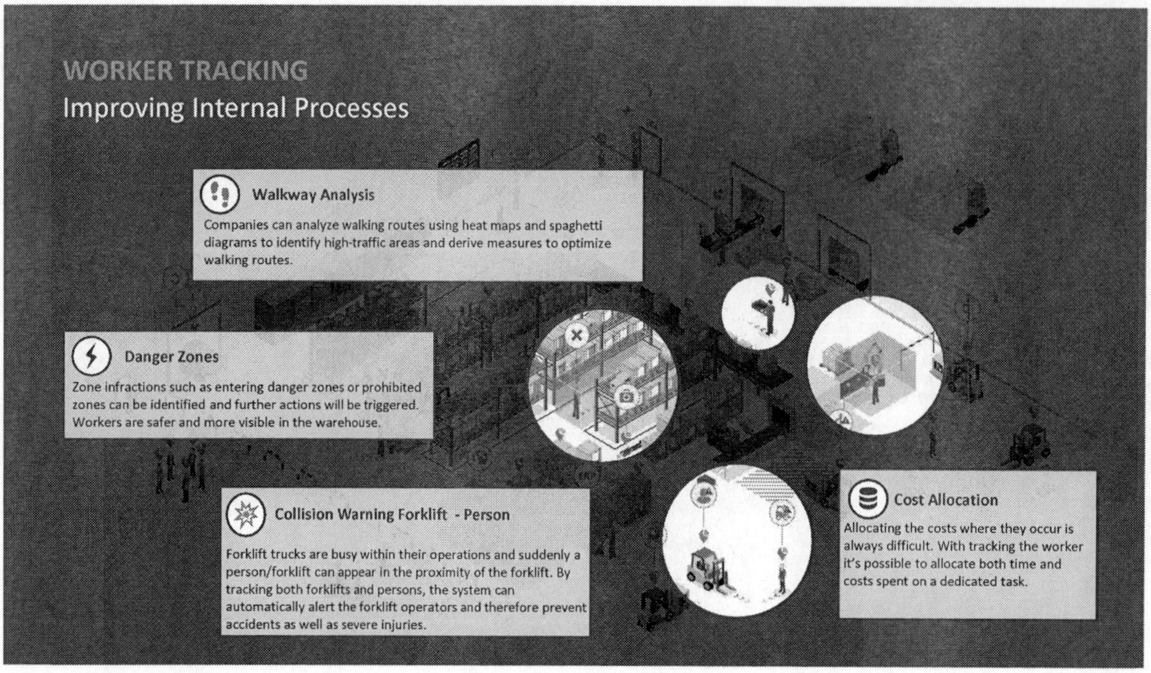
WORKER TRACKING
Improving Internal Processes
Walkway Analysis
Companies can analyze walking routes using heat maps and spaghetti diagrams to identify high-traffic areas and derive measures to optimize walking routes.
Danger Zones
Zone infractions such as entering danger zones or prohibited zones can be identified and further actions will be triggered. Workers are safer and more visible in the warehouse.
Collision Warning Forklift - Person
Forklift trucks are busy within their operations and suddenly a person/forklift can appear in the proximity of the forklift. By tracking both forklifts and persons, the system can automatically alert the forklift operators and therefore prevent accidents as well as severe injuries.
Cost Allocation
Allocating the costs where they occur is always difficult. With tracking the worker it's possible to allocate both time and costs spent on a dedicated task.

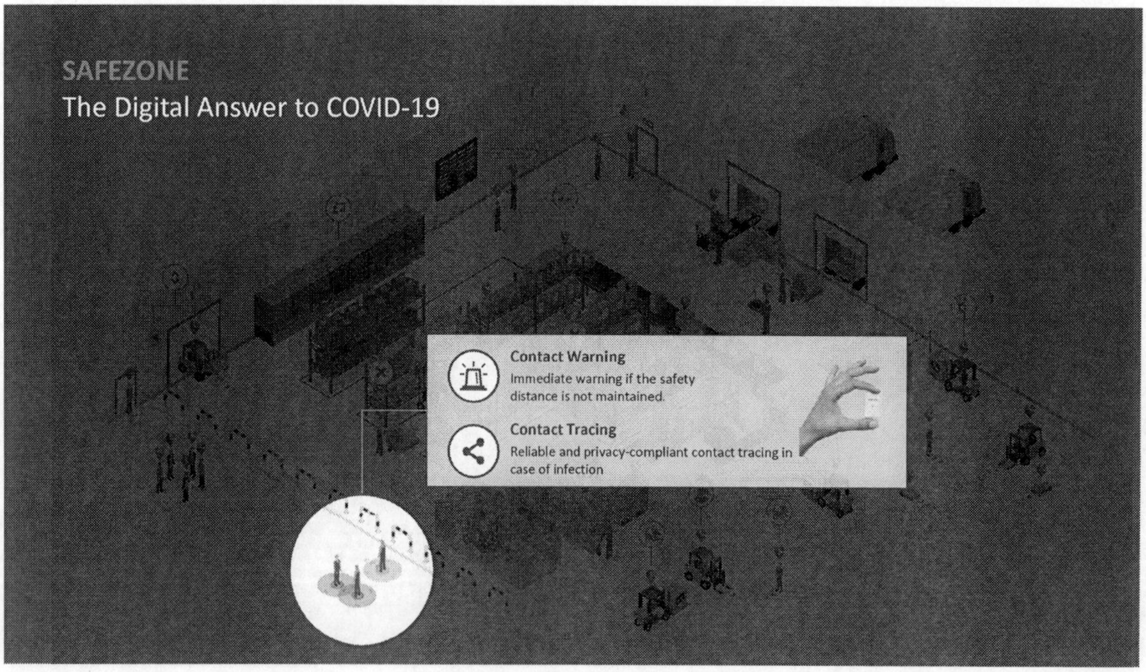
SAFEZONE
The Digital Answer to COVID-19
Contact Warning
Immediate warning if the safety distance is not maintained.
Contact Tracing
Reliable and privacy-compliant contact tracing in case of infection

KINEXON X Continental: A Case Study

KINEXON + Continental

#SensorsConverge

Sensors Converge

SMART FACTORY @ CONTINENTAL

4 Steps to a Fully Autonomous Material Flow

① Localization & Connectivity

All objects are localized and connected – relevant process information is immediately available.

② Location-based Automation

Live-location data creates new opportunities to automate regularly occurring processes in the material flow.

③ Real-time & Predictive Analytics

Automated and digitalized processes are analyzed and evaluated with state-of-the-art technology – in real-time.

④ End-to-End Autonomous Material Flow

Maximum throughput time and minimal delays are achieved, once the entire material flow is localized, connected, automated and self-optimized.

KINEXON RTLS

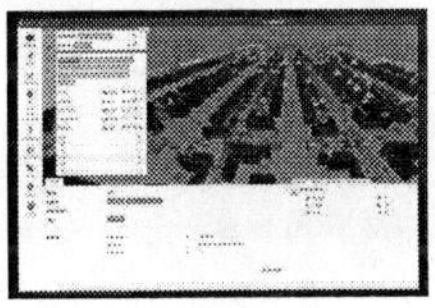

KINEXON RIoT

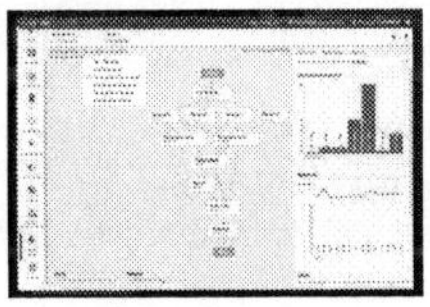

KINEXON PROCESS MANAGEMENT

KINEXON CONSULTING

18

CONTINENTAL 4.0

Benefits of Location-based Automation

Improvement	Increase	Reduction
... in the adherence to lean, kanban, and FIFO principles	... in production quality	... in expensive storage areas for buffer zones
... in the utilization of areas, load carriers and equipment	... in throughput rate	... in manual scans, logging, and search processes
... in transparency of material flow (24/7)	... in production data and information	... of machine downtime

22

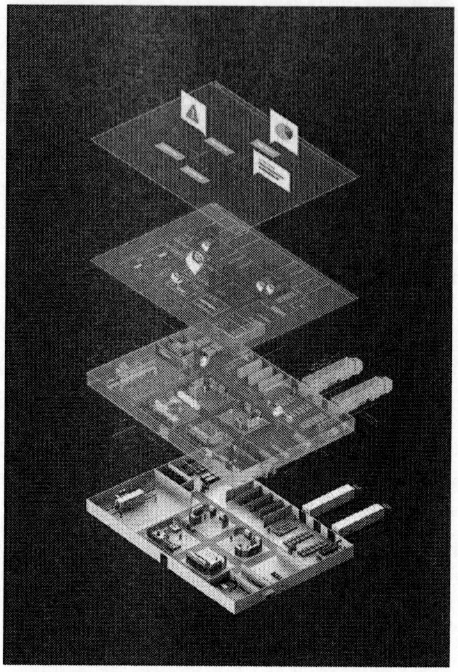

THE LATEST INNOVATION IN UWB INDOOR LOCALIZATION

Cost-Efficient UWB Precision

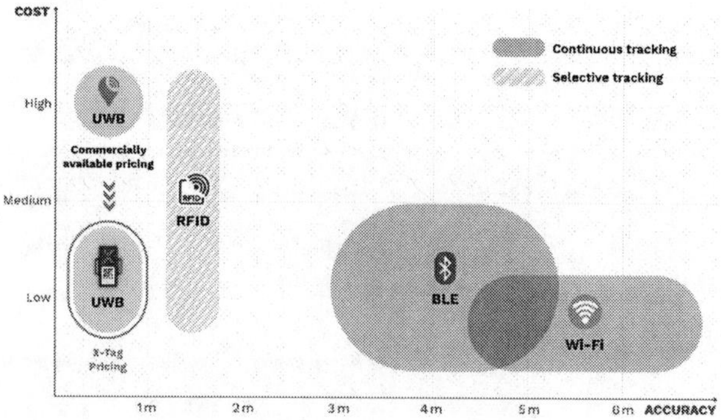

"KINEXON's X-Tag enables use cases that were previously unprofitable for Continental. Large-scale use of ultra-precise yet affordable UWB-technology allows us to gain better real-time data and a faster RoI."

Rafael Hymon, Head of Logistics at Continental Automotive

23

KINEXON

About KINEXON

- Fast growing, agile and innovation driven tech company with international footprint – 600 projects in 12 countries

3 locations: Munich | Chicago | New York

>200 employees: 2018 – **100** employees, 2019 – **164** employees, 2020 – **218** employees

PORSCHE · zalando · SCHENKER · Henkel · ASM · Continental · oerlikon · wilo · AEROTEC

Strong, international customer portfolio – 600 projects in 12 countries

KINEXON is the most trusted partner for location-based automation by market leaders across industries.

Largest single industrial contract worldwide for real-time location tech in 2020/21

KINEXON end-to-end technology (RTLS & IoT SW platform) in global plants of BMW.

Airbus/Premium Aerotec

Global frame contract. RTLS and IoT platform in roll-out and operational at serveral site.

Automated supply chain provider

Automation of entire supply chain, from planning to product delivery. Global frame contract for geolocation project rollout.

#SensorsConverge

Sensors Converge

Explore Location-based Automation with KINEXON

MEHDI BENTANFOUS
CEO - North America, KINEXON Inc.

KINEXON

Visit us at BOOTH 432

KINEXON Industries
200 S Wacker Drive, Suite 3100
Chicago, IL 60606

Tel. +1 (347) 630-0208

info@kinexon-industries.com

#SensorsConverge

Sensors Converge

Sensors Converge

Smart home Usability and implementation challenges

September 21-23, 2021 | San Jose, CA

Neomar Giacomini
Hardware Development Engineering Senior Manager
Whirlpool Corporation

#SensorsConverge

In short words...

- Smart home vs heavy connected
- Does it work?
- Setup
- The unexpected factors and effects
- Are we looking at the big (bigger) picture?
- Recommendations

#SensorsConverge

Sensors Converge

The Smart Home today

- What is a smart home?
- What do "most" consumers have at home today?
- What experience does this scenario provide to the consumer?

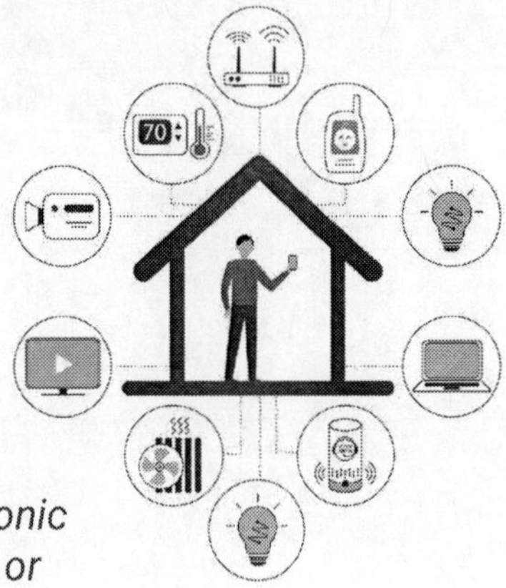

"a home equipped with lighting, heating, and electronic devices that can be controlled remotely by phone or computer." Google/Oxford Languages

#SensorsConverge

Sensors Converge

Where are we heading to?

Number of Smart Homes forecast worldwide from 2017 to 2025 (in millions)

Smart homes, not # devices!

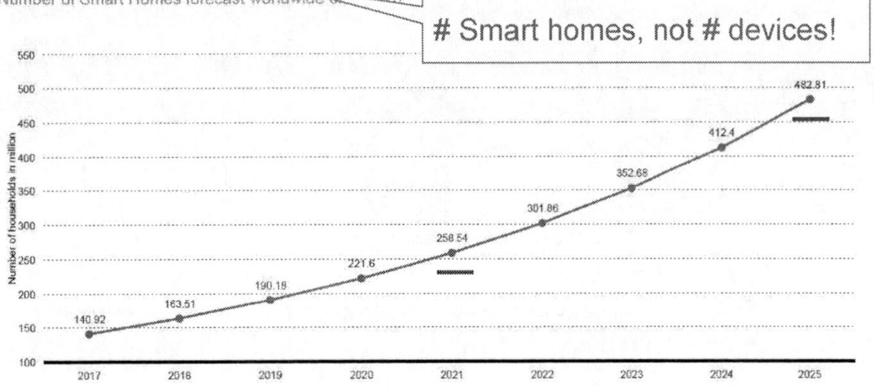

#SensorsConverge

Source: Statista Smart home dossier 2020

Sensors Converge

Where are we heading to?

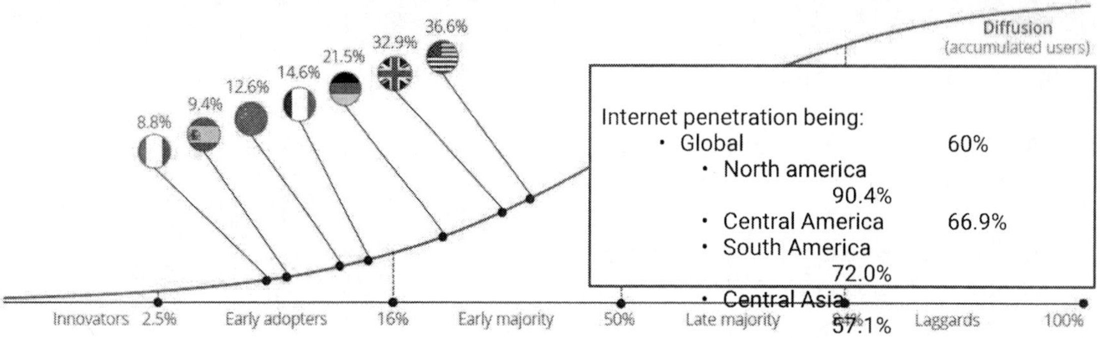

Internet penetration being:

- Global 60%
  - North america 90.4%
  - Central America 66.9%
  - South America 72.0%
  - Central Asia 57.1%
  - South Asia 42.2%

"Of this total, 92.6 percent accessed the internet via mobile devices."
(Broadband is near 22% in the Americas) 82~97%

#SensorsConverge

Source: Statista Digital market Outlook 2020
Source: Global internet penetration 2021

Sensors Converge

What exactly is ahead of us?

#SensorsConverge

Sensors Converge

Smart home versus Heavily Connected

- What is a reasonable #devices?
- What is a high #devices?
- What is too much?
- What is the reality we will face in 5..10 years?

#SensorsConverge

Smart home, Smart building… smart apartment?

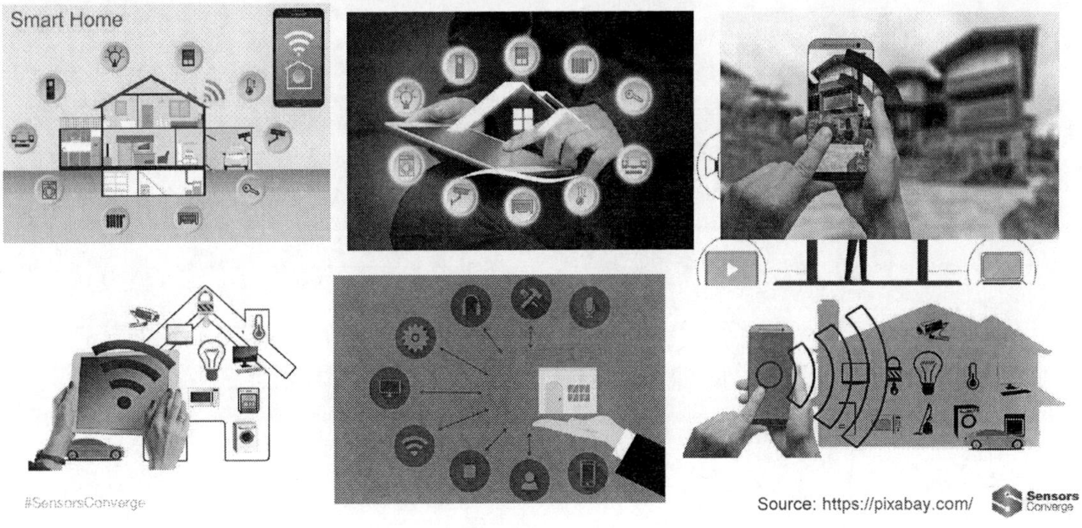

#SensorsConverge

Source: https://pixabay.com/

How far may our smart home reach?

#SensorsConverge

Sensors Converge

Can i build a Faraday cage around them?

#SensorsConverge

Sensors Converge

What can influence performance?

- Number of devices
- Structure of the house
- Quality of service
- Use of bandwidth

- High number of devices
- Router and Repeater limitations
- Neighbourhood
- Open shared WiFi networks

"[Manufacturer name removed] home routers can accommodate up to 32 clients per wireless band. If your router is dual band, the total wireless clients your router can handle is 64 (32 for the 2.4GHz and 32 for the 5GHz)."

#SensorsConverge

Sensors Converge

What can influence performance?

- Number of devices
- Structure of the house
- Quality of service
- Use of bandwidth

- High number of devices
- Router and Repeater limitations
- Neighbourhood
- Open shared WiFi networks
- Noise "overlap"

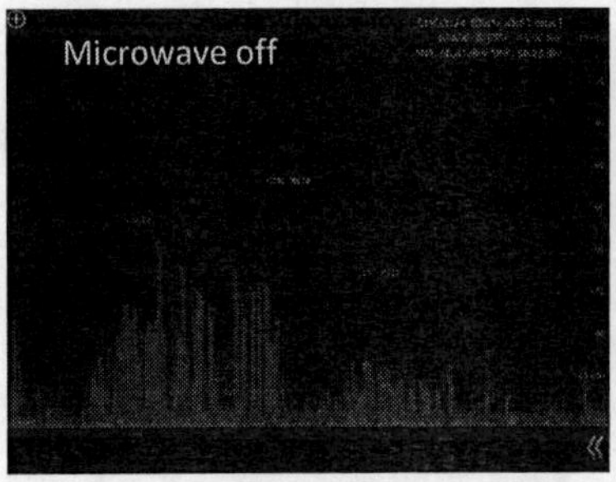

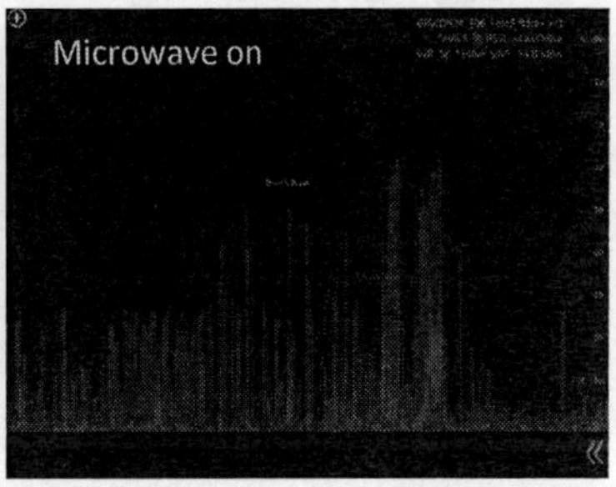

#SensorsConverge

Sensors Converge

What can influence performance?

- Number of devices
- Structure of the house
- Quality of service
- Use of bandwidth

- High number of devices
- Router and Repeater limitations
- Neighbourhood
- Open shared WiFi networks
- Noise “overlap”
- Power shortages
- Provider shortages
- Passing by cars with WiFi

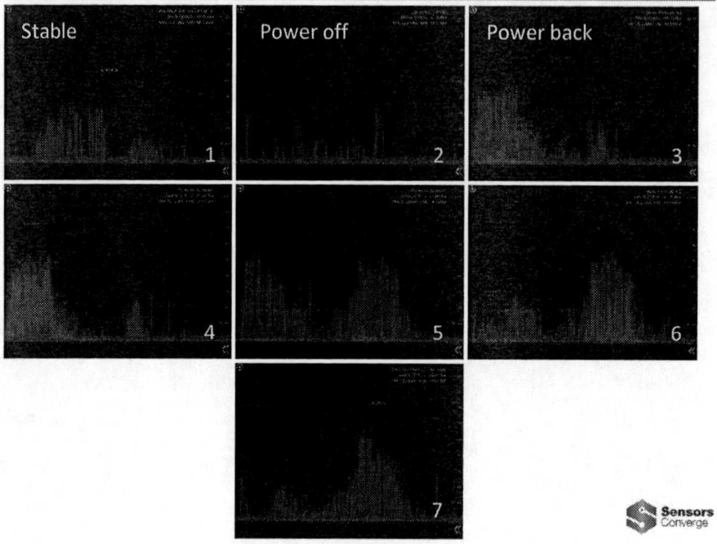

#SensorsConverge

Sensors Converge

What can influence performance?

- Number of devices
- Structure of the house
- Quality of service
- Use of bandwidth

- High number of devices
- Router and Repeater limitations
- Neighbourhood
- Open shared WiFi networks
- Noise “overlap”
- Power shortages
- Provider shortages
- Passing by cars with WiFi

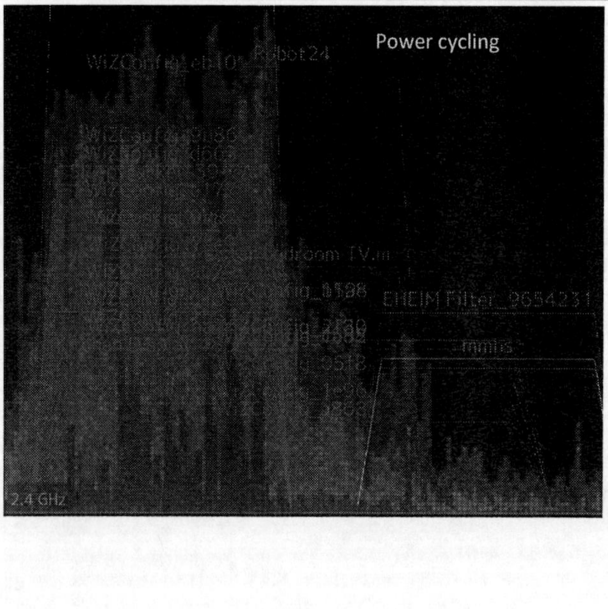

#SensorsConverge

Sensors Converge

What can influence performance?

- Number of devices
- Structure of the house
- Quality of service
- Use of bandwidth

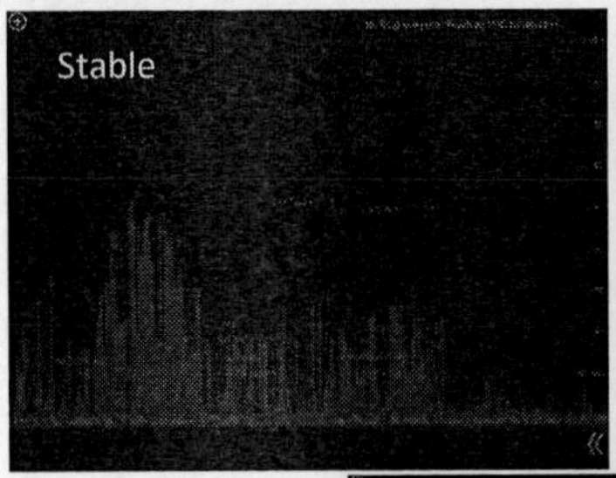

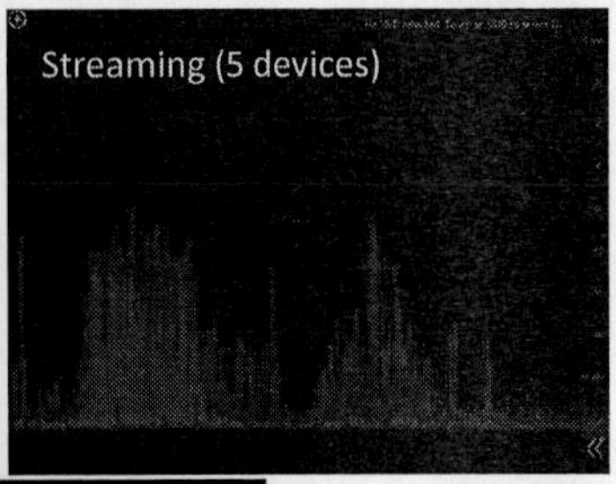

- High number of devices
- Router and Repeater limitations
- Neighbourhood
- Open shared WiFi networks
- Noise "overlap"
- Power shortages
- Provider shortages
- Passing by cars with WiFi
- Heavy streaming all around ("radio congestion")
- Weather

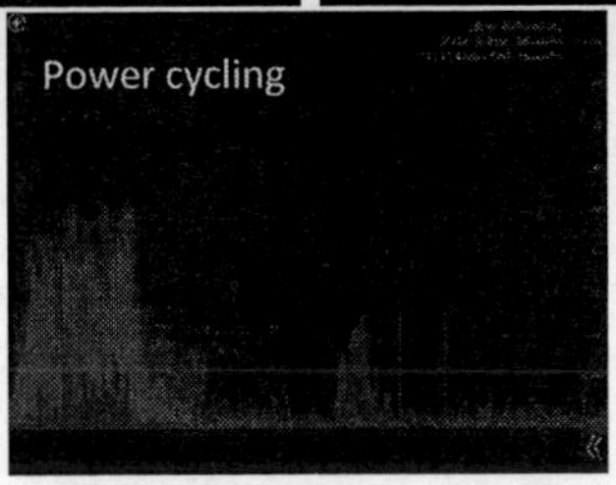

#SensorsConverge

Sensors Converge

What can influence performance?

- Number of devices
- Structure of the house
- Quality of service
- Use of bandwidth

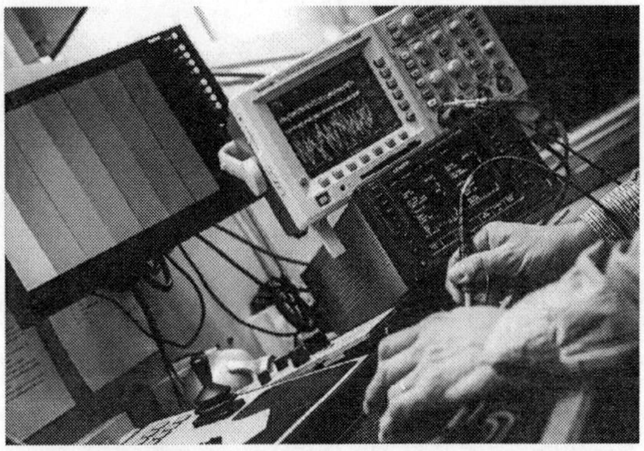

- High number of devices
- Router and Repeater limitations
- Neighbourhood
- Open shared WiFi networks
- Noise "overlap"
- Power shortages
- Provider shortages
- Passing by cars with WiFi
- Heavy streaming all around ("radio congestion")
- Weather
- **Design to my specification vs Design to the future use case?**

#SensorsConverge

Sensors Converge

The holistic* picture!

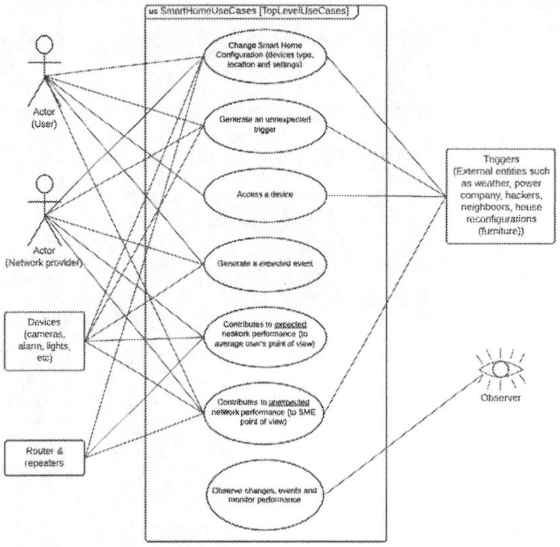

#SensorsConverge

Sensors Converge

Recommendation: Look further!

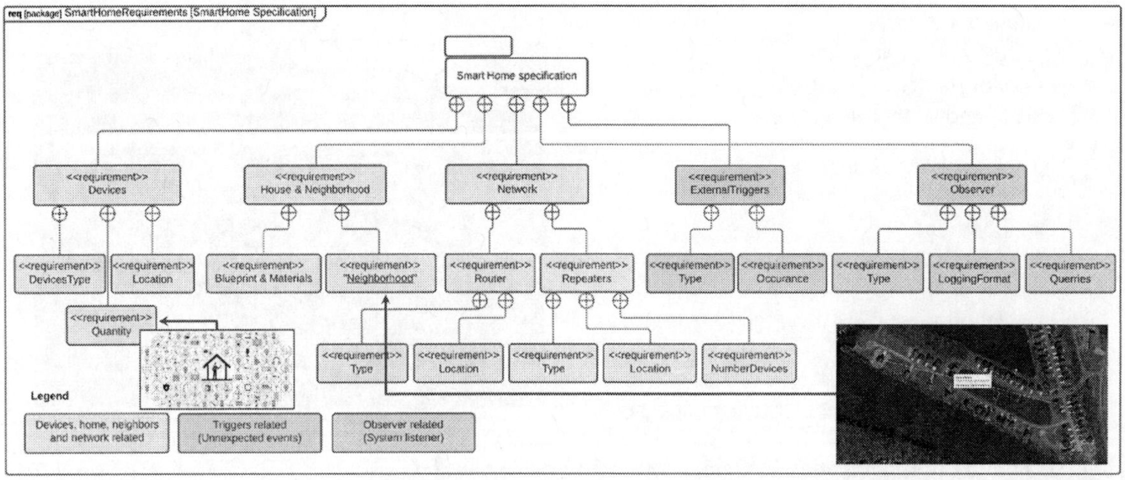

#SensorsConverge

Sensors Converge

Q&A

Neomar Giacomini, M.Sc. E.E., EMBA, AMA-CPM™

Hardware Development Engineering Senior Manager

Whirlpool Corporation

#SensorsConverge

Sensors Converge

Sensors Converge

MEMS Process and Supply Chain

Paul Carey, Ph.D.
SEMI Director of MEMS and Sensors Industry Group (MSIG)
1-1:30pm September 23, 2021 | San Jose, CA

#SensorsConverge

Outline

1. SEMI MSIG Introduction
2. MEMS Fabrication Technology
3. MEMS Device Types
4. MEMS Market
5. MEMS Supply Chain
6. Q & A

Photo: Micromotor and gears from Sandi National Labs

Photo: courtesy of DARPA's MTO Microsystems Technology Office

#SensorsConverge semi | MEMS & SENSORS INDUSTRY GROUP Sensors Converge

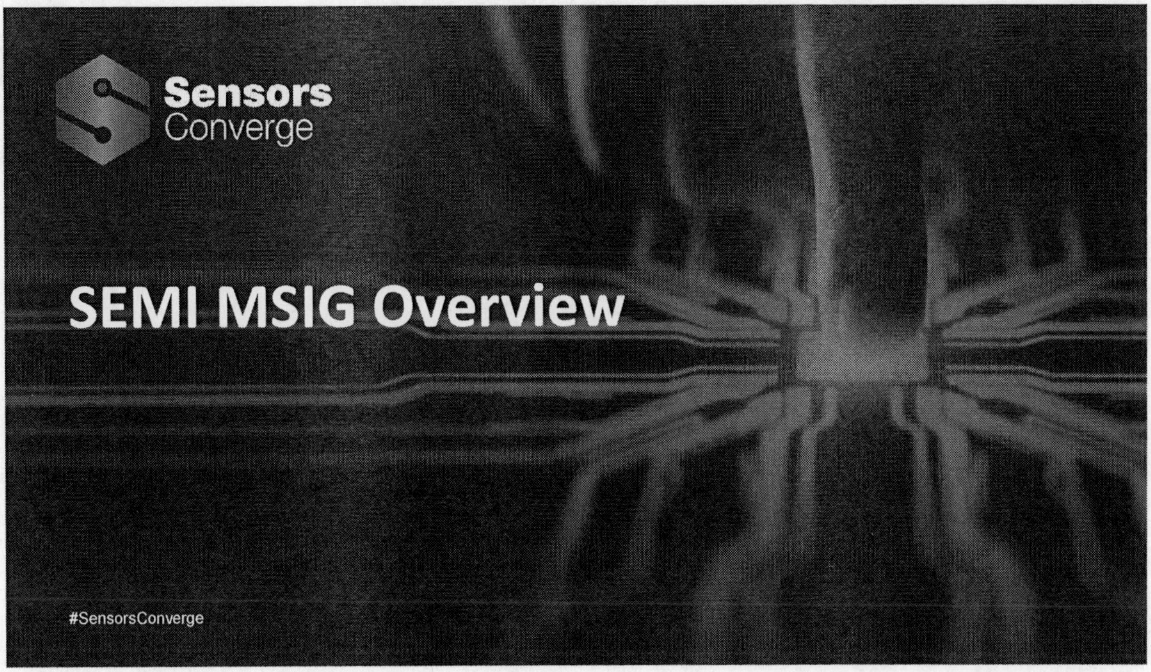
Sensors
Converge
SEMI MSIG Overview
#SensorsConverge

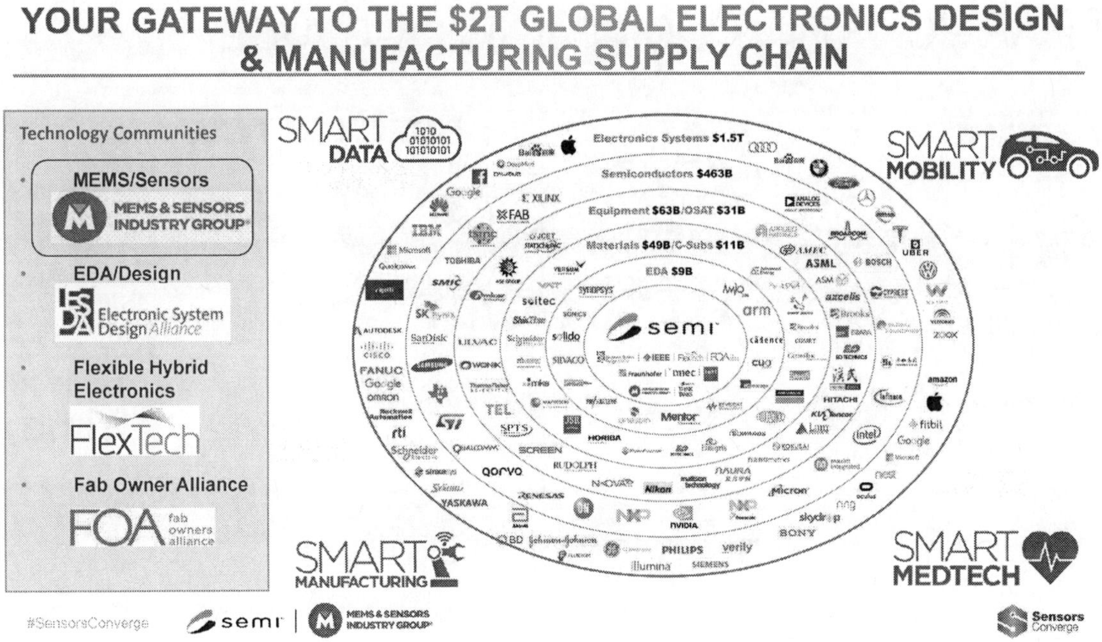
YOUR GATEWAY TO THE $2T GLOBAL ELECTRONICS DESIGN & MANUFACTURING SUPPLY CHAIN
Technology Communities
MEMS/Sensors
MEMS & SENSORS INDUSTRY GROUP
EDA/Design
Electronic System Design Alliance
Flexible Hybrid Electronics
FlexTech
Fab Owner Alliance
FOA fab owners alliance
SMART DATA
SMART MOBILITY
SMART MANUFACTURING
SMART MEDTECH
Electronics Systems $1.5T
Semiconductors $463B
Equipment $63B/OSAT $31B
Materials $49B/C-Subs $11B
EDA $9B
semi
#SensorsConverge
semi | MEMS & SENSORS INDUSTRY GROUP
Sensors Converge

MEMS & Sensors Industry Group (MSIG)
A SEMI Strategic Association Partner

MSIG Goal | **Help Member Companies Sensorize the World**

Example vertical markets served

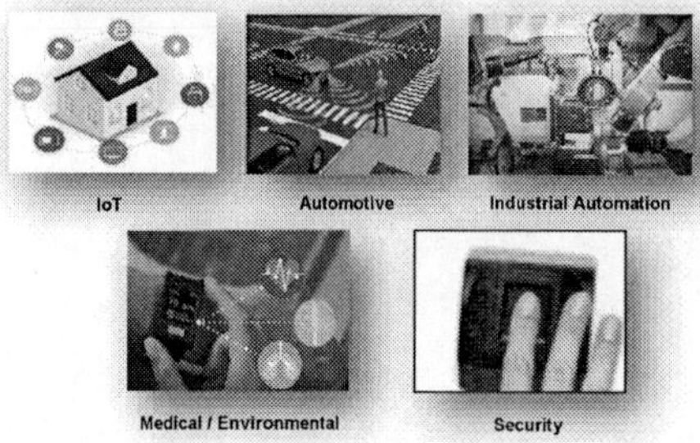

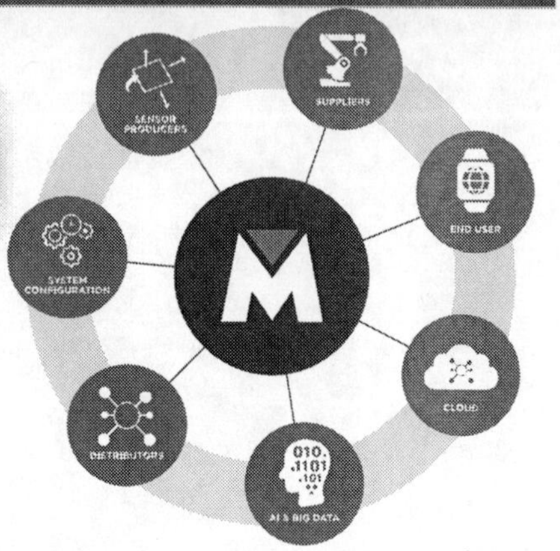

Mission
- Serve the entire MEMS and Sensor Supply Chain
- Expand market and global presences by leveraging SEMI's global reach

#SensorsConverge semi | MEMS & SENSORS INDUSTRY GROUP

Visit our web site www.msig.org

Sensors Converge

PARTICIPATING COMPANIES INCLUDE

NIST National Institute of Standards and Technology · Lam Research · BOSCH · TDK InvenSense · Nordson SONOSCAN · OKMETIC · softMEMS · infineon · GE · ST life.augmented · intel · APPLIED MATERIALS · EVG · SPTS An orbotech Company · IDT A Renesas Company · ANALOG DEVICES · NIST National Institute of Standards and Technology · Fraunhofer ENAS · AMFITZGERALD · ULVAC · TELEDYNE DALSA Everywhereyoulook Part of the Teledyne Imaging Group · onsemi · SiTime

And Over 100 More Companies!

#SensorsConverge semi | MEMS & SENSORS INDUSTRY GROUP

Join Us! Email to msig@semi.org

Sensors Converge

Sensors Converge

SEMI MSIG Sensor Solution Partnership

#SensorsConverge

Sensor Solution Partnership

- **New MSIG program started in 2021 aiming to:**
  - Establish better relationships between OEMs and sensor companies
  - Enabling discussion on value to products and sensor supply chain
  - Work together on non-differentiating items and standardization
  - Develop new and valuable opportunities

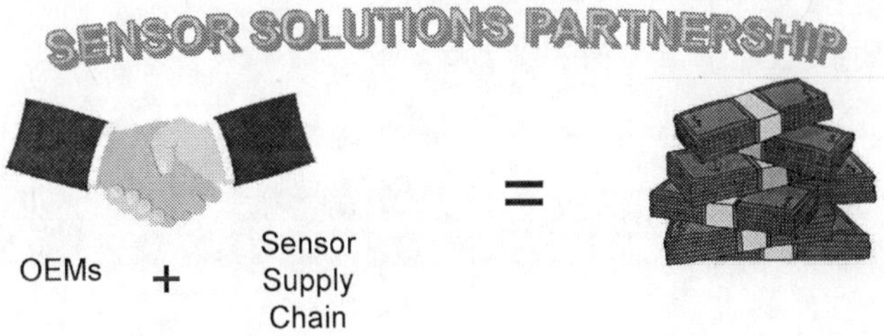

#SensorsConverge semi | MEMS & SENSORS INDUSTRY GROUP Sensors Converge

First Target Sector: Smart Cities

Market Size	$84B total market
Growth (whole market)	24.7% (CAGR 2020-2027)
Timeline	Now

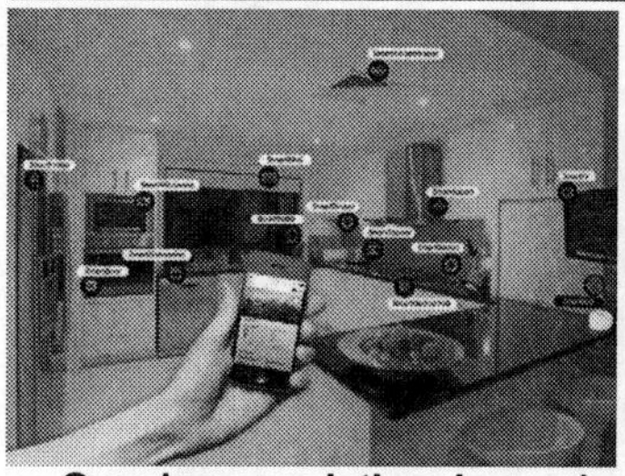

- Growing population demands cities become more advanced
- Must support more people safely and efficiently
  - ⇨ *Resource optimization is critical*
- Aligned to mega trends (IOT, 5G, AI, Climate Change)

Smart City Sensors Needs
Temperature
Motion
Occupancy
Water/leak detection
Humidity
Open/closed
AC current
Gas detection
Pressure
Air velocity
Ultrasonic (vehicle/person/package arrival)
Image sensors and cameras
Wireless sensors

OEM & Sensor Companies
Aclima, Aeroqual,Airthings, AMS, Apple, Atmotube, Awair, Blueair (A Unilever brand), Cepton, Cisco, CO2Meter, Columbia Weather System, Dynament, ecobee, ENVEA, EPA, Foobot, Google, Government Entities, HIVE (Centrica Hive Limited UK Company), Honeywell, Intel, IQ Air, Molekule , Nest , Netatmo, notAnotherOne, Plume Labs, PurpleAir, Qualcomm, Schneider, Sensirion, Temtop(subsidiary of Elitech Technology Inc), TI, TSI, uHoo, Vitesy, Eliko, Terranova, Fleetonomy, Harv, Woodoo, Aligned Energy, Alcatel-Lucent, BlocPower, Chordant, CIMCON Lighting, Choda Wireless, MER Group, MetroQuest, Monnit

#SensorsConverge semi | MEMS & SENSORS INDUSTRY GROUP

Contact us at msig@semi.org for details

Sensors Converge

Sensors Converge

SEMI MSIG R&D Funding

#SensorsConverge

SEMI MSIG Has Funding!

R&D projects: funded by Congress through SEMI/ARL

- 2020: $7M awarded for Positioning, Navigation and Timing (PNT). Funding is cost-shared up to 50%.

SEMI-MSIG PNT Projects: Budgets and Timelines

Item	Institution	Total Budget ($)	Project (2020 Q1 – 2022 Q3)
1	GE Research	$ 827,472	Low SWAP-C MEMS Gyrocompass Enabled by Electrostatic Carouseling Gyroscope
2	PARC	$ 1,424,883	On-chip UV/Blue Laser Sources for Integrated Photonics
3	Teledyne Scientific	$ 526,000	Low Cost, Battery Operated Chip Scale Atomic Clock (CSAC): Affordable Precision Timing for Denied Environments
4	Georgia Institute of Technology	$ 1,514,803	High-Aspect-Ratio Monocrystalline SiC-on-Insulator MEMS Platform for Ultra-High-Performance BAW Gyroscopes and Timing Resonators
5	Analog Devices Incorporated	$ 4,066,200	Nav Grade Synchronized Mass Gyroscope with System ID
6	SiTime	$ 4,590,196	MEMs Piezoelectric Resonators with Ultra-Stable Wafer Level Package
7	Teledyne Scientific	$ 357,863	Packaging and Integration for Compact, Nav-Grade MEMS IMUs
8	Carnegie Mellon University	$ 518,782	CMOS MEMS High-Stability Accelerometer through Machine Learning
9	Twinleaf	$ 350,000	Microfabricated, Self-Locking Light Source for Atomic Sensors
10	Honeywell	$ 684,096	Machine Learning for IMU Compensation (ML IMU)

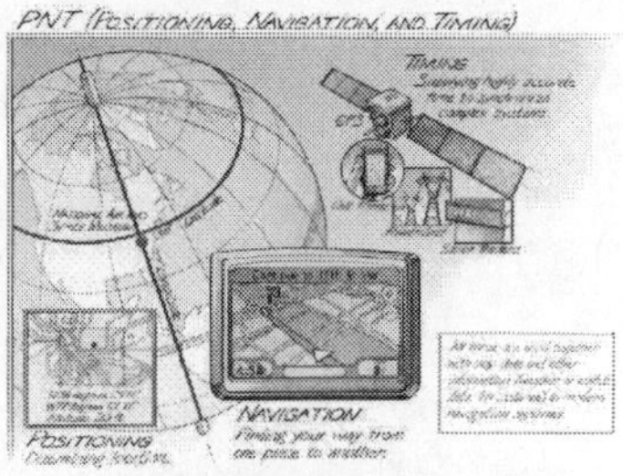

PNT: dual use technology good for both private and public sectors

Funding Roadmap:

- ☐ Fall 2021: $5M additional PNT related funding awarded for a follow-on PNT Program (New Money – RFP this Fall!)
- ☐ 2022: $10M proposed "Sensors to fight Pandemics"

#SensorsConverge semi | MEMS & SENSORS INDUSTRY GROUP Interested in Funding? https://discover.semi.org/rd-program.html Sensors Converge

Sensors Converge

SEMI MSIG Events

#SensorsConverge

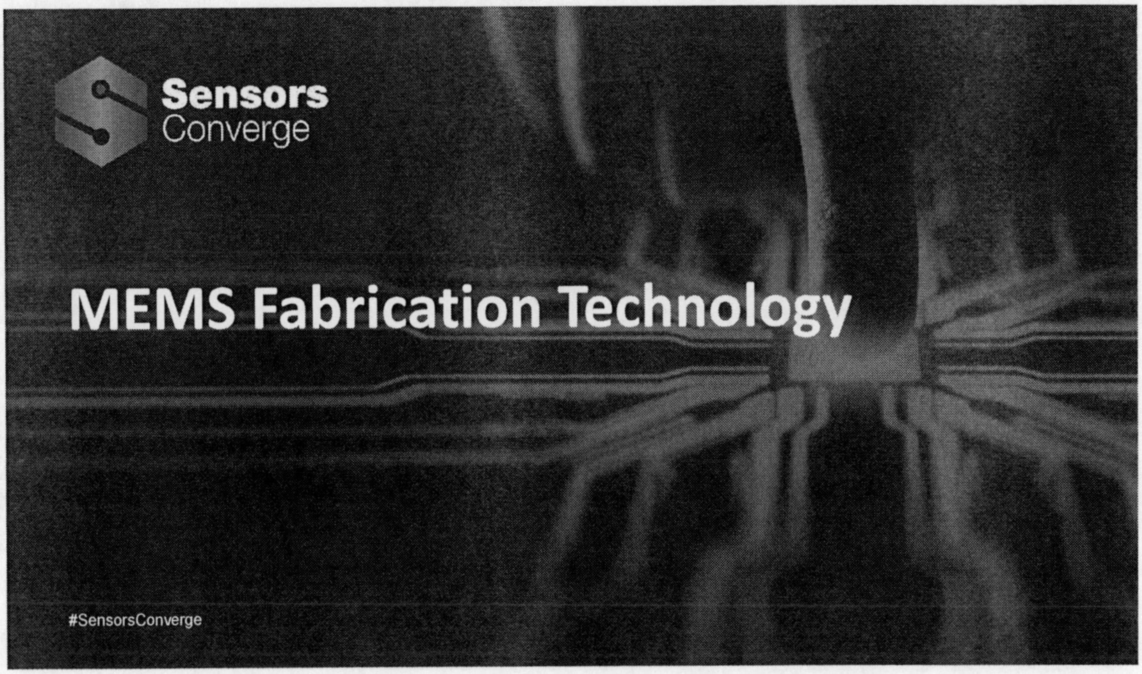
Sensors
Converge
MEMS Fabrication Technology
#SensorsConverge

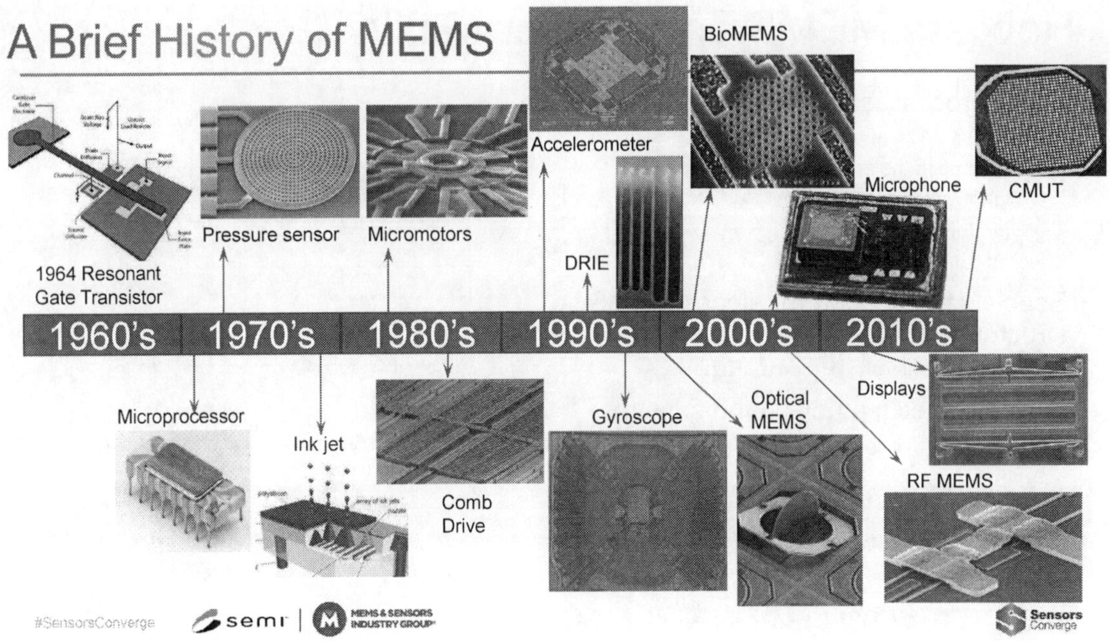
A Brief History of MEMS
1964 Resonant Gate Transistor
Pressure sensor
Micromotors
Accelerometer
DRIE
BioMEMS
Microphone
CMUT
1960's
1970's
1980's
1990's
2000's
2010's
Microprocessor
Ink jet
Comb Drive
Gyroscope
Optical MEMS
Displays
RF MEMS
#SensorsConverge
semi
MEMS & SENSORS INDUSTRY GROUP
Sensors Converge

How do MEMS Transducers Work?

- Goal: Convert physical phenomenon into electrical signal
  - Pressure, acceleration, force, flow, magnetic field, etc.
- MEMS Microphone example:
  - Step 1: Catch the pressure wave
    - All MEMS microphone transducers have a diaphragm that gets moved by the pressure changes
  - Step 2: Convert movement into an electrical signal
    - Capacitive, piezoelectric, piezoresistive, magnetics, etc.
    - Most common is using the diaphragm as one plate in a variable capacitor

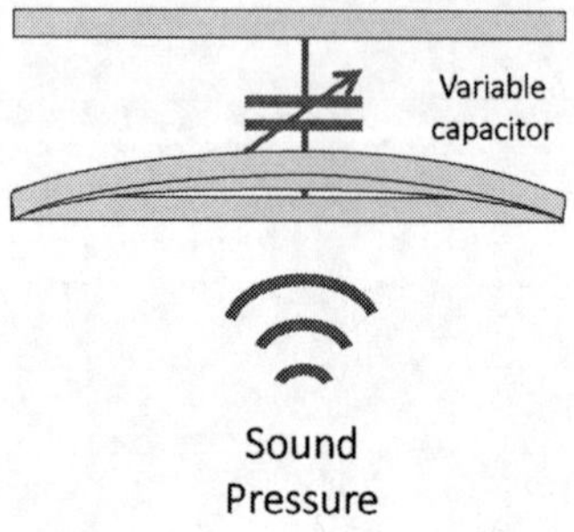

#SensorsConverge semi | MEMS & SENSORS INDUSTRY GROUP Sensors Converge

How are MEMS Transducers Built?

- Same processes used for integrated circuits
  - Deposit a film of material
  - Photomask the areas you want to keep
  - Etch away everything else
  - Strip the photoresist
  - Repeat
- Special step needed to release MEMS so structures can move
  - Sacrificial material "Release Etch"
- Could also etch a hole in the substrate

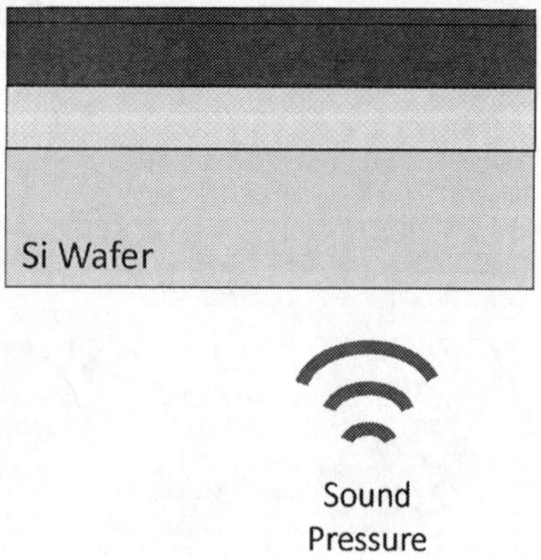

#SensorsConverge semi | MEMS & SENSORS INDUSTRY GROUP Sensors Converge

Designer substrates using SOI with with patterning and bonding technologies

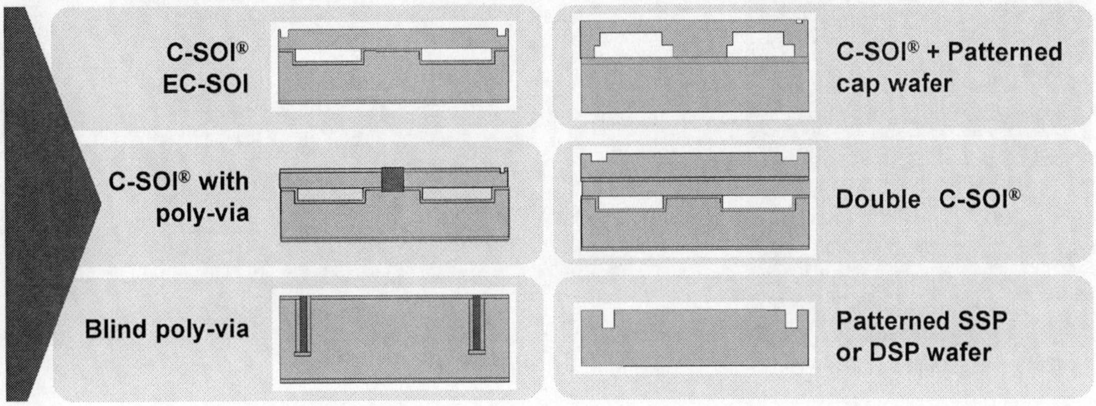

#SensorsConverge semi | MEMS & SENSORS INDUSTRY GROUP OKMETIC Sensors Converge

MEMS Created with Wafer Bonding

Wafer bonding equipment for MEMS

© EV Group (EVG)

Gyroscope cross-section – Schematic of bonding process

EVG®

Gyroscope cross-section – SEM view

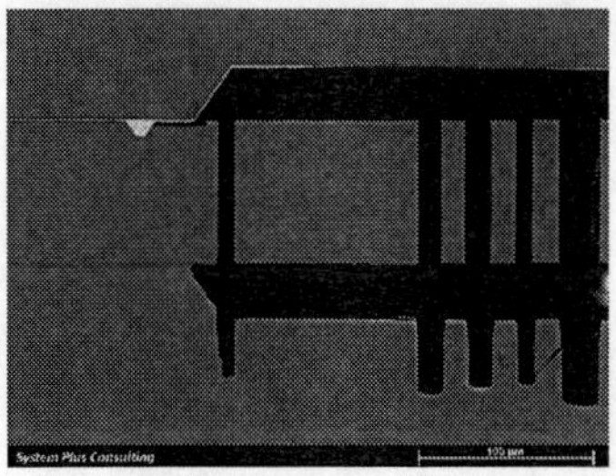

© System Plus Consulting / Courtesy of TDK Tronic's Microsystems

#SensorsConverge semi | MEMS & SENSORS INDUSTRY GROUP Sensors Converge

Alternate Substrate: Glass Wafers

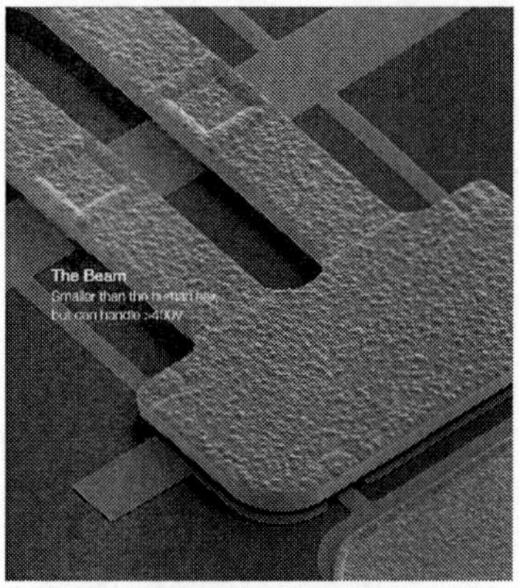

MEMS switch built on glass wafers
Courtesy of Menlo Micro

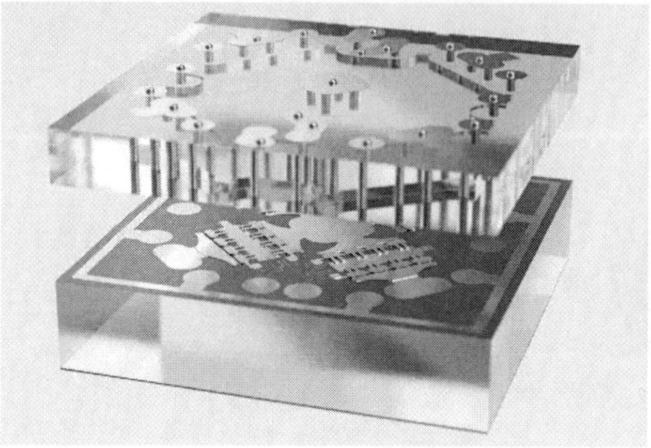

#SensorsConverge semi | MEMS & SENSORS INDUSTRY GROUP Sensors Converge

Deep Reactive Ion Etching of Silicon

High Aspect Ratio
8 x 180 µm trench/TSV
22:1 AR

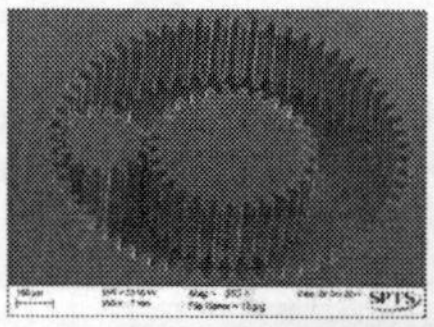

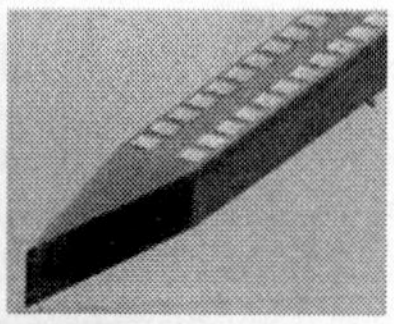

Complex shapes

1 x 40µm trench

Through Wafer Cavities
Microphones, Ink jets,
Capping wafers

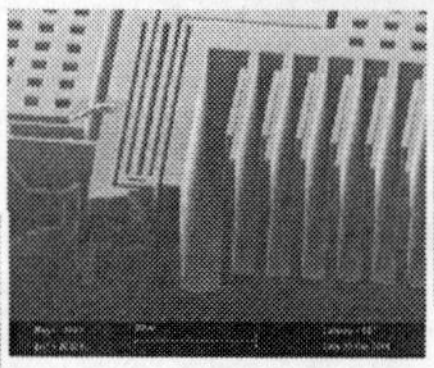

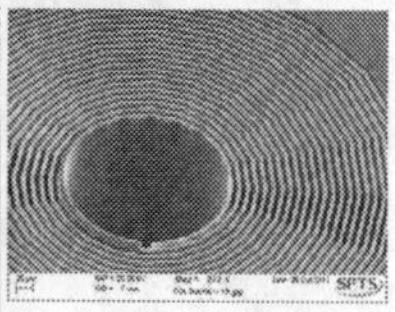

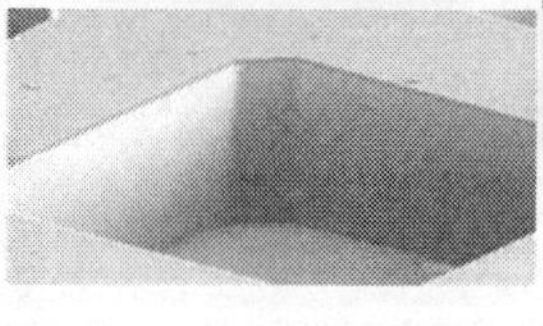

~0.4 µm trenches
~90:1 AR

SPTS
A KLA Company

#SensorsConverge semi | MEMS & SENSORS INDUSTRY GROUP Sensors Converge

Sacrificial Materials

Sacrificial Material	Variant	Release Etch
Silicon Oxide	Thermal SiO_2 PECVD oxide Spin-on glass	Wet etch: HF acid Dry etch: vapor HF
Silicon	Single crystal Polysilicon α-silicon	Wet etch: KOH, EDP Dry etch: XeF_2
Organics	Photoresist Polyimide Epoxy (SU-8)	Wet etch: resist stripper Dry etch: O_2 plasma

Microbolometer released using SPTS XeF_2 Etcher

Photoresist mold as sacrificial layer

#SensorsConverge semi | MEMS & SENSORS INDUSTRY GROUP Sensors Converge

MEMS Fabrications Re-cap

- **Mostly same as IC Fabrication**
  - **Same materials:**
    - silicon, silicon oxide, silicon nitride, aluminum, photoresist, etc.
  - **Same tools and processes:**
    - deposition, lithography, etch, strip
- **Key Process differences**
  - Wafer bonding
  - Etching features into wafers (e.g. DRIE)
  - Release etch
- **Specialty material options**
  - Glass wafers
  - Flexible substrates
  - Piezoelectric materials (e.g. AlN)
- **Key Challenges**
  - High topology
  - Wafer handling post release

#SensorsConverge semi | MEMS & SENSORS INDUSTRY GROUP Sensors Converge

MEMS Sensors Market

- The Global MEMS market:
  - **2020:** $10.92 billion
  - **2026:** $18.88 billion
  - **Forecast period 2021-2026:** CAGR of 8.71%
- Factors influencing the growth of MEMS market:
  - **Automotive:** Driven by advanced driver-assistance systems (ADAS)
  - **Industries and homes:** Growing adoption of automation and smart manufacturing
  - **Healthcare:** Increasing demand for smart consumer electronics and wearable devices
  - **Infrastructure:** increasing popularity of semiconductor IoT and sensor fusion in Smart Cities

ADAS

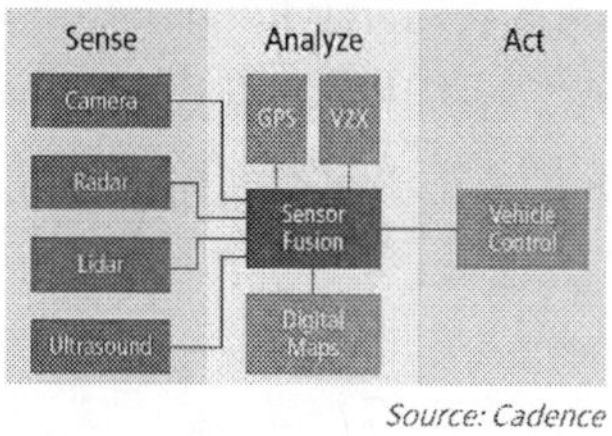

Source: Cadence

Source: MEMS Market - Growth, Trends, COVID-19 Impact, and Forecasts (2021 - 2026)

#SensorsConverge semi | MEMS & SENSORS INDUSTRY GROUP Sensors Converge

Total automotive sensor market will outgrow automotive sales primarily driven by strong growth in ADAS sensors

Estimates pre-covid

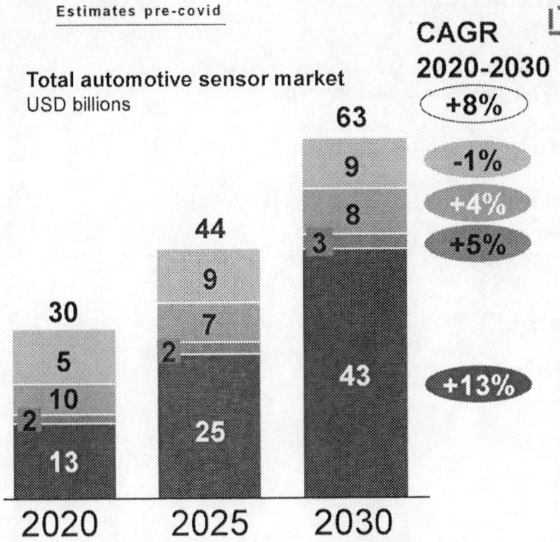

Traditional powertrain sensors with **increase** in line with growth of automotive market
New sensors for electric drives (e.g., current sensors) counterbalance the **decline of combustion sensors**

Increasing number of chassis sensors, e.g., due to **requirements for ADAS/AD systems** and **additional comfort features**, e.g., air suspension or back axle steering

Body sensors with positive outlook due to increase of comfort features offsetting decline of prices of commodity-type sensors

ADAS/safety as strongest growing domain due to adoption of ADAS and AD features
Growth primarily driven by **increasing demand for cameras, radars** and introduction of LiDAR sensors at scale

Source: McKinsey analysis, report: "Mapping the automotive software-and-electronics landscape through 2030"

#SensorsConverge semi | MEMS & SENSORS INDUSTRY GROUP Sensors Converge

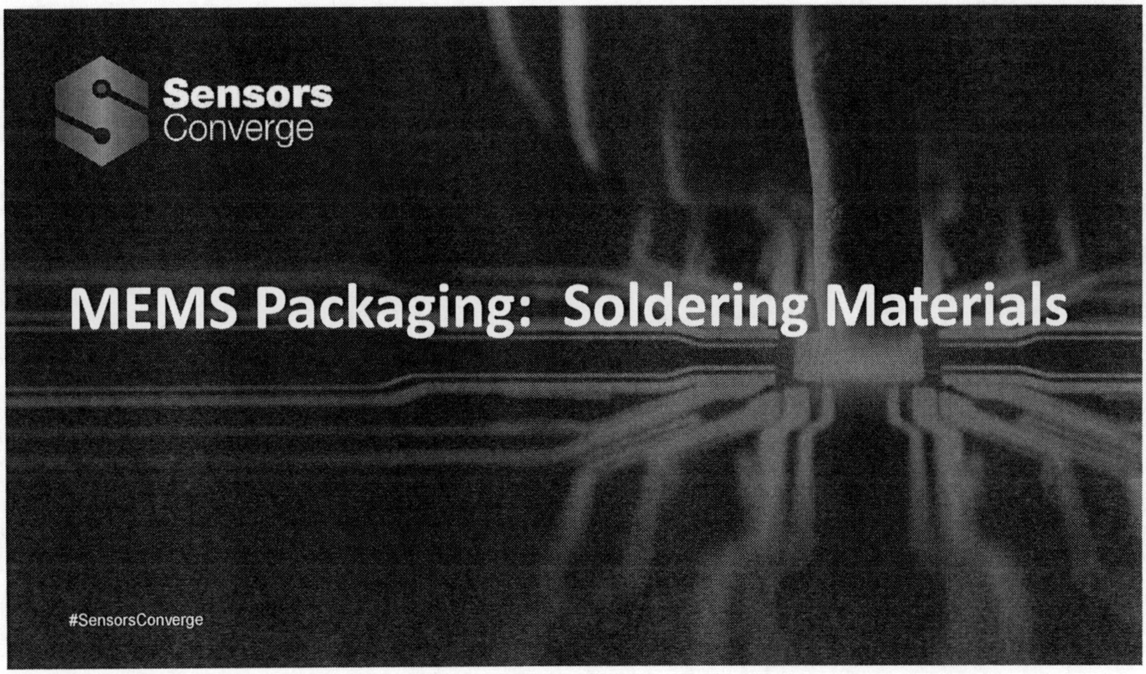

Wide range of materials available

- **Indium (ingots, compounds, paste, spheres, wire, preforms etc.)**
  - Bonds glass, quartz and glazed ceramics
  - Most attractive for sensors that have high I/O counts; in these applications a large number of solder balls need to be formed to inter-connect devices with signal processing logic chips via flip chip bonding, examples: pixel detectors/FPA, IR cameras, SWIR sensors
  - Deposition for wafer-scale indium bumping processes is either through electro-plating or (long-throw) evaporation
  - Also used as part of the active material in compound semiconductor-based architectures (InGaAs for SWIR, InP for some LIDAR)
  - Due to its softness, indium is an ideal material to create a compression seal. It remains malleable and ductile even at cryogenic temperatures
- **Gold-Tin, AuSn alloy (paste, spheres, wire, preforms etc.)**
  - Hermetic sealing, die attach etc.
  - LiDAR, VCSEL TOSA
  - Implantable medical devices
- **Soldering fluxes – liquid, tacky flux**

From One Engineer To Another

INDIUM CORPORATION

Solder Hierachy - Common Alloy List (Paste, spheres, wire, preform)

Alloy Composition	Melting Range (°C)	Comments
52In/48Sn	118	Lowest melting point practical solder
58Bi/42Sn	138	Good thermal fatigue performance; established history
57Bi/42Sb/1Ag	139-140	Ag addition makes alloy less brittle than 58Bi/42Sn
In	157	Soft, ductile metal, bonds to non-metallic, valuable for cryogenic application
77.2Sn/20In/2.8Ag	175-187	Not for use over 100C due to 118C Sn/In eutectic, replacement for SnPb
86.9Sn/10In/3.1Ag	204-205	No Sn/In eutectic problem
90.9Sn/3.8Ag/0.7Cu/3Bi/1.45Sb/0.15Ni	213-222	High reliability SAC alloy
SAC405	217-218	
SAC387	217-219	Original iNEMI recommended SAC alloy
SAC305	217-220	SPVC recommended alloy, most commonly used
96.5SnAg3.5	221	Binary solder, has history of used
SAC105	217-225	Low cost alloy with reasonable thermal cycling
SAC0307	217-227	Low cost SAC alloy
90.6Sn/3.2Ag/0.7Cu/5.5Sb	223-232	High reliability SAC alloy
99.3Sn/0.7Cu	227	Inexpensive; slightly higher temp than SAC
95Sn/5Sb	237-240	High temp Pb-free alloy
90Sn/10Sb	243-257	High temp Pb-free alloy
BiAgX®	260-320	High temp Pb-free alloy
BiAgX-HT®	270-320	High temp Pb-free alloy
80Au/20Sn	280	Strong solder with excellent thermal fatigue resistance, excellent when soldering to gold, high thermal conductivity

Low temp

Mid temp

High temp

From One Engineer To Another

INDIUM CORPORATION

Sensors Converge

MEMS Supply Chain Update

#SensorsConverge

Supply Chain: What is happening?

1. **[9/16/21 - Wall Street Journal] GM Plans to Idle Factories Longer Amid Chip Shortage**
   1. As the pandemic walloped the global economy last year, auto makers cut their production assumptions and underestimated their semiconductor needs when placing orders with suppliers.
   2. More recently, a new wave of Covid-19 infections in Malaysia and other Southeast Asian countries with a major role in chip production has set back manufacturing at factories that were already straining to run at full tilt.
2. [9/17/21] **The bad and (surprisingly) good of the global chip crisis, per industry honchos (Fierce Electronics]**
   1. The chip shortage is a "perfect storm and a perfect storm and crisis for the auto industry," said Jodi Shelton, CEO of the Global Semiconductor Alliance.
   2. "The reason we are here today is there was an acceleration of digitization by seven years from March 2020 to July 2021," she said. "New technologies because of the pandemic came into fruition... with demand for cloud .. and growth in 5G way more rapidly than expected."

#SensorsConverge semi | MEMS & SENSORS INDUSTRY GROUP Sensors Converge

Major Back-End Facilities in Southeast Asia and Their Respective Covid-19 Impact

September 2021 Status:

- 14% of global chip packaging and testing capacity located in Malaysia
- Only 47% of the workforce is currently running in those back-end facilities (as of 1h-Sept-21)

- Outlook: back-end vendors believe that chip output from Malaysia may improve significantly in November and December 2021

Global semi companies	Fab location city	Covid-19 impact	1H-Sep utilization	Remarks
Malaysia			*47%*	
Unisem	Ipoh	Serious	0%	Plant shut down again; to resume to operate on Sep 15
IDT	Penang	Moderate	60%	Operates with 60% man power
ASE P1/P2/P3	Penang	Moderate	60%	Operates with 60% man power
SanDisk WD	Penang	Moderate	40%	Suppliers need to do swab test weekly before enterance, 40% employee allowed to work in office
Intel	Penang	Serious	30%	Production operators and technicians, 30% employee allowed
Renesas Kulim	Penang	Moderate	40%	Production operators and technicians, 40% employee allowed
Resesas Penang	Penang	Moderate	40%	Production operators and technicians, 40% employee allowed
Osram	Penang	Moderate	40%	Production operators and technicians, 40% employee allowed
Ibiden	Penang	Moderate	60%	Operates with 60% man power
NXP KL	Kuala Lumpur	Moderate	60%	Operates with 60% man power
Renesas KL	Kuala Lumpur	Moderate	60%	Operates with 60% man power
Amkor	Kuala Lumpur	Moderate	60%	Operates with 60% man power
On-Semi	Seremban	Moderate	60%	Operates with 60% man power
Nexperia	Seremban	Moderate	60%	Operates with 60% man power
Infineon	Melaka	Serious	40%	Plant shut down on Aug 24
Vishay	Malaka	Serious	60%	Plant shut down; resumed to operate on Aug 11
Micron	Muar	Moderate	50%	Operates with 50% man power
STMicro	Muar	Serious	40%	Plant shut down; resumed to operate on Aug 18
Denso	Bangi	Moderate	40%	Production operators and technicians, 40% employee allowed
Hitachi Chemical	Shah Alam	Moderate	40%	Production operators and technicians, 40% employee allowed
Singapore			*80%*	
Micron Singapore	Bendemeer	Moderate	80%	Suppliers need to do ART weekly before entrance
Thailand			*80%*	
Microchip Thailand	Chachengsao	Moderate	80%	Suppliers need to do ART weekly before entrance
Hana Ayutthaya	Ayutthaya	Light	80%	Operates with 80% man power
Vietnam			*70%*	
Vishay	Hanoi	Moderate	50%	Operates with 50% manpower but does not accept vendors from other province go in
USI VN	Hanoi	Light	80%	Operates with 80% manpower but does not accept vendors from other province go in
Intel	Ho Chi Minh	Moderate	80%	Does not accept vendor in quarantine area; only accept when negative testing

Source: Morgan Stanley Research Report 9/14/21

#SensorsConverge semi | MEMS & SENSORS INDUSTRY GROUP Sensors Converge

Fundamental reality: semiconductor supply chain

Current Situation

- Idiosyncratic supply issues continue mostly related to COVID-19
- But not all:
  - Samsung Austin fab Feb-21 shutdown due to weather
    - $268 million product lost (weeks long shutdown, Yield hit on product when power was lost)
  - trade restrictions with China (ongoing)
- Overall effect: create both a ***real*** shortage and a ***general sense of*** shortage in the semiconductor supply chain.

Outlook

- Short Term (Sept-Nov): production of cars, computers, phones, and other devices (e.g. IOT) are negatively impacted
- Longer Term (Dec-21 +) production issues begin to ease.

#SensorsConverge semi | MEMS & SENSORS INDUSTRY GROUP Sensors Converge

Supply Chain Solution: Resilinc Software
resilinc
MAKING GLOBAL SUPPLY CHAINS RESILIENT, SUSTAINABLE, FAIR AND SECURE
150+ enterprise customers
4.2M+ news feeds monitored in 190 countries and 108 languages
Over 95% of global suppliers mapped
550K+ suppliers at 750K+ sites
Supply Chain Visibility Delivers Exponential ROI
People, Process Technology Alignment
Optimize inventory, Design products for Resiliency,
RESILIENT
EVENTWATCH
RISKSHIELD
MULTI-TIER
PREDICTIVE
End-to-End (E2E) Supplier Performance
Predict supplier delivery and price performance, lead time and inventory visibility
Proactive Visibility & Mitigation
Assess & mitigate supplier risks with deep network mapping and visibility
Supplier Monitoring & Assessments
24x7x365 monitoring, Scorecard, Collaboration
AWARE
$400,000-$2,000,000
PROACTIVE
$1,000,000
$2,000,000
INTEGRATED
$10,000,000
Hundreds of Millions in Long Term Savings & Value*
Technology
Data & Visibility
People Process Alignment & Maturity
*assumes mapping covers all suppliers, and best practices like inventory optimization, supplier mitigation, design for resiliency are implemented

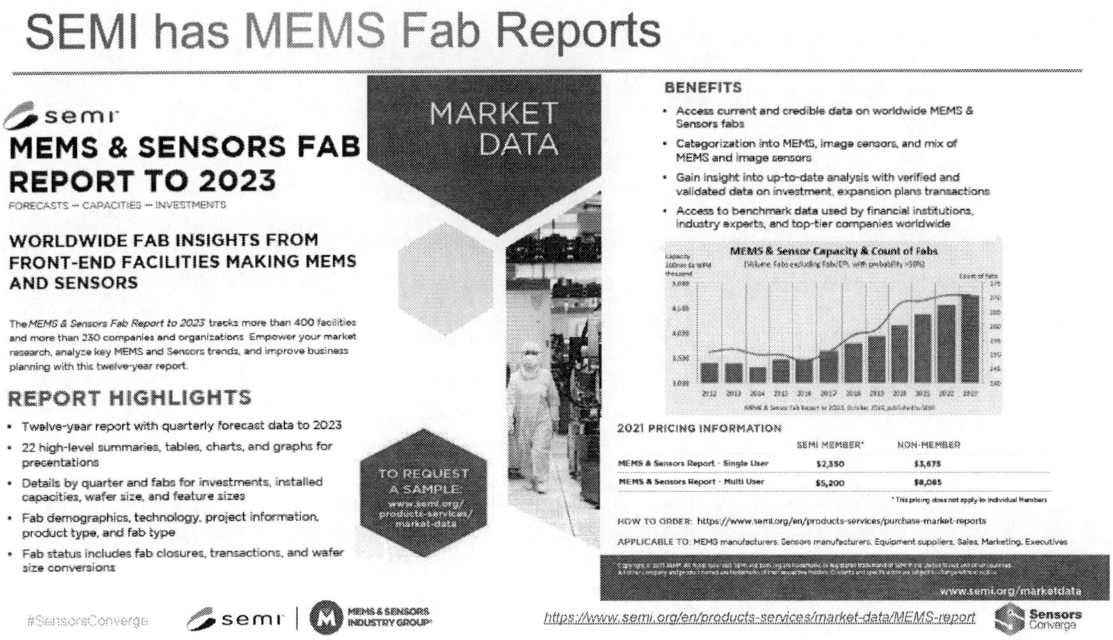
SEMI has MEMS Fab Reports
semi
MEMS & SENSORS FAB REPORT TO 2023
FORECASTS — CAPACITIES — INVESTMENTS
MARKET DATA
WORLDWIDE FAB INSIGHTS FROM FRONT-END FACILITIES MAKING MEMS AND SENSORS
The MEMS & Sensors Fab Report to 2023 tracks more than 400 facilities and more than 230 companies and organizations. Empower your market research, analyze key MEMS and Sensors trends, and improve business planning with this twelve-year report.
REPORT HIGHLIGHTS
• Twelve-year report with quarterly forecast data to 2023
• 22 high-level summaries, tables, charts, and graphs for presentations
• Details by quarter and fabs for investments, installed capacities, wafer size, and feature sizes
• Fab demographics, technology, project information, product type, and fab type
• Fab status includes fab closures, transactions, and wafer size conversions
TO REQUEST A SAMPLE: www.semi.org/products-services/market-data
BENEFITS
• Access current and credible data on worldwide MEMS & Sensors fabs
• Categorization into MEMS, image sensors, and mix of MEMS and image sensors
• Gain insight into up-to-date analysis with verified and validated data on investment, expansion plans transactions
• Access to benchmark data used by financial institutions, industry experts, and top-tier companies worldwide
MEMS & Sensor Capacity & Count of Fabs
2021 PRICING INFORMATION
SEMI MEMBER*
NON-MEMBER
MEMS & Sensors Report - Single User $2,350 $3,675
MEMS & Sensors Report - Multi User $5,200 $8,085
* This pricing does not apply to Individual Members
HOW TO ORDER: https://www.semi.org/en/products-services/purchase-market-reports
APPLICABLE TO: MEMS manufacturers, Sensors manufacturers, Equipment suppliers, Sales, Marketing, Executives
www.semi.org/marketdata
#SensorsConverge
semi
MEMS & SENSORS INDUSTRY GROUP
https://www.semi.org/en/products-services/market-data/MEMS-report
Sensors Converge

Summary

- **SEMI MSIG**
  - **Helping our member companies sensorize the world**
  - **Providing R&D funding for position, navigation, and timing (PNT)**
    - New $5M funding to be announced this Fall
- **MEMS Fabrication Technology**
  - **Similar to IC manufacturing (materials and equipment)**
  - **Fundamental differences: DRIE, sacrificial layers, glass and flexible substrates**
- **MEMS Market & Supply Chain**
  - **Market rapidly growing due to auto ADAS, Smart City (and building) Infrastructure & IoT, Healthcare, and Smart Manufacturing**
  - **Supply Chain Issues:**
    - COVID-19
    - Poor planning
    - Large demand: massive digitalization acceleration of technology caused by COVID-19

Backup

#SensorsConverge semi | MEMS & SENSORS INDUSTRY GROUP Sensors Converge

Outline

#SensorsConverge semi | MEMS & SENSORS INDUSTRY GROUP Sensors Converge

Outline

#SensorsConverge semi | MEMS & SENSORS INDUSTRY GROUP Sensors Converge

Abstract

Although early MEMS manufacturing originally leveraged existing semiconductor processes, there are now unique differences in virtually every step of the manufacturing process. Additionally, the MEMS Market for Sensors is growing rapidly, and the MEMS supply chain is trying to keep up. Growth areas such as sensors for Smart Cities, automotive applications, smart medical, environmental water and air monitoring, and bio-MEMS are adding complexity to the supply chain. The MEMS assembly and packaging presents additional complexity, and it is different and more complex than that used in semiconductor ASICs. This presentation will discuss the MEMS manufacturing process, materials, substrates, packaging, and specialized equipment used in the MEMS supply chain. It will feature slides from SEMI member companies that help to give a clear perspective on the supply chain challenges and some of the solutions.

2021 MEMS & Sensors Executive Congress (MSEC)

Our signature MSIG Event in the US will be LIVE in San Diego this year!

- **Who should attend:**
  MSEC 2021 is designed for senior executives across the MEMS and sensors supply chain and adjacent industries.
- **Date:** October 11-13, 2021
- **Location:** Marriott Coronado Island, San Diego, CA
- **Multiple socially-distanced face to face networking opportunities!**

Offering $500 off – come visit us at booth #435

Honeywell
ST life.augmented
iSono Health
RENESAS
infineon
BOSCH
U))) SOUND
TELEDYNE DALSA Everywhereyoulook™ Part of the Teledyne Imaging Group
MEMS

https://www.semi.org/en/connect/events/mems-sensors-executive-congress-msec

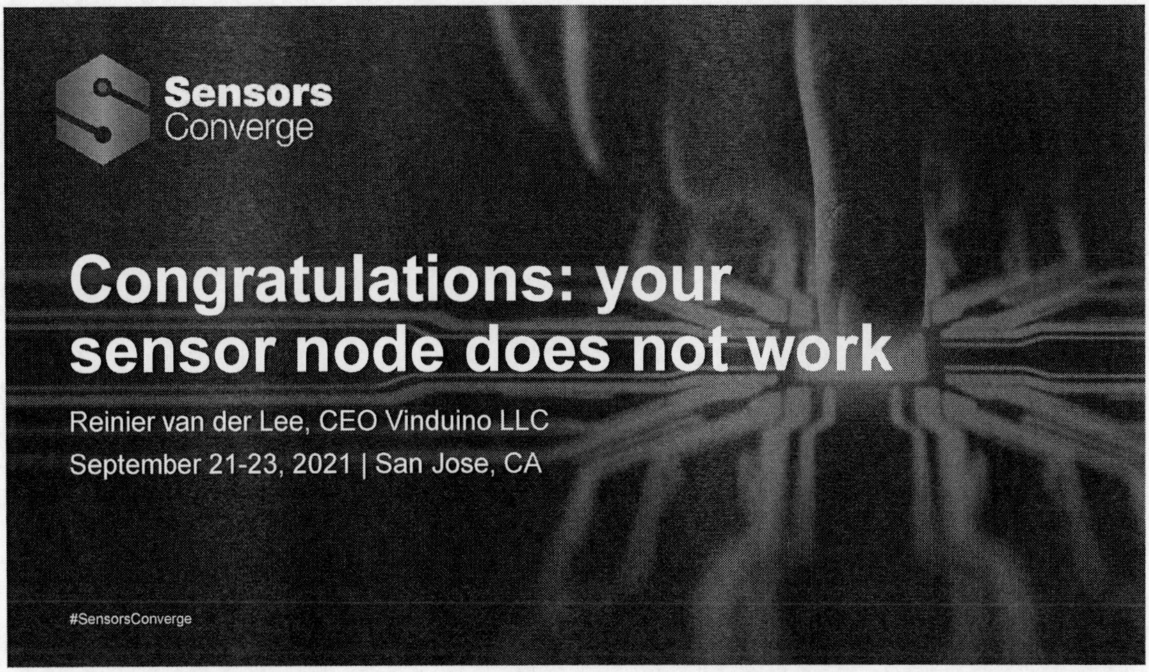
Sensors
Converge
Congratulations: your sensor node does not work
Reinier van der Lee, CEO Vinduino LLC
September 21-23, 2021 | San Jose, CA
#SensorsConverge

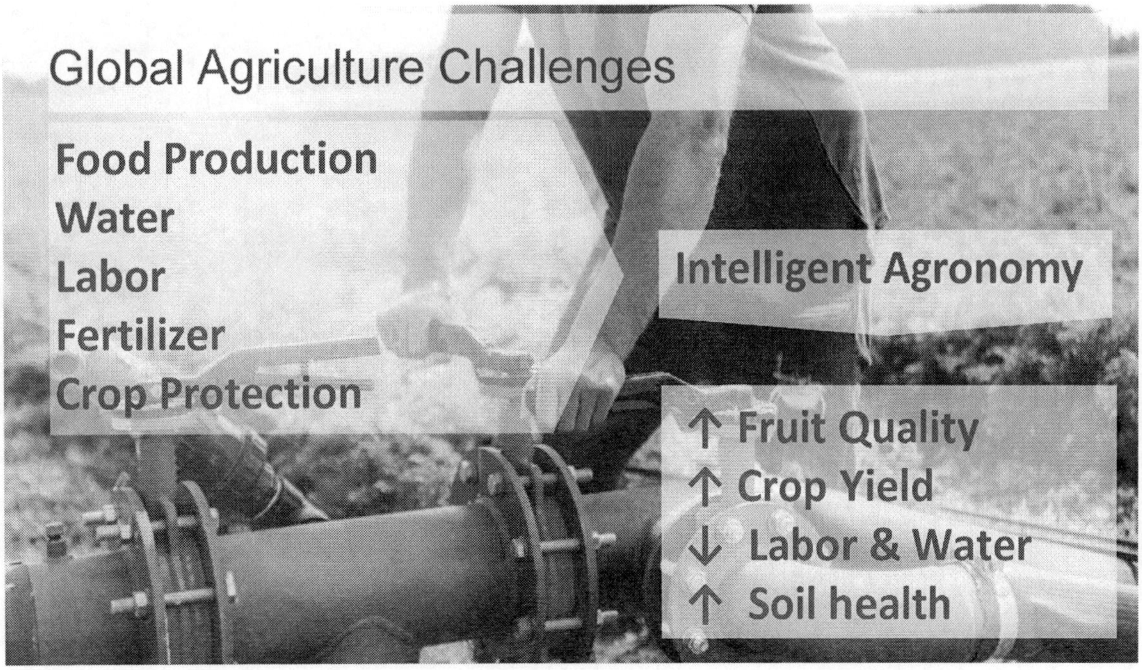
Global Agriculture Challenges
Food Production
Water
Labor
Fertilizer
Crop Protection
Intelligent Agronomy
↑ Fruit Quality
↑ Crop Yield
↓ Labor & Water
↑ Soil health

INTELLIGENT AGRONOMY SYSTEM

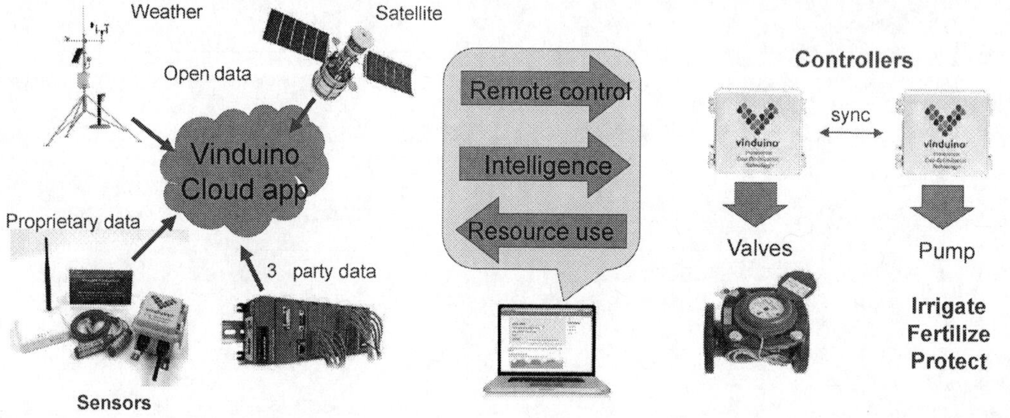

#SensorsConverge

Sensors Converge

LoRaWAN SUPERIOR FOR AG

GOOD

- 10-mile range, multi-path
- Low crop attenuation: no poles
- Low Power: small battery/solar
- Star topology: sleep mode
- Encrypted data: secure control

BAD

- Complexity, No LoRa analyzers
- Sub-optimal for control

UGLY

- LoRaWAN = developing standard
- Different frequency bands per country

#SensorsConverge

Sensors Converge

BRINGUP FIRST NETWORK

- Update and load software to gateway (luckily there was an installation script)
- 1 gen gateways did not have WiFi
- Connect gateway to LoRa provider (TheThingsNetwork)
- Register and connect your application @ LoRa provider
- Register your sensor node, and connect

..... nothing ......

First generation Lora gateway
Linux admin skills to setup

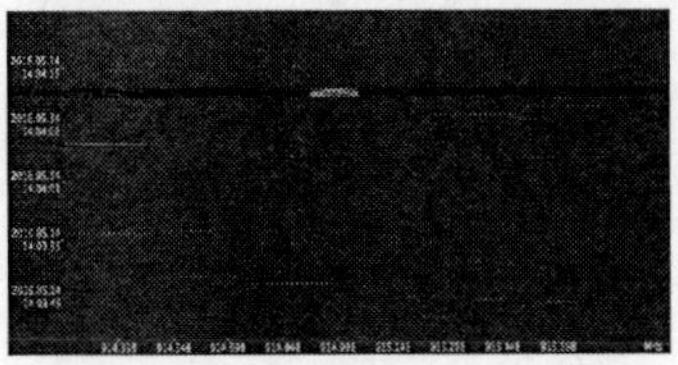

Checking radio signals with SDR (software defined radio):
Gateway and sensor node were transmitting and receiving on different frequency sub-bands

.... After two months SUCCESS!.....

Sensors Converge

ARDUINO MKR 1300, DEJA VU

- Arduino micro controller + Murata LoRaWAN
- Standard programming allows:
  - US-915 all channels (64 +8)
  - US-915 hybrid (sub-band 1, 8 channels)
- TheThingsNetwork uses sub-band 2, cannot connect
- Solved after 2 years:
- https://github.com/arduino/mkrwan1300-fw/
- modem.sendMask("ff000001f000ffff00020000");

"Hidden" library command

Sensors Converge

LoRaWAN ACTUATOR CONTROL

- LoRaWAN CLASS-A node:

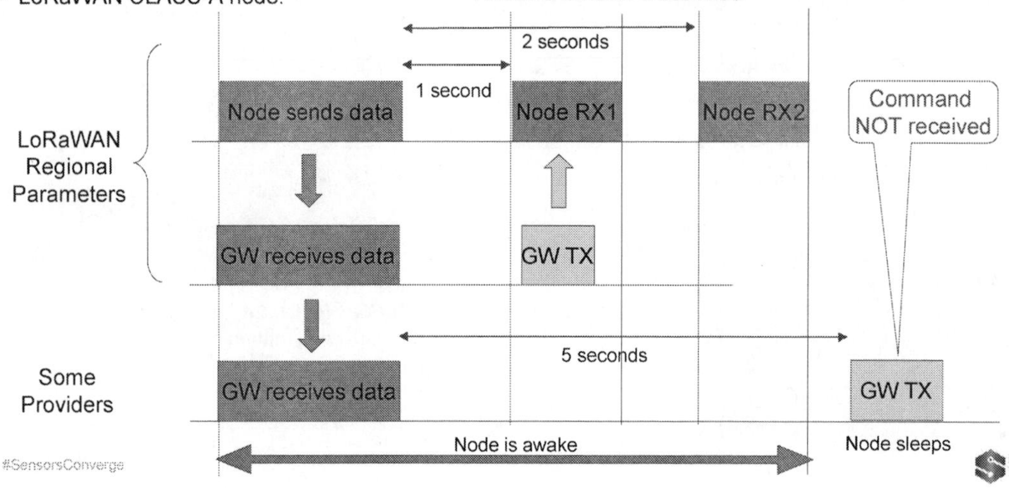

#SensorsConverge

Sensors Converge

LoRaWAN PROPAGATION

- Beyond line of sight
- Reflection
- Knife-Edge diffraction*

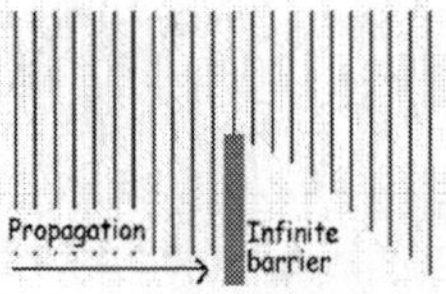

* http://www.mike-willis.com

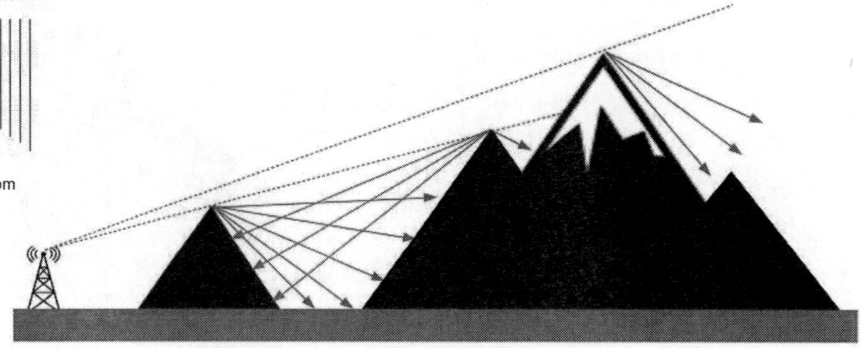

#SensorsConverge

Sensors Converge

LAST BUT NOT LEAST: ANTENNAS

- Range is all about the antenna
- Indoor gateway antennas = limited range
- Outdoor gateway antenna:
  - Omni-directional
  - Directional (beam)
- Node antenna performance
  - Radiation pattern
  - Unified Polarization (vertical = default)
  - De-tuning (enclosure, metal in proximity)

  - Consider the whole frequency band
  - Use an antenna analyzer!!

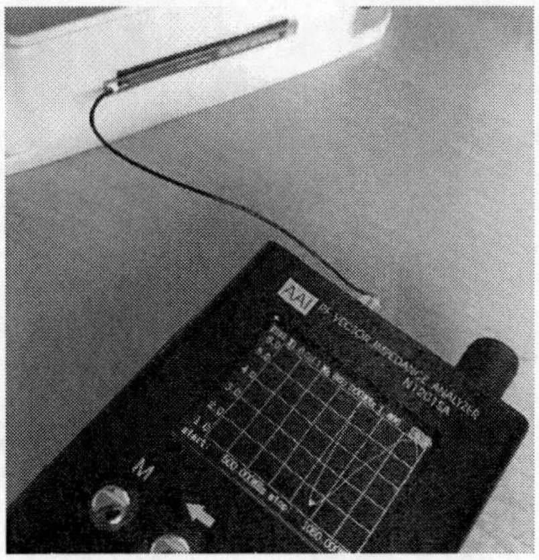

#SensorsConverge

Sensors Converge

Sensors Converge

Congratulations: your sensor node does not work

Reinier van der Lee, CEO Vinduino LLC
reinier@vinduino.com

#SensorsConverge

Single Pair Ethernet Reliable Sensor Connectivity for Smart Buildings

SPEAKERS

Ronna Davis — Strategy and Technology — COMMSCOPE

Bob Voss — Senior Principal Engineer — PANDUIT

TIA SPEC Single Pair Ethernet Consortium

TIA SPEC Single Pair Ethernet Consortium

Buildings and Connected Devices

The number of buildings worldwide is going to **DOUBLE** by **2060**

The number of connected devices will reach **75 BILLION IN THE NEXT 4 YEARS.**

5x More data will be created & processed outside the data center

BUILDING SYSTEMS CONVERGENCE

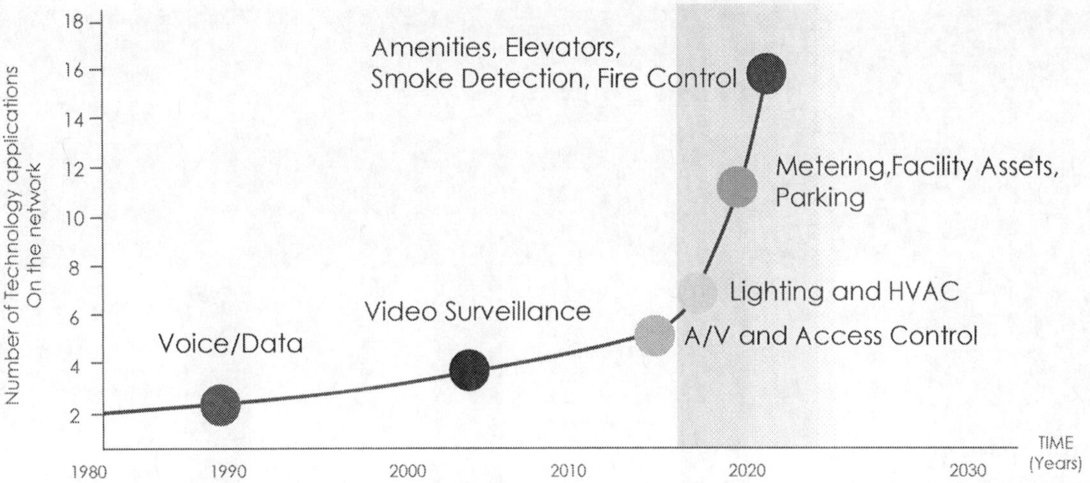

THE SHIFT FROM DISPARATE SYSTEMS TO OPEN PLATFORMS AND UNIFORM COMMUNICATION PROTOCOLS

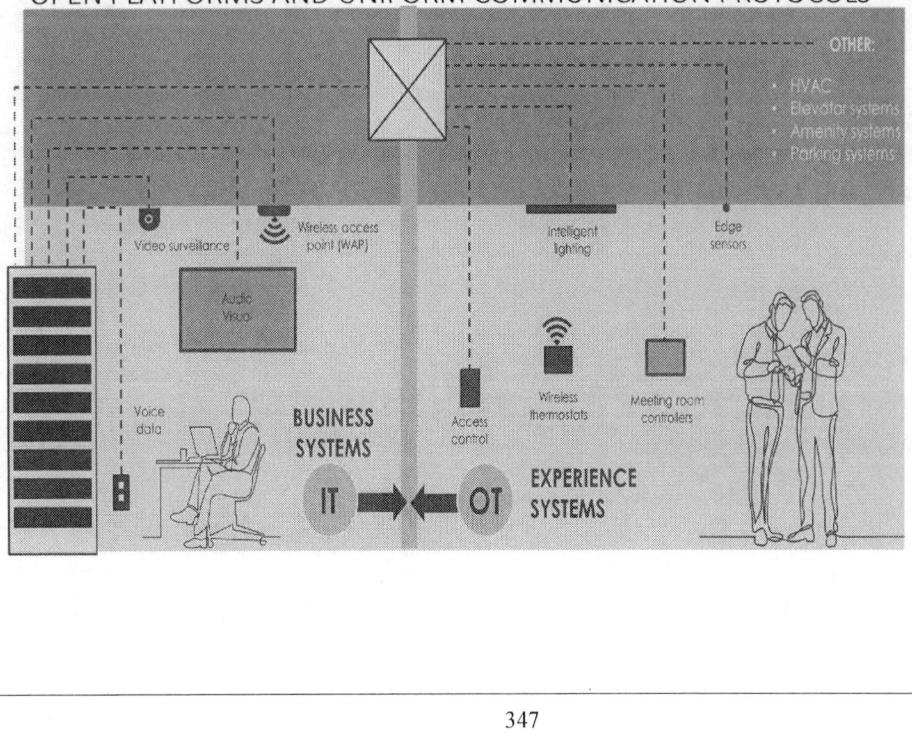

Why Single Pair Ethernet ?

TIA SPEC Single Pair Ethernet Consortium

It's about the DATA!

Accessing it.

Securing it.

Using it.

Need for a common communications protocol with a standardized interface

It's about the POWER!

OT devices need power

Batteries aren't scalable

OT devices are critical

PoE has significantly increased the availability of real-world deployable technologies for IT, Security and AV. SPE will do that for BAS.

It's about the TRAINING!

Skilled Labor Shortage

Disparate Systems

Knowledge Transfer

Standardization of infrastructure, connectivity and communication across multiple building systems has the potential to provide significant improvements in design velocity and installation.

It's about ADOPTION!

Expectations are changing.

OT wants the benefits of the IT evolution

System Optimization- SECURITY

Predictive Maintenance

Software Upgradability

Cloud Connected

Converged Management Layers

Single Pair Ethernet (SPE)

Ethernet with power over 2 Twisted Conductors (Single Pair) of cable and associated connectivity hardware and electronics.

- Low Power / Low Data *
- Developed to support IoT and OT conversion to common Ethernet communication protocol.
- Initially developed for Industrial Automation and Automotive Markets
- Not intended to replace 4 Pair but we should expect some overlap.
- More design flexibility than 4 Pair Ethernet to support various design conventions in Building Automation.
- Multiple connectors allowed under the standard. The -1 connector shown, it is the preferred connector for building IP20 applications because of its' familiar LC style, installation simplicity & field terminations.

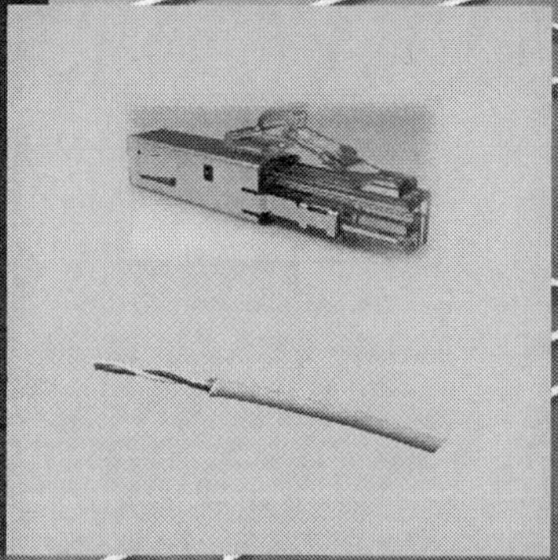

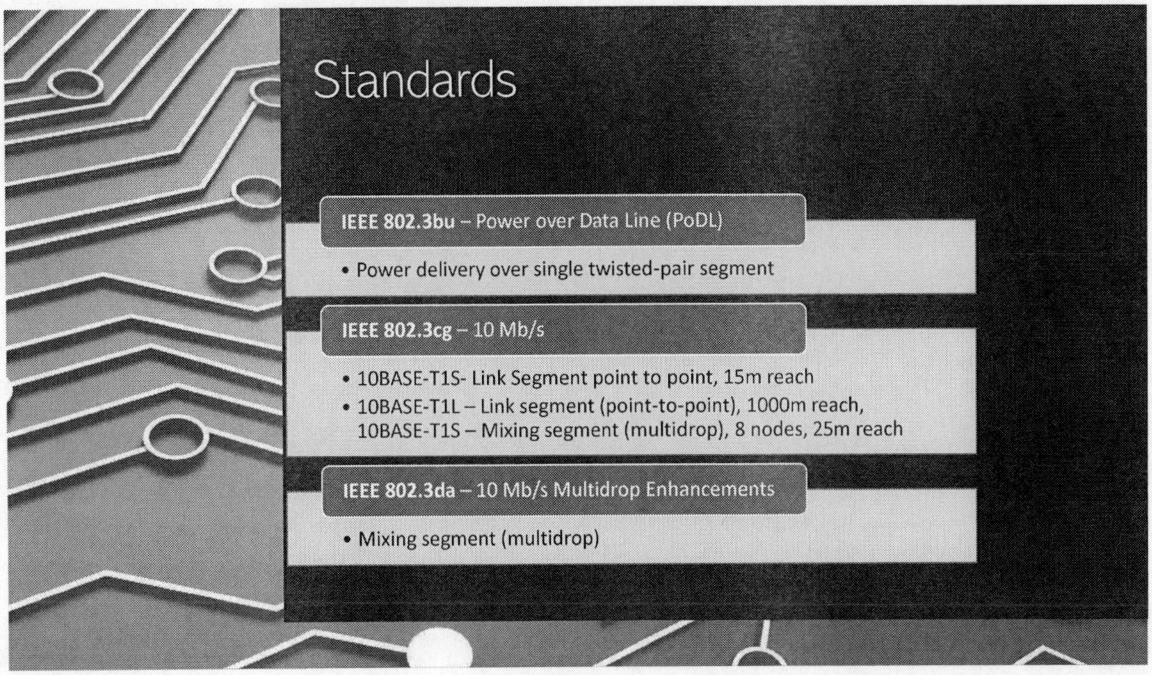
Standards
IEEE 802.3bu – Power over Data Line (PoDL)
• Power delivery over single twisted-pair segment
IEEE 802.3cg – 10 Mb/s
• 10BASE-T1S- Link Segment point to point, 15m reach
• 10BASE-T1L – Link segment (point-to-point), 1000m reach, 10BASE-T1S – Mixing segment (multidrop), 8 nodes, 25m reach
IEEE 802.3da – 10 Mb/s Multidrop Enhancements
• Mixing segment (multidrop)

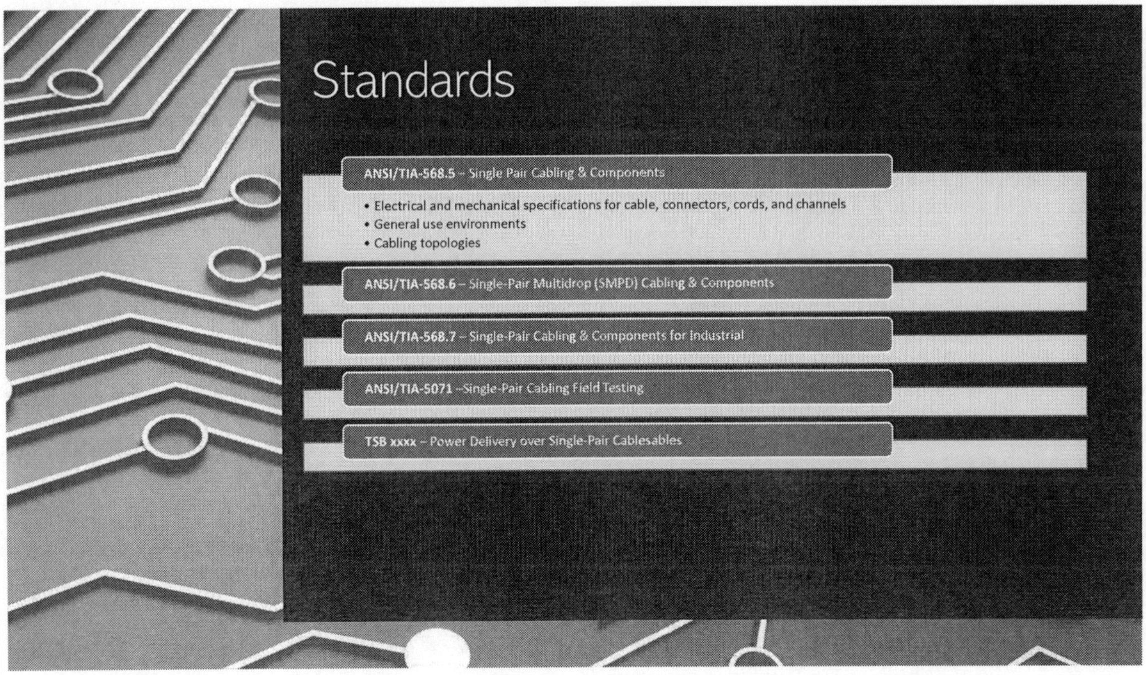
Standards
ANSI/TIA-568.5 – Single Pair Cabling & Components
• Electrical and mechanical specifications for cable, connectors, cords, and channels
• General use environments
• Cabling topologies
ANSI/TIA-568.6 – Single-Pair Multidrop (SMPD) Cabling & Components
ANSI/TIA-568.7 – Single-Pair Cabling & Components for Industrial
ANSI/TIA-5071 –Single-Pair Cabling Field Testing
TSB xxxx – Power Delivery over Single-Pair Cablesables

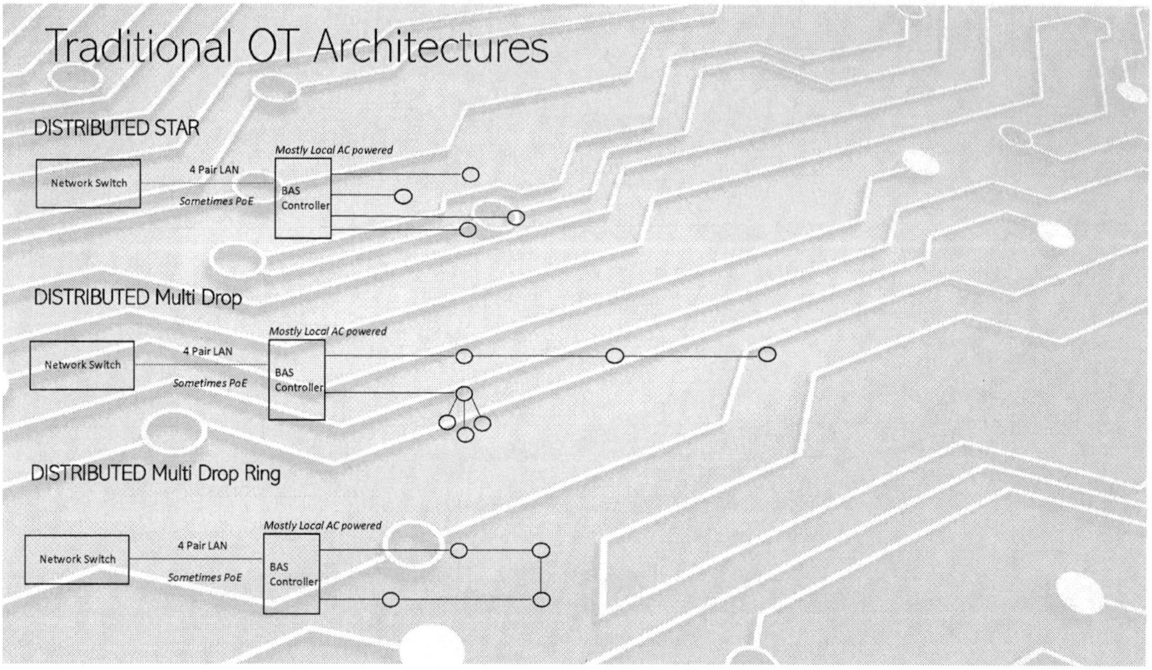
Traditional OT Architectures
DISTRIBUTED STAR
Mostly Local AC powered
Network Switch
4 Pair LAN
Sometimes PoE
BAS Controller
DISTRIBUTED Multi Drop
Mostly Local AC powered
Network Switch
4 Pair LAN
Sometimes PoE
BAS Controller
DISTRIBUTED Multi Drop Ring
Mostly Local AC powered
Network Switch
4 Pair LAN
Sometimes PoE
BAS Controller

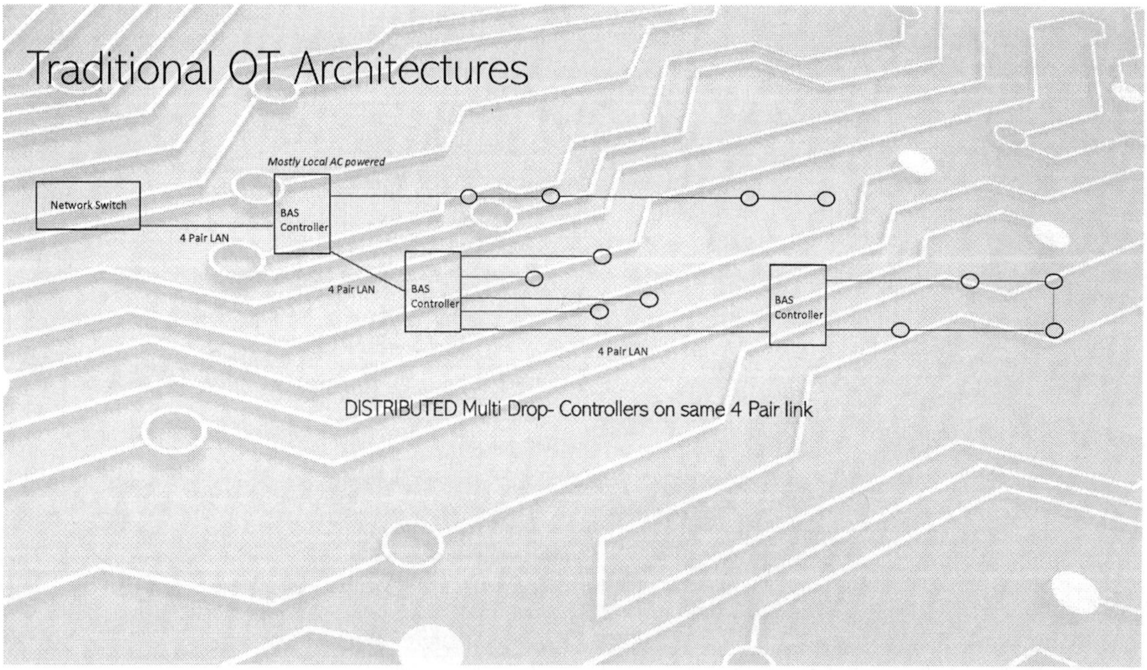
Traditional OT Architectures
Mostly Local AC powered
Network Switch
4 Pair LAN
BAS Controller
4 Pair LAN
BAS Controller
BAS Controller
4 Pair LAN
DISTRIBUTED Multi Drop- Controllers on same 4 Pair link

Most Likely SPE Architectures

STAR AND DISTRIBUTED STAR

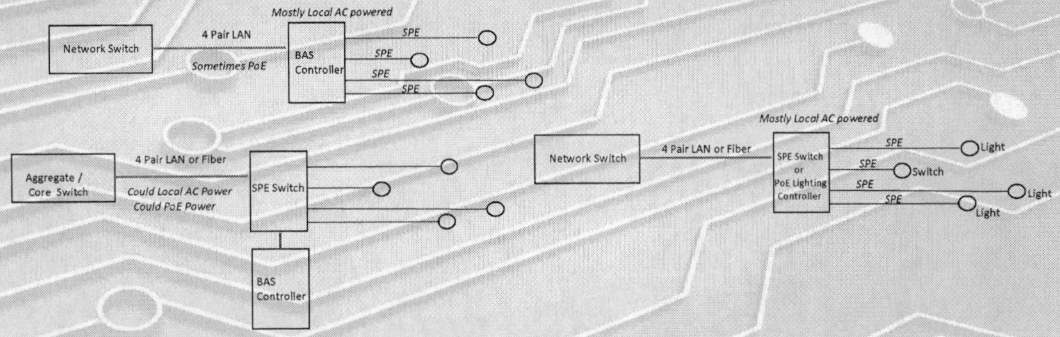

DISTRIBUTED Multi Drop

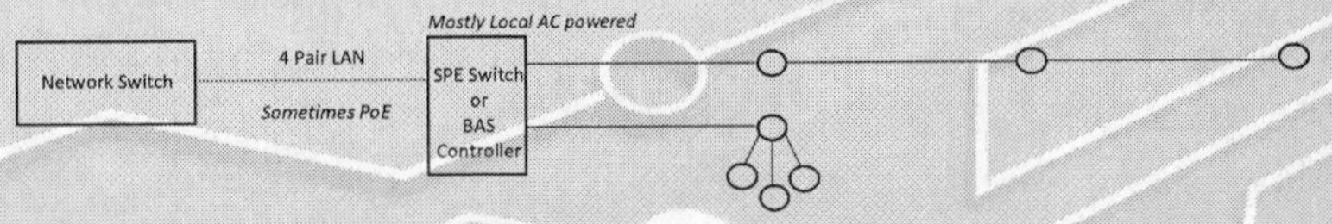

Single Pair Ethernet vs. Batteries for Sensors

TIA SPEC Single Pair Ethernet Consortium

- 75 billion connected devices around the world by 2025
  - These devices will all need power and data connections
- Batteries may last years, but the replacement effort is significant
  - Thousands of batteries, many behind walls or in other hard to reach locations
- Environmental impact
  - Single-use batteries must be disposed of responsibly
  - Not aligned with goals of reduced carbon footprint and sustainability

Power delivery over SPE is easier to maintain, more reliable, and more sustainable than batteries

12

Single Pair Ethernet vs. 4 Pair Ethernet for Sensors

- 50% more dense than RJ-45
- Low Power Low Data
- Support for Longer Distances
- Multidrop Capabilities

Parameter	4-pair  	Single Pair  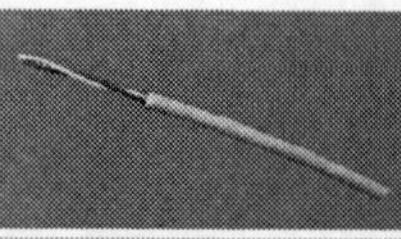
Data Rate	Up to 10 Gb/s (10GBASE-T)	10 Mb/s at 1000 m
Power Levels	Up to 71 W (PoE++)	7 W to 52 W *depending on cable length*
Reach	Up to 100 m	Up to 1000 m
Connector Type	RJ45	Modified LC

Small, Simplified and Standardized

- Small form factor makes it perfect for sensors. Less than ½ the size of RJ-45.
- Simplified connector is easy to field install.
- Standardization eliminates proprietary and non-compatible interfaces
- Standardization gives confidence to deploy for performance & safety

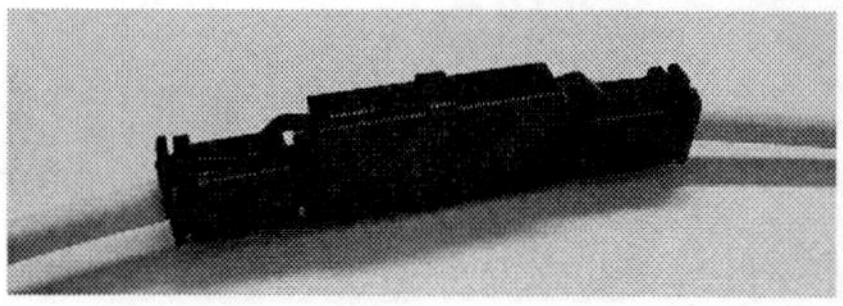

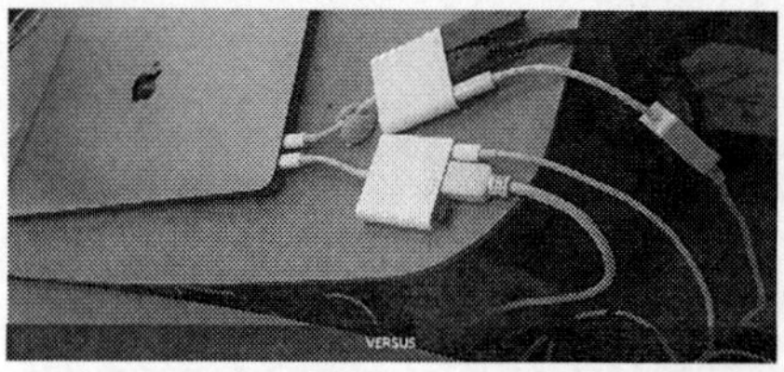

Delivering on SPE
• Roadmap
• Collaboration
• Industry Support
GO
TIA SPEC
Single Pair Ethernet Consortium

Thank you!

Sensors Converge

When Does Energy Harvesting Make Sense?

September 21-23, 2021 | San Jose, CA

#SensorsConverge

PowerFilm Brief

We design and manufacture custom solar cells, modules, panels and power solutions for energy harvesting and portable power applications using proprietary thin-film or high efficiency crystalline PV technology.

With over 200 staff years of engineering experience, we have provided rugged and high performance solar solutions across a wide range IoT, transportation, military, and consumer markets.

We take great pride in supporting our customers with the highest quality solar solutions. Located in Ames, Iowa, our products are completely designed and manufactured in the United States.

#SensorsConverge

Sensors Converge

Energy Harvesting (EH): 1000ft Level

Wiki Definition: The process by which energy derived from external sources is captured and stored for small, wireless autonomous devices, like those used in wearable electronics and wireless sensor networks.

PF Ext. Definition: A solar panel or PV module that is designed to supplement power to a specific device, often integrated into the product itself. Solutions are typically in the uW or mW range but can reach up to 100W+.

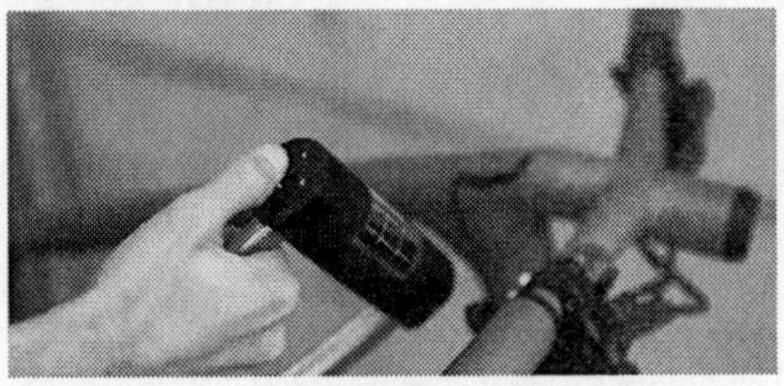

Smart bike lock. Maintenance free theft detection and crash notifications.

Custom Monocrystalline Panel For Refrigerated Trucking Unit

#SensorsConverge

Sensors Converge

What Does Energy Harvesting Mean for IoT?

- Minimal energy that solves massive battery problems.
- Minute power equals minute maintenance.
- Small energy that makes large networks of devices last forever.
- A negligible amount energy can significantly reduce e-waste.
- Devices have smaller batteries and bigger power budgets.
- Cool solar stuff that sometimes seems like magic.

#SensorsConverge

Sensors Converge

The Problem

Battery Life

Battery life is often measured in months, rather than years.

Dead batteries must be recharged or replaced, putting a heavy maintenance burden and cost on end users and hindering wider spread implementation of large IoT networks.

Limited Power

IoT solution providers are forced to cut features or reduce functionality based on the limited capacity of a battery.

Devices are also unable to recover from unexpected high power events, such as firmware updates and loss of connection.

Battery Bulk

Batteries take up significant physical space compared to the electronics they power.

This is problematic for wearables and other low profile electronics where reducing bulk volume is critical.

#SensorsConverge

Sensors Converge

Energy Harvesting Solution

Extend Battery Life with a perpetual source of light energy from outdoor or indoor, artificial sources.

Expand Functionality and Resilience with increased continual power available.

Enable Compact Low Profile Electronics with thin, flexible, high performance PV material.

#SensorsConverge

Sensors Converge

When Does Energy Harvesting Make Sense?

Answer: A complex function of value added, return on investment, and environmental compatibility -- You know it when you see it.

Key Indicators

- Significant extension of meaningful device lifetime.
- Available power is greater than power consumption.
- Significant reduction in battery related maintenance.
- Low power devices in bright environments.
- Significant reduction in e-waste.
- Enables significant increase in device functionality or resilience.
- Applications that have low price elasticity.

#SensorsConverge

Sensors Converge

When Does Energy Harvesting NOT Make Sense?

Answer: When value added does not justify increased cost.

Key Indicators

- Power available is negligible compared to device consumption.
- Device can reach 5-10 year battery life w/o energy harvesting.
- Applications with high price elasticity.
- EH for general power generation purposes. E.g. cellphones, battery banks, grid-tie, EVs.
- Devices that are not designed for low power / power efficiency. E.g. WiFi, wireless charging.
- Devices where PV integration is difficult.

#SensorsConverge

Sensors Converge

Putting Together an Energy Harvesting Solution

Case 1	Case 2	Case 3

Inventory Tracking	Pet Tracker	Electronic Price Tag

#SensorsConverge

Sensors Converge

Inventory Tracking Gateways

Application:

BLE gateways placed periodically throughout warehouse to track tagged items. Lights and tracking devices required to be on 24/7.

Setup:

- PV integrated on device enclosure installs directly under lights to support the high power consumption of the gateway.
- PV sized and paired with a supercapacitor to power the unit directly.
- No battery and no PMIC = cost savings.

Conclusion

Energy harvesting is a great fit for this application where a primary battery solution is not viable. Simplified installation does not require an electrician to route wire power to the unit, more than offsetting the cost of the solar solution. In this mild indoor environment, devices will easily achieve 10yr+ lifetimes.

- ✓ **No electrician needed for wired power!**
- ✓ **Significant increase in battery life compared to primary battery solution.**
- ✓ **No battery = No Maintenance!**
- ✓ **10yr+ estimated device lifetime!**
- ✓ **Low price elasticity!**

#SensorsConverge

Sensors Converge

Pet Tracker

Application:

Wearable device allowing end users to track and monitor there pets in case of emergency as well as collect data on everyday health and activity. Device is exposed to outdoor lighting on a regular basis and is relatively low power. Similar non-solar products have battery life of days to weeks.

Setup:

- Flexible single cell PV module embedded into device fabric.
- Single cell design eliminates shadowing effects and maximizes power collection.
- EH PMIC efficienctly boost low PV voltage to charge the Li battery.
- Lithium battery sized to last up to 2 weeks without solar input.

Conclusion

With a winning combination of value added, environment, and power requirements, this is a great fit for energy harvesting. End users benefit from significant reduction in manual charging and are much more likely to use the product long-term.

✓ **Significant increase in battery life compared to industry standard!**

✓ **Zero or reduced manual charging by end user!**

✓ **3-5yr estimated device lifetime!**

✓ **Nominal increase in cost offset by greatly increased convenience!**

#SensorsConverge

Sensors Converge

Electronic Price Tag

Application:

Electronic price tags placed on the edge of retail shelving with a 2-3 year typical battery life. Stores can update product prices dynamically giving them the opportunity to take advantage of cloud based analytics tools. This brighter indoor space pairs nicely with modern low power display technology.

Setup:

- Small PV cell supports multiple price updates per day.
- SMT mounted to PCB and exposed through the display frame.
- 95% power efficiency realized with high performance PMIC and multi-cell design.
- Lithium battery sized to last up to 2 weeks without solar input.

Conclusion

The bright retail enables a small PV cell to have a great impact on the functionality and performance of electronic price tags. With increased battery lifetime, daily function, and modest ROI, this is application is a good fit for solar energy harvesting.

✓ **Significant increase in battery life compared to industry standard!**

✓ **Eliminates battery related ongoing maintenance!**

✓ **10yr+ estimated device lifetime!**

✓ **ROI realized within 2-3 years!**

✓ **Allows more price updates per day!**

#SensorsConverge

Sensors Converge

Generic List of Well Suited Devices

Indoors

- BLE Devices
- Low Power Displays
- Thermostats
- Smart Locks
- Short Range Trackers

Bright Indoors

- Wearables (low latency)
- Force
- Acoustic
- Capacitive Touch

Outdoors

- Cameras
- Backlit Displays
- Lights
- Actuators
- Wearables (active)
- Long Range Trackers

#SensorsConverge

Sensors Converge

Summary

- Solar panels or PV modules can be designed and integrated into a wide range of low power IoT devices.
- Energy harvesting solves battery related industry pain points.
- Applications with the right combination of value added, cost, and environment are well suited.
- Getting started.

#SensorsConverge

Sensors Converge

Getting Started

Standard Products

Electronic Component • Semi-Flexible • Development Kits • Custom Design Tool

Whether you are designing a wireless sensor or setting up a remote base station, starting with a standard product can expedite the development process and get you up and running faster

Development Kits

Plug and play solar development kits make it easy to experiment with and explore the potential of indoor solar. These kits demonstrate that even in dimly lit environments, such as warehouses and industrial plants, Indoor Solar Panels can generate enough power to run sensors, beacons and other low power devices of the emerging IoT industry.

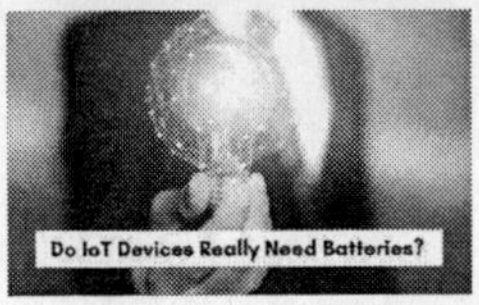

Learn More

The Horizon Blog: Simple to read technical content aimed at helping people learn more about solar, energy harvesting, and remote power.

Custom Solar Panel Design Tool

Contact Us: https://www.powerfilmsolar.com/explore/contact-us/

#SensorsConverge

Sensors Converge

Questions?

#SensorsConverge

Sensors Converge

Sensors Converge

Running tinyML on Sensors: Trends, Challenges, Applications, and Latest Technologies

September 21-23, 2021 | San Jose, CA

#SensorsConverge

Who We Are Qeexo

Replace with 2021 logo once available

- **Founded:** Spun out of Carnegie Mellon University in 2012
- **Key Product Lines**:
  - **Automated Machine Learning Platform**
    - **Qeexo AutoML** – Intuitive ML platform enabling efficient development of ML applications
    - **Qeexo Model Converter** – an API service that optimizes existing tree-based machine learning models to tinyML
  - **Machine Learning Applications** (400M+ devices in market)
    - **FingerSense** – Input-type classification for touchscreens
    - **EarSense** – Software-only proximity sensing solution

Best of sensors AWARDS 2019 FINALIST

CES Innovation Awards 2019 | CES Innovation Awards 2021 | The AI Awards

GLOMO Global Mobile Awards | sensors AWARDS 2019 FINALIST

Select Partners

BOSCH | ST | ARDUINO | arm | RENESAS

#SensorsConverge

Sensors Converge

Trend: Machine Learning is Moving to the Edge

North America AI Chipsets Market, By Processing Type, 2016-2026 (USD Million)

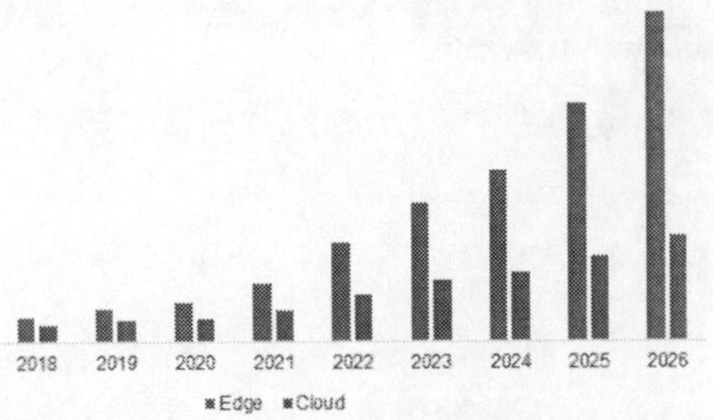

The edge compute market for AI chips is set to grow faster than cloud in North America over the next 6 years (Image: Global Market Insights)

tinyML Boom

- https://www.tinyml.org/
- founded in 2019, now boasts 6K+ members in 34 Meetup Groups across 26 countries
- "machine learning... at **extremely low power**, typically in the mW range and below... hence enabling a variety of **always-on use-cases**"

Industry leaders going "lightweight"

- Google's TensorFlow Lite & TF Lite Micro
- NVIDIA's Jetson Nano (ARM A57)
- ST Micro, NXP, Arm, QuickLogic, etc.

#SensorsConverge

Sensors Converge

tinyML Benefits

- **Reduces latency, bandwidth, and power usage** by eliminating data transfers (see Case Study 1)
- **Addresses privacy & security concerns** since data never leaves the premise
- **Achieves higher availability** without depending on the cloud or a centralized server

#SensorsConverge

Sensors Converge

Case Study 1: Smartphone Power Consumption

Component	Power Consumption (mW)
Active Cell Radio	800
Display	400
GPS	180
Gyroscope	130
Bluetooth	100
Accelerometer	20
Microcontroller	< 1

#SensorsConverge

Case Study 1: Smartphone Power Consumption

Component	Power Consumption (mW)
Active Cell Radio	800
Display	400
GPS	180
Gyroscope	130
Bluetooth	100
Accelerometer	20
Microcontroller	< 1

#SensorsConverge

tinyML Challenges

- **Resource-constrained environment lacks**
  - processing power (e.g. GPUs vs. Cortex-M0)
  - memory space
  - battery power
- **ML engineers are not experienced with embedded programming**
  - Python vs. C programming
  - focus is on performance, not on saving resources
  - difficulty in downsizing existing ML models for tiny devices
- **ML development process is labor-intensive**
  - requires quality data with correct labeling
  - lots of repetition in building and testing models for each environment

#SensorsConverge

Sensors Converge

Many Steps Required to Build Embedded ML Models

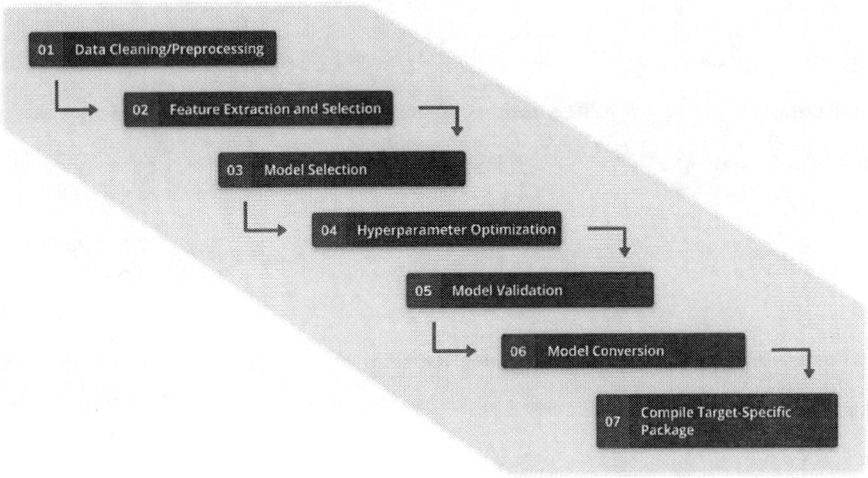

#SensorsConverge

Sensors Converge

Many Industries Benefits from tinyML

Empowering Sensors with tinyML

Motion Sensors:
accelerometer, gyroscope & magnetometer, radar, etc.

Acoustic Sensors:
microphone, ultrasonic, geophone, vibrometers

Environmental Sensors:
temperature, humidity, air pressure, indoor air quality, illumination, IR, etc.

Touchscreen Sensors:
capacitive & IR touchscreens

Image Sensors:
image & thermal cameras

Biometric Sensors:
fingerprint, heart rate, etc.

Case Study 2: Heart-Monitoring Wearable Device

- Current consumer ECG sensor patch only records data and cannot provide real-time data interpretation
- Data is later transferred to a computer for interpretation
- By downsizing existing ML models to run on low-power MCUs, wearable patches can interpret the data real-time and monitor patient's heart condition continuously on a small battery for days without sacrificing accuracy

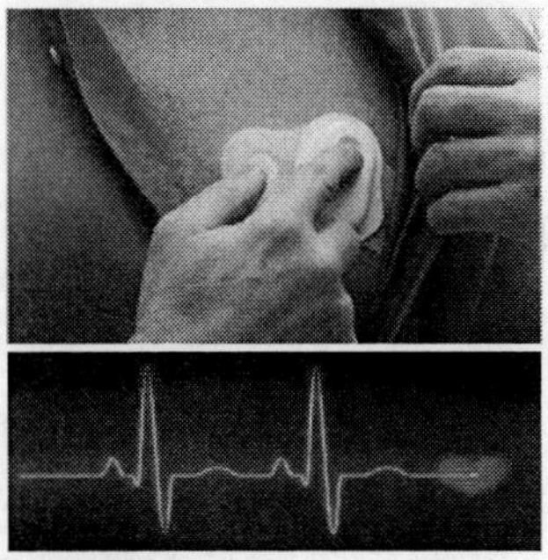

Model Type	Model Size	Latency
GBM on ARM Cortex M4 MCU	9 KB	3 ms

#SensorsConverge

Sensors Converge

Industrial Use Cases

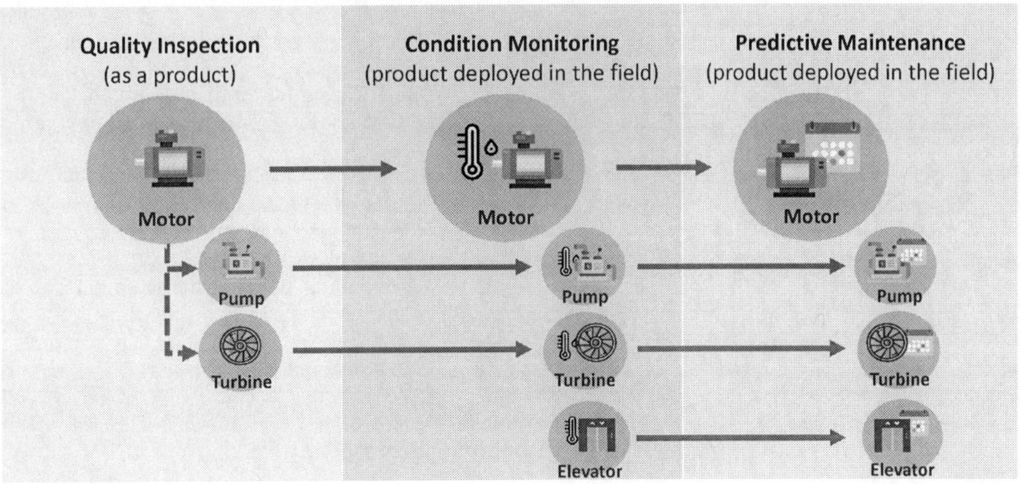

#SensorsConverge

Sensors Converge

Product Quality Inspection

Quality Inspection demo video

Place product on QA platform → Run product → ML solution checks product quality → Displays GOOD or BAD

- Must infer product quality based on data from **senses** or **sensors** (cannot disassemble end-product to check internal parts)
- Often done by humans using their eyes and ears
- **Machine learning + sensors** can replace humans, achieving higher accuracy and consistency with lower cost
- Replicable across different production sites, on a wide variety of products

#SensorsConverge

Sensors Converge

Product Condition Monitoring

- Built upon the quality inspection solution
- Can utilize **additional sensors** such as environmental sensors, acoustic sensors, etc.
- Ensure the product continues to function in the field, under various conditions
- With enough data, **predictive maintenance** can be achieved – knowing when the product is likely to fail and notify personnel for replacement

Condition Monitoring demo video

#SensorsConverge

Sensors Converge

Environmental Condition Monitoring

Monitor environmental conditions and detect anomalies

- **Anomaly detection** in known environments, sometimes used for **contextual awareness**
- **Sounds:** gunshot detection, baby-crying detection, etc.
- **Air quality monitoring:** vaping detection, indoor vs. outdoor detection, chemical safety alerts, etc.
- **Shipping & delivery conditions:** detect movement (e.g. drops/impact) and orientation

Indoor Air Quality Demo

#SensorsConverge

So How Do We Make ML Tiny?

Non-Neural-Network Models and Optimized Compression Methods Can Help:

Metrics	GBM	CNN (TensorFlow Lite)	GBM after Qeexo's Model Compression
Hyper-parameters	100 Estimators/class; Total 300 estimators Estimator depth-3	4-convolution layers 1-dense layer # Parameters 3357	14 Estimators/class; Total 42 estimators, 86% compression
Model Size	24 KB	19 KB	4 KB
Model Interpreter	1.6 KB	100KB	1.6 KB
Total Model Size	**25.6 KB (33KB)**	**119 KB (xx KB)**	**5.6 KB (13 KB)**
Classification Accuracy	97.40%	96.63%	97.40%
Latency	1.9 ms (featurization + classification)	2.4 ms (classification)	1.8 ms (featurization + classification)

* Human presence detection use case with 3-class classification, using Geophone (3KHz), Doppler Radar (3KHz), Microphone (16KHz)

#SensorsConverge

Sensors Converge

Qeexo Brings Machine Learning to ST MLC Sensors

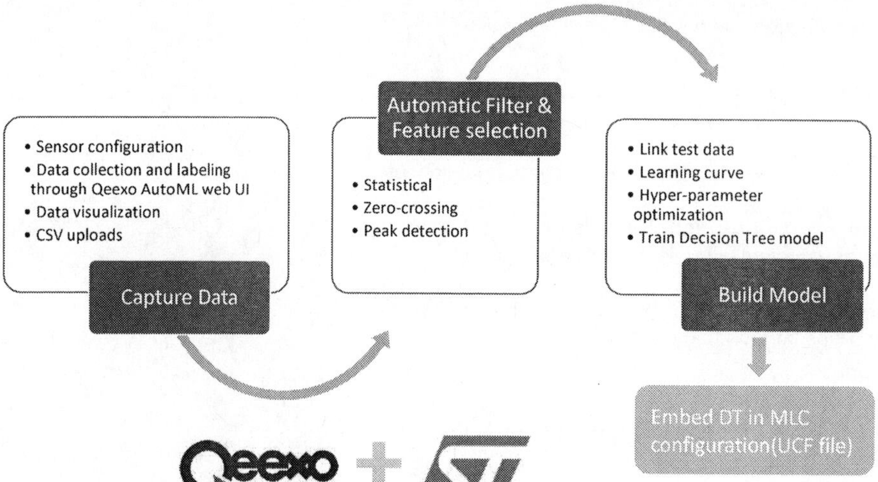

#SensorsConverge

Sensors Converge

Demo Video & Check Out Booth #738

Replace with Demo Video once available, similar to:

https://www.youtube.com/watch?v=1zZchmksAYs

#SensorsConverge

Sensors Converge

Qeexo AutoML for Embedded Devices

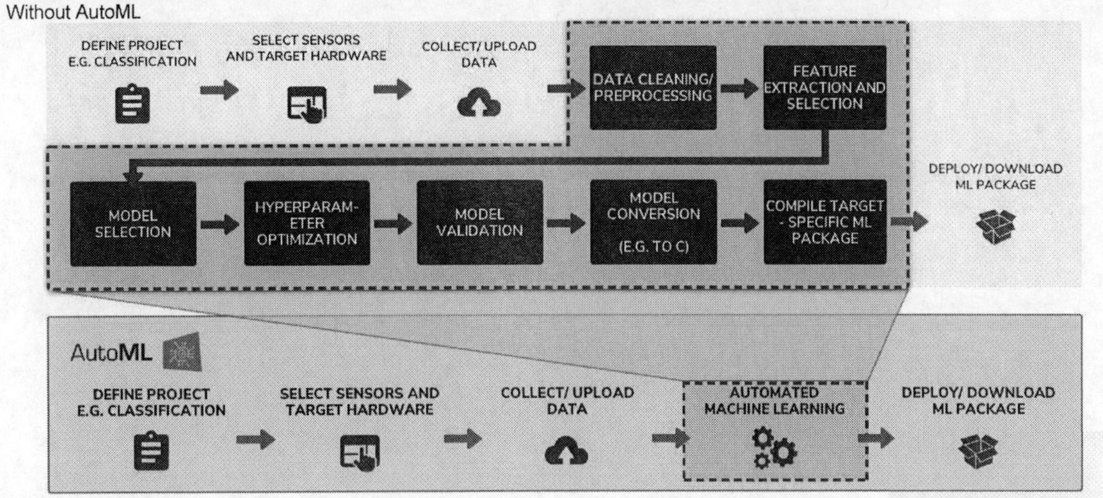

#SensorsConverge

Questions?

sang@qeexo.com

#SensorsConverge

Sensors Converge

Sensors Converge

Magnetoresistive Sensors for Non-Contact Measurements in Severe Environments

September 21 - 23, 2021 | San Jose, CA

#SensorsConverge

Agenda

- Background – Application Design Requirements
- Design Considerations – Eddy Current Sensors
- Overview – TMR Sensors
- Design Considerations – Kaman TMR-based Sensor
- Design Considerations – TMR Sensor Housing Material
- Resulting Kaman TMR Sensor – Advanced Magnetic Sensing (AMS)
- Sensor Technology Comparison AMS vs. Eddy Current
- Summary

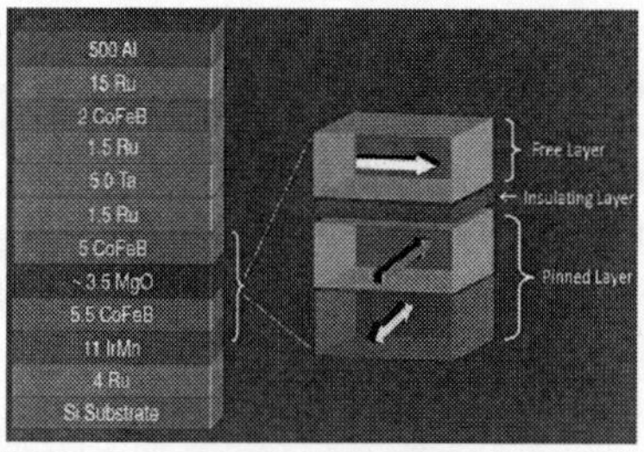

Material layers of a typical TMR magnetic tunnel junction detailing the pinned layer, the insulating layer, and the free layer

Sensors Converge

Background – Application Design Requirements

- **Non-contact displacement,** runout, speed sensing, event detection in caustic, abrasive, high pressure environment
- After successfully designing an eddy current sensor to meet a 16,500 psi (113 MPa) operating pressure, Kaman was tasked with designing a **new sensor capable of withstanding 22,500 psi (155 MPa)**
- **Requirements**:
  - 10 year life in nonhomogeneous fluid flow
  - Measurement Range >2 mm with a 0.5 mm offset
  - RMS Resolution < 5 µm
  - Temperature Range: -20°C to +120°C
  - 1.5% Non-linearity up to 2 mm
  - 22.5 ksi (155 MPa) operating pressure with a 1.5 minimum factor of safety
  - Resistance to a variety of working fluids
  - Output cannot be impacted by dynamic pressure

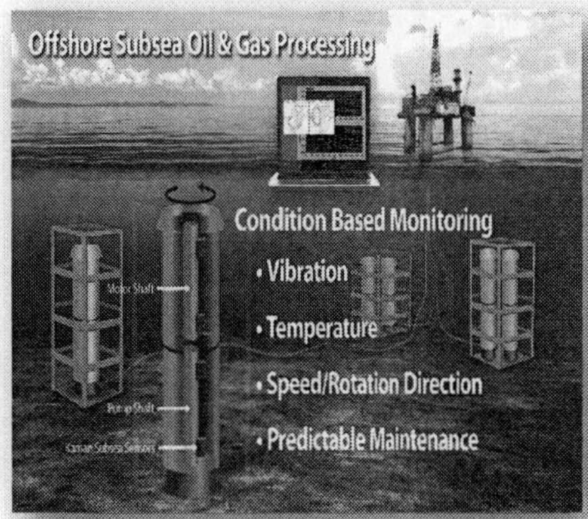

Design Considerations – Eddy Current Sensors

- **Material** requirements, **integration** constraints, and **performance** requirements **often conflict with sensor technology specific capabilities**. For example, according to Kaman's Inductive Technology Handbook [1]:
  - An **eddy current coil diameter** should be at least 2 times the measuring range
  - Ideally, there should be **no conductive materials near the coil** as they cause side loading
  - **Conductive side loading** can reduce measuring range by up to 50%

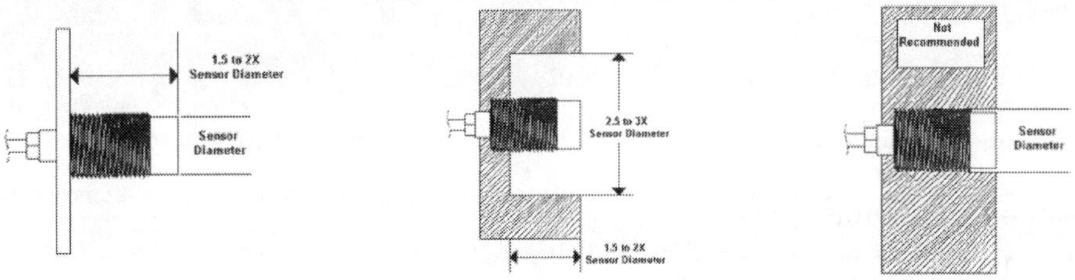

Design Considerations – Eddy Current Sensors, cont.

- An **electrically non-conductive sensor face (barrier) diameter of at least 15 mm was required** to meet the 16.5 ksi (113 MPa) pressure and performance requirements using eddy current technology
- At 22.5 ksi (155 MPa), with a 1.5 factor of safety, a non-conductive sensor barrier (housing face) material was required that:
  - Can survive at least 10 years
  - Can support a 9,250 lb (4,200 kg) load over a 0.275 sq in (177 mm^2)area
  - Will not deform and impact sensor output under static or dynamic loading conditions
  - Exhibits good fatigue strength
  - Exhibits excellent corrosion resistance
  - Has high yield strength and fracture toughness
- Engineered Plastics – not strong enough
- Ceramics – too brittle
- Ductile Metal Alloys – conductive

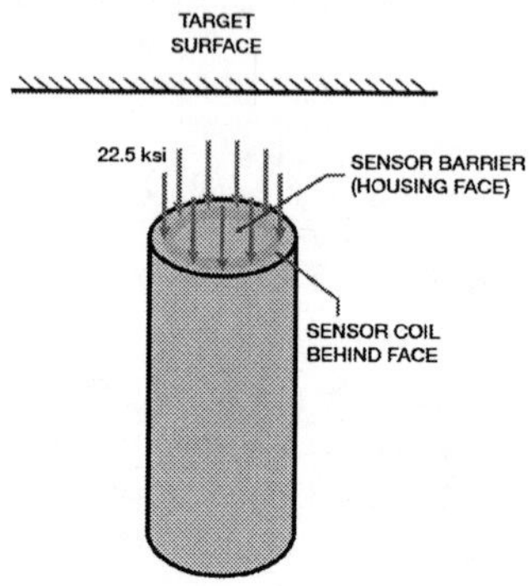

#SensorsConverge – Slide 5

Sensors Converge

Overview – TMR Sensor

- **Tunneling Magnetoresistive (TMR) IC** sensors offer a solution to help bridge the gap between robustness, reliability, and precision in high pressure environments
  - **Variable resistance device**
  - **Output (resistance change) varies with the magnitude and direction of an externally applied magnetic field**
- **Several advantages over other non-contact technologies**
  - Unlike eddy current sensors, **conductive *non-magnetic* side loading does not impact sensor output**
  - Unlike capacitive and optical sensors, **non-homogeneous working fluids do not impact sensor output**
- TMR sensors have the capability to **measure**

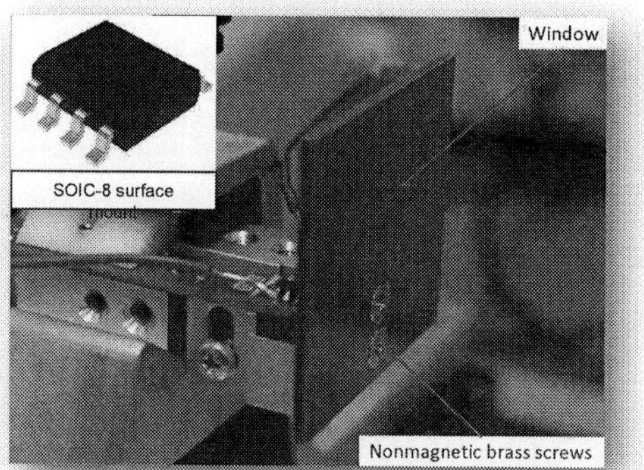

Lab prototype sensor holder assembly with the TMR sensor, magnet, and a 1.5mm thick non-magnetic metal barrier mounted in front of the sensor. (Target on right side, not shown).
The screws are made from brass (nonmagnetic) so as not to affect the measurement.

#SensorsConverge – Slide 6

Sensors Converge

Design Considerations – TMR-based Sensor

- With the **capability to detect magnetic targets through a nonmagnetic barrier** the design constraints are feasible
- At 22.5 ksi (155 MPa), with a 1.5 factor of safety, a **nonmagnetic** sensor barrier (housing) material is needed that:
  - Can survive at least 10 years
  - Will not deform and impact sensor output under static or dynamic loading conditions
  - Exhibits good fatigue strength
  - Exhibits excellent corrosion resistance
  - Has high yield strength or fracture toughness
- Engineered Plastics – not strong enough
- Ceramics – too brittle
- **Ductile Nonmagnetic Metal Alloys**

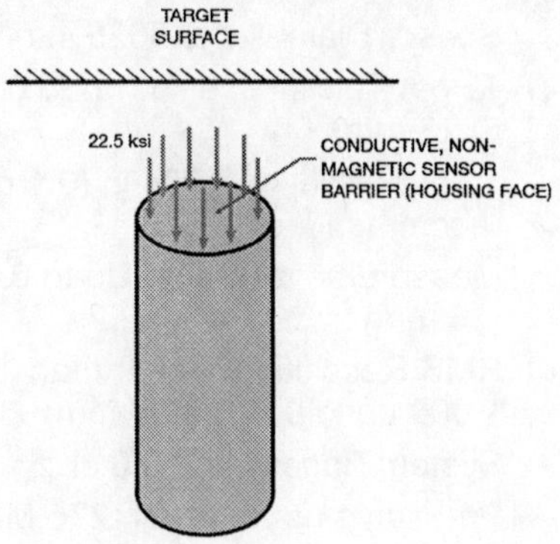

Design Considerations – TMR Sensor Housing Material

- Appropriate **nonmagnetic barrier materials include:**
  - **Inconel** – High strength, good to excellent corrosion resistance, and fair to good abrasion resistance. Commonly used in oil and gas extraction and subsea applications.
  - **300 Series Stainless Steels** – Low cost, moderate to high strength, good to excellent corrosion resistance commonly used in industrial, medical, and pharmaceutical applications
  - **Austenitic Manganese Steels** – Tough, cold working material with high wear resistance
  - **Aluminum** – Low cost light weight material commonly used in automotive and aerospace applications
  - **Ti**

TMR's feature of being unaffected by nonmagnetic barrier material significantly expands materials available for designing sensors for use in abrasive, corrosive, and high pressure environments

#SensorsConverge – Slide 8

Resulting TMR Sensor – "Advanced Magnetic Sensing" (AMS)

- **Preliminary System Specifications**
  - Sensor Diameter: 0.5625 in (4.3 mm)
  - Target Thicknesses down to 0.005 in (0.13 mm)
  - Target Offset: > 0.004 in (0.1 mm) recommended
  - Measurement Range: Up to 0.63 in (16 mm)
  - RMS Resolution: Better than 1 part in 1,000 up to 0.275 in (7 mm)
  - System Bandwidth: 5.0 kHz, -3dB
  - Pressures up to 40 ksi (275 MPa)
  - Temperature Range: -20°C to +12
  - Can be used as a turnkey sensor system or embedded directly into system barrier wall

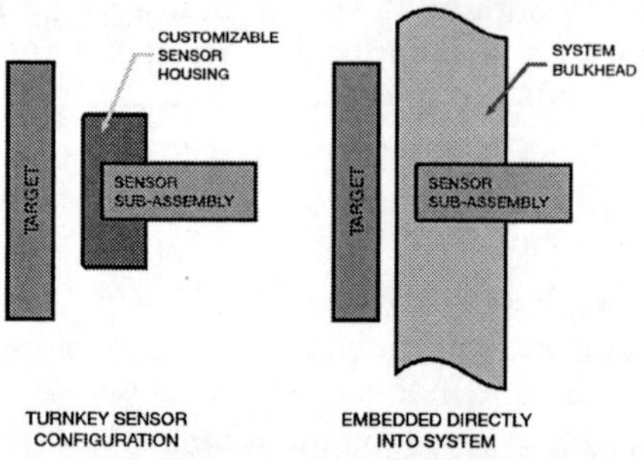

Target can be magnetic material or a permanent magnet. Can have a magnetic plating on a non magnetic target.

Sensors Converge

Sensor Technology Comparison AMS vs. Eddy Current

Advanced Magnetic Sensing	Eddy Current
Electromagnetic noncontact sensor	Electromagnetic noncontact sensor
Runs on DC power so no conversion is required to interpret the output	Runs on AC power and the output is converted to a DC signal
Sensor cable does not significantly impact the measurement; very long cables can be used between the sensor and signal conditioner	The sensor cable is part of the sensing circuit; frequency effects limit practical cable length
Responds only to magnetic materials in the neighborhood	Responds to all conductive materials in the neighborhood
Affected by nearby electromagnetic fields	Relatively immune to nearby electromagnetic fields
Conductive magnetic side loading matters	All conductive side loading matters
Exhibits hysteresis	Hysteresis not evident

Sensors Converge

Sensor Technology Comparison AMS vs. Eddy Current

Characteristic	Advanced Magnetic Sensing	Eddy Current
Measurement Range	Excellent	Good
Cable Length	Excellent	Good
Abrasion Resistance	Excellent	Fair
Corrosion Resistance	Excellent	Excellent
Pressure Capability	Excellent	Fair
Ideal Side Loading	Nonmagnetic	Nonconductive
Resolution	Good	Excellent
Linearity*	Excellent	Good
Repeatability	Good	Excellent
Reliability	Excellent	Excellent
Electrical Runout	Good	Good
Hysteresis	Fair	Excellent
EMI Resistance	Fair	Excellent
Target Conditioning Required	Application Dependent	No

*Without linearization circuitry

AMS-XHP [Extreme High Pressure] Displacement System Specifications

Sensor designed for this severe subsea environment application

- **AMS-XHP design**
  - Calibrated Range: 1.5 and 2.0 mm, with
    mm offset
  - Max Range: 5 mm
  - Full Scale Resolution at 2 mm: 0.009 m
    ppm)
  - Full Scale Resolution at 1.5 mm: 0.006 m
    (300 ppm)
  - Non-Linearity: < 0.7%
  - Temperature Range: -40°C to +120°C (application range: -1°C to +100°C)
  - Design Operating Pressure, max: 22,500 psi (155 MPa)
  - Design Proof Pressure: 40,000 psi (275 MPa)

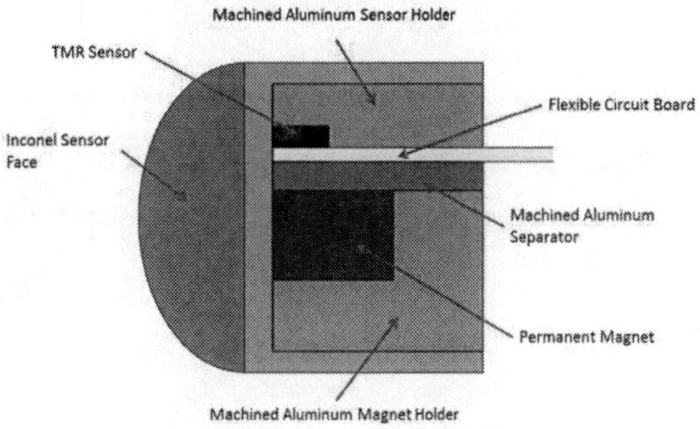

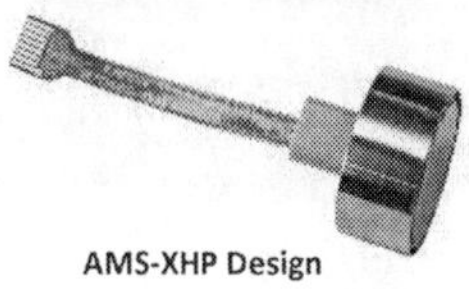

AMS-XHP Design

Summary

- **Kaman's TMR measuring system (AMS-XHP) provides for severe high-pressure noncontact displacement related machine condition monitoring**
- Comparison between Magnetoresistive and Eddy Current sensors for measuring rotating equipment in severe environments
- Because the **magnetoresistive sensor technology is insensitive to nonmagnetic materials, AMS systems are ideal when**:
  - **Sensor structural integrity** is critical
  - Operating in **abrasive environments**
  - **Edges or protrusions** into a flow may lead to increased **wear**
  - Operating in **corrosive environments**
  - **Sensors in harsh environments are inaccessible or difficul**
- **A few related applications**
  - Displacement and runout sensing in rotating equipment where s from nominal are expected
  - Rotor vibration monitoring
  - Machine health monitoring
  - Speed Sensing, RPM and Direction of Rotation can be calculated directly from sensor output by triggering on the extreme output values
  - Gear tooth condition monitoring

#SensorsConverge – Slide 13

Sensors Converge

Appendix

AMS Displacement Sensors

AMS System Specifications

References

#SensorsConverge – Slide 14

Sensors Converge

Kaman AMS Displacement Sensors – Five Sensor Configurations

AMS-XHP Sensor (22,500 psi / 155 MPa)

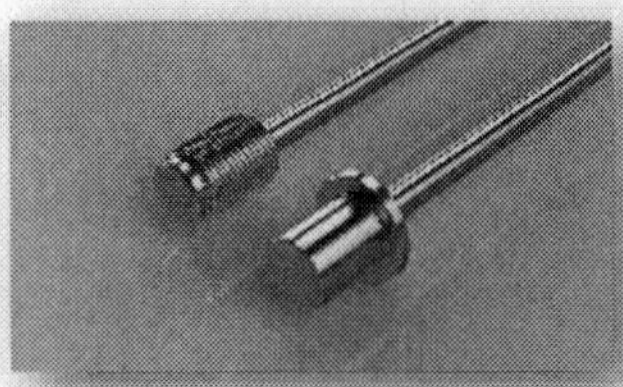

AMS-HP (4,900 psi / 34 MPa)
9/16" Threaded and Flanged Housings

AMS Commercial (500 psi / 3.4 MPa)
AS4320-06 Housing

AMS Commercial (500 psi / 3.4 MPa)
Straight 9/16-18 Threaded Housing

#SensorsConverge – Slide 15

Sensors Converge

Kaman AMS System Sensor Specifications

	Model and Part Number[1]				
	Threaded Body 856035-001D	AS-4320-06 856036-001D	AMS-HP 856037	AMS-HP 856038	AMS-XHP Custom
Thread	9/16–18 UNF 2A	9/16–18 UNF 2A	N/A	9/16–18 UNF 3A	Custom
Flange Diameter	N/A	N/A	0.825	N/A	Custom
Body Diameter	N/A	N/A	0.558	N/A	Custom
Pressure Rating	500 psi (3.4 MPa)	500 psi (3.4 MPa)	4,900 psi (34 MPa)	4,900 psi (34 MPa)	22.5 ksi (155 MPa)
Operating Temperature	-20°C to +80°C	-20°C to +80°C	-20°C to +80°C	-20°C to +80°C	-20°C to +120°C
Cable Connector[2]	IP-67 rated	IP-67 rated	IP-67 rated	IP-67 rated	N/A (integral mounted)
Shock	30 g				
Vibration[3]	1.125 g RMS				

Notes: 1. Custom form factor and hermetic sensors available
2. Integral (no connector) soft and hardline signal cables available
3. Rating for integral connector configuration only

#SensorsConverge – Slide 16

Sensors Converge

Kaman AMS-HP & AMS Commercial Conditioning Electronics Specifications [1]

Parameter	Specification
Operating Temperature	0°C to +50°C
Input Voltage	12 V to 28 V
Output Voltage Range	-10 V to +10 V
Power Consumption	< 1 W
Inrush Current	< 250 mA, 6 ms
Bandwidth [-3 dB]	5 kHz
Design Life	10 years
Shock	30 g
Vibration	1.125 g RMS
CE Mark Certification	Yes

[1] AMS-XHP electronics are custom

#SensorsConverge – Slide 17

Sensors Converge

References

1. Kaman Measuring and Memory Systems. "Inductive Technology Handbook". https://www.kamansensors.com/wp-content/uploads/2020/01/Kaman_Applications_Handbook_WEB.pdf
2. Wikipedia contributors. (2017, April 21). Magnetoresistance. In *Wikipedia, The Free Encyclopedia*. Retrieved 16:42, May 31, 2017, from https://en.wikipedia.org/w/index.php?title=Magnetoresistance&oldid=776487121
3. MultiDimension Technologies. "MR Effect Physical Explanation". Retrieved, May 31, 2017, from http://www.dowaytech.com/en/1777.html

#SensorsConverge – Slide 18

Sensors Converge

Sensors
Converge

Highlights of PARC's sensor research portfolio

September 21-23, 2021 | San Jose, CA

#SensorsConverge

Introduction to PARC
Overview of selected technologies
- Sensor floats
- Hyperspectral imaging
- Carbon nanotube gas sensors
- Colorimetric sensors

Q&A

#SensorsConverge

Sensors
Converge

Introduction to PARC

Overview of selected technologies

- Sensor floats
- Hyperspectral imaging
- Carbon nanotube gas sensors
- Colorimetric sensors

Q&A

#SensorsConverge

Sensors Converge

Introduction to PARC

- Subsidiary of Xerox, open-innovation business model
- 100+ researchers across hardware and software
- Work with academics, national labs, and companies from startup to Fortune 100

#SensorsConverge

Sensors Converge

Introduction to PARC

Overview of selected technologies

- **Sensor floats**
- Hyperspectral imaging
- Carbon nanotube gas sensors
- Colorimetric sensors

Q&A

#SensorsConverge

Sensors Converge

Sensor Float

Low-cost, flexible sensor platform for large-scale data collection

This research was developed with funding from the Defense Advanced Research Projects Agency (DARPA). The views, opinions, and/or findings expressed are those of the author and should not be interpreted as representing the official views or policies of the Department of Defense or the U.S. Government. Distribution Statement "A" (Approved for Public Release, Distribution Unlimited).

#SensorsConverge

Sensors Converge

Key features and differentiators

- Low cost: Thousands of floats can be deployed over a large area
- Robust: Can survive in harsh environments for up to one year. At end of life, glass float enclosure can scuttle on demand with minimal environmental impact
- Entirely self contained: Solar power + battery, sensors, onboard compute, and satellite modem
- Flexible, customizable architecture

#SensorsConverge

Sensors Converge

Float architecture

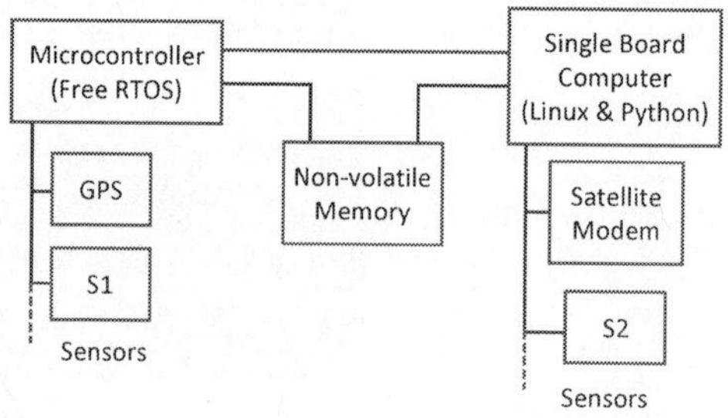

#SensorsConverge

Sensors Converge

Sensor float deployment data

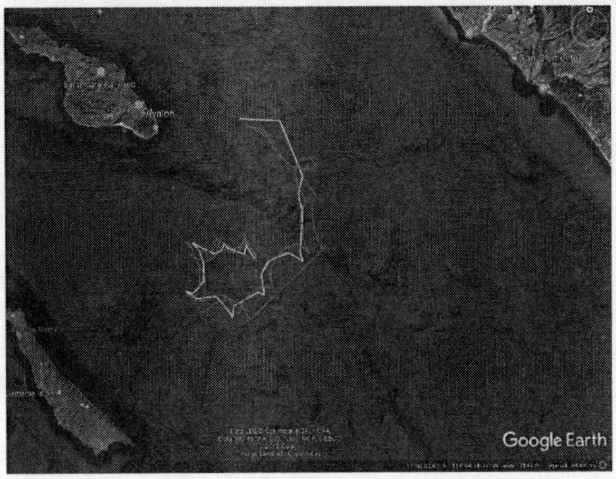

AIS Ship Detections

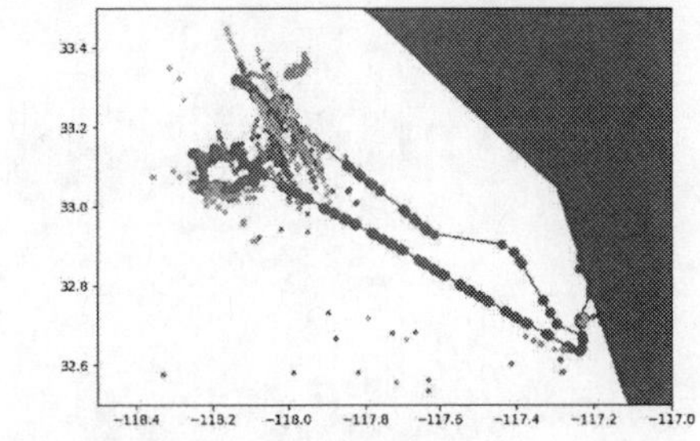

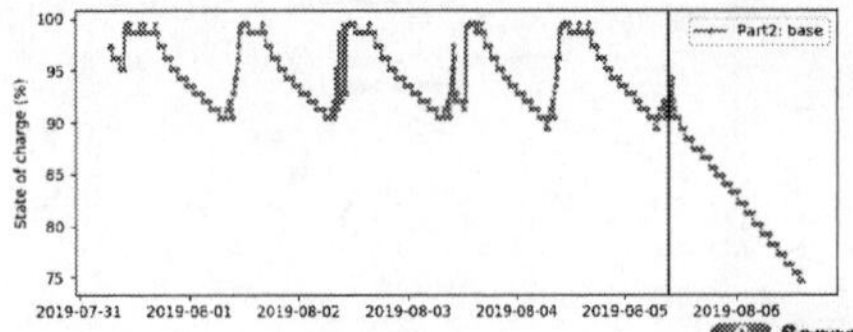

#SensorsConverge

Sensors Converge

Images and environmental data

Camera Images

Environmental Data

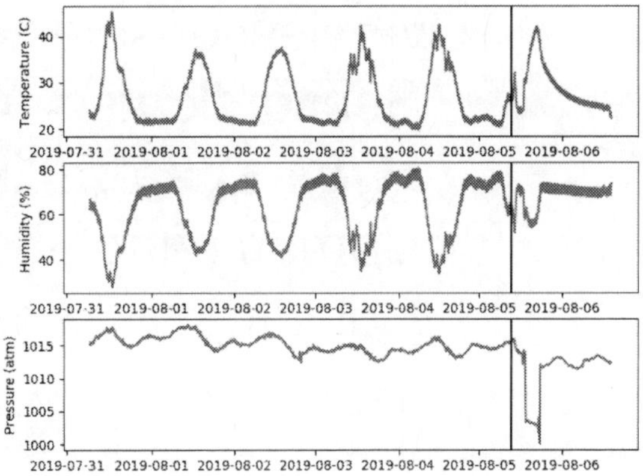

#SensorsConverge

Sensors Converge

Software-defined radio data

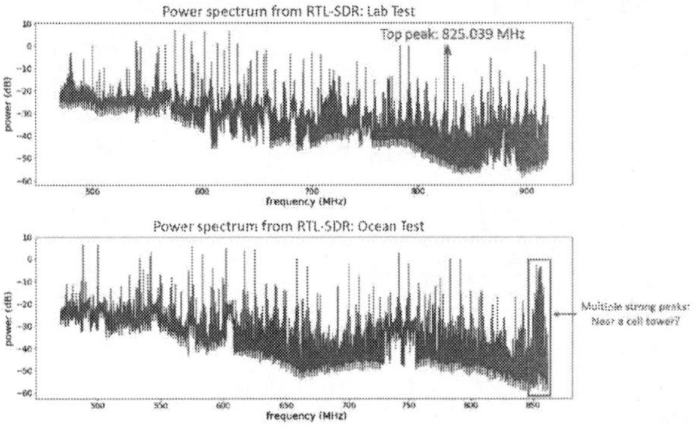

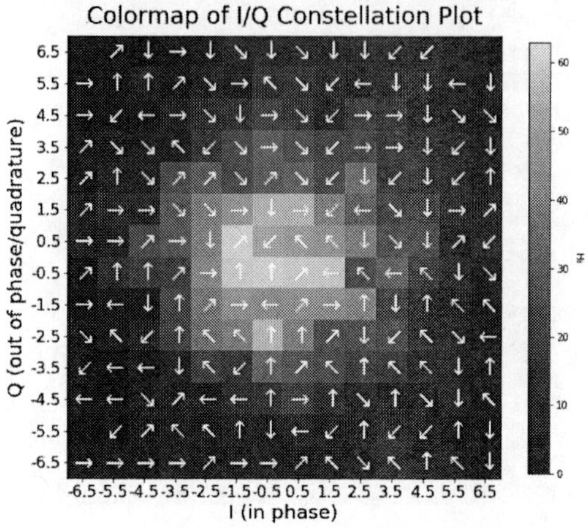

#SensorsConverge

Sensors Converge

Introduction to PARC

Overview of selected technologies

- Sensor floats
- **Hyperspectral imaging**
- Carbon nanotube gas sensors
- Colorimetric sensors

Q&A

#SensorsConverge

Sensors Converge

Hyperspectral imaging

Microscale, high-throughput hyperspectral imaging system that can be retrofitted into existing systems

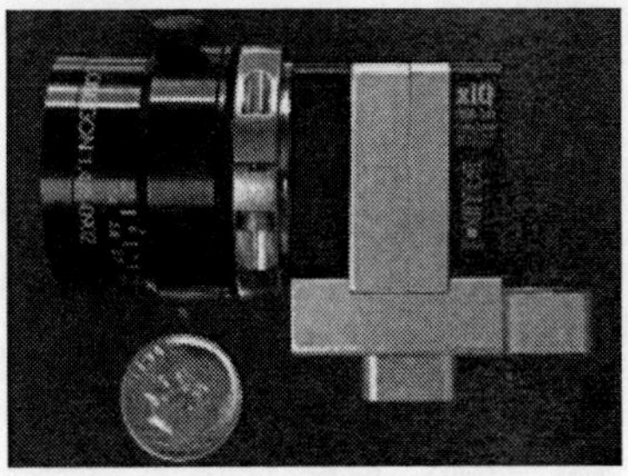

#SensorsConverge

Sensors Converge

What is hyperspectral imaging?

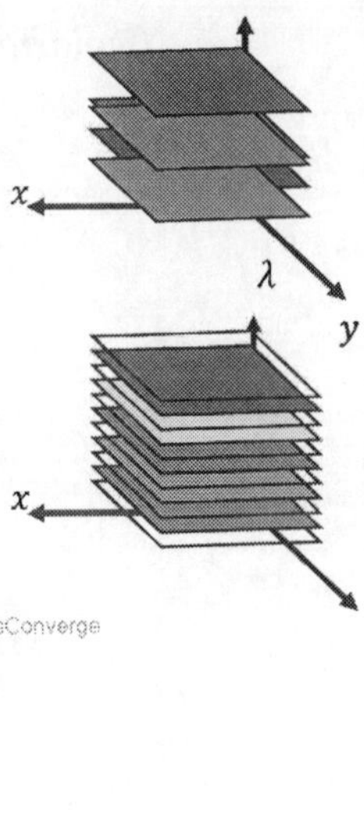

#SensorsConverge

Sensors Converge

Applications of hyperspectral imaging

For example:

- Precision agriculture with UAVs and tractors
- Product inspection
- Sorting
- Counterfeit detection
- Medical imaging

#SensorsConverge

Sensors Converge

Principle of operation

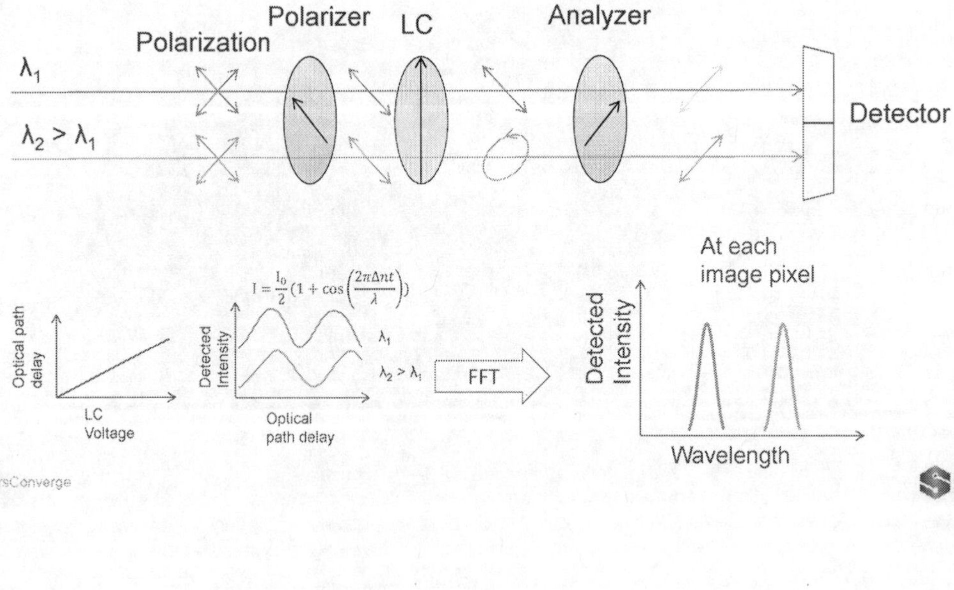

#SensorsConverge

Sensors Converge

Prototype hyperspectral imager

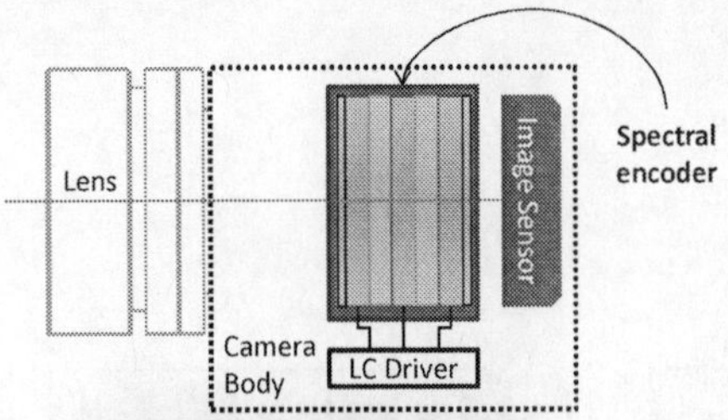

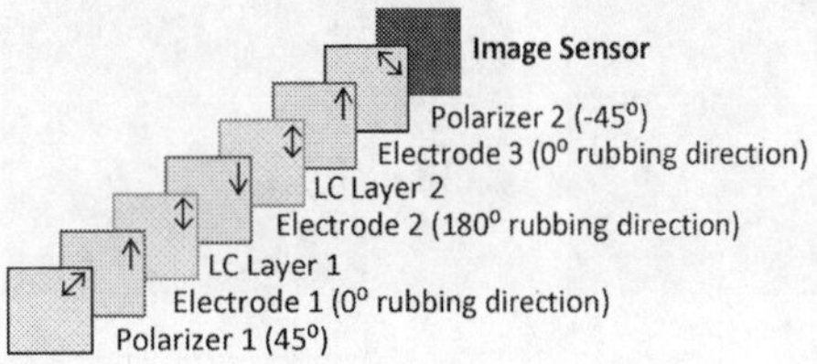

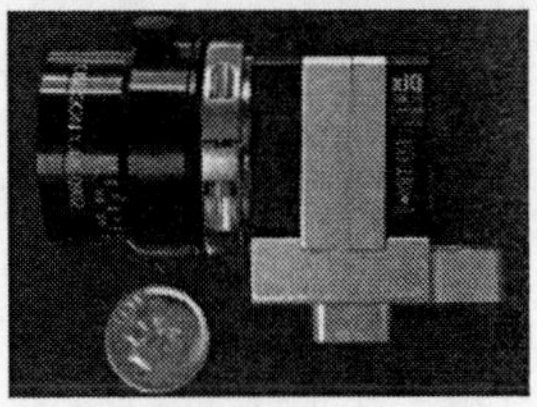

Specifications:
- ~1 s min. acquisition time at best spectral resolution (7 nm at 400 nm, 65 nm at 1000 nm)
- F/1.8 max. aperture
- 40 degree field of view
- 400 nm to 1000 nm (CMOS)

#SensorsConverge

Proof of concept with four lasers

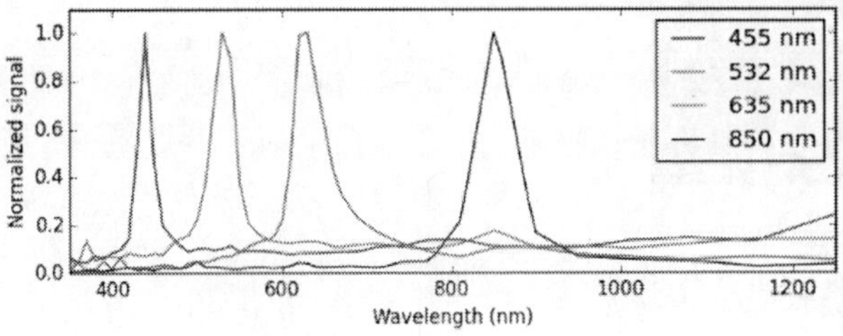

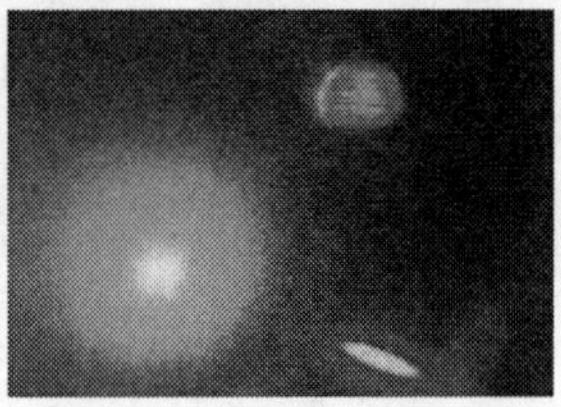

#SensorsConverge

Scan LC voltage to generate interferograms

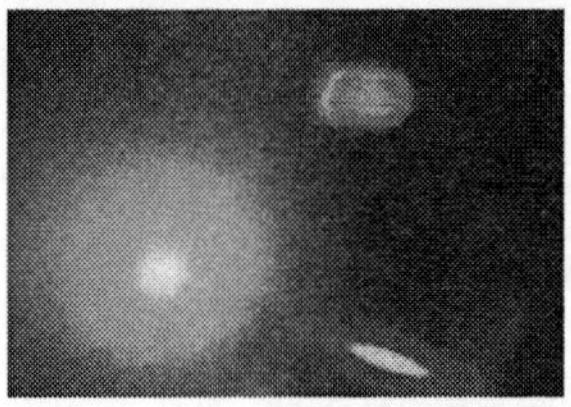

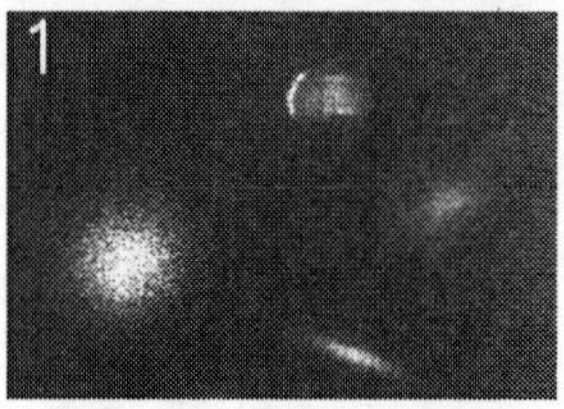

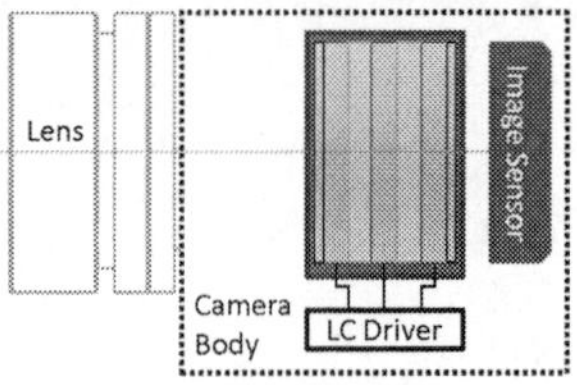

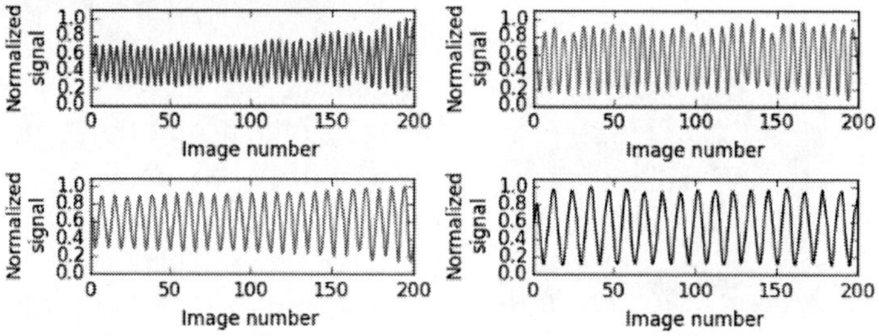

#SensorsConverge

Sensors Converge

FFT (at each pixel) to convert to frequency domain

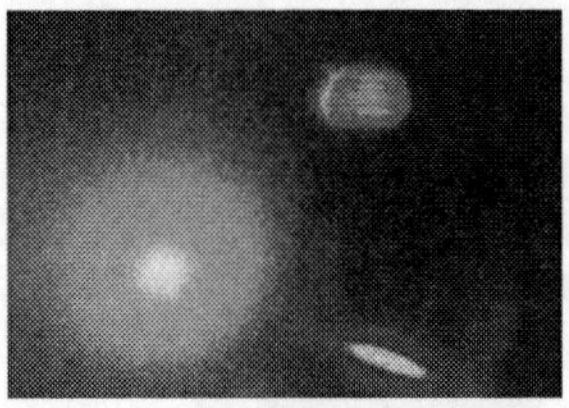

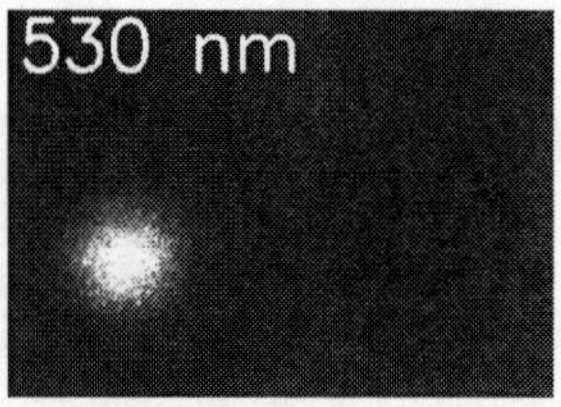

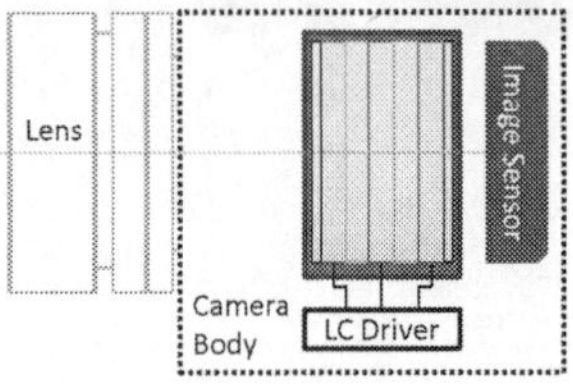

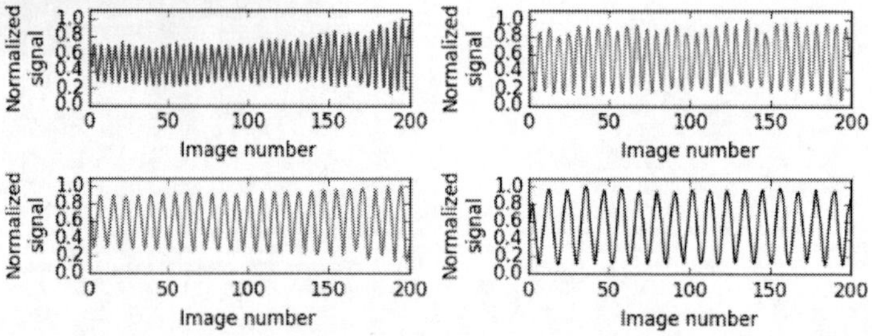

#SensorsConverge

Sensors Converge

Demo with real-world objects

US $20

Plants

Legos

#SensorsConverge

Sensors Converge

Demo with real-world objects

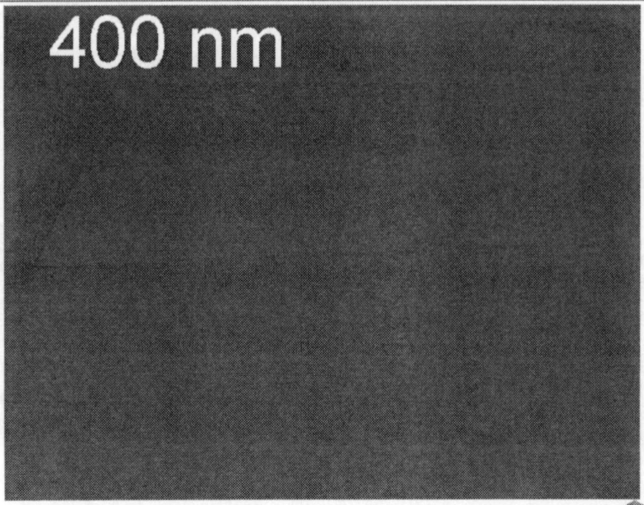

#SensorsConverge

Sensors Converge

Introduction to PARC

Overview of selected technologies

Sensor floats

Hyperspectral imaging

Carbon nanotube gas sensors

Colorimetric sensors

Q&A

#SensorsConverge

Sensors Converge

Carbon nanotube gas sensors

Arrays of functionalized carbon nanotube sensors coupled with PARC readout electronics and ML

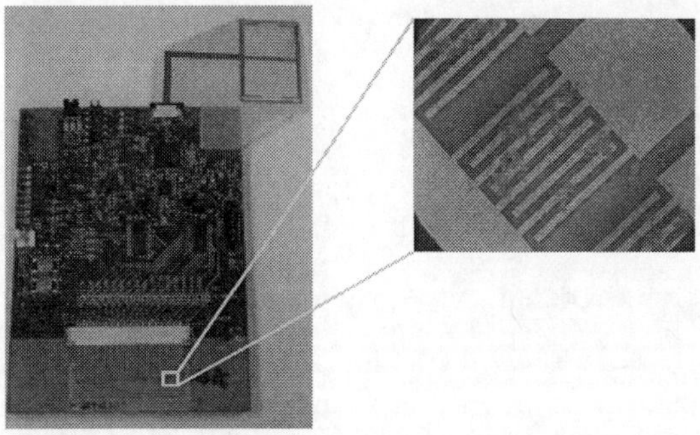

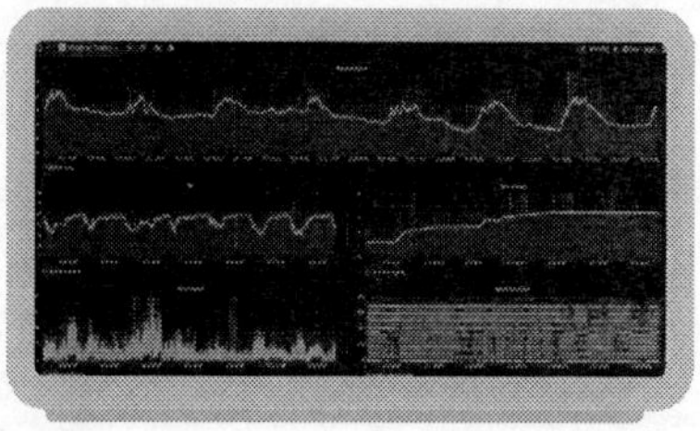

#SensorsConverge

Sensors Converge

Key Differentiators

Ultra-Low Cost: Pennies/sensor, <$15/sensor node

High Sensitivity: ppm-level detection in ambient conditions

Selectivity, robustness, and multi-analyte detection: Through machine learning applied to sensor arrays

#SensorsConverge

Sensors Converge

Application: Methane leak detection

- ARPA-E funded, partnered with NASA
- Methane is a potent GHG

#SensorsConverge

Sensors Converge

Methane sensors

Functionalized CNT inks printed on interdigitated electrodes

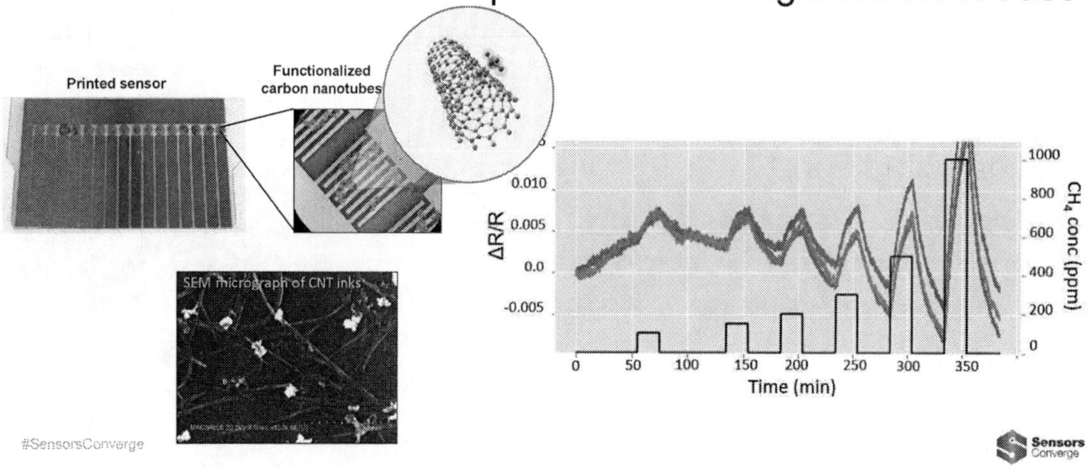

#SensorsConverge

Field deployment of methane sensor nodes

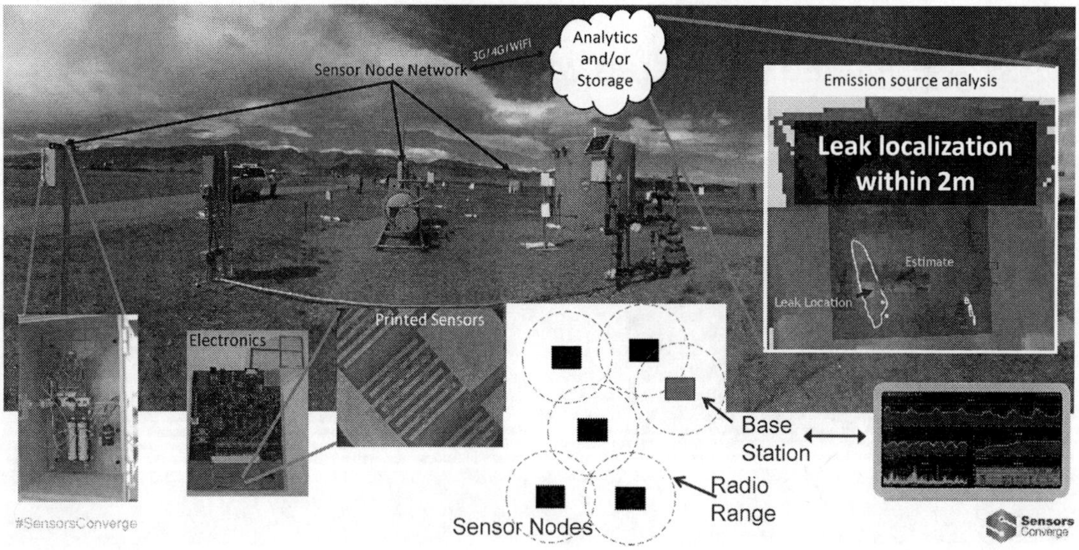

#SensorsConverge

Application: Air quality monitoring

Sense wide variety of gases at low concentration

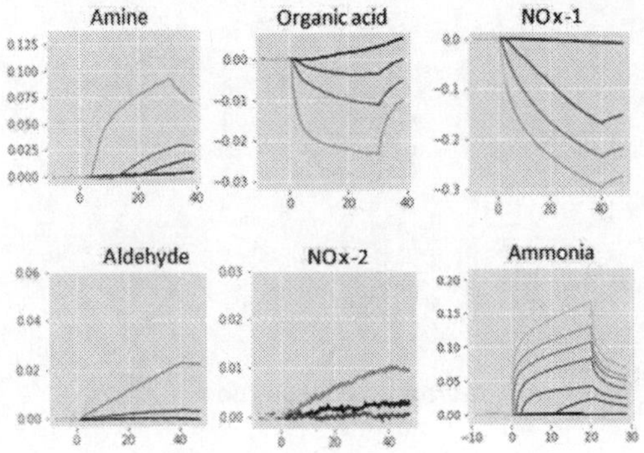

Portable sensor node

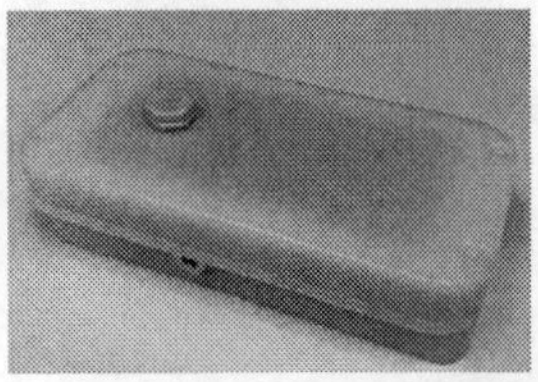

Base station for receiving and streaming data to cloud

#SensorsConverge

Sensors Converge

Specificity through fingerprinting

- CNT sensors with different modifications enable specificity through fingerprinting
- Low limits of detection (<ppm) for a variety of relevant gases

Specificity through response fingerprinting

Sensor Material	Amine	Organic acid	NOx-1	Aldehyde	NOx-2	Disulfide	Sulfide	Ammonia
A	+		-			+	+	+
B	+	-	-	+	+			+
C	+		+				+	+
D	+		-				+	+
E	+	+	-	+	+	+		+
F	+		-		+	+		+
G	+		+	+				+
H				-				
LoD (ppb)	50	50	50	100	100	TBD	10	50-100

Response type 1 | Response type 2 | Response type 3 | Response type 4

#SensorsConverge

Sensors Converge

Gas classification and quantification

Principal Component Analysis

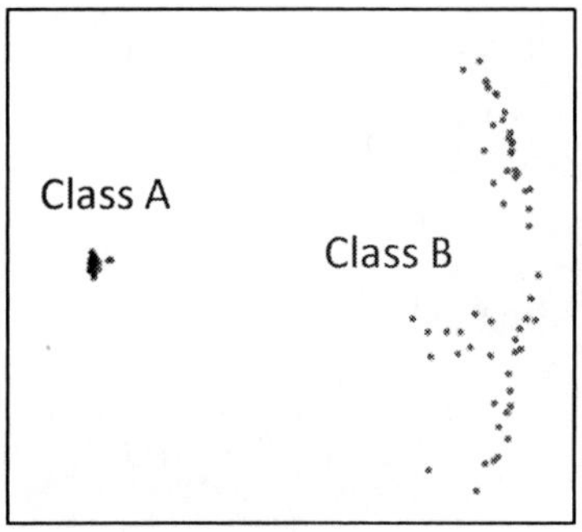

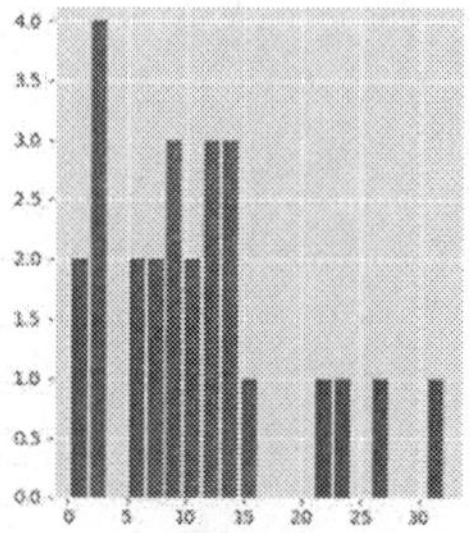

% error in concentration quantification

#SensorsConverge

Sensors Converge

Introduction to PARC

Overview of selected technologies

- Sensor floats
- Hyperspectral imaging
- Carbon nanotube gas sensors
- **Colorimetric sensors**

Q&A

#SensorsConverge

Sensors Converge

Colorimetric sensors

PARC aerogel technology enables sensitive colorimetric sensors with fast response-time

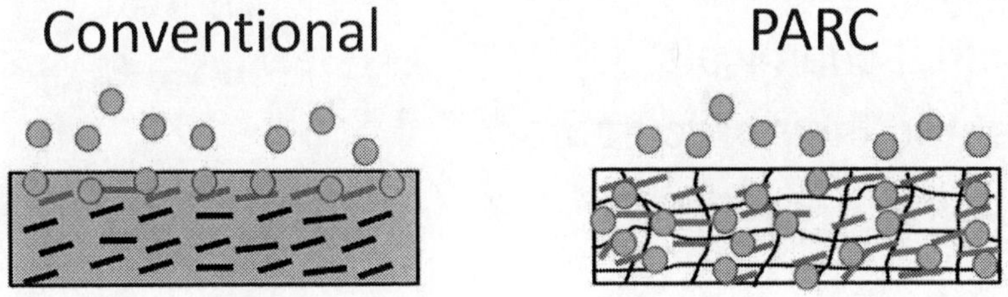

Sensors Converge

Sensor in action

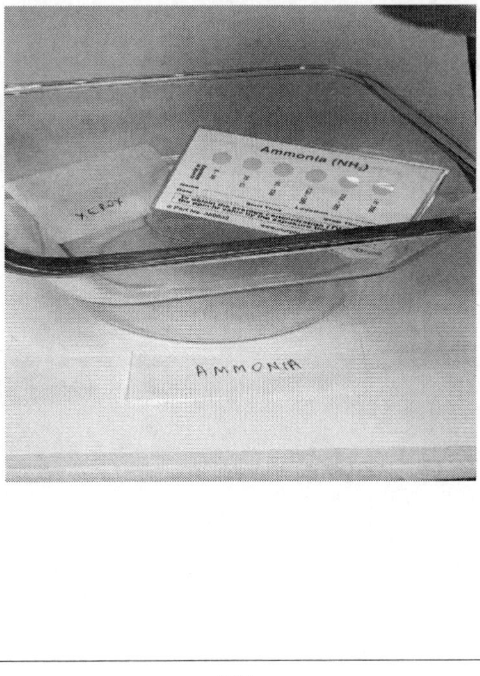

Sensors Converge

Exemplary applications

Transparent aerogel can serve as a host for any colorimetric sensing application. For example:

- Smart packaging
- Environmental monitoring
- Toxic industrial chemicals
- Explosives and their precursors
- Chemical warfare agents

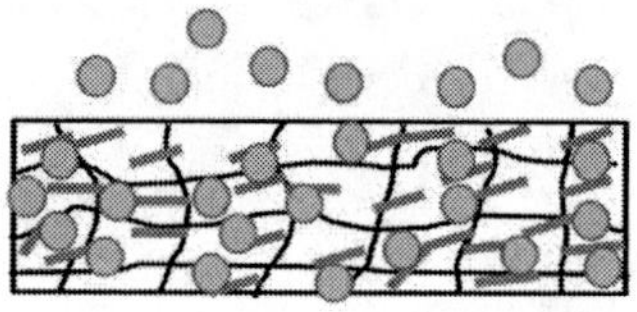

#SensorsConverge

Sensors Converge

Introduction to PARC

Overview of selected technologies

Sensor floats

Hyperspectral imaging

Carbon nanotube gas sensors

Colorimetric sensors

Q&A

#SensorsConverge

Sensors Converge

Conclusions and Q&A

I have shared four PARC technologies with you today: Sensor floats, hyperspectral imaging, carbon nanotube gas sensors, and colorimetric sensors

If you are interested in working with PARC (as a partner or an employee) please reach out: Sean.Doris@parc.com

#SensorsConverge

Sensors Converge

Sensors Converge

Doing Anomaly Detection Right

September 21-23, 2021 | San Jose, CA

Stuart Feffer, Reality AI
Gus Molina, Advantech

#SensorsConverge

Reality AI®

is for
non-visual sensing
with machine learning
in your product or factory

2

Reality AI combines advanced signal processing with artificial intelligence on inexpensive processors

RealityAI

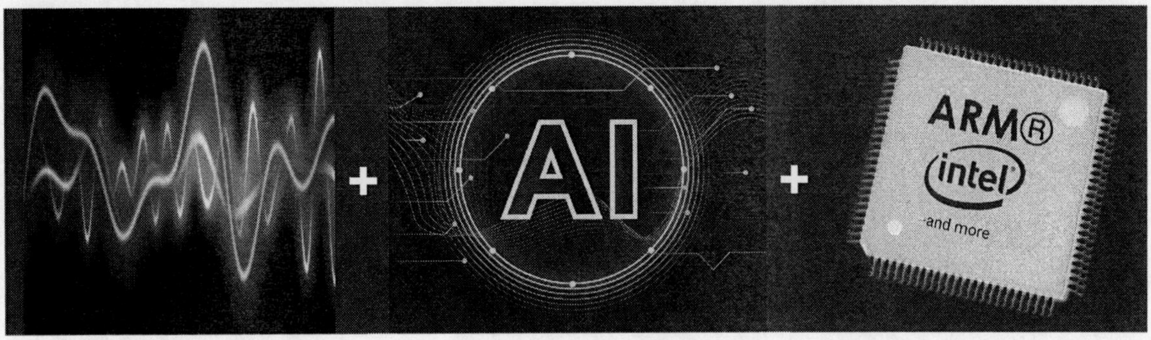

Advanced signal processing

Reality AI uses an algorithmic search of a wide range of feature spaces to derive a custom transform based on time and frequency.

Artificial Intelligence

Reality AI can automatically generate machine learning models, explanatory visualizations, and a variety of hardware analytics to aid product or solution design.

Inexpensive Processors

Reality AI code will run on ARM M- R- A-, and non-ARM microcontrollers, as well as on Intel processors and Linux. Runs on Infineon AURIX.

Just announced at Sensors Converge 2021:

RealityCheck AD, in partnership with Advantech

RealityAI

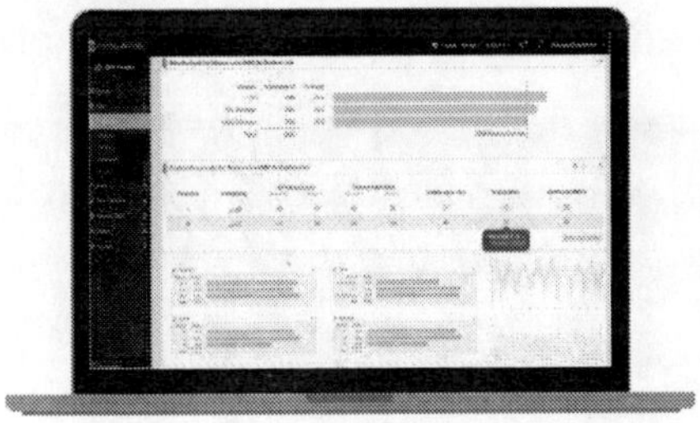

- Advanced anomaly detection for equipment monitoring and end-of-line testing
- Comes with Reality AI edge node firmware and machine learning software
- With edge node from Advantech and a range of sensors to choose from

Reality AI

Today's Topic:

How to do anomaly detection
(the right way)

Reality AI

What is "anomaly detection"?

- A "one-sided" model - learn what "normal" is, and report on deviations
- "Unsupervised" learning - no need for exhaustive data on all types of anomalies
- A "magic wand" for situations where data on the thing you really want to detect (the anomalies) is difficult or expensive to get.

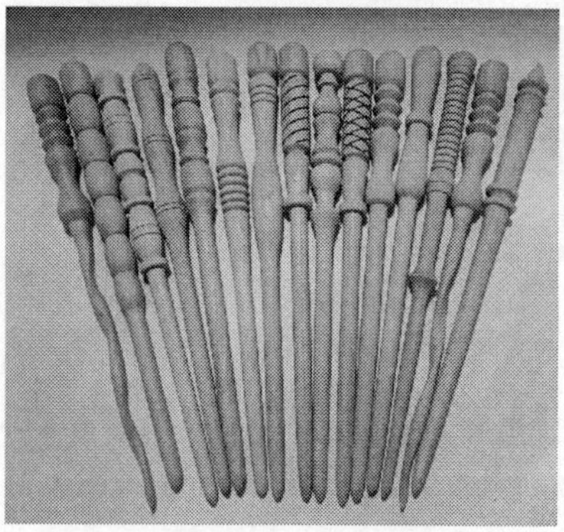

It's all about the baseline

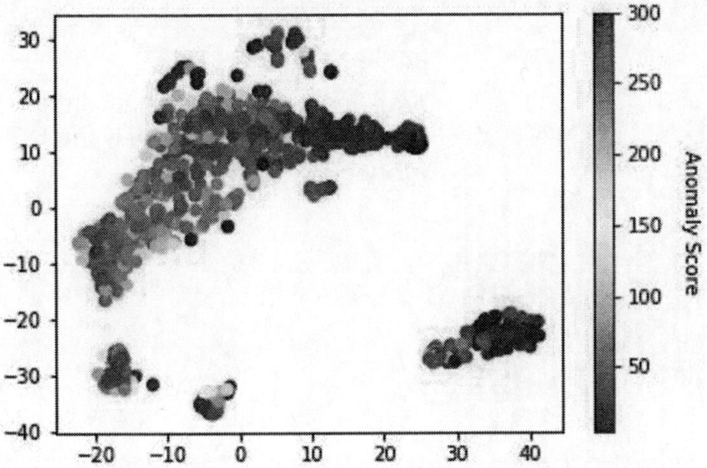

AD methods find a "baseline normal" region in feature space.

AD Scores tell you "how far" an observation is from the normal region.

The key is to choose the right feature space where:

a) The "baseline normal" region is compact, and tightly packed

b) All known anomalies are distant from the edges of the baseline.

Right Way and Wrong Way to do AD

The wrong way	The right way
Build with little or no data on known anomalies.	Collect or create anomalies for testing and "hints".
Gather and test in limited, controlled circumstances.	Gather and test data continuously, screening out false positives and false negatives.
Use instrumentation that misses the data that matters most.	Gather "rich data", including metadata wherever possible.

Wrong Way #1

No anomaly data - collect only "normal"

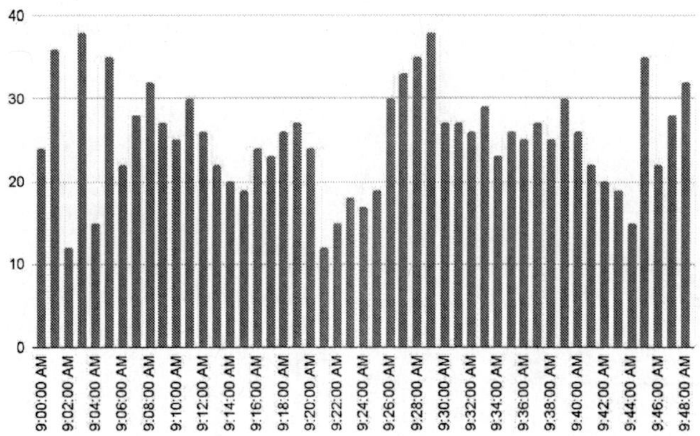

If all you have is "normal" data, how will you even know if the model is working?!?

Right Way #1

Collect (or create) enough anomalies to test the model, and to "hint" the algorithm

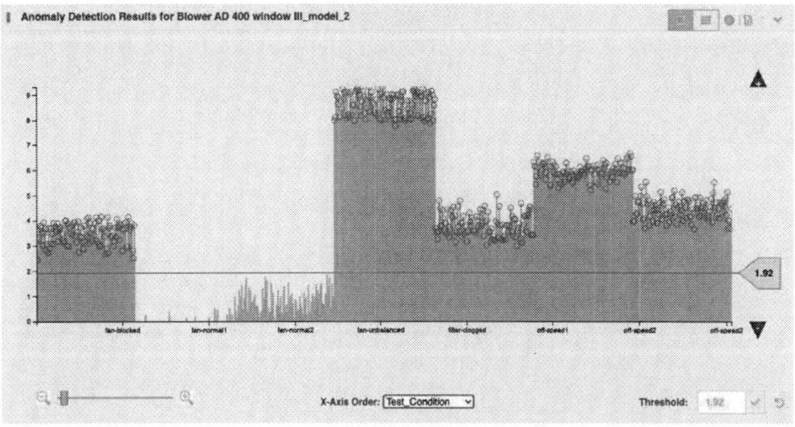

Wrong Way #2

Gather and test in limited circumstances

Machine learning is an exercise in overcoming variation with data.

Background	Machine States	Targets
Times of day, days of week, seasonal	Different operating modes	Natural variation
Background activities	Mechanical drift	Different makes/models
Nearby machines and processes		
People talking, etc.		

Right Way #2

Plan for continuous testing and iterative improvement

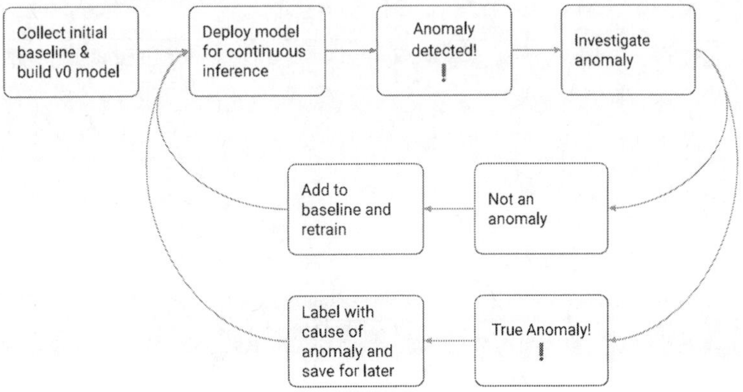

Wrong Way #3

Reality AI

Use instrumentation that misses the most important data

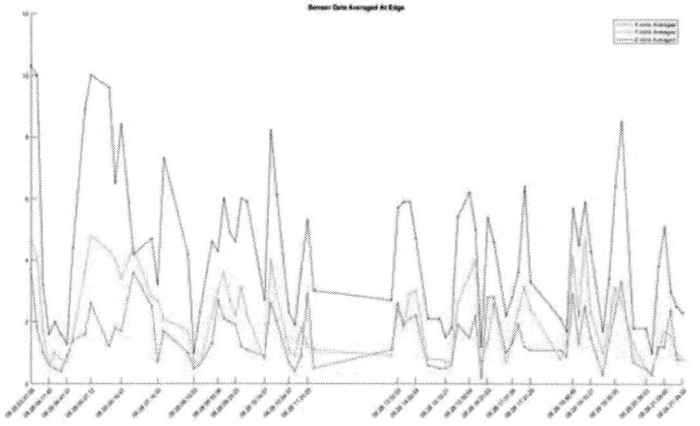

Accelerometer AD data based on RMS energy in X,Y,Z, collected periodically

Wrong Way #3

Reality AI

Use instrumentation that misses the most important data

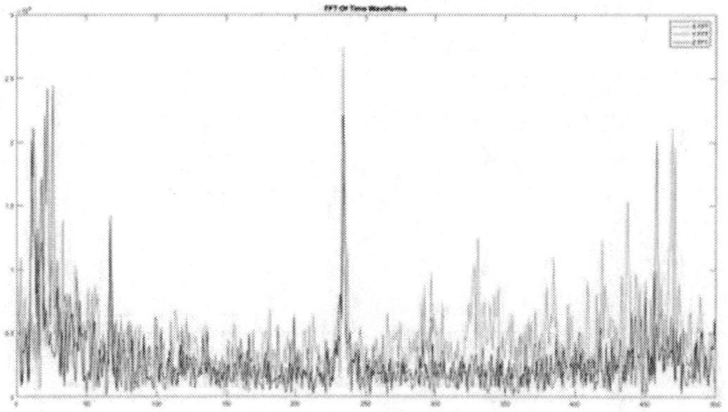

Accelerometer AD data processed with FFT

Wrong Way #3

Use instrumentation that misses the most important data

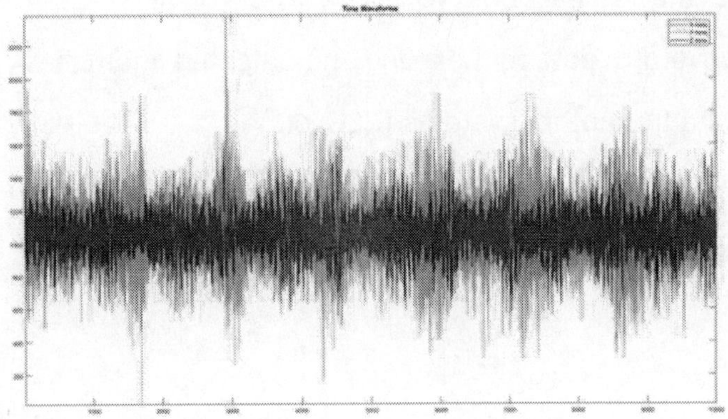

Accelerometer AD data time waveform

Wrong Way #3

Use instrumentation that misses the most important data

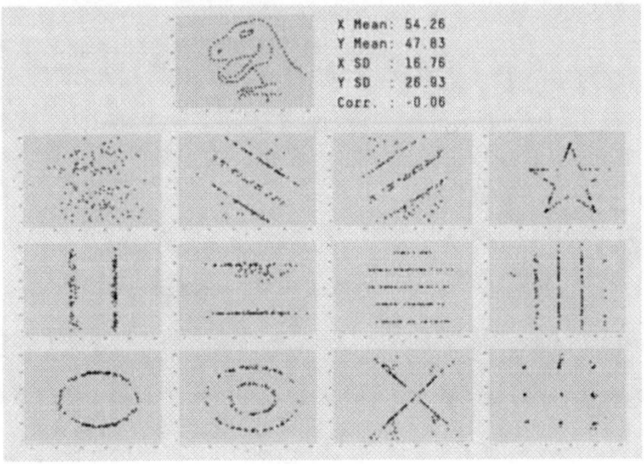

13 different plots with the same X and Y mean, X and Y standard deviation, and X-Y correlation.

With the wrong instrumentation, there could be a dinosaur in your data, and you'll never even see it!

Right Way #3

Reality AI

Use instrumentation and software that works with ***rich data***

- Highest possible sample rate - at least until you know what you need
- Collect and store time waveform data for baseline and detected anomalies
- Ability to capture metadata from other systems (PLC, etc)

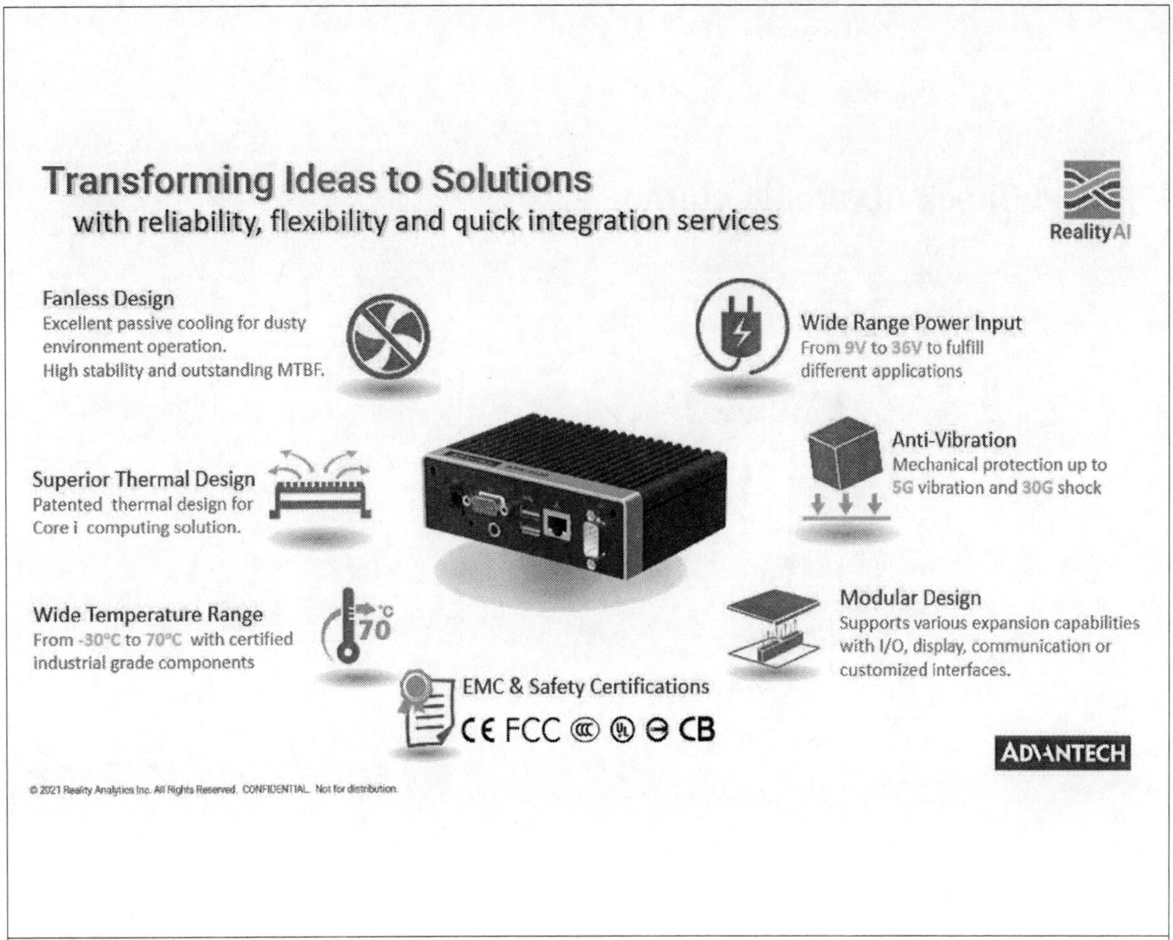
Transforming Ideas to Solutions
with reliability, flexibility and quick integration services
Reality AI
Fanless Design
Excellent passive cooling for dusty environment operation.
High stability and outstanding MTBF.
Wide Range Power Input
From 9V to 36V to fulfill different applications
Anti-Vibration
Mechanical protection up to 5G vibration and 30G shock
Superior Thermal Design
Patented thermal design for Core i computing solution.
Wide Temperature Range
From -30°C to 70°C with certified industrial grade components
Modular Design
Supports various expansion capabilities with I/O, display, communication or customized interfaces.
EMC & Safety Certifications
CE FCC CCC UL CB
ADVANTECH
© 2021 Reality Analytics Inc. All Rights Reserved. CONFIDENTIAL. Not for distribution.

Transforming Ideas to Solutions
with reliability, flexibility and quick integration services
Reality AI
Fanless Design
Excellent passive cooling for dusty environment operation.
High stability and outstanding MTBF.
Wide Range Power Input
From 9V to 36V to fulfill different applications
Anti-Vibration
Mechanical protection up to 5G vibration and 30G shock
Superior Thermal Design
Patented thermal design for Core i computing solution.
Wide Temperature Range
From -30°C to 70°C with certified industrial grade components
Modular Design
Supports various expansion capabilities with I/O, display, communication or customized interfaces.
EMC & Safety Certifications
CE FCC CCC UL CB
ADVANTECH
© 2021 Reality Analytics Inc. All Rights Reserved. CONFIDENTIAL. Not for distribution.

RealityCheck AD architecture

Reality AI

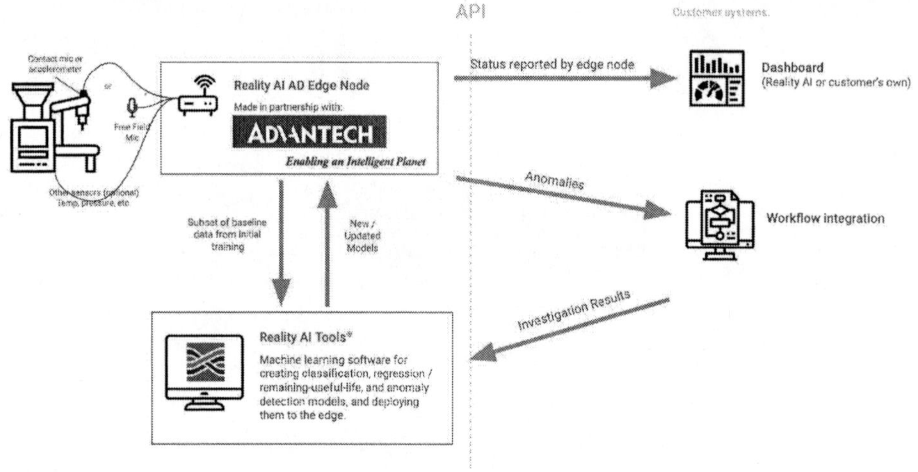

Reality AI®

https://reality.ai info@reality.ai @SensorAI Reality AI

ADVANTECH

22

Sensors
Converge
Rugged & Reliable Contactless Magnetic Proximity Sensing in Smart Building Applications
September 21-23, 2021 | San Jose, CA
#SensorsConverge

Sensors
Converge

Did you Know?

Amazon alone has more than 175 fulfillment centers globally

- Range in size up to 4,000,000 sq ft (~372k sq meters)
- 100 Loading Docks
- >1.6M packages a day (~50 while you read this bullet)

- ~1000 personnel
- 25% of warehouse injuries happen at the loading dock
- Automated & Semi-automated Freight Handling Equipment
- Automated Cleaning & Maintenance

How Can They Manage It All?

#SensorsConverge

Sensors Converge

DRIVEN
Sensors
Converge

DHL
Sensors
Converge

Magnetic Proximity Sensors

- Housed for Protection
- Paired with a magnet
- Wired or Wireless
- Customizable to fit different use cases

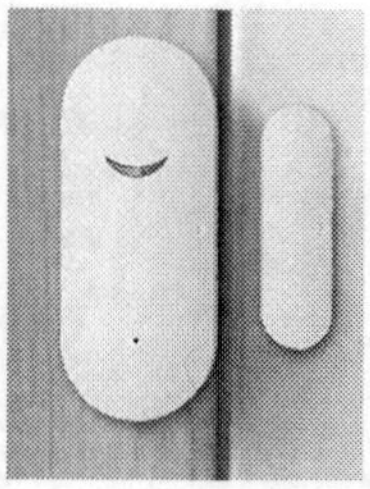

#SensorsConverge

Sensors Converge

Design Considerations for Choosing MPS

- Are you trying to monitor position/proximity of a movable interface like a door, window, lid, cover, or similar?
- Is the interface outside or otherwise exposed to harsh elements or contaminants that could compromise electronics or where electronics could pose a risk (e.g. spark/ignition risk)?
- Do you require a simple SPST form A type switch or changeover switching (SPDT/form C) functionality so you can toggle between two different circuit paths?
- Do you want to be able to switch signal level loads or higher power loads?
- Do you want to conserve as much power as possible?
- Do you want to minimize wiring (wire count, weight, etc...)?
- Do you want something that is easy to install?
- Are you looking for any kind of customization?

#SensorsConverge

Sensors Converge

Why You Want a Paired Magnet

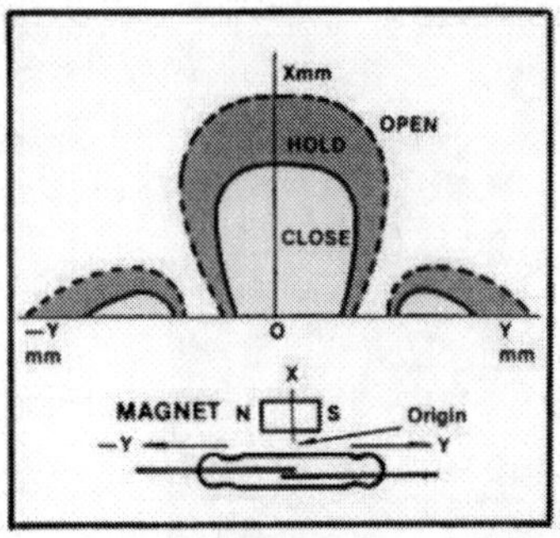

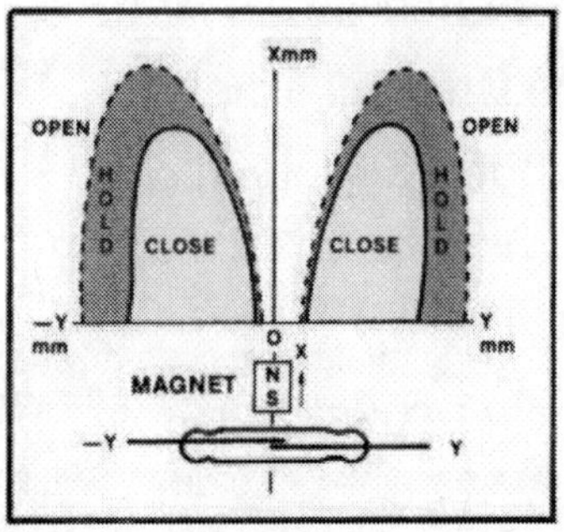

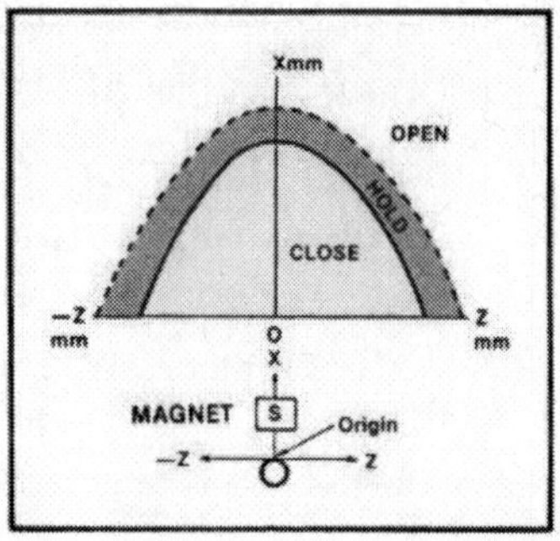

#SensorsConverge

Sensors Converge

C&K's Magnetic Proximity Sensors

MPS:

- Plastic housing, unsheathed wire
- SPST (Form A) switch contacts
- 30V 3W @ 300mA
- Minimum of 4M cycles

MPSR:

- Ruggedized aluminum housing & stainless-steel wire sheath
- SPDT (Form C) contacts
- 30V 3W@200mA
- Minimum of 2M cycles

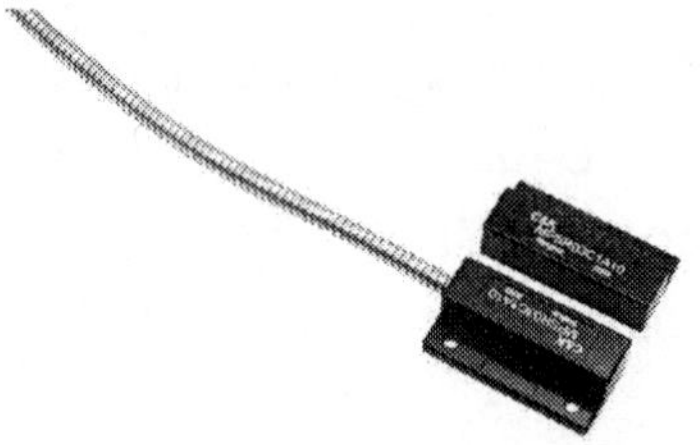

#SensorsConverge

Sensors Converge

Magnetic Proximity Sensor Uses & Applications

- Detect the Open/Close State of Doors, Windows, Gates, Loading Docks
- Detect Position of an Automated Sorter Arm
- Monitor the Lid of Remote Drop-off Point
- Docking Detection for Robots, Cobots, & Other Autonomous Vehicles

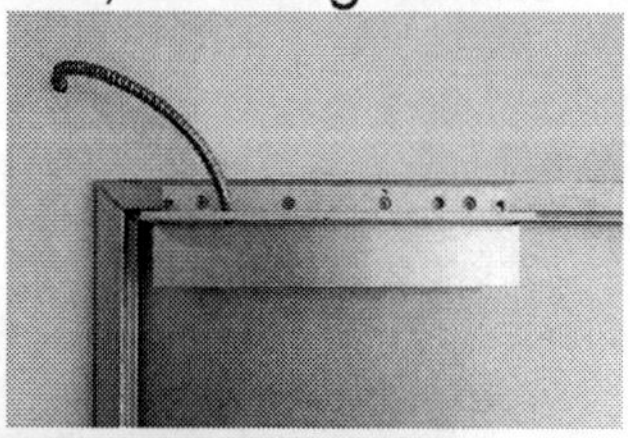

#SensorsConverge

Sensors Converge

Further Resources from C&K's Library

White Paper

- 5G and the Future of Smart Cities

Application Notes

- Magnetic Proximity Sensors
- Automated Guided Vehicles
- Barcode Scanning & Printing

Application Flyers

- Switch Solutions for Building & Home Automation Applications
- Factory Automation

All Freely Available at

CKSwitches.com

#SensorsConverge

Sensors Converge

THALES

How to Select an IMU for Extreme Challenging Conditions

September 2021

TEHMOOR DAR, PHD
PRINCIPAL ENGINEER - IMU

Introduction

- IMUs face uncertain and extremely varying environments such as shock and vibrations

- These shocks and vibrations
  - result in false output
  - degrade the IMU's performance
  - impact its accuracy and robustness.

- This presentation will focus on
  - parameters required for the extreme conditions
  - how to mitigate the impact of such conditions on IMUs during their use

THALES

Presentation Sequence

- MEMS IMU Background
- Theory of Operation
- Compensation and Calibration for IMU
- Sensors Common Specifications
- IMU Key Parameters for an IMU selection
- Vibration rejection – remedial measures
- Q&A

THALES

Inertial Sensing

- MEMS is a technology refers to miniaturization of mechanical and electro-mechanical elements.
- Inertial Sensors are the sensors based on inertia and relevant measuring principles.
- Inertial sensors typically come in the form of an Inertial Measurement Unit (IMU).
  - > accelerometers, gyroscopes and sometimes magnetometers.
- MEMS IMUs are ideal for smaller platforms (UAVs) and high-volume production units, as they can generally be manufactured with much smaller size and weight, and at lower cost.

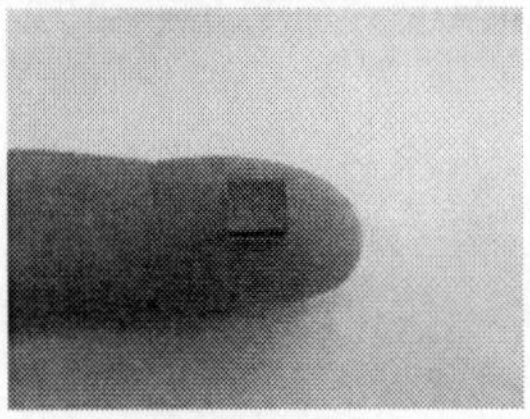

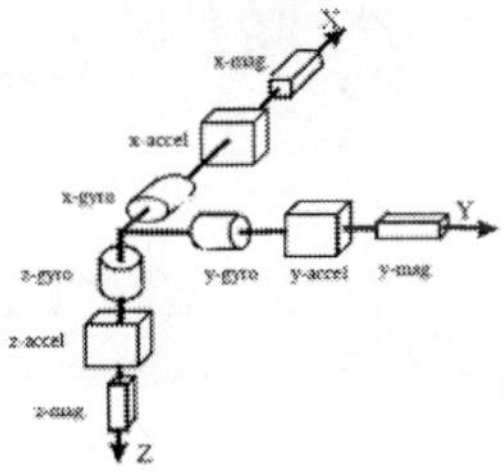

Use or disclosure of data contained on this page is subject to the restrictions of the title page of this presentation.

THALES

Inertial Measurement Unit

- IMUs are manufactured with a wide range of features, parameters, and specifications.
- The most suitable IMU selection will depend on the requirements for a specific application.
- There are many types of IMU
  - Quartz MEMS
  - FOG (Fiber Optic Gyro)
  - RLG (Ring Laser Gyro)
  - Silicon MEMS (Micro-Electro-Mechanical Systems),
    - Miniaturized sensors that measure the deflection of a mass due to movement.
    - Typically perform with higher noise, vibration sensitivity and instability parameters than FOG IMUs.
    - In recent years MEMS-based IMUs are becoming more precise as the technology continues to be developed.
- IMUs are typically available in these performance grades:
  - Tactical
  - Industrial
  - Consumer grade

THALES

IMU Performance Grades

- **Tactical-** and industrial-grade IMUs offer high levels of performance and accuracy. These are preferred for applications such as UAV navigation.
- Tactical-grade IMUs have gyroscopes with an extremely low in-run bias stability. This is a key specification for high-precision applications.
- **Industrial-grade** IMUs offer good tolerance to shock and vibration, and exhibit good repeatability over time and temperature.
- MEMS-based IMUs are commonly used for applications requiring small form factor.

THALES

IMU Functional block Diagram

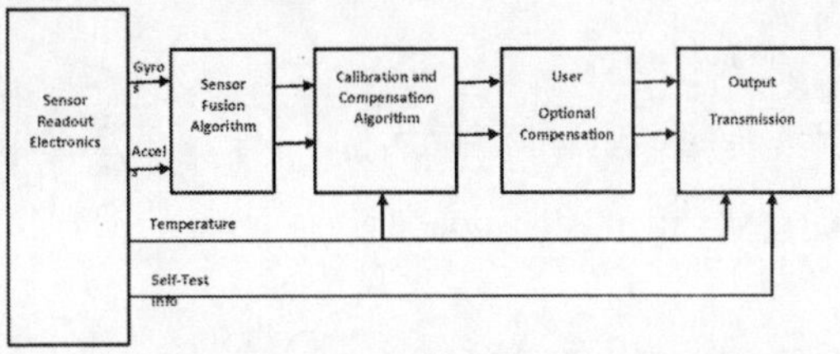

- A typical IMU includes a gyroscope, an accelerometer, temperature sensor and supporting algorithms
- An IMU typically includes A/D conversion to extract the measurements, temperature compensation and filtering to improve the output.
- Sensor fusion numerically integrates and solves the data for rotation angle (ΔΘ) and linear velocity (ΔV).
- Calibration and compensation corrects any misalignment or sensor biases
- A user, has an option to rotate (dΘ) and (dV) from IMU module internal axis to the mounted body (Vehicle's) frame of reference before transmitting the final data

THALES

Theory of Operation – Accelerometer

- An accelerometer is an electromechanical device used to measure acceleration
- Acceleration is the change in velocity, or speed divided by time
- Variation in MEMS process (etching , packaging etc) varies key parameters required to measure an acceleration
- Classical 2nd order acceleration equation:-

$$m\ddot{x} + c\dot{x} + kx = 0$$

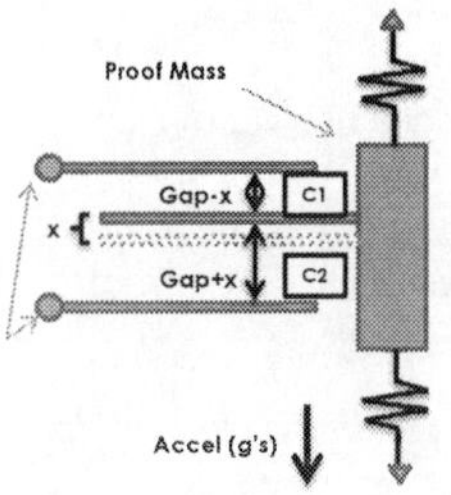

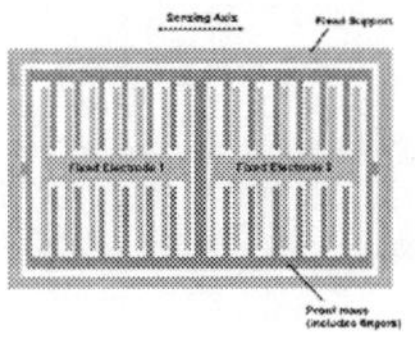

$$C \approx \varepsilon \frac{Area}{(gap + x)}$$

$$a \cong \frac{k.d^2}{\varepsilon.A.m} \Delta C$$

$$S = \frac{\varepsilon.A.m}{k.d^2}$$

THALES

Theory of Operation – Gyro's

- Gyro Sensors, Measure/sense angular velocity.
- Angular velocity is the change in rotational angle per unit of time.
- Gyros sense rotational motion and changes in orientation around a particular axis – X, Y or Z.
- For example: As an aircraft rolls, the gyro will measure non-zero values until the platform levels out
- Same as accelerometer, gyroscope output is dependent on calibration and compensation, post-assembly

THALES

Compensation, Calibration and Characterization

- Sensor calibration is a method of improving a sensor's performance by removing structural errors from the measurements of the sensor.
- Structural errors are differences between a sensor's expected output and its measured output, which show up consistently every time a new measurement is taken.
- By removing the structural errors, calibration provides a means of improving the overall accuracy of the underlying sensors.
  - > *Errors that are repeatable can be calculated during calibration and can be compensated in real-time to digitally remove any errors.*

THALES

Compensation, Calibration and Characterization

- Inertial measurement units (IMUs) are prone to various deterministic errors like:
  - Bias, scale factor, and non-orthogonality.

These errors are removed through various processes utilizing different equipment and test setups, including rate tables, and thermal chambers.

- These errors are removed through various processes utilizing different equipment and test setups, including rate tables, and thermal chambers.
- Sensor characterization incorporates a wide range of tests, including Allan Variance and vibration, to assess the inherent characteristics of the inertial sensors - specifications like noise that cannot be improved through a calibration process.
- Characterization testing can also be used to verify the post-calibration performance of a sensor to determine parameters such as scale factor error, using the same general testing process used for calibration.

MEMS Sensors - Common Specifications

- The performance and accuracy of an IMU are influenced by a variety of factors, including the sensor technology, the thermal properties of the packaging, and the software used.
- The following parameters are the most common and are generally included in the data sheet of the product:
- **Range:** The minimum and maximum input values a sensor can measure.
  - Accel: ±16g , Gyro: 2000 dps
- **Resolution:** The most precise unit of measure that can be outputted over a sensor's range. (µV, lsb/g etc)
- **Bandwidth:** The maximum frequency to which a sensor or system will respond. This frequency is typically defined at the point where the response has dropped to half power, or the -3 dB point on a Bode magnitude plot. Bandwidth defines the frequencies a sensor can measure.
- **Sample Rate:** the number of samples per second output by a sensor.
- **Noise:** any random variation of a measured output when a sensor is subjected to constant input at constant conditions; usually characterized by either a standard deviation value or a root-mean-square (RMS) value.
- **Noise Density:** outputting the signal at lower rate (down-sampling) reduces the measured noise of a sensor output. Some manufacturers specify standard deviation of noise at a particular sample rate, the more common measure is noise density which provides the noise divided by the square root of the sampling rate. (gyro: °/s/√hz)
- **Size, Weight and Power requirements (SWaP)** are key considerations in the design and development of any IMU

Critical Parameters For an IMU Selection

- These critical factors are dependent on the technologies used in the IMU and the physical properties of the accelerometers, gyroscopes and magnetometers.
- Several features to keep in mind before selecting an IMU for your application. Some key questions are:
  - what does the IMU output read when the input is zero? (Bias)
  - how similar is the IMU output when conditions have changed between measurements? (Bias Repeatability)
  - how much does the output change over time? (Bias stability)
  - how much random noise is present? (Random Walk)
  - how much does the output of the angular rate change per unit of vibration present in the system? (Vibration Sensitivity)

THALES

Bias

- The bias is a constant offset of the output value from the input value. There are many different types of bias parameters that can be measured
- **In-Run Bias Stability**, a.k.a. bias instability, is a measure of how the bias will drift during operation over time (due to noise) at a constant temperature. It is considered to be most critical specification as it represents the best possible accuracy with which a sensor's bias can be estimated.
  - The bias instability is expressed in degrees per hour for the gyro, and m/s^2 or milli-g for the accelerometer
  - Lower bias instability will lead to lower orientation, position, and velocity errors from the IMU
  - Bias instability is obtained by plotting an Allan-variance chart for a stationary gyro or accelerometer
  - The sensor fusion filter estimates the IMU biases to improve the state estimate. The IMU bias stability directly impact orientation estimation.
- **Turn-On Bias Stability,** or Bias Repeatability is an initial bias present in the IMU that can fluctuate in value from one turn-on to the next due to thermal, physical, mechanical, and electrical variations between measurements. This change in initial bias at constant conditions over the lifetime of the sensor is known as the turn-on bias stability, or bias repeatability. As it cannot be calibrated a smart algorithm can estimate it and account for it in the output measurement. This is very critical for unaided inertial navigation when it comes to faster tuning of the sensor fusion algorithms with less variable initial turn-on bias.
- **Bias Temperature Sensitivity**, the bias may respond differently to varying temperatures. This parameter is known as bias temperature sensitivity and can be calibrated after each of these biases are measured over the temperature range

THALES

Bias Error

- The impact of accelerometer and gyro bias on position error due to gravity misalignment

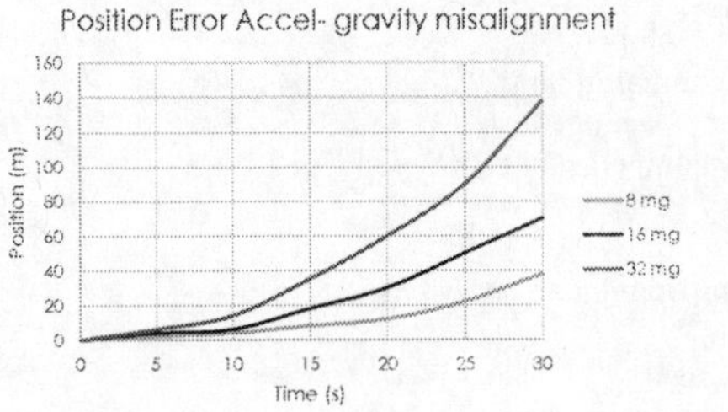

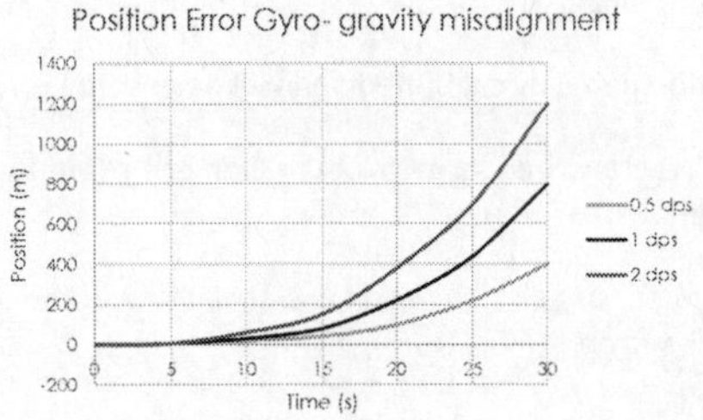

THALES

Random Walk

- If a noisy output signal from a sensor is integrated, for example integrating an angular rate signal to determine an angle, the integration will drift over time due to the noise.
- This drift is called random walk, as it will appear that the integration is taking random steps from one sample to the next.
- Two main types of random walk for inertial sensors
  - > angle random walk (ARW), which is applicable to gyroscopes, and
  - > velocity random walk (VRW), which is applicable to accelerometers.
- The specification for random walk is typically given in units of ∘/√s for gyroscopes, and m/s/√s

THALES

Scale Factor Error

- Scale factor or sensitivity is the ratio between the measured output and the change in sense input.
- SF typically varies over temperature and must be calibrated for over the operational temperature range
- SF will not be perfectly calibrated and will have some error in the estimated ratio.
- This error is categorized as parts per million error (ppm), or (equivalently) as an error percentage
- The scale factor can also have errors associated with the ratio being non-linear, known as nonlinearity errors
- The effect of accelerometer scale-factor error is similar to that of bias error, except that the error term increases as the input acceleration increases.
- Gyro scale-factor error contributes significant errors to the angle tracking of the IMU during dynamic motion. The scale-factor error term is worse under large angular velocities
- Scale factor error is usually a lesser contributor to total error as compared to bias error.

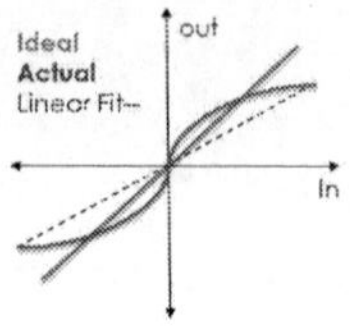

Orthogonality Error

- It is difficult to mount sensors perfectly orthogonal to each other. As a result, orthogonality errors are caused by a sensor axis responding to an input that should be orthogonal to the sensing direction.
- Two main types of orthogonality errors
  - Cross-axis sensitivity is an orthogonality error caused by a sensor axis being sensitive to an input on a different axis. In other words, an input in the x-axis may also be partially sensed in the z-axis.
  - Misalignment is an orthogonality error where the internal sensing axes do not align to the axes marked on the case of the IMU or case is not mounted perfectly to the platform (vehicle, camera etc.).

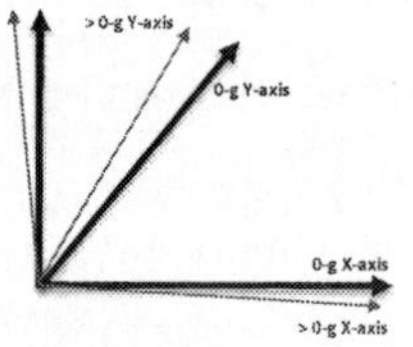

Allan Variance

- An Allan Variance test identifies the noise properties of an inertial sensor.
- Because of noise different asymptotic properties, they appear in the log-log plot of $\sigma^2(\tau)$ with the different slopes.
- A sensor is mounted statically inside a thermal chamber set to a constant temperature, with data logged at high rate for an extended period.
- The data is down-sampled at various time constants and the variances of each of these down-sampled measurements can be calculated at each of the different time constants.
- Despite its name, most of the time the results are plotted as standard deviations (square root of variance) versus the down-sampled time constants a log-log scale,
- The plot shown in Figure illustrates some key specifications for an inertial sensor:
  - **Angle Random Walk/White noise** (equivalent to noise density), Noise density is roughly equal to the standard deviation at an averaging time constant of one second.
  - **In-run bias stability,** the minimum standard deviation value on the plot is the in-run bias stability.
  - **Rate Random Walk** is characterized by red noise(Brownian noise) spectrum of the inertial sensor. Long term changes to bias off-set may be permanent in nature.

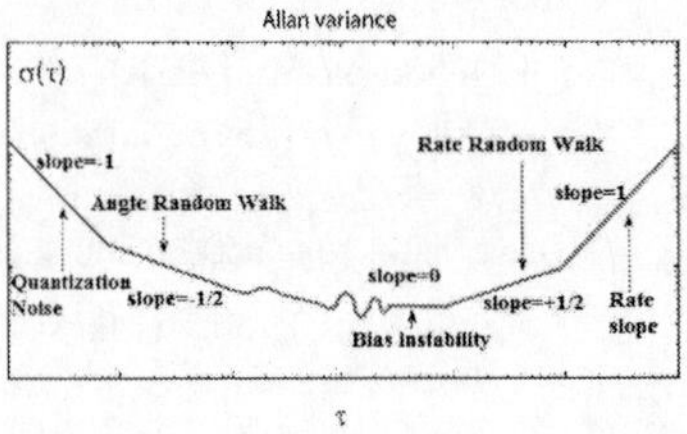

THALES

Acceleration Sensitivity For Gyroscopes

- In an ideal world, a gyroscope would only measure angular rate and would have no sensitivity to linear acceleration.
- In practice gyroscopes are susceptible to linear accelerations due to their asymmetrical design and manufacturing tolerances.
- Two types of linear acceleration sensitivities
  - G-Sensitivity: An acceleration sensitivity in which a gyroscope experiences a bias shift when subjected to a constant linear acceleration
    - Gyroscopes must be tested for sensitivity to linear accelerations both parallel and perpendicular to the sensing axis.
    - A gyroscope's bias sensitivity to linear acceleration can be calibrated in real-time using the measured (and calibrated) accelerometer values.
  - g^2 – sensitivity specification is an acceleration sensitivity that causes a bias shift in the output of a gyroscope due to oscillatory linear accelerations.
    - Gyroscopes' sensitivity to acceleration can be readily determined through vibration testing, both using sine-sweeps or random vibration profiles.

THALES

Vibration Rejection Under Extreme Conditions

Some key features to keep in mind while selecting and designing the IMU based application

- Selection of MEMS Gyro with specifically designed sense masses to reject external accelerations (unrelated to angular motion)
  - Quadruple mass design
  - Ability to measure Vibration rectification
- Use of filter to reject the shock using MEMS accelerometer data avoiding any latency in the signal output.
  - MEMS accelerometer logic should be sensitive enough to distinguish between sudden rotation vs a shock/vibration
  - Design of anti-alias and decimation filter
  - Use of Kalman filter to estimate sudden angular rate error and bias shift.
- Design and place the IMU in the middle of application board to reject any vibration
- Design of package and mounting to reject shock/vibration
- Choosing inertial sensor with bandwidth designed to reject high frequency vibration

THALES

The End

THALES

Sensors Converge

Using Metrics to Monitor IoT Devices at Scale

Tyler Hoffman (Memfault)

#SensorsConverge

Speaker

Tyler Hoffman

Co-founder, Memfault

tyler@memfault.com | @ty_hoff

Previously a Firmware Engineer @ Pebble & Fitbit

Split time between writing firmware and building internal services to help monitor millions of devices

Can find my thoughts and content on Memfault's Interrupt blog (interrupt.memfault.com)

pebble. fitbit Memfault

#SensorsConverge

Sensors Converge

Firmware is *hard* and *pervasive*

- Last Quarter Alone - 4.4 billion Cortex M's shipped!
- Software issues lead to:
  - Bricked devices, RMA's, and security exploits
- Software is becoming more complex

We need proper tools to help us build quality products

#SensorsConverge

What are we trying to do today?

- "Simple" firmware on embedded systems
- Speed from development to testing to mass production
- Find and fix (quickly) 1 in 10,000 hour bugs in production
- Prevent issues from being released to 100% of devices
- Establish measurable stats to track progress on goals

#SensorsConverge

A favorite quote

"These techniques are not necessary because experienced firmware engineers do not introduce bugs in their code"

- A (real) Firmware Engineer

#SensorsConverge

Sensors Converge

Agenda

1 State of the union

2 Quantifying current issues

3 Investigating the issues

4 Make decisions with metrics

5 Best Practices

#SensorsConverge

Sensors Converge

State of the union for firmware

Firmware is *complex*

#SensorsConverge

Complex Topologies

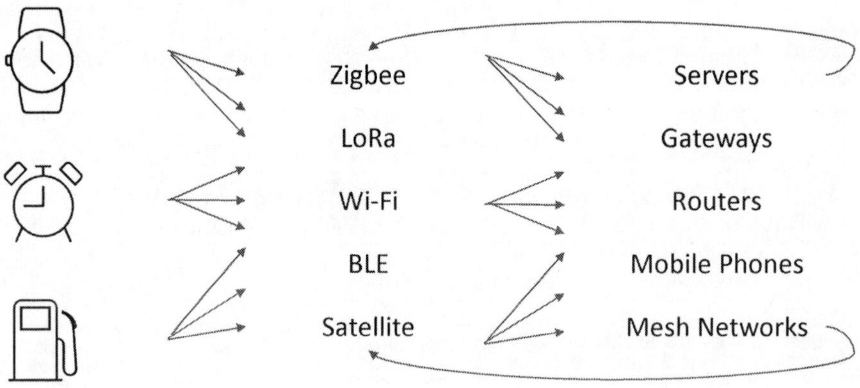

#SensorsConverge

Complex Software

Firmware no longer is complete isolated

- Must communicate to mobile phones & gateways
- Protocols, devices, and security issues constantly changing
- Libraries are *massively complicated* (e.g. mbedTLS)

Even the simplest sensors-only firmware is complex.

For example, Zephyr RTOS

Expectations are growing

- Everything connects to Internet
- Must enable firmware updates
- Competition is growing

#SensorsConverge

Limited Debugging Tools

```
***** MPU FAULT *****
  Instruction Access Violation
***** Hardware exception *****
Current thread ID = 0x20000074
Faulting instruction address = 0xe0000000
Fatal fault in thread 0x20000074! Aborting.
```

```
[I][1605794400] Wi-Fi connected
[W][1605796200] Wi-Fi disconnected, reason: -2
[I][1605796500] Wi-Fi connected
[W][1605797100] Wi-Fi disconnected, reason: -2
[I][1605798000] Battery status: 67%, 3574 mV
```

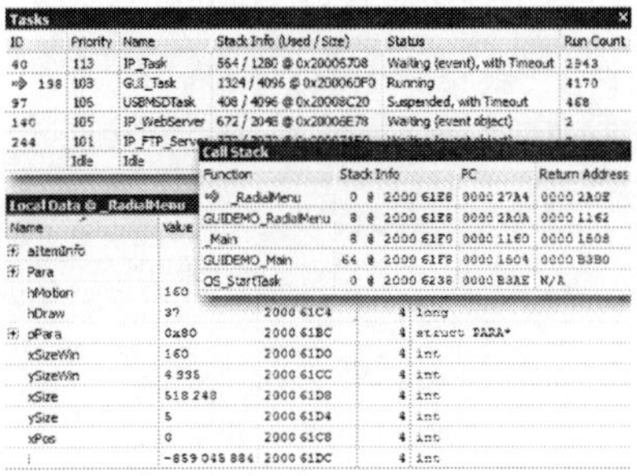

The existing tools are decent, but only when connected using JTAG

#SensorsConverge

Debugging Data Sent to ???

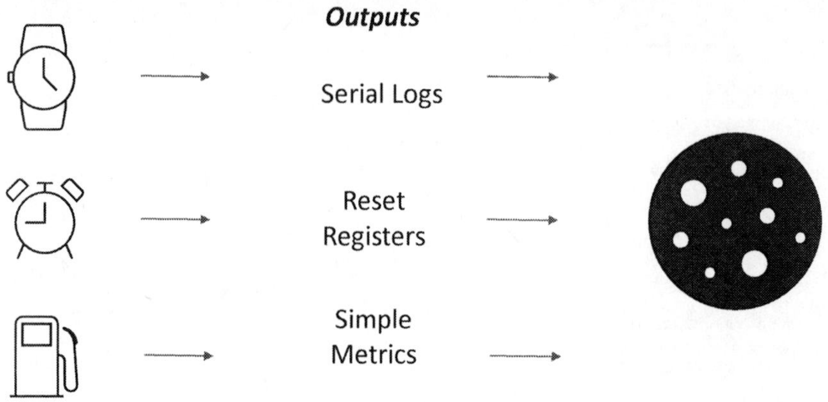

#SensorsConverge

Sensors Converge

Not much exists to help us

Existing software solutions won't work

- We aren't monitoring 10-100 servers, rather 10k – 1m+ devices
- We don't have MB's and GB's of RAM lying around
- Assembly, C, C++
- Symbol files (.elf's) required for interesting debugging

Firmware lacks a "sharing" mentality. It's also hard to.

Whatever we need, we have to build ourselves

#SensorsConverge

Sensors Converge

Some issues only happen in the field

"a third of all software faults take more than 5000 execution-years to manifest themselves."

*Source: http://www.ganssle.com/tem/tem417.html

#SensorsConverge

Sensors Converge

Agenda

1 State of the union

2 Quantifying current issues

3 Investigating the issues

4 Make decisions with metrics

5 Best Practices

#SensorsConverge

Sensors Converge

Detecting Current Issues

Do we have issues in the field?

Detecting Current Issues

If you don't know if or how often devices have issues…

They're likely having issues

#SensorsConverge

Sensors Converge

Detecting Current Issues

Fundamentally, we need to know if and how many times devices are experiencing issues.

Once we have this information:

- Can assess whether further work is needed.
- Can make assumptions about whether a firmware update improved stability
- Can guide business & product decisions
- *Leaders know whether it's time to fix bugs and tech debt or build new features*

#SensorsConverge

Sensors Converge

Detecting Current Issues

Reset

{
 "reason": "watchdog",
}

Watchdogs: 67
Hardfaults: 23
Shutdowns: 17

BLE Disconnect

{
 "reason": -5
}

Number Disconnects: 83
Common Reason: State Error

Ping

{
 "uptime": 86345
}

Number devices: 890
Average Uptime: 90,234 seconds

#SensorsConverge

Sensors Converge

Detecting Current Issues

Sending & Parsing logs

- Log important device events
- Log resets and registers
- ***Hard and doesn't scale well***

Assumes:

- Path to the Internet
- Some central repository for device data

Tracking simple metrics:

- # device issues (user & error resets)
- # devices alive and well
- Average uptime of devices
- ***Scalable, but less information***

#SensorsConverge

Sensors Converge

Agenda

1. State of the union
2. Quantifying current issues
3. Investigating the issues
4. Make decisions with metrics
5. Best Practices

#SensorsConverge

Sensors Converge

Debugging in Production

We don't have access to our normal toolset.

- No UART & serial logs
- No JTAG and quick re-flashing
- No IDE, GDB, or step-through debugging

We need tools specifically for debugging in production

- Build these tools **as early as possible**
- Having them early will pay off 10x. (Speaking from experience)
- If you have no interest in building them, check out Memfault.

#SensorsConverge

Sensors Converge

Using Logs to Analyze Issues

```
[I][1605794400] Wi-Fi connected
[W][1605796200] Wi-Fi disconnected, reason: -2
[I][1605796500] Wi-Fi connected
[W][1605797100] Wi-Fi disconnected, reason: -2
[I][1605798000] Battery status: 67%, 3574 mV
```

2 Wi-Fi disconnect events

1 Battery level event

```
***** MPU FAULT *****
  Instruction Access Violation
***** Hardware exception *****
Current thread ID = 0x20000074
Faulting instruction address = 0xe0000000
Fatal fault in thread 0x20000074! Aborting.
```

1 crash due to MPU violation

Program Counter:
`0xe0000000`

#SensorsConverge

Metrics

A **metric** is a measurement captured at runtime

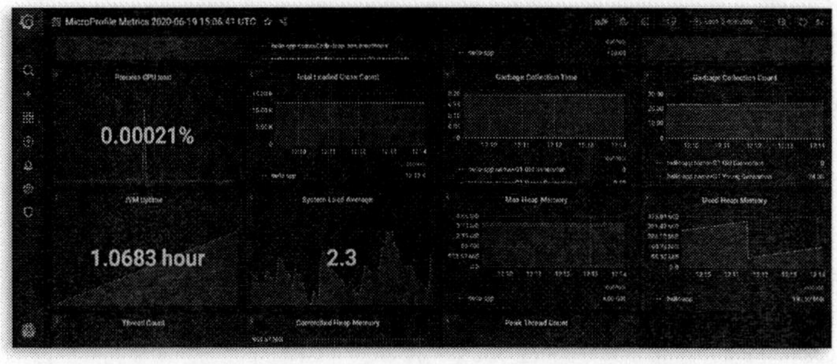

Combing large numbers of metrics and calculating statistics is called an **aggregation**

#SensorsConverge

Metrics

Uncover trends on anything that is numerical

Common metrics are:

- Task runtimes
- Heap information
- Connectivity statistics
- Frequency of errors
- Peripheral utilization and power states

```
Example App Booting
Metric ID: 1 -- Value: 15000  # elapsed ticks
Metric ID: 2 -- Value: 8531   # Main Task ticks
Metric ID: 3 -- Value: 8223   # Timer Task ticks
Metric ID: 4 -- Value: 14     # Timer Task count
Metric ID: 5 -- Value: 3593   # "sensor on" ticks
Metric ID: 6 -- Value: 4696   # heap-free low watermark
```

Pinpoint **power**, **connectivity**, and **performance** issues and regressions

#SensorsConverge

Sensors Converge

Metrics

1. View device's vitals over time

Battery Life %:

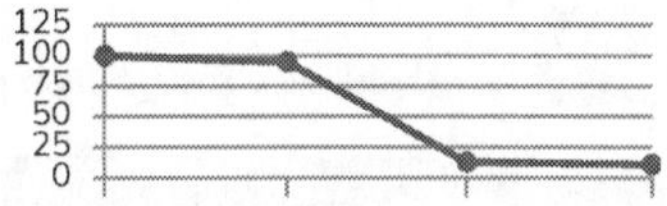

2. Assessing the collective health of all devices

% Time Connected per Hour: 95% -> 77%

3. Enable comparing metrics between firmware versions

Average Battery Life:

v1.0 - 5.5 days

v1.1 - 4.1 days

#SensorsConverge

Sensors Converge

Using Logs to Analyze Issues

```
void flash_sector_erase(uint16_t sector) {
    ...
    device_metrics_incr(kDeviceMetric_FlashSectorErases);
}

void flash_write_bytes(uint32_t addr, void *buf, size_t n) {
    ...
    device_metrics_incr_by(kDeviceMetric_FlashWriteBytes, n);
}
```

#SensorsConverge

Sensors Converge

Individual Device Insights

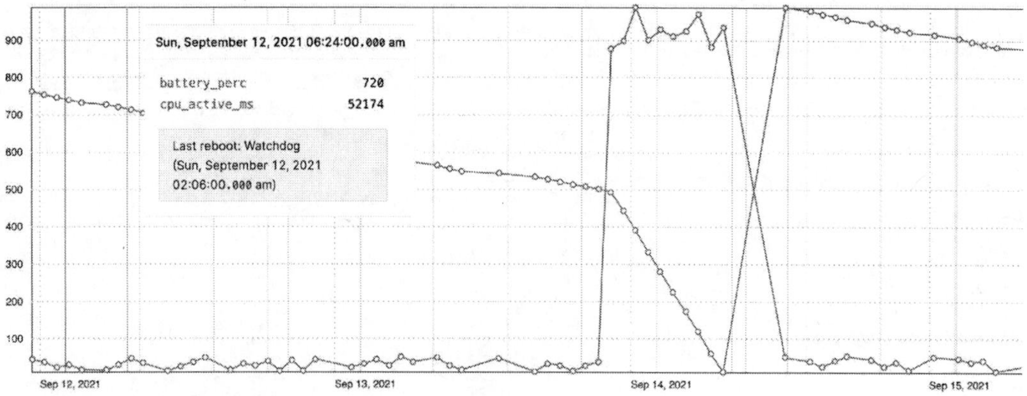

#SensorsConverge

Sensors Converge

Using Logs to Analyze Issues

Per Device

Counts
Averages
Min/Max

Entire Fleet

Counts
Averages
Min/Max

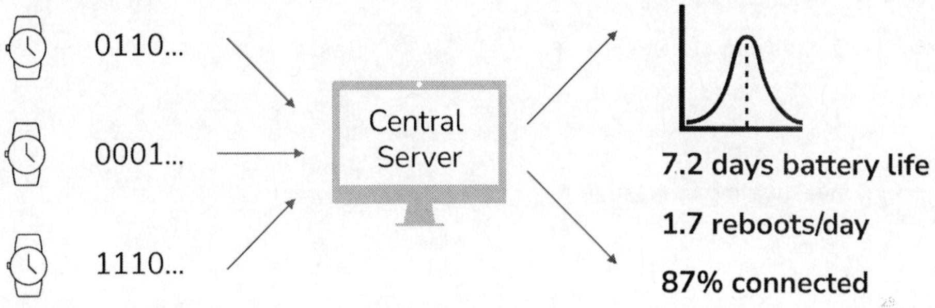

Using Logs to Analyze Issues

We can compare metrics between firmware versions

	v1.0.0	v1.1.0	Improvement?
CPU sleep time	83%	96%	✓
Average Uptime	1.3 days	1.32 days	⚠
Stack bytes free – low water mark	150 bytes	72 bytes	✗

Agenda

1. State of the union
2. Quantifying current issues
3. Investigating the issues
4. Make decisions with metrics
5. Best Practices

#SensorsConverge

Sensors Converge

Making Decisions with Metrics

Listen to the metrics

Go / No-Go Metrics

Are we good to ship this firmware?

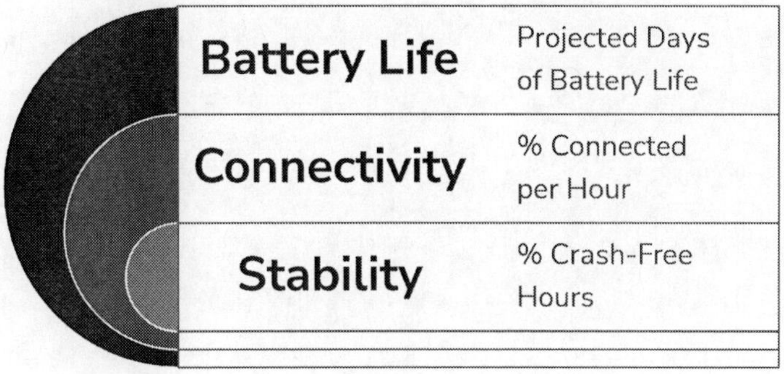

*Do **not** ship firmware **without** hitting your metrics.*

#SensorsConverge

Battery Life Drain

```
void device_metrics_flush(void) {
    ...
    static int32_t s_prev_battery_pct;

    const int32_t current_battery_pct = battery_get_pct();
    const int32_t battery_delta =
        current_battery_pct - s_prev_battery_pct;

    device_metrics_set(kDeviceMetricId_BatteryLifeDrain,
                       battery_delta);
}
```

#SensorsConverge

Measure Task Utilization

```
static void prvAltTask(void *pvParameters) {
    uint32_t task_tick;
    while (1) {
        unsigned long received;
        xQueueReceive(xQueue, &received, portMAX_DELAY);

        device_metrics_timer_start(&task_tick) {

        // Do work

        device_metrics_timer_stop(kDeviceMetricId_AltTaskTime,
                                  &task_tick) {
    }
}
```

#SensorsConverge

Connectivity Time

```
static uint32_t s_wifi_ticks;

void wifi_connected_callback(void) {
    // Start timer when Wi-Fi connects
    device_metrics_timer_start(&s_wifi_ticks);
}

void wifi_disconnected_callback(void) {
    // Stop timer when Wi-Fi connects
    device_metrics_timer_end(kDeviceMetricWifiConnectedDuration
                             &s_wifi_ticks);
}
```

#SensorsConverge

Agenda

1. State of the union
2. Quantifying current issues
3. Investigating the issues
4. Make decisions with metrics
5. Best Practices

#SensorsConverge

Sensors Converge

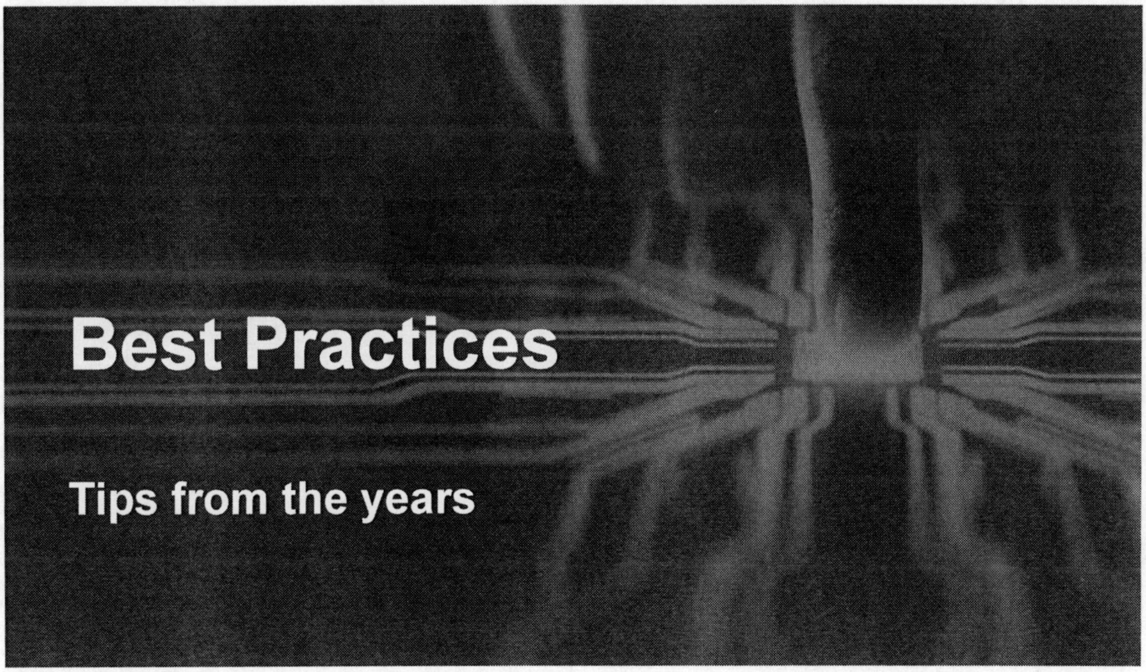

Creativity with Metrics

An int32_t can store a lot of data!

- Register Values
- Hardware Readings
- 4 ASCII chars
- Bitfields
- Device Configuration
- 32 booleans

Litter your codebase with them

#SensorsConverge

Sensors Converge

Internal Testing

You *must* be testing the devices internally

- Catch and fix as many bugs before production as possible
- Firmware team, QA, engineers, and other employees
- Ask biggest fans of your product to be beta testers
- Encourage users to report bugs

Build and deploy nightly or regular firmware updates to devices

- Constantly be fixing and verifying fixes
- Perform experiments!

Your device just reset. Please submit a support ticket!

Unfortunately, some bugs will only be caught in production.

#SensorsConverge

Sensors Converge

The End

Happy to connect!

https://www.linkedin.com/in/tyhoff/

https://memfault.com/webinars/

https://interrupt.memfault.com

Email: tyler@memfault.com

#SensorsConverge

Sensors Converge

haydenAI
Vaibhav Ghadiok
Executive Vice President Engineering
100 GOVTECH COMPANY 2021
CONFIDENTIAL | DO NOT DISSEMINATE | PROPERTY OF HAYDEN AI TECHNOLOGIES, INC.

HOW DO WE MAKE OUR CITIES MORE EFFICIENT?
ONLY
MTA

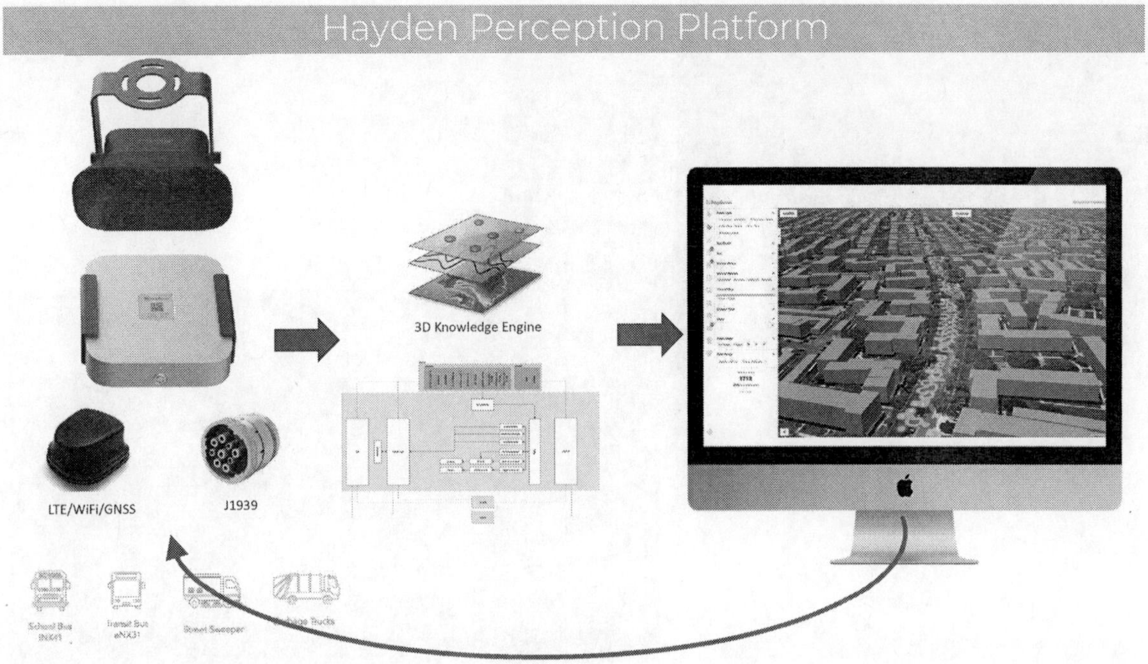
Hayden Perception Platform
3D Knowledge Engine
LTE/WiFi/GNSS
J1939

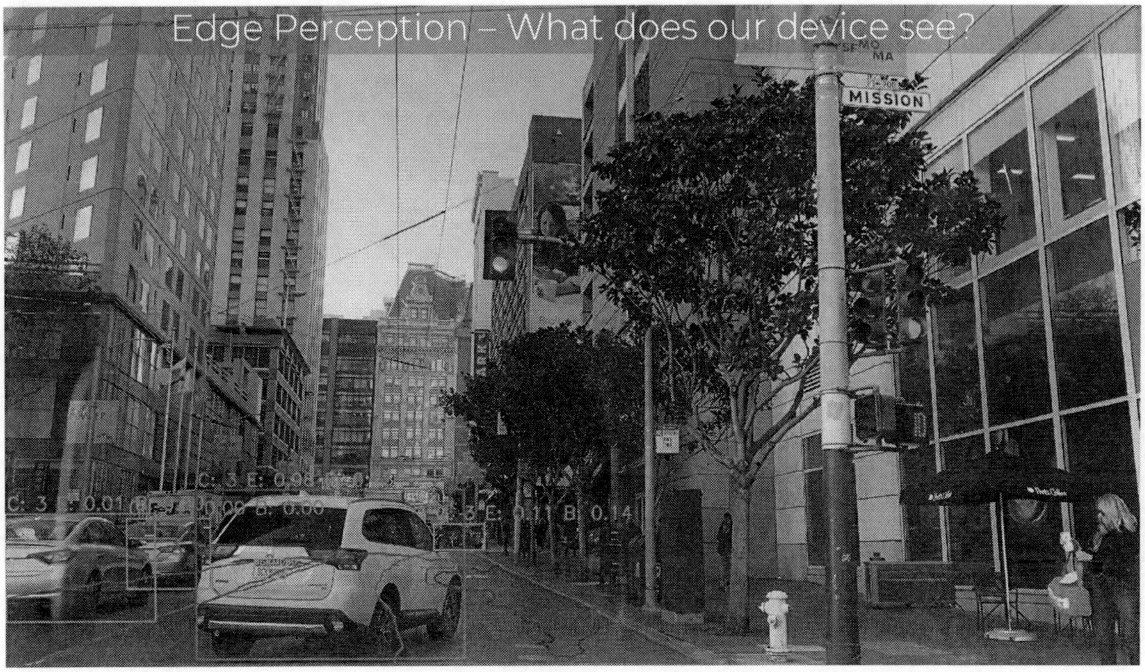
Edge Perception – What does our device see?
MISSION

Geometry
MISSION
Semantics
MISSION

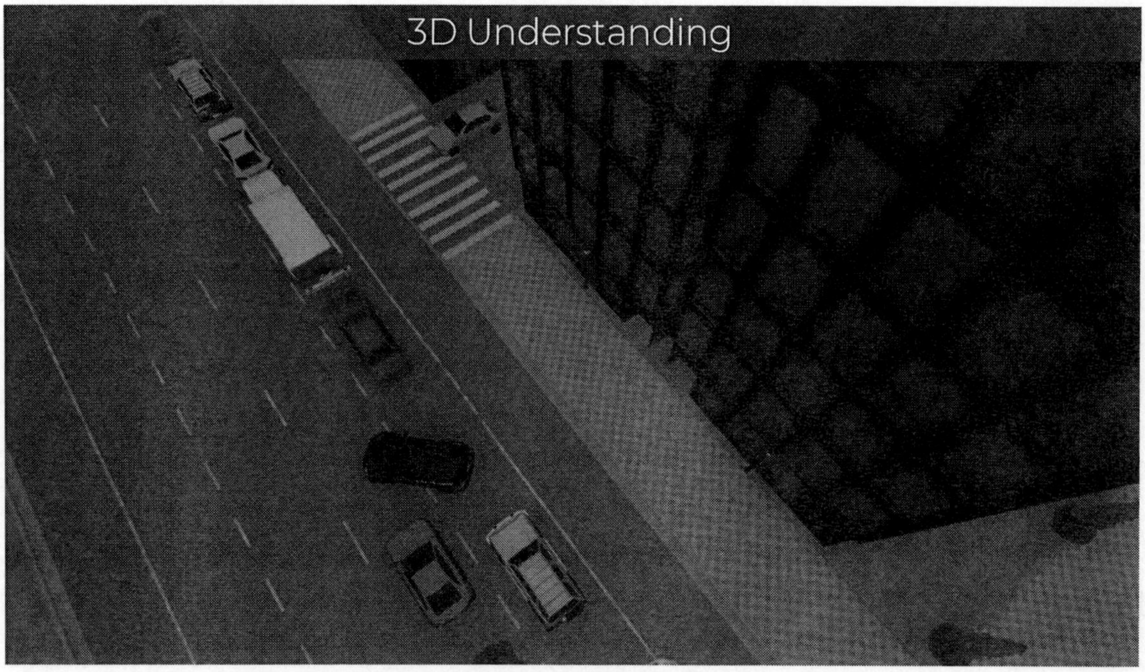
3D Understanding

On the inside

Highest Performance – Day, Night, Rain or Snow

Smallest Form Factor

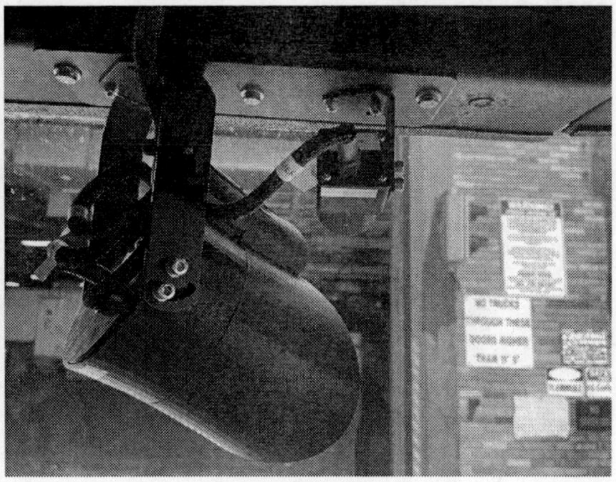

Think inside the bus!

Hayden iNX31 in action

Operate in Day, Night, Rainfall, or Snow

- Context Camera
  - HDR
  - ISP

- LPR Camera
  - Lens
  - SNR
  - Active vs Passive

Robust Localization - Sensor Fusion enabled cross-calibration

Camera - Scale ambiguity and drift

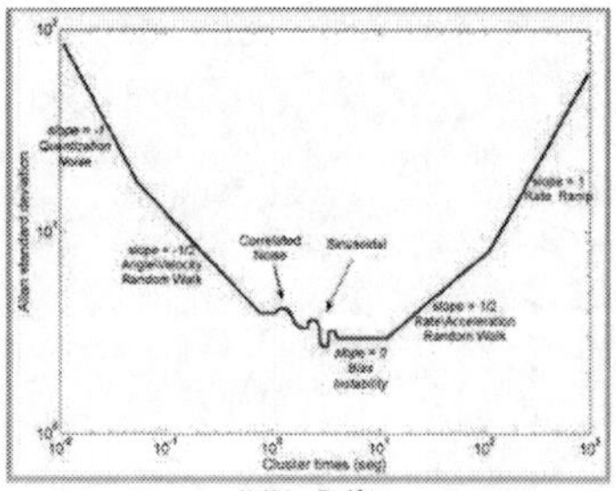
IMU - Drift

Wheel Odometry - Wheel Slip

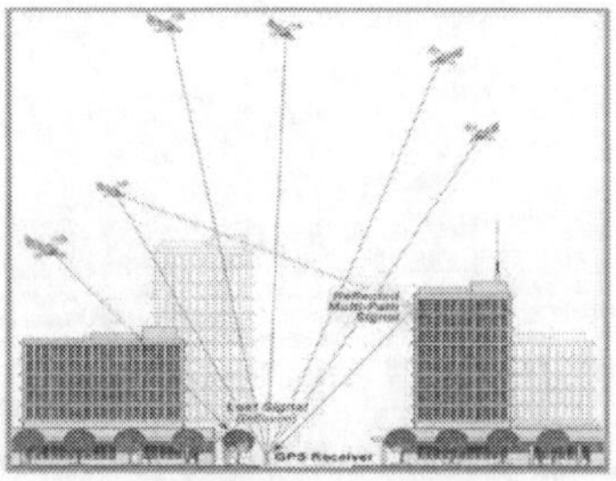
GNSS - Multipath

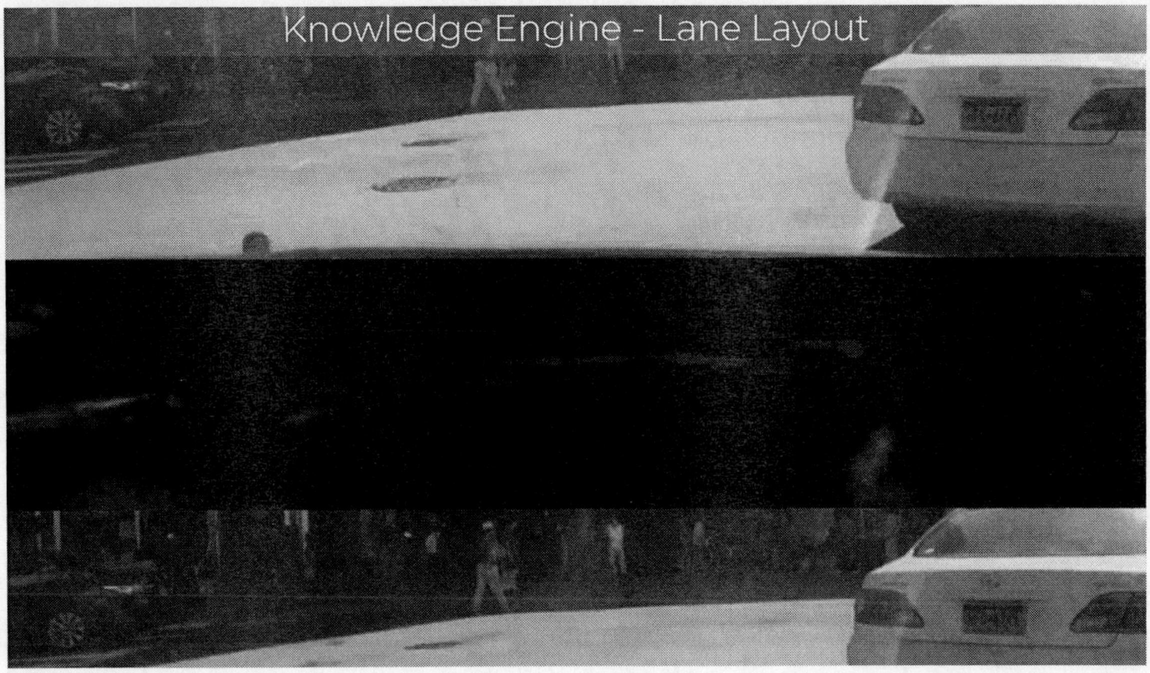
Knowledge Engine - Lane Layout

Semantic Layer
hayden.ai
Trajectory file:
Video file:
Selected 1 point(s)

Layered Perception Stack

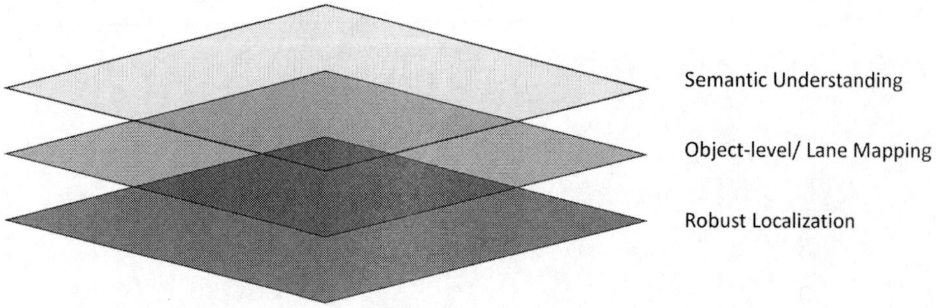

What else can we do?

hayden AI

Safety first - Is there a Bus Stop?
sky
building
traffic light
building
tree
truck
person
car
car
handbag
hayden.ai
road
pavement

Passengers waiting at a Bus Stop
sky
building
traffic light
building
traffic light
tree
person
car
car
person
hayden.ai
road
pavement

State-of-the-art Parking Management

Parking Management with Hayden AI – Software Update Away
2021/05/24 15:58:28
ProcFPS: 20 RecFPS: 13 LonErr: 0.000000 LatErr: 0.000000 LaneDist: 10000.000000

Protect the Cyclists

Data Driven Smart City Insights
sky
RIGHT LANE
BUSES
TAXIS
ONLY
building
Questions
tree
truck
person
person
car
vaibhav.ghadiok@hayden.ai
hayden.ai
road
pavement

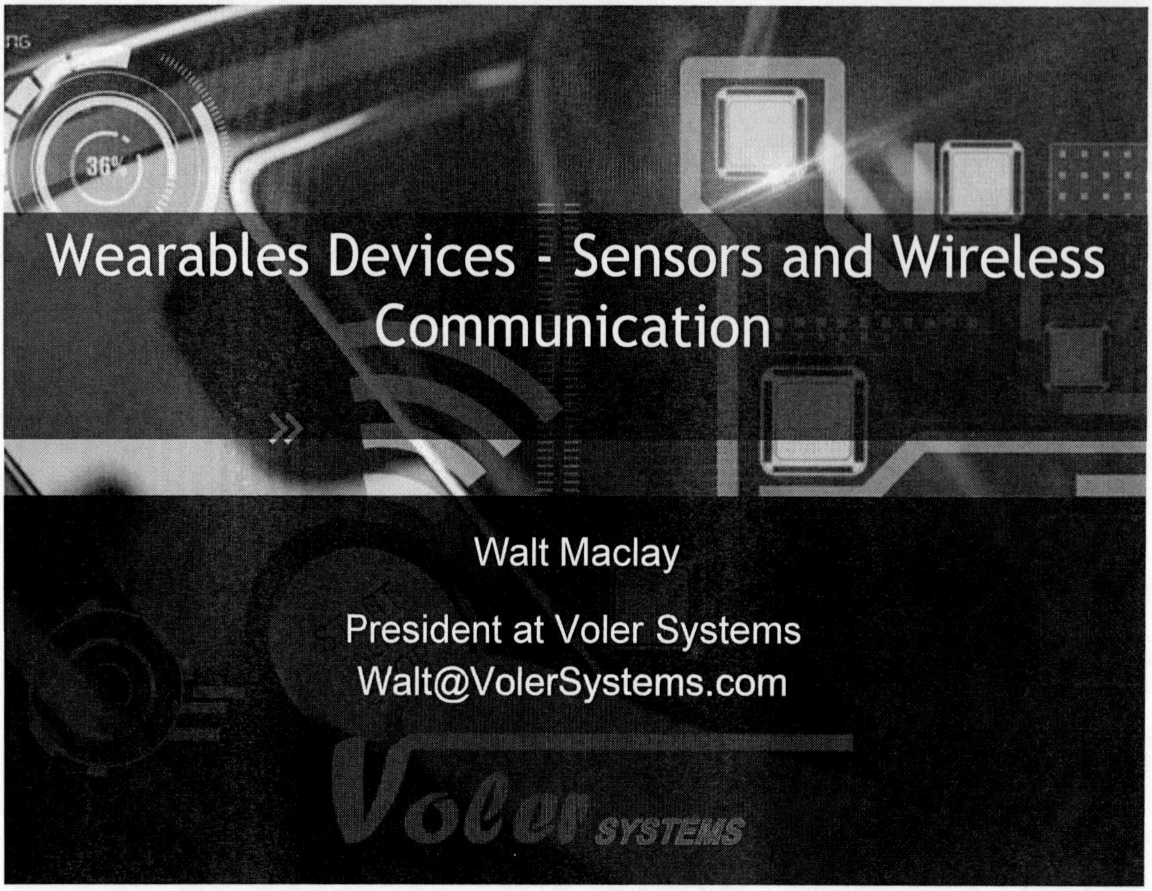
Wearables Devices - Sensors and Wireless Communication
Walt Maclay
President at Voler Systems
Walt@VolerSystems.com
Voler
SYSTEMS

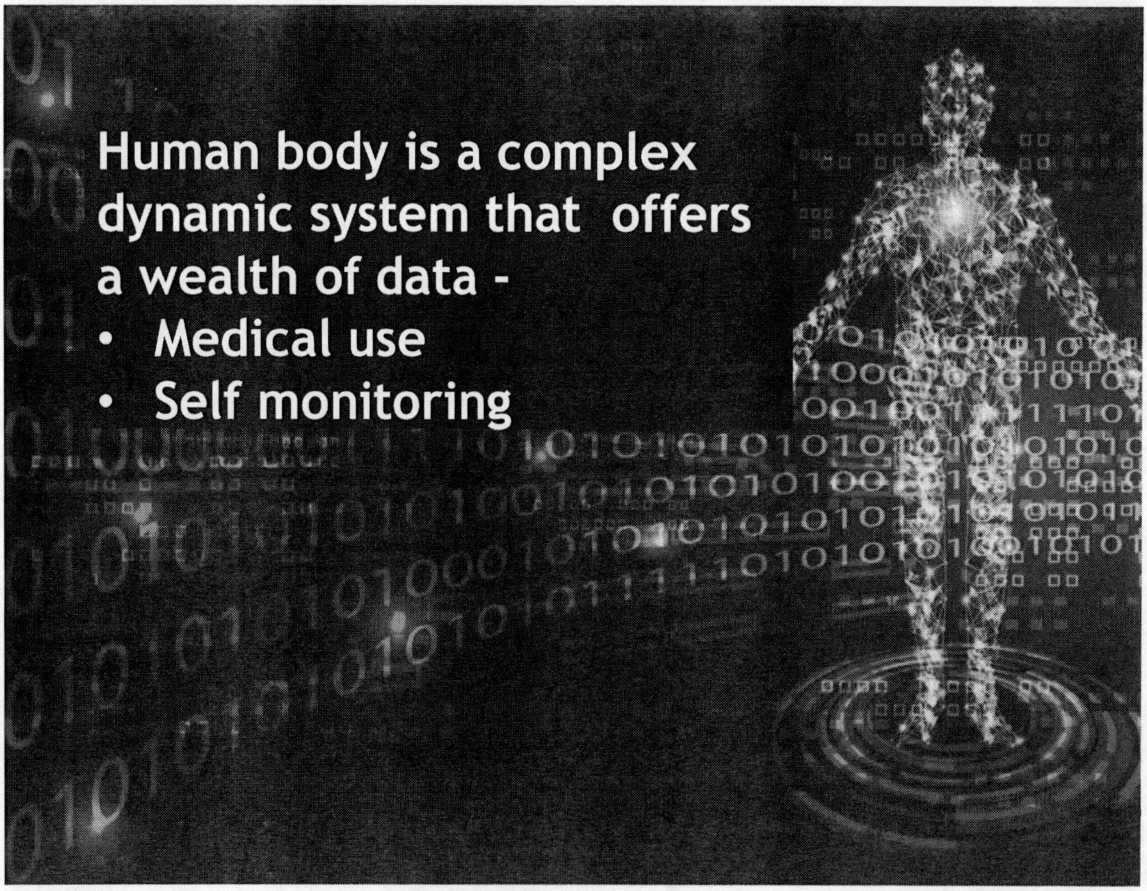
Human body is a complex dynamic system that offers a wealth of data -
• Medical use
• Self monitoring

< Slide 4 >

What kind of data would you like to have?

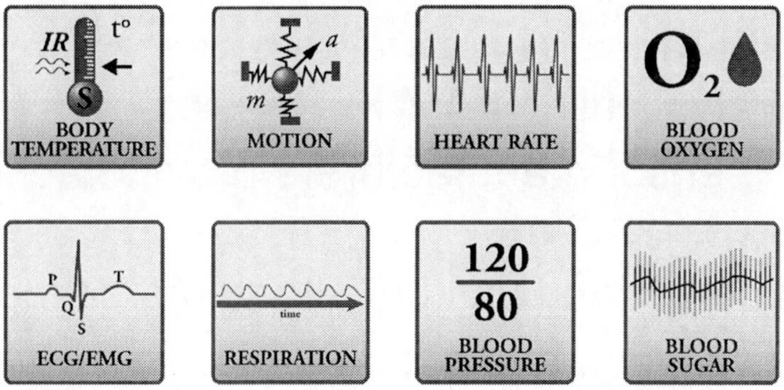

Voler SYSTEMS

< Slide 5 >

Body Temperature

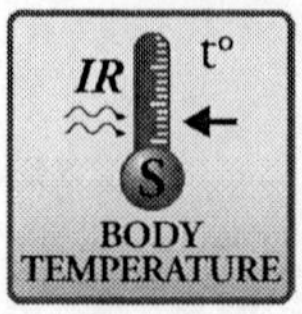

- Few good locations to measure core temperature
  - Axilla (under arm), ear, or forehead are best locations
  - Not convenient for most wearable devices
- Extremeties (eg wrist) have variable temperature
- Algorithms can partially adjust over time
- Good contact is important – heat flow causes errors

Voler SYSTEMS

< Slide 6 >

Motion

- The most studied and used parameter
- Step counts
- Gait analysis (illness)
- Motion sensor manufacturers provide advanced software algorithms
- Types of motion (walking, standing, sitting)
- Works on wrist, ankle, torso, etc.
  - Different algorithms at different locations
- Dead reckoning (9-axis motion)

Voler SYSTEMS

< Slide 7 >

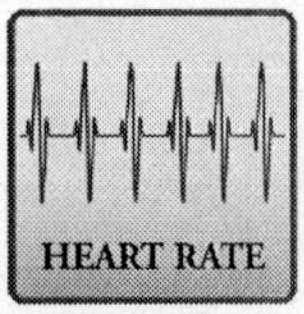

Heart Rate

- Measured by
  - ECG electrodes – two are sufficient
  - Pulse oximeter (PPG) sensing – transmissive
    - Transmitted works on finger and ear
  - Pulse oximeter (PPG) – reflected
    - Works more places on body
  - Pressure sensing of the pulse in the wrist
- Wrist measurement works well for Heart Rate, but not for ECG

Voler SYSTEMS

< Slide 8 >

Blood Oxygen

- Oxygen saturation in blood or SpO2
- Measured by pulse oximeter (PPG) sensor
  - Measure loss through body of 2 light wavelengths
  - Detects Oxygen content of red blood cells
  - Separates changes in blood from pulse
  - Measure pulse at the same time
- Transmissive or reflective measurement
  - Reflective for more places on body
  - Transmissive for better accuracy – on finger or ear only

Voler SYSTEMS

< Slide 9 >

ECG / EMG / EEG

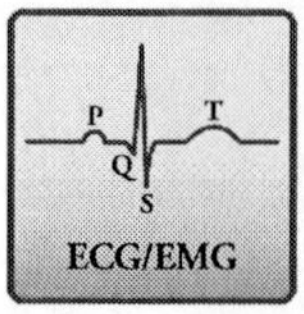

- Measure electrical signal using electrodes
- ECG measurement points have to be rather far apart
  - At least one and a half inches – larger devices needed
  - More leads is better (up to 12 for standard ECG)
- EMG requires accurate placement (millimeters)
  - Measure the wrong muscle
- EEG must use electrodes on the head

Voler SYSTEMS

< Slide 10 >

Respiration Rate

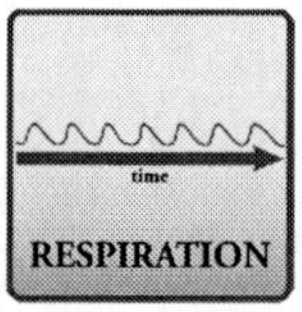

- Number of breaths per minute
  - Few good locations to measure
- Movement of chest
  - Chest strap
  - Not convenient for a wearable device except shirt
- Nasal Canula
  - Not comfortable or convenient
- Thoracic Impedance eliminates chest strap
  - Device can be small
  - Difficult on wrist
- ECG signal – filter out heart signal – experimental

Voler SYSTEMS

< Slide 11 >

Blood Pressure

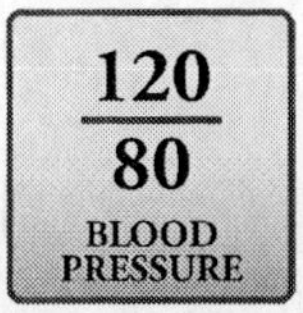

- Pressure cuff that is compressed and released
  - Does not work as well on wrist
- Pulse Transit Time – measure at ear, finger, or wrist
- PPG with software algorithm
  - Finally medically accurate without calibration
  - Study results published by Valencell, Inc., May 2021
- Others
  - Direct pressure measurement at artery
  - ECG – using neural network
  - Not medically accurate
- Other technologies in development

< Slide 12 >

Blood Sugar (Glucose)

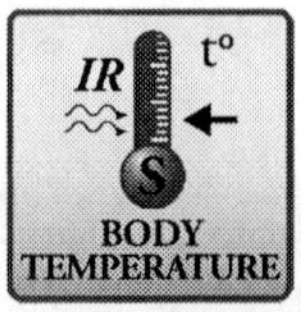

- Measure of glucose level in blood sample
- Continuous Glucose Monitoring (CGM) Use Growing
  - With small needle, microneedles, or implanted
- Calibration required
- Not accurate on wrist
  - Need good blood perfusion
- Closed loop system replaces the pancreas
  - Measure and control glucose with a pump

< Slide 13 >

Cameras on Wearable Devices

- Camera chips are small: 1x1 to 8x10 mm
- Wide field of view – depends upon lens
- Fixed focus has very good depth of field
  - A few centimeters to infinity
- Single images are easy to store and transmit
- Streaming video requires WiFi or cellular
  - High power consumption
- Camera consumes a lot of power

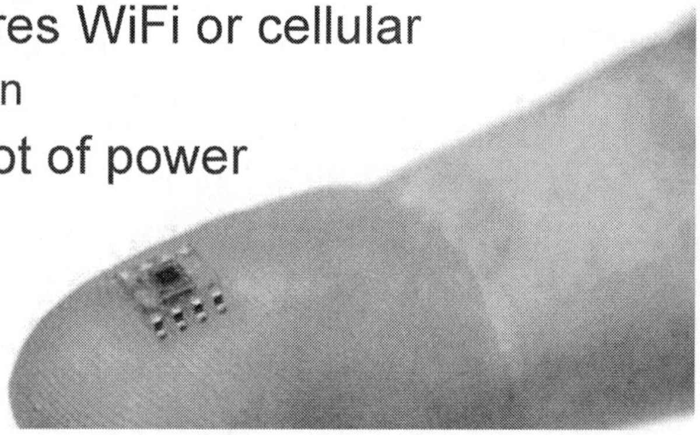

< Slide 14 >

Battery Limitations

- Slow pace of improvement
  If improved like semiconductors:
  Size of a pin head, could power your car, cost 1 cent
- Chemical energy storage is approaching the limit of its efficiency
- Must always work around limitations

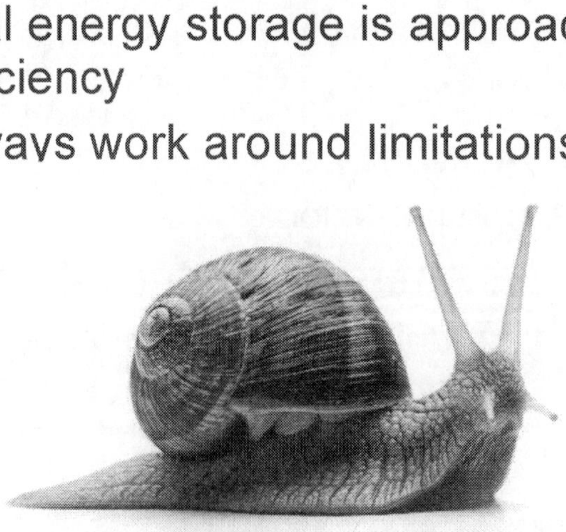

Voler SYSTEMS

< Slide 15 >

5 Areas That Impact Power

- Wireless transmission
- Sensors
- Displays
- Microprocessors
- Software

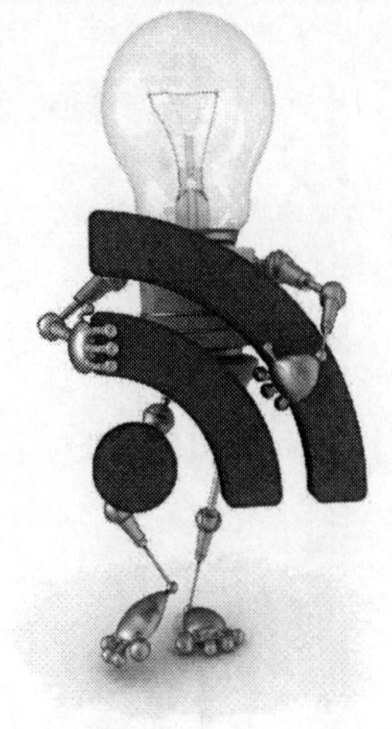

Let's focus on the first two

Voler SYSTEMS

< Slide 16 >

Comparison of IoT Wireless Standards

	LTE-M	NB-IOT	Sigfox	LoRa	BTLE Mesh	Zigbee	WiFi	Cellular
Range	1-50 km	1-50 km	10-50 km	2-50 km	10 m	50 m	100 m	10 km
Data rate	1 Mbit/s	20-250 Kbit/s	300 bit/s	200-50 K bit/s	20 Kbit/s	40 Kbit/s	50 Mbit/s	100 Mbit/s
Supports Audio	Yes	Yes	No	No	No	Yes	Yes	Yes
Network	Public	Public	Public	Public or Private	Private	Private	Private	Public
Available	Good coverage	Good coverage	Limited coverage	Yes Limited public	Limited	Mature	Mature	Mature

Voler SYSTEMS

Power- How Much? How Far?

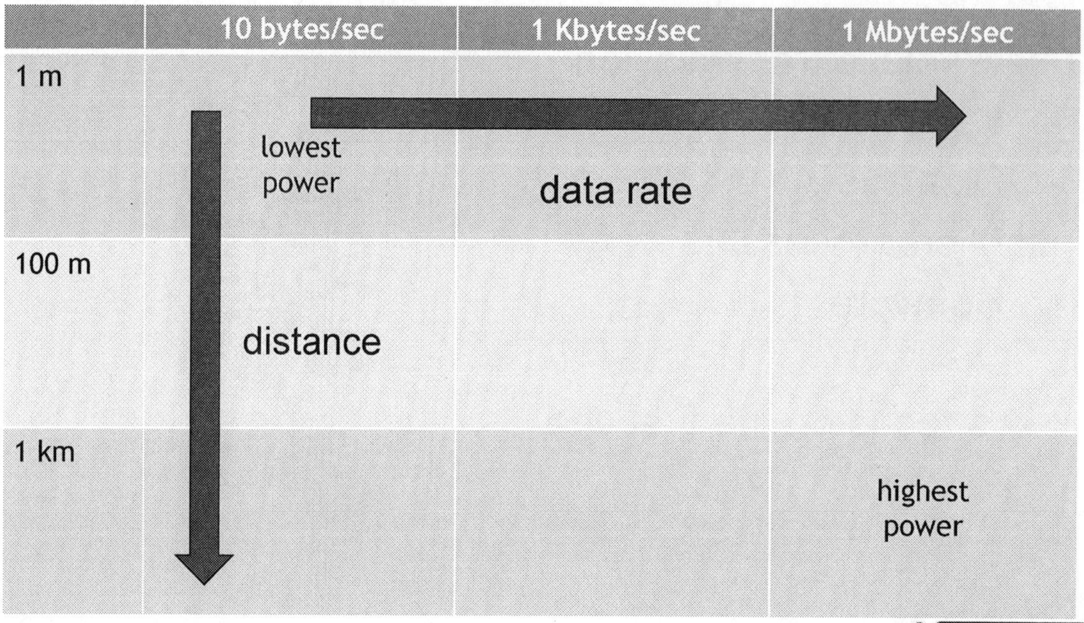

Voler SYSTEMS

Various Wireless Technology for IoT

	100 bps	10K bps	40K bps
1 m	BLE4/Zigbee 0.15 BLE Mesh 0.15 Bluetooth 25 WiFi 50 LoRa 0.5	BLE4/Zigbee 7.5 BLE Mesh 7.5 Bluetooth 25 WiFi 50 LoRa 10	Zigbee 30 Bluetooth 25 WiFi 50 LoRa 20
50 m	Zigbee 20 WiFi 100 LoRa 0.5 Sigfox 0.5 NB-IoT, LTE-M 1.0 LTE, 5G Cellular 100	Zigbee 30 WiFi 100 LoRa 20 NB-IoT, LTE-M 30 LTE, 5G Cellular 150	WiFi 200 NB-IoT, LTE-M 200 LTE, 5G Cellular 200
1 km	LoRa 30 Sigfox 30 NB-IoT, LTE-M 20 LTE, 5G Cellular 120	NB-IoT, LTE-M 100 LTE, 5G Cellular 200	NB-IoT, LTE-M 400 LTE, 5G Cellular 400

All units in mW

Voler SYSTEMS

< Slide 19 >

How Much Power Do Sensors Use?

150mW	200mW	20mW	10mW	50 uW to 50mW
Camera chip	Illumination for camera at night	GPS (Position)	Pulse Oximeter (Blood Oxygen)	Pressure Sensor
1mW	0.5mW	0.1 to 10mW	0.1 to 10mW	0.01 to 0.1mW
EKG/Heart Rate	9-axis Motion Sensor	Microphone	Light Intensity	3-axis Accelerometer

Voler SYSTEMS

< Slide 21 >

The Concern: Devices in Healthcare

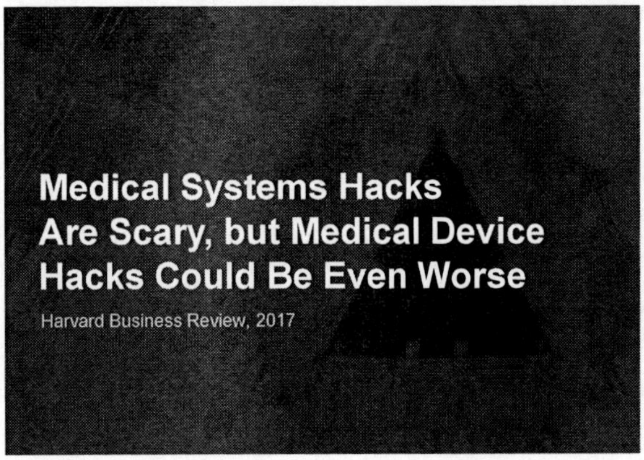

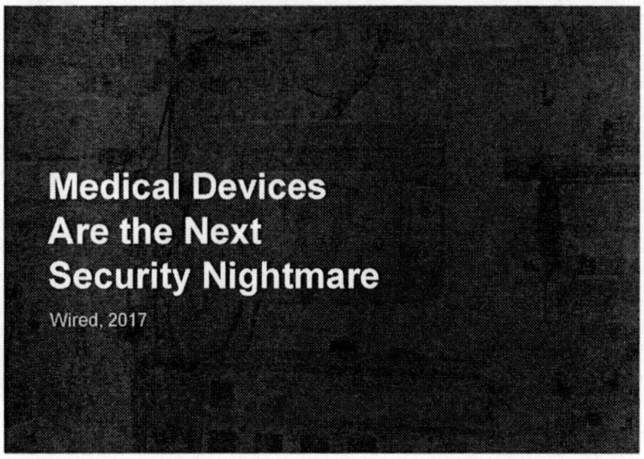

Voler SYSTEMS

< Slide 22 >

Consumer product companies are open to lawsuits

Quick Facts:

- Recent Incident: December 2019
- Hackers broke into Ring security cameras of two families
- Hackers used device speakers to broadcast racial slurs
- Ring advised customers to enable two-factor authentication, use strong passwords on their accounts

(Source: Vice)

Now:

- Ring has faced growing criticism over its security practices
- Two couples who had their devices hacked initiated class action lawsuits against Ring

(Source: Business Insider)

Voler SYSTEMS

< Slide 23 >

Security Recommendations for Medical Devices are Changing

Food and Drug Administration's (FDA) Guidance Document

Issued on Oct. 18, 2018	**Defined by FDA**	**Final release is still pending**	**Non-binding later guidance is advisable for use**
"Content of Premarket Submissions for Management of Cybersecurity in Medical Devices"	*Security requirements*	*Draft guidance only*	*2014 version applies for now*

Voler SYSTEMS

< Slide 24 >

FDA Cybersecurity Recommendations

- Based on NIST Cybersecurity Framework
- Two Tiers
  - Tier 1 – higher level of security if
    - Device connects to another product or network
    - A cybersecurity incident could directly result in harm to multiple patients
  - Tier 2 – other devices, standard security

Voler SYSTEMS

Medical Devices Needing High Security, Based on NIST Cybersecurity Framework

Tier 1 recommends the following:

A **Prevent unauthorized use**
- Limit access to trusted users and devices only
- Authenticate and check authorization of safety-critical commands

B **Ensure trusted content by maintaining code, data, and execution integrity**

C **Maintain confidentiality of data**

D **Design the device to detect cybersecurity threats in a timely fashion**

E **Design the device to respond to and contain the impact of a potential cyber security incident**

F **Design the device to recover capabilities or services that were impaired due to a cyber security incident**

25

< Slide 26 >

Walt Maclay, Voler Systems
Walt@VolerSystems.com
408-245-9844

Wearable Devices and IoT

Sensors
Converge

Energy Harvesting Design Techniques in Wireless Sensors for IIoT, Manufacturing and Environmental Sensing

Wenli Yu
CEO, Archimedes Controls Corp.

September 21-23, 2021 | San Jose, CA

#SensorsConverge

Why Energy Harvesting?

- Wiring is not convenient or impractical (hidden places, nearby connection not available, not desirable, etc.)
- Battery is not suitable (devices need steady power supply, battery life is too short, cold and hot weather conditions cause de-rating, voltage and capacity drop over time,)
- Replacing battery or charging is not possible (too often, too many spread out, hard to reach, cold and hot weather conditions, etc.)
- Extremely low average power consumption applications
- Invisible, concealed
- IP68 devices
- Nice to have

#SensorsConverge

Sensors Converge

Where Can Energy Harvesting Be Used

- IoT, IIoT, OT
- Energy management – power consumption monitoring, power quality monitoring,
- Industry control – temperature, humidity, real time current, motor operation, air/liquid flow rate, objet displacement, object movement, gas concentration level, vibration,
- Environmental – temperature, humidity, air quality, gas concentration, vibration, , disaster detection, object fall, mudslide and landslide, tunnel security, flood monitoring,
- Security – unauthorized access detection, motion detection, bank ATM security, theft detection, vandalism ,
- Assets management – assets tracking, assets protection,
- Communications – OSP monitoring, unauthorized access, water leak, power conditions,
- IT and IT equipment – data center environmental monitoring, network infrastructure protection, differential air pressure, AC monitoring,
- Cloud data centers – colocation security monitoring, biometric, environmental, power usage,
- Healthcare – vital sign monitoring, remote diagnostic and medicine, medical devices, wearables, emergency alert,
- Building management – environmental, AC units, security, power usage, fire and smoke detection, connected assets,
- Home appliances – energy usage monitoring, automatic sensing and on/off control,
- Smart cities – security, environmental, public safety, disaster detection, object recognition and classification,

#SensorsConverge

Sensors Converge

Other Potential Applications

- Transportation – parking space management, traffic monitoring and management, railroad and highway safety, disaster monitoring, object fall, mudslide, landslide, side hills, tunnel security, flood monitoring, autonomous, connected vehicles,
- Energy and utilities – fuel usage monitoring, fuel transport, fuel delivery, power sub-station monitoring, water leak,
- Agriculture and food safety – granary monitoring, transportation tracking, greenhouse monitoring, CO2 and brightness monitoring, soil moisture level, water level,
- AR,
- Drones,
- Digital adherence (glasses, helmets, eye protection, PPP, medical monitoring and alerting devices),
- Digital tracking (crucial and low visibility material tracking, waste tracking and monitoring),
- ML, AI,
- Packaging, tracking, warehouses,
- Digital performance,
- Material tracking,
- Visualization, inspection,
- Test and measurement,
- Sensing probes,
- And more

#SensorsConverge

Sensors Converge

Five Most Important Aspects

- Energy need types (burst, short term, long term, average)
- How will the energy be consumed
- Power consumption style (current mode, voltage mode, burst rate, duty cycle, on time and off time)
- Use environment
- Energy source(s)
- Power quality requirements (voltage stability, voltage range, burst current, average current)

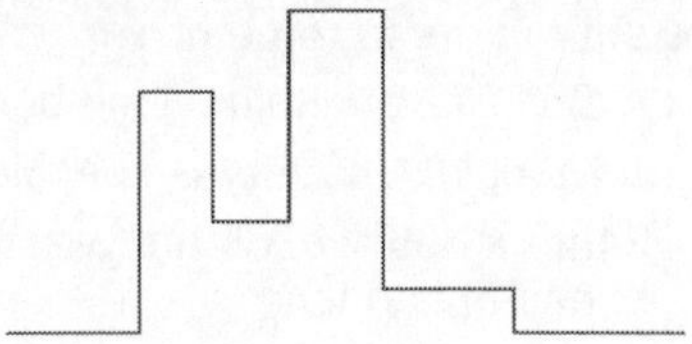

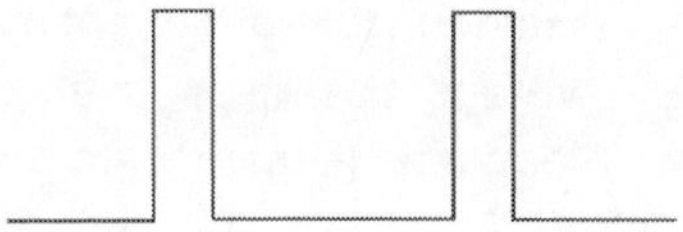

System Power Requirements

- Gross sanity check
  - ✓ What will be the peak power consumption?
  - ✓ Current type or voltage type?
  - ✓ What are the voltage and current needed?
  - ✓ For how long?
  - ✓ Duty cycle?
  - ✓ Connection time? Continuous on? Instantaneous on?
  - ✓ Latency requirement
  - ✓ Average power consumption?
  - ✓ Use environment (outdoor open field or indoor, stationary or in motion, at day time or night time, etc.)

- Double check all the above in time scale + safety margin

Power Requirements Summary

- Important factors to remember:
  - A CR2032 3V lithium coin battery is specified typically 225mAH
  - A typical AA battery is specified as 1500mAh
  - 24hrs x 365 = 8760 hrs/year, sleep time could be the most significant power consumption time

- Working power source:
  - ✓Voltage & current
  - Voltage mode, or current mode, or mixed
  - Average, peak high, peak low, duty cycle, etc.
  - Sleep time (sensor, data acquisition, MCU, RF transmitter, etc.)

#SensorsConverge

Sensors Converge

Needs Analysis

- What's needed - estimated requirements, implementation feasibility, negotiation, back n forth
- # of power sources needed:
  - ✓ 1.8VDC
  - ✓ 3.3VDC
  - ✓ 5.0VDC
  - ✓ 12VDC
  - ✓ USB
  - ✓ Min working voltage – important to know from power efficiency perspective
  - ✓ Try to minimize the number of different voltages
  - ✓ Linear regulator might be the most efficient approach for voltage conversion
- From each functional blocks (using both typical and max from datasheets for the entire working temperature ranges):
  - ✓ MCU
    - During sleep, standby, wake up, active cycles: from <100nA to a few hundred mA, duration, duty cycle;
  - ✓ Sensors (temperature, gas, environmental, MEMS, optical, power, ultra sound, etc.)
    - During sleep or off, heater up, wait period, measurement, turning off cycles: from a few nA to a few mA, duration, duty cycle;
  - ✓ Communication modules (WiFi, BT, LoRA, 4/5G, Ethernet, radio)
  - ✓ Others (GPS, USB, biometric, actuate, etc.)
- Sum all the above in time scale + safety margin
- Is it feasible and reasonable?

#SensorsConverge

Sensors Converge

Possible Energy Sources

- Solar
- Environment light
- Kinetic
- Thermal
- Magnetic
- Current transformer (for AC power line)
- Potential energy
- Chemical
- EM wave
- There is always a long life battery for power supplement

Converting Native Energy Source to Needed

- No need with DC energy pick up
- Rectifier for AC energy pick up
  - ✓ Low voltage drop diode
  - ✓ Full wave rectifier, half wave rectifier
  - ✓ MOSFET, but requires a control IC to achieve ultra low voltage drop.

Battery Capacity Considerations & Estimate

- System needs (V & mWh or V & mAh)
  - ✓ Check all components datasheets
  - ✓ Take into account low, high, typical, worst scenario of possible combinations
  - It's too easy to miss system current during power up and reset
- Working environment (hot summer, cold winter, indoor, outdoor)
  - Determines battery type (lithium, disposable, super cap)
  - Determines battery capacity needs, charging method, temperature de-rating factor
  - Battery type determines self discharging rate
- Capacity
  - Total need
  - x n to compensate all de-ratings
- Temperature de-rating
  - ✓ Low temperature causes significant capacity drop
- Charge/discharge cycle de-rating
  - ✓ Batteries, super caps all have life cycle limits
- Supercap/electrolytic cap/re-chargeable battery
  - ✓ Which one is the right one?

Building Blocks

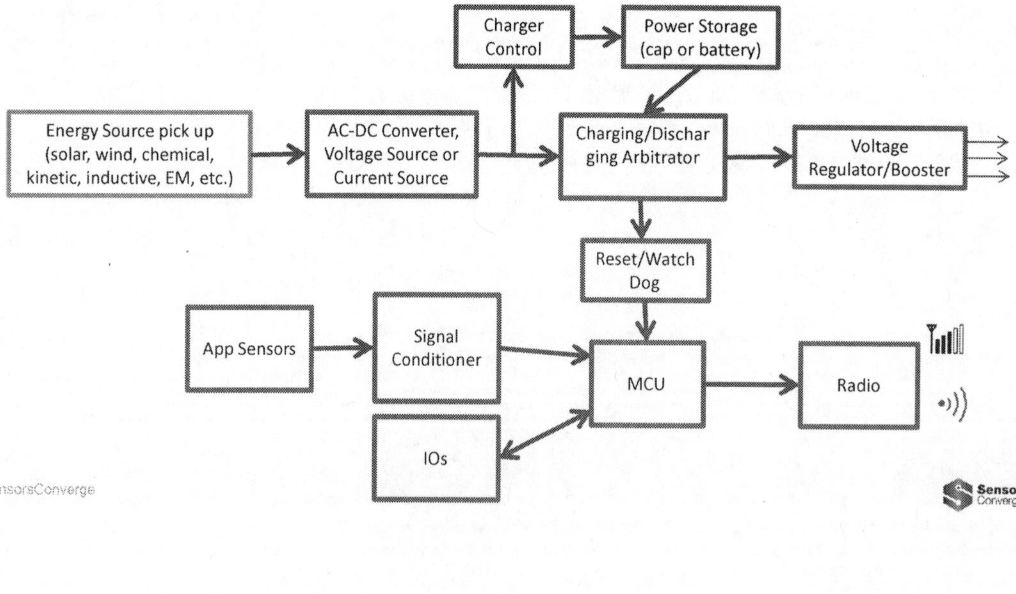

Final – Testing and Manufacturing

- Measuring actual current
- Calculate power usage against design using actual measurements
- DFx
- Cross margin check
- Considering components variation from min to max, from different manufacturers, parts aging,
- MTBF
- Sole-source parts
- Components lead time
- Muti footprint on PCB
- HASS and HALT
- etc.

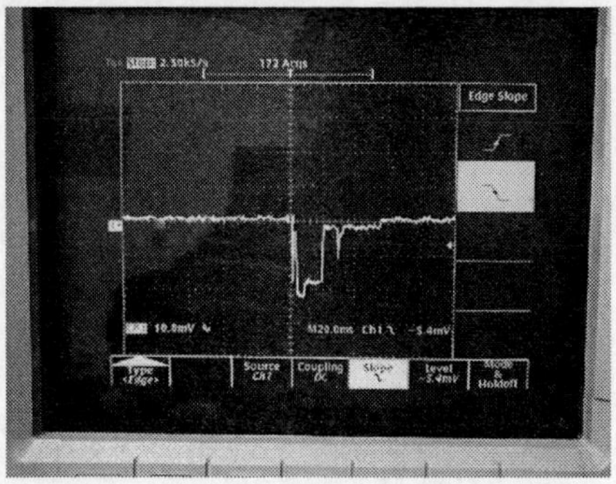

#SensorsConverge

Sensors Converge

Thank you

#SensorsConverge

Sensors Converge

Sensors Converge

zipline

Saving Lives with Autonomous Drone Deliveries

Whitney Huang
Embedded Systems Engineer, Zipline International Inc.

September 23, 2021

Outline

- Background
- Operations and Impact
- Technology Overview
- Testing
- Upcoming Technology

3

Background

4

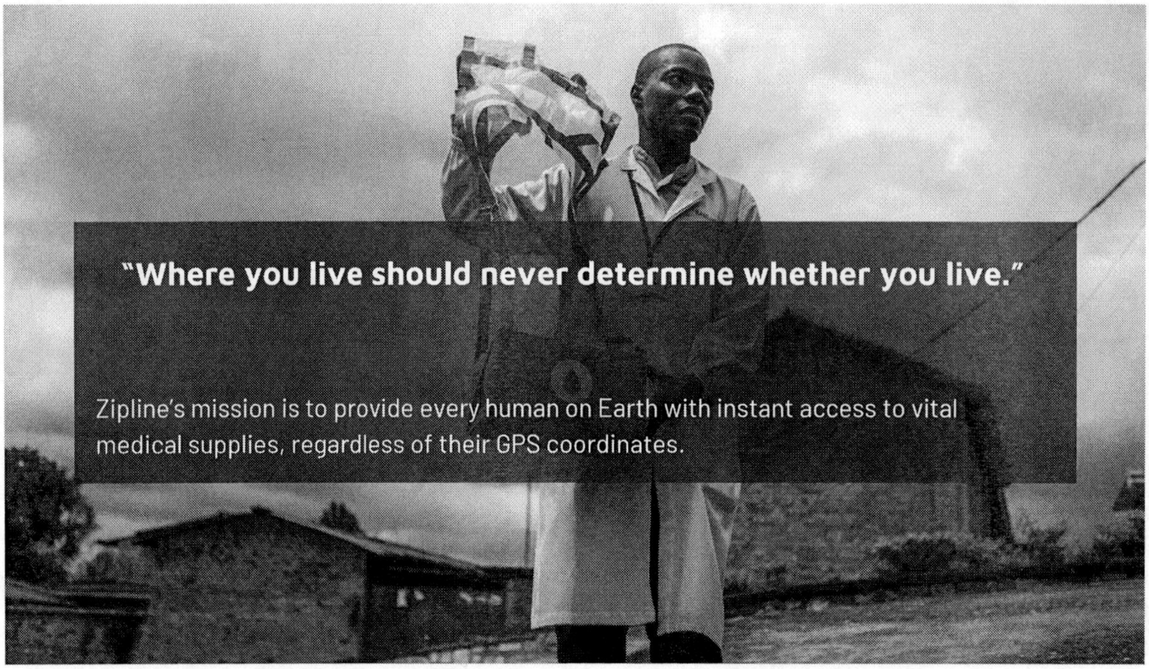
"Where you live should never determine whether you live."
Zipline's mission is to provide every human on Earth with instant access to vital medical supplies, regardless of their GPS coordinates.

zipline

Operations and Impact

8

Background (Operations)

9

Fast Facts

- 195,000 commercial deliveries
- 2 million vaccine doses delivered, including COVID-19 vaccines
- 9 million miles flown - zips fly enough to circle the world in 24 hours!
- Serve ~2,500 health facilities globally
- Operate in all weather conditions: rain, snow, storms

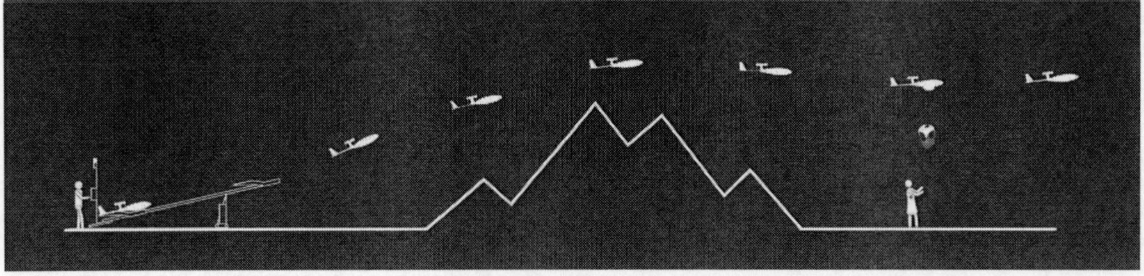

History

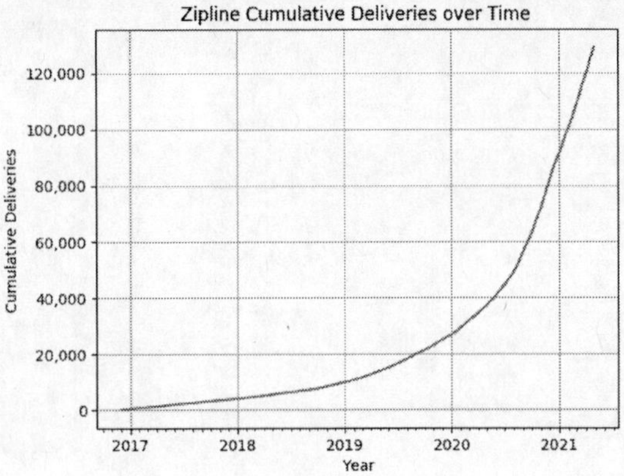

- 2013 → Zipline is founded.
- 2016 → The first delivery is made to Kabgayi Hospital in Rwanda.
- 2018 → Zipline expands to Ghana.
- 2020 → Zipline begins delivering PPE in North Carolina.
- 2021 → The 100,000th operational delivery is made.
- 2021 → COVID-19 vaccine distribution begins in Ghana.
- 2022 → Zipline Launches in Nigeria and Japan

11

Impact - Rwanda

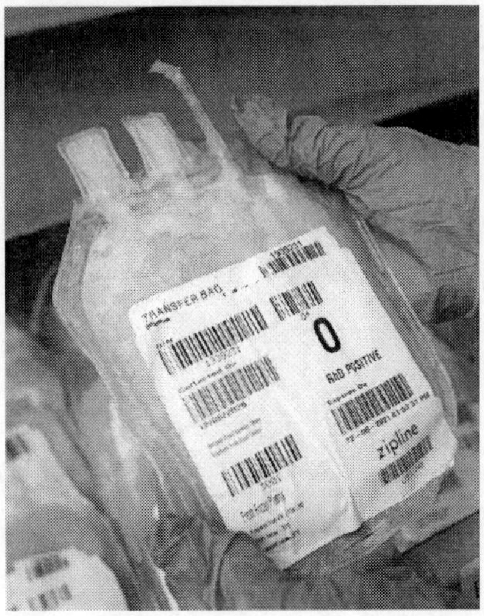

- **Increased access** to new blood products for transfusing facilities (platelets & cryoprecipitate)
- **Enabled central processing** to increase throughput by 2-3x while reducing maintenance costs and increasing quality control
- **Increased fill rate** from 70% to 95%
- **Decreased wastage** by over 90%
- **Reduced fulfillment time** from an average of 3.5 hours to under 1 hour

12

Technology Overview

13

Technology

- Safety and reliability
- Customer-driven requirements
- Cost effectiveness
- Operational scalability

14

Technology - Actuators

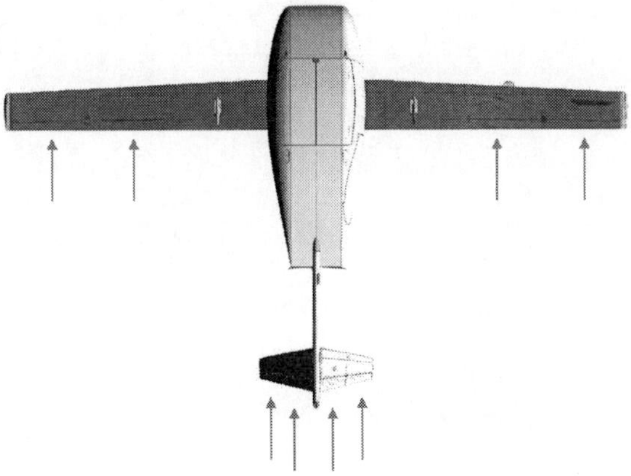

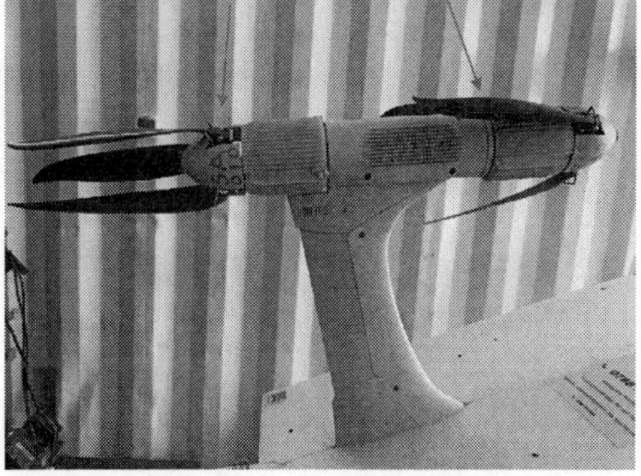

16

Technology - Distributed nodes

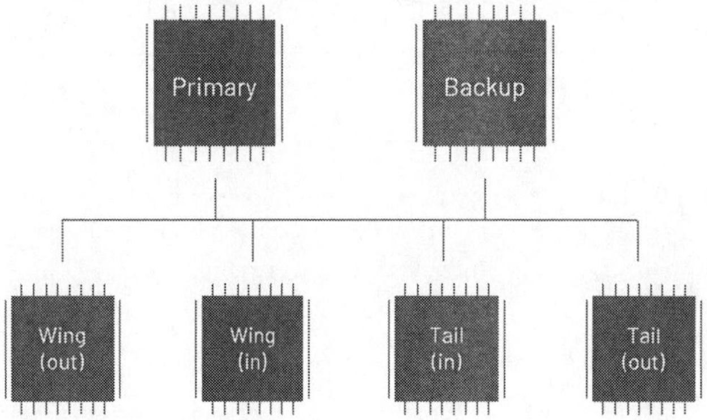

17

Technology - Communications

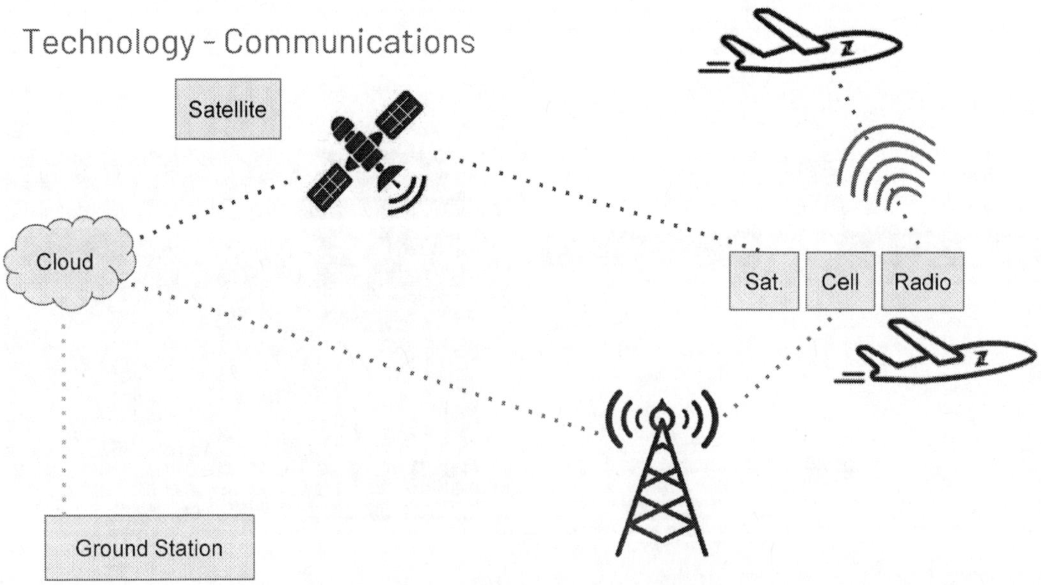

18

Technology - Autonomy, Path planning

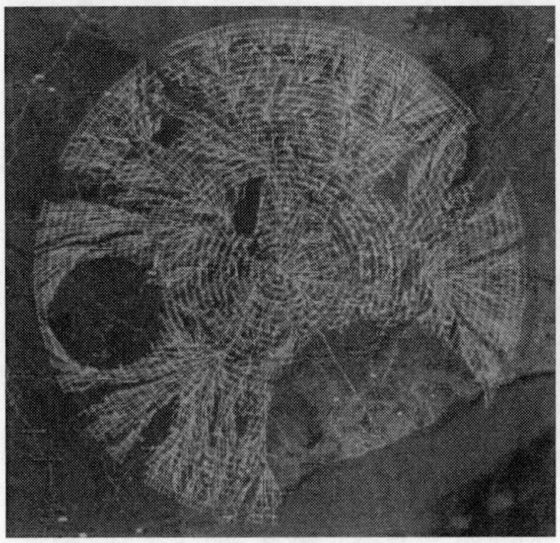

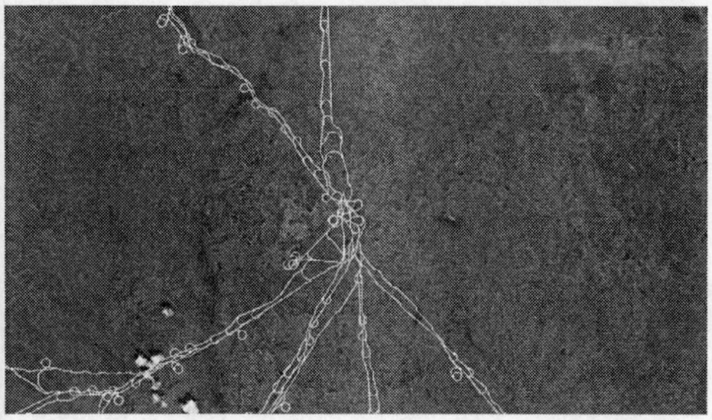

19

Technology - Behaviors, GNC

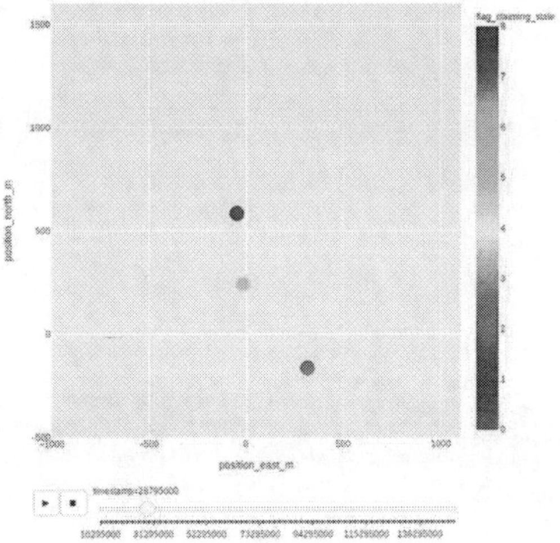

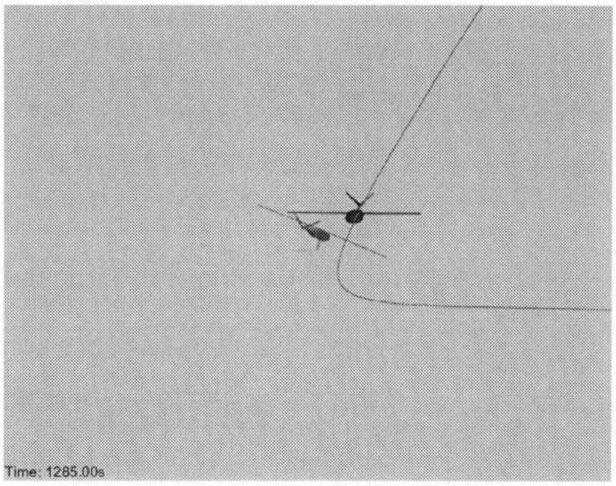

20

Technology - Launcher
21

Technology - Delivery

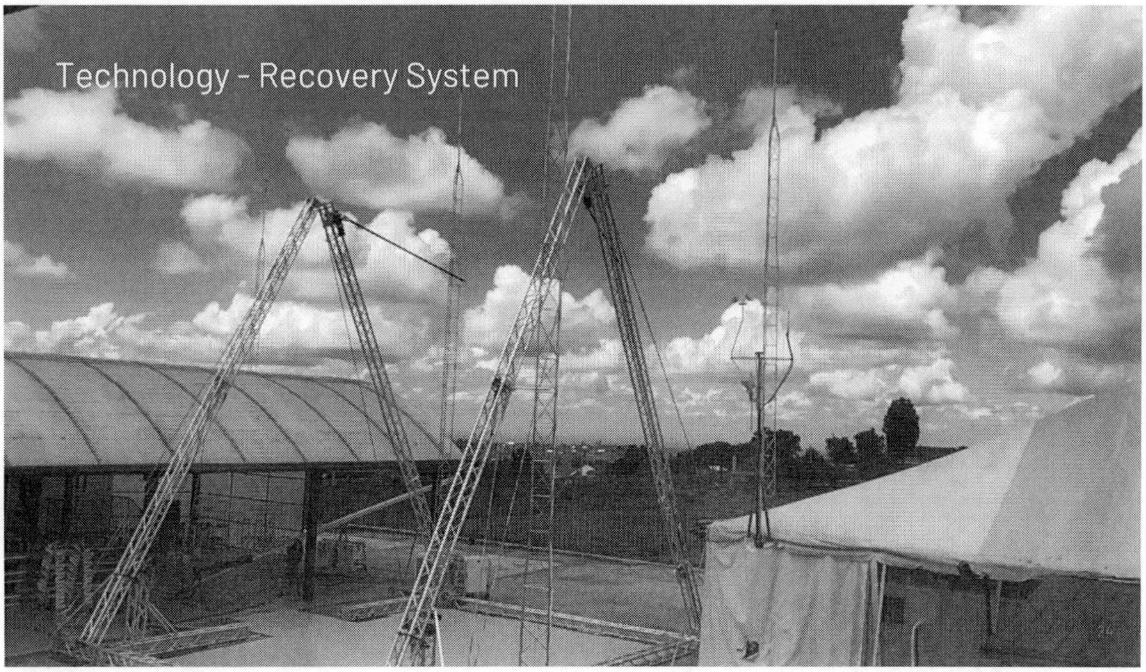
Technology - Recovery System

2 cm
zipline

RTK GPS

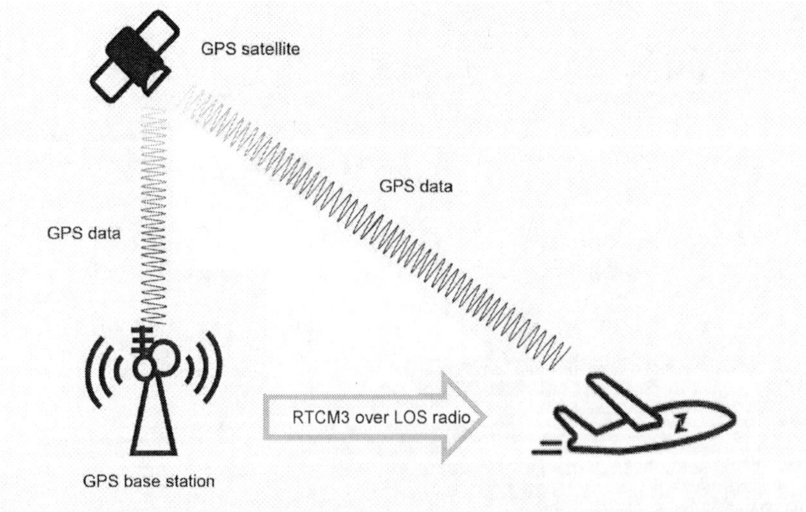
GPS satellite
GPS data
GPS data
RTCM3 over LOS radio
GPS base station

26

Technology – Paraland system

28

Technology - Chargers

29

Technology - Logs and Data Analysis

30

Testing

31

Testing – Test Facilities

Testing - HITL

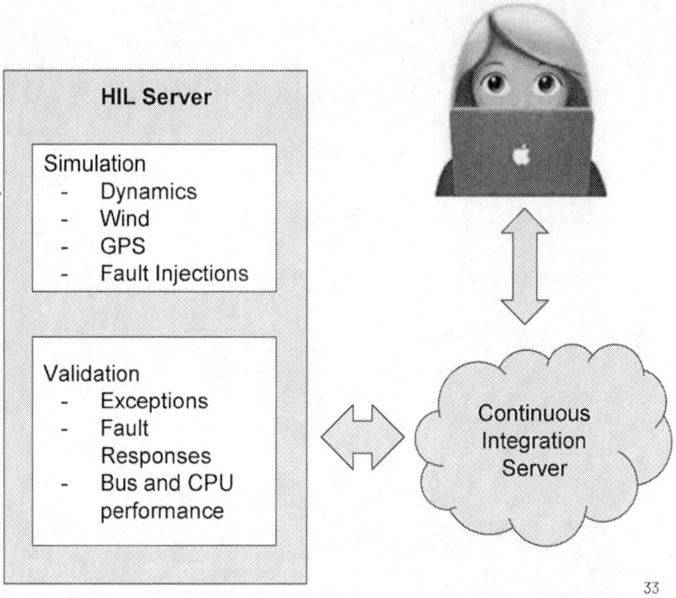

33

Future of Embedded Systems at Zipline

34

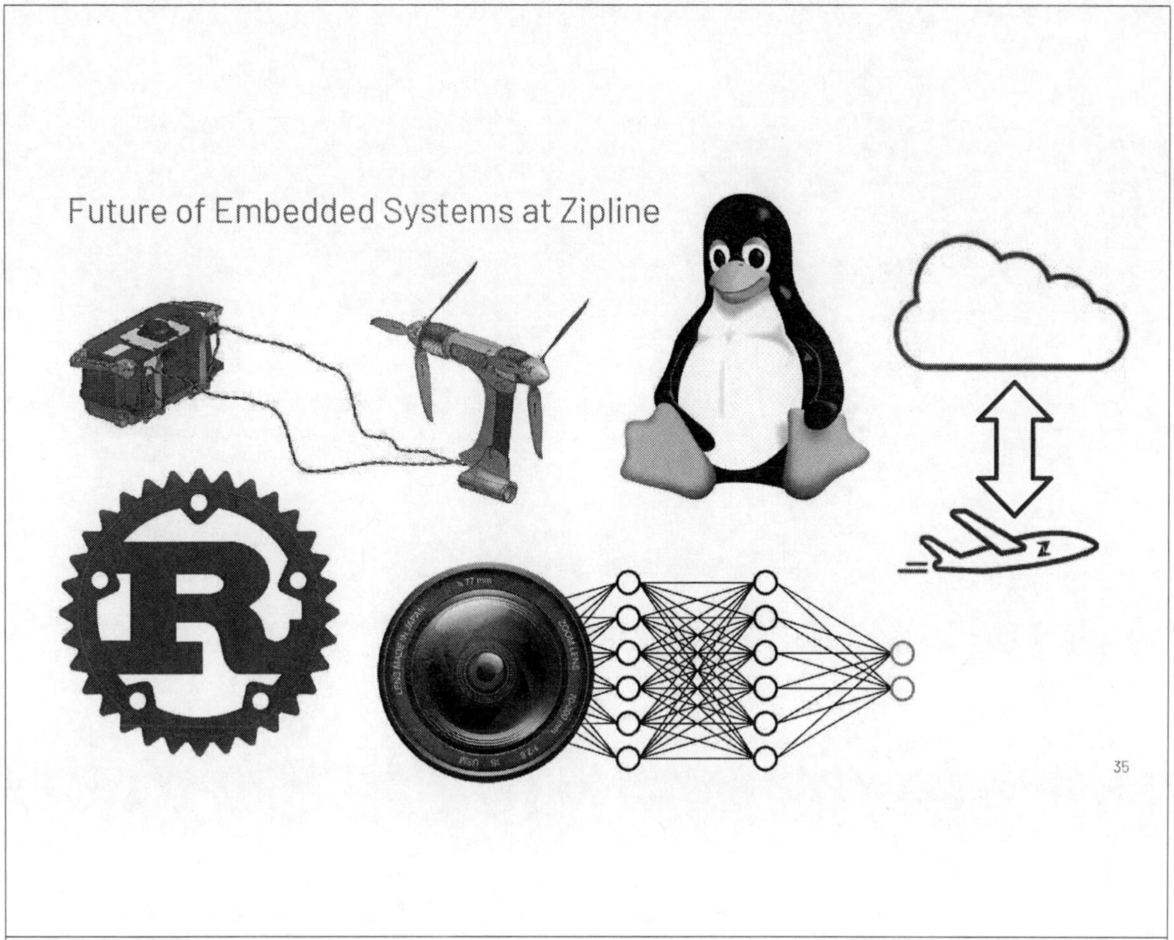
Future of Embedded Systems at Zipline
35

Q&A
zipline

AUTHOR INDEX